KENKYUSHA'S GUIDE TO QUANTITATIVE EXPRESSIONS IN ENGLISH

研究社
英語の数量表現辞典

増補改訂版

研究社辞書編集部 編
監修 トム・ガリー

© 2017　KENKYUSHA Co., Ltd.

PRINTED IN JAPAN

まえがき

　本書は 2007 年に刊行した『研究社　英語の数量表現辞典』の増補改訂版となります。読み物と辞書の両方を兼ね備える書籍という基本の構成を維持しつつ用例および（第 2 部での）見出しの増強を図り、また初版から 10 年がたつ現在の状況・事情に照らし初版での記述の見直しも行ないました。結果として本それ自体としてはもちろん（総ページ数は初版の 1 割増）内容の上でも一層の厚みをもつことができたと自負しております。

　本書の特色は初版から変わらず、簡単にまとめると次のようになります。

① 前半の第 1 部は 64 の章立て（トピック）で、日本人には難しい英文法上の事柄から日常・社会生活のさまざまな場面における数字や「多少」「増減」などの概念にまつわる表現、さらに数式の読み方から自然科学分野まで、幅広い内容をカバー。
② トピックごとの解説中で折に触れ「トリビア」として付随的な情報にも言及。
③ 後半の第 2 部は和英辞典の形式で、約 1500 の日本語見出しを収録。
④ 第 2 部は単体で辞書として使用することはもちろん、第 1 部と相互参照を行なっているので第 1 部の索引として利用することも可能。

　検索の便を考えてトピック別・辞典形式それぞれの強みを生かす 2 部構成としてありますが、今回は第 2 部の索引機能の強化も図り、求める語句・表現へのアクセスのしやすさは増したものと考えております。

　本書の編集には、『新和英大辞典』第 5 版（2003 年）を土台とした初版から引き続き、同辞典で編集委員のトム・ガリー［Tom Gally］氏（現東京大学大学院総合文化研究科・教養学部教授）と、かつて辞書編集部に在籍の友清理士（ともきよ・さとし）氏（現特許技術者）とがあたり、作業は友清氏が作成した原稿をガリー氏が監修する形の協働により進行しました。今回の増補改訂について特筆すべき点として、紙やファイルをやりとりするにとどまらず、編集部の担当も交え膝を突き合わせて意見を直接交換する機会を数度にわたり持てたことがあります。お二方のご尽力に記して深

く感謝申し上げます。

　なお、本書の刊行に向けて関係者一同、遺漏なきよう努めたつもりでありますが、不備不足の点については、本書をご利用くださる皆様から忌憚のないご意見を頂戴できれば幸いでございます。

2017 年 2 月

研究社辞書編集部

目　　次

まえがき iii
本書の見方 xvii

第1部 トピック別編　　　　　　　　　　　　　　　　　　　　　　　　　　　　1

1. 基数　　　　　　　　　　　　　　　　　　　　　　　　　　　　　　　　　　2
1-1 0〜99 2
　● 1-1-1「十五」と「五十」　● 1-1-2 fourteen と forty
1-2 100以上の数 3
　● 1-2-1 -s の有無　● 1-2-2 and の使用　● 1-2-3 3桁, 4桁の数の読み方
　● 1-2-4 コンマの使用　● 1-2-5 数の区切り　● 1-2-6 数詞が複合形容詞をつくる場合

2. 数え方　　　　　　　　　　　　　　　　　　　　　　　　　　　　　　　　6
　● 2-1 基本的な数え方　● 2-2 不可算名詞の数え方
　● 2-3 数え方に注意を要する可算名詞　● 2-4 数値を呈示する各種表現

3. ローマ数字　　　　　　　　　　　　　　　　　　　　　　　　　　　　　10
　● 3-1 ローマ数字を使うさまざまな場合　● 3-2 ローマ数字の字体

4. 序数　　　　　　　　　　　　　　　　　　　　　　　　　　　　　　　　13
　● 4-1 表記上の注意　● 4-2 the first と a first

5. アラビア数字で書くかスペルアウトするか　　　　　　　　　　　　　15
　● 5-1 桁数が多ければ数字に　● 5-2 続き番号は数字に　● 5-3 単位付きの数値の場合
　● 5-4 出現環境による使い分け　● 5-5 文頭の扱い　● 5-6 単位のスペルアウト

6. 数字の読み方　　　　　　　　　　　　　　　　　　　　　　　　　　　18
　● 6-1 基本的な読み方　● 6-2 電話番号の読み方　● 6-3 ハイフンの読み方
　● 6-4 その他

7. 大きな数　　　　　　　　　　　　　　　　　　　　　　　　　　　　　　20
　● 7-1 英米の違い　● 7-2 戯語　● 7-3 SI 接頭語　● 7-4 日本語の大きな数・小さな数

8. 漠然とした大きな数　　　　　　　　　　　　　　　　　　　　　　　　23
　● 8-1「何十」など　● 8-2「数十」など　● 8-3「うん十」など

9. 概数　　　　　　　　　　　　　　　　　　　　　　　　　　　　　　　　26
9-1「約」「およそ」.. 26
9-2「…何」「…数」「…余り」など 26
9-3「…台」... 27

9-4 「…足らず」 30
9-5 「二,三個」など 30
9-6 「数個」「いくつか」 31
9-7 「n個」など 31

10. 位取りと四捨五入・切り上げ・切り捨て 32
10-1 位取り 32
10-2 四捨五入 33
10-3 切り上げ 35
10-4 切り捨て 35

11. 数値範囲の表現 36
● 11-1「…から…まで」など区間を表わす表現　● 11-2 betweenの用法
● 11-3「…以上…以下」　● 11-4「…を超えて…まで」　● 11-5「…以上…未満」

12.「以上」「以下」等の表現 39
12-1 基本 39
● 12-1-1 more than … と「以上」の違い
● 12-1-2 規定を表わす no fewer than …　● 12-1-3 overの多義性
12-2 「…以上」「…より大きい」 40
● 12-2-1 基本　● 12-2-2 量を直接指す場合と間接的に指す場合
● 12-2-3「…以上である」　● 12-2-4「…が…以上の…」　● 12-2-5 その他
12-3 「…以下」「…より小さい(…未満)」 42
● 12-3-1 基本　● 12-3-2 その他

13. 比較・差・増減 44
13-1 比較の基本 44
● 13-1-1 比較級など　● 13-1-2 最上級など　● 13-1-3 その他の比較表現
13-2 差・増減 46
● 13-2-1 差　● 13-2-2 増減の程度
13-3 比較の基準の表現 47
13-4 増加・上昇を表わす各種表現 48
● 13-4-1 基本　● 13-4-2 急増・急上昇　● 13-4-3 相関　● 13-4-4 傾向
● 13-4-5 右肩上がり　● 13-4-6 増加率・上昇率　● 13-4-7 その他
13-5 減少・低下を表わす各種表現 52
● 13-5-1 基本　● 13-5-2 急減・急落　● 13-5-3 傾向　● 13-5-4 低下率・減少率
● 13-5-5 反落
13-6 横ばい 55

14. 最高と最低 56

- 14-1 最高　● 14-2 過去最高　● 14-3 自己ベスト　● 14-4 頭打ち　● 14-5 最低
- 14-6 過去最低　● 14-7 底　● 14-8 最上級と複数形

15. 順位・順番の表現 　61

15-1 …番目 61
15-2 順位 61
- 15-2-1 順位一般　● 15-2-2 スポーツ　● 15-2-3 ヒットチャートなど

15-3 格付けと星 67
15-4 順番 69
- 15-4-1 …順に　● 15-4-2「高い順」「低い順」　● 15-4-3 明示的に順番を言う例

16. 投票・選挙の表現 　71
- 16-1 票数　● 16-2 キャスティングボート　● 16-3 過半数　● 16-4 3分の2の多数
- 16-5 投票権　● 16-6 投票率　● 16-7 定数　● 16-8 定定数　● 16-9 票の動向
- 16-10 再選・多選

17. …倍 　78
- 17-1 基本　● 17-2 …倍になる　● 17-3 …倍以上　● 17-4 差・変化
- 17-5 希釈の倍率　● 17-6 拡大・縮小の倍率　● 17-7 again を使った表現
- 17-8 数値以外の「…倍」　● 17-9 半分

18. 同等・相当 　84
- 18-1「同じ」「等しい」　● 18-2「同数の」　● 18-3 相当　● 18-4「ちょうど」「ぴったり」

19. 多少の表現 　87

19-1 多数 87
- 19-1-1「多数の…」「たくさんの…」　● 19-1-2「…は多い」「たくさんある」
- 19-1-3「数多く」「たくさん」

19-2 多量 89
- 19-2-1「多量の…」　● 19-2-2「…は多い」「たくさんある」
- 19-2-3「大量に」

19-3 少数 90
19-4 少量 91

20.「…も」「…しか」「たった」 　93

20-1「…も」 93
20-2「…しか」「たった」 93
20-3 no more than …, no less than …, no fewer than … の用法 94

21. 過不足の表現 　96

21-1 不足 96

- ●21-1-1「…だけ足りない」 ●21-1-2「…に足りない」 ●21-1-3 欠乏
21-2 過剰 97
- ●21-2-1「…だけ…すぎる」 ●21-2-2 過剰

22. 割合　99
22-1 割合 99
- ●22-1-1 歩合 ●22-1-2 百分率／パーセント ●22-1-3 パーミル
- ●22-1-4 ppm / ppb / ppt ●22-1-5 分数 ●22-1-6 各種表現 ●22-1-7 疑問文
- ●22-1-8 変化率 ●22-1-9 ポイント ●22-1-10 重量比・体積比など
- ●22-1-11「割合」を表わす語句 ●22-1-12 パーセント表示

22-2 単位量当たりの割合 104
22-3 相対比率 104
22-4 定性的な割合 105
- ●22-4-1 半分 ●22-4-2 一部 ●22-4-3 ほとんど ●22-4-4 全部

22-5 部分否定と全否定 106

23. 確率と可能性　108
- ●23-1 確率を表わすさまざまな表現 ●23-2 可能性を表わす副詞
- ●23-3 定性的な可能性

24. 合計・累計・延べ　111
24-1 合計・総計・総額 111
24-2 小計 112
24-3 累計 112
24-4 延べ 112

25. 平均　114
- ●25-1 平均値を述べる表現 ●25-2 平均との比較 ●25-3 平均の算定
- ●25-4 平均の対象 ●25-5 平均からの偏差 ●25-6 平均点 ●25-7 平均年齢
- ●25-8 平均寿命 ●25-9 平均的 ●25-10 その他の術語

26. 数量に関する疑問文　118
26-1 数 118
26-2 量 119
- ●26-2-1 物の量 ●26-2-2 長さ・距離 ●26-2-3 身体計測 ●26-2-4 重さ
- ●26-2-5 各種物理量 ●26-2-6 過不足

26-3 単位付きの疑問文 121
26-4 単位の換算 122
26-5 時間・時刻 122
- ●26-5-1 暦と時刻 ●26-5-2 所要時間 ●26-5-3 いつ ●26-5-4 いつまで

- ●26-5-5 いつまでに　●26-5-6 時間の長さ

26-6 年齢 125

26-7 値段・金額・為替 126

26-8 計算 127

26-9 無名数・番号 128

26-10 何番目 129
- ●26-10-1「いくつ」の応用　●26-10-2「その前にいくつあるか」式
- ●26-10-3「どこ」「いつ」「どれ」の応用　●26-10-4 順位としての表現

26-11 その他 130

26-12 複数の疑問詞を含む構文 131

27. 単位　132
- ●27-1 一般的な注意事項　●27-2 SI基本単位　●27-3 SIと併用される非SI単位
- ●27-4 SI接頭語　●27-5 組立単位　●27-6 SI以外の単位

28. 伝統単位　137
- ●28-1 長さ　●28-2 面積と体積　●28-3 常衡　●28-4 英国の液量・乾量単位
- ●28-5 米国の液量・乾量単位　●28-6 組立単位　●28-7 温度
- ●28-8 日本の伝統単位

29. 年・年度・元号・世紀　144
- ●29-1 基本　●29-2 年号の読み方　●29-3 紀元前と紀元後　●29-4 年度
- ●29-5 元号　●29-6 …年代　●29-7 世紀

30. 日付と曜日　151

30-1 月名 151

30-2 月日 151

30-3 基本例 152

30-4 曜日 155

30-5 …付け 155

30-6 その他 156

31. 年・月・週・日　157

31-1 年 157
- ●31-1-1 長さ　●31-1-2 頻度・割合　●31-1-3 その他

31-2 月 158
- ●31-2-1 長さ　●31-2-2 頻度・割合　●31-2-3 月末　●31-2-4 今月　●31-2-5 時期

31-3 週 159
- ●31-3-1 長さ　●31-3-2 頻度　●31-3-3 時期　●31-3-4 週末　●31-3-5 期間

31-4 日 161

●31-4-1 長さ　●31-4-2 日数　●31-4-3 1泊2日　●31-4-4 中…日

31-5「来…」「先…」.. 162
　●31-5-1「来…」　●31-5-2「先…」　●31-5-3 next … の使用例
　●31-5-4 last … の使用例

31-6「翌…」「前…」.. 164
　●31-6-1「翌…」　●31-6-2「前…」　●31-6-3 使用例

31-7「…前」「…後」.. 165
　●31-7-1「…前」　●31-7-2「…後」

32. 時刻と時間　　167

32-1 時刻 167
　●32-1-1 時刻の言い方　●32-1-2 午前と午後　●32-1-3 24時制
　●32-1-4 零時と12時

32-2 時計 170
32-3 時差 170
　●32-3-1 基本　●32-3-2 日本時間・現地時間　●32-3-3 標準時

32-4 時間 172
　●32-4-1 時間の長さ　●32-4-2 単位時間

33. 時間を表わす句・節　　174

33-1 簡単な前置詞句など 174
　●33-1-1 …に　●33-1-2 …から　●33-1-3 …まで　●33-1-4 その他

33-2「初頭」「末」「旬」.. 176
33-3 同時 177
33-4 時間を表わす副詞的な名詞句 178
　●33-4-1 副詞的な名詞句　●33-4-2 副詞節を導くことのできる名詞句

34. 期間の表現　　180

　●34-1 期間の長さ　●34-2「…以内」　●34-3 契約期間　●34-4 有効期間

35. 期日・期限の表現　　182

35-1 …まで... 182
35-2 …までに... 182
　●35-2-1 締め切り／期限　●35-2-2 期日まであと…　●35-2-3 期限オーバー

35-3 時間差 185
35-4 賞味期限・消費期限 185

36. 回数・頻度の表現　　187

　●36-1 回数　●36-2 …回目　●36-3 頻度　●36-4 …年ごとの　●36-5 …周年
　●36-6 …回忌　●36-7 頻度の多寡

37. 伝統暦　　192
- 37-1 月名　●37-2 太陰太陽暦と閏月　●37-3 二十四節気　●37-4 十二支
- 37-5 十干　●37-6 十干十二支　●37-7 気象用語

38. 年齢　　200
- 38-1 基本　●38-2 年齢の比較など　●38-3 …代　●38-4 満年齢と数え年
- 38-5 妊娠・出産　●38-6 馬齢

39. 通貨と為替　　206
39-1 通貨単位　　206
- 39-1-1 円　●39-1-2 ドル　●39-1-3 ユーロ　●39-1-4 ポンド　●39-1-5 その他

39-2 外国為替　　208
- 39-2-1 換算・為替取引　●39-2-2 為替相場　●39-2-3 相場変動　●39-2-4 円高
- 39-2-5 円安

39-3 株　　211
- 39-3-1 株価　●39-3-2 株価指数・平均株価　●39-3-3 株価の水準と変動
- 39-3-4 値幅制限・ストップ高・ストップ安　●39-3-5 売買　●39-3-6 保有・持ち株比率
- 39-3-7 時価総額　●39-3-8 配当・利益　●39-3-9 発行　●39-3-10 公開
- 39-3-11 株式分割　●39-3-12 その他

39-4 入札・オークション　　217

40. 料金・価格・収支　　219
40-1 料金　　219
- 40-1-1 rate, chargeを中心に訳す例　●40-1-2 feeを中心に訳す例
- 40-1-3 fareを中心に訳す例　●40-1-4 その他

40-2 価格・値段　　221
- 40-2-1 価格の表現　●40-2-2 価格の高低　●40-2-3 価格帯
- 40-2-4 価格にまつわる術語　●40-2-5 単価　●40-2-6 時価　●40-2-7 物価
- 40-2-8 その他

40-3 費用　　227
40-4 割引　　228
40-5 収入と支出　　229
- 40-5-1 収支　●40-5-2 収入　●40-5-3 支出

40-6 日常的な各種表現　　231
- 40-6-1 基本　●40-6-2 支払いに関係する表現　●40-6-3 小銭　●40-6-4 おつり

41. 英文会計　　235
41-1 用語　　235
- 41-1-1 財務諸表　●41-1-2 貸借対照表　●41-1-3 損益計算書
- 41-1-4 キャッシュフロー計算書　●41-1-5 収益性指標　●41-1-6 安全性指標
- 41-1-7 効率性指標・その他

- 41-2 決算の表現 239
  - ●41-2-1 決算報告の各種表現　●41-2-2 用語

42. 大きさ・重さ　　241

42-1 長さ 241
42-2 幅 241
42-3 奥行き 242
42-4 深さ 242
42-5 高さ 243
42-6 縦・横・高さ 244
- ●42-6-1 二次元　●42-6-2 三次元
42-7 厚さ 245
42-8 面積 245
42-9 体積・容積 246
42-10 重さと質量 246

43. 身体計測　　248
- ●43-1 身長　●43-2 体重　●43-3 胸囲　●43-4 ウエスト　●43-5 ヒップ
- ●43-6 スリーサイズ　●43-7 股下　●43-8 指を表わす番号

44. 服のサイズ　　253

44-1 靴のサイズ 253
- ●44-1-1 日本　●44-1-2 ISO9407　●44-1-3 ヨーロッパ　●44-1-4 イギリス
- ●44-1-5 アメリカ　●44-1-6 関連表現
44-2 ブラジャーのサイズ 254
- ●44-2-1 日本　●44-2-2 英米
44-3 婦人服のサイズ 255
- ●44-3-1 日本　●44-3-2 欧米　●44-3-3 関連表現

45. 温度・気象・地震　　258

45-1 温度 258
- ●45-1-1 温度の単位　●45-1-2 温度の表現　●45-1-3 気温　●45-1-4 体温
45-2 気圧 262
45-3 湿度 262
45-4 降水・積雪 262
45-5 風速 263
45-6 震度とマグニチュード 264
- ●45-6-1 震度　●45-6-2 マグニチュード　●45-6-3 耐震強度

46. 住所と電話番号　　　　　　　　　　　　　　　　　　　　　　　　267
46-1 住所 267
46-2 郵便番号 267
46-3 住居 268
46-4 電話番号 269
- ●46-4-1 電話番号の読み方　●46-4-2 局番　●46-4-3 海外向けの番号表記
- ●46-4-4 アメリカの特殊な電話番号　●46-4-5 電話の関連表現

47. 学校　　　　　　　　　　　　　　　　　　　　　　　　　　　　　　　273
- ●47-1 学年　●47-2 …年生　●47-3 学級　●47-4 学期

48. 法律・条約　　　　　　　　　　　　　　　　　　　　　　　　　　　276
- ●48-1 法令番号　●48-2 条項　●48-3 articleとsection　●48-4 条[節]・項・号
- ●48-5 枝番　●48-6 訳例

49. 野球の数字表現　　　　　　　　　　　　　　　　　　　　　　　　280
- ●49-1 回／イニング　●49-2 延長　●49-3 ゲーム差　●49-4 点　●49-5 点差
- ●49-6 打順　●49-7 カウント　●49-8 アウト　●49-9 三振・三者凡退
- ●49-10 四球　●49-11 塁　●49-12 打率　●49-13 打数・安打　●49-14 打点
- ●49-15 防御率　●49-16 記録　●49-17 背番号　●49-18 守備位置

50. その他の競技・勝敗の数字表現　　　　　　　　　　　　　　　　292
50-1 勝敗 292
- ●50-1-1 …勝…敗　●50-1-2 連勝・連敗

50-2 サッカー 293
50-3 ゴルフ 294
- ●50-3-1 ホール　●50-3-2 ハンデ　●50-3-3 その他

50-4 トランプ 296

51. 電池・テレビ　　　　　　　　　　　　　　　　　　　　　　　　　297
- ●51-1 電池　●51-2 バッテリー・充電・放電　●51-3 テレビ・ディスプレイ
- ●51-4 チャンネル　●51-5 録画　●51-6 その他

52. 小数　　　　　　　　　　　　　　　　　　　　　　　　　　　　　　300
- ●52-1 小数の読み方　●52-2 小数点vs.コンマ　●52-3 小数点と複数形
- ●52-4 小数と分数　●52-5 各種表現

53. 分数　　　　　　　　　　　　　　　　　　　　　　　　　　　　　　302
- ●53-1 基本　●53-2 分数の読み方　●53-3 「…分の…拍子」の言い方
- ●53-4 ハイフンの使用　●53-5 分数の用法　●53-6 いろいろな分数
- ●53-7 分母と分子　●53-8 通分　●53-9 約分　●53-10 各種表現
- ●53-11 何分の一

54. 加減乗除   308

54-1 足し算 ... 308
- 54-1-1 足し算 ● 54-1-2 加算 ● 54-1-3 和 ● 54-1-4 術語

54-2 引き算 ... 309
- 54-2-1 引き算 ● 54-2-2 差 ● 54-2-3 術語

54-3 かけ算 ... 310
- 54-3-1 かけ算 ● 54-3-2 積 ● 54-3-3 術語

54-4 割り算 ... 312
- 54-4-1 割り算 ● 54-4-2 商 ● 54-4-3 余り ● 54-4-4 整除

54-5 累乗 ... 314
- 54-5-1 2乗 ● 54-5-2 3乗 ● 54-5-3 …乗 ● 54-5-4 累乗・冪乗 ● 54-5-5 何乗

54-6 累乗根 ... 316
- 54-6-1 平方根 ● 54-6-2 立方根 ● 54-6-3 累乗根 ● 54-6-4 …乗根

55. 式の読み方   317
- 55-1 式の読み方の原則 ● 55-2 大文字と小文字 ● 55-3 添え字
- 55-4 四則演算, 累乗根 ● 55-5 関数 ● 55-6 関係 ● 55-7 応用例
- 55-8 極限・微積分

56. 式の書き方   321
- 56-1 記号と複数形 ● 56-2 変数記号と複数形 ● 56-3 記号と冠詞
- 56-4 所有格と冠詞 ● 56-5 複数行にわたる式 ● 56-6 式と句読点

57. 式変形の英語   324
- 57-1 変数の定義 ● 57-2 式の呈示 ● 57-3 式の導出 ● 57-4 論理
- 57-5 その他文中の式 ● 57-6 懸垂分詞

58. 図形の基本表現   327
- 58-1 基本用語 ● 58-2 …角形 ● 58-3 …面体 ● 58-4 基本的な図形の性質
- 58-5 面積の公式 ● 58-6 体積の公式

59. 方向・向き   333

59-1 左右 ... 333
- 59-1-1 基本 ● 59-1-2 向かって右, 向かって左 ● 59-1-3 上下左右 ● 59-1-4 前後

59-2 縦・横 ... 334

59-3 道順 ... 335
- 59-3-1 基本動作 ● 59-3-2 曲がる ● 59-3-3 位置

59-4 将棋の駒の動き ... 337

59-5 東西南北 ... 337
- 59-5-1 基本方位 ● 59-5-2 基本例

59-6 内外 ... 339

59-7 各分野での方向・向きの表現 339
- 59-7-1 日常   ●59-7-2 乗り物・機械   ●59-7-3 物理   ●59-7-4 医学
- 59-7-5 舞台

60. 有名な科学の法則　344
- 60-1 ニュートンの運動の法則 Newton's laws of motion
- 60-2 万有引力の法則 the law of gravitation
- 60-3 ケプラーの法則 Kepler's laws   ●60-4 電荷の法則 the law of charges
- 60-5 フックの法則 Hooke's law   ●60-6 熱力学の法則
- 60-7 メンデルの法則 Mendel's laws   ●60-8 ボイルの法則 Boyle's law
- 60-9 シャルルの法則 Charles' law
- 60-10 気体反応の法則 the law of combining volumes

61. ギリシア語／ラテン語系の数を表わす接頭辞　347
61-1 基本的な数を表わす接頭辞 347
61-2 化合物名の倍数接頭辞 348
61-3 重複を表わす倍数接頭辞 349
61-4 新元素名 350
61-5 数字を造語要素として含む単語のいろいろ 351
- 61-5-1 …年ごとの   ●61-5-2 …周年   ●61-5-3 …角形   ●61-5-4 …面体
- 61-5-5 …次   ●61-5-6 …つ子   ●61-5-7 重奏、…重唱   ●61-5-8 …倍
- 61-5-9 重項   ●61-5-10 …重極、…極子   ●61-5-11 …個組   ●61-5-12 …進法
- 61-5-13 経妊婦   ●61-5-14 同姓同名の区別   ●61-5-15 …折判
- 61-5-16 法律・規格文書の枝番   ●61-5-17 トランプやさいころ   ●61-5-18 その他

61-6 付録：各国語の数詞 355

62. 数の一致　357
- 単数語形なのに複数扱いする名詞（集合名詞）
- the + 形容詞の形の集合名詞   ●単複両様の扱いがある集合名詞
- 複数語形なのに単数扱いするもの   ●グループ名について
- 通例複数形でのみ使うもの（絶対複数）   ●単数形と複数形がまぎらわしいもの

63. 不定代名詞と単数／複数　362
63-1 数詞 362
63-2 all 362
- 63-2-1 形容詞のall   ●63-2-2 代名詞のall   ●63-2-3 副詞のall

63-3 each 363
- 63-3-1 形容詞のeach   ●63-3-2 代名詞のeach   ●63-3-3 副詞のeach

63-4 either / neither 363
- 63-4-1 形容詞のeither / neither   ●63-4-2 代名詞のeither / neither
- 63-4-3 副詞のeither / neither

63-5 both 364
- ●63-5-1 形容詞のboth　●63-5-2 代名詞のboth　●63-5-3 副詞のboth

63-6 every 364

63-7 everybody / everything / everyone / anybody / anything / anyone / nobody / nothing / no one 365

63-8 any 365
- ●63-8-1 形容詞のany　●63-8-2 代名詞のany

63-9 none 366

63-10 no 366

63-11 most of 〜 / half of 〜 / part of 〜 / the rest of 〜 367

63-12 anotherとother 367
- ●63-12-1 形容詞のanotherとother　●63-12-2 代名詞のanotherとother

63-13 「それぞれ」の用法 368

64. 各種構文と単数／複数　370
- ●64-1 修飾句　●64-2 A and B　●64-3 A as well as B
- ●64-4 A or B / either A or B / neither A nor B　●64-5 one or more
- ●64-6 at least one　●64-7 more than one
- ●64-8 half of … / more than half of …　●64-9 one of + 複数名詞
- ●64-10 a + 名詞 + of + 複数名詞　●64-11 複数名詞 + of + 単数名詞
- ●64-12 仮定法

第2部 和 英 編　375

本書の見方

本書が使用する主な記号類

- 　　　用例を示す.

[　]　　語句の言い換えを示す.
　　　　英訳中で [　] を用いるときは，後述する場合を除き，[　] 内の語句と置き換え可能な語句（語が複数のときは最初の語）の左肩に「という記号を付し，言い換えの対象範囲が明確になるようにした.
　　　　　1 巻のテープ　a ⌈reel [spool] of tape
　　　　　1 個の石鹸　a ⌈cake [bar, piece] of soap
　　　　すぐ上は cake の言い換えとして bar と piece の 2 語があることを示している.
　　　　　1 切れ [1 本] のテープ　a ⌈piece [roll] of tape
　　　　この場合は日本語の言い換えに対応する形で roll の語を示している.
　　　　次のケースでは「の記号は用いていない.
　　　　ⅰ) 言い換えの対象範囲が訳の最初からであるとき.
　　　　　　物価の上昇　① a rise [an increase] in prices　② a price ⌈rise [increase] …
　　　　ⅱ) 同一訳中に [　] を複数含む場合で，後の [　] の対象範囲がその前の [　] の直後からであるとき.
　　　　　　5 歳以下の小児　① children of five years ⌈and [or] under [younger] …
　　　　ⅲ) ハイフンで結ばれた語の前部要素または後部要素どうしの言い換え.

(　)　　省略可能な部分を表わす.
　　　　　3 位に落ちる　① drop to (the) third place　② slip into third(-ranking) place
　　　　補足の説明に用いた場合もある.
　　　　　…も　（中略）③（距離）as far as …　④（長さ）as long as …

〔 　〕　　語義などを示す.

〈 　〉　　〈人が主語〉のように英訳の用法を示す.

《 　》　　下記のスピーチラベル以外に，次の 2 つの用途に用いる.
　　　　ⅰ) 訳の英語のコロケーションを例示する.
　　　　　　低下する　…　⑥ go down 《in price》 …
　　　　　　低下させる　…　③ make [let] 《prices》 fall　④ bring down 《prices》 …
　　　　上から順に訳の動詞（句）が従える前置詞句，目的語の例.

　　　　　　ii) 補足の説明.
　　　　　　　《物価などの》上昇を抑える　curb an increase

《米》　「米国英語［語法］(では)」の意.
　　　　　hundred の後の and は《米》ではしばしば省かれる.
　　　　　1 本のズボン　a pair of「trousers [《米》pants]」

《英》　「英国英語［語法］(では)」の意.

《口》　口語

《文》　文語

⇨　　　後に参照先を示す.
　　　　《　》内で発想指示に用いる場合もある.
　　　　　100 メートルを 10 秒台で走る　①《⇨ 11 秒未満》run the hundred meters in 「less than [under] 11 seconds」②《⇨ 10 秒 + α》run the hundred meters in ten something

=　　　後に同義の参照先を示す.

one など　人を指す語・代名詞が入る可変部分を表わす.
　　　　　票を読む　① estimate the number of votes *one* could get …
　　　　　得票数　① the number of votes「obtained [cast for *one*]」② *one's* poll
　　　　　対立候補との得票差　the difference between votes cast for *one*self and for *one's* rival candidate
　　　　上から順に主格, 目的格, 所有格, 再帰代名詞を表わす.

do　　　動詞が入る可変部分を表わす.

〖　〗　　当該語句が使用される分野を示す. 下は分野名を表わす略語の例.
　　　　〖数〗(数学), 〖物〗(物理学), 〖化〗(化学), 〖生物〗(生物学), 〖生態〗(生態学), 〖天〗(天文学), 〖医〗(医学), 〖機〗(機械工学), 〖結晶〗(結晶学), 〖法〗(法学), 〖電算〗(電算［コンピューター］用語), 〖文法〗(文法用語)

第 2 部　和英編での見出しの配列について

　五十音順で濁音・半濁音は清音の後に置く. 同音語のうち接辞の類は後回しにした (接辞類どうしでは前に付くもの, 後に付くものの順).
　　　かいせき【解析】, がいせき【外積】
　　　きょう【今日】, …きょう【…強】, ぎょう【行】

じゅん【順】，じゅん…【純…】

だい…【第…】，…だい【…大】

拗音など小さく書かれる字は直音の後に置く．

ひよう【費用】，ひょう【表】

表記が同一の語については，【　】の中に示した漢字表記の字数，字数が同じ場合は頭字の画数，のそれぞれ少ない順となっている．

にち【日】，にち【二値】

…かい【…回】，…かい【…階】

かいしゅうごう【開集合】，かいしゅうごう【解集合】

長音符（ー）を含む語は長音符を直前のカナの母音に読み替えて置き場所を決定した．

こえる【超える】，コード，ごかくけい【五角形】

「コード」は「コオド」と読み替えられて「こえる」と「ごかくけい」の間に来る．

第 **1** 部

トピック別編

1. 基数

■ 1-1 0〜99

0 zero	15 fifteen	30 thirty
1 one	16 sixteen	31 thirty-one
2 two	17 seventeen	32 thirty-two
3 three	18 eighteen	⋮
4 four	19 nineteen	
5 five	20 twenty	40 forty
6 six	21 twenty-one	50 fifty
7 seven	22 twenty-two	60 sixty
8 eight	23 twenty-three	70 seventy
9 nine	24 twenty-four	80 eighty
10 ten	25 twenty-five	90 ninety
11 eleven	26 twenty-six	⋮
12 twelve	27 twenty-seven	
13 thirteen	28 twenty-eight	
14 fourteen	29 twenty-nine	99 ninety-nine

1-1-1 「十五」と「五十」

fifteen (15) と fifty (50), sixteen (16) と sixty (60) などの発音は日本人はよく聞き間違えるので注意が必要である．fiftéen は後にアクセントがあり，fífty は前にアクセントがあるのが原則ではあるが，実際には fífteen のアクセントもめずらしくない．アクセントよりもむしろ，fifteen の場合には -ee- も鼻から空気を出して鼻母音で発音することが重要で，この鼻母音がないと英米人に正しく聞き取ってもらえないことがある．逆にこのような発音上の違いを頭に置いておくと聞き取りの間違いも減らすことができる．ほかに twenty の -en- もよく一つの鼻母音として発音される．

1-1-2 fourteen と forty

forty (40) は fourteen (14) と違って綴りに u がないことに注意．

■ 1-2 100以上の数

100	one hundred
101	one hundred (and) one
102	one hundred (and) two
110	one hundred (and) ten
111	one hundred (and) eleven
120	one hundred (and) twenty
121	one hundred (and) twenty-one
200	two hundred
300	three hundred
400	four hundred
999	nine hundred (and) ninety-nine
1,000	one thousand
2,000	two thousand
10,000	ten thousand
16,000	sixteen thousand
100,000	one hundred thousand
1,000,000	one million
2,000,000	two million

▶ 口語では 100 は one hundred より a hundred と読むことが多い．one thousand, one million についても同様．

- 26,751,987
  twenty-six million, seven hundred and fifty-one thousand, nine hundred and eighty-seven
- 5 万人　fifty thousand people
- 26 万語　two hundred and sixty thousand words
- 123 万円　①one million two hundred and thirty thousand yen ②¥1.23 million　★one point two three million yen と読む．
- 1,678 万色　sixteen million seven hundred and eighty thousand colors
- 1 億 3 千万人　one hundred and thirty million people

関連項目 ⇨ 7. 大きな数

1-2-1 -s の有無

two hundred (200), two thousand (2000), two million (200万) などというときに -s がつかないことに注意．several hundred, a few hundred（数百）なども普通は -s をつけない．million については以前は -s がつくこともあったが，現在では two millions などは古風とされる．hundreds of …（何百もの…）などの表現では -s がつく（⇨ 8. 漠然とした大きな数）．

1-2-2 and の使用

hundred の後の and は《米》ではしばしば省かれる．ただし，口頭では《米》でも and を入れることが多い．

thousand の後には and をつけないが，100 の位が 0 のときは and を入れる．これも《米》では略されることが多い．

- 2,624　two thousand six hundred (and) twenty-four
- 2,024　two thousand (and) twenty-four
- 2,004　two thousand (and) four

1-2-3 3桁，4桁の数の読み方 [⇨ 6. 数字の読み方]

3 桁の数に hundred を使わないことがしばしばある．

- 789　seven eighty-nine
- 904　nine-oh-four

4 桁の数は thousand を使わずに 2 桁ごとに区切っていうことがしばしばある．

- 1,234　twelve (hundred (and)) thirty-four
- 1,600　sixteen hundred

1-2-4 コンマの使用

4 桁以上の数字は 3 桁ずつコンマで区切る（例：12,300）．ただし，年号・ページ番号・番地などではコンマは用いない．また，科学技術分野では 4 桁の場合はしばしばコンマは省かれる．

イギリス以外のヨーロッパ諸国ではコンマと小数点が英語と逆なので（⇨ 52. 小数）桁区切りにコンマもピリオドも使わず，空白（通常の語間スペースの半分）を空けることが推奨されることもある．コンマでなく空白を使うことには小数点以下の桁にも使えるという利点がある．

1-2-5 数の区切り

英語で数の 3 桁ごとにコンマを打つのは英語の数の数え方における thousand や million という単位に合わせたもので，表やグラフで大きな数を扱うときにも千や百万を単位とする．日本語では英語式に千や百万を単位とすることもあるが，万や億を単位とすることも多い．そうした文書を英語に直すときには単位も英語式に直すのがよい．なお，単位の表示は英語では次のように 1 を付けないこともある．

- 単位: 千円　① units: ¥1,000　② units: ¥000　③ units: ¥000s
- 単位: 千人　① units: 1,000　② units: 000　③ units: 000s

［⇨第 2 部・たんい］

1-2-6 数詞が複合形容詞をつくる場合

two, three などの数詞がついていても次のように形容詞句をつくる場合には名詞は複数形にせず単数形となる．

- a two-column layout　2 段組レイアウト
- a three-part series　3 作シリーズ
- a three-gun turret　3 連装砲塔
- a four-component spinor　4 成分スピノル
- a five-year plan　5 か年計画
- a six-digit number　6 桁の数
- an eight-bit byte　8 ビットのバイト
- a 20-cent stamp　20 セント切手
- a 40-watt bulb　40 ワットの電球

ただし，通常複数形でしか使わない名詞や複雑な名詞句については複数形になる場合もある．

- a two-pants suit　ツーパンツスーツ
- a three-bottles-of-wine-for-$20 sale　20 ドルでボトル 3 本のワインが買えるセール

2. 数え方

2-1 基本的な数え方 [⇨第2部・かず]

英語では日本語のように助数詞を使い分けることはなく,「3 冊」「3 頭」などみな three といえばよい.

- 3人の人　① three people　② three persons [⇨第2部・にんずう]
- 3個のナシ　three pears
- 3冊の本　three books
- 3頭の馬　three horses
- 3台の車　three cars
- 3本の鉛筆　three pencils
- 3隻の船　three ships
- 3機の飛行機　three airplanes
- 3枚の葉　three leaves

2-2 不可算名詞の数え方

一方,英語には可算名詞(数えられる名詞)と不可算名詞(数えられない名詞)の区別があり,不可算名詞を数えるには単位となる助数詞が必要になる.日本語の感覚では数えられそうなものが不可算名詞であることもあるので注意が必要である.たとえば紙は英語では不可算名詞とされ,1枚なら a sheet of paper, 2枚なら two sheets of paper のようにいう.同じ paper でも「新聞」「論文」などの意味では可算名詞になるなど,語義によって扱いが異なることもある. glass が「ガラス」なら不可算,「グラス」なら可算となるのも同様である.

- 1枚の紙　a「sheet [piece] of paper
- 1個の荷物　a piece of「baggage [luggage]
- 1台の装置　a piece of equipment
- 1点の家具　a piece of furniture
- 1つのニュース　a piece of news
- 1つの助言　a piece of advice
- 1曲の音楽　a piece of music
- 1本のチョーク　a piece of chalk
- 1枚の(板)チョコレート　a bar of chocolate
- 1個の石鹸　a「cake [bar, piece] of soap
- 1枚のガム　a stick of chewing gum

2. 数え方 2-3

- 1切れのケーキ　a「piece [slice] of cake　★全体 (cake) から切り分けた1片など.
- 1切れのピザ　a「piece [slice] of pizza　★全体 (pizza) から切り分けた1片など.「1枚のピザ」(円形の全体) なら a pizza でよい.
- 1斤のパン　a loaf of bread
- 1枚 [1切れ] のパン　a slice of bread
- 1枚のハム　a slice of ham
- 1本の糸　a piece of string
- 1切れ [1本] のテープ　a「piece [roll] of tape
- 1巻のテープ　a「reel [spool] of tape
- 1本のフィルム　a roll of film

次は容器によって数える例.

- 1杯のコーヒー　a cup of coffee
- 1杯の紅茶　a cup of tea
- 1杯の水　a glass of water
- 1杯のジュース　a glass of juice
- グラス1杯のビール　a glass of beer
- 1缶のビール　a can of beer
- 6本パックのビール　a six-pack of beer
- ボトル1本のワイン　a bottle of wine
- 1箱の牛乳　a carton of milk
- 1杯のご飯　a bowl of rice
- 大さじ1杯の砂糖　a tablespoon of sugar
- 小さじ1杯の砂糖　a teaspoon of sugar
- 1個の角砂糖　a lump of sugar

2-3 数え方に注意を要する可算名詞

可算名詞ではあっても，日本語では1つのものが英語では左右一対ととらえられるものも多い．

- 1本のジーンズ　a pair of jeans
- 1本のズボン　a pair of「trousers [《米》pants]
- 1枚のパンティー　a pair of panties
- 1足のストッキング　a pair of stockings
- 1足の靴下　a pair of socks
- 1足の靴　a pair of shoes

このため数えるときでなくても複数形で言わなければならないので注意が必要である．また，代名詞の one は使えず，pair を使う．

- それは私の靴下だ．　Those are my socks.
- このズボンは合わない．新しいのが欲しい．　These pants don't fit. I want a new pair.　★セーターの場合は普通に This sweater doesn't fit. I want a new one. となる．

左右の一方のみを指すときには単数形が使える．

- 靴下に穴が空いた．　I have a hole in my sock.

衣類以外では次のような例がある．

- 1 丁のはさみ　a pair of scissors
- 1 本の眼鏡　a pair of glasses
- 1 台の双眼鏡　a pair of binoculars

2-4 数値を呈示する各種表現

「数値が…である」という内容を表現するには be 以外にもさまざまな表現がある．

- 犠牲者の数は 113 人だ．
  ① The number of victims was 113.　★犠牲者が出たのは過去のことなので，英語では過去形が普通．
  ② Victims「numbered [totaled] 113.
  ③ There were 113 victims.
  ④ One hundred and thirteen people were killed. [⇨ 5-5 文頭の扱い]
- 駐車している車の数は 60 台に近い．
  ① The number of parked cars is close to 60.
  ② There are close to 60 parked cars.
  ③ The parked cars number nearly 60.
  ④ The parked cars are nearly 60 in number.
- 参加者数は 2015 年には 53 名だった．
  ① The number of participants was 53 in 2015.
  ② The number of participants stood at 53 in 2015.
  ③ There were 53 participants in 2015.
  ④ Fifty-three people participated in 2015.
- 鉄の融点は 1538°C だ．
  ① The melting point of iron is 1538°C.
  ② Iron has a melting point of 1538°C.
  ③ Iron melts at 1538°C.
- コストは数億円だ．
  ① The cost is several hundred million yen.
  ② The cost amounts to several hundred million yen.

③ The cost ⌈runs [comes, adds up]⌋ to several hundred million yen.
④《The project》costs several hundred million yen.
- その船の長さは 256 メートルだ．
  ① The length of the ship is 256 meters.
  ② The ship is 256 meters ⌈long [in length]⌋.
  ③ The ship measures 256 meters in length.
- 日本では女性研究者の比率は 14% でしかない．
  ① The ratio of women among Japanese researchers is only 14 percent.
  ② Women account for a mere 14 percent of researchers in Japan.
  ③ Only 14 percent of researchers in Japan are women.
- 落札率が 90% を超えていた．〔落札額が予定価格の 90% 超〕The winning bid price was above 90% of the bid ceiling.

3. ローマ数字

1	I	**11**	XI	**21**	XXI	**100**	C
2	II	**12**	XII	**22**	XXII	**200**	CC
3	III	**13**	XIII	⋮		**300**	CCC
4	IV	**14**	XIV	**30**	XXX	**400**	CD
5	V	**15**	XV	**40**	XL	**500**	D
6	VI	**16**	XVI	**50**	L	**600**	DC
7	VII	**17**	XVII	**60**	LX	⋮	
8	VIII	**18**	XVIII	**70**	LXX	**900**	CM
9	IX	**19**	XIX	**80**	LXXX	**1,000**	M
10	X	**20**	XX	**90**	XC	**2,000**	MM

- CI   101
- MCMLXXXVI   1986
- MMXVII   2017

　ローマ数字の C (100) や M (1000) が century (1 世紀 = 100 年) や milli- (ミリ = 1000 分の 1) との関連をうかがわせるのに対し，L (50) や D (500) は不規則に見える．実は L や D はもちろん，C や M も含めてローマ数字はラテン語に由来するわけではなく，本来アルファベットとは関係なかった記号が起源となっている．L(50) – C(100) – D(500) – M(1000) の順番は Lucy Can't Drink Milk. という覚え方がある．

> **トリビア** 時計の文字盤の IIII
>
> 　ローマ数字の 4 は時計の文字盤などではしばしば IV ではなく IIII となっている．この由来についてはどこそこの王様が決めたというまことしやかな伝説もいろいろ伝わっているが，実は IV (4) とか XC (90) のように引き算をする方式が導入されたのはルネサンス時代であり，むしろ IIII のほうが歴史が古い．

3-1 ローマ数字を使うさまざまな場合

ローマ数字は時計の文字盤や銘文の年号表示のデザインに見られるほか，次のようなときに用いられる．

君主

- Elizabeth II　エリザベス2世　★Elizabeth the second と読む

なお豪華客船 Queen Elizabeth 2 の 2 は Queen Elizabeth（イギリスのエリザベス女王の母でジョージ6世の王妃だった Elizabeth にちなむ）の後継であることを表わし，two と読む．

続編

- The Godfather: Part II　ゴッドファーザー PART II
- Back to the Future Part II　バック・トゥ・ザ・フューチャー PART 2
- Superman II　スーパーマン 2—冒険編
- Men in Black II　メン・イン・ブラック 2
- Rocky V　ロッキー 5／最後のドラマ

書物の前付け

目次や凡例といった前付けの部分はしばしば本文からは独立して，ローマ数字の小文字のページ番号が割り当てられる．

箇条書き

項目の番号付けに使われることがある．スタイルは I I. i (i) i) などさまざまである．

聖書の章，劇の幕，雑誌の巻

- *Luke* VIII 14　『ルカ伝』第 8 章 14 節　★Luke 8:14 と書くことも多い．Luke, chapter eight, verse fourteen などと読む．
- *Hamlet*, III, i　『ハムレット』第 3 幕第 1 場（Act III Scene 1）
- *Scientific American*, LXXX, 12　『サイエンティフィック・アメリカン』第 80 巻第 12 号　★vol. 80, No. 12 のようにアラビア数字を使うことも多い．
▶ 学術誌で巻を通したページ番号がある場合には号数なしに直接ページ数（アラビア数字）を示すことが多い．

その他

- World War II　第二次大戦
▶ World War two と読み，無冠詞．the Second World War というときには the がつく．

3. ローマ数字 3-2

> **トリビア** George III は「ジョージ・パート3」?
> 　イギリスの劇作家アラン・ベネット（Alan Bennett）の戯曲に The Madness of George III という作品があるが，これは映画版では The Madness of King George となった（邦題は『英国万歳!』）．原作者によるとこれは商売上の都合で，The Madness of George III というタイトルではアメリカの観客が The Madness of George と The Madness of George II を見ていないといって敬遠するかもしれないと指摘されて改名したのだという．もちろん George III はイギリス国王ジョージ3世の意味なのであるが，ローマ数字が「パート3」の意味ととられることを心配したのである．

3-2　ローマ数字の字体

　日本語ではⅢⅧⅨのようにローマ数字の横線を続けて書くことがよくある．一方，英米ではかつての碑文などにはそのような例もあるが，現在の印刷物やパソコン文書では I, V, X を別々に書く．また，日本語の文字コードにはローマ数字用の特別のコードがあるが，これは機種依存文字といわれるもので，文字化けの原因になるので注意が必要である．ましてや日本語未対応のパソコンでは表示できないので，英語では「II」のように普通のアルファベットの I, V, X を使って書く必要がある．

4. 序数

1st	first	21st	twenty-first
2nd	second	22nd	twenty-second
3rd	third	23rd	twenty-third
4th	fourth	⋮	
5th	fifth	29th	twenty-ninth
6th	sixth	30th	thirtieth
7th	seventh	31st	thirty-first
8th	eighth	⋮	
9th	ninth	40th	fortieth
10th	tenth	50th	fiftieth
11th	eleventh	60th	sixtieth
12th	twelfth	70th	seventieth
13th	thirteenth	80th	eightieth
14th	fourteenth	90th	ninetieth
15th	fifteenth	100th	(one) hundredth
16th	sixteenth	101st	(one) hundred (and) first
17th	seventeenth	200th	two hundredth
18th	eighteenth	1,000th	(one) thousandth
19th	nineteenth	2,000th	two thousandth
20th	twentieth	10,000th	ten thousandth
		16,000th	sixteen thousandth
		100,000th	(one) hundred thousandth
		1,000,000th	(one) millionth
		2,000,000th	two millionth

4-1 表記上の注意

nine [nain] (9の) と ninth [nainθ] (第9の) は綴りの上では wide [waid] (幅広い) と width [widθ] (幅) と同じ関係だが，短母音化は起こらないので注意．five → fifth, eight → eighth の綴りも変則的になっている．

1の位が1, 2, 3の場合はアラビア数字を使う場合に 21st, 22nd, 23rd のようになる．21th, 22th, 23th は誤り．

4. 序数 4-2

4-2 the first と a first

すでに序列が決まっているものについて「…位」「第…」というときは定冠詞 the がつくが,「ある第…の」というときには不定冠詞 a がつく.

- 恒久的な月面基地は火星への有人飛行の**第一歩**となりうる. A permanent base on the Moon could be **a first step** toward a manned mission to Mars.
- 有名なその二人の科学者に加えて実は**第三の人物**がその発見に重要な役割を果たした. In addition to those two celebrated scientists, **a third person** played an important role in the discovery.
- 第1の信号と第2の信号にそれぞれ**ある第3の信号**が乗算される. The first and the second signals are each multiplied by **a third signal**.

関連項目⇨ 15. 順位・順番の表現

5. アラビア数字で書くかスペルアウトするか

　数字をアラビア数字で書くか単語として綴りで書くかは微妙な問題で，どちらでも誤りではないものの，一定の方針を定めておくことが望ましい．いくつかの判断基準がある．

5-1 桁数が多ければ数字に

- ▶3桁以上の数は数字にする．
- ▶2桁は科学技術分野では数字が，新聞などでは綴りが好まれる．
- ▶1桁は綴りが好まれる．
- ▶いくつかの数が続けて出てくるときには上記の基準で1つでも数字で書くものがあればみな数字で統一する．
  - A cube has 6 faces, 12 sides, and 8 vertices.　立方体は6つの面，12の辺，8つの頂点をもつ．
- ▶同じカテゴリーでない数は統一する必要はない．上の例文の直前にThere are only five regular polyhedrons.（正多面体は5つしかない）のような文があっても five は綴りのままでよい．
- ▶百万以上できりのいい数の場合，特に概数であれば，末位まで数字で書いて 13,000,000 とするよりも，thirteen million または 13 million が好まれる．thirteen とするか 13 とするかは上記の2桁の数の基準に準じればよい．

5-2 続き番号は数字に

- on page 3　3ページに　★前付けにはローマ数字の小文字を使うことが多い．⇨ 3. ローマ数字
- device 15　装置15
- (No.) 36 Craven Street　クレーヴン通り36番

5-3 単位付きの数値の場合

- ▶単位が記号なら数は数字にする．
- ▶単位を記号にするかスペルアウトするかが決まっていない場合には twelve meters, 12 meters, 12 m の形が考えられる（twelve m の形はよくない）．

- ▶ 単位がスペルアウトされていても科学技術分野では数字が好まれる傾向がある．百分率や a 40-watt bulb（40 ワットの電球），200 volts（200 ボルト）などやや専門的な感じの数値や数値の換算を表現するような場合には日常的な文脈で単位がスペルアウトされていても数字が好まれる．

5-4　出現環境による使い分け

- ▶ 数値がたくさん出てくる文章では数字にしたほうが読みやすい．
- ▶ 次に数字で始まる語がくるときはその前の数字はスペルアウトする（3 桁以上の数字にはこれを適用しないこともある）．
  - fifteen 3-meter telescopes　15 台の 3 メートル望遠鏡
  - twenty 60-cent stamps　60 セント切手 20 枚
  - eight 32-bit registers　8 つの 32 ビットレジスタ
- ▶ 組み合わせによっては逆に前の数を数字で書くほうがいいこともある．
  - 200 sixty-cent stamps　60 セント切手 200 枚

5-5　文頭の扱い

　文頭を数字で始めるのは好ましくないとされ，数字をスペルアウトするか，構文を変えて数字が文中になるようにする．たとえば 159 countries sent delegates to the convention.（159 か国が会議に代表を送った）という文を例にとって書き換えパターンの可能性を以下に示す．

数字をスペルアウトする例：
One hundred and fifty-nine countries sent delegates to the convention.

構文を変える例（数字が大きすぎるなどスペルアウトが好ましくないとき）：

(i) 修飾句を文頭に出す

　　To this convention, 159 countries sent delegates.（この会議には 159 か国が代表を送った）

(ii) 言葉を加える

　　A total of 159 countries sent delegates to the convention.（合計 159 か国が会議に代表を送った）

　　In all, 159 countries sent delegates to the convention.（全部で 159 か国が会議に代表を送った）

　　As many as 159 countries sent delegates to the convention.（159 か国もが会議に代表を送った）

No less than 159 countries sent delegates to the convention.（159 もの国が会議に代表を送った）

(iii) 態を変える

Delegates were sent by 159 countries to the convention.（会議へは 159 か国から代表が送られた）

Delegates from 159 countries were sent to the convention.（159 か国からの代表が会議に送られた）

(iv) 態変換以外の仕方で主語を変える

Delegates from 159 countries met at the convention.（159 か国からの代表が会議に集った）

The number of countries that sent delegates to the convention was 159.（会議に代表を送った国の数は 159 だった）

The convention drew delegates from 159 countries.（会議には 159 か国から代表が集まった）

5-6 単位のスペルアウト

　数値の単位を meter, inch のように綴りで書くか m, in. のように記号や略語で書くかについてもいくつかの判断基準がある．ただし，単位によっては略語が好まれないこともあり，yr. (year), m. (month), wk. (week), t (ton), a. (acre) などは略語を使わず必ずスペルアウトする方針をとることもある．逆に専門的で複雑な単位は記号のほうがわかりやすい．以下は綴りと記号・略語のどちらも使える単位の表記についての判断基準である．

▶ 数値をスペルアウトするときには単位もスペルアウトする（three centimeters を three cm と書くのは美しくない）．

▶ 文頭にきたため数字がスペルアウトされたときには単位もスペルアウトする．

▶ 数値を数字で書くときには科学技術分野では単位も記号にするが（例：256 m），それ以外の分野では単位は綴りが好まれる（例：256 meters）．

▶ every twelve meters（12 メートルごとに），weigh to the nearest kilogram（四捨五入してキログラム単位で測る）のような表現では単位を綴りで書く．

6. 数字の読み方

6-1 基本的な読み方
次の3通りの読み方がある．
(i) 数字として読む．

 789   seven hundred (and) eighty-nine
 1600   one thousand six hundred

(ii) 1桁ずつ読む．シリアル番号，電話番号など特に桁数が多い場合に使われる．

 789   seven eight nine
 1600   one six oh oh

▶ 0 の読み方は《米》では zero, oh, 《英》では zero, nought, nil, nothing がある．

▶ 同じ数字が続くときはしばしば double を使い，たとえば one one の代わりに double one という．

(iii) 3桁，4桁の数字の場合，2桁の単位に区切って読むこともある．

 789   seven eighty-nine
 3461   thirty-four (hundred (and)) sixty-one
 1600   sixteen hundred
 725号室 Rm. 725 / Room 725 room seven twenty-five
 900号室 Rm. 900 / Room 900 room nine hundred
 1217号室 Rm. 1217 / Room 1217 room twelve seventeen
 126条   Art. 126 / Article 126 article one twenty-six

6-2 電話番号の読み方 [⇨ 46-4 電話番号]
03-3288-7711

oh three, three two eight eight, seven seven one one

oh three, three two double eight, double seven double one

▶ 1桁ずつ分けて読むのが基本だが，区分の中に同じ数字があれば eight eight とせずに double を使うことが多い．3288 を three two double eight, 3882 を three double eight two のように読むのである．

▶ oh は zero と読んでもよい．

6-3 ハイフンの読み方

　日本語ではしばしば「-」を「の」と読むが，英語では電話番号の「-」は読まず，間をとるだけである．

　住所の 2-11-3 のような場合はしばしば「-」を dash と読む（⇨ **46-1** 住所）．

6-4 その他

$12 million　　twelve million dollars
¥25 billion　　twenty-five billion yen
36°C　　　　　thirty-six degrees「Celsius［centigrade］

関連項目⇨ **29-2** 年号の読み方，**55.** 式の読み方

7. 大きな数

	《米》	《英》
thousand	10^3	10^3
million	10^6	10^6
billion	10^9	10^{12}
trillion	10^{12}	10^{18}
quadrillion	10^{15}	10^{24}
quintillion	10^{18}	10^{30}
sextillion	10^{21}	10^{36}
septillion	10^{24}	10^{42}
octillion	10^{27}	10^{48}
nonillion	10^{30}	10^{54}
decillion	10^{33}	10^{60}
undecillion	10^{36}	10^{66}
duodecillion	10^{39}	10^{72}
tredecillion	10^{42}	10^{78}
quattuordecillion	10^{45}	10^{84}
quindecillion	10^{48}	10^{90}
sexdecillion	10^{51}	10^{96}
septendecillion	10^{54}	10^{102}
octodecillion	10^{57}	10^{108}
novemdecillion	10^{60}	10^{114}
vigintillion	10^{63}	10^{120}

たとえば 10^{24} は 1 のあとに 0 が 24 個続く数を表わす.

7-1 英米の違い

　billion 以上の数の意味は本来アメリカとイギリスで異なる.《米》では million 以降, 3 桁ずつ増えていく.《英》では million を 2 乗, 3 乗したものが billion, trillion なので 6 桁ずつ増えていく. 10 の指数は, 接頭辞が語源的に表わす数を k として,《米》では $3+3k$,《英》では $6k$ になっている. たとえば octillion の oct- は語源的には 8 を表わしているが,《米》では $3+3\times8=27$ 個,《英》では $6\times8=48$ 個 0 が並ぶ数を表

わす．近年ではイギリスでもアメリカ式が使われることも多い．

- ▶ 金融報道などでは k (thousand), m (million), b, bn (billion), t, tn (trillion) のような略記を使うこともある（k は kilo- より）．たとえば £6.5 m で 650 万ポンド，$5.5 tn で 5.5 兆ドルを表わす．

7-2 戯語

俗語で「膨大な数」の意味で zillion, gazillion, bazillion, squillion といった語もある．

- He is worth **zillions of** dollars.　彼は**何億何兆ドルとも知れない**資産の持ち主だ．

7-3 SI 接頭語

科学技術で使われる単位には mega- (10^6), giga- (10^9) のような米式・英式にとらわれない独自の接頭辞が使われる（⇨ **27-4 SI 接頭語**）．

7-4 日本語の大きな数・小さな数

日本語の大きな数としては，江戸時代の数学書『塵劫記』に下記のように記されているものがある．ただし，『塵劫記』には多くの版があり，命数法に関しても万進でなく万万進としたり，恒河沙以降のみ万万進としたりする版もある．

10^{68}	無量大数	10^{40}	正 (せい)	10^{12}	兆
10^{64}	不可思議	10^{36}	澗 (かん)	10^{8}	億
10^{60}	那由他 (なゆた)	10^{32}	溝 (こう)	10^{4}	万
10^{56}	阿僧祇 (あそうぎ)	10^{28}	穣 (じょう)	10^{3}	千
10^{52}	恒河沙 (ごうがしゃ)	10^{24}	秭 (じょ)	10^{2}	百
10^{48}	極 (ごく)	10^{20}	垓 (がい)	10	十
10^{44}	載 (さい)	10^{16}	京 (けい)	1	一

小さな数は次のようなものがある．

10^{-1}	分 (ぶ)	10^{-5}	忽 (こつ)	10^{-9}	塵 (じん)
10^{-2}	厘 (りん)	10^{-6}	微 (び)	10^{-10}	埃 (あい)
10^{-3}	毛 (もう)	10^{-7}	繊 (せん)		
10^{-4}	糸 (し)	10^{-8}	沙 (しゃ)		

7. 大きな数 7-4

> **トリビア** 大きな数
>
> 1人の人間の細胞の数…数十兆
> 高額紙幣…10兆マルク札（第一次大戦後のドイツ），1垓ペンゲー札（第二次大戦後のハンガリー）
> 世界各国のGDPの合計…77兆ドル
> 銀河系に含まれる恒星数…1000億
> 宇宙の年齢…138億年
> 空気1 cm³ 中の分子の数…2.5×10^{19} = 2500京
> 地球の重さ…6×10^{24} kg = 6秄 kg

8. 漠然とした大きな数

8-1 「何十」など

- 何十（も）の… tens of …
- 何百（も）の… hundreds of …
- 何千（も）の… thousands of …
- 何万（も）の… tens of thousands of …
- 何十万（も）の… hundreds of thousands of …
- 何百万（も）の… millions of …
- 何千万（も）の… tens of millions of …
- 何億（も）の… hundreds of millions of …
- 何十億（も）の… billions of …

「何十」は上記のように tens of … と言えるものの，hundreds of … や thousands of … ほど日常的に使う表現ではない．「何十」には dozens of …，scores of … も可能であるが，dozen は 12，score は 20 の意であるので日本語の「何十」よりも大きい数字を指すこともありうる．tens of thousands（何万）や tens of millions（何千万）などは普通に使うことができる．

また，英語では 1600 を sixteen hundred と表現することがあるので hundreds of…の指すものの数が1000を超えることもある．thousands of … は数万程度まで，millions of … も数千万程度まで含みうる．また，桁にとらわれず漠然と「膨大な数の」の意味でこれらの表現を使うこともある．

▶その他の表現例

- **何十年もの decades of** …
- それは**何百万ドルもかけた**研究プロジェクトだった．It was a **multimillion-dollar** research project.
- **天文学的**数字に達する ① reach an **astronomical**「figure［sum］② run (in)to astronomical「figures［numbers］③ be astronomical
- 彼女は**億に上る**財産を作った．She made a fortune **running into nine figures**.
- その病気に苦しむ患者はすでに**万をもって数える**．Patients suffering from the disease「already **number**［**can** already **be counted**］**in the tens of thousands**.
- **大量の**宿題 《口》**tons of** homework

8-2 「**数十**」など

- 数十の… several [a few] tens of …
- 数百の… several [a few] hundred …
- 数千の… several [a few] thousand …
- 数万の… several [a few] tens of thousands of …
- 数十万の… several [a few] hundred thousand …
- 数百万の… several [a few] million …
- 数千万の… several [a few] tens of millions of …
- 数億の… several [a few] hundred million …
- 数十億の… several [a few] billion …
- デモ行進に加わる者は数千人に達するだろう．① The number of demonstrators will probably be in the thousands. ② There will probably be several thousand demonstrators. ③ Thousands of demonstrators are expected.

日本語でも多さを強調する「何百」に比べると「数百」は控えめなニュアンスがあるが，英語でも上限が不定の hundreds of … に比べると several [a few] hundred … のほうが少ない語感がある．ただし，文脈によっては上の「何百」などで挙げた表現を「数百」などの英訳に使えることもある．

- ▶ several [a few] tens of … も tens of …（⇨ 8-1）と同様あまり使われない．意味的に少しずれるが，several [a few] dozen のほうが一般的である．（例：several dozen eggs, a few dozen eggs）
- ▶ a few は少なさを含意することがあるが，several にはそのような含みはない．
- ▶ 科学では「数十億 K の温度」の代わりに数字を使って「数 10^9 K の温度」といった書き方をすることがある．これは a few 10^9 K (a few ten to the ninth kelvin などと読む；⇨ 55. 式の読み方）でよい．
- ▶「数百分の一」などについては ⇨ 53. 分数 53-10

8-3 「**うん十**」など

- 私も **50 うん歳**になりました． I've turned **fifty-something**.
- **うん十万円**　**some hundreds of thousand** yen
- **うん百万円**のダイヤの指輪　a diamond ring worth **X million** yen
- 彼の年収は**うん千万円**だ． His annual income is **somewhere in the tens of millions of** yen.

英語にも口語で「うん…」に似た次のような表現がある．

- the **umpty-fifth** meeting　**何十五回目の**会議
- After failing **for the umpteenth time**, he eventually gave up.　**何度目かの**失敗でようやくあきらめた．

umpty, umpteen はいずれも多さを強調する表現である．

9. 概数

■ 9-1 「約」「およそ」

- **約** 100 冊の本　① **about** 100 books　② **approximately** 100 books　③ **roughly** 100 books　④ **around** 100 books
- **約** 950°C の温度　a temperature of「**about** [**approximately**] 950°C
- **大ざっぱにいって** 1,000°C の温度　temperatures of **roughly** 1,000°C
- 室温を 20 度**前後**に保つ　keep the room temperature **around** 20°C　★前置詞 around の例
- 数字でいうと**およそ** 75 万ドルです．　In figures, it comes to **around** $750,000.　★この around は副詞

ほかに次のような言い方がある

- 100 **に近い値**　① a value **close to** 100　② a value **near** 100
- **ほぼ** 100 パーセントの　① **nearly** 100 percent　② **almost** 100 percent
- **100 本ほどの柱**　① **some hundred** pillars　② **around 100** pillars
- 100 cm **くらい**　① 100 cm **or thereabout(s)**　② 100 cm **or so**　③ **something like** 100 cm
- 100 cm **くらいだ**　be somewhere「**around** [**near**] 100 cm
- 3 時間**そこそこ**で　in **a matter of** three hours (or so)
- 若干の**前後**はあるとして 100　100, **more or less**
- **きりのいい数値でいうと**　① **in round numbers**　② **in round figures**
- その男は 40 歳**くらい**だった．　He was「**around** [**about**] forty.
- **プラスマイナス** 3 歳くらいの違いはあるとして，その男は 27, 8 歳に見えた．　The man looked 27 or 28, **give or take** about three years.　[⇨第 2 部・プラスマイナス]
- 出席者は当日になって 2, 3 人の**出入り**があるかもしれません．　When the day comes, there may be two or three people **more or less** (than planned).
- 季節によって**多少の出入りはあるが**，販売量は月に 100 ケース程度です．　Sales are about a hundred cases a month, **though they go up or down slightly depending on the season**.

関連項目　⇨第 2 部・…くらい，…ぜんご，…ごろ，…ほど

■ 9-2 「…何」「…数」「…余り」など

「+ 若干の端数」をいうときには次のような表現がある．
① -odd　② -plus　③ -some　④ … and some　⑤ -something　⑥ something over …　⑦ just over …　⑧ a little over …

文脈によっては「…超」を意味する over や more than も使うことができる．

- 50 **何**年前　① fifty-**some** years ago ② fifty-**odd** years ago
- 2 千**何**百万　① twenty-**some** million ② twenty-**odd** million
- 20 年**余り**　① twenty-**odd** years ② twenty-**plus** years
- 1,000 円**余り**　1,000-**odd** yen
- 100 **何**冊かの本　① a hundred **and some** books ② **something over** a hundred books ③ a hundred-**odd** books ④ a hundred-**plus** books
- 1 世紀**余り**にわたって　for **something over** a century
- 1 億円**余り**　**just over** 100 million yen
- この万年筆は 1 万**いくら**で買った．　I paid **something over** ¥10,000 for this fountain pen.
- この会社には関連会社が 40 **いくつ**あります．　This corporation has「forty-**plus** [forty-**odd**, forty-**some**, forty-**something**] related firms.
- 私がこれまでに作曲した曲は 100 **いくつ**です．　Up to now I've composed 「a hundred **and some** [**something over** a hundred, a hundred-**odd**] pieces.
- 50 **何**歳かのときに　① when 《he》 was fifty-**something** ② in 《his》 fifty-**somethingth** year
- 90 歳**余り**の女性　① a woman **over** 90 ② a woman of 90-**plus**
- それは 5 ドル**何セントか**した．　It cost five **something**.
- 4 時**何分か**の列車　① a train at **something after** four ② a four-**something** train
- 10 キロメートル**強**　① **a bit longer than** ten kilometers ② **a little over** ten kilometers
- 人口はその期間に 300 万**強**から 400 万**強**へと増加した．　The population grew from **over** three million to **over** four million during that period.

■ 9-3 「…台」

「…台」は次のような訳し方がある．

(i) 複数形の数詞を使う．「…年代」「…歳代」(⇨ 38-3 …代) というときと同じ表現で，日本語に最も近いが，単位を付けられないので応用範囲は広くない．

(ii) 境目になる値を level や mark で表現する．「突破した」「割った」などの文脈ではこの方法で問題ない．

(iii)「ある値 + a」または「ある値より小さい」と表現する (⇨ 9-2「…何」「…数」「…余り」など)．

(iv) range を使って範囲を示す．

9. 概数 9-3

(v) between を使って値の範囲を明示する．最も芸がないが曖昧さがなく，応用範囲も広い．

(1) 数詞の複数形

- **50 台の数字**　a number **in the fifties**
- **70 台のスコア**　a score **in the seventies**
- 会員数は **7 万人台**だ．　Our membership is「**in the seventy thousands**［**in the 70,000s**］．★下記 (3) の訳例も参照．
- 砂漠の気温は日中の **40 度台**から夜間の氷点下まで幅がある．　Desert temperatures range from **the 40s** during the day to below zero at night.
- 夏は気温が **40 度台**になる．　Summer temperatures reach **the 40s**.
- **50 台前半の数字**　① a figure **in the low fifties**　② a figure **in the**「**first [lower] half of the fifties**
- **50 台なかばの数字**　a figure **in the mid fifties**
- **50 台後半の数字**　① a figure **in the high fifties**　② a figure **in the**「**second [upper] half of the fifties**

★low, high は日本語の「前半」「後半」に正確に対応するものではない．

(2) 境界値に着目する訳例

- **15,000 円台に達する**　① touch［rise to］**the level of 15,000 yen**　② reach [hit] **the 15,000-yen**「**mark [level]**　③ rise above **15,000**　④ rise above **the 15,000 mark**
- **インフレ率は 30 パーセント台に達した**．　The rate of inflation **topped 30%**.
- **平均株価は 13,000 円台を回復した**．　The average stock price index **has**「**recovered [regained] the ¥13,000 level**.
- そのニュースで株価は **1 万円台**に戻って 10,104 となった．　The news brought the stock prices **back above the 10,000 mark** to 10,104.
- **1,000 円台割れする**　fall [drop] below **the thousand yen**「**level [mark]**
- 男子スピードスケート 500 メートルで **35 秒台の壁**を突破する新記録が出た．　The **35-second barrier** has been broken with a record time in the 500-meter men's speed skating event.
- 1 ドル＝**114 円台前半**の円ドル為替相場　a yen-dollar exchange rate in **the lower 114-yen level**　★下記 (4) の類例も参照．

(3) 「…＋a」「…より小さい」「…より大きい」などと訳す例

- **50 台の数字**　① a number **of fifty-something**　② **a fifty-something** number　③ **fifty-something**
- **700 台の数字まである**．　① There are figures **above 700**．② The figures continue **beyond 700**．★どちらの英語も厳密には 700 を含まない．
- **200 メートル台の長さ**　a length of **two hundred and something meters**

9. 概数 9-3

- **1分30秒台**のタイム　a time of **1 minute 30 seconds**「**plus**［**and a fraction, and change**］
- スピードスケートの男子500メートルで**35秒台**を出した．　He did the men's 500-meter speed skating race in **a fraction over 35 seconds**.
- 100メートルを**10秒台で**走る　①《⇨11秒未満》run the hundred meters **in**「**less than**［**under**］**11 seconds** ②《⇨10秒+α》run the hundred meters **in ten something**
- 会員数は**7万人台**だ．　Our membership is **over 70,000**.
- ★厳密には over 70,000 は 8万以上の数も含むが，普通は 8万以上のことにあえて over 70,000 とは言わないので「7万人台」の訳として使うことができる．
- **20万円台**の中古車　《30万円未満》a used car for **less than ¥300,000**
- こんないいホテルに**1万円台**で泊まれるなんて（安いね）．　《⇨2万円未満》① Imagine being able to stay in a hotel as nice as this for **less than twenty thousand yen**. ② **Less than twenty thousand yen** for a hotel as nice as this — what a bargain!

(4) range を使った訳例

- 100メートル**10秒台**で　in **the 10-second range** for the 100 meters
- **40秒台前半**の記録を出す　record a time in **the lower half of the 40-second range**
- コンスタントに**90メートル台**を飛ぶ地力がある．　He has the ability to jump consistently in **the 90-meter range**.
- **39秒台**を記録する　① post a time in **the 39-second range** ②〔ゴールする〕finish in **the 39-second range**
- 為替は**1ドル120円台前半**で推移している．　The yen-dollar exchange rate is fluctuating **around the lower end of the 120-yen range**. ★上記(2)の類例も参照．

(5) between を使って範囲を明示する例

- **夜9時台**の航空便　a flight leaving **between 9 and 10 p.m.**
- **朝8時台**の電車は非常に混む．　**Between 8 and 9 a.m.** the trains are extremely crowded.
- 上位**10番台**のランナー　runners **between tenth and nineteen place**

(6) 以下に「大台」の訳例を挙げておく．境界値に着目する上記(2)と同様に訳せる場合が多い．

- その新聞は発行部数を**300万の大台に乗せた**．　The circulation of the paper has **hit the three million mark**.
- この国の女性の平均寿命は，やがて**90歳の大台に乗る**かもしれない．

The average life span for women in this country might eventually **reach the landmark figure of ninety or over**.

- 株価が…円の**大台乗せ**となった．　Stock prices **rose above the benchmark「level [figure] of** … yen.
- 予算が**1兆円の大台を超えた**．　The budget **topped the 1 trillion yen mark**.
- このままではこの国の人口は早晩**2億の大台を超える**であろう．　If things go on this way, this country's population sooner or later will **pass the 200 million mark**.
- ロンドン市場では円は一時1ドル**120円の大台に乗りました**．　On the London exchange the yen at one point **broke the 120 yen barrier** against the dollar.
- その会社の累積債務は昨年度ついに**5億円の大台を突破した**．　The company's accumulated debt ended up **breaking through the 500 million yen mark** last fiscal year.
- 業績は見る間に悪化し，翌年の売り上げは**10億の大台を割った**．　Business results suddenly worsened, and the following year's sales「**fell [dropped] below the 1 billion mark**.
- 来年は私も（**40 [50, etc.]の）大台**だ．　Next year I'll **be into my「forties [fifties, etc.]**, too.

■ 9-4 「…足らず」

① a little less than …　② a little under …　③ (just) short of …　④ (just) inside of …

- 1,000円**足らずの**金しか持ちあわせがない．　I have with me only **a little under** ¥1,000.
- 1キロ**足らず**　①**just inside** a kilometer　②**a little short of** a kilometer　③**just under** a kilometer
- 半年**足らずで**　in **just under** half a year
- 1時間**足らずで**　in **a little under** an hour
- そこにはひと月**足らず**しかいなかった．　I stayed there for only「**less than [under]** a month.

■ 9-5 「二，三個」 など

orで結ぶのが基本．

- 二，三　**two or three**
- 三，四冊の本　**three or four** books
- 十二，三の少年　①a boy **of twelve or thirteen**　②a boy **twelve or thirteen years old**

- 七,八十人　① seventy or eighty people　② between seventy and eighty people　③ (from) seventy to eighty people
- 百四,五十人　one hundred and forty or fifty people
- 五,六千円　five or six thousand yen
- 一つ二つの誤りが見つかった.　**One or two** errors were found.　★one or two の次にくる名詞は two に合わせて複数形で,動詞もそれに一致する（⇨ 64. 各種構文と単数／複数 64-4）.
- 1日に2時間から4時間　for two to four hours a day
- 1か月から3か月［1か月ないし3か月］の治療ののちに　after one to three months of treatment

「二,三の」「四,五人の」などは「若干数の」を表わす a few, several, 《口》a couple of で代用できる場合もある.

　　関連項目 ⇨ 8. 漠然とした大きな数

■9-6 「数個」「いくつか」

① some　② a few　③ a number of　④ several　⑤《口》a couple of

▶ a number of は「たくさん」の意味にもなるので注意.また,a few は少ないことを含意するが several にはそのような含みはない.

- 何個かのボール　① some balls　② several balls　③ a few balls　④ a number of balls

■9-7 「n個」など

- n個の点　n points
- n番目の　the nth
- n角形　an n-gon
- n進法　the n-ary system
- n次方程式　①an equation of degree n　②an equation of the nth degree
- n項組　an n-tuple

10. 位取りと四捨五入・切り上げ・切り捨て

■ 10-1 **位取り**

- 位取り記数法　positional notation
- 位　① a place　② a position　③ a column
- 1の位　① the ones place　② the units place　★ the ones' place のようにアポストロフィを入れることもある．
- 10の位　the tens place
- 100の位　the hundreds place
- 1000の位　the thousands place
- 10000の位　the ten-thousands place
- ★「小数第…位」については⇨ 52. 小数
- 1の位の数字　① the units digit　② the ones digit　③ the last digit
- 10の位の数字　the tens digit
- 100の位の数字　the hundreds digit
- 1の位が0だ．　① The digit in the units place is 0.　② The units digit is 0.　③ 《The number》 has 0 in the units place.　④ 《The number》 ends in 0.
- 5412の4は100の位にあるので100が4つあることを［400を］表わしている．　Since the 4 in 5412 is in the hundreds place, it「shows there are four hundreds [represents four hundred]．★ four hundred (400) と four hundreds (4つの100) の違いに注意．
- 2199の2は何の位ですか．— 1000の位です．　What is the place value of the 2 in 2199? — It is in the thousands place.　★ 2という数字の値は2000だが place value は桁の値を表わし，この場合1000である．
- 整数は1の位の数が偶数であれば2で割り切れる．　A whole number is divisible by 2 if the「units [last] digit is even．
- 四捨五入して100の位まで求めなさい．
  ① Round (off) to the nearest hundred.
  ② Round to the nearest hundreds place.
- この暗号書では各番号の1の位と10の位は単語のすぐ左に印刷されており，100の位，1000の位，10000の位は列の上部にある．　In this codebook, the units and tens of each number are printed to the left of the word and the hundreds, thousands, and tens of thousands are at the top of the column.

■ 10-2 四捨五入

- **四捨五入する**   **round (off)**
▶ round (off) は「(数値を) きりのいい数 (round number) にする」「丸める」という意味で，普通は日本の四捨五入と同じ操作を意味する．

- **四捨五入して整数にする** [小数第1位を**四捨五入する**，小数点以下を**丸める**]
  ① round (off) 《fractions》 to「whole numbers [integers, units]
  ② round (off) 《3.45》 to the nearest「whole number [integer, unit]

★日本語では捨てる桁を目的語にして「小数第1位を」ということもできるが，英語では残される「きりのいい」部分に着目する．

- **四捨五入して10の位までの数字にする** [1の位を**四捨五入する**]   ① round (off) to the nearest ten ② round (off) to tens ③ round (off) to the nearest multiple of ten

- 10の位を**四捨五入する** [**四捨五入して**100の位までの数字にする]
  ① round (off) to the nearest hundred ② round (off) to hundreds

- 1000の位を**四捨五入する** [**四捨五入して**1万単位にする]   ① round (off) to the nearest ten thousand ② round (off) to ten thousands

- 小数第3位以下を**四捨五入する** [**四捨五入して**小数第2位までにする]
  ① round (off) to two decimal places ② round (off) to the nearest hundredth
  ③ round (off) to hundredths

- **四捨五入して**有効数字3桁まで求める   ① round (off) to three「significant figures [s.f.] ② round (off) to three「digits [places]

- 9.45を小数第2位で**四捨五入する**と9.5になる．   9.45 **rounded** to one decimal place is 9.5.

- 測定値を**四捨五入して**メートル単位にする   round (off) the measurement to the nearest meter

- 1/4インチ未満を**四捨五入する**   round (off) … to the nearest「quarter [1/4] inch ★ ⇨ 28. 伝統単位

- 3.43を**四捨五入して**小数第1位まで求めるときにはまず小数第2位の数字に着目します．その数字が5以上であれば切り上げ，小数第2位の数字が4以下であれば切り捨てます．   When you **round (off)** 3.43 to one decimal place, look at the second digit to the right of the decimal point. You round up if it is 5 or「more [greater] and round down if it is 4 or less.

★測定値をやや多めに出したいときに「三捨四入」，少なめに出したいときに「五捨六入」といった変則的な丸めが行なわれることがあるが，上の表現を応用して説明できる．

- 値は誤差の有効数字と同じ桁まで**四捨五入する**．   The value should be **rounded off** to the same place value as the significant figure in the error.

- 平均は切り捨てではなく**四捨五入**によって小数第1位まで出す．   The average is **rounded (off)** rather than truncated to one decimal place.

- **四捨五入すべき桁**

① 《⇨四捨五入して残される数字の次の数字》 the digit following the one **to be rounded (off) to**
② 《⇨四捨五入して残す数字の次の数字》 the digit next to the one you are **rounding to**
③ 《⇨四捨五入して残す数字の右の数字》 the digit to the right of the one that you are going to **round to**
④ 《⇨残す最後の数字の次の数字》 the digit following the last digit to be kept
⑤ 《⇨落とすべき最初の桁》 the first digit to be dropped

★上の訳例に現われる the digit to be rounded (off) to; the digit you are going to round to; the digit you are rounding to (代名詞 one が digit を表わしている) は「四捨五入してきりのいい数字にして残す桁」を表わす．よって四捨五入すべき桁はその次の数字である．

- 丸め誤差　a rounding error　★英語の rounding error は「小さな相違」の意味で比喩的にも使う．例：Compared to the total cost of the project, the secretary's salary is no more than a rounding error.（プロジェクトの総コストに比べれば秘書の給与などたかが知れている．）

round (off) the second decimal place の意味

英語の round は「きりのいい数にする」という意味なので，上記の英語は「小数第 2 位まで残して小数第 3 位を四捨五入する」の意味になるのが普通．round (off) at the second decimal place は「小数第 2 位を四捨五入する」の意味に使われることもなくはないが，「小数第 2 位まで残す」ことを意味するほうが多い．

> **トリビア　偶数への丸め**
>
> 英語では四捨五入をしばしば nearest（最も近い）を使って表現するが，たとえば 3.5 は 3 からも 4 からも同じだけ離れているので，英語話者にはこのような場合に切り上げになることに釈然としない思いを抱く人もいる．たとえば 4.00 から 4.99 までの 0.01 きざみの 100 個の数が均等に出現するなら 4.00 から 4.49 の 50 個は切り捨て，4.50 から 4.99 までの 50 個は切り上げということでフェアな方法と言えるのであるが，××.5 のような数字が多いデータだと普通に四捨五入すると切り上げが多くなってしまう．この例のような場合，ぴったり××.5 であったら 1 の位が奇数であれば切り上げる（普通の四捨五入と同じ）が，1 の位が偶数だったら切り捨てる（「五捨」）というようにして切り上げと切り捨てが均等に起こるようにすることがある．これは××.5 を丸めた結果が必ず偶数になるので rounding to even（偶数丸め方式，偶数への丸め）と呼ばれている．

■ 10-3 切り上げ

- **切り上げる**　① round up　② round (off) upwards
- 2.1 を**切り上げて** 3 にする　　round 2.1 **up** to 3
- **切り上げて**整数にする　　① **round up** to whole numbers　② **round up** to the nearest「whole number [integer]
- 小数第 2 位を**切り上げる**　　① **round up** to one decimal place　② **round up** to the nearest tenth　★英語では切り上げて残す桁（今の場合は小数第 1 位）に着目する．
- 誤差は**切り上げて**有効数字 1 桁にしなさい．　**Round up** the error to one significant figure.
- 利息の 1 円未満を**切り上げる**　　round up the interest to the nearest yen
- 誤差範囲は通常は絶対誤差の最大値を有効数字 1 桁に**切り上げて**求める．The error range is usually found by **rounding up** the maximum absolute error to 1 significant figure.

■ 10-4 切り捨て

- **切り捨てる**　① omit　② discard　③ drop　④ disregard　⑤ ignore　⑥〔切り捨てにより数値を丸める〕truncate　⑦ round down
- **切り捨て**　① omission　② rounding down　③ truncation
- 端数を**切り捨てる**
  ① **omit [ignore, discard]** fractions
  ② **round** ⟪a number⟫ **down** to the nearest whole number
  ③ **reduce** ⟪a number⟫ to the nearest whole number
★②③では切り捨てて残る桁に着目して whole number で表現している．
- 小数第 3 位以下を**切り捨てる**
  ① **omit** the figures below the second decimal place
  ② **discard [drop, disregard]** all numbers after the second decimal place
  ③ **round down** to two decimal places
  ④ **truncate** to two decimal places
★①②において，below や after はその桁自身は含まないので英語は「小数第 2 位より下」という表現になっている．
- 1 の位を**切り捨てる**　　① **round down** to the nearest ten　② **disregard** units
- 100 円未満の端数は**切り捨てます**．　Any fractional sum (of) less than ¥100 **is disregarded**.
- 小数第 2 位（まで）で**打ち切る**　　truncate … at the second decimal place
- 打切り誤差　　a truncation error

11. 数値範囲の表現

11-1 「…から…まで」など区間を表わす表現

- 50 から 100 までの値　① values **from** 50 **to** 100　② values **from** 50 **through** 100《米用法》　③ values「50 **to** 100 [50-100]　④ values **from** 50 **up to** 100　⑤ values **ranging from** 50 **to** 100　⑥ values **between** 50 **and** 100

★日本語の「50 から 100 まで」と同様，上記の英語表現は両端の数値を含めるのが普通．

次のようにして両端の扱いを明示することもできる．

- 50 **以上** 100 **未満**　values **from** 50 (**inclusive**) **to** 100 (**exclusive**)
- 50 **以上** 100 **以下**　values **from** 50 **to** 100 (**both inclusive**)

日本語では「50 から 100 まで」をしばしば「50～100」のように波ダッシュで表わすが，英語では半角ダッシュ（n dash）を使って 50-100 とする．これは 50 to 100 の代わりの表記であって，読むときも fifty to one hundred と読む．ただし，from 50 to 100 の場合には - を使うのは好ましくない．between 50-100 のように and の代わりに - を使うのもよくない．また，科学技術文書ではマイナス記号とまぎらわしいのでそもそも - の使用が好ましくないとされることもある．

- 10 歳**から** 15 歳**までの**子供　① children **between** the ages of ten **and** fifteen　② children (**ranging**) **from** ten **to** fifteen years of age
- 長さ 150 m **から** 250 m **まで**　① **from** 150 **to** 250 m in length　② **between** 150 **and** 250 m in length　③ 150-250 m in length
- 初任給は 20 万円**から** 25 万円です．
  ① Starting salaries are **between** ¥200,000 **and** ¥250,000.
  ② Starting salaries **range from** ¥200,000 **to** ¥250,000.
- 選挙人の数は最も小さな数州の 3 人**から**カリフォルニア州の 55 人**まで**幅がある．　The number of electors ranges **from** three for the smallest states **to** fifty-five for California.
- 野党の議席数は 350 **から** 400 だった．
  ① The number of opposition members was **between** 350 **and** 400.
  ② The opposition numbered **between** 350 **and** 400.
- 2 万円**から** 3 万円くらいなら出せる．　We can pay (from) about twenty **to** thirty thousand yen.
- 液滴のサイズは体積で 2～25 ピコリットル**程度**だ．　The size of the drop「is [measures] **somewhere between** 2 **and** 25 picoliters in volume.
- **上は** 70 歳**から下は** 15 歳**まで**いろんな人が集まった市民合唱団
  ① a city chorus **ranging** in age **from** seventy (**at the top**) **to** fifteen (**at the**

bottom)
② a municipal chorus including singers **as old as** seventy **and as young as** fifteen

- 1時**から**4時**まで**　**from** one o'clock「**to** [**until**, 《口》 **till**] four
- 祭りは7月10日**から**14日**まで**です．　The festival is **from** July 10 **to** 14.
- 月曜**から**水曜**まで**休みます．　I'll be off **from** Monday「**to** [**until**, 《口》 **till**, 《米》 **through**] Wednesday.

▶ 日本語で「月曜から水曜まで」といえば普通は月曜日と水曜日も含む．英語の from Monday to Wednesday, from Monday through Wednesday も同じである．from Monday until Wednesday の場合には曖昧さが残る．[⇨第2部・…まで]

11-2　between の用法

英語の numbers between 100 and 200 は「100 から 200 までの間の数」，つまり両端を含めた範囲を表わすのが普通．日本語で「100 と 200 の間の数」というと「101 から 199 まで」のように聞こえるので注意が必要である．曖昧さを避けるためには both inclusive などを使うことができる．

- an integer **between** 1 and N　1 **から** N **まで**の整数
- children **between** the ages of ten **and** fifteen　10 歳**から** 15 歳**まで**の子供
- wages **between** $500 **and** $2,000 a week　週給 500 ドル**から** 2,000 ドルの賃金
- years **between** 1980 **and** 1985　1980 年**から** 1985 年**まで**の間
- stations **between** Shinjuku **and** Shibuya　新宿**と**渋谷**の間の**駅　★この場合は両端（新宿と渋谷）は含まない．

また，連続量の場合には必ずしも両端を含むとは限らない．次の例では 1 以上 10 未満が意図されているので厳密に言うとすれば a number 1 or more and less than 10 または a number between 1 (inclusive) and 10 (exclusive) となる．

- 科学的記数法では値は 1 **から** 10 **の間**の数と 10 の冪との積で表わされる．
  In scientific notation, a value is expressed as a number **between** 1 **and** 10 times some power of 10.

11-3　「…以上…以下」

これも「…から…まで」と同様に訳せる．

- A **以上** B **以下**　① **from** A **to** B　② **between** A **and** B　③ **more than or equal to** A **but not more than** B　④ **at least** A **and at most** B　⑤ **neither less than**

11. 数値範囲の表現 11-4

A **nor more than** B ⑥ **no「fewer [less] than** A「**and [but] no more than** B

- スイッチは床面から0.8 m **以上** 1.5 m **以下**の高さに設ける.　　The switch is installed **between** 0.8 **and** 1.5 meters above the floor.
- 《課目の》12 単位**以上** 16 単位**以下**
  ① **no fewer than** 12 **and no more than** 16 units of credit
  ② **at least** 12 **but no more than** 16 units of credit
- 1,000 語**以上** 1,200 語**以下**の小論文を書きなさい.　　Write an essay **no fewer than** 1,000 **and no more than** 1,200 words in length. ★英語では文章の長さを字数でなく語数でいう.

11-4 「…を超えて…まで」

- この収入印紙代は契約金額が100万円**を超えて** 500万円**まで**の場合である.　　This revenue stamp fee is「used [applied, applicable]」when the amount of the contract is **more than** a million yen and **less than or equal to** five million yen.

11-5 「…以上…未満」

- A **以上** B **未満**　① **more than or equal to** A **but less than** B　② **at least** A **but less than** B　③ **no「fewer [less] than** A「**and [but] less than** B
- 従業員数が 50 人**以上** 100 人**未満**の会社　　a company with 50 **or more but fewer than** 100 employees
- 我々は会社を従業員 1,000 人以上の会社,従業員 100 人以上 1,000 人未満の会社,従業員 100 人未満の会社の 3 つのグループに分類した.　　We divided companies into three groups: those with 1,000 or more employees, those with at least 100 but fewer than 1,000 employees, and those with fewer than 100 employees.

12.「以上」「以下」等の表現

■ 12-1 基本

- **…より大きい** ① more than … ② greater than … ③ higher than … ④ larger than … ⑤ above … ⑥ over … ⑦ in excess of …
- **…より小さい（未満）** ① less than … ② fewer than … ③ lower than … ④ smaller than … ⑤ below … ⑥ under …
- **…以上** ①… or [and] more ②… or [and] greater ③… or [and] above ④… or [and] over ⑤… or [and] up ⑥ not less than … ⑦ no fewer than … ⑧ greater than「or [and] equal to … ⑨ equal to「or [and] greater than … ⑩〔少なくとも〕at least … ⑪ at least equal to …
- **…以下** ①…or [and] less ②… or [and] fewer ③ not more than … ④ not exceeding … ⑤ no more than … ⑥ less than「or [and] equal to … ⑦ equal to「or [and] less than … ⑧〔高々〕at most … ⑨〔…まで〕up to …

12-1-1 more than … と「以上」の違い

たとえば英語の more than three は「3 より大きい」であって 3 を含まないことに注意．したがって，「4 以上」は数字を一つずらして more than three と表現することもできる．

英語では「以上」「以下」に直接対応する表現がないが，境界の値を含むかどうかが重要でない文脈では「…より大きい」「…より小さい」に対応する英語を「以上」「以下」の訳に使ってさしつかえない．境界の値を含むことを明確にするには…or more や greater than or equal to … などの表現を使う．

12-1-2 規定を表わす no fewer than …

no fewer than … は「…も」と多さを強調する表現だが，規定を述べた文では「以上」を表わすこともある．同様に，no more than … も「…しか」と少なさを強調する表現だが，「以下」を表わすこともある．（⇨ 20.「…も」「…しか」「たった」20-3）

12-1-3 over の多義性

over は多義なので誤解がないよう気をつける必要がある．たとえば a bridge spanning over 200 meters といった場合に，「200 m 超にまたがる橋」（span は他動詞）の意味と「（ちょうど）200 m にまたがる橋」（span は自動詞）の 2 つの意味に解釈できる．「200 m 超」なら a bridge over

200 meters「long [in length]」あるいは a bridge longer than 200 meters など，「200 m」なら a bridge spanning over a length of 200 meters あるいは a bridge 200 meters long などというほうが明確である．

■ 12-2 「…以上」「…より大きい」

12-2-1 基本

- 100 以上の整数
  ① an integer **greater than or equal to** 100
  ② an integer **equal to or greater than** 100
  ③ an integer **not less than** 100
- 100 ボルト以上の電圧　a voltage of 100 volts **or**「**more**［**higher**］
★純粋な数値の比較には greater を使うが，単位が付く数値に対しては数の多さを表わす more を使う．
- 100 メートルを超える長さ　a length of **more than** 100 meters
- 100 冊を超える本　① **more than** 100 books　② **over** 100 books
- 500 冊以上の本　① 500 books **or more**　② **not less than** 500 books　③ **more than or equal to** 500 books
- 総投票数の 5% 以上の票　a number of votes **equal to or greater than** 5% of the total votes cast
- 100 万ドル超　① **more than** a million dollars　② **over** a million dollars
- 10 kg 以上のプルトニウム　① 10 kg **or more** of plutonium　② **not less than** 10 kg of plutonium　③ **more than or equal to** 10 kg of plutonium
- 500 ギガバイト以上の容量　① a capacity of 500 gigabytes **or more**　② a capacity **more than or equal to** 500 gigabytes
- 1,000°C 以上の温度　① temperatures **higher than** 1,000°C　② temperatures **above** 1,000°C　③ temperatures of **more than** 1,000°C
- 100 万人以上の人口　① a population of **more than** a million　② a population「**greater than**［**larger than**, **over**］a million
- バージョン 2.3 以上　version 2.3 **or**「**above**［**later**, **higher**, **beyond**］
- 5 歳以上の小児
  ① children five years old **and above**
  ② children of five years **and**「**over**［**up**, **upward(s)**］
  ③ children aged five **and**「**over**［**up**, **upward(s)**］
  ④ children (of) five **and**「**over**［**up**, **upward(s)**］
  ⑤ children from five years (old) **and**「**up**［**upward(s)**］
- 5 歳より上の小児　children **above** five (years of age)

12-2-2 量を直接指す場合と間接的に指す場合

- 300 メートル**を超える**高さ　①a height of **more than** 300 meters　②a height of **over** 300 meters
- 300 メートル**を超える**塔　①a tower「**higher**［**taller**］than 300 meters　②a tower **more than** 300 meters in height　③a tower **exceeding** 300 meters in height
- ▶「高さ」の数値に直接言及する場合は more でよいが，高さという属性をもつ「塔」に言及するときは「塔」に合わせて higher や taller を使うのがよい．tower を more than で修飾する場合には in height を付けるとよい．
- 10 トン**を超える**荷重　①a load of **more than** 10 tons　②a load **heavier than** 10 tons
- 500 g **以上の**本　①a book which weighs 500 g **or more**　②a book weighing 500 g **or more**　③a book of weight **equal to or more than** 500 g　④a book **more than or equal to** 500 g in weight
- 重さ 500 g **を超える**本　①a book that weighs **more than** 500 g　②a book that weighs **over** 500 g　③a book weighing **over** 500 g　④a book of **more than** 500 g　⑤a book of **over** 500 g　⑥a book **heavier than** 500 g

12-2-3 「…以上である」

- N は 2 **以上である**．
  ①N **is equal to or greater than** 2.
  ②N **is greater than or equal to** 2.
  ③N **is** 2 **or greater**.
- その幅は 10 cm **以上**でなければならない．
  ①It must **be no less than** 10 cm wide.
  ②It must **be at least** 10 cm wide.

12-2-4 「…が…以上の…」

- メンバーが 10 人**以上の**グループ　a group of 10 **or more** members
- 従業員数が 100 人**以上の**会社　①a company with 100 **or more** employees　②a company that has 100 **or more** employees
- それらの銀行は自己資本比率が8% **以上**であることが求められる．Those banks are required to have a capital adequacy ratio of「8% **or more**［8% **or higher**, **at least** 8%］.

12-2-5 その他

- 売り上げ額は目標を 20% **以上**も上回った．The sales figures were **more than** 20% above the target.

- 牛肉の価格が1週間で2倍**以上**になった． The price of beef **more than** doubled within the space of one week.
- その数が閾値**以上**になったとき… When the number **equals or exceeds** the threshold, ...
- 消費する**以上**に生産する ① produce **at least as much as** 《it》 consumes ② produce **more or as much as** 《it》 consumes
- 1,000億ドル**超**の対米貿易黒字　a $100 billion-**plus** trade surplus with the U.S.

■ 12-3 「…**以下**」「…**より小さい（…未満）**」

12-3-1 基本

- 100**以下**の整数　① an integer **less than or equal to** 100　② an integer **equal to or less than** 100　③ an integer **not more than** 100
- xを超えない最大の整数　the「greatest [largest] integer **not exceeding** x
- 10人**未満**の生徒　① **fewer than** 10 students　② **less than** 10 students
▶ 量ではなく数の場合には less よりも fewer が好まれる．
- 5ミリ**未満**の長さ　a length of **less than** 5 millimeters
▶ 量を表わす単位は可算名詞であっても fewer より less が普通．
- 5センチ**未満**の棒　① a bar **shorter than** 5 centimeters　② a bar **less than** 5 centimeters long　③ a bar **less than** 5 centimeters in length
▶ 「長さ」の数値に直接言及する場合は less でよいが，長さという属性をもつ「棒」に言及するときは「棒」に合わせて shorter を使うのがよい．bar を less than で修飾する場合には long や in length を付けるとよい．
- 厚さ3センチ**未満**の板　① a board **less than** 3 centimeters thick　② a board **thinner than** 3 centimeters
- 100 mg **未満**の青酸カリ　**less than** 100 mg of potassium cyanide
- 500 g **未満**の小包　① a package **lighter than** 500 g　② a package **less than** 500 g in weight
- 4℃**未満**の温度　① temperatures **below** 4℃　② temperatures **lower than** 4℃　③ temperatures **less than** 4℃
- 0℃**以下**　zero degrees and「**below**［**lower**］
- 5歳**未満**の小児　children **under** five (years of age)
- 5歳**以下**の小児
① children of **five years**「**and**［**or**］**under**［**younger**］
② children aged **five**「**and**［**or**］**under**
③ children (of) five「**and**［**or**］**under**

12.「以上」「以下」等の表現 12-3-2

- 従業員の平均年齢が30歳**未満の**会社　① a company in which the average age of the employees is **less than** 30　② a company with employees averaging **under** 30 in age
- 1,000万円**未満の**所得　an income **under** ¥10 million

12-3-2　その他

- 原価**以下**で売る　sell **at or below** cost
- 30秒**未満**で走る　run in **less than** 30 seconds
- 500万円**以下**では売るまい．　He wouldn't sell it **under** five million yen.
- 1,000円**未満**切り捨て．　Omitting **fractions** of ¥1,000.
- 4年生**以下**　fourth graders **and**「**below**［**under**］
- 信号はクリッピング・レベル**以下**だ．　The signal is **at or below** the clipping level.

関連項目⇨第2部・いない

13. 比較・差・増減

■ 13-1 比較の基本

13-1-1 比較級など

- A は B よりも長い． A **is longer than** B.
- A は B と同じくらいの長さである． A **is as long as** B.
- A は B よりも **5 メートル**長い． ① A is **five meters** longer than B. ② A is longer than B **by five meters**.
- A は B よりも**はるかに**長い． ① A is **much** longer than B. ② A is **far** longer than B.
- A は B より**十分**大きい． A is **sufficiently** greater than B.
- A は B より**わずかに**大きい． ① A is **a little** greater than B. ② A is **slightly** greater than B.
- 平均**よりかなり高い**［低い］ well ｢**above** [**below**] the average
- 2 つの値のうち**大きいほう** **the larger** of the two values ★2 つのうちの比較では一つに決まっているので比較級に the が付く．

13-1-2 最上級など ［⇨ 14. 最高と最低］

- これらの値のうちで**最大のもの** **the largest** of these values
- 世界で**最も深い**湖 **the deepest** lake in the world
- この湖はこのへんが**いちばん深い**． This lake is **deepest** around here. ★一つのものの中で「いちばん…」という場合の最上級には普通は the が付かない．
- 直径が最大になるところの断面 the cross-section at which ⟪its⟫ diameter is greatest
- ウエストを**いちばん細い**ところで測る ① measure ⟪a person's⟫ waist where it is **narrowest** ② measure ⟪a person's⟫ waist at its **narrowest** point
- 融点が**最も高い**元素はタングステンだ． The chemical element with **the highest** melting point is tungsten.
- 世界で産油量が**最も多い** 10 か国 the ten **biggest** oil producing countries in the world ［⇨ 15. 順位・順番の表現 15-2-1］
- 青森県は**他のどの都道府県よりも**りんごの生産量が**多い**．
  ① Aomori Prefecture produces **more** apples **than any other** prefecture.
  ② Aomori Prefecture is **the top** producer of apples in Japan.
  ③ Aomori Prefecture produces **the most** apples (among the prefectures) in Japan.
- 米の生産量が**最も多い**県はどこですか．［⇨ 26. 数量に関する疑問文 26-2］

① What is **the biggest** rice producing prefecture?
② Which prefecture produces the「**most** [**greatest amount of**]」rice?

13-1-3　その他の比較表現 [⇨第２部・のぼる, こえる, たっする, わる]

- **上回る**　① exceed　② surpass　③ top　④ be「**more** [**better**]」than　⑤ be in excess of　⑥ be above　⑦ outdo
- 重さが**上回る**　① outweigh　② be heavier than
- 平均を**大きく上回る**年収　an annual income **far above** (the) average
- 損失の総額は 100 万円を**はるかに上回っている**．
  ① The total loss is **far in excess** of a million yen.
  ② The total loss「**far** [**greatly**]」**exceeds** a million yen.
- 輸出額が輸入額を 20 億ドル**上回った**．　Total exports **exceeded** imports by two billion dollars.
- 今月の美術展の入場者数は, 先月を**上回る**勢いだ．　Attendance at this month's art exhibition is on its way to **surpassing** last month's.
- 彼女の新作アルバムは自身の前作を**凌駕する**売り上げを記録した．　Her newly released album has **outstripped** her previous album in sales.
- 売り上げが 1 億円に**達した**．　Sales **reached** a hundred million yen.
- 売り上げがやっと**目標額に達した**．　① At last sales have **reached the target**.　② We have finally hit our sales target.
- **下回る**　①「be「**less** [**lower**]」than　② be [fall] below　③ be [fall] short of　④ be under
- 売り上げが予想額に**届かなかった**．　Sales **fell short of**「expected totals [(*one's*) expectations]」.
- 世界記録には**届かなかった**．　It **didn't reach** the world record.
- 入場者数は予想を**はるかに下回った**．
  ① Attendance was **much lower than** anticipated.
  ② **Far fewer** people came than expected.
- **あとわずかのところで**合格点に**達しなかった**．
  ① His score was **just under** the pass mark.
  ② He **didn't quite reach** the pass mark.
- 死者は 300 人を**下らない**．　**No fewer than** 300 were killed.
- この絵が 500 万円を**下ることはないだろう**．
  ① I **doubt** that this painting would sell for **less than** five million yen.
  ② This painting should be **worth** five million yen **at the very least**.
- 労働組合加入率は 2014 年には男性の 22% に対して女性は 28% だった．
  The proportion of female workers who were in a trade union was 28% in 2014, compared with 22% for male employees.

■ 13-2 差・増減

13-2-1 差 [⇨ 54-2 引き算, 49-5 点差]

- AとBの高さの**差** ① the **difference** in height between A and B ② the height **difference** between A and B
- AとBには**差がある**.   ① **There is a difference** between A and B. ② A **differs** from B. ③ A **is at variance with** B. ④ A and B are「different [not the same].
- 著しい高低**差**がある   there is a considerable **difference** in height《between …》
- 当地は季節による寒暑の**差**が大きい.   ① Seasonal temperature **variation** is quite wide here. ② Temperatures vary widely here by season.
- トップとびりの**差**   the **gap** between the top and bottom「positions [scores, records]
- ある閾値量より大きい幅だけ最高値より小さい
  ① be less than the highest value by more than a threshold amount
  ② be less than the highest value by an amount greater than a threshold amount
  ③ be more than a threshold amount less than the highest value
- **かなりの差で**当選する   be elected **by a**「**wide** [**handsome**] **margin** [⇨ 16-1 票数]
- ゴールでは2位以下に**大きく差を**つけていた.   He had **a big lead** over the other runners at the finish.
- 敵の人数はこちらの**倍以上**だ.   ① The enemy outnumber us **by more than two to one**. ② The enemy have **more than double** our numbers.
- 二人の能力はほとんど差がない.   There is hardly any「difference [disparity] in their ability.

13-2-2 増減の程度 [⇨ 22-1-8 変化率]

- 昨年に比べ**1割の増加**   a gain [an increase] **of 10 percent** over last year
- **3割**増加する [**3割**増になる]   increase (**by**) **30 percent**
- θ が **2π** 増加する. θ increases **by 2π** (**radians**)
- 年に**3%**増加する   ① increase **by 3% per year** ② increase **at** (**the rate of**) **3% per year**
- **5% 減**は驚きではない.   **A decrease of 5%** is not surprising.
- この数字は前年比 15.3 パーセント増だ.   ① This figure is up 15.3 percent from the year before. ② This figure is 15.3 percent higher than in the previous year.
- 売り上げは第4四半期では**5%**増, 通年では**4%**増となった.   Sales increased (**by**) **5%** for the fourth quarter and (**by**) **4%** for the full year.

- **3〜4倍に増加する** ①increase **by a factor of three to four** ②increase **by three to four times**
- **3分の1に減少する** be reduced [fall (off), drop (off), dip] **to one third**
- 人口が**1万人**増加して15万人になった．The population increased **by 10,000** to a total of 150,000.
- 失業率は**0.5ポイント**上がって6.4パーセントになった．The unemployment rate increased **0.5 percentage point** to 6.4 percent.
- 石油価格は**1.2ドル上がって**[**1.2ドル高の**]1バレル当たり64ドルになった．Oil prices increased **$1.20** to $64 a barrel.
- 中国の2015年のGDPの**伸びは6.9%**で2014年の7.3%より下がった．China's GDP **expanded by 6.9 percent** in 2015, less than the 7.3 percent growth in 2014.
- 15%**速い**速度で ①at a 15% **higher** speed ②15% faster
- その会社は今年は23%**多く**採用した．The company hired 23 percent **more** people this year. ★moreは「より多い」の意．
- その会社は**さらに**20人採用した．The company hired 20 **more** people. ★moreは「さらなる」の意．
- **もう**1万円借りる ①borrow 10,000 yen **more** ②borrow **another** 10,000 yen ③borrow **an additional** 10,000 yen
- 大きく変化する ①change greatly ②change by a large amount ③〔質的に〕undergo a「major [sea] change

■ 13-3 比較の基準の表現

- 彼の収入は**去年より**増えている．
  ① His income has increased **over last year**.
  ② His income has increased (**as**) **compared with last year**.
  ③ His income has increased (**as**) **compared to last year**.
  ④ He has「more [a better] income **than he did last year**.
  ⑤ He earns more **than he did last year**.
- **1985年の**3倍の石油を輸入している．They import three times as much oil **as** (**they did**) **in 1985**. ★英語ではas 1985のように比較対象を直接「1985年」とするのは口語などでは使うが，厳密な文章では避けるべきとされる．as in 1985なら問題ない．
- 本年度の収益は**昨年度と比較して**2割減だ．
  ① This year's profits are 20 percent lower **than last year's**.
  ② This year's profits are down 20 percent **from last year's**.
  ③ **Compared with last year**, profits this year are down 20 percent.
- 参加者数は**前回の**半分だった．The number of participants was half (that **of**) last time.
- 彼女の収入は**10年前の倍**だ．

13. 比較・差・増減 13-4

① Her income is **twice as large as it was ten years ago**.
② Her income is **twice what it was ten years ago**.
③ Her income is **twice as large as**「her income [the amount, that]」**ten years ago**.

- 中国の2015年の実質GDPは**前年比**6.9%増で，25年ぶりの低い伸びだった． China's real gross domestic product grew 6.9 percent「**year on year [year over year, on a year-on-year basis, on a year-over-year basis]**」in 2015, the lowest growth in twenty-five years.

- 売り上げは2007年の第1四半期には**2006年の同期比で**5%増加した． Sales grew 5% in the first quarter of 2007「**from [over, (as) compared with, (as) compared to] the same quarter** in 2006.[⇨第2部・どうき]

- 売り上げは相変わらず好調で**昨年同期比で**5パーセント増となった．
① Sales remained brisk and increased (by) 5%「**from [over, (as) compared with, (as) compared to] the same quarter a year ago**.
② Sales remained brisk and increased (by) 5%「**year on year [year over year, on a year-on-year basis, on a year-over-year basis]**」. ★②は「前年の同じ時期に比べて」の意味で，話題にしている売り上げが四半期の売り上げであれば前年同期比の意になる．

- **前期比で** ① on a quarter-on-quarter basis ② quarter on quarter ③ compared to the previous quarter ④ compared to the immediately preceding quarter ⑤ over the previous quarter

- わが社の業績は**前期比で**10ポイント上昇した． Our performance rose 10 points **over the previous period**.

- **4年前の同期に比べて**売り上げは5パーセント増加している． **In comparison with figures for the same quarter four years ago**, sales have increased (by) 5%.

- 売り上げは123億円で，**前年同期比で**5%増であった． Sales were ¥12.3 billion, a 5% increase **compared「with [to] the same quarter of the previous year**.

- 売り上げは123億円で，**前年同期の**119億円**より**増えた． Sales were ¥12.3 billion, up **from** ¥11.9 billion **for the same quarter of the previous year**.

- **2010年の**300万から2015年には200万に減った． 《The figure》declined from 3 million **in 2010** to 2 million in 2015.

- 参加者は**2015年の**560名から増えて780となった． There were 780 participants, up from 560 **in 2015**.

- 会員数は2015年には53名で，**2010年から**10名減った． The number of members stood at 53 in 2015,「**a decrease of 10 [down by 10] from 2010**.

■ 13-4 増加・上昇を表わす各種表現

13-4-1 基本

- 増加[上昇] ① (an) increase ② (a) gain ③ augmentation ④ (a) rise

- 増加する　①increase ②rise ③grow ④swell ⑤multiply ⑥be augmented
- 増加させる　①increase ②raise ③multiply ④augment
- …の温度上昇を引き起こす　①cause the temperature of … to「increase [rise]」②cause「an increase [a rise]」in the temperature of …
- 数が増える　increase in number
- 重さが増す　increase in weight
- 人口の増加　①(an) increase in population ②population growth
- 会員数の増加　①(an) increase in the number of members ②(an) increase in the membership
- 温度の上昇　①(an) increase「in [of]」temperature ②a rise in temperature ③(a) temperature increase ④rising temperatures
- 物価の上昇　①a rise [an increase] in prices ②a price「rise [increase]」③rising prices
- 地価の高騰　①a rise in land prices ②soaring land prices
- 高騰市況　①a rising market ②an appreciating market

13-4-2　急増・急上昇

- 急上昇［急騰］　①a jump ②a「sudden [sharp]」rise ③a surge ④a sharp upswing
- 《数の》急増　a「sudden [rapid]」increase in numbers
- 物価の急騰　a「sudden [sharp]」rise in prices
- 急騰する物価　①booming prices ②soaring prices ③surging prices ④skyrocketing prices
- 最近のドルに対する円の急騰　the yen's recent surge against the dollar
- 一時的急騰　①a spike ②a blowoff
- 急上昇［急騰］する　①jump ②rise suddenly ③shoot up suddenly ④skyrocket ⑤rocket ⑥soar《(to …)》⑦run up sharply ⑧zoom
- 急騰させる　①send … soaring ②send up sharply ③send … sharply higher ④cause … to「rise suddenly [shoot up suddenly, etc.]」
- 600円に急騰する　jump [soar, (sky)rocket] to 600 yen
- その会社の株価は過去1年間で50％の急騰を遂げた．　The company's stock price has soared 50% in the past year.
- 物価がはなはだしく高騰している．　Prices are「rising dramatically [skyrocketing, surging]」.

13-4-3　相関［⇨第2部・…ほど］

- 気体の温度が上がると体積も増す．
  ①As the temperature of a gas increases, so「will [does]」the volume.

13. 比較・差・増減 13-4-3

② Increase in the temperature of a gas 「results in [leads to, causes]」an increase in the volume.
③ As the temperature of a gas rises, the volume increases.
④ The volume of a gas increases with increasing temperature.

- 絶対等級が同じなら星が地球に**近いほど**明るく見える．**The closer** a star is to Earth, the brighter it appears, provided that the absolute magnitude is the same.
- その値が大きいほど時間がかかる．The greater the value (is), the more time (is) required.
- 絶対等級 M が**小さいほど**星は明るい．① **Smaller** absolute magnitude M 「indicates [means]」brighter stars. ② The star is brighter for **smaller** absolute magnitude M.
- 粒子衝突の数が**多いほど**新発見の確率が高まる．**The greater the number** of particle collisions, the greater the chances for new discoveries.
- 含まれる磁性材料が**多いほど**磁気による引力は強くなる．The magnetic attraction is stronger **the more** magnetic material it contains.
- アリストテレスは物体は**重いほど**速く地面に落下すると考えた．Aristotle believed that **the heavier** a body is, the faster it falls to the ground.
- カーボンナノチューブの直径が**大きいほど**その物質はグラファイトのように振舞う．**The greater** the diameter of the carbon nanotubes (is), the more the material behaves like graphite.
- そのデバイスは小さいほど高い．The smaller the device (is), the more expensive it 「is [becomes]」.
- 早く手を打つほど損害を小さく抑えられる．The sooner you take action, the smaller the damage will be.
- 関与する人が増えるほど秘密漏洩の危険は高まる．As the number of people involved grows, there will be a 「greater [higher]」risk of secrets being leaked.
- この結果は温度が高いほど収率が高くなることを示している．These results show higher yields for higher temperatures.
- 温度の低下**につれて**急激に増加する　increase steeply **with** decreasing temperature
- 開口の大きさが光の波長に近づく**につれて**回折の効果は増大する．Diffraction effects increase **as** the dimension of the aperture approaches the wavelength of the light.
- 成層圏では，酸素やオゾンによる紫外線の吸収のため，気温は高度**とともに**上昇する．In the stratosphere, temperature increases **with** altitude due to the absorption of ultraviolet light by oxygen and ozone.
- 託児所の必要性は働く女性の増加**とともに**増した．The need for day-care centers increased **in accordance with** the increase in the number of working women.

13. 比較・差・増減 13-4-4

- 光によって照らされる面の面積は光源からの距離の**二乗で**［**に比例して**］増大する．　The surface area illuminated by the light increases ｢**as**［**with**, **in proportion to**］ the square of the distance from the light source.

13-4-4　傾向

- 上昇傾向　① an upward tendency　② a rising trend
- 物価は上昇傾向にある．　Prices are ｢**on the rise**［**on the advance**, **going up**］.
- 増加しつつある［に向かっている］　be on the increase
- 増加の一途をたどっている　① be ever increasing　② increase steadily
  ③ keep on rising
- 売り上げは**4期連続で**増加した．［⇨第2部・れんぞく］
  ① Sales increased **for four consecutive periods**.
  ② Sales increased **for four periods in a row**.
  ③ Sales increased **for four periods in succession**.
  ④ Sales increased **for four periods running**.
- 失業率は**ここ4か月続けて**上昇している．　The unemployment rate has been **steadily** rising (**for**) **the past four months**.
- 売り上げは**4期目の**増加となった．　Sales increased **for the fourth consecutive period**.
- 物価は日々**急騰を続けている**．　Prices **are skyrocketing** every day.
- その会社との取り引きは**年々増加している**．　Our trade with that company **grows larger every year**.
- 海水の温度が**年々上昇している**．　The temperature of sea water **rises year by year**.
- 株価は**じりじり上昇している**．　Stock prices **are showing a steady advance**.
- 2007年には2億円増え，2010年にはさらに3億円増えた．　It increased by 200 million yen in 2007 and by another 300 million yen in 2010.
- 家賃は今や年額700万円になっていた．月額約60万円である．　The rent had now become seven million yen a year, about 600,000 yen a month.

13-4-5　右肩上がり

- 右肩上がりで増加する　increase steadily
- 右肩上がりの　① continuously increasing　② steadily increasing　③ ever increasing
- **右肩上がりの**経済成長　a **continuously growing** economy
- **右肩上がりの**時代は終わった．　The days of a **continuously growing** economy ｢are over［are history］.

13-4-6 増加率・上昇率

- 増加率［上昇率］　① a rate of increase　② an increasing rate
- 物価上昇率　the rate of increase in commodity prices
- 地価上昇率　the rate of increase in land prices
- 賃金上昇率　the rate of increase in wages
- **増加の度合い**は著しく低下した．　**The rate of increase** has narrowed significantly.
- 交通事故が**猶予がならないペースで**増加している．　The number of traffic accidents is increasing **at an alarming rate**.

13-4-7 その他

- 《株価などの》上昇のきざし　signs of a rise
- 上昇に転じる　① start rising　② shift to an upward trend　③ rebound
- 売り上げは半年ぶりに**上昇に転じた**．　Sales **turned around and rose** for the first time in six months.
- 《1日の取引のうちで》**一時は15ドルにまで上がった**　rose **to an intraday high of $15**
- 人口はその後100年間で**3倍になり**，1950年代には60万人**に達した**．　The population **tripled** in the next hundred years, **reaching** 600,000 in the 1950s.
- 今期決算は**急騰した**石油価格に足を引っ張られた．　The latest results were weighed down by the **sharply higher** oil prices.
- 反騰　① a rally　② a rebound
- 反騰する　① rally　② rebound
- 株価の急反騰　a sharp rebound in stock prices
- 金利の上昇に歯止めをかける　put the brake on rising interest rates
- 《物価などの》上昇を抑える　curb an increase
- 株価の**乱高下**　① erratic ［violent］ fluctuations in stock prices　② violent ［wild］ ups and downs ［swings］ of stock prices
- わずかとはいえ統計的に有意に増大した．　There was a small but statistically significant increase.

■ 13-5 減少・低下を表わす各種表現

13-5-1 基本

- 低下［減少］　① a fall　② a decline　③ a drop　④ a dip　⑤ (a) decrease　⑥ lowering　⑦〔価値・値段の〕depreciation
- 低下する　① fall (off)　② drop (off)　③ decrease　④ sink　⑤ decline　⑥ go

down 《in price》 ⑦ come down ⑧ depreciate
- 低下させる　①lower ②decrease ③make [let]《prices》fall ④bring down《prices》 ⑤〔相場などを〕depreciate
- 金利の低下　a fall in interest rates
- 出生率の低下　a「decline [drop, fall] in the birthrate
- 発行部数の低下　① a drop in the number of copies「published [issued] ② a fall in circulation
- 視力の低下を食い止める　① check [halt] a decline in *one's* eyesight ② check [halt] the deterioration of *one's* eyesight
- 円の下落　a「decline [fall] in the yen
- 株価の下落　a fall in share prices
- 前年よりも 50 万円の**減少**　a「**decrease** [**drop**] of 500,000 yen compared with the previous year
- 多少の**減少**を示す　show a slight「**decrease** [**decline**]
- ここの地価は昨年より**大きく下落した**．　Land prices in this area have **fallen sharply** from last year.
- 株が**下落して**ただ同然となった．
  ① Share prices have **fallen** to (virtually) nothing.
  ② Shares have **sunk** so much that they are now virtually worthless.
- その方策では物価は**下落**すまい．　I doubt that the measure would **bring down** prices.
- 給料が **2 割減**になった．　My salary has been **cut** (**by**) **20 percent**.
- …の大きさの半分ほどにまでスケールダウンする　scale down to about half the size of …
- 最初のレベルより 70dB 下まで減衰させられる　be attenuated to 70 dB below the initial level
- 原子を絶対温度で 100 万分の数度以内まで冷却する　cool atoms to within a few millionths of a degree above absolute zero
- その面積はもっと小さくできる．　The area can be made smaller.

13-5-2 急減・急落

- 急落　①a「sudden [sharp] drop [decline, fall, plunge] ② a precipitate drop ③ a steep decline ④ (a) free fall ⑤〔大量売りによる〕a sell-off
- 急落する　① drop [decline, fall] suddenly ② decline「sharply [heavily] ③ drop sharply ④ plunge ⑤ plummet ⑥ go into (a) free fall
- 急落させる　① throw 《the stock market》 into a「steep [sharp] decline ② cause … to「drop [decline, etc.] suddenly [sharply]
- 血圧が**急激に低下した**．　Her blood pressure **dropped fast** [**suddenly sank, suddenly fell**].

13. 比較・差・増減 13-5-3

- 株価が**急落している**.
  ① Share prices are「**dropping sharply**[**declining sharply**, etc.]．
  ② Share prices are「**plummeting**[**plunging**]．
- 物価の**急落を引き起こす** **cause a sharp drop** in prices
- その株は**急落して**終値は 890 円，前日比 20 円安となった．The stock「ended [closed] **sharply lower** at 890 yen, down 20 yen from the day before.
- **暴落** ① a slump ② a (sharp) break ③ a crash ④ a heavy「fall [decline]
  ⑤ a tremendous drop ⑥ a nosedive
- **暴落する** ① decline「heavily [sharply] ② slump ③ drop suddenly
  ④ plunge ⑤ plummet ⑥ nose-dive ⑦ tumble ⑧ go into (a) free fall ⑨ free-fall
- 276 円から 150 円に暴落する tumble from 276 yen to 150 yen
- 円の暴落 a heavy decline in the yen
- 株の暴落 a「slump [crash, sharp decline, heavy decline] in「stocks [share prices]
- 地価の暴落 a「slump [crash, etc.] in land「prices [values]
- 金の暴落 a heavy fall in the gold market
- 大暴落 ① a big fall ②〔株の〕a great crash

13-5-3 傾向

- 下落傾向 ①(a) downward movement ② a「falling [downward] trend
- 小売価格は依然下落傾向にある．Retail prices are still tending downwards.
- 減少しつつある ① be on the decrease ② be on the ebb ③ be decreasing ④ be diminishing ⑤ be dropping (off) ⑥ be falling (off) ⑦ be dipping ⑧ be dwindling
- 相場は **3 か月連続で**下落している．
  ① Market prices have「fallen [declined, dropped] **(for) three months in succession**.
  ② Market prices have「fallen [declined, dropped] **(for) three consecutive months**.
  ③ Market prices have「fallen [declined, dropped] **(for) three months in a row**.
  ④ Market prices have「fallen [declined, dropped] **(for) three months running**.

13-5-4 低下率・減少率

- 下落幅 an extent [an amount, a degree] of「decrease [reduction, decline, fall]
- 下落率 a rate of「decrease [reduction, decline, fall]

- 減少率　① a rate of「decline [decrease, reduction]　② a「decline [reduction] rate　③ a percent reduction
- 減少率が小さくなった．　The rate of「decline [decrease, reduction] has narrowed.
- 5 年間で 75% の削減　(a) reduction of 75% in (a period of) five years

13-5-5　反落

- 反落　① a fallback 《in stock prices》　② a correction　③ a setback
- 反落する　① fall [drop, slip] back　② fall [drop, retreat] after 《hitting a record high》
- 反落がある　there is a correction 《in stock prices》
- 急反落　a sharp correction
- 小反落　① a slight setback　② a small correction

■ 13-6　横ばい

- 横ばいである　① remain at the same level　② show no (marked) fluctuations
- 株価の横ばいが続いている．　Stocks remain steady.
- 物価は横ばいを続けている．　There are hardly any noticeable fluctuations in commodity prices.
- 鉄の生産は横ばい状態である．
  ① The output of iron remains at the same level.
  ② The output of iron shows no marked fluctuations.
- 横ばいになる　① level off　② stabilize [⇨ 14-4 頭打ち]
- インフレ曲線は横ばい状態になりつつあるようだ．　The inflation curve seems to be leveling off.
- **高止まり**する　be stuck at a high level
- 原油価格の高止まり　continuing high crude oil prices
- 失業率は 10% 台の高止まりが続いている．　The unemployment rate has stayed above the 10-percent level.
- 円相場は（対ドルで）当面 120−125 円で推移するだろう．　The exchange rate will probably hover around 120 to 125 yen to the dollar for the time being.

14. 最高と最低

14-1 最高 [⇨ 13-1-2 最上級など，第2部・さいこう，さいだい]

- **観測史上の最高気温**を記録した．
  ① We recorded **the highest temperature on record**.
  ② It was **the hottest day on record**.
  ③ **The temperature hit a record high**.
- 最高気温が30℃以上の日　a day on which the temperature reaches 30℃ or above [⇨ 37-7 気象用語]
- 最高気温が0℃未満の日　a day on which the temperature stays below 0℃ [⇨ 37-7 気象用語]
- 大会の参加者数が**最高**だったのは1985年だった．
  ① The year **with the highest** number of convention participants **was** 1985.
  ② The convention **had the highest** number of participants in 1985.
- 1970年代初頭**以来最も急速な**成長
  ① **the fastest** growth **since** the early 1970s
  ② **faster** growth **than at any time since** the early 1970s
- 平均株価が**今年最高**を記録した．　The stock average rose to its **highest level this year**.
- 株価は1989年に**ピークに達した**．　Share prices「**peaked** [**reached a peak**] in 1989.
- **最高値**(さいたかね)　① an **all-time high** (price) ② a **record high** (price)
- この日の**最高値**　① the day's **highest price** ② the day's **high** ③ the **highest price** of the day
- 戦後最高値　① 《hit》a postwar high ② the highest price since the Second World War
- この株は**先月つけた最高値**のほぼ半値にまで落ち込んだ．　The stock has fallen from **last month's all-time high** to about half (price).
- 株価が**最高値を更新した**．
  ① Share prices **reached a record high**.
  ② Share prices **reached a new high**.
- 5年ぶりの**高水準**　① **the highest level** in five years ② a five-year **high**

14-2 過去最高

次の基本形またはそれに level (水準) を付けた形が使える．

all-time high (これまでの最高)
all-time record (これまでの記録)
all-time record high (これまでの最高記録)

record（記録的）

record high（記録的高さ）

- 過去最高値にある　①be at a record high ②be at an all-time high ③be at an all-time record (high)
- 過去最高を記録する　①hit [set, mark] a record high ②hit [set, mark] an all-time high ③hit [set] an all-time record ④hit [set] a new record ⑤hit [set] a new high
- 過去最高水準にある　①be at record highs ②be at record high levels ③be at all-time highs ④be at all-time high levels ⑤be at all-time record highs
- 過去最高水準に達する　①reach [rise to, increase to] record levels ②reach [rise to, increase to] record highs ③reach [rise to, increase to] record high levels ④reach [rise to, increase to] all-time highs ⑤reach [rise to, increase to] all-time high levels
- 過去最高の10億ドル　①an all-time high of $1 billion ②an all-time record of $1 billion ③a record high of $1 billion
- 過去最高水準の10億ドル　①a record level of $1 billion ②a record-high level of $1 billion ③an all-time high level of $1 billion ④an all-time record level of $1 billion
- 過去最高水準の価格　①record-high prices ②record prices ③all-time high prices
- 過去最高の歳入　①record-high revenue ②record revenue ③all-time high revenue
- 過去最高益　①《its》best ever profits ②the best profits ever ③unprecedented profits
- 過去最大の月産量　①the largest-ever monthly output ②the largest amount ever produced in a month
- 過去最多の年間事故件数　①the largest number of accidents ever to happen in a year ②the largest-ever number of accidents in one year ③the most accidents in one year
- 過去最高の気温　①the highest temperature ever registered ②the highest-ever temperature ③the record-high temperature
- 過去最大規模の軍事演習　①the「largest [largest-scale] military (training) exercise ever held ②the largest-ever military (training) exercise
- 石油価格は**過去最高の**1バレル75ドルに達した．　①Oil prices「hit [reached] **a record high of** $75 a barrel. ②Oil prices「hit [reached] a **record** $75 a barrel.
- 日本の貿易黒字は**過去最高の**1,209億ドルになった．　Japan's trade surplus reached **an all-time high of** $120.9 billion.

14-3 自己ベスト

- 自己最高[ベスト]記録　①*one's* best record　②*one's* best performance　③a [*one's*] personal best
- 自己ベストを更新する　① better [beat] *one's* previous「best [record, time, height, distance]　② better *one's* best performance　③ improve on *one's* best score

14-4 頭打ち [⇨ 13-6 横ばい]

- 頭打ちになる　①reach [come to] a limit [an upper limit]　②reach a ceiling　③ hit a ceiling　④ reach a maximum　⑤ peak　⑥ level off
- 大学進学率が**頭打ちになっている**．　The percentage of students going on to university「**has peaked [has stopped increasing]**.
- 住宅の建設は**頭打ち気味**だ．
  ① Housing construction **seems to have「peaked [hit a ceiling]**.
  ② **It looks as though there isn't going to be any further increase** in the building of houses.
- 自動車に対する国内の需要は目下**頭打ちの傾向が強い**．　Domestic demand for cars is now **moving strongly toward the saturation point**.
- **上げ止まる**　① stop rising　② stop increasing　③ top out　④ hit a ceiling　⑤ reach a ceiling
- 上げ止まり　a halt in the rise 《of …》
- 株価が**上げ止まって**下落に転じる気配を見せている．　Stock prices **have topped out** and are now showing signs of retreat.
- ダウ平均株価が1万ドルの大台を突破し，市場の**上げ止まり感**が強まっている．　With the Dow-Jones Industrial Average having broken through the 10,000-point benchmark, there's a growing **feeling that the market has「hit a ceiling [topped out]**.

14-5 最低 [⇨第2部・さいてい，さいしょう]

- 歴代内閣で**最低の**支持率　the **lowest** level of support for any cabinet in history
- 3年来の**低水準**　①**the lowest level** in three years　②a fresh three-year **low**
- **最安値** (さいやすね)　①**an all-time low (price)**　②**a record low (price)**
- 株価が**最安値**をつけた．
  ① Share prices have reached **an all-time low**.
  ② The stock market has registered **an all-time low**.
- 株価が**最安値を更新した**．
  ① Share prices have **reached a record low**.
  ② Share prices have **reached a new low**.
- 最低気温が25°C以上の日　a day on which the temperature does not fall

below 25°C [⇨ 37-7 気象用語]

14-6 過去最低

次の基本形またはそれに level（水準）を付けた形が使える．このほか，文脈から最高ではなく最低記録であることが明らかなら単に all-time record, record ということもできる．

all-time low（これまでの最低）
all-time record low（これまでの最低記録）
record low（記録的低さ）

- 過去最低値にある　①be at a record low ②be at an all-time low ③be at an all-time record low
- 過去最低を記録する　①hit [set, mark] a record low ②hit [set, mark] an all-time low ③hit [set] a new low
- 過去最低水準にある　①be at record lows ②be at record low levels ③be at all-time lows ④be at all-time low levels ⑤be at all-time record lows
- 過去最低水準まで低下する　①fall to [drop to] record lows ②fall to [drop to] record low levels ③fall to [drop to] all-time lows ④fall to [drop to] all-time low levels
- 過去最低の55%　①an all-time low of 55% ②a record low of 55%
- 過去最低水準の10億ドル　①a record-low level of $1 billion ②an all-time low level of $1 billion
- 過去最低水準の価格　①record-low prices ②all-time low prices
- 過去最低の歳入　①record-low revenue ②all-time low revenue

14-7 底

- 底値　①a (rock-)bottom price ②a bedrock price
- 底値に達する　①reach (the) bottom ②strike (the) bottom
- 底を打つ［底入れする］　①reach (the) bottom ②strike (the) bottom ③hit (the) bottom ④bottom out ⑤touch [reach] the (rock-)bottom price
- 底入れ　①reaching bottom ②bottoming out
- 物価は目下底値だ．　Prices are now **at rock bottom [at their bottom]**.
- 鉄鋼株は今が底値だ．　Steel stocks **have bottomed out**.
- 鉄道株は底値安定．　Railway stocks remain near **the bottom**.
- 消費低迷は底を打った．　The consumption slump **has hit bottom**.
- 景気は底を打ったと見ていいだろう．　It is probably fair to say that the economy **has bottomed out**.
- 市況はおそらく底入れしている．　The market has probably **reached bottom [bottomed out]**.

- 底入れ感　a sense that the market has bottomed out
- 底を割る　〔底値より下がる〕① break the bottom　② go [sink] below the bottom line　③ go through the floor
- 底割れ　① breaking the bottom　② sinking even deeper　③ a double recession
- 株価が底割れした．　Stock prices hit new lows.
- **下げ止まる**　① stop falling　② bottom out　③ hit rock bottom
- 今月に入って株価がようやく**下げ止まった**．　Stock prices finally 「**stopped falling** [**bottomed out**] this month.
- 景気が回復傾向にあり，失業率も**下げ止まった**ようだ．　The economy is in a recovery, with the unemployment rate showing signs of **no further worsening**.
- 人口は減少したが，1900 年には**下げ止まった**．　Population declined until it **leveled off** by 1900.

14-8　最上級と複数形

　たとえば 80 点，78 点，75 点，70 点とあったときに日本語の「最高の得点」も英語の the highest score も「80 点」を指すが，英語では複数形にして the highest scores というと 80 点と 78 点など，上位のいくつかを指すこともある．このように，英語の最上級＋複数形は日本語でいう「上位」に対応することがある．

- 企業ランキング上位 20 社　① the top twenty companies　② the twenty highest-ranking companies
- 世界で最も高い 3 つの建物　the three tallest buildings in the world
- 上位 3 名の入札者　① the three highest bidders　② the top three bidders
- 上位 3 ビット　the three most significant bits　★単数形の the most significant bit なら「最上位ビット」の意．

15. 順位・順番の表現

■ 15-1 …番目

- **5番目の人**　the fifth person
- **右から3番目の人**　the third person **from the right**
- **行列の3番目**にいる　be (**the**) third in line
- **2番目に来たのは**田中さんでした．　Ms. Tanaka was (**the**) **second** to come.
- 世界で**2番目に高い山**　the **second highest** mountain in the world
- 富士山に次いで日本で**2番目に高い山**　①**the second highest** mountain in Japan after Mt. Fuji ②Japan's **second highest** mountain after Mt. Fuji
- **2番目に重要な問題**　the **second most important** problem
- **次に大きな値**　the **next highest** value ★the next highest（2番目に高い）は highest（最高）より低いが，the next higher … は普通は「その前に言及されたものより高い，次の」という意味．
- **下から数えて4番目だ**　be fourth **from the bottom**
- **下から2番目の水準**　the **second lowest** level
- **最後から2番目の走者**　①**the second** runner **from the end** ②**the second** runner **from the last** ③**the second-to-last** runner
- **下から3行目**　**the third line from the bottom**〔⇨第2部・ぎょう〕
- **下から2番目の弟**　①*one's* **second youngest** brother ②*one's* **youngest** brother **but one**
- **何番目**　⇨ 26. 数量に関する疑問文 26-10 何番目

■ 15-2 順位

15-2-1 順位一般

(1) 特定の順位

- **1位**　①(the) first place ②the top position ③(the) first rank ④No. 1〔⇨(2) トップ，第2部・いちばん〕
- **2位**　①(the) second place ②No. 2
- **1位である**　①occupy [hold, have] (the) first place ②come [be, rank, stand, be ranked] first ③be in the first rank ④be at the「top [head] of《a class》⑤head [top] the list《of …》⑥lead ⑦be No. 1 ⑧hold [have] the「No. 1 [top] ranking
- **2位である**　①rank [be, stand, be ranked, be placed] second ②hold (the) second place ③be (the) runner-up ④be No. 2
- 彼は57.25点で**4位**だった．　①He placed fourth with 57.25 points. ②He

was in fourth place with 57.25 points.
- 20人中3位である　rank [be, etc.] (the) third out of twenty
- 1位になる　① reach [attain, win, take, get, secure] (the) first place ② be the top ③ come out on top ④ gain the No. 1 position ⑤〔コンテストなどで〕win the first prize ⑥〔規模などが〕become the largest 《market, exporter, etc.》 ⑦〔競走などで〕finish first ⑧ come in first ⑨ come out (at the) top ⑩〔順位の上昇〕rise to first place
- 2位になる　①〔競技で〕finish second ② come in second ③ finish 《a race》in second place ④〔コンテストで〕win (the) second prize ⑤〔規模などが〕become the second largest 《market, exporter, etc.》
- **3位**に落ちる　① drop to (**the**) **third place** ② slip into **third**(-**ranking**) **place**
- 4位は佐々木君だった．　Fourth place went to Sasaki.
- 世界**第1位の**自動車メーカー　the world's「**largest**［**No. 1**］automobile manufacturer
- 日本で**2位の**携帯電話会社　Japan's「**second biggest**［**No. 2**］cellular phone「provider［operator］
- 売上高で世界**2位の**自動車メーカー　the world's **second largest** automobile manufacturer「by sales［in terms of sales］
- 売れ筋**2位の**商品　the **second biggest** seller
- サウジアラビアに次ぐ世界**2位の**石油輸出国　the world's **second largest** oil exporter「following［after, behind］Saudi Arabia
- ランキング1位の米国を破る　defeat the top-ranked United States
- 世界ランキング4位の鈴木を破る　beat the world No. 4-ranked Suzuki
- ヨーロッパでの市場シェア**2位**を占める　hold the **second largest** market share in Europe
- そのページのヤフーでの検索順位は**6位**だ．　The page is ranked「**sixth**［**number six**］in Yahoo.
- この買収によりB社はA社に次いで**2位**になる．　The acquisition will make B Corp. **second largest** after A Corp.
- この業界で世界**2位**の会社と**3位**の会社を合併させる　① merge the world's **No. 2** and **No. 3** companies in this industry ② merge the world's **second** and **third largest** companies in this industry
- 1位と2位の差が**広がった**［**開いた**］．　The gap has **widened** between first and second place.
- オリンピックのメダルは1位から3位までにだけ授与される．　Olympic medals are awarded only for the first three places.

(2) トップ

- 人口が**最も多い**州はカリフォルニア州で3,900万人．**その次**はテキサス州

15. 順位・順番の表現 15-2-1

で 2,700 万人だ．　**The largest** state「in [by]」population is California with 39 million residents, **followed** by Texas with 27 million.
- **先着** 200 名　**the first** 200 (people) to arrive
- 癌は日本人の死亡原因の**第1位を占めている**．
  ① Cancer **is the leading** cause of death among Japanese.
  ② Cancer **tops** the list of causes of death among Japanese.
  ③ **The most common** cause of death for Japanese is cancer.
- 電車内の忘れ物の**1位**は傘だ．
  ① Umbrellas are **top** of all lost property left behind on trains.
  ② Of all lost property left on trains, **first place** goes to umbrellas.
- 彼の新著は5週連続で売り上げ**1位**を記録している．
  ① His new work has been **the top** seller for five weeks running.
  ② His new work has been at **the top** of the best-seller list for five consecutive weeks.
- このキーワードについてグーグルでの検索順位**トップの**サイト　① **the top-ranked** site in Google for this keyword　② the site **ranked first** in Google for this keyword　③ the site **ranked number one** in Google for this keyword
- **世界一**である　① be the「best [greatest, top]」… in the world　② be the world's best [greatest, top, etc.]　③ beat [lead] the world in …
- 世界一の富豪　① the richest person in the world　② the wealthiest person in the world
- 世界一のレーサー　① the top racer in the world　② the number one racer in the world
- 世界一の長寿国　the country that tops the longevity list
- 栃木県はいちごの生産量が**日本一**だ．　① Tochigi Prefecture is the top producer of strawberries in Japan.　② Tochigi Prefecture produces the most strawberries in Japan.
- ここ4年間ずっと市場シェア1位だ．　It has led in market share for four years now.
- **業界トップ**の会社　the top firm in the field
- **断トツの1位**　in first place by a「decisive [runaway, clear]」lead
- **ぶっちぎりの優勝**　winning [a win, a victory] by a huge margin
- **歴代1位[トップ]**　①(the) all-time number one　②(the) all-time first place [⇨第2部・れきだい]
- **史上最高**　① the highest 《level》 in history　②《米口》《hit》 a historical high
- **史上最大の…**　① the greatest 《victory》 in history　② the worst 《disaster》 in history　③ the biggest 《army》 in history
- **最年少[最年長]記録**　a [the] record for being the「youngest [oldest]」《world champion》[⇨ 38. 年齢 38-2]

15. 順位・順番の表現 15-2-1

- **一番**で合格する　pass an examination with the highest score
- 期末試験で学年の一番は彼女だった．　She was the one who had the top score in her「《米》grade [《英》form] on the end-of-term examination.
- 英語では彼がクラスで一番だ．　He leads the class in English.
- トップに躍り出る　① jump into first place　② leap into the top position
- **首位**を奪う　take over first place
- 首位を守る　hold onto first place
- 首位から転落する　drop out of first place
- 首位の座を明け渡す　surrender first place 《to …》
- 日本人の平均寿命は世界一を維持した．　Japan retained the top spot in average life expectancy.
- 佐藤が加藤に追いついて1位で並んだ．　Sato caught up with Kato to share the top spot.

(3) 同順

- 日本は6位で，フランスと**同順**だった．　Japan ranked 6th, **tied** with France.
- アリスはボブとともに2位[首位]タイだった．　Alice「**tied** [was tied] with Bob for「second place [the lead]．[⇨第2部・タイ]
- 4位はイギリス・フランス・オランダの**三者同率**となった．
  ① **There was a three-way tie** for fourth place among Britain, France, and the Netherlands.
  ② Britain, France, and the Netherlands **tied** for fourth place.

(4) 上位

- 上位50名の高得点者　① the top 50 scorers　② the 50 highest scorers
- 上位にランクされる　① be highly ranked　② be ranked high
- **上位**3社　**the top** three companies
- これら3つの病気が**上位3位を占めて**いた．
  ① These three diseases **topped the list**.
  ② These **were the top three** diseases.
- グーグルでの**上位**10位の検索順位を得る　① get a **top** 10 ranking in Google's search results　② get a **top** 10 Google ranking　③ rank in the **top** 10 in Google
- 彼なら悪くても**6位**入賞は堅いだろう．　I should think he's certain of **sixth place**, at (the very) worst.
- **10位**以内にはいりたい．　I want to be somewhere in **the top ten**.
- 上位10位以内にゴールする　finish in the top ten
- 私は学年で10番より下に落ちたことがない．
  ① I've never been below 10th in my year.
  ② I've always managed to stay among the top ten in my year.

- 彼はクラスの上から3分の1以内の成績で卒業したいと思っていた． He hoped to graduate in the top third of his class.
- その検索エンジンで検索順位**上位**になる　get ranked **high** in the search engine
- ウェブサイトのMSNでの検索**順位**を上げる　improve the search engine **ranking** of a website in MSN
- アメリカ人の**上位**1パーセントの富は下位95パーセントの富よりも多い． The wealth of the **top** one percent of Americans is greater than that of the bottom 95 percent.
- **ベストテン**　① the top ten　② the ten best … [⇨第2部・ベスト]
- 今年度映画［小説］のベストテン　the year's top ten in「film [fiction]」
- ベストテンから消える　disappear from [fall from, drop out of] the top ten
- ベストテンに入る　come out [be] among the top ten
- 日本**最大級**のショッピングセンター　**one of the largest**「shopping centers [《米》malls] in Japan
- その城の**最古級**の写真　**one of the**「**oldest**[**earliest**] photographs of the castle

(5) 下位

- 我がチームはここ数年リーグの**下位**に低迷している． For the last few years our team has「remained stuck in a low position [trailed behind]」in the league.
- **最下位**　① last place　② the lowest「rank [position]」③ the tail end
- 最下位である　① rank lowest　② be lowest in rank　③〔競技で〕be at the bottom《of the league》④『野球』《米》be in the cellar
- 最下位から抜け出す　① escape [break out] from the bottom　② get out of last place
- 最下位から2位に上がる　rise [climb] from the bottom of the standings up to second place
- 最下位に転落する　go [fall, drop] to「the bottom [last place]」
- 最下位のチーム　① the team in bottom place　② the team at the bottom《of the league》③ the bottom team　④《米》the last-place team　⑤《米》the cellar team　⑥《米》the tailender
- 万年最下位のチーム　the perennial last-place team
- 最下位争い　①《be in》a race for the bottom《of the league》② a race for last place
- 私は**びり**だった．　① I「was [came] last.　②〔成績で〕I「was [came] at the bottom　③ I was the last person.　④〔競走で〕I「came in [finished] last.
- びりで卒業する　① graduate at the bottom of *one's* class　② graduate with the lowest grades　③ have the worst score among the graduates

15. 順位・順番の表現 15-2-2

- びりから2番目〔3番目〕 the「second [third] from the bottom
- **ブービー賞** 〔びりから2番目の賞〕a prize for the second from the last place ★英語では a booby prize は「最下位賞」の意.
- 《成績が悪くて》下から数えたほうが早い.
① It would be easier to count up from the bottom (than down from the top).
② 《My grades》are closer to the bottom (than the top).
- 先進国で**最悪**の財政赤字 the worst fiscal deficit among industrialized countries
- 今年の米は最悪のできだった. This year's rice crop was the worst ever.
- 財政状態は過去最悪だ. Financial conditions are as bad as they have ever been.
- 今年の防御率は過去最悪だった. His earned run average this year was the worst of his career.
- 交通事故死全国**ワースト**ワン〔ワースト1位〕の県 the worst prefecture「for [with regard to] traffic fatalities
- 日本はその30か国中, ワースト3位だ.
① Japan is ranked third from the bottom among the thirty countries.
② Japan is ranked third lowest among the thirty countries.
③ Japan is ranked after all the thirty countries but two.
- ワーストテンにはいっている ① be among the worst ten ② be in the bottom ten ③ be one of the ten《worst-performing countries, most disliked actors, etc.》
- 何位, 何番目 ⇨ 26. 数量に関する疑問文 26-10

15-2-2 スポーツ

- わずかの差で**2位**になる make [come] a close **second**《in a race》
- 彼女は**5位**にわずかに遅れてゴールした. She finished just behind the **fifth-place** finisher.
- 彼女は**2位**の走者に対して大きく差をつけていた.
① She had a big lead「on [over] the **second-place** runner.
② She was far ahead of the runner **in second**.
- 彼は**先頭**走者との差を縮めた. He closed (in) on the **top** runner.
- 彼は4分12秒のタイムで**2位**だった. He came in **second**, with a time of 4 minutes 12 seconds.
- 1997年にヒンギスは16歳で最年少の**世界ランキング1位**になった.
① In 1997, at the age of 16, Martina Hingis became the youngest **world No. 1**.
② In 1997, at the age of 16, Martina Hingis became the youngest **No. 1 ranked player** in tennis history.
③ In 1997, sixteen-year-old Martina Hingis became the youngest player to

「attain [achieve, reach] **the world No. 1 ranking**.
④ In 1997, Martina Hingis「attained [reached] **the No. 1 position in the world ranking** at the age of 16, the youngest ever in tennis history.
- 世界ランキング2位である　be ranked second in the world
- 彼は世界フライ級の第3位にランクされている．　He is ranked the No. 3 flyweight in the world.
- 世界ランキング40位に上がる　rise to No. 40 in the world

15-2-3　ヒットチャートなど

- イギリスのシングルヒットチャート**第1位になる**　hit [reach] No. 1 on the UK singles charts
- そのCDはたちまちヒットチャート**1位**に躍り出た．　The CD immediately「leapt [shot] to「**No. 1** [**the top** of the charts].
- そのアルバムで**2度目の1位**になる　get「a [*one's*] **second No. 1** with the album
- ビルボード・ホット100・シングルチャート**の1位**に留まる
① remain **No. 1 on** the Billboard Hot 100 Singles chart
② remain **atop** the Billboard Hot 100 Singles chart
- かろうじて**上位50位**に食い込む　barely make **the top 50**
- その歌は**4位でヒットチャート入りして**3か月間チャートに留まった．　The song **entered the charts at No. 4** and stayed on the charts for three months.
- ランクアップ　a rise in *one's* ranking
- そのアルバムは**3ランク**上がって**4位**になった．　The album has gone up **three places** to **fourth place**.
- この映画は先週の20位から**一挙にランクアップし**2位に躍り出た．　This movie has「**shot** [**leapt, jumped**] **up** to second place from last week's 20th.
- ランキング入りしている　be included in the ranking
- ヒットチャートにランクインする　make the hit charts
- 彼女の歌が今年のベストテンにランクインした．　Her song was one of this year's ten most popular songs.
- ランクが下がる　go down in *one's* ranking
- 3位に落ちる　fall [drop] to No. 3
- トップテンから外れる　drop out of the top 10
- ヒットチャートの圏外に落ちる　drop [fall] out of [off] the charts

■ 15-3　格付けと星

- わが社はAAに**格付けされています**．
① Our company has **been rated AA**.

15. 順位・順番の表現 15-3

- ② We have **been given an AA rating**.
- ムーディーズによる銀行の格付け一覧　Moody's table of bank credit ratings
- 格付けの引き上げ　① a ratings upgrade　② upgrading　③ a boost in *one's* rating
- 格付けの引き下げ　① a ratings downgrade　② downgrading　③ a drop in *one's* rating
- 新たに発表された格付けを見ると日本の銀行は軒並み**ランクダウンしている**．　The newly announced ratings reveal that Japanese banks have all **been downgraded**.
- 格付けの変更が相場を左右する．　Changes in rating(s) affect the market.
- ホテルの格付け　a hotel's rating
- このホテルのほうがあちらよりも**数段ランクが上だ**．　This hotel is **several notches「above [better than]** that one.
- **三つ星の**ホテル［星三つのホテル］　① a **three-star** hotel　② a hotel **with three stars**　③ a hotel **with a three-star rating**
- そのガイドブックで**五つ星の**レストラン　a restaurant **with a「five-star [top] rating** in the guidebook
- **五つ星**を獲得する　get [attain, be awarded] **five stars**
- **四つ星**の評価を得る　① be rated (as) **four stars**　② be given (a rating of) **four stars**
- このホテルはミシュランガイドで**三つ星**がつけられている．　This hotel has **three stars** in the Michelin Guide.
- この国ではホテルは**一つ星から五つ星までの星の数で**評価される．　In this country, hotels are rated **on a scale of one to five stars**.
- 星をつける　① rate　② give 《a hotel》 a star rating
- 新作映画に星をつける　rate a new movie
- このリンゴは B ランクに**等級を下げられた**．　These apples **have been downgraded to grade B**.
- どうせ大学に行くなら**もっと上のランク**を目指せ．　If you're going to go to college, you should at least「try [aim] for「one of **higher standing**「a **higher-ranked** one］．
- 品質に応じて**ランク付けされる**　be「**rated [graded]** according to quality
- テストの成績によって**ランク付けされる**　be「**rated [graded]** by [according to] *one's* exam results

■ 15-4 順番

⇨第2部・じゅんじょ，じゅんばん

15-4-1 …順に

- …順に　①**in (the) order of** …　②**in the order in which** …　③**according to**…　★①は順序を説明して表現するような場合は order に the を付け，決まり文句のように使うときには無冠詞とする傾向がある．
- 申し込み（受け付け）順に　①**in order of application**　②**in the order of applications received**　③**in the order in which applications are received**
- アルファベット順［ABC 順］に　①《arrange a list》**alphabetically**　②**in alphabetical order**　③**in the order of the alphabet**　④**in ABC order**
- 逆アルファベット順に　**in reverse alphabetical order**
- レコードを先頭フィールドの**数値の逆順**にソートする　sort records in **reverse numerical order** of the first field
- 五十音順［アイウエオ順］に　①《arrange a list》**in the order of the Japanese syllabary**　②**in kana order**　③**in *a-i-u-e-o* order**
- 背の順に並ぶ　line up **in order of height**
- 登場順に　**in order of appearance**
- 先着順に　①**in (the) order of arrival**　②〔申込書などの〕**in (the) order of receipt**　③**on a first-come-first-served basis**
- 〔メールなど〕**到着時刻順**に　①**in the order received**　②**in (the) order of arrival**
- 化石は**年代順**に展示してある．　The fossils are exhibited **in chronological order**.
- その表は**年齢順である**．　①The list is arranged **in order of age**.　②The list is arranged **according to age**.　③The list is **ordered by age**.
- 日付順に　①**in order of date**　②**by date**
- **画数順**の漢字表　a table of kanji **ordered by stroke count**
- 名前を**リストに現われる順**に印字する　①print the names **in the order in which they appear in the list**　②print the names **in the same order as they appear in the list**
- 右から順に　①**in order from the right**　②**starting from the right**　③〔写真などの説明〕**from the right**　④**(R–L)**
- オランダの国旗は**上から順番に**赤，白，青だ．　The national flag of the Netherlands is, **in order from the top**, red, white, and blue.

15-4-2 「高い順」「低い順」

- 重要度**の高い順**に　①**in order of most** important **to least** important　②**in order of most** important **first**　③**in order of decreasing** importance　④in a descending order from most to least important

- 元素を原子番号**の（増加する）順に**並べる　①arrange the elements **in order of increasing** atomic numbers　②arrange the elements **according to increasing** atomic numbers
- リクエストの**多かった順に**挙げると　①to name them **in the order of most** requests　②to name them **according to the decreasing number of** requests
- 点数の**高い順に**　in the order **from highest** score **to lowest** (score)
- **人口の多い順に**都市の名を一覧にする　①list the names of cities **in (the) order of population rank**　②list the names of cities **in the order of population from the largest to the smallest**　③list cities **ordered by population**
- メーカーは成分を製品に含まれる割合の多い順に表示する必要がある．Manufacturers have to list ingredients in the order of the ratio of their content in the product, from highest to lowest.
- 単語［数字］を昇順に並べる　arrange「words [figures] in ascending order
- 降順になっている　be in descending order
- x の昇冪の順で　in ascending powers of x

15-4-3　明示的に順番を言う例

- 国語，数学，英語**の順に**　**in the order of** Japanese, mathematics, and English
- 続いてイギリス，スイス，カナダ，ドイツ**の順に**ゴールインした．Britain, Switzerland, Canada, and Germany were runners-up **in the order named**.
- 就職が決まった学生の専門は工業が88％と最も高く，**次いで**商業，水産，農業**の順である**．The specialties of those students who have found jobs are **in the order of** engineering—the highest at 88%—**followed by** commerce, fisheries, and agriculture.

16. 投票・選挙の表現

16-1 票数

- 票数　①〔票の数〕the number of votes　②〔票決力〕(a) voting strength

16-1-1 採決

- **賛成** 3, **反対** 6 だった．　There were three votes **for** and six **against**.
- その法案は **200 票対 150 票**で可決された．　The bill was passed **by a vote of 200 to 150**.
- 予算案は **331 票対 76 票**(の大差)で下院を通過した．　The budget bill passed the Lower House by (a landslide of) **331 votes to 76**.
- 議案は 108 票対 141 票，すなわち **33 票の差で**否決された．　The bill was defeated **by** (**a vote of**) 141 to 108 — **a margin of 33**.
- 多数決　①(a) decision by the majority　②(a) majority vote　③majority rule

16-1-2 選挙

- その候補者は **20 万票**を得た．　The candidate「got [obtained, polled] **two hundred thousand votes**.
- 彼女は**過去最高得票**の 42,000 票を獲得して当選した．　She was elected with her **highest ever poll** of 42,000 votes.
- その政党は**総投票数**の 4 分の 1 を得ただけであった．　The party only polled a quarter of **the votes cast**.
- **わずかの差で勝つ**　win **by a narrow margin**
- **かなりの差で**当選する　be elected **by a「wide [handsome] margin**
- 彼女は次点の候補者より **400 票以上上回っていた**．　She was **more than 400 votes ahead of** the second-place candidate.
- 彼は彼女より 50 票下回っていた．　He was 50 votes behind her.
- アリスが 340 票を取ったのに対し，ボブはたったの 180 票だった．　Alice polled 340 votes against only 180 for Bob.
- (2 位と) **1,500 票の差で**当選する
  ① win an election **by a margin of 1,500** (**votes**)
  ② win an election **by 1,500** (**votes**)
  ③ win an election **by a majority of 1,500** (**votes**)
  ④《米》win an election **by a plurality of 1,500** (**votes**)
★majority, plurality は相手［次点］より多いときの差を表わすときに使う．
- **1,500 票の差で**落選する
  ① lose an election **by a margin of 1,500** (**votes**)
  ② lose an election **by 1,500** (**votes**)

16. 投票・選挙の表現 16-1-2

- 彼女の予測は労働党 352, 保守党 196, その他 98 だった.　Her forecast was: Labour 352, Conservative 196, and others 98.
- 3 人が出馬した知事選で彼は**次点であった**.　He **was the runner-up** in the gubernatorial election, in which three candidates had run.
- (得票数)**上位 2 名**の候補者
  ① the top two (leading) candidates
  ② the top two finishers
  ③ the top two vote「getters [receivers]」
  ④ the top two vote-receiving candidates
  ⑤ the two candidates who receive(d) the「greatest [highest]」number of votes
  ⑥ the two candidates who receive(d) the most votes
  ⑦ the two candidates receiving the highest vote
  ⑧ the two candidates with the highest number of votes
  ⑨ the two highest-polling candidates
- どの候補者も過半数の得票がない場合には**上位 2 者**の間で決選投票が行なわれる.
  ① If no candidate receives a majority, **the top two candidates** compete in a run-off election.
  ② If no candidate receives a majority, a run-off election is held between **the two candidates who receive the「greatest [highest]」number of votes**.
  ③ If no one wins a majority, **the two candidates with the most votes** hold a run-off.
- **得票数**　① the number of votes「obtained [cast for *one*]」② *one's* poll
- 法定得票数　the legally required minimum number of votes
- (相対)**得票率**　① the percentage of 《a candidate's》 votes relative to the total vote(s) cast　② the「ratio [proportion]」of votes 《for a「candidate [party]」》 to the total vote(s) cast
- 全有権者に対する絶対得票率　the absolute proportion of votes (cast [received]) 《for a「candidate [party]」》 against the total number of eligible voters
- その政党は小選挙区では 48% の**得票率**で 76% の議席を獲得した.
  ① The party won 76% of the single-constituency seats with 48% of the vote(s) cast.
  ② In the single-member districts, the party won 76% of the seats with its share of the popular vote at 48%.
- 開票結果は佐藤 68%, 加藤 32% だった.　① The「tally [final result]」was Sato 68% and Kato 32%.　② The「tally [final result]」was 68% for Sato and 32% for Kato.
- 佐藤は 43% 対 41% で加藤を上回った.　Sato led Kato (at) 43% to 41%.
- 彼は彼女を 3% 上回っていた[に 3% 後れを取っていた].　He「placed [was placed]」3%「above [behind]」her.
- クリントンとサンダーズは約 50%[49.9% 対 49.6%]で引き分けだった.

Clinton and Sanders were tied at「about 50% [49.9% to 49.6%].

- 目下オバマ 53%,マケイン 46% だ.　Now, it's Obama at 53%, McCain at 46%.　★開票の途中経過. it は漠然と状況を指す.
- 最新情報ではブッシュは 28% となっている.　The latest numbers have Bush at 28%.
- **得票差**　the difference in votes polled
- 対立候補との**得票差**　the difference between votes cast for *one*self and for *one's* rival candidate
- **議席占有率**　the 《party's》 share of seats 《in the House of Representatives》
- **開票率** 30% で　① with 30% of the vote(s) counted　② with 30% of the vote(s) in　③ with 30% of the total vote(s)　★選挙区単位で結果を集計する場合には with 30% of「(electoral) districts [《米》 precincts] reporting (results) のような表現もある.
- まだ 3 分の 1 の票が未開票だ.　One third of the vote is yet to be counted.
- 26,000 票以上が無効票と判定された.　More than 26,000 ballots were「invalidated [ruled invalid].
- 12 票差で勝負がついた争いで 134 の白票があった.　There were 134 blank ballots in a race decided by 12 votes.

16-2　キャスティングボート

- 賛否同数　① a tie(d) vote　② an equal number of votes for and against
- 両議院の議事は出席議員の過半数でこれを決し, **可否同数**のときは議長の決するところによる.　All matters shall be decided, in each House, by a majority of those present, and in case of **a tie**, the presiding officer shall decide the issue.
- キャスティングボートを握っている　① hold the casting vote　② hold the deciding vote
- (議長が)キャスティングボートを行使する　exercise *one's* casting vote

16-3　過半数

- 過半数　① a majority　② the greater「part [number]《of …》　③ more than half　④ a plurality
- 組合員 123 名の**過半数**がその計画に反対している.　**A majority** of the 123 members are opposed to the plan. ★a majority of … の…が複数形の時は動詞は複数扱いするのが普通. More than half (of) … も同様 (⇨ 64. 各種構文と単数／複数).
- 衆議院における**過半数**の賛成により　with the support of **a majority** in the House of Representatives
- **過半数**の議席を得る　get [obtain, gain, win] **a majority** (of seats)
- 彼女の得票は**過半数**に達した [満たなかった].　She「got [failed to get] a

16. 投票・選挙の表現 16-4

majority of the vote(s).

- 現職候補に**過半数**の票が集まった．
  ① The incumbent candidate got **a majority** of the vote(s).
  ② **A majority** of the votes went to the incumbent candidate.
- 与党の議席は**過半数**に届かなかった． The ruling party didn't「get [obtain]」**a majority**.
- 保守勢力は国会で**過半数**を占めている． Conservative forces have **a majority** in the Diet.
- ぎりぎりの**過半数** ① 《get》a「bare [tiny]」**majority** ② just **over half**《of the citizens》
- かろうじて**過半数**を獲得する　narrowly obtain **a majority** (**vote**)
- 賛成票は**過半数**に2票足りなかった． Votes in favor fell two (votes) short of **a majority**.
- **過半数**を割る　① fall (to) below **half**　② fall below **a majority**

★《米》では plurality を相対的な多数の意に使う．ほかに得票差(⇨16-1-2)を表わすのにも用いる．

- 最多数の投票を得て当選する[**トップ当選**する]　① be elected with the「**highest number** [**plurality**]」**of votes**　②《英》be returned **at the head of the poll**
- 投票で**多数**になったが過半数には至らなかった． They **won a plurality of votes** but fell short of a majority.
- 共和党支持者では賛成が**わずかに多かった**が(44%)，反対も同じくらいだった(40%)． A「**small** [**slight**]」**plurality** of Republicans (44%) approved but nearly as many (40%) were opposed. ★ a「small [slight]」plurality で「わずかな差での最多数」の意．

16-4 3分の2の多数

- 出席者の**3分の2**以上の多数票　a majority vote of **two thirds** or more「of those in attendance [of the members present]」
- 全会員の**3分の2**の承認が必要とされる． Approval by **two thirds** of the total membership is required.
- **3分の2**の多数によって承認される　① be approved by a **two-thirds**「**vote** [**majority**]」② be approved by a majority of **two thirds**
- 委員会の**3分の2**の同意を得られないときは動議は否決される． The motion will be defeated if it fails to secure the support of **two-thirds** of the committee.
- この憲法の改正は，各議院の総議員の**三分の二**以上の賛成で，国会が，これを発議し，国民に提案してその承認を経なければならない． Amendments to this Constitution shall be initiated by the Diet, through a concurring vote of **two-thirds** or more of all the members of each House and shall

thereupon be submitted to the people for ratification. ★日本国憲法より.
- 得票数は拒否権をくつがえすのに必要な**3分の2**の得票に6票足りなかった.
  ① The tally fell six votes short of the **two-thirds** (majority) necessary to overturn the veto.
  ② The vote fell six short of the「necessary [needed] **two-thirds** majority.

16-5 投票権

- 投票権　① the right to vote　②《women's》suffrage
- わが家には5票ある.
  ① There are five「votes [voters] in our family.
  ② Five people in the family are entitled to vote.
- ドイツの持ち票は29だ.
  ① Germany is assigned 29 votes.
  ② Germany has 29 votes.
- 国連内でアジア・アフリカ諸国の占める票数の比重は大きなものである.
  The Afro-Asian bloc has「a large vote [substantial voting strength] in the United Nations.
- 有権者数　① the number of eligible voters　② the size of the electorate

16-6 投票率

- 投票率　①(a) voter turnout　② a turnout (of voters)　③ a turnout rate　④ a voting rate
- 投票率は49.16%だった.　Voter turnout stood at 49.16%.
- 高い[低い]投票率　① a「high [low] turnout　② a「good [poor] turnout
- 北海道の投票率が特に高いという情報が入った.　We got word that Hokkaido was voting exceptionally heavily.
- 投票率はかなりよかった.　The (voter) turnout was quite good.
- 投票率は戦後最低であった.　The (voter) turnout was the lowest since the war.

16-7 定数

- 議員定数　an [the] allotted number of「members [seats]《in the Diet》
- 両議院の議員の**定数**は,法律でこれを定める.　**The number** of the members of each House shall be fixed by law. ★日本国憲法より.
- 英国の下院は646名の議員からなる.
  ① The British House of Commons「**consists of** [**has, is composed of**] 646「members [Members of Parliament, MPs].
  ② **There are** 646「members [seats] in the British House of Commons.
  ③ **The membership** of the British House of Commons is 646.

- 参議院では3年ごとに**定数の半数**が改選される．
  ① There is an election for **half the seats** in the House of Councillors every three years.
  ② **Half the seats** in the House of Councillors come up for election every three years.
- その選挙区の定数　the number of seats of the「constituency［(electoral) district］
- 定数1の選挙区　a single-member「constituency［(electoral) district］
- 定数2の選挙区　a two-member「constituency［(electoral) district］
- 定数配分　(an) apportionment《of seats in the Diet》
- 定数格差　malapportionment of seats
- 一票の格差　inequity［disproportion］in the value of a single vote
- 一票の格差は是正されるどころか広がっている．　Rather than being resolved, the weight differential among individual votes (in different electoral districts) has in fact spread.
- 当時の日本の国政選挙では一票の重みに最大4倍もの格差があった．　In Japanese national elections at the time, the differential in the value of a single vote varied by up to a factor of four.
- 定数是正　(a) reapportionment《of seats in the Diet》
- 定数削減　① (a) reduction in the number of seats　② a reduction of《fifty》seats
- 定数削減法案　a bill to reduce the number of seats

16-8 定足数

- 定足数　a quorum
- 定足数に達する　① constitute a quorum　② form a quorum
- 定足数に満たない　① fail to meet the quorum《required for the session》　② do not come up to a quorum　③ be short of a quorum
- 定足数を確認する　check that「there is［*one* has］a quorum
- 過半数の理事が出席していなければならない．　More than half of the directors must「be present［attend］．

16-9 票の動向

- 彼女は30代から50代の有権者の票を**さらって**当選した．
  ① She got in by **attracting** the votes of people in their thirties, forties, and fifties.
  ② The **support of most** people in their thirties, forties, and fifties secured her election.
- 県知事選挙では与党支持層の票が**割れた**．　In the gubernatorial election,

votes cast by ruling-party supporters **were split**.
- かなりの票が対立候補に**流れた**.
  ① A substantial number of votes「**went**［**were lost**］to the rival candidate.
  ② A substantial part of the electorate **changed colors and voted for** the rival candidate.
- あの失言で票が逃げた. That slip of the tongue **cost**「him［her］a lot of votes.
- 票を読む ① estimate the number of votes *one* could get ②〔全体の〕predict voting ③ predict the outcome of「an election［a vote］④ predict how people will vote ⑤ predict how the vote will go
- その種の活動をしても票にはならない.
  ① That sort of activity won't「get (you)［attract］votes.
  ② You don't win support by doing that kind of thing.
  ③ You don't get people to vote for you by doing that kind of thing.

16-10 再選・多選

- 再選 reelection
- 再選される ① be reelected《mayor, to the Diet》② win reelection
- 三選 election for a third term
- 三選される be (re)elected for a third (consecutive) term
- 三選市長 a mayor elected for a third term
- 大統領は三選が禁止されている. ① The President cannot serve for more than two terms. ② One cannot be elected to the office of President more than twice.
- 多選 ① election many times ② frequent reelection ③ multiple election
- 多選首長 a many-times-elected head of local government
- 多選制限 ① a limitation on the number of times a person can be elected ②《employ［place, impose, etc.］》a term limit《of two terms》
- 多選制限のある職 an office subject to a term limit
- 多選を制限する動きが強まっている. The campaign to limit the number of times a person can be elected has gained momentum.

17. …倍

17-1 基本

- …倍 ① … times ② -fold ③ by a factor of … ④ multiplied by …
- 2倍 ① two times ② double ③ twice ④ twofold ［⇨第 2 部・ばい］
- 3倍 ① three times ② threefold ③ treble ④ 《文》thrice
- 1,000倍 ① a thousand times ② a thousandfold
- 3 の 2 倍は 6.《3×2＝6》
  ① Two times three is (equal to) six.
  ② Three multiplied by two［Two multiplied by three］is (equal to) six.
- ある数を**4倍**して 3 を足すと 31 になります. **Multiply** a (certain) number **by four** and add three and you will get thirty-one.
- その金額は町の年間予算の**3倍**だ. The sum is **three times** (as much as) the annual budget of the town.
- 市場価格の **2.5倍**で at **2.5 times** the market price
- その数の倍あった.
  ① There were twice that many.
  ② There were twice that number.
  ③ There were twice as many (as that number).
- サンプリングレートは信号に含まれる最高周波数の少なくとも**2倍**でなければならない. The sampling rate must be at least **twice** the highest frequency present in the signal.
- その 3 倍の町が 5,000 人を超える人口を有していた. Three times as many towns had populations over 5,000.
- 1985 年の**3倍**の石油を輸入している. They import **three times as much** oil as (they did) in 1985. ★英語では as 1985 のように比較対象を直接「1985 年」とするのは口語などでは使うが，厳密な文章では避けるべきとされる．as in 1985 なら問題ない.
- 彼女の収入は **10 年前の倍**だ.
  ① Her income is **twice as large as it was ten years ago**.
  ② Her income is **twice what it was ten years ago**.
  ③ Her income is **twice as large as**「her income［the amount, that］**ten years ago**.
- A は B の 2 倍の長さである.
  ① A is twice as long as B.
  ② A is twice the length of B.
  ③ A is twice longer than B.
- A は B の 3 倍の長さである.
  ① A is three times as long as B.

17. …倍   17-1

  ② A is three times the length of B.
  ③ A is three times longer than B.
- A は B の 3 倍の大きさである．
  ① A is three times as large as B.
  ② A is three times the size of B.
  ③ A is three times larger than B.
- A は B の 3 倍の重さである．
  ① A weighs three times as much as B.
  ② A weighs three times the weight of B.
  ③ A is three times heavier than B.
  ④ A is three times more massive than B.
- A は B の 3 倍の時間がかかる．
  ① A takes three times as long as B.
  ② A takes three times longer than B.
- A は B の 3 倍の値段だ．
  ① A costs three times as much as B.
  ② A is three times the price of B.
- A は B の 3 倍の量がある．
  ① There is [We have, etc.] three times as much A as B.
  ② A is three times as abundant as B.
- それは B の 3 倍の量の A を含む．
  ① It contains three times as much A as B.
  ② It contains three times more A than B.
  ③ It contains three times more A compared「with [to] B.
- それはオレンジの 3 倍のビタミン C を含む．
  ① It contains three times as much vitamin C as an orange (does).
  ② It contains three times more vitamin C than an orange (does).
  ③ It contains three times the vitamin C of an orange.
- それは B の 2 倍の量の A を消費する．
  ① It consumes twice as much A as B.
  ② Its consumption of A is「twice [double] that of B.
- それは B の 2 倍の数の A を有する．
  ① It has twice as many A as B.
  ② It has「twice [double] the number of A as B.
- 予想の **3 倍の**応募者があった．
  ① There were **three times as many** applicants as had been expected.
  ② The number of applicants was **three times as many** as had been expected.
  ③ **Three times more** people applied than had been expected.
- その新しい電池は古いものより **2.5 倍**長持ちする．　 The new battery lasts **2.5 times** longer than the old one.
- 1 等星は 6 等星の **100 倍の明るさだ**．　First-magnitude stars **are 100 times brighter** than sixth-magnitude stars.

17. …倍 17-2

- A は B よりたった 5 倍程度速いだけだ　A is only about five times faster than B.

17-2 …倍になる

- 10 倍になる　① increase by a factor of ten　② increase (by) ten times　③ increase tenfold　④ show [achieve, etc.] a tenfold increase　⑤ show [achieve, etc.] a ten times increase　⑥ be [get] multiplied by ten　⑦ become [get] ten times「bigger [larger, etc.]　⑧ become [get] ten times as「big [large, etc.]
- 平均の **40 倍**から **110 倍**に増加した.　It has increased from **40** (**times** the average) to **110 times** the average.

17-3 …倍以上

- その金額は町の年間予算の **3 倍よりも大きい**.
  ① The sum is「**more** [**larger**, **bigger**] **than three times** the annual budget of the town.
  ② The sum is **more than three times**「**greater** [**larger**, **bigger**] **than** the annual budget of the town.
- A は B の 5 倍以上である.
  ① A is five or more times larger than B.
  ② A is five or more times as large as B.
  ③ A is more than or equal to five times as large as B.
  ④ A is more than five times as large as B.
  ⑤ A is more than five times larger than B.
- ★④⑤は厳密には「5 倍」ちょうどは含まない表現だが通例問題ない.

17-4 差・変化

- それらは 10 倍異なる.　They differ by a factor of 10.
- 20 倍の差 [相違]　① a difference by a factor of 20　② a 20-fold difference
- たった 3 倍の違いしかない.　① There is only a factor-of-three difference.　② There is only a difference of a factor of three.
- 10 倍以内の差で　within a factor of 10
- 5 倍の増収　a「**fivefold** [**five-times**, **500-percent**] increase in revenue

17-5 希釈の倍率

- 溶液を 3 倍に薄める　dilute a solution three times
- 1,000 倍の…溶液 2ml　2 ml of a 1:1,000 solution of …　★1:1,000 は one「in [to] a [one] thousand と読む.
- 10% の…を 100 倍に薄めた希釈溶液　a 1:100 diluted solution of 10% …
- 酸素の同位体 ^{18}O は 100 倍に濃縮されている.　The ^{18}O isotope of oxygen

is enriched by a factor of 100.

17-6 拡大・縮小の倍率 [⇨第2部・ばいりつ, しゅくしゃく, あっしゅくりつ]

- 1,500 倍の顕微鏡　① a 1,500-power microscope　② a 1,500X microscope
- 1 万倍で撮影した顕微鏡画像　① a microscopic image taken at 10,000 power　② a 10,000X microscopic image　③ a microscopic image magnified 10,000 times
- 100 倍に拡大する　magnify … 100 times
- 図を 25%［4 分の 1］に縮小する　reduce [shrink] an illustration to「25%[one fourth, one quarter] (of its original size)

17-7 again を使った表現

times の「倍」の意味は「…回」から派生したもの．これと同じように again (2 回) で 2 倍の意味になることもある．

- …の 2 倍の大きさ［長さ］で　as「large [long] again as…
- …の 1.5 倍の大きさ［長さ］で　① half as「large [long] again as …　② half again as「large [long] as …
- …の 1/3 増し［＝4/3 倍］の大きさ［長さ］で　a third again as「large [long] as …

17-8 数値以外の「…倍」

- 整数倍　① an integral multiple 《of …》　② an integer multiple 《of …》　③ a whole number multiple 《of …》［⇨第2部・せいすう］
- 偶数倍　an even multiple 《of …》
- 奇数倍　an odd multiple 《of …》
- 電子電荷の厳密な整数倍　an exact multiple of the electron charge
- 単位行列のスカラー倍　a scalar multiple of the identity matrix
- 処理速度は接続されるコンピューターの**台数倍**になる．
① The processing speed「is [gets] **multiplied by the number of** computers connected.
② The processing speed increases **by a factor equal to the number of** computers connected.

17-9 半分

- その金の半分　① half of the money　② half the money
★② は歴史的には ① の of が省略されたもの．
★half of … の half には修飾語がつくとき以外は a はつかない．
- リンゴの半分は腐っていた．
①〔半分の個数〕Half (of) the apples were rotten.

17. ···倍 17-9

② 〔1個の半分〕 Half (of) the apple was rotten.
★動詞の単複に注意 (⇨ 64. **各種構文と単数／複数**). a good half of the apples だと「それらのリンゴの半分も」の意.

- 半マイル　half a mile　★冠詞 (a, the) や所有格の人称代名詞 (my, etc.) は half の後が標準だが単位の場合は a half mile の語順もある.「2マイル半」の場合, two and a half miles が普通だが, two miles and a half の語順もある.
- 半分の人はそれに反対だ.　Half (of) the people are against it.

▶ 英語の half は日本語の「半」「半分」を使う場合と一致しないことがある. たとえば「半年」というときには half a year だけでなく six months もよく使われる. 逆に英語では「30分」を half an hour,「500グラム」を half a kilogram と half を使って表わすことも多い.

- もう半世紀の成長　another half-century of growth
- A は B の半分の長さである.
  ① A is half as long as B.
  ② A is half the length of B.
- A は B の半分の大きさである.
  ① A is half as large as B.
  ② A is half the size of B.
- A は B の半分の重さである.
  ① A weighs half as much as B.
  ② A is half the weight of B.
  ③ A's weight is half that of B.
- A は B の半分の時間がかかる.　A takes half as long as B.
- A は B の半分の値段だ.
  ① A costs half as much as B.
  ② A is half the price of B.
- AはBの半分しか本を持っていない.　A has only half as many books as B (does).
- 経費を半分にする　① cut expenditures by half　② reduce expenditures by a factor of two　③ halve expenditures
- 半分に減らす　① reduce by「half [50 percent]　② cut by「half [50 percent]　③ halve　④ make a reduction of 50% 《in the price》　⑤ reduce to half (of) what 《it》 was
- 半分に減る　① be halved　② be cut in half　③ be reduced by half　④ decrease by half　⑤ be reduced to half what 《it》 was
- 半分 (ずつ) に分ける　① divide [split, cut] ··· into (two) halves　② divide [split, cut] ··· in half　③〔分け合う〕share ··· half-and-half　④ split evenly
- ひもを半分のところで切る　cut a「cord [string] in the middle

- 株価が5年前の半分になった． ① Stock prices are half what they were five years ago. ② Stock prices have fallen by half「from [since] five years ago.
- 金を半分使う　spend half (of) the money
- まだ半分しか読んでいません．
  ① I have only read half the book.
  ② I am only halfway through the book.
- 小麦粉を半分ずつ加える　add flour half at a time
- それぞれが敷地全体の約半分［をほぼ半分ずつ］占めている． Each occupies about half of the entire premises.
- 費用は半分ずつ持ちましょう．
  ① Let's pay half of the expenses each.
  ② Let's「share [split] the expenses「fifty-fifty [half-and-half].

18. 同等・相当

18-1 「同じ」「等しい」

- …と同じである ①be the same as … ②be equal to … ③equal … ④be identical「to [with]」…
- 1センチは10ミリに等しい.
  ① A centimeter is ten millimeters.
  ② A centimeter is the same as ten millimeters.
  ③ One centimeter is equivalent to ten millimeters.
  ④ One centimeter is the equivalent of ten millimeters.
  ⑤ There are ten millimeters in a centimeter.
- それらは同じ値段だ.
  ① They are the same price.
  ② They have the same price.
  ③ They cost the same.
  ④ Their prices are the same.
  ⑤ The price is the same for both of them.
- どちらの店でも値段は同じだった. The price was the same at both shops.
- 線分AとBは長さが等しい.
  ① Line A is the same length as line B.
  ② Line A is of the same length as line B.
  ③ Line A has the same length as line B.
  ④ Lines A and B are equal in length.
- 日本は面積ではドイツにほぼ等しい.
  ① Japan and Germany are roughly the same「size [area].
  ② Japan is roughly the same size as Germany.
  ③ Japan has roughly the same area as Germany.
  ④ Japan is more or less equivalent to Germany in area.
  ⑤ Japan is more or less as big as Germany.
- 彼は私と**同じくらいの**背の高さだ. He is **about as** tall「as I am [as me].
- このネックレスは**ほぼ同じ大きさの**真珠でできている. This necklace is made from pearls that are **all about the same size**.
- 広島型原爆100発と同じ量のエネルギー the same amount of energy as 100 Hiroshima-type atomic bombs
- 平均的な家庭が1か月に消費するのと同じ電気エネルギー
  ① the same amount of electric energy「as [that] an average household consumes in a month
  ② the same amount of electric energy as consumed by an average household in one month
- 与えられた円と同じ面積の正方形を作図する construct a square with the

same area as a given circle
- 図形を同じ面積になるように二つに分ける　divide a figure into two parts with the same area

18-2 「同数の」

- …と同数の…　① as many … as …　② the same number of … as …
  ③ … equal in number to …　④ … of the same number as …
- この辞書はあの辞書と**同じ数**の項目がある．
  ① This dictionary has **as many** entries as that one.
  ② This dictionary has **the same number of** entries as that one.
  ③ The entries in this dictionary are **equal in number** to the entries in that one.
  ④ The entries in this dictionary are **of the same number** as those in that one.
- 今年は去年と同じ台数の新車販売は望めそうにない．　There is little hope of selling **the same number of** new vehicles this year **as** last year.
- 未知数の数と**同じ数の**方程式
  ① **the same number of** equations as (the number of) unknowns
  ② **an equal number of** equations as (the number of) unknowns
  ③ as many equations as unknowns
- 日本の総人口の 80% **に当たる**人がその地域に住んでいる．　A number of people **equal to** 80 percent of Japan's total population live in that region.
- 本を延滞したのと**同じ日数だけ**　for **the same number of** days「that [as, by which] a book is overdue
- パラメーターによって指定された値に等しい数の格納位置　storage locations「of [with] a number equal to the value specified by the parameter
- 同量の…　① the same「amount [quantity] of …　② an equal「amount [quantity] of …

18-3 相当

- 3 か月**分**の給料に相当するボーナス　a bonus **equivalent to** three months' pay
- ちょうど九州**に相当する**くらいの面積
  ① an area **just about the same as**「Kyushu [Kyushu's, that of Kyushu]
  ② an area **just about equivalent to**「Kyushu [Kyushu's, that of Kyushu]
- 3 万円**相当**の商品券　shopping coupons **to the value of** ¥30,000
- 総額 2,000 万円**相当**の宝石　jewels **to a** total **value of** ¥20 million
- 1 万円**相当**の品物　¥10,000 **worth of** goods
- 500 円**分**の切手　five hundred yen('s) **worth of** stamps

18-4 「ちょうど」「ぴったり」

- ちょうど　① just　② exactly　③ precisely
- ちょうど 1 時間　① just an hour　② exactly one hour　③ one hour to the

18. 同等・相当 18-4

minute
- 5時ぴったりに　①exactly at five o'clock　②precisely at five o'clock　③just at five o'clock　④at five o'clock sharp　⑤at five sharp o'clock on the dot　⑥at five to the minute
- ちょうど3メートル　①exactly three meters　②three meters on the mark
- 彼女は100メートルを11秒きっかりで走った．　She ran the hundred meters in eleven seconds flat.

19. 多少の表現

■ 19-1 **多数**

19-1-1 「多数の…」「たくさんの…」

① many ② a large number of ③ a number of ④ numbers of
⑤ a great number of ⑥ an enormous number of ⑦ a huge number of
⑧ a vast number of
⑨ a lot of ⑩ lots of ⑪ plenty of ⑫《口》loads of
⑬ a good many ⑭ a great many
⑮ a multitude of ⑯ multitudes of ⑰ multitudinous ⑱ numerous
⑲ a host of ⑳ hosts of ㉑ a myriad of ㉒ quite a few ㉓《文》many a

- ▶ ① many と ② a large number of が書き言葉で最も普通に用いられる表現.
- ▶ ② の a large number of は a very large number of (非常に多数の), a relatively large number of (比較的多数の), a larger number of (より多数の) などの変形もでき応用のきく表現である. 単に ③ a number of とすると「たくさんの, いくつもの」の意味のほかに「若干の, いくつかの」の意味もあるので注意. ⇨第2部・かず
- ▶ 口語では ① の many よりも ⑨〜⑫ のような表現が好まれるが, 否定文・疑問文で, また肯定文でも too many, so many などの形では many も普通に使われる.
- ▶ 上記のうち many a だけは次に単数形の名詞が続き, 動詞も単数形で受ける (例: Many a day has passed. 何日もたった).

- 数え切れない (ほどたくさん) ① countless ② uncountable ③ numberless ④ innumerable ⑤ incalculable ⑥ untold《number》⑦ beyond count ⑧ without number ⑨ infinite ⑩ too many to count ⑪ so many as to be impossible to count
- 数え切れないほど何度もそこへ足を運んだ. I've been there「countless times [more times than I can count].

19-1-2 「…は多い」「たくさんある」

英語でも「多い」を述語にした表現は可能だが,「多数の…」として訳したほうが自然になる場合が多い. また, number を主語にすれば large を述語にして受けることができる.

19. 多少の表現 19-1-3

- 可能な組み合わせは**たくさん**ある．
  ① There「are [is]」**a large number of** possible combinations.
  ② The number of possible combinations is (**very**) **large**.
  ③ The possible combinations are「**many** [**numerous**]」.
- 今日は来客が**多かった**．　We **had**「**a lot of** [**a large number of**, **a number of**, **many**]」visitors today.
- その質問に答えられない大学生が**多かった**．
  ① **Many** college students were unable to answer the question.
  ② **There were many** college students who could not answer the question.
- 日本人でこの町の名前を知っている人は**多くはない**．
  ① **Not many** Japanese know the name of this town.
  ② **There are not many** Japanese who know the name of this town.
- そのクラスは日本人**よりも**外国人学生が**多い**．　There are **more** foreign students **than** Japanese in that class.
- 2004 年のロシア人 1 人当たりのビール消費量は日本人よりも **1 割多かった**．
  ① Per capita beer consumption of Russians in 2004 was **10 percent more** than that of Japanese.
  ② In 2004, Russians drank **10 percent more** beer per capita than Japanese.
- 日本人の死因で**最も多い**のが癌だ．　The **most common** cause of death for Japanese is cancer.
- この町を訪れる外国人観光客で**一番多い**のはアメリカ人で，**その次に多い**のはドイツ人だ．
  ① Among the foreign tourists who visit this town, **the most numerous** are Americans, with Germans **second**.
  ② Americans **rank first** and Germans **second** among the foreign tourists visiting this town.
  ③ Among the foreign tourists visiting this town, **the largest number** are American, **followed by** Germans. ★the largest number は the largest number of the foreign tourists の略なので複数扱いになっている．
- その病気には薬が効かない**ことが多い**．
  ① Medicines **often** have no effect against that disease.
  ② Medicines are「**seldom** [**rarely**]」effective against that disease.
- 酒気帯び運転による交通事故は**数え切れない**．　There are **too many** drunk driving accidents **to count**.
- 枚挙にいとまがない　① be too「**numerous** [**many**] to「**mention** [**list**, **count**]」② be too many to enumerate　③ be virtually impossible to exhaust the list of …　④ the list (of …) could go on (and on)

19-1-3 「**数多く**」「**たくさん**」

- バッグをたくさん持っている　　have a lot of bags
- 本をたくさん読む　　read a lot of books

- 多数当選する　be elected in large numbers
- 多すぎる　⇨ 21. 過不足の表現

■ 19-2　**多量**

19-2-1　「**多量の…**」

① much　② a large amount of　③ a large quantity of　④ a large volume of
⑤ large amounts of　⑥ (large) quantities of　⑦ (large) volumes of
⑧ a great amount of　⑨ an enormous amount of　⑩ a huge amount of　⑪ a vast amount of
⑫ great amounts of　⑬ enormous amounts of　⑭ huge amounts of　⑮ vast amounts of
⑯ a good deal of　⑰ a great deal of
⑱ a lot of　⑲ lots of　⑳ plenty of
㉑ 《口》tons of　㉒ 《口》loads of　㉓ 《口》masses of　㉔ 《口》piles of

▶ ①～④が書き言葉で最も普通の表現.

▶ ②の a large amount of は a very large amount of (非常に多量の)、a relatively large amount of (比較的多量の)、a larger amount of (より多量の)などの変形もできる. ③の a large quantity of や④の a large volume of についても同様. また、⑧ a great amount of から⑮ vast amounts of については amount を quantity, volume で置き換えた表現も可能. ⇨第2部・かず

▶ ① much は不可算名詞に付く. ②～⑰も amount, quantity, volume, deal といった語が量を表わすので原則は不可算名詞に付く. ⑱の a lot of 以下は不可算名詞の多量のほか、可算名詞(複数形)の多数にも使うが、数という意識は薄れている.

▶ large quantities of water のような場合は quantities に合わせて複数扱いするのが本則とされるが、a lot of books を books に合わせて複数扱いにするのと同じように water に合わせて単数扱いすることもある. lots of water では lots of が much と同じような形容詞のように感じられて単数扱いが普通.

- たくさんの仕事　① much work　② a large amount of work
- **大量の**データを記憶するのに好適な記憶媒体　a storage medium suitable for storing **large volumes of** data
- タンカーの座礁事故で**大量の**原油が湾内に流出した.　When the tanker ran aground, **a huge「volume [quantity] of** crude oil spilled out into the bay.

- **多量**の毒薬を飲む　take [swallow] **a large「dose [amount] of** poison
- 南アフリカはダイヤモンドを**多量**に産出している．　South Africa yields **great quantities of** diamonds.

19-2-2 「…は多い」「たくさんある」

英語でも「多い」を述語にした表現は可能だが，「多量の…」として訳したほうが自然になる場合が多い．

- この理論を支持する証拠は**たくさん**ある．
  ① There is **much** evidence to support this theory.
  ② There is **a lot of** evidence supporting this theory.
- その国は石油の埋蔵量が**多い**．
  ① The country has **rich** oil reserves.
  ② The country is **rich** in oil.
- この地域は雨が**多い**．
  ① It rains **a lot** in this area.
  ② There is「**much** [**plentiful**, **copious**] rain in this area.
- 金がたくさんある　have「a lot [lots, plenty] of money
- やるべきことがたくさんある　have「much [a lot, many things] to do
- 宿題がたくさんある　have a「lot [mountain] of homework (to do)

19-2-3 「大量に」

- 大量に　①abundantly ②plentifully ③amply ④in abundance ⑤in profusion ⑥in large「amounts [quantities]
- O 型の血液が大量に不足している．　There is a massive shortage of type O blood.
- 多すぎる　⇨ 21. 過不足の表現

■ 19-3　**少数**

① few　② a small number of

▶ few は「ほとんどない」という含意だが，a few とすれば「少しはある」という意味合いになる．「若干」を表わす語に several があるが，これは a few と違って少ないという含意はない．

▶ a small number of は a very small number of（非常に少数の），a relatively small number of（比較的少数の），too small a number of（少なすぎる数の），a smaller number of（より少数の）のような変形もできる．　⇨第 2 部・かず

▶ 科学技術文では a small number of を冗長として a few の使用が推奨

されることもある．これも very few（きわめて少ない），relatively few（比較的少ない），too few（少なすぎる），fewer（より少ない）のような応用が可能．
▶ 比較級で「より数が少ない」というときには less も使われるが，fewer のほうが正しいとされている．ただし，単位の場合には可算名詞でも less が普通（例：less than 30 minutes）．

- 反対者は**少数だけ**だった． **Only a handful** were against it.
- 雨のため参加者は**ごく少数**だった． The attendance was **very「small［low］**owing to the rain.
- そんな人は**数えるほどしかいない**．①There are **only a handful of** people like that. ② There are **very few** people like that.
- それは**少数**だが今日でも生産されている． It is still「produced［manufactured］today, though **in small numbers**.
- この時代の史料は**少ない**．
 ① There are **few** documents from this period.
 ② **Few** documents survive from this period.
- その病気で助かる人は**少ない**． **Few** people survive the disease.
- このごろは仕事の口が**少ない**． There are **not many** job openings these days.
- こういう正直者は**少ない**．
 ① Such honest people are **rarely (to be) found**.
 ② **Not many** people are so honest.
 ③ **Few** people are so honest.
- こういう例は少ない．
 ① Such instances are **few and far between**.
 ② Such instances are **rare**.
- 少なすぎる　⇨ 21. 過不足の表現

■ 19-4 少量

① little ② a small amount of ③ a small quantity of ④ a slight amount of ⑤ a minute amount of ⑥ a tiny amount of
⑦ small amounts of ⑧ small quantities of
⑨《口》a bit of
⑩〔微量の〕a trace amount of ⑪ trace《impurities》
⑫〔乏しい〕scarce ⑬ scanty ⑭ scant ⑮ meager

▶ ① の little は「ほとんどない」という含意だが，a little とすれば「少しはある」という意味合いになる．little の比較級は less，最上級は

19. 多少の表現 19-4

least.

▶ a small amount of は a very small amount of (非常に少量の)，a relatively small amount of (比較的少量の)，too small an amount of (少なすぎる量の)，a smaller amount of (より少量の) のような変形もできる．

- 少量存在する　be present in small quantities
- 微量の不純物　① small amounts of impurities　② trace impurities
- これらの新元素はその瀝青ウラン鉱には**きわめて微量に**しか存在していなかった．
  ① These new elements were present in the pitchblende only **in extremely small quantities**.
  ② There were only **minute traces of** these new elements in the pitchblende.
- その牛乳から**微量の**農薬が検出された．　A「**minute [tiny, trace] amount of** pesticide was found in the milk.
- ほとんど知覚できないほど少量　in almost imperceptible quantities
- カロリー [鉄分] が少ない　be「low [poor] in「calories [iron]
- 在庫が少なくなった．　The stock has run low.
- 彼女は家にいることが少ない．　She is「seldom [hardly ever] at home.
- 食べる量を少なくする　① reduce the「quantity [amount] of food *one* eats
  ② eat less
- 少なすぎる　⇨ 21. 過不足の表現

20.「…も」「…しか」「たった」

■ 20-1 「…も」

- …も ① as「many [much] as … ② no「fewer [less] than … ③ (距離) as far as … ④ (長さ) as long as …
- ★many, fewer は可算名詞に，much, less は不可算名詞に使う．
- 10個もある． ① There are **as many as** ten． ② There are **no fewer than** ten．
- 80% もの高支持率　an approval rating **as high as** 80%
- 100万円もする腕時計　a wristwatch that「is [costs] **as much as** ¥1 million
- 5 年も　① **as long as** five years　② for five **long** years
- 5 回も落選する　be defeated in elections「**as often as** five times [**no less than** five times]
- 彼女の店では 10 人も人を使っている． **No fewer than** ten people are employed in her store.
- 負債は 5,000 万円**にもなる**． The debt **amounts to** ¥50 million.
- 温度が 60 度**にも達した**． The temperature **reached as high as** 60°C.
- 500 キロメートル**にも達する**
  ① **extend as far as** 500 kilometers
  ② **extend to a length of** 500 kilometers
- 5,000 万円**も**借金がある　be in debt **to the「extent [tune] of** ¥50 million
- 1 億円もの大金　the enormous sum of 100 million yen
- 7.9 テラバイトもの記憶容量を消費する　① consume as much as 7.9 terabytes of storage　② 《口》 consume a whopping 7.9 terabytes of storage
- **まるまる** 1 週間　① a **full** week　② a **whole** week　③ an **entire** week
- **まるまる** 3 時間　① three **whole** hours　② three **full** hours　③ three **entire** hours

■ 20-2 「…しか」「たった」

- …しか　① only　② but　③ no more than …　④ as few as …　⑤ as little as … ★few は可算名詞に，little は不可算名詞に使う．
- 10 個**しかない**．
  ① There are **only** ten.
  ② There are **but** ten.
  ③ There are **no more than** ten.
  ④ There are **as few as** ten.
- 200 人**しか**収容できない．
  ① **Only** 200 people can be accommodated.

② **No more than** 200 people can be accommodated.
③ 《The hall》 can hold **only** 200 people.
④ 《The hall》 can hold **no more than** 200 people.

- GDP［国内総生産］の**たった**0.1%　**no more than** 0.1% of「GDP [the gross domestic product]
- **たった**3日間　① for **just** three days　② for **only** three days　③ for **no more than** three days　④ for **a mere** three days　⑤ for **but** three days
- 会員の30パーセント**しか**その計画に賛成しなかった．　**Only** 30 percent of the members approved the plan.
- **これっぱかりの金では何も買えない．**
  ① **Such a**「**small** [**paltry**, **tiny**] sum won't buy anything.
  ② You can't buy anything for「**this much** [**so little**].
- 1,000円や2,000円の**はした金**　**a paltry sum** of one or two thousand yen
- 設立から**やっと**半年たったところだ．
  ① It is **barely** half a year since it was established.
  ② It was established **only** six months ago.
- 売り上げは**かろうじて**前年を上回った．
  ① The sales were **barely** above the amount of the previous year.
  ② The sales **barely** exceeded the amount a year earlier.
- 一度**しか**ない人生　a life one can live「**only** [**but**] once.
- これだけしか持ってません．　This is all I have.
- **たった**1分の差で列車に間に合わなかった．　I missed the train by **just**「a [one] minute.
- ほんの少しのところで　① by **just** a little　② 《lose the game》 by the slimmest of margins
- ほんのちょっとの間　① **just** a minute　② **just** a moment　③ **just** for a little while
- ほんの少し前まで　until **just** a short while ago
- ほんの数分の間に　① in the space of **just** a few minutes　② in a matter of minutes

■ 20-3　no more than …, no less than …, no fewer than … の用法

　no more than … は「…より少したりとも多くない」という少なさを強調する表現であるのに対し，not more than … は「…よりも多くない」という客観的な事実を表わす．

- その場には8人**しか**いなかった．　**No more than** eight people were present.
- その場にいた人は8人を**超えなかった**．　**Not more than** eight people were present.

ただし，規定を述べる文などでは主観的な色合いなしに no more than … を「…よりも多くない」の意味で使う．

- 報告は事件から 15 日**以内に**提出すること．　Reports must be submitted **no more than** 15 days after an incident.

同様に，no less than …，no fewer than … は「…より少したりとも少なくない」という多さを強調する表現であるが，規定を述べる文などでは主観的な色合いなしに「…よりも少なくない」の意味で使う．

- 12 単位**以上** 16 単位**以下**　**no fewer than** 12 and **no more than** 16 credits

21. 過不足の表現

■ 21-1 不足

21-1-1 「…だけ足りない」

- 1,000 円足りない　be ¥1,000 short
- 10 万円以上足りない　be more than 100,000 yen short
- (お金が) いくら足りないの？　How much is it short (by)?
- 重さが 1 ポンド足りない　be one pound short in weight
- プレイする人が 1 人足りない．
  ① We are short one player.
  ② We are one player short.
- いすが 2 つ足りない．
  ①〔必要である〕We need two more chairs.
  ②〔あるはずのものがない〕Two chairs are missing.
- 長さが 10 センチ足りない
  ① be 10 centimeters (too) short
  ② be too short by 10 centimeters

21-1-2 「…に足りない」

- 1,000 円に 10 円足りない．　I'm ten yen「short [shy]」of a thousand (yen).
- 規定の寸法に 2 センチ足りなかった．　It was two centimeters「short [shy]」of the regulation measurement.
- 3,000 円では電車代にも足りない．　Three thousand yen isn't enough even for the train fare.

21-1-3 欠乏

- 不足している
  〈対象物が主語〉① be not enough　② be insufficient　③ be deficient　④ be inadequate　⑤ be lacking　⑥ be in short supply
  〈人などが主語〉⑦ be short of …　⑧ be shy of …　⑨ be deficient in …　⑩ lack　⑪ be lacking in …
- 少なすぎる…　①〔数が〕too few　②　too small a number of　③〔量が〕too little　④ too small an amount of　⑤ too small a quantity of
- 深さが足りない　① be not deep enough　② be too shallow
- 使える色数が少なすぎる．
  ① There are too few colors available.
  ② There aren't enough available colors.
  ③ The available colors are not enough.

- 参加者が少なすぎる．
  ① There are too few participants.
  ② We have too few participants.
  ③ The number of participants is too small.
  ④ There aren't enough participants.

■ 21-2 過剰

21-2-1 「…だけ…すぎる」

- 0が1つ多すぎる
  ① There is one zero too many.
  ② There is one too many zero.
- それでは2人多すぎだ． That's two people too many.
- 10ドル払いすぎる　pay ten dollars too much
- 少し[かなり]大きすぎる　be「a little [much] too large《for …》
- xの値が1大きすぎる． The value of x is too large by 1.
- 3センチ長すぎる　be three centimeters too long
- 20分早く来すぎる　come twenty minutes too early
- 外国貿易は40億円の輸入超過を見た．
  ① The balance of foreign trade has shown an excess of four billion yen in imports over exports.
  ② The foreign trade deficit has exceeded ¥4 billion.

21-2-2 過剰

- 多すぎる…　①〔数が〕too many　② too large a number of　③〔量が〕too much　④ an excessive amount of　⑤ an excessive quantity of　⑥ too large an amount of　⑦ too large a quantity of
- このプログラムには誤りが多すぎる．　There are too many errors in this program.
- 1日3回のミスは多すぎる．　Three errors in a day is「too many [too much]．★「3回のミス」を一つのデータとして見ているので動詞は単数の is になる．too much は数の多さよりも「あまりにひどい」ことに重点を置いている．文語では Three errors in a day is more than can be tolerated. なども可能．
- ビール何杯なら多すぎか．　How many beers is too many?
- 多すぎるくらいのチップ　a more-than-adequate tip
- 過剰な　①〔数量が〕surplus　② overabundant　③ superabundant　④ redundant　⑤ superfluous　⑥ bloated　⑦〔程度が〕excessive　⑧ exaggerated
- 過剰に　①〔数量が〕too much　② excessively　③ in excess　④ in too great「quantity [quantities, amounts]　⑤ overabundantly　⑥〔程度が〕too much

21. 過不足の表現 21-2-2

⑦ excessively ⑧ in excess ⑨ unduly ⑩ overly
- 設備過剰　overcapacity
- 過剰生産能力［設備］　① excess (production) capacity ② overcapacity
- 在庫過剰　overstock
- 過剰在庫　① surplus stock ② excess stock ③ an excessive inventory
- 供給過多　① an excess(ive) supply ② an excess of supply ③ an oversupply
- 労働力の過剰　a surplus of labor
- 生産過剰　overproduction
- 人口過剰の都市　an overpopulated city
- 人員過剰の省庁　① overstaffed ministries and agencies ② a bloated bureaucracy
- 胃酸過多　① gastric hyperacidity ② hyperchlorhydria
- 債務超過　liabilities in excess of assets
- 債務超過額　net liabilities

22. 割合

■ 22-1 割合

22-1-1 歩合

- 1 割　① 10 percent　② a tenth　③ one tenth
- 2 割 7 分　27 percent
- 2 割 3 分 5 厘　① 23.5 percent　② 0.235　③ 〔打率〕《a batting average of》.235
  ★小数 0.235 は zero 〔naught〕 point two three five と読むが，打率の場合は 0 を書かず two thirty-five と読む．
- 1 割未満　① below 10 percent　② under 10 percent　③ less than 10 percent
- 有権者の 7 割以上　more than 70 percent of the eligible voters
- 8 割の確率で　① with a probability of 80 percent　② with an eight-in-ten chance
- 8 分の利子　8% interest
- 5 分利付き公債　five-percent bonds
- 日歩 5 厘の利子　interest of 0.5 percent per day
- 1900 年にはアフリカ系アメリカ人の約 **9 割**が南部に住んでいた．　In 1900, about「**nine tenths〔ninety percent**〕of all African-Americans lived in the South.

22-1-2 百分率／パーセント

- パーセント　① percent　② per cent　★《記号 %》英語の cm, kg などの単位は数字との間にスペースを空けるが，% 記号はスペースを空けずに数字の次に書く．
- 65 歳以上が人口**の 10% を占めている**．　Those 65 years old or above **account for 10 percent of** the population.　★ percent は「100 当たり」が原義であり，percents のように -s を付けることはしない．
- **80% 以上**の票　① **80 percent or more** of the votes　②〔80% 超〕**more than 80 percent** of the votes
- 利率は **3%** だ．　The interest rate is **3 percent**.
- **約 30% の濃度**の硫酸　sulfuric acid of **about 30 percent concentration**
- **70% の**削減　a **70 percent** reduction

22-1-3 パーミル

- パーミル　① per mil　② per mill《記号 ‰》
- **パーミル**で表わした濃度　concentration expressed **in permillage**
- その値は **2 ないし 3 パーミル**の範囲にある．　The value ranges **from 2 to**

22. 割合 22-1-4

3 per mil.

22-1-4 ppm / ppb / ppt

ppm (parts per million) は 10^6 分の 1, ppb (parts per billion) は 10^9 分の 1, ppt (parts per trillion) は 10^{12} 分の 1 を表わす．

- 水銀含有量が **10ppm** である． The mercury content《of the waste》is 「**10 ppm [10 parts per million]**．
- 窒素酸化物の濃度が **0.031ppm** を超える． Nitrogen oxide concentration levels exceed **0.031 ppm**.

22-1-5 分数 [⇨ 53. 分数]

- 会員の 3 分の 2　　two thirds of the members
- 全体の 8 分の 1　　one eighth of the whole
- 参加者の 4 分の 3　　three quarters of the participants
- **3 軒に 2 軒**の家庭にテレビがあった． **Two thirds** of the households had a TV set.
- **100 人のうち 99 人**までが賛成するだろう． **Ninety-nine people out of one hundred** will approve.
- **5 人のうち 4 人**までもが電気のない暮らしをしている． As many as **four out of every five people** live without electricity.
- **5 人に 1 人**が病気だった． **One out of five** was sick.
- 受験者 **10 人に 1 人の割合**で合格者が出た．
  ① **One out of ten** examinees passed the test.
  ② The pass rate was **one in ten**.
- **100 個に 1 つ**が故障していた．
  ① **One in a hundred** was out of order.
  ② **One in every hundred** was out of order.
- この病気は **1,000 人に 1 人の割合**で現われる．
  ① This disease occurs **in one in a thousand**.
  ② This disease occurs **in one in every thousand**.
  ③ This disease affects **one in a thousand people**.

22-1-6 各種表現

- 地球の表面の**約 70%** は海だ．
  ① **About 70 percent of** the Earth's surface is covered by oceans.
  ② Oceans cover **about 70 percent** of the Earth's surface.
- EU は世界人口の 7% 余りを**占めていた**． The EU **accounted for** just over 7 percent of the world's population.
- わがチームは 20 歳未満が 3 割を**占めている**．

① Those under 20 years of age **account for** 30 percent of this team's players.
② Thirty percent of the players on this team are under 20 (years of age).
- 大気は体積比ではほぼ **80%** が窒素，**20%** が酸素だ． The atmosphere is roughly **80%** nitrogen and **20%** oxygen by volume.
- 最も古い部類の星は約 **75%** の水素と **25%** のヘリウムからなる． The oldest stars are made up of about **75 percent** hydrogen and **25 percent** helium.
- グラウンドには 500 人ほどの児童がいたが，**そのうち約 6 割**が男子だった．
  ① There were about 500 children on the playground, **of which around 60 percent** were boys.
  ② **Of the** approximately 500 children on the playground, **about 60 percent** were boys.
- **少なくとも 3 分の 1** がブローカーに取られ，現地の住民に残るのは 20 トンだけだ． **At least a third** is taken by the broker, leaving only 20 tons for the local inhabitants.
- 近隣の星**の 85% 近く**がなんらかの伴星を伴っている． **Nearly 85 percent of** nearby stars have some kind of companion. ★stars に合わせて動詞は複数語形の have になっている．
- 太陽のエネルギー放出**の約 50%** が可視光の領域にあたる． **About 50 percent of** the energy output of the sun falls within the visible spectrum. ★output に合わせて動詞は単数語形の falls になっている．
- 鋼は**何パーセントかの**炭素を含む． Steel contains **several percent of** carbon.
- ウインドーのできるだけ多くの部分を表示する　display as large an area of the window as possible

22-1-7　疑問文

- 大気中の酸素の割合は**何 %** ですか． **What is the percentage** of oxygen in the atmosphere?
- 物理を取っている生徒の**何 %** が女子ですか． **What percentage** of students taking physics are girls?
- 大気の**何 %** が酸素ですか． **What percent** of the atmosphere is oxygen?
- **何 %** の学生が試験に合格しましたか． **What percent of** the students passed the examination?
- 25 は 125 の**何 %** ですか．
  ① 25 is **what percent** of 125?
  ② **What percent** of 125 is 25?
- 職場の女性の**割合**はどれくらいですか． What is the ⌈**percentage** ⌊**proportion, ratio**⌋ of women at your workplace?
- 可動端子の位置が，入力電圧のうち**どれくらいの割合**が回路に加えられる

かを決める. The position of the movable terminal determines **what percentage** of the input voltage is applied to the circuit.
- 定期預金の利子は今**何パーセント**ですか. **What is** the interest rate on time deposits?

22-1-8 　**変化率** [⇨ 13-2-2 増減の程度]

- 気温の **1%** の上昇　　a **1 percent** increase in temperature
- 現在の値より **25%** 低い　　be **25 percent** lower than the present value
- **30%** 以上増加する　　increase by more than **30%**
- 年 **5%** を超える成長　　growth at more than **5%** per year
- **20〜30%** 減少する　　decrease by **20 to 30 percent**
- 歳入は前年より **6%** 上がった.　　The revenue was up by **6%** 「over [compared with] the previous year.
- 失業率が **0.3%** 上がった.　　The unemployment rate went up 「**0.3 percent** [**0.3 point**, **0.3 percentage point**].
- 金利目標値を **0.25%** 上げて 1.25% にする　　raise the target for the money rate **by a quarter point** [**by a quarter of a percentage point**] to 1.25%
- 目標金利の **0.25%** の上昇　　a **quarter-point** increase in the target rate

22-1-9 　**ポイント**

- ポイント　　a (percentage) point
- 割合は **10 ポイント**上がって 70% から 80% になった.　　The percentage rose **(by) 10 points**, from 70 percent to 80 percent. ★70% に対して 10% 上昇して 77% になったという誤解を避けるため, percent でなく point を用いている.
- 割合は **4 ポイント**上がった [下がった].　　The percentage went 「up [down] **four points**.
- 大統領の支持率は **2 ポイント**下がった.　　The popularity rating of the president dropped **two percentage points**. ★point は多義語なのでしばしばこのように percentage point という.
- 利率の **1 ポイント**の低下　　a **one-percentage-point** drop in the interest rate

22-1-10 　**重量比・体積比など**

- 重量パーセント　　① percent by weight　② weight percent
- 体積パーセント　　① percent by volume　② volume percent
- ある成分の重量百分率または体積百分率　　a component's percentage by weight or volume
- **重量パーセント**で表わした濃度　　concentration (expressed) 「**in percent by weight** [**in weight percent**]

- 岩石中の SiO₂ の**重量パーセント**　**the weight percentage** of SiO_2 in the rock
- それらの元素の**重量パーセント濃度**を求める　determine **the weight percent concentrations** of those elements
- 重元素の存在比は，これまでに調べられた星の中で**質量比にして 4%** 程度までの変動がある．　The heavy-element abundances vary up to about **4 percent by mass** among all stars so far studied.
- この鉱物のカルシウムの含有率は，**モル比にして 16 から 40% まで**ある．　The calcium content in this mineral ranges **from 16 to 40 mole percent**.
- 表の数値は**総重量に対する百分率**で表わしてある．　The values in the table are expressed **in percentage of the total weight**.

22-1-11　「割合」を表わす語句

- 割合　①a proportion ②a ratio ③a rate ④a percentage ⑤〔受け取る割合など〕a share
- ★母数の中で占める比率を表わすのは percentage, proportion, ratio, rate (⇨第2部・りつ)．a:b のような相対比率を表わすのは proportion, ratio, 単位量当たりの大きさを表わすのは rate．
- 経費の総収入に対する割合　the「percentage〔ratio〕of expenses to gross receipts
- 全人口に対する割合　a percentage relative to the total population
- **割合**は，その要素の大きさを基準としている．　**Percentages** are relative to the size of the element.
- この会社は女性社員の**割合**が高い．　There is a high **proportion** of women employees in this company.
- 合格者のうち男性の**比率**が年々高くなってきている．　**The percentage** of men among successful examinees has been increasing yearly.
- 参加者の大きな**割合**を中高年が占めている．　A large **proportion** of participants are middle-aged and elderly people.
- もとの長さに対して**所与の割合**だけ変形する　deform … **by a given percentage** of the original length

22-1-12　パーセント表示

- **百分率**で表わしたその同位体の割合　the proportion of the isotope expressed「**in percentage**〔**in percent, as a percentage, as a percent**〕
- 相対湿度は普通**パーセント**で表わされる．　The relative humidity is usually expressed「**in percent**〔**in percentage, as a percentage, as a percent**〕.
- 実際の蒸気圧を飽和蒸気圧で割って，それに 100 をかけて**パーセント**にする　divide the actual vapor pressure by the saturation vapor pressure and then multiply by 100 to convert to **a percent**

- **百分率**から小数に直す ① convert from 「**percent** [**percentage**]」 to decimal ② write a percent as a decimal

■ 22-2　**単位量当たりの割合**
[⇨第2部・…あたり]

- 1秒当たり100ギガビットの割合で　at the rate of 100 gigabits per second
- 月に1度の割合で　① at the rate of once a month ② as often as once a month
- 1ドル100円の割合で換算する　convert at the rate of ¥100 to the dollar
- 1時間当たりの料金　an hourly rate 《of 200 yen》
- 1kg増すごとに100円の割合で加算する　add ¥100 for every additional kilogram
- ★使用量との関係などで考える料金はしばしば rate で表現する．a flat rate (固定料金), a freight rate (貨物料金), water rates (水道料金) など．
- 導出された値を一定の割合だけ下げる　reduce the derived value by a 「fixed [predetermined]」 percentage
- その学校ではパソコンは**クラスに1台**しかなかった．　The school had only **one** PC **for each class**.
- 看護師**1人当たり**患者が10人いる．　There are ten patients **for** 「**each** [**every**]」 **nurse**.

■ 22-3　**相対比率**

- A と B の比 [A の B に対する比]　① the ratio of A to B ② the ratio between A and B ③ the ratio $A{:}B$ ★$A{:}B$ は A to B または A B と読む．
- 3対2の比率である．
  ① They are in a ratio of three to two.
  ② They are in the ratio 3:2.
- 3対1の比率を示す　indicate a ratio of three to one
- 5:5:3 の比率　① 《at》 a five-five-three ratio ② 《at》 a ratio of 5:5:3
- 油と酢を2対1の割合で [油2, 酢1の割合で] 混ぜる
  ① mix oil and vinegar 「in [at]」 「a [the]」 ratio of two to one
  ② mix two parts (of) oil and one part (of) vinegar
- 三角形の3辺の比を2対5対7とする．　Assume the sides of the triangle are in the ratio two to five to seven.
- 乗客は日本人**10に対して**外国人は**3**の割合だった．　The ratio of Japanese to foreign passengers was **ten to three**.
- 6対4で男子が多かった．
  ① There were more boys by a ratio of 6:4.
  ② There were more boys by a proportion of 6:4.

③ Boys outnumbered girls by 6 to 4.
- 社員の男女比は男が6で女が4だ．
  ① The ratio of men to women in the company is six to four.
  ② There are six men to every four women in the company.
- その植民地の男女の不均衡は**女1人に男が6人**から2.5人にまで縮小した． The gender imbalance of the colony decreased from **6** to 2.5 **males for each woman**.
- メンバーの男女比はどのくらいですか．
  ① What is the ratio of male to female members?
  ② What is the ratio of men to women among the members?

■ 22-4 定性的な割合

22-4-1 半分 [⇨ 17-9 半分]

- リンゴの半分が腐っていた．
  ①〔半分の個数〕Half (of) the apples were rotten.
  ②〔1個の半分〕Half (of) the apple was rotten.

22-4-2 一部

- 一部　① a part　② a portion　③〔小部分〕a fraction
- **一部の**患者にはその薬は効かなかった．　The medicine did not work for **some** patients.
- その意見に反対した人は**ごく一部**にすぎない．　**Only a few** people disagreed with that opinion.
- 1秒の何分の1という短い瞬間　a tiny fraction of a second
- 部分修正　(a) partial revision

22-4-3 ほとんど

- ほとんどの　① almost all (of)　② nearly all (of)　③ the vast majority of　④ most
- 廃熱のほとんどが回収される．　Almost all [Nearly all] (of) the waste heat is recovered.
- メンバーのほとんどが初心者だった．　The vast majority of the members were beginners.
- 金はほとんど残っていない．
  ① There is hardly any money left.
  ② I have almost no money left.
  ③ I am nearly out of money.

22-4-4 全部

- 全部 ① all ② the whole
- すべての ① all ② the entire ③ the whole ④ every ⑤ each and every
- 所持金全部 ① all *one's* money ② the whole of *one's* money
- すべてがうまくいかなかった． ① Everything went wrong. ② Nothing went right.
- 最初の3ブロックを除いて全部のブロック all but the first three blocks

■ 22-5 部分否定と全否定

英語では all を否定文で使うと，all と not の前後関係にかかわりなく普通は全否定ではなく部分否定の意味になる．

All did **not** go right. すべてがうまくいったわけではなかった．（部分否定）

Nothing went right. 何もうまくいかなかった．（全否定）

They did **not** fix **all** of the bugs. バグを全部直したわけではなかった．（部分否定）

They did **not** fix **any** bugs. バグを一つも直さなかった．（全否定）

ただし，all と not が離れている場合などには全否定の意味になることもある．not all の形にすれば部分否定を表わすことができる．

All the members present in that room were **not** satisfied with the proposal. その部屋に集まっていたメンバーはみなその提案に満足していなかった．（全否定）

Not all members present in that room were satisfied with the proposal. その部屋に集まっていたメンバーがみなその提案に満足したわけではなかった．（部分否定）

every, both についても否定文では普通は部分否定の意味になる．

Everyone can**not** be satisfied. 全員を満足させることはできない．（部分否定）

Not a single person can be satisfied. 誰一人満足させることはできない．（全否定）

It does **not** satisfy **both** conditions. それは両方の条件は満足しない．（部分否定）

It does **not** satisfy **either** condition. [It satisfies **neither** condition.] それ

はどちらの条件も満足しない．（全否定）
  ▶ or は否定語のあとで使うと「どちらも…でない」の意味になる．
  Pigments do **not** dissolve in water **or** oil. 顔料は水にも油にも溶けない．
  ＝Pigments do **not** dissolve in **either** water **or** oil.
  ＝Pigments dissolve **neither** in water **nor** in oil.

23. 確率と可能性

23-1 確率を表わすさまざまな表現

- 確率 ① (a) probability ② odds ③ chances ④〔見込み〕(a) likelihood
- 彼が勝つ確率は 1000 に一つだ.
  ① The probability that he wins is one in 1000.
  ② The probability of「his [him]」winning is one in 1000.
  ③ The「odds [chances]」of「his [him]」winning are one in 1000.
  ④ The「odds [chances]」that he wins are one in 1000.
  ⑤ The likelihood of「his [him]」winning is one in 1000.
  ⑥ The likelihood that he wins is one in 1000.
  ⑦ The odds are 1000 to 1 against him.
  ⑧ There is a one-in-a-thousand chance of「his [him]」winning.

▶ この意味の odds は常に複数で使う. chances は特定の値をいうときには単数形でいう.

▶ likelihood は統計学では「尤度 (ゆうど)」を表わすが, 日常的な文脈で「見込み」「可能性」という意味での「確率」を表わす場合には使える.

- 彼女は 99% の確率で勝つだろう. She has a 99% chance of winning.
- その判定アルゴリズムは誤りの確率が 10^{-5} だ.
  ① The determination algorithm has an error probability of 10^{-5}.
  ② The error probability of that determination algorithm is 10^{-5}.
- それは 3/4 の確率で起こる. It occurs with a probability of 3/4.
- **50%** の確率で吸収される可能性がある. There is a **50 percent** chance of being absorbed.
- それは 9 割以上の確率でスパムだろう.
  ① It is more than 90% likely to be spam.
  ② It has more than a 90% chance of being spam.
  ③ It has a probability of more than 90% of being spam.
- 彼女が勝つ確率は五分五分といったところだ.
  ① Chances are even that she will win.
  ② She has a fifty-fifty chance of winning.
- 表が出る確率 ① the probability of getting heads《when tossing a coin》 ② the probability (that)《the coin》lands heads up ③ the probability of heads
- 3 つの硬貨を投げたときに, 少なくとも 1 つ表が出る確率 the probability of getting at least one head when three coins are tossed.
- 2 つの硬貨が同じ面になる確率 the probability (that) two coins show the same face
- 2 人の人物が同一の指紋をもつ確率はほとんど 0 だ.

① The probability of two persons having identical fingerprints is almost zero.
② The probability that two persons have identical fingerprints is almost zero.

- ハートのエースを引く確率　the probability of drawing the ace of hearts 《from a「pack [《米》deck] of cards》》
- その事象の確率を求める　find the probability「for [of] the event.
- 奇数の目が出る確率は2分の1である．　There is a one-in-two「probability [chance, likelihood] of an odd number (turning up).
- 彼が成功する確率は10に1つもない．　There isn't even a one-in-ten「probability [chance, likelihood] of his succeeding [of him succeeding, that he will succeed].
- N人のグループで2人以上の人が同じ誕生日である確率はどれくらいですか．　What is the「chance [probability] of two or more people having the same birthday in a group of N people?
- 23人以上いれば少なくとも2人が同じ誕生日である確率は50%以上になる．　When there are 23 or more people, there is a more than 50% chance that at least two people have the same birthday.
- 成功する確率は0.1よりずっと少ない [低い]．　The probability of success is much「less [lower] than 0.1.
- **100%の確実性**　a **100 percent** certainty
- **90%の精度**　**90 percent** accuracy
- 彼女が正しいと**100%**確信している．　I'm **100 percent** sure that she is right.

23-2 可能性を表わす副詞

probably おそらく…だろう，まず…だろう《可能性が高い》
perhaps, maybe …かもしれない《可能性の大小は問わない》
possibly …の可能性もある《可能性は高くないがありうる》

23-3 定性的な可能性

- たばこを吸う人は吸わない人よりも肺がんになる**確率が高い**．
  ① Smokers **have a greater likelihood** of getting lung cancer than nonsmokers.
  ② Smokers **are more likely** than nonsmokers to get lung cancer.
- 彼の死は自殺の**可能性が高い**．　There is a strong「**likelihood** [**possibility**] that his death was suicide.
- この動物はすでに絶滅している**可能性が高い**．
  ① **It is highly「probable** [**likely**] that this animal is already extinct.
  ② **There is a high probability** that this animal is already extinct.
  ③ This animal is **very probably** already extinct.
  ④ 《口》 **(The) chances are** (that) this animal is already extinct.

23. 確率と可能性 23-3

- その計画が成功する**可能性は十分ある**.
  ① **It is perfectly possible** that the plan will ⌈succeed [work, come off]⌋.
  ② The plan **may well** succeed.
- その計画は成功する**可能性がある**.
  ① The plan **may** succeed.
  ② **There is a possibility** that the plan will succeed.
  ③ **It is** ⌈**possible** [**conceivable**]⌋ that the plan will succeed.
- その計画が成功する**可能性は依然残されている**.
  ① **There is still** ⌈**some** [**a**] **possibility**⌋ that the plan will succeed.
  ② **It is still** ⌈**possible** [**conceivable**]⌋ that the plan will succeed.
- その計画が成功する**可能性は低い**.
  ① **The chances** that the plan will succeed **are low**.
  ② **It is unlikely** that the plan will succeed.
- その計画が成功する**可能性はまずない**.
  ① **It is extremely unlikely** that the plan will succeed.
  ② **There is little likelihood** that the plan will succeed.
  ③ **There is little** ⌈**likelihood** [**possibility**]⌋ of the plan working.
- 彼女が再選される**見込みはどのくらいありますか**.
  ① **What are the chances that** she will be reelected?
  ② **What are the chances of** her reelection? ★against her reelection とすると「再選されない見込み」.
  ③ **What are her chances of** ⌈reelection [getting reelected]⌋?
  ④ **What chances are there of** her reelection?
  ⑤ **How likely** is she to be reelected?
  ⑥ **How are things going for** her reelection?

24. 合計・累計・延べ

■ 24-1 合計・総計・総額

- 合計　① the total　② the total「amount [sum]」　③ an aggregate 《of …》　④〔小計に対する総計〕the「sum [grand, full]」total
- 合計する　① add up　② sum up　③ add together　④ total
- 合計して，合計すると　① in total　② altogether　③ in all　④ all told　⑤ in the aggregate
- **合計** 12,000 円　① 12,000 yen **in total**　② **a total of** 12,000 yen
- 流動資産**合計**　**the total** current assets
- **合計** 100 冊の本　① **a total of** 100 books　② 100 books **all told**　③ 100 books **in all**　④ books numbering 100 **in total**
- 合計…になる　① amount to … in all　② total …　③ make a total of …　④ add up to …
- 合計 100 になる．　① The total is one hundred.　② The total amounts to one hundred.　③ They are one hundred in all.　④ They total a hundred.
- **合計では** GDP［国内総生産］の 25% **にもなる**．　① It **totals no less than** 25% of「GDP [the gross domestic product]．　② **In total**, it **accounts for no less than** 25% of「GDP [the gross domestic product]．
- 参加者の**合計**は 500 名を超えた．
  ① **The total number** of participants surpassed 500.
  ② More than 500 people attended **altogether**.
- 同機には**合計** 75 名が搭乗していた．　There were **a total of** 75 people aboard the plane.
- 同機に搭乗していた**合計** 75 名が救助された．　**All** 75 people aboard the plane were rescued.
- 乗組員**合計** 30 人であった．　The crew consisted of 30 **all told**.
- 過去半年間にトラクター 100 台，**総額** 10 億円が同国に輸出された．　During the past six months 100 tractors「**totaling** one billion yen [amounting to one billion yen **in total**, **with a total value of** one billion yen] were exported to that country.
- 月額費用の**合計**　**the total** of monthly expenses
- 合計いくらになりますか．
  ① How much does it come to?
  ② What does it amount to「in all [altogether, in total]?
  ③ What does the total come to?
- 前方に 3 つ，後方に 2 つで合計 5 つのスピーカーがある．　① There are three speakers in the front and two in the rear, making a total of five speak-

ers. ② There are five speakers in total, three in the front and two in the rear.

■ 24-2 小計

- 小計　a subtotal
- 小計 5,000 円になる．　It subtotals five thousand yen.

■ 24-3 累計

- 累計　① the cumulative「total [number, amount]」《to date》 ② the accumulated「total [number, amount]」　★ number は個数・回数など，amount は量・額などの場合．
- その辞書は**累計部数**が 1,000 万部を超える．
  ① **The cumulative number of copies** of that dictionary exceeds ten million.
  ② More than ten million copies of that dictionary **have been printed since its first publication**.
  ③ **The total print run** of that dictionary has been over ten million.
- 全 7 巻のそのコミックは**累計販売部数** 300 万部を突破した．　**The cumulative sales** of that comic, complete in seven volumes, exceeded three million copies.
- 累計…に達する　① total … 　② amount to … 　③ run up to … 　★文脈により「合計」（⇨ 24-1）に対する英語をそのまま使えることも多い．
- 乗客数の**累計**　the cumulative total number of passengers
- **累計**売上高　① **cumulative** sales　② **accumulated** sales
- 減価償却**累計額**　① **accumulated** depreciation　② **the cumulative amount** of depreciation
- 剰余金**累計**　**accumulated** surplus
- **年初からの累計**売上高　the **year-to-date gross** sales
- **今年にはいってからの累計**申請件数　① the **year-to-date** filings　② the **year-to-date** applications　③ the number of applications filed so far this year

■ 24-4 延べ

- 延べ数　① a total　② an aggregate
- **延べ** 35,000 人　**a total of** 35,000 people
- その庭園は完成するのに**延べにして** 150 人日かかった．　It took **a total of** 150 man-days to finish the garden.
- 看護職員全員の**月延べ勤務時間**　① **the monthly total number of** hours worked by the entire nursing staff　② **the monthly total** working hours of all nursing employees
- 作業者全員の**延べ就労日数**　the **total** man-days of all the workers

- 延べ日数　① a total number of (working) days　② total man-days
- 延べ出撃回数は 3000 回を超えた．　A total of 3,000 missions were flown.
★mission は「任務を帯びた飛行」の意．
- 延べ語数　① a total number of words used　② the number of tokens
★同じ単語は 1 回しか数えない「異なり語数」は the number of types という．
- 延べ視聴率〔複数回コマーシャルを出したときにそれぞれの視聴率の合計〕a gross rating point《略 GRP》

25. 平均

25-1 平均値を述べる表現

- 平均　① an average　② a mean
- 平均値　① the mean value　② the average value
- 平均では [平均して，平均すると]　① on average　② on an average　③ on the average
- 平均では…となる　① be [come to, amount to, etc.] … on average　② average …
- このサイトは**平均して**1日に1,000件ほどのアクセスがある．
  ① This site is accessed **on average** 1,000 times a day.
  ② This site receives **an average of** 1,000 hits a day.
  ③ This site **averages** 1,000 hits a day.
- **1日平均**10時間働く　① **work** 10 hours **a day on (the) average**　② **average** 10 hours **a day at work**
- 成人は一晩に**平均**コップ2杯程度の汗をかく．　An adult sweats **an average of** two cups per night.
- 昨年は地価が**平均して** 1.2% 下がった．　Land prices fell by **an average of** 1.2% last year.
- 2001年から2005年の経済成長率は**年平均** 3.2% だった．　The economy grew at **an average annual rate of** 3.2 percent from 2001 through 2005.
- 3か月の平均　a three-month average
- 去年の平均　the average for last year
- ここ5日間の平均取引高　the average trading volume over the last 5 days
- 彼は多い日には100通近く，**平均でも**毎日50通ほどのメールを受け取っている．　On some days he receives as many as 100 e-mails, and **even on an average day** he gets about 50.
- **そのぐらいが平均**だろうね．　I suppose **that's about average**.

25-2 平均との比較

- 平均以上 [以下] である　① be「above [below] (the) average」② be「above [below] par」
- **平均より**離乳の早い子供　a child weaned earlier **than average**
- **平均より上の**成績を維持する　maintain **above-average** results
- **平均を上回る [超える]**　① exceed **the average**　② be above **average**
- **平均を下回る**　① fail to reach **the average**　② be below **average**
- この町の下水道普及率は**全国平均を下回っている**．　This town **is below the**

national average in terms of the number of households served by a sewage system.

25-3　平均の算定

- 平均する　average
- ブロック内の全ピクセルを**平均する**　**average** all the pixels in a block
- **平均**を出す　① calculate **an average**　② work out **an average**
- **平均**を取る　① take **an average**　② strike **an average**
- 正確な数値を知るためには，何回か計測して**平均を取る**必要がある．　To get an accurate value, you need to take measurements a number of times and **calculate the mean**.

25-4　平均の対象

- 上位10名の得点の平均　① the average of the scores of the top ten 《students, examinees, etc.》　② the average of the top ten scores
- 最高価格と最低価格の間の平均を取る　① take an average「of [between] the highest and the lowest prices ② average the highest and lowest prices
- 各従業員の残業時間の**平均**　**the average** overtime for every employee
- ★日本語も英語も1人について日々の残業時間を平均するのか，1日について全従業員の残業時間を平均するのかを明確にするには下記のようにいえる．
- 1人の従業員について日々の残業時間を**平均した値**　① the overtime for one employee **averaged** over days 《during a certain period》　② **the average** of daily overtime for one employee
- 1日の残業時間を全従業員について**平均した値**　the overtime per day **averaged** over all employees

25-5　平均からの偏差

- 分散は**平均値のまわりのばらつき**の指標である．　The variance is a measure of **the spread「about [around] the mean**.
- 標準偏差は**平均値からの偏差**の2乗の平均として計算される．　The standard deviation is calculated as the average squared **deviation from the mean**.

25-6　平均点　[⇨第2部・てん，へんさち]

- 平均点　〔試験の得点〕the average「grade [《英》mark]
- 平均点を出す　① work out an average「grade [《英》mark]　② calculate an average「grade [《英》mark]
- 平均点を上回る[下回る]　score「above [below] the average「grade [《英》

mark]
- 息子の今学期の全教科の試験得点の**平均点は** 78 点だった．　My son's **average** ⌈**grade** [《英》**mark**]⌋ for all his exams this term was 78.
- 私たちのクラスの平均点は学年の**平均点より高かった**．　Our class average was **higher than the average** for students of our year as a whole.
- 本校では**平均点** 60 点未満は落第とする．　A student who fails to ⌈get [score]⌋ **an average** ⌈**grade** [《英》**mark**]⌋ **of** 60 will be failed at this school.

25-7　平均年齢

- 平均年齢　the average age 《of the members》
- あのチームは**平均年齢**が低い [高い]．
  ① **The average age** on that team is ⌈low [high]⌋．
  ② That team has a ⌈low [high]⌋ **average age**.
  ③ The team is ⌈young [old]⌋ **on average**.

25-8　平均寿命

- 平均寿命　①〔人の〕the average life span 《of Japanese people》　② the average longevity 《of coal miners》　③ the average life expectancy (at birth)　④〔放射性核種などの〕the mean lifetime
- ★③ の life expectancy は平均余命の意味であり，平均寿命は 0 歳児の (at birth) 平均余命に等しい．ただし，年齢を指定せずに life expectancy といえば普通は 0 歳児の平均余命，すなわち平均寿命を指す．
- 日本人男性の**平均寿命**　the life expectancy (at birth) for ⌈Japanese men [male Japanese]⌋
- 日本人の平均寿命は世界一だ．　① Japan leads the world in average life expectancy.　② Japan ⌈places [ranks]⌋ first in average life expectancy.
- 男性の平均寿命は 83 歳だ．　①Men's average life expectancy is 83.　②The average life expectancy for men is 83 years.　③Men live to an average age of 83.
- **平均寿命**まで生きる　① live until **the average age of life expectancy**　② reach **the average age of life expectancy**
- 日本人の**平均寿命**が伸びた．　**The average life expectancy** of Japanese people has risen.
- 一般に女性のほうが男性より**平均寿命が長い**．　In general, women **have a longer life expectancy** than men.
- 男女の**平均寿命**の差　the difference in **average life expectancy** between men and women
- 犬の**平均寿命**は人間の 7 分の 1 だと言われる．　**The average life span** for dogs is said to be about one-seventh that for human beings.

25-9 平均的

- 平均的　① 〔平均値の〕mean　② average　③ 〔普通の〕ordinary　④ normal　⑤ general
- 平均的な家庭　an average「family [household]
- 平均的日本人　① an average Japanese (person)　② an ordinary Japanese (person)
- 自分では平均的なサラリーマンだと思っています．　I think of myself as an ordinary「salaryman [office worker].

25-10 その他の術語

- 幾何［相乗］平均　the geometric mean
- 算術［相加］平均　the arithmetic mean
- 調和平均　the harmonic mean
- 月平均　the monthly「mean [average]
- 年平均　① the annual「mean [average]　② the yearly「mean [average]
- 平均温度　the mean temperature
- 平均価格　① the average price　② 〔実勢料金〕the going rate
- 平均株価　a stock price average
- 平均気温　the mean「air [atmospheric] temperature
- 平均距離　the mean distance
- 太陽からの平均距離　the mean distance 《of a planet》 from the sun
- 平均重合度　the「mean [average] degree of polymerization
- 平均速度　the「mean [average] velocity
- 全国平均値　the national average
- 平均値の定理　① the mean value theorem　② the law of the mean
- 平均賃金　the average wage

26. 数量に関する疑問文

ここでは特定の見出し語に分類しにくい表現を中心に扱う．第2部の「なん…」の各項目も参照．

■ 26-1 数

- テーブルの上にコップは**いくつ**ありますか． **How many** glasses are there on the table?
- CDを**何枚**持っていますか． **How many** CDs do you have?
- **何人**が完走しましたか．
  ① **How many people** ran the whole distance?
  ② **How many runners** (were there who) completed the course?
- 玉ねぎは**いくつ**で100円ですか． **How many** onions will I get for 100 yen?
- ケーキは**いくつ**にお切りいたしましょうか． **How many pieces** shall I cut the cake into?
- **もういくつ**欲しいですか． **How many more** do you want?
- 「**100いくつ**って言いました？」「138だよ」 "A hundred and how many did you say?" — "A hundred and thirty-eight."
- この格子中の点Aから点Bまでは**何通り**の経路がありますか． **How many** paths are there from point A to point B in this grid?
- そのたばこは一箱**何本**入りですか．
  ① **How many** of those cigarettes come in one box?
  ② **How many** of those cigarettes does one box contain?
- この箱には本が**何冊**入るでしょう． **How many** books will this box hold?
- **何人**出席していましたか． ① **How many** people were there? ② **How many** people were present?
- 被災地救援に必要な人数は**何人**ですか． **How many** people will be needed to help at the scene of the disaster?
- このエレベーターの定員は**何人**ですか． **What** is the maximum number of passengers for this elevator?
- デモの**人数**[**規模**]はどのくらいか． **How big** is the demonstration? ★答えは It is 3,000 (people) strong. など．
- 〔レストランで〕**何名**様ですか． **How many** (people) are in your party?
- その図柄は**何色**(なんしょく)ですか． **How many colors are used** in that pattern?
- あなたの国では虹の色は**何色**ですか． In your country, **how many colors** are (said to be) in a rainbow? ★英国や日本では虹の連続スペクトルは7色ということになっているが，米国その他では5色，6色など一定しない．
- アリスとボブはどちらが本をたくさんもっていますか． Who has more

books, Alice or Bob?
- 箱の中には赤い玉と白い玉のどちらがたくさんありますか． Are there more red balls or (more) white balls in the box?
- アメリカとロシアのどちらが核ミサイルを多く保有しているかを調べる
  ① investigate which country, America or Russia, has more nuclear missiles
  ② investigate whether America or Russia has more nuclear missiles
- 日本人の間でいちばん多い血液型は何ですか． What is the most common blood type among Japanese?
- 日本人留学生がいちばん多いのはどの国ですか． What country has the most number of students from Japan?
- 日本にいる外国人でいちばん多いのはどの国の人ですか． Which nationality comes first among foreign residents in Japan?

■ 26-2 量

26-2-1 物の量

- 油はあと**どのくらい**残っていますか． **How much** oil is left?
- **どのくらいの量**が必要か計算してみなさい． Calculate **how much** you need.
- この大きなタンクには**どのくらい**はいりますか．
  ① About **how much** will go into this big tank?
  ② About **how much** will this big tank hold?
- そのワイン（のボトル）は**何ミリリットル**入りですか．
  ① **How many milliliters** of wine does that bottle contain?
  ② **What is the size** (**in milliliters**) of that bottle of wine?
- 米の生産量が**最も多い**県はどこですか．
  ① What is **the biggest** rice producing prefecture?
  ② Which prefecture produces the [**most** [**greatest amount of**] rice?
- 鋼鉄の生産量がいちばん多い会社はどこですか． ① Which company is the biggest producer of steel? ② Which company produces the most steel?

26-2-2 長さ・距離

- 長さはどのぐらいですか．
  ① How long is it?
  ② What length is it?
  ③ What is its length?
- その木は直径いくらありますか．
  ① What is the diameter of the tree?
  ② What does the tree measure across the middle?
  ③ What does the tree measure from one side to the other?
- この川の幅はどれぐらいあるか．

26. 数量に関する疑問文 26-2-3

① How wide is this river?
② What is the width of this river?

- 厚さは**いくら**ありますか.
  ① How thick is it?
  ② What is its thickness?

- ここから仙台までの距離は**どのくらい**ですか.
  ① **How** far is it from here to Sendai?
  ② **What** is the distance from here to Sendai?

- この山は**海抜どのくらい**ありますか.   **How high above sea level** is this mountain?

- 箱根は小田原の何キロぐらい先ですか.   About how many kilometers beyond Odawara is Hakone?

- どのくらいの大きさのテレビを買ったらいいでしょうか.
  ① How big a TV should I buy?
  ② What size of TV should I buy?

26-2-3 身体計測　　[⇨ 43. 身体計測]

- **身長**はいくらありますか.   How tall are you?
- **体重**はどのぐらいですか.
  ① How much do you weigh?
  ② What is your weight?
- **胸囲**はいくつですか.
  ① What's your chest measurement?
  ② How much [What] do you measure around the chest?
- **ウエスト**はおいくつですか.   What's your waist size?
- **スリーサイズ**はいくつですか.   What are your「measurements [vital statistics]?
- 靴の**サイズ**はおいくつですか.
  ① What size shoes do you wear?
  ② What size do you take in shoes?

26-2-4 重さ

- 目方は**いくら**ありますか.   **How much** does it weigh?
- 水1リットルの重さはいくらですか.
  ① What is the weight of a liter of water?
  ② How much does a liter of water weigh?

26-2-5 各種物理量

- 10メートルの深さで**水圧**はどれくらいになりますか.   What is the water pressure at (a depth of) 10 meters?

- その部屋の**湿度**はどのくらいですか．
  ① How high is the humidity in the room?
  ② What is the room's humidity?
  ③ How humid is the room?
- 加えられた力によってなされる**仕事**はいくらか． How much work is done by the applied force?
- その抵抗を流れる電流は**何アンペア**か．
  ① How many amperes flow through the resistor?
  ② What is the current in amperes「flowing [running]」through the resistor?
- その抵抗が消費する電力は**何ワット**か．
  ① How much power in watts does the resistor「use [consume]」?
  ② What is the power in watts used by the resistor?
- 1gの水素が燃焼すると**何モルの**水が発生しますか． **How many moles of** water will be produced when 1 g of hydrogen is burned.
- どのくらいの**縮小率**でコピーしますか． How much do you want the copy reduced?
- その溶液の**pH**はいくらですか． What is the pH of the solution?

26-2-6 過不足

- (お金が) **いくら**足りませんか． **How much** is it short (by)?
- **どのくらい**長すぎますか． **How much** is it too long by?
- 彼女は制限速度を**どれくらい**超えたのですか． **How「fast [much, far]** over the speed limit did she go?

■ 26-3 単位付きの疑問文

- 「この湖の**深さは何メートル**ですか」「423 メートルです」
  ① **How deep** is this lake (**in meters**)? — It is 423 meters deep.
  ② **How many meters deep** is this lake? — 423.
- 「その空母の**全長は何メートル**ですか」「317 メートルです」
  ① **How long** is that aircraft carrier (**in meters**)? — It is 317 meters long.
  ② **How many meters long** is that aircraft carrier? — 317.
- 2M の NaCl 溶液を 1.5 リットル作るには**何グラムの** NaCl が必要ですか．
  How many grams of NaCl「are [is]」needed to make 1.5 liters of a 2M NaCl solution? ★ ⇨ 64. 各種構文と単数／複数 64-11
- 1日に**何時間**テレビを見ますか． **How many hours** per day do you watch TV?
- この船は何トンですか． What is the tonnage of this ship?
- 木星の平均軌道半径は何天文単位か． What is the average radius of Jupiter's orbit in astronomical units?
- 「グラスの何分目まで入れましょうか」「7分目くらいまで入れてください」

26. 数量に関する疑問文 26-4

"How full do you want your glass?" — "Fill it about seven-tenths full."
- 何 % ⇨ 22. 割合 22-1-7

■ 26-4 単位の換算

- 1 インチは**何センチ**ですか.
  ① **How many centimeters** are there in an inch?
  ② **How many centimeters** make an inch?
  ③ **How long** is an inch **in centimeters**?
  ④ **What** is one inch **in centimeters**?
- 1 インチは 2.54 センチです.
  ① One inch is (equal to) 2.54 centimeters.
  ② There are 2.54 centimeters in an inch.
- 1 ポンドは**何グラム**ですか.
  ① **How many grams** are there in a pound?
  ② **How many grams** make a pound?
  ③ **How much** is a pound **in grams**?
  ④ **What** is one pound **in grams**?
- 体重 120 ポンドというのは**何キロ**ですか.
  ① **How much** does a person of 120 pounds weigh **in kilograms**?
  ② **What** is a weight of 120 pounds **in kilograms**?
- 1 年は**何日**ですか.
  ① **How many days** are there in a year?
  ② **How many days** make a year?

■ 26-5 時間・時刻

26-5-1 暦と時刻

- **何時**ですか.　① What time is it? ② What's the time? ③ Do you have the time? ★③は時計を持っていますかという形で婉曲的に時間を聞く表現で, 通りすがりの人に聞く場合などにおいて比較的ぶしつけでないとされる.
- 今日は**何日**ですか.
  ① **What day** of the month is it?
  ② **What's the date** today?
  ③ **What date** is it today?
- 誕生日は**何日**ですか.
  ① **What day** ((in April)) is your birthday?
  ② **When** is your birthday?
- 憲法記念日は**何月何日**ですか.
  ① **When** is Constitution Day?
  ② **What date** is Constitution Day?

- 今日は**何曜日**ですか.
  What day of the week is it today?
- 明日は**何曜日**ですか.
  ① **What day of the week** is it tomorrow?
  ② **What day** is tomorrow?
- ピアノのレッスンは**何曜日**ですか.　**What day of the week** is your piano lesson?
- 今**何月**だっけ？
  ① Hey, **what month** (**of the year**) is it now?
  ② **What's the month** now?
- 誕生日は**何月**ですか.　**What month** is your birthday (in)?
- 今年は (西暦) **何年**ですか.　**What year** is this?
- 今年は平成**何年**ですか.　**What year** of Heisei is this?
- モーツァルトは**何年**生まれですか.　**In what year** was Mozart born?
- **何年**（<ruby>年<rt>えと</rt></ruby>）生まれですか.［**干支**は何ですか.］
  ① **In what year of the Oriental zodiac** were you born?
  ② **In which year** were you born **in terms of the Oriental zodiac**?
  ③ **What is your sign in the Oriental zodiac**?
- そのワインは**何年**物ですか.　**What year** is that wine (**from**)?

26-5-2　所要時間

- **あとどのくらい**でできあがりますか.
  ① **How much longer** will it take before it's ready?
  ② **How soon** will it be ready?
- 到着まで**あと何時間**かかりますか.
  ① **How many hours** will it be till we arrive?
  ② **How**「**many more hours**［**much more time**］will it take before we arrive?
  ③ **How much longer** will it take for us to get there?
- 一つの作品を仕上げるまでに**どのくらい**かかりますか.　**How long** does it take to complete one work?
- それを達成するのに**何年**かかりますか.
  ① **How many years** will it take to achieve it?
  ② **How long** will it take to achieve it?
- その苗木が実をつけるまでに**何年**かかりますか.
  ① **How many years**［**How long**］does it take for the seedlings to bear fruit?
  ② **How many years**［**How long**］does it take before the seedlings bear fruit?
- このパスタは**何分**ゆでますか［ゆで時間は**何分**ですか］.
  ① **How long** should I boil this pasta?
  ② **How long** does it take to cook this pasta?
  ③ **What** is the cooking time for this pasta?

26. 数量に関する疑問文 26-5-3

- 彼は**どのくらいで**退院できますか．　**How soon** can he leave the hospital?

26-5-3 いつ

- 中央線の運転再開は**いつ**になりますか．　**When** [**How soon**] will the Chuo Line be running again?
- 出発は**いつ**ですか．　**When** are「we [you] leaving?
- 引っ越しは**いつ**にしようか．　**When** [**How soon**] shall we move?
- お訪ねするのは**いつ**がいいですか．　① **When** [**How soon**] would it be okay for me to visit you? ② **When** would you like me to come?
- お届けは**いつ**にいたしましょう．　① **When** would you like it delivered? ② **When** shall we deliver it?
- 予定日はいつですか．　① When is your baby due? ② When are you expecting your baby? ③ When is your due date? [⇨ 38-5 妊娠・出産]
- 今朝家を出たのは**何時**ごろですか．　About **what time** did you leave the house this morning? [⇨第２部・なんじ]
- 明日の打ち合わせは**何時**からにしましょうか．　**What time** should we start the meeting tomorrow?
- 新学期は**何日**からですか．
  ① **When** will the new (school) term begin?
  ② **On what date** will the new (school) term begin?
- **いつから**ピアノを習っていますか．　① **How long** have you been learning the piano? ② **When** [**How long ago**] **did you start** learning the piano?
- 電話料金が安くなるのは**いつから**ですか．　① **When** are telephone charges going down? ② **When** is it that charges for phone calls are going down?
- お茶を飲むようになったのは**いつの時代から**ですか．　When did people start drinking tea?
- **いつから**私にそんな質問ができる身分になったのかね．　**Since when** have you had the right to ask me such questions?
- **何月**に実施されますか．
  ① **In what month** will it take effect?
  ② **When** will it take effect?
- あなたが宝石の盗難に気づいたのは，帰宅なさってから**どのくらい後の**ことですか．　**How long** was it **after** you returned home that you noticed the jewels were missing?
- 彼は**どのくらい前に**家を出ましたか．　**How long ago** did he leave the house?
- **どのくらい前に**予約しなければなりませんか．　**How long in advance** do I have to make a reservation?
- それは**何か月前**のことですか．
  ① **How many months** has it been **since** then?

② **How many months ago** did it happen?
③ **How long ago** did it happen?
- 体育の授業は**何時間目**ですか. **What period** is「PE [physical education]」?

26-5-4 いつまで

- **いつまで**東京にご滞在ですか. **How long** are you going to stay in Tokyo?
- **いつまで**逗留できますか. **How long** can you stay?
- この戦争は**いつまで**続くのだろう.
  ① **How long** will this war last?
  ② **When** will this war end?
- 「この本**いつまで**借りられますか」「いつまででもどうぞ」 "**How long** can I borrow this book?" — "Keep it as long as you like."
- 消費期限は**いつまで**ですか.
  ① **When** does the use-by date expire?
  ② **When** is the use-by date?
- どのくらい持ちますか. **How long** will it keep?

26-5-5 いつまでに

- これは**いつまでに**やればいいの？
  ① **By when** should this be done?
  ② **When** do you want this finished?
- 明日は**何時までに**来ればいいですか. **(By) what time** should I be here tomorrow?

26-5-6 時間の長さ

- どのくらい遅刻したのですか.
  ① **How long** were you late?
  ② **By how long** were you late?
- その時計は**何分**遅れているの？ **How many minutes** behind is that clock?
- 日本へ来てから**どのくらい**になりますか. **How long** have you been in Japan?
- 「開演まで**何時間**ありますか」「あと2時間あります」 "**How**「**many more hours** [**much longer**] before the curtain goes up?" — "Two (more) hours."
- このディスクに**何分**はいりますか.
  ① **How many minutes** (of video) can I record on this disc?
  ② **How many minutes** (of video) can be stored on this disc?

■ 26-6 年齢

- お子さんは**おいくつ**ですか. **How old** is your child?

26. 数量に関する疑問文 26-7

- 娘さんは今年のお誕生日で**何歳**になりますか. **How old** will your daughter be on her birthday this year?
- あの人は**いくつ**だと思いますか.
  ① **How old** do you think he is?
  ② **How old** do you take him to be?
- この猫, **何歳**ぐらいかな. I wonder **how old** this cat is.
- これ, **いくつ**の時の写真？
  ① **How old** are you in this photo?
  ② **How old** were you when this photo was taken?
- 兄さんは君より**いくつ上**ですか. **How many years older** than you is your brother?
- あなたたち兄弟は**いくつ違い**ですか. **What's the age difference** between you and your brother?
- 初めてお酒を飲んだのは**何歳**の時でしたか. **How old** were you when you had your first drink?
- 日本では**何歳**で車の免許が取れますか.
  ① In Japan, **at what age** can people get driver's licenses?
  ② In Japan, **how old** do you have to be to get a driver's license?

■ 26-7　値段・金額・為替

- これは**いくら**ですか. **How much** is this?
- 値段は**いくら**ですか. ① **How much** does it cost? ② **What**'s the price?
- そのハンドバッグ**いくら**しました？
  ① **How much** did that handbag cost?
  ② **What did you pay** for that handbag?
- これ**いくら**だったと思う？
  ① **How much** do you think this「was [cost]？
  ② **How much** do you think I paid for this?
  ③ Guess **how much** this was!
- 費用はどのぐらいだろうか.
  ① What will it cost?
  ② How much will it come to?
  ③ What will the「cost [expenditure]」be?
- 砂糖は1キロで**いくら**ですか. **How much**「would [will]」one kilogram of sugar be?
- この商品は1個**いくら**で売ればもうけが出ますか. **At what price** would I have to sell each item of this merchandise in order to make a profit?
- ここの通行料金は**いくら**ですか.
  ① **How much** is the toll on this road?
  ② **What**'s the toll on this road?

- 原宿まで（の切符）は**いくら**ですか．
  ① **How much** is the fare to Harajuku?
  ② **What**'s the fare to Harajuku?
- この車が**いくら**なら買いますか．
  ① **How much** would you give for this car?
  ② **How much** would you buy this car for?
- **値段はどのくらい**まで大丈夫ですか．
  ① **What price** would you wish to go to?
  ② **What price range** are you thinking of?
  ③ **How much** are you「ready [prepared]」to pay?
  ④ **How much** can you afford?
- 財布に今**いくら**ある？　**How much** do you have in your wallet at the moment?
- 1日**いくら**で働いているの？　**How much**「a [per]」day are you working for?
- (お金が)**いくら**足りないの？　① **How much** more (money) do you need?
  ② **How much** are you short (by)?
- 《パーティーの》会費は**いくら**にしましょうか．
  ① **How much** shall we make the (participation) fee?
  ② **What** shall we set the (participation) fee at?
- 自分の給料から所得税を**いくら**引かれているか知っていますか．　Do you know **how much** income tax is deducted from your salary?
- あの銀行に預金すると利子はどれくらいですか．　How much interest do they give at that bank?
- 定期預金の利子はいくらですか．
  ① What is the interest rate on time deposits?
  ② What interest is「paid [allowed]」on time deposits?
- 300ドルは**日本円**で**いくらに相当**しますか．
  ① What is $300 equivalent to in Japanese yen?
  ② How many yen is $300?
  ③ How much is $300 worth in yen?
- 今，**円相場**はどのくらいですか．
  ① What is the current exchange rate for the yen?
  ② How is the yen doing now?
  ③〔ドルに対して〕What is the current exchange rate for the yen to the dollar?

■ 26-8 計算

- 16に**何を足すと**35になりますか．　What number added to 16 gives 35?
- ロシアの面積は日本の**何倍**ですか．
  ① **How many times** larger is Russia than Japan?
  ② **How much** larger is Russia than Japan?

26. 数量に関する疑問文 26-9

- 2等星は1等星に比べて何倍の明るさですか. How many times brighter is a first-magnitude star than a second-magnitude star?
- 木星は地球の何倍の重さですか. How many times「more massive [heavier] is Jupiter than the Earth?
- 三角形の辺の長さを5倍したとき, 面積は**何倍**になるか. **By what factor** does the area of a triangle **increase** if the lengths of all sides are multiplied by five?
- 26を**何倍**すれば100を超えるか. **By what factor** should 26 **be multiplied** to get a number greater than 100?
- xを求めるには, 方程式の両辺に**どんな数をかけ**たらいいですか. **By what number** would you **multiply** both sides of the equation to find the value of x?
- 2を**何乗**すれば1024になりますか.
  ① **To what power** must 2 **be raised** to get 1024?
  ② **2 raised to what power** gives 1024?
- 1分は1時間の**何分の一**か. What fraction of an hour is one minute?
  [⇨ 53-11 何分の一]
- 和が36となる3つの**連続する整数**を求めよ.
  ① Find the three **consecutive integers** whose sum is 36.
  ② What three **consecutive integers** add up to 36?

■ 26-9 無名数・番号

- 3足す5は**いくつ**になりますか.
  ① **What** does 3 plus 5「make [come to, add up to]?
  ② **What** is 3 plus 5?
- メーターは**いくつ**を指していますか.
  ① **What** is the reading on the meter?
  ② **What** does the meter indicate?
- 《間違い電話に対して》何番におかけですか.
  ① What number are you trying to reach?
  ② What number are you calling?
- ファクスは何番ですか. What is your fax number?
- 長嶋の背番号は何番ですか. What's Nagashima's number?
- 《ゴルフで》何番のアイアンを使いますか. What number iron will you use?
- 「成田行きは**何番線**ですか」「10番線です」
  ① **Where** does the train for Narita leave from? — Track [Platform] (No.) 10.
  ② **Which track** is the train for Narita on? — No. 10.
- **何号室**に行けばいいですか. **What (number) room** should we go to?

26-10 何番目

「何番目」はストレートに英語に訳せない日本語の代表例であり，いろいろな工夫が必要になる．

26-10-1 「いくつ」の応用

- それは本文の何番目の単語ですか． How many words from the beginning of the text is it located? ★答えは It is the 23rd word. または It is located 23 words from the beginning of the text. など．23 words というのは 23rd word とは異なるが，23 words from the beginning なら「先頭から 23 語のところに」の意味になる．
- あなたが犯行現場で見た男というのは**右から何番目**ですか． **How many people from the right** is the man you saw at the scene of the crime?
- あなたの病名を言い当てた医者は**何人目**でしたか． **How many** doctors did you see to find out the name of your illness?
- 来日は**これで何度目**ですか． **How many times** have you come to Japan, **including this time**?
- 新横浜は**いくつめ**の駅ですか．―4つめです． **How many stops are there to** Shin-Yokohama? — It's the fourth stop. [There will be four.]
- ★今どこかの駅に停車中である場合，日本語，英語とも，停車中の駅は数えないが，いずれも誤解の余地はある表現である．「次から数えて4つめです」なら It's the fourth stop,「counting [starting] from the next one. または There will be four, not counting this station. などといえばよい．
- 今妊娠何か月目ですか． How many months pregnant are you? [⇨ 38-5 妊娠・出産]

26-10-2 「その前にいくつあるか」式

▶ before を使った問いはその回自身を数えないので，答えるときに日本語の「…番目です」とは数字がずれることに注意．

- その人物は列の中で**何番目**ですか．―17番目です． **How many persons are there** in the line **before** that person? — Sixteen. ★26-10-3 の訳例も参照．
- リンカーンは**何代目**の大統領ですか．―16代目です． **How many** presidents were there **before** Lincoln? — Fifteen. ★26-10-3 の訳例も参照．
- 採用したのは**何人目**の応募者ですか．―5人目です． **How many** applicants did you reject **before** you hired one? — Four.
- 何フレーム後にメタデータをデータストリームに挿入するかを決める determine the number of frames after which metadata is included in the data stream

26-10-3 「どこ」「いつ」「どれ」の応用

- その人物は列の中で**何番目**ですか．—17番目です． **Where** is that person in the line? — He is the seventeenth. ★26-10-2の訳例も参照．
- リンカーンは**何代目**の大統領ですか．—16代目です． **Where**「is Lincoln [does Lincoln come] **in the**「**list**[**order**] of American presidents? — He's the sixteenth. ★26-10-2の訳例も参照．
- あなたの発表は**何番目**ですか．—3番目です． **When** is your presentation? — I'm third.
- パスポートは**何番目**の引出しに入っていますか． **Which** drawer is your passport in?

26-10-4 順位としての表現

- わが県の人口は全国で**何番目**ですか． **How** does the population of our prefecture **rank** nationwide?
- 彼は娘がクラスで**何番**かをいつも気にしている． He always worries himself about **where** his daughter **ranks** in her class.
- そのレースで彼女は**何位**[**何着**]でしたか．
  ① **Where** did she「**place**[**finish**] in that race?
  ② **What** was her **final position** in that race?
  ③ **What place** did she「**finish**[**come in**] in that race?
- マリナーズは今何位ですか． **What place** are the Mariners in?
- 彼は今（ランキングが）**何位**ですか． ① **What rank** is he now? ② What is his rank now? ③ How is he ranked now?
- **何等賞**だった？ **What prize** did you get?
- 彼らの辞書暗号では，最初の数字が辞書のページを，2番目の数字がそのページの上から何番目の単語かを表わす． In their dictionary code, the first number represents the page of the dictionary and the second number represents the number of the word counting from the top of the page.
- 印を付けた文字が何番目の文字かを書き留める　write down the number of letters from the beginning to the marked letter

■ 26-11 その他

- 今何**アウト**？ How many outs?
- ハンデはいくつですか． What is your handicap?
- それは何チャンネルでやっていますか．
  ① What channel is it on?
  ② What channel can you see it on?
  ③ On what channel is it aired?
  ④ What's the channel for it?

- 何チャンネルで何時から何がやっているかを載せた雑誌　a magazine showing what programs are on what channel at what time
- 彼女は何段ですか．　What 「*dan* [grade, rank] is she?
- どういう順番にこれらの町を訪問するのがいちばんいいですか．　What is the best order (in which) to visit these towns?
- 何を基準として誤差を推定していますか．
  ① **With respect to what** did you estimate the error?
  ② **What is the reference point of** your error estimate?
- 何年生　⇨ 47-2 …年生
- それは何調ですか．　What key is it in?
- それは何調で始まりますか．　What key does it start in?
- ドからミは何度ですか．　**What is the interval** from C to G.
- そこへはどのくらいよく行きますか．　**How often** do you go there?
- 一年に何回出張しますか．　**How many** business trips do you take a year?

■ 26-12　複数の疑問詞を含む構文

- その列車はどこからどこへ行きますか．　① Where does the train start and end its run? ② Where does the train come from and where to? ★②は列車の行程の途中で尋ねる場合．
- どっちがどっちだか見分けがつかない．　I can't tell **which is which**.
- 何から何を引くのか明記しなさい．
  ① Specify **what is subtracted from what**.
  ② Specify **the minuend** and **the subtrahend**．★minuend が引かれる数，subtrahend が引く数（⇨ 54. 加減乗除）．
- 何と何の差を取るのか明確にしなさい．　Clarify **between what and what the difference is taken**.
- 何と何の位相を比べているのか．　**What** phases are considered in the comparison?
- 何と何をどのように比べるのかが明確でない．　It is not clear **what is compared with what in what way**.
- ここでは何のどのような状況をいっているのか明確にしなさい．　Clarify what kind of situation is 「referred to [meant] here．★「何のどのような」は普通は what で十分．
- その値が何からどのようにして求められるのか説明しなさい．
  ① Explain **how and from what** that value can be derived.
  ② Explain **from what** that value can be derived **and in what way**.

27. 単位

単位の表示は原則としてメートル法が使われる．メートル法は歴史的にCGS (centimeter-gram-second) 単位系，MKS (meter-kilogram-second) 単位系，MKSA (meter-kilogram-second-ampere) 単位系などとして整備されてきたが，現在ではSI単位系が国際的な標準になっている．SI単位系は国際単位系（フランス語でSystème International d'Unités）の略で，英語ではthe International System of Units という．

専門的な詳細は国際度量衡局（BIPM）公式資料第8版（2006）の日本語版『国際文書 国際単位系（SI）』（独立行政法人産業技術総合研究所 計量標準総合センター，https://www.nmij.jp/library/units/si/R8/SI8J.pdf）やその後の更新を反映したホームページ（英文，http://www.bipm.org/en/publications/si-brochure/）を参照．

27-1 一般的な注意事項

▶ メートル法の単位にピリオドは付けない．伝統単位（⇨ 28. 伝統単位）ではft. やlb. のようにピリオドを付けることが多い．

▶ 単位記号は複数形にならない．例外として，科学技術分野でない一般的な文章ではlbs.（ポンド），yrs.（年），hrs.（時間），secs.（秒）といった複数形が使われることがある．

▶ 単位をスペルアウトするときは人名に由来するものも含めて小文字で書く．

 例） newton, pascal, coulomb, …
 例外） Celsius, Fahrenheit

▶ 数字と単位記号の間は英語ではスペースを空ける．ただし，25°C，$200，40%，640K（640 kilobytesの意）などはスペースを空けない．

▶ 単位付きの量を並べるときには単位は1回のみ記すこともある．ただし，スペースを空けない単位の場合は両方の数字に単位を付ける．

 例） 200–300 m 40×50 cm
   25°C–30°C 8 1/2″×13″
   70%–80% $500–$1,000

27-2 SI 基本単位

物理量	名称		記号
長さ	メートル	meter	m
質量	キログラム	kilogram	kg
時間	秒	second	s
電流	アンペア	ampere	A
温度	ケルビン	kelvin	K
光度	カンデラ	candela	cd
物質の量	モル	mole	mol

27-3 SI と併用される非 SI 単位

時間	分	minute	min
	時	hour	h
	日	day	d
平面角	度	degree	°
	分	minute	′
	秒	second	″
面積	ヘクタール	hectare	ha
体積	リットル	liter	l, L
質量	トン	ton	t
比	ベル	bel	B
	ネーパー	neper	Np

トリビア　今も健在なキログラム原器

　現在，SI 基本単位のうち，メートルはある時間（1 秒の 299792458 分の 1）に光が進む距離として定義されている．秒はセシウム 133 の原子が出す特定の放射の周期を基準として決められている．キログラムはパリの国際度量衡局（BIPM）に国際キログラム原器（kilogram prototype）が保管されており，1889 年以来その質量が 1 kg であると定義されているが，2011 年に普遍的な物理定数であるプランク定数に基づいてキログラムを定義しなおすことが決議され，検討が続けられている．

27-4 SI 接頭語

大きさ	名称	記号	大きさ	名称	記号
10^{24}	yotta- (ヨタ)	Y	10^{-1}	deci- (デシ)	d
10^{21}	zetta- (ゼタ)	Z	10^{-2}	centi- (センチ)	c
10^{18}	exa- (エクサ)	E	10^{-3}	milli- (ミリ)	m
10^{15}	peta- (ペタ)	P	10^{-6}	micro- (マイクロ)	μ
10^{12}	tera- (テラ)	T	10^{-9}	nano- (ナノ)	n
10^{9}	giga- (ギガ)	G	10^{-12}	pico- (ピコ)	p
10^{6}	mega- (メガ)	M	10^{-15}	femto- (フェムト)	f
10^{3}	kilo- (キロ)	k	10^{-18}	atto- (アト)	a
10^{2}	hecto- (ヘクト)	h	10^{-21}	zepto- (ゼプト)	z
10^{1}	deca- (デカ)	da	10^{-24}	yocto- (ヨクト)	y

▶ zetta-, yotta-, zepto-, yocto- は 1991 年に導入されたものだが,将来の拡張時には x, w, v, … と逆アルファベット順に頭文字を選んでいく方針をうかがわせる命名となっている.

例)
terabyte テラバイト
terahertz テラヘルツ
gigabyte ギガバイト
megawatt メガワット
megahertz メガヘルツ
hectopascal ヘクトパスカル
nanometer ナノメートル
picoliter ピコリットル
picofarad ピコファラド
femtometer フェムトメートル
attosecond アト秒

▶ kilo- は kilobyte などコンピューターで扱うデータ長に関して使う場合は $10^3 = 1000$ ではなく $2^{10} = 1024$ の意で用いることが多い.mega-, giga- なども同様である.同じコンピューター分野でもデータ長に関係ない megaflops などでは十進法が普通.

27-5 組立単位

　基本単位を組み合わせて作られる単位を組立単位または誘導単位（derived unit）という．固有の名称が与えられている組立単位もあり，それを別の組立単位を作るのに使うこともできる．

　速度の単位 m/s（または $m \cdot s^{-1}$）はスペルアウトすると meter per second（メートル毎秒）となる．加速度の単位 m/s^2（または $m \cdot s^{-2}$）は meter per second per second または meter per second squared（メートル毎秒毎秒）となる．力積の単位 $N \cdot s$ は newton second（ニュートン秒）となる．

固有の名称をもつ SI 組立単位

物理量	名称		記号	他の SI 単位との関係
平面角	ラジアン	radian	rad	無次元
立体角	ステラジアン	steradian	sr	無次元
振動数	ヘルツ	hertz	Hz	$= s^{-1}$
力	ニュートン	newton	N	$J \cdot m^{-1} = m \cdot kg \cdot s^{-2}$
圧力，応力	パスカル	pascal	Pa	$N \cdot m^{-2} = m^{-1} \cdot kg \cdot s^{-2}$
エネルギー，仕事，熱量	ジュール	joule	J	$N \cdot m = m^2 \cdot kg \cdot s^{-2}$
仕事率，電力	ワット	watt	W	$J \cdot s^{-1} = m^2 \cdot kg \cdot s^{-3}$
電気量，電荷	クーロン	coulomb	C	$A \cdot s$
電圧，電位	ボルト	volt	V	$J \cdot C^{-1} = m^2 \cdot kg \cdot s^{-3} \cdot A^{-1}$
電気抵抗	オーム	ohm	Ω	$V \cdot A^{-1} = m^2 \cdot kg \cdot s^{-3} \cdot A^{-2}$
コンダクタンス	ジーメンス	siemens	S	$A \cdot V^{-1} = m^{-2} \cdot kg^{-1} \cdot s^3 \cdot A^2$
静電容量	ファラド	farad	F	$C \cdot V^{-1} = m^{-2} \cdot kg^{-1} \cdot s^4 \cdot A^2$
磁束	ウェーバー	weber	Wb	$V \cdot s = m^2 \cdot kg \cdot s^{-2} \cdot A^{-1}$
磁束密度	テスラ	tesla	T	$Wb \cdot m^{-2} = kg \cdot s^{-2} \cdot A^{-1}$
インダクタンス	ヘンリー	henry	H	$Wb \cdot A^{-1} = m^2 \cdot kg \cdot s^{-2} \cdot A^{-2}$
光束	ルーメン	lumen	lm	$cd \cdot sr$
照度	ルクス	lux	lx	$lm \cdot m^{-2}$
放射能	ベクレル	becquerel	Bq	$= s^{-1}$
吸収線量	グレイ	gray	Gy	$J \cdot kg^{-1} = m^2 \cdot s^{-2}$
線量当量	シーベルト	sievert	Sv	$J \cdot kg^{-1} = m^2 \cdot s^{-2}$
酵素活性	カタール	katal	kat	$mol \cdot s^{-1}$
セルシウス温度	セルシウス度	degree Celsius	°C	

27-6 SI 以外の単位

実験的に決定される基礎定数に関連する単位

下記は SI との併用が認められているもの．このほか分野によっては自然界の基本定数（電子質量，換算プランク定数など）に基づく自然単位系や原子単位系の単位が用いられる．

物理量	名称		記号	およその値
エネルギー	電子ボルト	electronvolt	eV	1.602177×10^{-19} J
質量	ダルトン	dalton	Da	1.66054×10^{-27} kg
	統一原子質量単位	unified atomic mass unit	u	1u=1Da
長さ	天文単位	astronomical unit	AU	1.4960×10^{11} m

その他の非 SI 単位

長さ	海里	nautical mile		1852 m
	オングストローム	ångström	Å	10^{-10} m
速さ	ノット	knot		(1852/3600) $m \cdot s^{-1}$
面積	バーン	barn	b	100 fm^2
圧力	バール	bar	bar	10^5 Pa
	水銀柱ミリメートル	millimeter of mercury	mmHg	133.322 Pa

CGS 単位系および CGS ガウス単位系に属する非 SI 単位

エネルギー	エルグ	erg	erg	10^{-7} J
力	ダイン	dyne	dyn	10^{-5} N
粘性率	ポアズ	poise	P	1 $dyn \cdot s \cdot cm^{-2}$
動粘性率	ストークス	stokes	St	1 $cm^2 \cdot s^{-1}$
磁束密度	ガウス	gauss	G, Gs	10^{-4} T
磁界の強さ	エルステッド	oersted	Oe	$(1000/4\pi) A \cdot m^{-1}$
磁束	マクスウェル	maxwell	Mx	10^{-8} Wb
輝度	スチルブ	stilb	sb	1 $cd \cdot cm^{-2}$
照度	フォト	phot	ph	10^4 lx
加速度	ガル	gal	G	$cm \cdot s^{-2}$

28. 伝統単位

　フランス革命でメートル法が導入される以前から欧米で伝統的に使われていた単位が各種ある．十進法でない上に同じ物理量（長さ，質量など）を表わすのにいくつもの単位を併用するなど繁雑だが，長い歴史を通じて日常生活と密着していた側面もある．20世紀後半に世界各地でメートル法への切り替えが進んだが，アメリカ，イギリスは伝統単位への執着が強い．アメリカは科学技術分野や政府・軍関係ではメートル法が使われているものの，一般社会でメートル法に背を向けている残り少ない国の一つとなっている．イギリスもヨーロッパ諸国に比べて遅れていたが，EU の後押しもあって 1990 年代に商品表示や店頭の秤のメートル法化が進んだ．ただし，パブで売られるビールの「1 パイント」や道路標識の「マイル」の切り替えは日程に上っていない．イギリスでは体重をストーンで表わすことも一般的である（⇨ 43-2 体重）．

　アメリカもメートル法化の努力をしなかったわけではない．1975 年に Metric Conversion Act（メートル法転換法）が成立して「合衆国におけるメートル法の使用の増加を調整・計画する」ために Metric Board（メートル法局）が設置されたが，メートル法使用の義務づけはされなかったこともあって一向に進捗せず，1982 年には廃止された．1988 年の Omnibus Trade and Competitiveness Act（包括通商・競争力法）により政府省庁やその関係先（建築業界を除く）ではメートル法が導入された．日常生活でも一部の単位にはメートル法が使われるようになっている．2 リットル入りのソフトドリンクもあるし，酒類もかつて 1/5 ガロン（757 ml）だったのがいつのまにか 750 ml が一般的になった．

28-1 長さ

インチ	inch	in. または ″	1 in.＝2.54 cm
フィート	foot	ft. または ′	1 ft.＝12 in.＝30.48 cm
ヤード	yard	yd.	1 yd.＝3 ft.＝0.9144 m
マイル	mile	mi.	1 mi.＝1760 yd.＝約 1.609 km

28-2 面積と体積

エーカー	acre	a.	1 a.＝4840 sq. yd.≒4047 m^2
平方インチ	square inch	sq. in.	
平方フィート	square foot	sq. ft.	
平方ヤード	square yard	sq. yd.	
平方マイル	square mile	sq. mi.	
立方インチ	cubic inch	cu. in.	
立方フィート	cubic foot	cu. ft.	
立方ヤード	cubic yard	cu. yd.	

▶ 伝統単位の記号はピリオドをつけることが多いが，ピリオドをつけず，平方インチなどの記号も sq. in. ではなく in^2 と書くなど，メートル法の単位 (⇨ 27-1) に倣った表記をすることもある．

トリビア　定規の目盛りは 1/16 きざみ

英米ではインチで表わす靴のサイズや紙のサイズなど，5 1/2 のように分数を使った表示がよく見られる．日本語なら小数で表わすところを分数で表わすこうした伝統を反映してコンピューター表示用のユニコードでも 1/4, 1/2, 3/4 には 00BC, 00BD, 00BE という特別なコードが割り当てられている．そもそもインチ式の定規では 1 インチの 1/2, 1/4, 1/8, 1/16 が目盛られている．このため四捨五入するときにも「1/4 インチ未満を四捨五入する」こともある (⇨ **10-2** 四捨五入)．

株式相場でもかつては分数表示が一般的だった．NYSE（ニューヨーク証券取引所）では当初は 1/8 単位で，1997 年にはさらに細かく 1/16 単位となったが，2001 年にはこれも十進法に切り替えられた．

28-3 常衡

名称	略	概算値	相対値
grain	gr.	0.0648 g	1/7000
dram	dr.	1.772 g	1/256
ounce	oz.	28.35 g	1/16
pound	lb. または #	453.6 g	1
stone	st.	6350 g	14
hundredweight	cwt.	50.80 kg	112
(long) ton	tn.	1016 kg	2240

▶ 常衡（avoirdupois weight）のほかに薬衡（apothecaries' weight），金衡（troy weight）がある．avoirdupois は古フランス語の「重さの品」の意味で，「アヴァドポイズ」またはイギリスではフランス語式に「アヴワールデュポワー」のように読む．常衡なら lb. av. と，金衡なら lb. t. または lb. tr. と，薬衡なら lb. ap. または lb. apoth. と書いて区別することもできる．

▶ ポンドの記号 lb. はラテン語の libra に由来する．通貨のポンドの記号 £ も同様である（⇨ 39-1-4 ポンド）．

28-4 英国の液量・乾量単位

名称	略	概算値 (cm^3)	相対値
minim	min.	0.05919	1/9600
fluid dram	fl. dr.	3.55163	1/160
fluid ounce	fl. oz.	28.413	1/20
gill	gi.	142.065	1/4
pint	pt.	568.261	1
quart	qt.	1136.522	2
gallon	gal.	4546.088	8
peck	pk.	9092.176	16
bushel	bu.	36368.704	64

28-5 米国の液量・乾量単位

米国の液量単位

名称	略	概算値 (cm³)	相対値
minim	min.	0.06161	1/7680
fluid dram	fl. dr.	3.69669	1/128
fluid ounce	fl. oz.	29.5735	1/16
gill	gi.	118.29	1/4
pint	pt.	473.176	1
quart	qt.	946.35	2
gallon	gal.	3785.41	8

▶ 缶飲料でよく見られる 355 ml というのは 12 fl. oz. からきている (ちなみに日本のビールの大瓶の 633 ml というのはかつて大瓶の容量を統一したとき,調査した 10 工場の瓶の最小値であった 3.51 合が採用されたもの).

米国の乾量単位

名称	略	概算値 (cm³)	相対値
dry pint	dry pt.	550.610	1
dry quart	dry qt.	1101.22	2
peck	pk.	8809.76	16
bushel	bu.	35239.0	64

28-6 組立単位

伝統単位でも組立単位を構成してさまざまな物理量を表わすことができる.ヤードポンド法で使われる組立単位の例を示す.

pound-force ポンド重 ▶ 記号 lbf. 力の単位で,SI 単位系では newton.
pound-force per square inch ポンド重毎平方インチ ▶ 記号 psi. 圧力の単位で,SI 単位系では pascal. 絶対圧の psia と大気圧との差で示されるゲージ圧の psig がある.

> **トリビア** 単位の換算ミスによる火星探査の失敗
>
> 1999年に米国の火星探査機Mars Climate Orbiterが火星まで到達しながら近づきすぎて大気との摩擦熱で燃え尽きてしまうという事故があった．調査の結果，ヤードポンド法からメートル法への換算のミスが原因だったことがわかった．バーニア（vernier）噴射後に推力と噴射時間の積に基づいて速度変化を計算するのだが，この力の数値をpound-forceからnewtonに換算する際にミスが生じたのである．1ポンド重＝4.45ニュートンなので桁外れの異常値ではなかったが，探査機制御に致命的となるには十分だった．

28-7 温度

SI単位系でも使われるセルシウス（セ氏）温度はSI基本単位のケルビンの原点をずらしただけのものである．一方，英米では伝統的にカ氏が使われてきた．イギリスではメートル法の採用と並んでセ氏への移行が進み，今では天気予報でもセ氏が使われるが，アメリカは一般社会ではカ氏を使い続けている．

セ氏温度Cとカ氏温度Fは次の関係がある．

$C = (5/9)(F - 32)$

カ氏は18世紀初頭にドイツの物理学者ファーレンハイト（Fahrenheit, 中国語で華倫海）が考案した温度目盛りであるが，ファーレンハイトはこれに基づいて初めて信頼できる市販の水銀温度計を作成したため，カ氏は広く普及した．セ氏は1742年にスウェーデンの天文学者セルシウスが考案した．セ氏は水の氷点と沸点を100等分する目盛りであるためcentigradeと呼ばれていたが，1948年にSI単位系のcenti-の用法との関係もあってCelsiusに変更された．ただし，今でもcentigradeが使われることも少なくない．

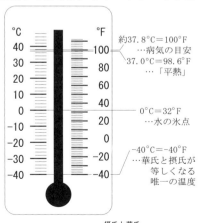

摂氏と華氏

28. 伝統単位 28-7

トリビア　英米人の平熱は 37.0°C?

アメリカの映画やドラマを見ていると，体温を測って平熱で安心するといったシーンでは98.6°Fという温度がよく使われる（たとえばテレビドラマ『フレンズ』第8シリーズ23話，映画『アップタウン・ガールズ』）．これはちょうど37.0°Cにあたり，日本人の感覚では高熱である．実はこれは19世紀に統計を取ったドイツの医師がセ氏の小数点以下を四捨五入して発表したものが人口に膾炙してしまったためらしく，英米では実際の平熱は36.5°C〜37.2°C程度の間と言われている．これでも高いように思えるが，実は日本とは測定法の違いがある．上記の値は口で測った体温の平熱であり，日本のように脇の下で測る場合にはさらに0.2°C〜0.5°C低くなるのである．近年赤外線を使って数秒で検温できる耳式体温計も登場しているが，やはり脇の下とは異なる値になるので，測る部位ごとに平熱を把握することが必要である．

アメリカの体温計は98.6°Fや37°Cのところに赤で印がついていることもある．デジタル式になっても商品写真に37°Cと示されることもしばしばある．

トリビア　文豪たちの華氏使用

日本でも明治時代から昭和初期にかけて華氏が使われていた．気象観測では一貫して摂氏を使っていたが，市販の温度計は輸入品が多かったため，市井では華氏がしばしば使われたのである．摂氏と華氏が併記されている温度計もあった．正岡子規，寺田寅彦，永井荷風，石川啄木，芥川龍之介，宮本百合子といった文人たちの著作や書簡にも華氏への言及がある．

トリビア　単位の誤解

ヘミングウェイのA Day's Waitという短編小説は温度の単位の誤解が落ちになっている．フランスに住むアメリカ人の少年が102度の熱を出すのだが，友だちが44度でも死ぬと話すのを聞いて落ち込むという筋である．

28-8 日本の伝統単位

- 尺貫法　① the traditional Japanese system of measurement　② (the system of) measuring length by *shaku* and weight by *kan*　③ the *shakkan-ho* system
- 尺は長さの単位だ．　(The) *shaku* is a unit of length.
- 合は酒を出す升の一般的なサイズだ．　(The) *gō* is a common size「for a sake cup [of a cup for serving sake].
- 長さを測る基本になるのは尺だ．　The basis for measuring length is (the) *shaku*.
- 鯨尺は曲尺の 1.25 倍だ［より 25% 長い］．　① One *kujirajaku* equals 1.25 *kanejaku*.　② A *kujirajaku* is 25% longer than a *kanejaku*.
- 尺八は一尺八寸ということからそう呼ばれる．　The *shakuhachi* is called that because it is one *shaku* and eight *sun* in length.　★英語にとって外国語である日本語の単位は単複同形とすることが多い．
- 九十九里浜や七里ヶ浜はそれぞれ 99 里，7 里あったことから名付けられたと言われている．　Kujukuri Beach and Shichiri Beach are said to have been named for being 99 *ri* and 7 *ri* long, respectively.
- 面積を坪単位で記入する　write the area in *tsubo*

29. 年・年度・元号・世紀

29-1 基本

- 1945 年に　in 1945
- 1945 年以前は　before 1945
- 1945 年は日本にとって新しい出発点だった．　The year 1945 was a new starting point for Japan.
- 来年は 2018 年だ．　Next year will be 2018.
- 45 年に　in '45　★英語でも西暦の下 2 桁だけをいうことはあるが，書くときにはアポストロフィを付ける．
- 1945 年はじめに　① at the beginning of (the year) 1945　② early in 1945
- 1945 年も終わりに近づくころ　① as the year 1945 drew to a close　② towards the end of (the year) 1945　③ in late 1945
- 2007 年版　the 2007 edition
- 1955 年の暴動　① the riots of 1955　② the 1955 riots
- 2016 年オリンピック金メダリスト　the 2016 Olympic [champion [gold medalist]　★特定の競技の文脈では一人なので the が付く．

トリビア　2000 年問題

西暦の 2 桁表示のために世界中のコンピューターシステムの誤動作が懸念されたことがあった．20 世紀には社会のインフラから電子機器まで多くのシステムでは年号の管理を下 2 桁だけで行なっていたため，西暦 2000 年になると下 2 桁の「00」では 1900 年と解釈されてしまい，システムの誤動作や非常停止が起こると予想された．これが 2000 年問題というもので，英語では the Year「2000 [Two Thousand] Problem; the Millennium bug; the Millennium problem; the Y2K problem などと呼ばれた (Y2K の K は kilo- の意で 1000 を表わす)．

各方面で対策が進められたが，古いプログラミング言語で書かれたシステムも多く残っていて多大な負担となった．1999 年の大みそかから 2000 年にかけては社会インフラに関係する部署では不測の事態に備える特別態勢が敷かれ，日をまたぐ航空便には変更・欠航となったものもあった．結果的には一部でちょっとした不具合が生じただけで大事には至らなかった．

29-2 年号の読み方

1945 nineteen forty-five ▶ 2 桁ずつに区切って読むのが基本.
1900 nineteen hundred
1904 ① nineteen oh-four ② nineteen hundred and four ③ nineteen 「naught [ought] four
2000 two thousand ▶ in 2000 は in the year two thousand と読める.
2001 two thousand (and) one
2010 ① two thousand (and) ten ② twenty ten
2199 twenty-one ninety-nine
800 eight hundred
476 four seventy-six

> **トリビア** 年号の読み方が決まるまで
>
> 20 世紀の終わりごろまで,2001 以降の年が英語でどう呼ばれるかはっきりしなかった.たとえば2001 年のことは,1990 年代には two thousand one という人もいれば twenty oh-one という人もいた.それが 21 世紀になってみると, two thousand (and) one (《米》では and なし) が主流で, twenty oh-one はほとんど聞かれなかった.
>
> 2010 年以降は 1945 年 (nineteen forty-five と読む) などと同様に 2 桁ずつに分けて読み,たとえば2016 は twenty sixteen と読む.このような言い方が耳になじんでくるにつれて,最初の 10 年間についても,たとえば 2001 を twenty-oh-one と呼ぶことも出てきている.

29-3 紀元前と紀元後

紀元前を表わす B.C. または BC, 紀元後を表わす A.D. または AD は通例小型大文字で書く.

B.C. は before Christ の略で数字の後に置く.

A.D. は anno Domini (「主の年で」の意味のラテン語) の略で数字の前に置くのが本来だが,主に年号が大きい場合,また《米》で数字の後とすることもしばしばある.また,「年」でなく世紀に拡大して使われることもあり,その場合は A.D. は後置が普通.

- 紀元前 7 年に in 7 B.C.
- 紀元 67 年に   ① in A.D. 67 ② in 67 A.D.
- 西暦 4 世紀に in the fourth century A.D.

トリビア　西暦

　西暦が考案されたのはユスティニアヌス帝時代の6世紀のことであった．それまでは執政官の任期や皇帝の在位に基づく年表記が用いられていた．新しい方式の年号はラテン語で anno Domini（主の年で）と表現され，イギリスでは近世になっても公文書の年号に in the year of our Lord 1688 のような表現がされることがめずらしくなかった．西暦は名前の通りイエス生誕を元年にしたつもりだったのだが，現在ではイエス生誕は西暦1年より数年前のこととされている．A.D. という略形が英語の文献に残っているのは16世紀以降のことである．

　西暦は世界的に使われているようになっているが，キリスト教に関係ない中立的な名称としてADの代わりにCE（= Common Era），BCの代わりにBCE（= Before Common Era）を使うこともある．

トリビア　西暦以外の暦

　西暦以外の暦といえばイスラム諸国で使われるヒジュラ暦がある．これは西暦622年のムハンマドの聖遷（ヒジュラ）を紀元とする太陰暦である．純粋な太陰暦であるため太陽暦とは毎年11日ほどずれていき，たとえばラマダン（断食月）も年によって季節が一定しない．また，1年の長さも太陽暦より短いため，たとえば622年の1400年後は西暦では2022年だが，イスラム年の1400年はほぼ西暦1980年にあたる．イスラム暦の暦年は AH（= anno Hegirae）で示す．なお，聖遷を紀元としつつ太陽暦を採用したペルシア暦もイランなどで使われている．

　ユダヤ教は太陰太陽暦であるユダヤ暦を使っている．紀元前3761年を紀元としてその年号は A.M.（= anno mundi 世界暦）と表示される．台湾では1912年を紀元とする中華民国暦がしばしば使われている．北朝鮮でも金日成の生年1912年を主体1年とする主体暦（Juche calendar）が1997年に導入されて西暦と併記されている．

　日本の皇紀（神武紀元）は『日本書紀』に基づく神武天皇即位の年である紀元前660年を紀元とする．1940年が皇紀2600年に当たり，零式艦上戦闘機（ゼロ戦）の「零」はこの00を指している．神武紀元が制定されたのは1872年（明治5年）のことである．

> **トリビア　B.C. ならぬ B.P.**
> 考古学の放射線年代測定では B.P. という原点が使われる．これは before present の意味である．ただし，「現在から」という名前ではあるが，測定年により変わっては都合が悪いので 1950 年を基準として何年前かを表わすことになっている．このため before physics（物理以前）ということもある．

29-4　年度

- 会計年度　①《米》a fiscal year　②《英》a financial year
★米国政府では会計年度の 2017 年度は暦年（calendar year）の 2016 年 10 月 1 日に始まる．英国政府は日本と同じで 4 月 1 日からだが，個人の税務に関しては 4 月 6 日から始まる．これは 1752 年までイギリスの公式年初だった 3 月 25 日がグレゴリオ暦では 19 世紀に 4 月 6 日に相当し，これが固定化されたのだという．

- 2017 年度　① the 2017 fiscal year　② (the) fiscal year 2017　③ fiscal 2017　④ FY 2017

- 日本では会計年度は 4 月 1 日に始まり 3 月 31 日に終わる．　① In Japan, the fiscal year begins on April 1 and ends on March 31.　② In Japan, the fiscal year runs from April 1 to March 31.

- 平成 29 年度予算　① the budget for the 29th fiscal year of Heisei　② the budget for fiscal 2017　★新年度が 4 月から始まることになじみのない外国人向けには fiscal 2017 starting in April のようにいうこともできる．

- 2016 年度決算　(financial) results for the fiscal year 2016　[⇨ 41-2 決算の表現]

- 6 月 30 日までの会計年度の決算　the results for the fiscal year「ending [ended] 30 June　[⇨ 第 2 部・…まで 2]

- 年度初めに　at the beginning of the fiscal year

- 年度末に　at the end of the fiscal year

- 年度が変わると新法が適用される．　The new law goes into effect at the turn of the fiscal year.

- 学校年度　① a school year　② an academic year

- 2018 年度入学試験　the entrance examination for the 2018 academic year

- その会社はまだ累積損失が残っているが，単年度では 2 年連続黒字になった．　That company still has a cumulative loss, but it has been in the black for two consecutive fiscal years.

- 単年度予算　a one-year budget

29-5 元号

- 平成 10 年に　① in the 10th year of Heisei　② in the 10th year of the Heisei era　★実務上は in 1998 のように西暦に直すことが多い.
- 平成 15 年は西暦 2003 年にあたる.
  ① Heisei 15 is the same as (AD) 2003.
  ② The 15th year of the Heisei era is the same as (AD) 2003.
- 去年は平成 28 年だ.　Last year was「Heisei 28 [2016].
- 昭和 60 年の本学卒業生　a graduate of this university in「Showa 60 [1985]
- 今年は平成何年ですか.　What year of Heisei is this?
- 昭和 20 年代に　① in the 20s of the Showa period　② from 1945 to 1954
  ③ from the mid-1940s to the mid-1950s
- 昭和一桁生まれの人　a member of the generation born in the first nine years of the Showa period (from 1926 to 1934)　★厳密さを求めなければ the first nine years は the first decade または the first years としたほうがすっきりする.

> **トリビア**　治世による年号表示
>
> イギリスでもかつては君主の治世年による表記は法律文などに多く見られ, 長年, 議会法に付ける番号に君主の治世で数えた年号 (regnal year) を付けていた. たとえば 1752 年にグレゴリオ暦を導入した法律は 25 Geo 2 c.30 と表わされる (ジョージ2世の治世第 25 年の法第 30 号の意). しかし, 1963 年以降はこれも西暦になった.

29-6 …年代

- 1930 年代に　in the「1930s [1930's]　★-s [-'s] は所有格ではなく複数形の語尾.
- 1990 年代のはじめに　in the early 1990s
- 1990 年代の半ばに　in the mid-1990s
- 1990 年代の終わりに　in the late 1990s
- 1990 年代の後半に　① in the second half of the 1990s　② in the latter half of the 1990s
- 1960 年代 [60 年代] は高度経済成長の時代だった.　The 1960s「was [were] a period of rapid economic growth.
- 1660 年代のロンドンでは　① in London「in [of] the 1660s　② in 1660s London　★② は in sixteen sixties London と読む.
- 50 年代　① the fifties　② the '50s

- 昭和 30 年代に　① in the 30s of the Showa period　② from 1955 to 1964　③ from the mid-1950s to the mid-1960s
- 1900 年代　the 1900s　★文脈により 1900～1999 年を指す場合と 1900～1909 年を指す場合があるのは日本語と同様である．
- 2000 年代　the 2000s　★the two thousands と読むことが多いが，the twenty hundreds, the twenty-ohs などと読むこともある．また，文字通りには 2000 年からの最初の 10 年，最初の 100 年，2999 年までの 1000 年の 3 通りの意味があるが，100 年なら the 21st century のような表現があるので，2000-2009 年の意で使うことが多い．

トリビア　00 年代

日本語で「ゼロ年代」とも言われる「00 年代」は the '00s と書くことはできるが，英語でこれをどう読むかとなるとコンセンサスはない．イギリスでは the noughties という言い方がある一方，アメリカでは the aughts, the double-ohs, the oh-ohs などの言い方があるが完全には定まっていない．nought は「ゼロ」の意があるが，「いたずら好きな」という意味の naughty が想起されることも普及の障害になっているかもしれない．the 2000s を流用して口頭では the two thousands, the twenty hundreds, the twenty-ohs などと言うこともあるが，上記のように必ずしも「最初の 10 年」を指さないという曖昧さが残る．

英語では「10 年代」も問題になる．the teens, the one-and-some-things, the one-ies という表現が提案されているが定着していない．

29-7 世紀

- 21 世紀　① the twenty-first century　② the 21st century
- 20 世紀に　① in the twentieth century　② in the 20th century
- 今世紀　① this century　② the present century
- 前世紀　the last century
- 世紀の変わり目に　at the turn of the century

★at the turn of the nineteenth century のような表現は，文脈によって 19 世紀初頭を指す場合と 19 世紀から 20 世紀への移行期を指す場合がある．

- 20 世紀初頭まで　until the early 20th century
- 19 世紀の中ごろに　① in the middle of the nineteenth century　② in the mid-nineteenth century
- 20 世紀の最初の四半期に　in the first quarter of the twentieth century

- 18 世紀の後半に　① in the second half of the eighteenth century　② in the latter half of the eighteenth century
- それは2世紀の間忘れられていた．　It was forgotten for two centuries.　★「世紀」を絶対的な時代ではなく「100年間」という時間の単位として使っている例．

▶「××00年」が世紀の最初の年か最後の年かについては議論がある．西暦に0年がなく1年から始まっていることで1〜100年が1世紀，101〜200年が2世紀…と考えていくと，たとえば21世紀は2001年から2100年までで，2000年は20世紀最後の年となる．一方，数字が繰り上がって2000年になったときが新しい世紀の始まりと感じる人も多い．概して，世紀は「1年に始まる」という規範的な考え方が強い日本に比べ，英米では0年からを世紀とする考えも受け入れられている．The Chicago Manual of Style は the first decade of a century（世紀の最初の10年）という表現の場合，00〜09年を指すと例で示した上で，「01〜10年と考える人もいる」としている．

30. 日付と曜日

■ 30-1 月名

1月	January	Jan.	**7月**	July	Jul.
2月	February	Feb.	**8月**	August	Aug.
3月	March	Mar.	**9月**	September	Sep., Sept.
4月	April	Apr.	**10月**	October	Oct.
5月	May	May	**11月**	November	Nov.
6月	June	Jun.	**12月**	December	Dec.

- 月の大小　how many days each month has
▶ 日本では小の月を「にしむくさむらい（2・4・6・9・11）」と覚えるが，英米では次のような詩による覚え方がある．Thirty days hath September, / April, June, and November; / All the rest have thirty-one, / Excepting February alone, / And that has twenty-eight days clear / And twenty-nine in each leap year.

■ 30-2 月日

英語の日付の表現は多様で，しかも文書と口頭とで一致しないこともある．

▶ 口頭での日付の表現

April the eighth, twenty seventeen（2017年4月8日）

これは英米共通だが，アメリカでは日付の the を言わないこともある．略式には序数でなく基数を使って April eight のようにいうこともある．特にイギリスでは the eighth of April ともいう．年号の読み方については⇨ 29-2. 年号の読み方を参照．

▶ 文書での日付の表現

米式では口頭表現そのまま，英式は小さい単位からの順に整理したものとなる．

米式：April 8(th), 2017　　4/8/2017
英式：8(th) April 2017　　8/4/2017

ただし，イギリスでも米式の April 8(th), 2017 の形は使われる．逆に

アメリカでも科学・軍関係では英式の 8 April 2017 の形が好まれる.

▶ 単位の小さい順になっていない米式では年号の前にコンマを打つ. また, 文中では年号の後にもコンマを打つのがよいとされる.
- The resolution adopted on July 15th, 2006, was ….(2006年7月15日に採択された決議は…)

▶ 月を数字で表わすのは, 口頭では 9/11 (nine eleven) のような歴史的事件の名称を別にすればほとんどないが, 文書ではめずらしくない. 読み上げるときには April などに置き換えて読むのが普通だが, 状況によっては機械的に数字として読むこともある.

▶ 日付を数字で表わす場合, 年・月・日の順序に気をつける必要がある. たとえば 2016 年 8 月 10 日の場合, DD/MM/YY と指定されていれば 10/08/16, MM/DD/YY なら 08/10/16, DD/MM/YYYY なら 10/08/2016 などと書く.

■ 30-3 基本例

「…に」というときの前置詞は「年」「月」は in, 「日」まで特定されれば on である.

- 2017 年に　in 2017
- 2017 年 4 月に　① in April 2017　② in April of 2017
- 2017 年の春に　in the spring of 2017
- 6 月から 9 月にかけて　from June to September
- その会社は 8 月のいつかに渋谷に引っ越した.　The company moved to Shibuya some time in August.
- 2009 年 8 月の総選挙　① the general election of August 2009　② the August 2009 general election
- 2007 年 4 月 8 日に　① on April 8(th), 2007　② on 8(th) April 2007
- 4 月 8 日は私たちの記念日です.
  ① April 8(th) is our anniversary.
  ② The 8th of April is our anniversary.
- 3 月 10 日の午後 3 時に　① at three p.m. on March 10　② at three o'clock (in the afternoon) on March 10
- 3 月 10 日の火曜日に　① on Tuesday, March 10　② on Tuesday 10 March
- 3 月 10 日の朝に　on the morning of March 10　★「朝に」というときは in the morning だが, 日付や曜日で限定された場合は前置詞は on になる. afternoon, evening, night も同様.

30. 日付と曜日 30-3

- 3月10日の新聞　① a newspaper「from [dated] March 10　② a March 10 newspaper
- 3月10日の会議　① the meeting「on [of] March 10　② the March 10(th) meeting　③〔過去〕the meeting held on March 10　④〔予定〕the meeting scheduled for March 10
- 10月10日に子供の運動会がある．　Our kids' field day is October 10.
- 3月10日と11日に　on March 10 and 11
- 16日に　on the 16th　★日付だけをいうときには the＋序数を省かずに書く．
- 来月の16日に　on the 16th of next month
- 16日の午後3時に　at three p.m. on the 16th
- 16日の火曜日に　on Tuesday the 16th
- 2000年1月1日現在　as of January 1, 2000
- 3月末日　①《by》the end of March　② the last day of March
- 末日締め　closing accounts on the last day of the month

▶ 箇条書きなどで単にデータとして示すときには前置詞 on を省くことがある．

- 2016年8月1日に完成した報告書　the report completed (on) August 1, 2016
- 1918年9月13日に出願され，1919年7月22日に発行された米国特許第1,310,719号を参照．　See US Patent No.1,310,719, filed (on) September 13, 1918, and issued (on) July 22, 1919.

トリビア　**国情と月名**

慣れ親しんだ月の名が政治的な事情で変更された例としてはフランス革命暦が有名だが，2002年には終身大統領ニヤゾフ（2006年没）が絶大な権力を握ったトルクメニスタンが月と曜日の名を変更した．採用された月の名には，歴史上の人物や大統領の著書名と並んで大統領の母の名（Gurbansoltan Eje）もあった．だがニアゾフ大統領没後の2008年には変更前に戻された．

30. 日付と曜日 30-3

> **トリビア**　October はなぜ「8月」でないか
>
> 英語の月名 September（9月），October（10月），November（11月），December（12月）を見れば，語源的な意味である 7，8，9，10 と 2 か月ずれているのがわかる．しかし，考えてみれば January が年の始まり，すなわち「1月」である必然性もないはずである．人類が初めて 1 年という周期を認識するとき，自然な基点として考えられるのは春に向かうころである．実は古代ローマでも最初は今でいう 3 月が年初であり，そのため 9 月を「7の月」，10 月を「8 の月」などと呼んでいたのである．
>
> なぜ 1 月が年初になったかというと，3 月が年初だった時期にはそもそも 1 月，2 月という冬のさなかは月が割り当てられていなかった．それが紀元前 700 年ごろに January, February が導入され，前と後の両方を見る顔をもち物事の始まりを意味する門を司る神であるヤヌスにちなんだ January がその後年初とされたことで，月名が 2 か月ずれる現在の形になったのである．
>
> ユリウス・カエサルが紀元前 45 年に太陽暦（ユリウス暦）を実施した時には，7 月，8 月も Quintilis（5 の月），Sextilis（6 の月）と呼ばれていたが，紀元前 44 年に 7 月がカエサルにちなんで Julius と改称され，紀元前 8 年には後継者アウグストゥスにちなんで 8 月が Augustus と名付けられた．次のティベリウス帝は 9 月をティベリウスとする提案を「皇帝が 13 人になったらどうするのだ」と言って固辞した．その後も名前を月名に残そうとする皇帝は出たが，みな当人が没するとすぐ撤回されて定着をみなかった．
>
> なお，月名のずれの原因になった年初にはさらに波乱がある．キリスト教の時代になると 3 月 25 日（受胎告知日），12 月 25 日（イエス降誕日）などの年初が使われるようになったのである．ただし，1 月 1 日を New Year's Day などと呼ぶ例は中世にすでに見られ，16 世紀から 18 世紀にかけて 1 月 1 日が公式な年初となっていった（主要国ではイギリスの 1752 年が最も遅い）．

■ 30-4 曜日

日曜日	Sunday	Sun.	木曜日	Thursday	Thu.
月曜日	Monday	Mon.	金曜日	Friday	Fri.
火曜日	Tuesday	Tue.	土曜日	Saturday	Sat.
水曜日	Wednesday	Wed.			

- 月曜日に　on Monday　★前後関係により直前の月曜日のできごと，次の月曜日の予定，毎月曜日の習慣を表わすことができる．
- 16日の火曜日までに返信します．　I will respond by Tuesday the 16th.
- 翌3月15日月曜日…　the next day, Monday, March 15, …
- 翌15日月曜日…　the next day, Monday the 15th, …
- 今日は何曜日ですか．　What day of the week is it today?
- 明日は何曜日でしょう．
  ① What day of the week is it tomorrow?
  ② What day is tomorrow?
- 次の月曜日　next Monday
- 先の月曜日　last Monday

★next Monday, last Monday については⇨31-5「来…」「先…」の項目も参照．

- 毎週水曜日に　① every Wednesday　② on Wednesdays
- 毎週同じ曜日に　on the same day every week
- 隔週で同じ曜日に　on the same day every other week
- 隔週の水曜日に　(on) every other Wednesday
- 毎月第2土曜日に　① (on) the second Saturday of every month　② (on) every second Saturday
- 毎月第1と第3木曜日に　on the first and third Thursdays of each month
- そのドラマの放送時間は月曜から金曜までの午後5:30から6:00までだ．
  ① The drama is aired from 5:30 p.m. to 6:00 p.m. Monday to Friday.
  ② The drama is aired from Monday to Friday from 5:30 p.m. to 6:00 p.m.
  ③ The air time of the drama is from 5:30 p.m. to 6:00 p.m. Monday to Friday.
  ④ The time slot of the drama is from 5:30 p.m. to 6:00 p.m. Monday to Friday.

■ 30-5 …付け

- 今月5日付けの手紙　a letter dated the fifth of this month
- 本日付けのお手紙　your letter of today

30. 日付と曜日 30-6

- 6月30日付け官報　the Official Gazette「for [dated] June 30
- 人事異動は本月1日付けで発令された．　The personnel reassignments were announced as of the first of this month.
- 本規則は10月20日付けをもって施行された．　The rule took effect「on [as of] October 20.
- 6月10日付けで配属される　be「assigned [moved] (to …) as of June 10
- 6月10日付けで退職する　① resign as of June 10　② leave [quit] on June 10　★退職辞令の日である6月10日まで在籍．

■ 30-6 その他

- 毎年の支払いは各年の応答日に行なわれる．　The annual payment shall be made on the corresponding date in each year.
- 公布の日から起算して1年を経過した日　the day on which one year has elapsed from the date of promulgation
- 公布の日から起算して1年を超えない範囲において政令で定める日　the day specified by Cabinet Order within a period not exceeding one year from the date of promulgation

31. 年・月・週・日

■ 31-1 年

31-1-1 長さ

- 3 年 5 か月　three years and five months
- 半年　① half a year　② a half year　③ six months
- 四半期　a quarter［⇨第 2 部・しはんき］
- 1 年は 365 日だ.
  ① One year has 365 days.
  ② One year consists of 365 days.
  ③ There are 365 days in a year.
- 10 年間　① for ten years　② for a decade
- 被告に禁固 10 年の判決が下った.　The defendant was sentenced to ten years' imprisonment.
- 何年　⇨第 2 部・なんねん

31-1-2 頻度・割合

- 年に 1 度　① once a year　② annually
- 年に 2 度　① twice a year　② biannually　③ semiannually
- 2 年に 1 度　once every two years
- 年に 1 度の　① yearly　② annual
- 2 年に 1 度の　① biennial　② biyearly　③ biannual
- 1 年に 2 度の　① biannual　② semiannual　③ half-yearly　④ twice-a-year　⑤ twice-yearly　⑥ biyearly　★ biyearly は「2 年に 1 回」の意味になることも多いので注意.［⇨ 36. 回数・頻度の表現 36-3］
- 年 5 分の利息　① interest of five percent「per annum [a year]　② annual interest of five percent

31-1-3 その他

- 25 年物のワイン　① wine 25 years old　② 25-year-old wine
- 1935 年物のロマネコンティ　①《a bottle of》Romane Conti of 1935 vintage　② 1935 Romane Conti
- あの建物は築何年ですか.　How old is that building?
- 満 20 年をもって成年とす.
  ① Majority is reached on attainment of the twentieth birthday.
  ② Adulthood is reached on the twentieth birthday.
  ③ Adulthood is reached at age 20.

31. 年・月・週・日 31-2

- 年々増加する　① increase every year　② increase from year to year　③ increase year by year　④ increase year after year　⑤ increase with years
- ここ数年は　①〔過去〕for some years (now [past])　② for the「last [past] 」few years　③ for the「last [past]」several years　④ in recent years　⑤〔未来〕for some years ahead　⑥ for some years to come
- 通年の　① year-round　② year-around　③ full-year
- 売り上げは通年で30億に上る見込み.
  ① Sales for the (whole) year are estimated at over ¥3 billion.
  ② Full-year sales are estimated at over ¥3 billion.

■ 31-2　月

31-2-1　長さ

- 1年は12か月だ.
  ① A year is twelve months (long).
  ② One year「consists of [has]」twelve months.
  ③ There are twelve months in a year.
- 半月　① half a month　② a half month
- 何か月　⇨第2部・なんかげつ

31-2-2　頻度・割合

- 月に1度　① once a month　② monthly
- 毎月数回　several times a month
- 月に2回の　① twice-monthly　② semimonthly　③ bimonthly　★bimonthlyは「2か月に1回」の意味にもなるので注意.［⇨ 36. 回数・頻度の表現 36-3］
- 2か月に1回の　bimonthly
- 毎月　① every month　② monthly
- 毎月の　monthly
- 毎月毎月　① month after month　② month by month　③ month in, month out
- 月にいくらという計算で　at so much per month

31-2-3　月末

- 月末ごろ　① towards the end of the month　② near the end of the month
- 月末に　at the end of the month
- 月末までに　by the end of the month
- 月末の払いが多い　have a lot of payments to make at the end of the month
- 月末残高　① the end-of-month balance　② the monthly balance
- 月末締め　① the settlement of accounts at the end of the month　② the

monthly settlement of accounts
- 3月末日　① the end of March ② the last day of March
- 3月末日現在　as of March 31
- 支払期日は翌月末日だ．　(The [My, etc.]) payment is due on the last day of the following month.
- 支払期日は請求書の日付の翌月の末日だ．　(The [My, etc.]) payment is due on the last day of the month following the date of the「invoice [bill]．

31-2-4　今月

- 今月　① this month ② the current month ③ the present month
- 10年前の今月　① this month ten years ago ② ten years ago this month
- 今月13日付の貴信　your letter of the 13th (of this month)
- 今月いっぱい　① until the end of「this [the] month ② throughout this month ③《米》through the end of this month ④《米》for the whole month ⑤《英》for the whole of this month
- 今月中に　① (in the course of) this month ② before [by] the end of this month ③ before the month is out
- 今月号　① the current「issue [number]《of the magazine》 ② this month's issue
- 今月分の新聞代　① this month's newspaper bill ② the newspaper bill for this month
- 今月分の給料　① this month's「salary [pay, wages] ②《my》salary for the month ③《my》pay for「this [the current] month

31-2-5　時期　[⇨ 31-5「来…」「先…」]

- 来月　① next month ② the coming month
- 来月1日に　on the first of next month
- 先月　last month

■ 31-3　週

31-3-1　長さ

- 2週間　① two weeks ②《主に英》a fortnight ★ fortnight は語源的には fourteen nights（14夜）の意．
- 3週間にわたって　① for three weeks ② over three weeks
- 3週間の休暇　① three weeks off ②《米》a three-week vacation ③《英》a three-week holiday
- この1週間に　① in the past week ② in the last week
- その日から4週間目に　① four weeks after that day ②《英》four weeks that

day
- 今日から4週間後に　four weeks from today
- 2週間前の日曜日に　two weeks ago (on) Sunday
- 4週間で作業を終える　finish the work in four weeks
- 4週間以内に作業を終える　finish the work within four weeks

31-3-2 頻度

- 2週間に1度　① every two weeks　②《主に英》fortnightly
- 2週間に1回の　① biweekly　②《主に英》fortnightly
- 1週間に2回の　① semiweekly　② twice-weekly　③ biweekly　★biweekly については⇨ 36. 回数・頻度の表現 36-3
- ここの部屋代は週200ドルです．　The rent for this room is 200 dollars a week.
- この工場では週40時間5日制です．　We work a 40-hour, five-day week at this factory.
- 週当たりの労働時間　① the number of working hours per week　②《米》one's workweek　③《主に英》one's working week
- 週休2日　⇨第2部・しゅうきゅう…

31-3-3 時期

- 今週　this week
- 来週　next week ［⇨ 31-5「来…」「先…」］
- 先週　last week
- 毎週　every week
- 毎週水曜日に　① every Wednesday　② on Wednesdays
- 毎週同じ曜日に　on the same day every week
- 隔週で同じ曜日に　on the same day every other week
- 隔週の水曜日に　(on) every other Wednesday
- 子供たちは2週間交代で父親と過ごす．　The children stay with their father every other「two weeks [two-week period]. ★「1週間交代」なら every other week.
- 4月の第1週に　in [during, etc.] the first week of April
- 来月の第2週から　from the second week of next month
- 24日の週に　in [during, etc.] the week of the 24th
- 週の半ばに　① in the midde of the week　② at midweek
- 週の前半［後半］に　in the「first [second] half of the week

31-3-4 **週末**

- この週末に　①〔今度の〕this (coming) weekend　②〔過ぎた〕this past weekend
- この週末の予定　plans for this weekend
- 週末の過ごし方　①how *one* spends the weekend　②how to spend the weekend
- 週末を鎌倉で過ごす　①spend the weekend in Kamakura　②stay in Kamakura over the weekend

31-3-5 **期間**

- 5月10日から16日までは愛鳥週間である．　Bird Week is「observed [held] from May 10 to 16.
- 週間天気予報　①a weather forecast for the coming week　②a seven-day weather forecast

■ 31-4 **日**

31-4-1 **長さ**

- 2, 3日で　①in two or three days　②in a couple of days
- 15日ごとに　①every fifteen days　②once in every fifteen days　③once every fifteen days
- 15日おきに　〔16日に1回〕①every sixteenth day　②with fifteen intervening days
- 10日間の名古屋出張　a ten-day business trip to Nagoya
- 半日　①half a day　②a half day
- 一両日中に　①in a day or two　②within the next couple of days

31-4-2 **日数**

- 稼働日数　〔生産設備などの〕the number of days in operation
- 就労延べ日数　the total number of working days
- 出席日数　the number of days present
- 欠席日数　the number of days absent
- 完成には日数がかかる．　It will require many days to complete.
- どのくらい日数がかかりますか．　How「long [many days] will it take?
- 何日　⇨第2部・なんにち
- 週休2日　⇨第2部・しゅうきゅう…

31-4-3 １泊２日

- ４泊５日の旅行　① a trip of five days and four nights　② an excursion over four nights　③ a「five days'［five-day］trip
- １泊２日のセミナーに参加した．　I participated in a seminar that ran two days with an overnight stay.
- 新作 DVD は１泊２日 450 円です．　The overnight rental for new-release DVDs is 450 yen.
- 駐車料金１泊２日 7,400 円．　〔掲示〕Overnight parking: 7,400 yen.
- 一泊 8,000 円のビジネスホテルに泊まった．　I stayed at an ¥8,000-a-night business hotel.

31-4-4 中…日

- 中２日あれば仕上げます．
  ① Two full days will be enough to finish it.
  ② It will take three days to finish it.
- 中１日おいて　① leaving one day (in) between　② after「a gap［an interval］of one day
- 中３日で登板する　① come in to pitch after an interval of three days
  ② come back to the mound after「three days off［three days without pitching, three days' rest］

■ 31-5 「来…」「先…」

31-5-1 「来…」

- あした　tomorrow
- あさって　① the day after tomorrow　② two days from now
- しあさって　three days from now
- 来週　next week
- 再来週　① the week after next　② two weeks from now
- 来月　next month
- 再来月　① the month after next　② two months from now
- 来月か再来月　next month or the month after
- 来年　① next year　②《in》the coming year
- 再来年　① the year after next　② two years from now
- 来年か再来年　next year or the year after

31-5-2 「先…」

- きのう　yesterday

- おととい　① the day before yesterday　② two days ago
- さきおととい　three days ago
- 先週　last week
- 先々週　① the week before last　② two weeks ago　★《米》では ① の the は省略可能．
- 先月　last month
- 先々月　① the month before last　② two months ago
- 昨年［去年］　last year
- 一昨年［おととし］　the year before last
- おととしの夏　the summer before last　★秋以降には last summer はその年の夏．the summer before last は「去年の夏」の意味になってしまう．「おととしの夏」というには (in) the summer two years ago などという必要がある．
- 一昨昨年［さきおととし］　three years ago

31-5-3　next … の使用例

- 来月の 10 日に　① on the 10th (of) next month　② next month on the 10th
- 来週の木曜日に　① on Thursday (of) next week　② next Thursday　③《英》Thursday week
- 来年の 8 月に　① in August (of) next year　② next August

★next Thursday（次の木曜日）に類する表現は曖昧になることがある．言ったのが金曜日なら「来週の木曜日」の意味であるが，月曜日に言うとその週の木曜日を指すか来週の木曜日を指すか不明な場合もある．ただし，その週の木曜日であれば on Thursday といえばすむ．また水曜日なら翌日の木曜日のことを next Thursday とは言わずに tomorrow と言うので，next Thursday といえば来週の木曜日と解釈されることが多い．

★next August も同様で 8 月より前に使うと論理的にはその年の 8 月を指すが，その年の 8 月なら in August でよく，next August が来年の 8 月の意味になることもある．

- 来年の今ごろ　about this time next year
- 来年の今日　① this day next year　② a year from today

31-5-4　last … の使用例

- 先月の 10 日に　① on the 10th (of) last month　② last month on the 10th
- 先々月の 10 日に　① on the 10th (of) the month before last　② two months ago on the 10th
- 先週の木曜日に　① on Thursday (of) last week　② last Thursday
- 去年の 8 月に　① in August (of) last year　② last August

31. 年・月・週・日 31-6

★last にも next と同様の問題がある．金曜日に last Tuesday（この前の火曜日）と言えば先週の火曜日ではなくその週の火曜日を指すこともある．前日の木曜日のことは last Thursday とは言わずに yesterday と言うので，あえて last Thursday というと先週の木曜日だと解釈されることが多い．last August も 9 月以降に使っても前年の 8 月の意味になることが多い．

- 去年の 8 月 25 日に　① on August 25 (of) last year　② last August 25
- 去年の今日　① this day last year　② a year ago today

■ 31-6 「翌…」「前…」

日本語と同様，英語でも，過去のある時点を起点にして「翌月」「前月」などという場合は，原則として現在を起点にした「来月」「先月」などとは別の表現を使う．

31-6-1 「翌…」

- 翌日　① the next day　② the following day　③ the day after
- 翌々日　two days later
- 翌週　① the next week　② the following week
- 翌々週　two weeks later
- 翌月　① the next month　② the following month
- 翌々月　two months later
- 翌年　① the next year　② the following year　③ the year after
- 翌々年　two years later
- その請求があった日の属する月の翌月　the month following the month「of [containing, including] the day when the request is made

31-6-2 「前…」

- 前日　① the day before　② the previous day　③ the preceding day
- 前々日　① two days before　② two days earlier
- 前週　① the week「before [earlier]　② the previous week
- 前々週　two weeks「before [earlier]
- 前月　① the month「before [earlier]　② the previous month
- 前々月　two months「before [earlier]
- 前年　① the year「before [earlier]　② the preceding year　③ the previous year
- 前々年　two years「before [earlier]

31-6-3 **使用例**

- 火事のあった翌日に　on the day 「after [following] the fire
- (旅行から) 帰宅した翌日　① the day after reaching home　② the day after 《we》 came home
- 試合を翌日に控えたある日，…
  ① It was on a day with a game coming the next day when …
  ② It was on the day before a game when …
- 結婚式の前日に　on the day before the wedding
- それは第二次大戦が勃発する前日だった．　It was the day before World War II broke out.

▶ 決算報告などで前の年と比較する場合，その年がすでに終わって過去の結果とみなせば「前年」だが，終わってまもないころであれば「昨年」ということもある．日本語でも英語でもこの使い分けは曖昧な部分がある．

- 昨年同期比で　① compared「with [to] (the figures for) the same period「a year ago [last year]　② compared with the year-ago period　③ on a year-on-year basis [⇨第 2 部・どうき]
- 前年同期比で　① compared「with [to] (the figures for) the same period the previous year　② compared with the year-before period　③ on a year-on-year basis

■ 31-7　「…前」「…後」

31-7-1　「…前」

- 数日前　①〔今から〕a few days ago　②〔その時から〕a few days「before [previously, earlier, prior to 《that》]
- 3 日前の新聞　① a newspaper of three days「ago [before]　②《looking for》the newspaper from three days ago
- 5 年前の金融危機　the financial crisis of five years ago
- 10 年前の今日　ten years ago today
- 100 年前の東京の地図　a map of Tokyo from 100 years ago
- この建物は 300 年前のものだ．　① This building dates back 300 years.　② This building is 300 years old.
- 我々が見ているその星の姿は約 600 年前のものだ．　That star as we see it now is from about 600 years「ago [in the past].
- ほんの 3 ページ前に出てきた．　《The word》 occurred just three pages earlier.
- 数フレーム前に写っていたオブジェクト　an object that appeared a few

frames earlier
- それは明治維新の10年前のことだ. ① It was ten years before the Meiji Restoration. ② It antedates the Meiji Restoration by ten years.
- それはお前が生まれるずっと前のことだよ. It happened long before you were born.
- 彼の死ぬ3日前に会った. ① I saw him three days before he died. ② I saw him three days prior to his death.
- 彼は1週間**前から**病気です. He's been ill for a week.
- ずっと前から ① for a long time now ② from long ago ③ from way back
- 1か月前から予約を受け付けます. We accept「reservations [bookings]」starting a month prior to 《the performance》.
- それは**どれくらい前**のことですか. About how long ago「was that [did that happen]」? [⇨ 26. 数量に関する疑問文 26-5-3]

31-7-2 「…**後**」[⇨第2部・さき]

- それから2年後 ① after two years ② two years after (that) ③ two years afterward(s) ④ two years later ⑤ two years on
- 今から3年後 ① three years from now ② three years on ③ in three「years [years' time]」④ three years hence
- 開始後5分で five minutes「after [from]」the start
- 何日かあとに ① a few days later ② a few days after ③ after a few days
- その後 ① after that ② afterward(s) ③ later ④ subsequently ⑤ since then
- その後ずっと ① ever after (that) ② ever afterward(s) ③〔今まで〕ever since (then)
- 革命後のイラン ① Iran「after [since]」the revolution ② postrevolution(ary) Iran
- これから50年後の世界 ① the world in 50「years [years' time]」② the world 50 years「from now [in the future, on, hence]」
- 100年後の東京から来ました I'm from (the) Tokyo of 100 years from now.
- 工事の完成はその2年ほどあとになる. The construction work will be completed about two years「later [after that]」.
- その値は初期化がされるまで定義されない. The value is not defined until after the initialization is run.

32. 時刻と時間

■ 32-1 時刻

32-1-1 時刻の言い方

7:10 を seven ten というように時間と分をそれぞれ数字として読むのが基本.

7:00 ① seven o'clock ② seven
7:05 ① seven (oh) five ② five past seven
7:10 ① seven ten ② ten past seven
7:15 ① seven fifteen ② quarter past seven
7:30 ① seven thirty ② half past seven
7:45 ① seven forty-five ② quarter to eight ③《米》quarter of eight
7:50 ① seven fifty ② ten to eight ③《米》ten of eight

▶ 正時は… o'clock であるが, o'clock を付けずに数字だけいうことも多い.
▶ 30 分までは past (…分過ぎ), それ以降は to (…分前) を使うこともできる.《米》では to の代わりに of を使うこともある. 30 分は half (1 時間の半分), 15 分は quarter (1 時間の 1/4) という.

- 何時ですか. ① What time is it? ② What's the time? ★⇨第2部・なんじ
- 10 時 30 分です. It is 10:30.
- 11 時に ① at eleven ② at 11:00
- 8:00 の電車に乗る take the 8:00 train
- 毎正時に every hour on the hour
- 毎時 10 分に ① every hour at ten minutes past the hour ② at ten minutes past each hour
- 3 月 7 日の 8 時 10 分に at 8:10 on March 7
- 火曜日の 11 時に予約する make an appointment for Tuesday at eleven
- 皆既食は 22 日の午前 9 時 34 分 59 秒に始まった. Totality started at 9:34:59 on the morning of the 22nd. ★9:34:59 は nine thirty-four and fifty-nine seconds と読む.

32-1-2 午前と午後

午前 8:00 ① 8:00 in the morning ② 8:00 a.m.
午後 5:00 ① 5:00 in the afternoon ② 5:00 p.m.

- 午後でも遅い時間は 10:00 in the evening, 10:00 at night のようにいう．「午前2時」は 2:00 in the morning でよい．
- a.m. は A.M., AM, p.m. は P.M., PM とも書く．a.m. は ante meridiem（ラテン語で「正午より前」の意），p.m. は post meridiem（ラテン語で「正午より後」の意）に由来する．日本語では AM, PM を時刻の前に付けることもあるが，英語では必ず後に書く．
- a.m. [p.m.] は o'clock と一緒には使わない．よって 8:00 a.m. は eight o'clock a.m. ではなく，eight a.m. と読む．eight o'clock in the morning などは可．

トリビア　うるう秒

原子時計で時間が精密に測定できるようになると，地球の自転のむらが時刻の決定の際に問題となってくる．そのずれを調整するために不規則な間隔でうるう秒（leap second）が挿入される．1972年〜2017年の間に27回挿入され，直近では（日本時間で）2017年1月1日8時59分59秒の次に8時59分60秒がきたあと9時00分00秒となった．ただし，近年は不規則なうるう秒の挿入がコンピューターシステムにとって不便であるため，うるう秒の廃止も議論されている．

32-1-3　24 時制

24 時制はイギリスや非英語諸国では使われているが，アメリカでは軍隊や一部業界を除いて一般的でない．読み方は 12 時制に準じるが，05:10 のような先頭の 0 を読み，後に hours（常に複数形）を付けることもある．特に軍隊では oh, hours を省かずに読み，時と分の間にコロンを入れずに 0510 のように書く．

00:00	zero hours
00:30	① oh oh thirty hours　② zero thirty hours
05:01	oh five oh one hours
05:00	oh five hundred hours
21:00	twenty-one hundred hours
21:40	twenty-one forty hours または twenty-one hundred and forty hours

> **トリビア** 「25 時」
> 日本では，深夜営業・深夜放送などに関して夜中の零時を過ぎた時間を 25 時などと表記することもある．これは英語圏では普通使わない．

> **トリビア** 軍の数詞呼称法
> 日本でも旧軍や自衛隊でヒト (1)，フタ (2)，サン (3)，ヨン (4)，ゴー (5)，ロク (6)，ナナ (7)，ハチ (8)，キュウ (9)，マル (0) という数字の読み方があり，時刻を 0120（まるひとふたまる）のように読む．時刻のほかに方位，距離などのデータの読み上げにも使われる．口頭の連絡の際に聞き間違えを減らすためのものと言われている．

32-1-4 零時と 12 時

12 時制では「12 時」の扱いが問題になる．午前 11 時半の 1 時間後は午後零時半というのならわかる．だが，英語の 12 時制では「零時」の表現は一般的でない．そのため午後 12 時半ということになるが，これは午前 11 時半の 13 時間後というちぐはぐなことになってしまう．数字の連続性からは昼の 12 時半が午前 12 時半となるはずで，午前・午後を付けずに文脈に任せるのであれば 12:30 で問題ない．だが，正午過ぎの 12:30 に午前を付けるのは矛盾しており，機器やパソコンでは昼なら 12:30 p.m. と表示されることも多い．

さらに微妙なのは 12 時ちょうどの問題である．これも日本では昼の 12 時は「午後零時」，夜の 12 時は「午前零時」を使って誤解を避けることができ，12 時というにしても数字の連続性から午前 12 時なら昼，午後 12 時なら夜と考えることが多い．しかし，英語では上記の 12:30 p.m. との整合性のため昼の 12 時を 12:00 p.m. と，夜の 12:00 を 12:00 a.m. と称することが少なくない．ただし，12 時は「正午より前 (a.m.)」でも「正午より後 (p.m.)」でもないので語源的には矛盾しているとして英米でもよく議論になる問題である．誤解を避けるには昼なら 12:00 noon (twelve noon)，夜なら 12:00 midnight (twelve midnight) といえばいい．

32. 時刻と時間 32-2

> **トリビア** 夜の 12 時は翌日か
>
> 法的に 12 時の帰属が大きな問題になることがある．日本の著作権法改正により映画の著作権保護期間が 50 年から 70 年になったが，2004 年の施行以前に 50 年の保護期間が切れていたものは対象とならない．著作権保護期間が過ぎた映画は格安 DVD などで大きなビジネスになるので保護期間延長の対象となるかどうかは重要である．問題とされたのが 1953 年の作品で，2003 年までが旧法による保護期間であることから，映画会社は改正法施行の瞬間には著作権保護期間が切れておらず，20 年延長の対象になると主張したのである．文化庁著作権課も「2003 年 12 月 31 日午後 12 時と 2004 年 1 月 1 日午前 0 時が接着している」として映画会社の主張を支持する見解を発表していたが，2006 年 7 月と 10 月に，東京地裁は格安 DVD 販売差し止めを求める仮処分申請を相次いで却下した．保護期間を把握する単位は「日」であるなどというのがその理由である．

■ 32-2 時計

- この時計は 3 分進んでいる．　This「clock [watch]」is three minutes fast.
  ★以下の訳例では，簡単のため clock のみ示す．
- この時計は 2 分遅れている．　This clock is two minutes slow.
- この時計は進んでいる．　This clock is (running) fast.
- この時計は遅れている．　This clock is (running) slow.
- その時計は何分遅れているの？　How many minutes behind is that clock?
- この時計は 1 日に 2 秒進む．　This clock gains two seconds a day.
- この時計は 1 日に 10 秒遅れる．　This clock loses ten seconds a day.
- 時計を合わせる　set a clock (right) 《by the「radio [telephone time signal]」》
- 時計を進める　put [set] the clock「ahead [forward]」
- 時計を遅らせる　put [set] the clock「back [backward]」
- タイマーを 6 時にセットする　set a timer for six (o'clock)

■ 32-3 時差

32-3-1 基本

- **時差**　① (a [the]) difference in time　② a [the] time difference　③ a [the] time differential
- 東京とロンドンでは夏は 8 時間の**時差**がある．　Between Tokyo and London

there is an eight-hour **time difference** in summer.
- 日本の時間はグリニッジ標準時より9時間**進んでいる**．　(The time in) Japan is nine hours **ahead of** Greenwich Mean Time.
- モンタナ州の地方時はニューヨークより2時間**遅れている**．　The local time in Montana is two hours **behind** New York.
- 時差を考慮する　① take into account the time difference　② consider the time zone difference
- その試合は時差の関係で深夜に放送された．　The game was broadcast late in the night due to the difference in time zones.
- 時差に順応する　adjust to the time zone「change［difference］
- まだ**時差ぼけ**が抜けない．
  ① I'm still suffering from **jet lag**.
  ② I'm still recovering from **jet lag**.
  ③ I still have **jet lag**.
- 国境も時差もない世界　a world where borders and time differences do not matter

32-3-2 日本時間・現地時間

- 真珠湾攻撃は**日本時間**で12月8日に行なわれたが，**現地時間では**12月7日だった．
  ① The attack on Pearl Harbor took place on December 8 (**by**) **Japanese time** but on December 7 **locally**.
  ② The attack on Pearl Harbor occurred on December 8 **Japan time**, which was December 7 **local time**.
- **日本時間**で2月15日の正午までにこの電子メールに返事をください．
  Please respond to this e-mail by noon, February 15, **Japan time**.
- **そちらの時間**で15日の朝10時ごろ電話します．　I will call you on the 15th at around 10 o'clock in the morning **your time**.

32-3-3 標準時

イギリス

Greenwich Mean Time グリニッジ標準時 (GMT)　　　西経 0°

アメリカ

Atlantic time 大西洋標準時 (AST)	西経 60°	GMT－4時間
Eastern time 東部標準時 (EST)	西経 75°	GMT－5時間
Central time 中部標準時 (CST)	西経 90°	GMT－6時間
Mountain time 山地標準時 (MST)	西経 105°	GMT－7時間
Pacific time 太平洋標準時 (PST)	西経 120°	GMT－8時間
Alaska time アラスカ標準時 (AKST)	西経 135°	GMT－9時間

Hawaii-Aleutian time
　ハワイ・アリューシャン標準時 (HST)　　西経 150°　　GMT－10 時間
Samoa time サモア標準時　　　　　　　　　西経 165°　　GMT－11 時間

▶ 略称の ST は standard time に由来するが，S を省いて ET, CT などとすることもある．Eastern standard time のように呼称に standard を入れることもある．

▶ サマータイム（daylight saving time）期間中は EDT (eastern daylight time 東部夏時間) のように表示する．

▶ EST, CST, MST, PST がアメリカ本土に当たる．

日本
Japan Standard Time 日本標準時 (JST)　　東経 135°　　GMT＋9 時間

■ 32-4　時間 [⇨第2部・じかん]

32-4-1　時間の長さ

- 2 時間 34 分 56 秒　① 2 hours, 34 minutes, (and) 56 seconds　② 2 hr. 34 min. 56 sec.　③ 2:34:56
- 1 時間は 60 分である．
  ① There are 60 minutes in an hour.
  ② One hour has 60 minutes.
- 24 時間　⇨第2部・にじゅうよじかん
- 15 分　① fifteen minutes　② a quarter (of an hour)
- 30 分　① thirty minutes　② half an hour　③《米》a half hour
- 30 分番組　① a thirty-minute program　② a half-an-hour program　③《米》a half-hour program
- 8 時間の睡眠　eight hours of sleep
- 5 時間で　in five hours
- 制限時間は 2 時間．
  ① There is a two-hour time limit.
  ② The time limit is two hours.
  ③ You have two hours《to *do*》.
- 時間を 5 分延長する　extend the time「by [for] five (more) minutes
- 時間を 10 分短縮する　shorten [reduce] the time by 10 minutes
- (シャッタースピード) 100 分の 1 秒で写真を撮る　take a「photograph [picture] at a hundredth of a second
- 1 秒の何分の 1 まで正確な時計　a watch that is accurate to (within) a fraction of a second

32-4-2 単位時間

- 毎時　①every hour　②per hour　③an hour
- 毎時 20 マイルの速力で　①at a speed of 20 miles an hour　②at 20 mph
- 毎分　①every minute　②per minute　③a minute
- 毎分 45 回転で回転する　rotate (at) 45「rpm [revolutions per minute]
- 成人では安静時に心臓は毎分約 70 回鼓動する．　In adults, the heart at rest beats about 70 times per minute.
- 毎秒　①every second　②per second　③a second
- 毎秒 100 m の速度で　at 100 meters per second
- 毎秒 1 万回転で回転する　rotate (at) 10,000「rps [revolutions per second]
- 動画を毎秒 25 フレームの速度で表示する　display video at a rate of 25 frames per second

33. 時間を表わす句・節

■ 33-1 簡単な前置詞句など

33-1-1 …に

- 10 時に ① at ten (o'clock) ② at 10:00
- 10 日に on the 10th
- 午前中に in the morning
- 10 日の午前中に on the morning of the 10th
- 日曜日に on Sunday
- 10 月に in October
- 2010 年に ① in 2010 ② in the year 2010
- 21 世紀に in the 21st century
- 現時点において ① now ② at the moment ③ at present ④ at this point (in time) ⑤ currently
- 今日の時点で ① (as of) today ② as things stand today
- 8 月 15 日の時点において ① on August 15 ② as of August 15
- この時点で at this point (in time)
- 今から 20 年たった時点で ① in twenty years ② twenty years from now ③ when [after] twenty years have passed
- 衆議院が解散された時点で at the time (when [that]) the House of Representatives is dissolved
- 10 月(の間)は during October

33-1-2 …から

- 10 月から 12 月まで from October「to [until, till] December [⇨ 34. 期間の表現]
- 10 月から始まる start [begin] in October ★英語では「10 月に始まる」と発想する.
- 10 月から手が空く ① be free beginning in October ② be free from October
- 10 月 1 日以降 ① beginning on October 1 ② from October 1 ③ from October 1 on ④ on and after October 1
- この時点以降 from this point on
- 10 月から, 10 月以来(現在まで) 《have been working》 since October
- 父が死んで 5 年になる.
  ① My father has been dead for five years.
  ② My father died five years ago.

③ It is [It has been] five years since my father died.

33-1-3 …まで

- 10月まで（は）　① until October　② before October ［⇨第2部・…まで］
- 10月までに　by October ［⇨ 35. 期日・期限の表現］
- 遅くとも10月には　① by October at the latest　② no later than October
- 10月いっぱい　①《continue》until the end of October　②《it will take》all October
- 10月いっぱいで　《quit》at the end of October
- 10月いっぱいまでに　《finish》by the end of October

33-1-4 その他

- 3週間（の間）　for three weeks ［⇨ 34. 期間の表現］
- 3週間で　in three weeks
- 3週間以内に　① within three weeks　②《米口》in three weeks ［⇨ 35. 期日・期限の表現］
- 3週間もしないうちに　in less than three weeks
- 3年そこそこで　in little more than three years
- さらに3週間延期される　be「delayed [put off, set back] for another three weeks
- 3週間後に　①〔今から〕three weeks from now　② in three weeks　③〔過去または未来のある時点から〕three weeks later
- 3週間前に　①〔今から〕three weeks ago　②〔過去または未来のある時点から〕three weeks earlier
- 試験の2日前に　two days before the examination
- 両チームは決勝戦を3日後に控えている．
  ① The teams have three days until the finals.
  ② It is [There are] (only) three days till the two teams face each other in the finals.
  ③ The teams (are to) play each other in the finals in three days.
- 3週間前から　①〔今から〕since three weeks ago　②〔過去または未来のある時点から〕since three weeks earlier　③〔3週間の間〕for three weeks
- ★**ago と earlier:**「…前」というときの ago は現在を基準にするときの表現．過去または未来のある時点を基準にして「…前」というときは earlier を使う．
- 予約は1年前から承ります．　We begin accepting reservations a year in advance.
- 出発日の7日前以降のキャンセル　① cancellation less than 8 days before the departure date　② cancellation up to 7 days before the departure date　③ cancellation 0 to 7 days before the departure date

33. 時間を表わす句・節 33-2

- 10 日前以降に　① less than 11 days before 《the date》　② no sooner than 10 days before 《the date》
- 3 週間の努力の末　① after 《her》 effort over three weeks　② after three weeks of effort　③ after three weeks' effort
- 続く数週間にわたって　over the next few weeks
- 続く数週間で　within the next few weeks
- 続く数週間の間　during the next few weeks
- 1950 年から 2000 年までの間に　① between 1950 and 2000　② during the period from 1950 to 2000
- 3 年ぶりに　① for the first time in three years　② for the first time since three years ago ［⇨第 2 部・…ぶり］
- 今年の米は何年来の不作だった．　This year's rice crop was the worst in many years.
- 20 年来の大雪　① the heaviest snowfall in twenty years　② the heaviest snowfall that「we [they] have had for the past twenty years
- 1955 年以来　since 1955
- 女性参政権が認められたのは 1945 年になってのことだった．
  ① It was only in 1945 that women obtained「suffrage [the right to vote]．
  ② It was not until 1945 that women obtained「suffrage [the right to vote]．

■ 33-2　「初頭」「末」「旬」

- 6 月のはじめに [6 月初頭に]　at the beginning of June
- 6 月はじめごろ [6 月初旬に，6 月上旬に]　① in early June　② early in June
- 6 月中ごろ [6 月中旬に]　① in the middle of June　② in mid-June
- 6 月遅くに [6 月下旬に]　① in late June　② late in June
- 6 月の終わりごろ　towards the end of June
- 6 月の終わりに [6 月末に]　at the end of June
- 6 月の上旬から中旬にかけて　from early to mid-June
- 6 月の前半に　in the first half of June
- 6 月の後半に　in the「second [latter] half of June

▶ June (6 月) の代わりに 2007 (2007 年) などを使う場合も同様．

▶ 上旬，中旬，下旬という区切りは英語圏では普通は使われない．定義に沿った訳を考えることもできるが，厳密を要さない文脈では「はじめ」「中ごろ」「終わり」程度の英語にしたほうが自然である．

- 6 月の上旬　① early June　② the first ten days of June　③ the first third of June
- 6 月の中旬　① the middle of June　② mid-June　③ the second ten days of

June　④ the second third of June
- 6月の下旬　① late June　② the last ten days of June　③ from the 21st to the end of June　④ the last third of June
- 18世紀のはじめに [18世紀初頭に]　at the beginning of the eighteenth century
- 18世紀はじめごろ [18世紀の初期に]　① in the early eighteenth century　② early in the eighteenth century
- 18世紀中葉に　① in the middle of the eighteenth century　② in the mid-eighteenth century
- 18世紀遅くに [18世紀後期に]　① in the late eighteenth century　② late in the eighteenth century　③ in the latter part of the eighteenth century
- 18世紀の終わりごろ　towards the「end [close] of the eighteenth century
- 18世紀の終わりに [18世紀末に]　at the「end [close] of the eighteenth century
- 18世紀の前半に　in the first half of the eighteenth century
- 18世紀の後半に　in the「second [latter] half of the eighteenth century

▶ eighteenth century（18世紀）の代わりに 1990s（1990年代），Meiji period（明治時代）などを使うこともできる．

- 縄文（時代）草創期　the Incipient Jomon period
- 縄文（時代）早期　the Initial Jomon period
- 縄文（時代）前期　the Early Jomon period
- 縄文（時代）中期　the Middle Jomon period
- 縄文（時代）後期　the Late Jomon period
- 縄文（時代）晩期　the Final Jomon period

■ 33-3　同時

- …するとき　① when …　② at the time when …
- …する間　① while …　② in 《calculating》　③ during 《heating》
- …するやいなや　① as soon as …　② no sooner than …
- …したとたんに　① just as …　② the moment (that) …　③ the minute (that) …
- …するのと同時に　at the same time as …
- 彼は私の姿を見るやいなや出ていった．
  ① As soon as he caught sight of me, he went out.
  ② He no sooner caught sight of me than he went out.
  ③ No sooner had he caught sight of me than he went out.
  ④ The moment he saw me he went out.

- その光子が放出されるのと同時に　① at the same time as the photon is emitted　② on [upon] emission of the photon
- イベントが発生するのと同時に検出する　detect events as they occur
- ナポレオンの没落と同時に長い戦争が終わりを告げた．　With Napoleon's fall ended the long war.
- …と同時またはそれより前に　prior to or simultaneously with …
- 同時に　① at the same time　② simultaneously 《with …》　③ in the same instant　④ concurrently 《with …》　⑤ in concurrence 《with …》　⑥ synchronously
- 同時に走る（複数の）プログラム　programs that run concurrently
- 画質を維持すると同時にスピードを改善しなければならない．
  ① It is necessary to improve the speed while maintaining the image quality.
  ② It is necessary to improve the speed and, at the same time, maintain the image quality.
  ③ It is necessary to improve the speed as well as to maintain the image quality.

■ 33-4　時間を表わす副詞的な名詞句

33-4-1　副詞的な名詞句

次のような句は前置詞なしで副詞的に用いる．

毎…

every morning / every night / every Friday / every week / every August / every summer

この前の…

yesterday morning / yesterday afternoon / last night / last Friday / last week / last August / last summer

- ▶ last morning, last afternoon とはいわずに yesterday を使う．
- ▶ last Friday, last August のたぐいの表現の曖昧さについては⇨ 31-5「来…」「先…」

次の…

tomorrow morning / tomorrow night / next Friday / next week / next August / next summer

- ▶ next morning, next night とはいわずに tomorrow を使う．
- ▶ next Friday, next August のたぐいの表現の曖昧さについては⇨ 31-5

「来…」「先…」

この…

this morning / this Friday / this week / this August

▶ this Friday は場合により過去の金曜日を指す場合と未来の金曜日を指す場合がある．this August も同様である．

33-4-2 副詞節を導くことのできる名詞句

each time ...　…する都度
every time ...　…するときは毎回
any time ...　…するときはいつも
(the) next time ...　次に…するときは
(the) last time ...　この前…したときは
(the) first time ...　初めて…したときには

▶ いずれも time のあとに that を入れてもよい．that は関係副詞 when と同義だが省略可能．

34. 期間の表現

34-1 期間の長さ

- 5年間　① for five years　② for the「space [period] of five years
- この1か月[1週, 1年]間　the past「month [week, year]
- 過去20年の間に　during [in] the past twenty years
- 30分の運動　half an hour of exercise
- 5分間の休憩　a five-minute「recess [break, breather]
- 3か月間の闘病生活　a three-month struggle against illness
- 1週間のキャンプ旅行　a week-long camping trip
- 展覧会は明日から10日間開かれる．　The exhibition will be held for ten days beginning tomorrow.
- 日本へ来てからどのくらいになりますか．　How long have you been in Japan?
- 一つの作品を仕上げるまでにどのくらいかかりますか．　How long does it take to complete one work?
- 彼はどのくらい前に家を出ましたか．　How long ago did he leave the house?
- あなたが宝石の盗難に気づいたのは，帰宅なさってからどのくらい後のことですか．　How long was it after you returned home that you noticed the jewels were missing?
- 彼はどのくらいで退院できますか．　How soon can he leave the hospital?

34-2 「…以内」

- 3日以内に　within three days [⇨第2部・いない]
- 3日で仕上げる　finish … in three days
- あとどのくらいでできあがりますか．
  ① How much longer will it take before it's ready?
  ② How soon will it be ready?
- 購入**から**1週間**以内に**　**within** a week「**after** [**from, of**] purchase
- 本条約の批准書の交換**の日から**3か月**以内に**
  ① **within** three months **from the date of** the exchange of the ratifications of this treaty
  ② **within** three months **from the date**「**when** [**that**] the instruments of ratification of this treaty are exchanged
- (過去)6か月**以内に**撮影された写真　a photograph taken **within the**「**last** [**past**] six months

34-3 契約期間

- 契約の**有効期限**　①〔期間の長さ〕the term of a contract　② the term of validity of a contract　③〔期間満了日〕the time limit of a contract　④ the expiry date of a contract　⑤ the expiration date of a contract
- この契約の**期間**は 1 か年である．
  ① This contract is for「a one-year period [one year].
  ② This contract holds good for「a one-year period [one year].
- あと 5 日で契約の**期限**が切れる．　The contract expires in five days.
- この契約が**期限**を迎えるのは 2011 年 3 月 31 日だ．　This contract expires on March 31, 2011.
- 東宝との契約は**まだ 2 年以上**ある．
  ① My contract with Toho has more than two years left to run.
  ② I still have more than two years on my contract with Toho.
- 契約（の**期限**）が切れた．　The contract has「expired [run out].
- その契約は 1997 年に**期限**が切れて更新されなかった．
  ① The contract expired in 1997 and was not renewed.
  ② The contract was not renewed on its expiry in 1997.
- 契約の**期限**が切れるまで　until [through] the expiration of a contract
- 合意は今月末までに契約が成立しなければ**期限切れとなる**．　The agreement will **be canceled** if it is not finalized by the end of this month.
- 社長は**契約期限の** 1 か月前に退任した．　The president resigned one month **before her contract was to end**.

34-4 有効期間

- 有効期間　①〔期間〕the term of validity　② the period of validity　③ the period for which《a ticket》is「valid [good]　④〔期限〕the expiry date　⑤ the expiration date
- 有効期間内に　① within the term of validity of《the ticket》　② within the period covered by《the ticket》
- 有効期間は 3 日間だ　① be valid for three days　② be good for three days
- 有効期間の満了　the expiration of the validity period
- 期限の切れたパスポート　an expired passport
- パスポート［運転免許証］の有効期間　the period of validity of a「passport [driver's license]
関連項目⇨第 2 部・まんき，にんき

35. 期日・期限の表現

■ 35-1 …まで

- 水曜まで休みます． I'll be off「until [till]」Wednesday.

▶ 日本語でも英語でも水曜日に来るかどうか曖昧な表現である．英語の「until [till]」は続いていたことがそうでなくなる時点を表わす語なので，終端は含まない（水曜日は「休み」に含まれない）ことが多い．I'll be off from Monday to Wednesday.（月曜日から水曜日まで休みます）なら日本語でも英語でも水曜日も休む意味になる．

- 水曜まで来ません． I won't come till Wednesday.

▶ 日本語でも英語でも水曜日は来ることが含意される．このように否定文では終端を含まない（水曜日は「来ません」に含まれない）原則が成り立つ．

▶ 終端を含むことを明示するには until and including Wednesday, 終端を含まないことを明示するには until but not including Wednesday または until but excluding Wednesday といえる．

- ゆうべは 11 時**まで**起きていた． I was up **until** eleven last night.
- 10 時**過ぎ**まで帰らなかった． He didn't come back **till after** ten.
- この戦争は**いつまで**続くのだろう．
  ① **How long** will this war last?
  ② When will this war end?
- 「この本**いつまで**借りられますか」「いつまででもどうぞ」 **How long** can I borrow this book? — Keep it as long as you like.
- **いつまで**東京にご滞在ですか． **How long** are you going to stay in Tokyo?
- **いつまで**逗留できますか． **How long** can you stay?

■ 35-2 …までに

35-2-1 締め切り／期限

- …までに ① by … ② no later than … ③ not later than … ④ before …
- 3 時までに ① by three (o'clock) ② before three
- 日曜までに by Sunday
- 明日の朝までに by tomorrow morning
- イベントの前または直後に before or immediately「after [following]」the event

35. 期日・期限の表現 35-2-1

- 期限までに　① by the deadline　② by the due date
- 遅くとも明日のこの時間までには着くはずだ．　At the latest it should be here by tomorrow at this time.
- 予約の**締め切り**は3月10日です．
  ① The deadline for reservations is March 10.
  ② Reservations close on March 10.
  ③ Reservations will not be accepted after March 10.
- デザイン募集の**締め切り**は3月10日だ．
  ① **The deadline** for (sending in) designs is March 10.
  ② Competitors must send in their designs no later than March 10.
- 支払**期日**は6月30日だ．　① (The [My, etc.]) payment is **due** on June 30.
  ② The payment due date is June 30.
- 応募**締め切り**は2月20日 (**消印有効**).　Entries must be postmarked [by [no later than] February 20.
- 10月3日が**締め切り**の宿題　homework [an assignment] **due** on October 3
- 願書は1月31日までに**必着**のこと．　The application must [reach us [arrive, be received] no later than January 31st [by January 31st without fail].
- 3月3日**までに**このメールにお返事ください．
  ① Please respond to this e-mail **by** March 3.
  ② Please let us have your answer to this e-mail **by** March 3.
  ③ We would appreciate it if you could reply to this e-mail **by** March 3.
★日本語，英語とも3月3日に返事をするのでもよい．
- 応答期限：3月3日　〔表示〕Response due: March 3
- いつまでに　① by what [time [day]　② by when　③ how soon
- これはいつまでにやればいいの？
  ① By when should this be done?
  ② When do you want this finished?
- この仕事にはいつまでという期限はない．　This job does not have to be done by a specific time.
- 出発の15分前**までに**　**by** fifteen minutes before departure
- テスト開始10分前**までに**着席しなさい．　Be in your seats **no later than** 10 minutes before the test begins.
- 予約は3日前**までに**お願いします．　Please make reservations **at least** three days **in advance**.
- **締め切り**を8月30日に設定する　① make August 30 **the deadline**　② set August 30 as **the deadline**　③ set **the deadline** [at [to, for] August 30
- 我々には**締め切り**がある．
  ① We have **a deadline** to meet.
  ② We are on **a deadline**.
- **締め切り**を守る　① meet **a deadline**　② meet **a time limit**

- **締め切り**を延ばしてもらう　① get **a deadline** put off　② get **a deadline** postponed
- **締め切り**が迫っている．
  ① **The deadline** is approaching.
  ② **The deadline** is almost here.
  ③ **The deadline** is drawing near.
- 食品が望ましい品質を保持する期限　① the date after which a food product may not have the desirable quality　② the end of the period during which a food product retains the desirable quality [⇨ 35-4 賞味期限・消費期限]

35-2-2　期日まであと…

- 試験はまだ2週間先だ．　The examination is still two weeks「off [away].
- 試合まであと2日しかない．
  ① The「game [match] is only two days「off [away].
  ② We have only two days left before the「game [match].
- 締め切りまであと何日ありますか．
  ① How many days are left before the deadline?
  ② How many days do I have before the deadline?
- 大学を卒業するまであとまだ2年あります．　I still have two more years to go before I graduate from college.
- その100問を解く時間は100分ある．　You will have 100 minutes to complete the 100 questions.

35-2-3　期限オーバー

- **締め切り**が過ぎてしまった．
  ① The deadline「is past [has passed].
  ② I have missed the deadline.
- 電気料金を2か月分**滞納**している．
  ① I'm two months overdue with my electricity bill.
  ② My electricity bill is two months overdue.
  ③ My electricity bill is overdue by two months.
- 税金を**滞納**したことはない．
  ① I have never been in arrears with my tax.
  ② I have always paid my tax on time.
- 家賃が3か月**滞納**になっている．
  ① The rent is three months overdue.
  ② The rent is three months in arrears.
- 借金の**返済期限**を越えた場合には延滞金を支払わなくてはならない．
  You have to pay a delinquency charge if you miss the deadline for repayment of your debt.
- 督促後20日間**滞納**の際は　upon [in case of] delinquency 20 days after (a)

reminder

■ 35-3 時間差

- 出発時間の **10 分前に**　**ten minutes before** departure time
- (予定の時刻より) **10 分早く着く**　arrive at 《a place》 **ten minutes ahead of time**
- 電車は **20 分遅れ**ていた．　The train was (running) **twenty minutes** 「**late** [**behind schedule**]．
- 列車は **1 時間遅れ**で大阪に着いた．
  ① The train reached Osaka 「**an** [**one**] **hour** 「**late** [**behind schedule**]．
  ② The train was **delayed** (**by**) **an hour** in reaching Osaka.
- 駅での友達との待ち合わせ時間に **30 分遅れた**．　**I was thirty minutes late** meeting my friend at the station.
- 経営者側からの回答はもう 2 週間も **遅れ**ている．　Management's response is now two weeks **overdue**.
- 今年は予想より 3 日 **遅れて**桜が咲いた．　This year the 「cherries [cherry trees] blossomed [came into bloom] three days **later** than predicted.
- 光の往復時間だけ **遅れる**　**be delayed** by a time equal to the round-trip time of the light
- どのくらい遅刻したのですか．
  ① How long were you late?
  ② By how long were you late?

■ 35-4 賞味期限・消費期限

「賞味期限」の語は食品の風味なども含めた期待される品質が損なわれない期限．かつて「品質保持期限」が同義に使われていたが，2003 年に「賞味期限」に一本化された (2005 年に移行期間も終了)．一方，短期間 (5 日程度以内) で品質が劣化する食品に表示される「消費期限」は食べても問題がない期限である (通例若干の余裕は見てある)．「販売期限」は消費者宅による貯蔵期間をさらに見込んだ日付．

- **賞味期限**　① a "best before" date　② a "best if used by" date　③ a date of minimum durability　④《俗に》an expiry date　⑤ an expiration date
  ★①③がヨーロッパで使われる表現．③は「最小限それだけはもつ」という意味の称．⑤はヨーロッパでは次の「消費期限」の意とされる．アメリカでは全国的に統一的な公式表現はない．
- **消費期限**　① a use-by date　② an expiration date　③ an expiry date
- **販売期限**　① a sell-by date　②《米》a pull-by date
- 賞味期限 2008 年 8 月 31 日　〔表示〕Best [Consume] by Aug. 31, 2008.
  ★ヨーロッパでは比較的日持ちしない食品について月日で表示する場合

は best before，日持ちする食品について年月を表示する場合は best before end と表示することになっている．

- この牛乳は販売期限を過ぎている．　This milk is past its sell-by date.
- 消費期限はいつまでですか．
  ① When does the use-by date expire?
  ② When is the use-by date?
- **どのくらい**持ちますか．　How long will it keep?
- この食品は**日持ち**がよい［**日持ち**する］．
  ① This food keeps (well [for a long time]).
  ② You can keep this food for a long time (without it going bad).

36. 回数・頻度の表現

36-1 回数 [⇨第2部・…かい【回】, いっかい, いちど, にど, さんど]

- 1回　① once　② one time
- 2回　① twice　② two times
- 3回　three times
- 1, 2回　once or twice
- 2, 3回　two or three times
- 日本選手権4回優勝者　a four-time Japan national champion
- 過去100年の間に3度　three times during the「last [past] (one) hundred years
- 1度ならず (2度3度)　① more than once　② on more occasions than one　③ repeatedly
- もう1回　① once more　② one more time　③ again
- 2回以上　① more than once　② twice or more　③ two or more times
- 何回も　① many times　② over and over again　③ again and again
- 何十回も, 何十回となく　dozens [scores] of times
- 何百回も, 何百回となく　hundreds of times
- 何千回も, 何千回となく　thousands of times
- 彼とは学内で1, 2回顔を合わせたことがある．　I've met him once or twice on campus.
- 朝晩2回食後に服用のこと．　Take twice a day, in the morning and evening after「eating [meals].
- 7回繰り返す　repeat … seven times
- 同じ文字の4回の繰り返し　repetition of the same letter four times
- その事象が5回発生するたびにカウンターがインクリメントされる．　The counter is incremented「every five times the event occurs [once for every five instances of the event].
- 回数　the number of times
- アクセス回数　the number of accesses
- スキャンが行なわれる回数　the number of times scans are made
- 的に当たった回数　the number of times the target was hit
- 命令を所定の回数実行する　〖電算〗execute an instruction a predetermined number of times
- 何回さいころを振れば, 少なくとも1回1が出る確率が1/2を上回りますか．　How many times do you have to throw a die in order for the proba-

bility of getting one at least once to be greater than 1/2?
- 何回使えるか　the number of times it can be used
- 彼女はこのごろ遅刻の回数が増えた［減った］．　She has been late「more [less]」often recently.
- 彼の無断欠勤の回数はどれほどですか．　How「often [many times]」has he missed work without permission?

36-2 …回目

- 初めて　for the first time
- 生まれて初めて　for the first time in *one's* life
- 歴史上初めて　for the first time in history
- 記録のある歴史上初めて　for the first time in recorded history
- 人類の歴史で初めて　for the first time in the history of human beings
- 初めての沖縄訪問　《her》first visit to Okinawa
- 初めてアメリカに行ったとき…
  ① The first time 《I》went to America, ...
  ② When 《I》went to America for the first time, ...
- 初めて投票する人たち　first-time voters
- 私は演壇に立ったのはこれが**初めてです**．
  ① **This is the first time** (that) I have ever stood at the rostrum.
  ② **This is the first time** for me to stand at the rostrum.
- 彼に金を貸したのはその時で**2度目**だった．
  ① I lent him money **for the second time**.
  ② **That was the second time** I had lent him money.
- もし彼女が勝てば一昨年以来**2回目**になる．　If she wins, it will be **her second time** since (she won) the year before last.
- **3度目**に行ったら帰宅していた．　He had come home when I went by **for the third time**.
- もし**3度目**にドイツを訪れるとすれば　if I am to visit Germany **for a third time**
- 来日はこれで**何度目**ですか．　How many times have you come to Japan, including this time?［⇨ 26-10 何番目］
- **5回目**で成功した．
  ① I succeeded **the fifth time (I tried)**. ★for the fifth time だと「5回目の成功」（前の4回も成功）の意味になる．
  ② I succeeded「**on [at] my fifth attempt**」.
- 1回目で成功した．　I succeeded on my first try.

36-3 頻度

- 1 日 3 回　three times a day
- 年に 5 回も　as often as five times a year
- 週に 2, 3 回　① two or three times a week　② several times a week
- 4 年に 1 度　① once every four years　② once in four years　③ every four years
- 数か月に 1 度　once every few months
- 3 日に 1 度　every three days
- 2 日に 1 度［1 日おきに］　every other day
- 3 度に 1 度は　① one time out of three　② once in three times
- 5 回に 1 回は失敗した．
  ① I failed every five times.
  ② I failed once in every five times.
  ③ I failed「once［one］out of five times.
- 4 割（の場合）は失敗した．　① I failed 40 percent of the time.　② I failed four times out of ten.
- この現象は 100 万回に 1 回の割合で起きる．
  ① This phenomenon occurs once every million times.
  ② The frequency of this phenomenon is one in a million.
- そこへはどのくらいよく行きますか．　How often do you go there?
- 一年に何回出張しますか．　How many business trips do you take a year?
- 毎日　① every day　② daily
- 毎週　① every week　② weekly
- 毎月　① every month　② monthly
- 毎年　① every year　② annually　③ yearly
- 1 週間に 2 回の　① semiweekly　② twice-weekly　③ biweekly

▶ biweekly は「2 週間に 1 回」「1 週間に 2 回」の両方の意味があるが，特に刊行物では「2 週間に 1 回」の意が普通であり，「週 2 回」の意味では semiweekly, twice-weekly などの代替表現が好まれる．下記の bimonthly, biyearly についても同様である．一方，輸送スケジュールなどでは biweekly を「週 2 回」の意味に使うのが普通．また，年については通例「年 2 回」の意味で使う biannual という語がある．

- 2 週間に 1 回の　① biweekly　②《主に英》fortnightly　★fortnightly は語源的には「14 日に 1 回」の意．
- 月 2 回の　① twice-monthly　② semimonthly　③ bimonthly　★bimonthly については上記の注を参照．
- 2 か月に 1 回の　bimonthly

36. 回数・頻度の表現 36-4

- 1年に2回の　① biannual ② semiannual ③ half-yearly ④ twice-a-year ⑤ twice-yearly ⑥ biyearly ★biyearly については上記の注を参照.
- 2年に1回の　① biennial ② biyearly ③ biannual ［⇨ 36-4 …年ごとの］
- 隔週で　① every two weeks ② every「other ［second］ week ③ in alternate weeks ④ biweekly ⑤《主に英》fortnightly
- 隔週火曜日に　every「other ［second, alternate］ Tuesday
- 隔月で　① every two months ② every「other ［second］ month ③ in alternate months ④ bimonthly

36-4　…年ごとの

annual	1年	undecennial	11年
biennial	2年	duodecennial	12年
triennial	3年	quindecennial	15年
quadrennial	4年	vicennial [vigentennial, vigintennial]	20年
quinquennial [quintennial]	5年	semicentennial	50年
sexennial	6年	centennial	100年
septennial	7年	quasquicentennial	125年
octennial	8年	sesquicentennial	150年
novennial	9年	millennial	1000年
decennial	10年		

「50年」「150年」「125年」はみな100年を基本にした表現になっているが，semi- は「半分」，sesqui- はラテン語の「半分だけより多く」，quasqui- は同じく「1/4だけより多く」が語源になっている.

特に数字の大きなものは「…年ごと」というよりは「…周年」の意味で使われることのほうが多いが，「…周年」ならたとえば decennial anniversary ではなく 10th anniversary という言い方もある.

36-5　…周年

centenary	100年	quincentenary	500年
bicentenary	200年	sexcentenary	600年
tercentenary	300年	septcentenary	700年
quatercentenary	400年	octocentenary	800年

- **5 周年祭**　the fifth anniversary 《of …》
- **創立 100 周年記念日［祭］**
  ① the 100th anniversary of 《the「university's［company's］》 foundation
  ② 《the「university's［company's］》 100th anniversary
- 1997 年はブラームスの**没後 100 年**に当たる年だった．
  The year 1997「was［marked］ the「100th anniversary［hundredth anniversary, centennial, centenary］of Brahms' death.

関連表現：…婚式

paper wedding	1 周年	pearl wedding	30 周年
wooden wedding	5 周年	coral wedding	35 周年
tin wedding	10 周年	ruby wedding	40 周年
linen wedding	12 周年	sapphire wedding	45 周年
crystal wedding	15 周年	golden wedding	50 周年
china wedding	20 周年	emerald wedding	55 周年
silver wedding	25 周年	diamond wedding	60［時に 75］周年

36-6　…回忌

- 一周忌　〔死後満 1 年〕the first anniversary of 《my grandfather's》 death
- 三回忌　〔満 2 年〕the second anniversary of 《…'s》 death　★以下，満で数えた年数と 1 ずれることに注意．
- 七回忌　〔満 6 年〕the sixth anniversary of 《…'s》 death

36-7　頻度の多寡

- 常に　always
- ほとんどの場合は［たいていは］　most of the time
- 10 回中 8 回は［80％のケースでは］　① eight times out of ten　② 80％ of the time
- 非常に頻繁に　① very often　② very frequently
- 頻繁に　① often　② frequently
- 時々　① sometimes　② occasionally
- まれに　rarely
- ごくまれに　very rarely
- ほとんど…ない　① seldom　② hardly

37. 伝統暦

37-1 月名

月名	月	月名	月
睦月（むつき）	1月	文月（ふづき）	7月
如月（きさらぎ）	2月	葉月（はづき）	8月
弥生（やよい）	3月	長月（ながつき）	9月
卯月（うづき）	4月	神無月（かんなづき）	10月
皐月（さつき）	5月	霜月（しもつき）	11月
水無月（みなづき）	6月	師走（しわす）	12月

英訳としてはたとえば次のような可能性がある．

- 睦月　① the first month of the lunar calendar　② January

37-2 太陰太陽暦と閏月

明治維新で太陽暦が導入されるまで日本は太陰太陽暦を使っていた．これは月の運行に基づく太陰暦に太陽暦のような季節との対応を導入したものに当たる．閏月は太陰暦と季節とのずれを調整するために 32～33 か月ごとに挿入される月で，たとえば坂本竜馬と桂小五郎が下関で薩長同盟に向けた話し合いをもったのは慶応元年（1865 年）閏 5 月 1 日のことであった．この年は普通の 5 月のあとに「閏 5 月」があったのである．

- 閏 3 月 15 日　① the fifteenth day of the intercalary third month　② the fifteenth of intercalary March

37-3 二十四節気

- 二十四節気　the 24 seasonal divisions of the year in the old lunar calendar

閏月を導入した太陽太陰暦でも暦と季節のずれは生じるので，暦の上で正しい季節を示すための目印が二十四節気である．むしろ太陽の運行に基づく二十四節気は 1 月～12 月の暦日を決め，閏月の挿入を決める基盤だった．

春分 (the vernal equinox, the spring equinox)・秋分 (the autumnal equinox)・夏至 (the summer solstice)・冬至 (the winter solstice) 以外は英米には相当するものはない．詳細に立ち入らずに説明するには one of the twenty-four divisions of the four seasons（四季を 24 に分ける時点の一つ）

として太陽暦でいつごろに相当するかを around February 18 in the solar calendar（太陽暦の2月18日ごろ）などと付け足せばよい．二十四節気は次の通り．

```
立春 (りっしゅん) (2月4日ごろ)      立秋 (りっしゅう) (8月8日ごろ)
雨水 (うすい) (2月18日ごろ)       処暑 (しょしょ) (8月23日ごろ)
啓蟄 (けいちつ) (3月6日ごろ)      白露 (はくろ) (9月7日ごろ)
春分 (しゅんぶん) (3月21日ごろ)     秋分 (しゅうぶん) (9月23日ごろ)
清明 (せいめい) (4月5日ごろ)      寒路 (かんろ) (10月8日ごろ)
穀雨 (こくう) (4月20日ごろ)      霜降 (そうこう) (10月23日ごろ)

立夏 (りっか) (5月6日ごろ)       立冬 (りっとう) (11月8日ごろ)
小満 (しょうまん) (5月21日ごろ)     小雪 (しょうせつ) (11月23日ごろ)
芒種 (ぼうしゅ) (6月5日ごろ)      大雪 (たいせつ) (12月8日ごろ)
夏至 (げし) (6月22日ごろ)        冬至 (とうじ) (12月22日ごろ)
小暑 (しょうしょ) (7月7日ごろ)     小寒 (しょうかん) (1月6日ごろ)
大暑 (たいしょ) (7月23日ごろ)     大寒 (だいかん) (1月20日ごろ)
```

37-4 十二支

- 十二支　① the twelve (annual) zodiac signs　② the twelve signs of the 「Chinese [Oriental]」zodiac
- 何年 (なにどし) 生まれですか．［干支は何ですか．］
  ① In what year of the Oriental zodiac were you born?
  ② In which year were you born in terms of the Oriental zodiac?
  ③ What is your sign in the Oriental zodiac?
- 子年です．　I was born in the year of the Rat.
- 彼は私より（干支で）一回り上だ．　He's 「twelve years [one zodiac cycle]」 older than me.

子 (ね) 年 [ねずみ年]	the year of the Rat
丑 (うし) 年	the year of the Ox
寅 (とら) 年	the year of the Tiger
卯 (う) 年 [うさぎ年]	the year of the Rabbit
辰 (たつ) 年	the year of the Dragon
巳 (み) 年 [へび年]	the year of the Snake
午 (うま) 年	the year of the Horse
未 (ひつじ) 年	the year of the 「Ram [Sheep]」

申(さる)年		the year of the Monkey
酉(とり)年		the year of the「Cock [Rooster]
戌(いぬ)年		the year of the Dog
亥(い)年 [いのしし年]		the year of the「Boar [Pig]

★日本でいう「いのしし年」は中国や韓国では「ブタ年」と呼ばれる.

37-5 十干

- 十干　the ten calendar signs

甲・乙・丙・丁・戊(ぼ)・己(き)・庚(こう)・辛(しん)・壬(じん)・癸(き)であるが，陰陽五行説により木・火・土・金・水の五行，陽＝兄(え)，陰＝弟(と)と次のように関連付けられる．

	木	火	土	金	水
陽	甲(きのえ)	丙(ひのえ)	戊(つちのえ)	庚(かのえ)	壬(みずのえ)
陰	乙(きのと)	丁(ひのと)	己(つちのと)	辛(かのと)	癸(みずのと)

しいて説明的に訳せば下記のようになるが，序列だけに着目してたとえば甲[乙]を the「first [second] of the ten calendar signs と訳すこともできる．

- 甲(きのえ) the elder of the element wood
- 乙(きのと) the lesser of the element wood
- 丙(ひのえ) the elder of the element fire
- 丁(ひのと) the lesser of the element fire
- 戊(つちのえ) the elder of the element earth
- 己(つちのと) the lesser of the element earth
- 庚(かのえ) the elder of the element metal
- 辛(かのと) the lesser of the element metal
- 壬(みずのえ) the elder of the element water
- 癸(みずのと) the lesser of the element water

37-6 十干十二支

- 十干十二支　the「sixty-year [sexagenary] cycle of (the combination of) the ten calendar signs and the twelve zodiac signs

周期12の十二支と周期10の十干を「丙午(ひのえうま)」のように組み合わせた周期60 (10 と 12 の最小公倍数) の系列が十干十二支で，年を表わ

すのに用いる．戊辰戦争（1868年），甲午農民戦争（1894年），辛亥革命（1911～1912年）など歴史上の事件の名前にも使われる．甲子園球場は甲子の年（1924年）に完成したことから命名されたものである．

1 甲子	きのえね	21 甲申	きのえさる	41 甲辰	きのえたつ
2 乙丑	きのとうし	22 乙酉	きのととり	42 乙巳	きのとみ
3 丙寅	ひのえとら	23 丙戌	ひのえいぬ	43 丙午	ひのえうま
4 丁卯	ひのとう	24 丁亥	ひのとい	44 丁未	ひのとひつじ
5 戊辰	つちのえたつ	25 戊子	つちのえね	45 戊申	つちのえさる
6 己巳	つちのとみ	26 己丑	つちのとうし	46 己酉	つちのととり
7 庚午	かのえうま	27 庚寅	かのえとら	47 庚戌	かのえいぬ
8 辛未	かのとひつじ	28 辛卯	かのとう	48 辛亥	かのとい
9 壬申	みずのえさる	29 壬辰	みずのえたつ	49 壬子	みずのえね
10 癸酉	みずのととり	30 癸巳	みずのとみ	50 癸丑	みずのとうし
11 甲戌	きのえいぬ	31 甲午	きのえうま	51 甲寅	きのえとら
12 乙亥	きのとい	32 乙未	きのとひつじ	52 乙卯	きのとう
13 丙子	ひのえね	33 丙申	ひのえさる	53 丙辰	ひのえたつ
14 丁丑	ひのとうし	34 丁酉	ひのととり	54 丁巳	ひのとみ
15 戊寅	つちのえとら	35 戊戌	つちのえいぬ	55 戊午	つちのえうま
16 己卯	つちのとう	36 己亥	つちのとい	56 己未	つちのとひつじ
17 庚辰	かのえたつ	37 庚子	かのえね	57 庚申	かのえさる
18 辛巳	かのとみ	38 辛丑	かのとうし	58 辛酉	かのととり
19 壬午	みずのえうま	39 壬寅	みずのえとら	59 壬戌	みずのえいぬ
20 癸未	みずのとひつじ	40 癸卯	みずのとう	60 癸亥	みずのとい

たとえば「甲午（きのえうま）」を英語にするとしたら，周期60の中での序列に着目して the thirty-first year of the sexagenary cycle といったり，「き」「うま」に着目して the year of the Wood-Horse in the sixty-year cycle といったりできる（「きのとうま」という組み合わせは存在しないので「え」を訳さないことは組み合わせ的には問題ない）．もう少し説明的に「十二支では午年で十干で1番目の」という意味で the year that is the year of the Horse in the Chinese zodiac and the first of the ten calendar signs のようにもいえる．

「丙午（ひのえうま）」のような人口に膾炙したものは the year of the Fiery Horse

37. 伝統暦 37-6

のような特別な訳を考えることもできる．

- この前の**丙午**（1966 年）にも出生数は著しく低下した． The birthrate in Japan dropped dramatically in 1966, the most recent year of the Fiery Horse.
- **丙午**生まれの女は夫を殺すという迷信がある． A superstition holds that women born in the year of the Fiery Horse kill their husbands.

トリビア　日本の改暦

　明治維新政府が太陰太陽暦から太陽暦への移行を決めたのは 1872 年（明治 5 年）11 月のことだった．明治 5 年 12 月 2 日の翌日が明治 6 年 1 月 1 日になると決められたのである．改暦の布告がされてから 1 か月もたたず，師走になったと思ったら 2 日で正月という事態に庶民が戸惑ったのも無理はない．「三十日に月もいづれば玉子の四角もあるべし」（旧暦では毎月 15 日は満月で 30 日には月は出ないのが常識だったが，その常識が覆るようなら四角い卵もあるだろうという意）とのぼやきも聞かれるのだった．

トリビア　西洋の改暦〜ユリウス暦からグレゴリオ暦へ

　早くから太陽暦を導入していた西洋でも改暦の問題はあった．古代ローマのユリウス・カエサルが導入した太陽暦は 1600 年もたつと実際の季節とのずれが蓄積して無視できないほどになりつつあった．キリスト教で復活祭の日を決めるのに重要な意味のある春分の日が，実際から 10 日もずれていたのである．ローマ教皇グレゴリウス 13 世はこれを正すために閏年の回数を減らすことにした．ユリウス暦では年号が 4 で割り切れる年を閏年と定めていたのだが，100 で割り切れ，かつ 1000 で割り切れない年は閏年にしないと改めたのである．こうして 1582 年 10 月 4 日の次の日が 10 月 15 日とされた（『ティバルドと消えた十日間』は改暦のおかげで自分の誕生日が消えてしまうことになった少年ティバルドのほほえましい奮闘の物語である）．

　こうしてグレゴリオ暦が導入されたのは宗教対立のさなかのことだった．カトリック諸国はすみやかにグレゴリオ暦に移行したものの，プロテスタント諸国は旧暦を使い続けた．ドイツ，オランダ，デンマークといった大陸諸国がグレゴリオ暦に移行するのは 1700 年前後のことになる．しかし，イギリスとその植民地ではその後も旧暦を使い続けたため，10 月 18 日にパリを出発した使者が 10 月

11日にロンドンに到着するという状況が続いた．イギリスがグレゴリオ暦に移行するのは1752年である．ロシアの改暦もロシア革命で帝政が倒れたのちの1918年のことであった．二月革命，十月革命といった名称はユリウス暦に基づくもので，グレゴリオ暦ではこれらは三月革命，十一月革命となる．

37-7 気象用語

- **真夏日**　〔最高気温30°C以上の日〕① a "tropical day" ② a day on which the temperature reaches 30°C or above
- **真冬日**　〔最高気温0°C未満の日〕① a "midwinter day" ② a day on which the temperature stays below 0°C
- **猛暑日**　〔最高気温35°C以上の日〕① an "extreme tropical day" ② a day on which the temperature reaches 35°C or above
- **熱帯夜**　〔最低気温25°C以上の夜〕① a "tropical night" ② a night on which the temperature does not fall below 25°C
- **夏日**　〔最高気温25°C以上の日〕① a "summer day" ② a day on which the temperature reaches 25°C or above
- **冬日**　〔最低気温0°C未満の日〕① a "winter day" ② a day on which the temperature falls below 0°C
- **春一番**　① the first strong southerly wind of spring ② the first spring gale
- **木枯らし一号**　the first wintry blast of autumn

トリビア　縁起のいい数・悪い数

日本でもラッキーセブンなどとして7という数字が縁起がいいとされるが，これは第二次大戦後のアメリカ文化の流入によるものという．アメリカではそもそも1880年代なかばに野球界で the lucky seventh（幸運の7回）という表現がポピュラーになったらしい．その立役者はシカゴ・ホワイト・ストッキングズの大投手クラークソン（John Clarkson）．大事な試合でリードされていたとき，心配する監督アンソン（通称 Pop Anson）を余裕の態度で安心させ，"Remember, this is the lucky seventh."（だって今回は幸運の7回じゃないか）と言った．1889年にはニューヨークタイムズが別のチームの試合を報じる際に the lucky seventh の表現を使った次の例がある．

- For six innings the Indianapolis men held a lead over the Giants yesterday, but in the lucky seventh the latter forged to the front and held the lead during the remainder of the contest. 昨日，6回までインディアナポリスがジャイアンツをリードしていたが，幸運の7回にジャイアンツが挽回に成功し，そのまま試合終了までリードを守った．

19世紀末にはポーカーマシンからスロットマシンが発達するが，3つの鐘や3つのさくらんぼと並んでラッキーセブンを揃えた777が当たりであることは周知の通りである．

しかし，7という数を重視するルーツはもっと古い．そもそも7は聖書でも大切な数字であった．旧約聖書ではモーセの後継者ヨシュアがエリコを攻略する際，お告げに従って兵士たちに毎日城壁のまわりを回らせた．7日目に7周して7人の祭司が角笛を吹き鳴らし，兵士が鬨の声を上げると城壁が崩れ落ちた．また，創世記では神は6日かけて天地を創造したのち7日目に休んだことになっている．

さらにさかのぼれば1週間＝7日という単位は旧約聖書とも密接な関係のあるバビロニアでも使われていた．惑星の数（当時知られていた五惑星＋日，月）が7つだし，これが月の周期の4分の1に近いこともあって重視されていたものと想像される．

ところ変わって日本では，伝統的には8が縁起のいい数とされていた．これは「八」という漢字の形が「末広がり」につながるためとされる．一方，中国でも8は縁起のいい数であるが，こちらは発音（ba）が繁栄を意味する「発」（fa）に通じるためである．

一方，日本も中国も4は「死」と発音が同じため不吉とされる．ところが9については日本では「苦」に通じるとして縁起が悪いとされるが，中国では「久」と同音で縁起がよいとされる．台湾では中華民国建国（1912年）を元年とする暦の「民国99年」に当たる2010年の9月9日付の鉄道切符（「永康」発「保安」行）が人気を呼んだ．

西洋で縁起の悪い数といえば13である．イエスを裏切ったユダを含めた最後の晩餐の参列者が13人だったためなどと言われている（なお，イエス処刑の金曜日が13日だったとの記述も見られるが，史料的裏づけはない）．ただし，キリスト教登場よりはるか前のハムラビ法典でも13が欠番となっており，そのころから13を不吉とする見方があった可能性をうかがわせる．西洋ではホテルの13号室やビルの13階がないこともめずらしくなく，英語ではtriskai-dekaphobia（13恐怖症）という単語もある．これにならって日本や

中国で 4 を忌むことは tetraphobia ともいう．

トリビア　手書きの数字
　欧米人の手書き文字ではアラビア数字の七は7のような左の縦画を書かずに一筆で7のように書くことが多く，1のように見えることがある．1 を単なる縦棒で書けば区別に問題はないが，ヨーロッパの一部（ドイツなど）では 1 の上部のひげを長めに書くので，そのような 1 と区別するために 7 のように斜線を入れることもある．機械読み取り式の書式などではそうした斜線を入れないよう Do not cross sevens. などの注意書きがある場合がある．

38. 年齢

38-1 基本

- 彼は 25 歳です.
  ① He is twenty-five years old.
  ② He is twenty-five.
  ③ He is twenty-five years of age.
- その男の子は 3 歳 4 か月です.　　The boy is three years and four months old.
- その男の子は 3 歳半です.　　The boy is three and a half (years old).
- 娘は 1 歳 3 か月です.
  ① Our daughter is fifteen months old.
  ② Our daughter is「one [a]」year and three months old.
- ★英米では乳幼児の年齢は 2 歳くらいまでは月齢でいうことが多い.
- 息子は今年 20 歳になります.　　① Our son will be twenty this year.　② Our son is going on twenty this year.
- 息子は今日で 20 歳になります.　　Our son is twenty today.
- 息子は 20 歳になった.　　Our son has turned twenty.
- 息子は昨日で 20 歳になった.　　Our son turned twenty yesterday.
- 80 歳に手が届く　　① be nearing eighty　② be almost eighty　③ be just this side of eighty　★③は話者も 80 歳前である場合.
- 90 歳に達する　　① reach (the age of) ninety　② get to ninety (years old)　③ become ninety (years old)
- 彼は何歳ですか.　　How old is he? [⇨ 26. 数量に関する疑問文 26-6]
- 17 歳の少女　　① a seventeen-year-old girl　② a girl of seventeen (years)　③ a girl seventeen years old　④ a girl aged seventeen　★seventeen-year-old のように形容詞句をなす year は単数形
- 20 歳以上の男子　　①〔一人〕a man twenty or older　②〔複数〕men twenty「and [or]」older　③ men of twenty years「and [or]」more　④ men twenty years old and above　⑤ men of twenty years and「over [up, upward(s)]」　⑥ men aged twenty and「over [up, upward(s)]」　⑦ men (of) twenty and「over [up, upward(s)]」　⑧ men twenty years (old) and「up [upward(s)]」
- 5 歳より上の小児　　children above five (years of age)
- 80 歳を超えている　　① be more than eighty　② be over eighty
- 90 歳で死ぬ　　① die at (the age of) ninety　② die at age 90
- 30 そこそこで社長の座に就いた.　　She had barely reached 30 when she took over as president.
- 60 歳以下の人々　　① people of sixty years「and [or]」under [younger]　② people aged sixty and under　③ people (of) sixty and under　④ people

sixty years (old) and under ⑤ people up to sixty years old
- 65 歳未満の人　①〔一人〕a person under sixty-five　②〔複数〕people under sixty-five
- 20 歳から 60 歳までの人
  ①〔一人〕a person between twenty and sixty (years of age)
  ②〔複数〕people between twenty and sixty (years of age)　③ people from twenty to sixty (years old)　④ people of ages between twenty and sixty
  ⑤ people between (the) ages of twenty and sixty　⑥ people (ranging) from twenty to sixty years「in [of] age
- 100 歳以上の人　a centenarian
- 110 歳以上の人　a supercentenarian
- 最高齢の日本人男性　the oldest living man in Japan
- リヴァプールのジョン・スミス (20) もそんな若者の一人だ．　John Smith, 20, from Liverpool is one such young person.
- 「…」と 28 歳の加藤は言った．　"…," said the 28-year-old Kato.
- 会員の大部分は 20 歳から 35 歳の間です．
  ① Most members are between 20 and 35 (years of age).
  ② Most members range in age from 20 to 35.
  ③ The ages of most members range from 20 to 35.
- 13 歳のときに日本に来た．
  ① I came to Japan at (the age of) thirteen.
  ② I came to Japan when I was thirteen.
- 5 歳のときからピアノを習っている．　I have been taking piano lessons since I was five.
- 3 歳のときからピアノを習った．
  ① I took piano lessons from the age of three.
  ② I started taking piano lessons when I was three.
  ③ I began piano at three.
- 20 歳になるまでフィラデルフィアに住んでいた．
  ① He lived in Philadelphia until he was twenty.
  ② He lived in Philadelphia until twenty years of age.
- 5 歳さばを読む　① misrepresent *one's* age by five years　②《口》fudge on *one's* age by five years　③ take [trim] five years from *one's* age　④ knock five years off *one's* age
- 彼女は 20 歳だと言っても十分通用するだろう．　She could easily pass for 20.
- もう 10 歳若かったら言い寄るところだ．　If I were ten years younger, I would try to chat her up.
- 年がいっている　① be advanced in years　② be old　③ be an old「man [woman]　④ have reached an advanced age
- 孫のような年の娘と結婚した．　He married a girl young enough to be his

grandchild.

▶ 英語の … years old は動植物の年齢や物の古さにも使う.

- その木は樹齢 120 年だ. The tree is 120 years old.
- 僕の車は製造後 10 年たっている. My car is ten years old.
- その建物は築後 90 年だ. The building is ninety years old.

38-2 年齢の比較など

- アリスはボブより 3 歳年上だ. Alice is three years older than Bob.
- アリスはボブより 3 歳年下だ. Alice is three years younger than Bob.
- アリスとボブは 3 歳離れている. Alice and Bob are three years apart.
- 5つ年上の兄 ① a brother five years older ② a brother five years *one's* senior
- 彼らは同い年だ. They are the same age.
- 私は君と同い年だ. I am the same age as you (are).
- 会社に私と同い年の女性が 3 人いる. There are three women (of) my age at the office.
- アンはメアリーが結婚したときより 2 歳上だ. Anne is two years older than Mary was when she got married.
- アンもすぐメアリーが結婚したときの年になるだろう. Anne will soon be as old as Mary was when she got married.
- 彼は父親が今の彼の年だったときとそっくりだ. He looks remarkably like his father did at his age.
- 私もお前の年だった時がある. I was your age once.
- 現内閣では彼が最年少だ. He's the youngest member of the current cabinet.
- このグループの最年長は彼女だ. She is the oldest member of this group.
- 歴代最年少の囲碁名人 the youngest person ever to become a master of go
- 彼は史上最年少の 44 歳で首相となった. He became, at 44 years of age, the youngest prime minister in history.
- 最年少記録 a [the] record for being the youngest 《world champion》
- 最年長記録 a [the] record for being the oldest 《person to climb Everest》
- 彼女はオリンピック金メダルの最年少記録を塗り替えた. She set a new record as the youngest ever winner of an Olympic gold medal.
- ホームラン王の最年長記録は 45 歳だ. ① The record for the oldest home run king is 45. ② Forty-five is the oldest anyone has ever become a home run king.

38-3 …代

- 彼は50代だ．　He is in his fifties.
- 彼は50代に見える．　He looks (to be) in his fifties.
- 40代の男　a man in his forties
- 40代前半の男　a man in his early forties
- 40代半ばの男　a man in his middle forties
- 40代後半の男　① a man in his late forties　② a man in the latter half of his forties　③ a man between the ages of 45 and 49　★①は「40代の終わり」の意．
- 10代から20代にかけて　from *one's* (mid-)teens (in)to *one's* twenties
- 10代の若者　① a teenager　② a teenage(d)「boy [girl]」[⇨第2部・じゅうだい]
- 彼はまだ20代．　① He is still in his twenties.　② He is still under 30.
- 彼女は10代で結婚した．　She got married while she was (still) in her teens.
- 30代から40代の女性をターゲットに売り出す化粧品　cosmetics targeted at women in their thirties and forties
- 50前の働き盛り　the prime of life before fifty
- 彼はまだ40前だ．　① He is still under forty.　② He is still this side of forty.　③ He is still on the right side of forty.　★②は話者も40歳前の場合．

38-4 満年齢と数え年

満年齢は「年齢計算に関する法律」(1902)で定義されていたが，数え年からの切り替えが進んだのは1950年施行の「年齢のとなえ方に関する法律」による．

- 満年齢　*one's* age expressed in completed years　② *one's* age expressed in the Western style
- 数え年　*one's* age by the (traditional) East Asian system (of one year old at birth, with one year added at every New Year)
▶ 数え年は日本や中国，朝鮮など東アジアに特徴的な年齢の表わし方で，英語では特に断わらなければ満年齢である．日本でも第二次大戦後，中国では文化大革命後は満年齢が一般的になった．

- 満15歳になる　① turn fifteen (years old)　② attain *one's* fifteenth year　③ complete *one's* fifteenth year
- 彼は今月10日で満20歳になった．　He turned twenty (years old) on the 10th of this month.
- 来月祖父は満で89，数えで90になる．　Next month my grandfather will be 89, or 90 by the traditional calculation that makes you one year old at birth.

38. 年齢 38-5

- 年齢を満で数える　calculate age in completed years
- 数え年で7つの時に　①at [when *one* was] seven by the traditional counting system　②at [when *one* was] seven according to traditional Japanese reckoning
- 早生まれの人　a person born between January 1 and April 1　★学校教育法で満6歳に達した日の翌日以降における最初の学年の初めから就学させると規定されているが，法律上，4月1日生まれの人が満6歳になるのは3月31日の終わりなので，4月1日生まれの人も1月～3月生まれの人と一緒に入学することになる．根拠となる法律は「年齢計算に関する法律」の「年齢は出生の日より之を起算す」の記載と民法143条の期間が「起算日に応答する日の前日に満了する」との記載である．
- **喜寿**〔77歳；「喜」の俗字「㐂」から〕　①attaining seventy-seven years of age　②〔その祝い〕celebration of 《a person's》 seventy-seventh birthday　③〔祝う催し〕a celebration in honor of 《a person's》 seventy-seventh birthday　★このほか**傘寿**〔80歳；「傘」の俗字「仐」から〕，**米寿**〔88歳；「米」の字が「八十八」と分解できることから〕，**卒寿**〔90歳；「卒」の俗字「卆」から〕，**白寿**〔99歳；「白」の字が「百」から「一」を除いたものであることから〕なども同様に訳せる．

38-5 妊娠・出産

医学的には妊娠の月数は最終月経開始日から数える．排卵は月経の約14日後なので，受精の時点ですでに約2週間が経過していることになる．医学的には週が基本単位とされ，月数をいうときも4週間＝28日を1月とする．

日本では月数は数えで表わすので，「3か月」といったときには満3か月は経過しておらず「第3か月」の意となる．また国際的に満の週数でweek 1, week 2などと表わすのと整合性をもたせるために週は第0週，第1週…と数える．

出産までの妊娠期間は統計調査から40週間＝280日とされているが，英米ではその全体を3つの三半期（trimester：各三半期が約3か月）に分けて考えることが多い．

- 妊娠6か月である　①be six months「pregnant [《口》along, gone, on the way]　②be in the sixth month of pregnancy
- 妊娠20週目である　be in「the 20th week [week 20] of pregnancy
- 今妊娠何か月目ですか．　How many months pregnant are you?
- 予定日はいつですか．　①When is your baby due?　②When are you expecting your baby?　③When is your due date?
- 妊娠は3回目です．　This is my third pregnancy.
- （おなかの中の子は）3人目です．　This will be my third child.

- 妊娠3度目の妊婦 〚医〛① a 3-gravida ② a gravida「3 [III]」③ a terti-gravida ▶ nulligravida（未妊婦），primigravida（初妊婦），secundigravida（2回経妊婦），tertigravida（3回経妊婦），multigravida（経妊婦）などという．
- 2回経産婦 〚医〛① a para II ② a secundipara ▶ nullipara（未産婦），primipara（初産婦／1回産婦），secundipara（2回経産婦），multipara（2回以上の経産婦）などという．

> **トリビア　ヒトの妊娠期間**
>
> 　ヒトの妊娠期間は日本では「十月（とつき）」とか「十月十日（とつきとおか）」と言い習わしているが，英語圏では9か月として知られている．医学的な妊娠期間280日は最終月経開始日から数えるので，排卵が月経の約14日後であることを考えると受精から数えた妊娠期間は266日程度となる．これなら英語の9か月にほぼぴったりである．
>
> 　実は日本語の「十月十日」は数えで「10か月めの10日め」という意味（つまり満9か月＋10日）であり，しかも1か月というものを月経周期の28日で考えていた．これなら $9 \times 28 + 10 = 262$ で現在の知見とも一致する．

38-6　馬齢

イギリスの伝統的な馬文化を反映して英語では年齢ごとに細かく馬の名称がある．

1歳未満は foal（当歳馬），離乳前の仔馬は suckling，離乳後の仔馬は weanling，1歳馬は yearling，2-4歳は colt（雄），filly（雌），5歳以上は horse（雄），mare（雌）となり，さらに牡馬（ぼ）なら stallion（種馬），sire（父馬），牝馬（ひん）なら broodmare（繁殖牝馬），dam（母馬）もあり，去勢馬は gelding という．

39. 通貨と為替

■ 39-1 通貨単位

39-1-1 円

- 円　a yen
- 200 円　① 200 yen　② ¥200　★ yen は単複同形
- 5 億円　① 500 million yen　② ¥500 million
- 100 円玉　① a 100-yen coin　② a one-hundred-yen coin　③ a hundred-yen coin
- 1 万円札　①《米》a 10,000-yen bill　②《英》a 10,000-yen note
- ▶ ¥500 million は通貨記号が先頭についているが，500 million yen と同じように five hundred million yen と読めばいい．¥2.4 million のような場合も同様で，two point four million yen でよい．
- 102 円 95 銭　102.95 yen

39-1-2 ドル

- ドル　a dollar
- 50 ドル　① 50 dollars　② $50
- 50 セント　① 50 cents　② 50¢
- 4 ドル 99 セント　① four dollars and ninety-nine cents　② four ninety-nine
- ★会話では②が普通．記号は¢は使わず $4.99 とするのが普通．
- ★会話では 499 ドルのことも単に four ninety-nine ということがあるのでまぎらわしいが，2 桁も違うのでたいてい前後関係でわかる．
- 1 ドル札　① a one-dollar bill　② a dollar bill
- 1 セント貨　① a one-cent coin　② a penny　★硬貨の意味では penny の複数形は pennies
- 5 セント貨　① a five-cent coin　② a nickel
- 10 セント貨　① a ten-cent coin　② a dime
- 25 セント貨　① a twenty-five cent coin　② a quarter
- 50 セント貨　① a fifty-cent coin　② a half dollar
- 1 ドル貨　① a one-dollar coin　② a dollar coin
- ★米国では日常頻繁に使われる 1 セント貨から 25 セント貨までは，a one-cent coin, a five-cent coin のような説明的表現より a penny, a nickel などというのが普通．
- この自動販売機は 25 セント硬貨しか使えない．　This vending machine takes only quarters.

39. 通貨と為替 39-1-3

- 現在 1 米ドルは 1.18 カナダドルだ． The [One] US dollar is currently worth 1.18 Canadian dollars.
- その本はカナダドルで $20 だ． The book is $20 in Canadian dollars.
- ★ 米ドルは US$20，カナダドルは C$20 または Can$20，オーストラリアドルは A$20，$A20，AU$20，$AU20，ニュージーランドドルは NZ$20，シンガポールドルは S$20，香港ドルは HK$20 のように書く．

> **トリビア** アメリカの紙幣
> アメリカの紙幣の肖像はベンジャミン・フランクリン（100 ドル札），ユリシーズ・グラント（50 ドル札），アンドルー・ジャクソン（20 ドル札），アレグザンダー・ハミルトン（10 ドル札），エイブラハム・リンカーン（5 ドル札），トマス・ジェファソン（2 ドル札），ジョージ・ワシントン（1 ドル札）．20 ドル札の表面の肖像をハリエット・タブマンにするなど新デザインが 2020 年に発表される予定．

39-1-3 ユーロ

- ユーロ　a euro
- 50 ユーロ　① 50 euros　② €50　③ EUR 50
- 50 セント　① 50 cents　② €0.50　③ EUR 0.50　④ 50¢
- ★ 当初は公式文書では euro も cent もあらゆる言語で単複同形とされていたが，2011 年の欧州委員会による English Style Guide では普通に -s を付けるものとしている．
- ★ セントの公式記号は定められておらず，国により c，ct，またはアメリカ風に¢などの記号も使われる．
- 4 ユーロ 99 セント　① four「euros [euro] and ninety-nine「cents [cent]　② four ninety-nine　★記号は €4.99 または EUR 4.99

39-1-4 ポンド

- ポンド　a pound
- ペニー　a penny　★複数形は pence
- 50 ポンド　① 50 pounds　② £50
- 50 ペンス　① 50 pence　② 50P
- 4 ポンド 99 ペンス　① four pounds and ninety-nine pence　② four ninety-nine　★記号は £4.99
- 10 ポンド札　a ten-pound note
- ▶ イギリスで使われているポンドを特に pound sterling という．sterling

というのはもともとはノルマン朝時代のペニー銀貨のことで，ポンドは重さの単位だった．「重さ1ポンドのスターリング貨」という発想から転じてポンドが通貨単位として使われるようになり，スターリングのほうは形容詞として英ポンドを表わすようになった．

▶ 現在のイギリスの通貨は1ポンド＝100ペンスだが，十進法が1971年に導入される以前は1ポンド＝20シリング，1シリング＝12ペンスだった．1960年まではファージング (1/4ペニー; farthing)，1969年までは旧半ペニー (halfpenny)，1971年から1984年までは新半ペニーという小銅貨もあった．

- 10ポンド5シリング6ペンス　① ten pounds, five shillings, and sixpence　②《口》 ten pounds five and「six [sixpence]　★記号 £10 5s. 6d.

39-1-5 その他

- 元　a yuan　★単複同形
- ウォン　a won　★単複同形

為替表示などではしばしばUSD (米ドル)，GBP (英ポンド)，CAD (カナダドル)，AUD (豪州ドル)，NZD (ニュージーランドドル)，JPY (日本円)，CNY (人民元)，RUB (ルーブル) といった記号が使われる．これはISO4217で定められており，国名の2文字略称に通貨記号のイニシャルなどを付けたものになっている．元はRMB (renminbi (人民幣) の略) で表わすこともある．

■ 39-2 外国為替

39-2-1 換算・為替取引

- 円を米ドルに**両替する**　① exchange yen for US dollars　② change yen into dollars
- 円を米ドルに**換算する**　convert the yen to the US dollar
- 1ドル100円の**為替相場で**　at the (exchange) rate of 100 yen to the US dollar
- 1ドル100円で円をドルに**換算する**　convert yen at 100 to the dollar
- 300ドルは日本円で**いくらに相当**しますか．
  ① What is $300 equivalent to in Japanese yen?
  ② How many yen is $300?
  ③ How much is $300 worth in yen?
- 円を売る [買う]　sell [buy] (the) yen
- 円売り [買い]　selling [buying] (of) (the) yen
- ロンドン市場で円が売られている [買われている]．　The yen is being「sold

off [bought up] on the London market.

39-2-2 **為替相場**

- **円相場** ① the yen exchange rate ② the exchange rate [for [of] the yen ③ the [price [value] of the yen ④ the yen
- 今, **円相場**はどのくらいですか.
  ① What is the current exchange rate for the yen?
  ② How is the yen doing now?
  ③ [ドルに対して] What is the current exchange rate for the yen to the dollar?
- **1 ドル 120 円だ．** The [One] dollar is (worth) ¥120.
- 7 月 14 日時点での**為替レート**は 1 ドル 110 円だ．
  ① As of July 14th, the exchange rate is 110 yen to the dollar.
  ② As of July 14th, the dollar exchange rate is 110 yen.
- 輸出産業にとっての**採算レート**は 1 ドル 117 円程度と思われる．　The breakeven line for exporting industries is considered to be around 117 yen to the dollar.

39-2-3 **相場変動**

- 円の急落　a sharp fall [in [of] the yen
- 円の高騰　a sharp rise [in [of] the yen
- 円の強さ　the strength of the yen
- 東京市場で円が**下落** [**上昇**] している．　The yen is [falling [rising] on the Tokyo market.
- 円相場はドルに対して半日で 3 円**上がった** [**下落した**]．　The yen [rose [fell] 3 yen against the dollar in half a day.
- 円は 1 ドル 100 円に**まで上がった**．　The yen **rose to** 100 yen to the dollar.
- 円の為替レートが 1 ドル 100 円台を**割りそうな気配**である．　The exchange rate of the yen is **threatening to break below** the ¥100-per-dollar level.
- 一時 1 ドル 103 円を**割って** 102 円 95 銭となった．　The dollar briefly **dropped below** 103 yen to 102.95 yen.
- ドル相場は昨年 9 月以来初めて 1 ドル 110 円の**水準を超えた**．　The dollar **rose above** the 110-yen mark for the first time since last September.
- 先週ドルは**最安値を更新し**, 日本の当局によるさらなるドル買い介入を招いた．　The dollar **hit a record low** against the yen last week, prompting yet more dollar buying by the Japanese government.
- 1 ドル 110 円から 112 円**の範囲に保とうとする努力**　an effort **to keep** the dollar in the 110-112 yen **range**
- 日銀の**介入目標レンジ**は 1 ドル 110 円程度と思われる．　The Bank of Japan's **target range for its intervention** is thought to be around 110 yen to

the dollar.
- 円は20年間1ドル360円という相場に**固定されていた**．　The yen was **pegged** at the rate of 360 to the dollar for two decades.

39-2-4　円高

- 円高　①〔高いこと〕a strong(er) yen　②〔高くなること〕(an) appreciation of the yen 《against the dollar》　③ the yen's appreciation　④ a rise in (the value of) the yen
- 円高になった．　The yen「appreciated [rose]」(against the dollar).
- 円高が進行している．
  ① The yen is continuing to「appreciate [rise]」(against the dollar).
  ② The yen is still appreciating.
  ③ The yen is on the rise.
- 5円の円高　a 5-yen「appreciation [rise]」against the dollar
- 円高ドル安　① (an) appreciation of the yen against the dollar　② a strong yen and (a) weak dollar.
- 円が高すぎる．　The yen is too「high [strong]」.
- 円高ドル安の圧力が予想される．　Upward pressure on the yen against the dollar is expected.
- 円高に歯止めがかかった．
  ① A brake has been applied to the yen's appreciation.
  ② The yen's rise has been halted.
- 円高を食い止める　stem the yen's「rise [appreciation]」《against the dollar》
- 日銀は**急激な円高を阻止するために**介入した．　The Bank of Japan intervened **against a sharp appreciation of the yen**.
- 1月に日銀は**円高を食い止める**べく過去最大の670億ドルもの介入をした．　In January, the Bank of Japan spent a record $67 billion to **keep the yen from strengthening against the dollar**.
- 日銀の介入が当面の**急激な円高を抑えた**．　The Bank of Japan's intervention **stemmed the yen's sharp rise** for the present.
- **行き過ぎた円高**は日本経済を悪化させた．　**The excessive strengthening of the yen** damaged the Japanese economy.
- 円高のメリット　① the benefit of a stronger yen　② an advantage [the advantages] of a strong yen
- 円高で海外旅行が手軽になった．　The strong yen has made overseas travel more affordable.
- 円高差益　① a foreign exchange gain (resulting) from「the stronger yen [the yen's appreciation, the rise in the yen]」　② a profit「from [generated by]」the strong yen
- 円高差益の還元　passing on the benefit of the strong yen to consumers

- 円高差損　①a foreign exchange loss (resulting) from「the stronger yen [the yen's appreciation, the rise in the yen]　②a loss「from [generated by] the strong yen
- 円高不況　a recession caused by the strong yen

39-2-5　円安

- 円安　①〔安いこと〕a「weak [cheap, low] yen　②weakness「in [of] the yen　③a low (rate of exchange) for the yen　④〔安くなること〕(a) depreciation of the yen　⑤the yen's depreciation　⑥a「fall [drop, decline] in (the value of) the yen
- 5円の円安　a 5-yen「depreciation [fall] against the dollar
- 円安になった．The yen「depreciated [fell, dropped, weakened] (against the dollar).
- 円安が進んでいる．
①The yen is continuing to「depreciate [fall, weaken, lose ground] (against the dollar).
②The yen is still depreciating.
- 円安の進行　the yen's further「slide [fall, decline, downswing, depreciation]
- 円が急落した．The yen「plunged [dropped sharply, fell precipitately].
- 相場が円安に転じた．The market「turned [moved] against the yen.
- 為替相場は円安に終始した．The yen「fell [lost ground] throughout the entire trading session.
- 各国のドル買いが進み，**円安に歯止めがかからなかった**．
①**The yen continued to fall** on dollar buying in markets throughout the world.
②**There was no halt to the yen's decline** as traders in all markets continued to buy dollars.
- 日本政府は円安を容認している．①The Japanese government is letting the yen fall.　②The Japanese government is not intervening to protect the yen.

39-3　株

39-3-1　株価

- **株価**　the price of a「stock [share]　②a「stock [share] price
- P社の株は1株当たり12,000円で**取引されている**［12,000円が相場だ］．
①P Corp.'s stock **is trading** at ¥12,000 per share.　②P Corp.'s stock is quoted at ¥12,000 a share.　③The going rate for P Corp.'s stock is ¥12,000 a share.
- 株の値上がり　①〔平均株価の〕a rise in「stock [share] prices　②〔ある株式の〕a rise in the value of a「stock [share]

- **終値**　① the closing price　② the closing quotation　③ the closing market price　④ the close
- 午前の終値　《at》the morning close
- 昨日の平均株価は**終値**で 8,500 円だった．　Yesterday's average share price was 8,500 yen **at the close of trading**.
- 日経平均株価の**終値**は 55 円 55 銭安の 14,872.15 となった．　The Nikkei Stock Average **closed at** 14,872.15, down 55.55 points.
- 32 **銘柄**が今年の安値を更新した．　Thirty-two **stocks** slipped to new lows for the year.
- その株は公募価格の 2 倍の**初値**がついた．
  ① The stock **began trading at a price** that was double its offering price.
  ② The stock fetched **an initial price** double its offering price.
- その株はあまりの人気のため**初値**がつかなかった．　The stock's immense popularity sent demand through the roof, making it impossible to arrive at **an initial trading price**.

39-3-2 株価指数・平均株価

- **株価指数**　① a「stock [share]」price index　② a price index of stocks
- **日経平均株価[日経株価指数]**　① the Nikkei (stock) average　② the Nikkei index　③ the Nikkei
- **東証株価指数**　① the Tokyo Stock Price Index　② the TOPIX
- **ダウ・ジョーンズ工業平均株価[ダウ・ジョーンズ平均]**　① the Dow Jones Industrial Average　② the Dow Jones industrials　③ the Dow Jones「average [index]」
- 過去 6 か月の D 社の平均株価　the average stock price of D Corp. over the past six months

39-3-3 株価の水準と変動 [⇨ 13-4 増加・上昇を表わす各種表現, 13-5 減少・低下を表わす各種表現]

- **株価動向**　the trend「in [of]」stock [share] prices
- 株価が**上昇**した．　Stock [Share] prices have risen.
- 株価が**下落**した．　Stock [Share] prices have fallen.
- P 社の株価は 10% 下落した．　P Corp.'s stock (price) dropped by 10 percent.
- TOPIX は 0.5% 下落して 1720.18 となった．　The TOPIX index fell 0.5 percent to 1720.18.
- 株価が**急騰**した．
  ① Stock prices rose dramatically.
  ② Share prices shot up.

- 株価が**急落**した．
  ① Stock prices fell dramatically.
  ② Share prices plummeted.
- 株価は**低迷**している．　Stock prices are「flagging [hovering low]．
- 株価を**押し上げる**　drive up [push up, boost, lift] the「stock [share] price
- 株価を**支える**　① shore up the「stock [share] price　② prop up the「stock [share] price
- 日経平均株価は**16年来の低水準**に落ち込んだ．　The Nikkei Stock Average fell to **a sixteen-year low**.
- 日経平均株価はほぼ5年ぶりに**15,000円台を回復した**．　The Nikkei Stock Average **climbed above the 15,000 mark** for the first time in almost five years.
- 日経平均株価は1989年末には38,915円87銭だったが，1年もしない間に一時20,000円を割るほどに暴落した．　The Nikkei Stock Average **stood at** 38,915.87 at the end of 1989, but then it crashed and, less than a year later, dipped briefly below the 20,000 mark.
- 日経平均株価は2003年に1982年**以来の安値**である7,607円88銭を記録した．　In 2003, the Nikkei Stock Average hit a record low of 7,607.88, **the lowest since** 1982.
- 東証は2か月ぶりの高値で取引を終えた．　The「TSE [Tokyo Stock Exchange] closed trading on a two-month high.

39-3-4　**値幅制限・ストップ高・ストップ安**

▶ 日本の証券取引所では前営業日の終値を基準として価格帯ごとに制限値幅が設けられているが，ニューヨーク証券取引所やナスダック証券取引所は値幅制限はない．

- **ストップ高** ①《register, record, hit》a limit-up　② a limit high
- **ストップ安** ①《register, record, hit》a limit-down　② a limit low
- P社の株価は**ストップ高**の26,500円まで上がった．　P Corp.'s stock price「went up [rose, etc.] to **the limit high** of 26,500 yen (per share).
- J社の株価は**制限値幅**の10万円下落して572,000円となった．　J Corp.'s stock plunged by its **daily limit** of 100,000 yen to 572,000 yen.

39-3-5　**売買**

- K社の株を100 [1] 株買う　buy「100 shares [1 share] of K Company
- J社の株の1株を61万円で売る　sell one J Corp. share for 610,000 yen
- ABC社の株を16ドルで100株買う注文を出す　place an order to buy 100 shares of ABC Corp.'s stock at $16 (per share)
- ABC社の株100株に対するビッドを提示する [出す]　〔買い〕place [make,

put in] a bid for 100 shares of ABC Corp.'s stock
- ABC 社の株 100 株に対するオファー 〔売り〕 an offer for 100 shares of ABC Corp.'s stock
- 売り注文の株数　the number of shares offered
- 東京証券取引所の今日の**出来高**　today's「volume [turnover] on the Tokyo Stock Exchange

39-3-6　保有・持ち株比率

- N 社は M 社の株式の 20% を保有している．
  ① N Corp. owns 20% of M Corp.'s「equity [shares].
  ② N Corp. holds a stake of 20% in M Corp.
- 10 万株を追加取得する　acquire an additional 100,000 shares
- N 社は M 社の筆頭株主で**持ち株比率は 30%** だ．　N Corp. is M Corp.'s largest stockholder, **with a 30% stake**.
- これにより N 社の M 社株**持ち株比率**が 20% から 30% に増す．　This raises N Corp.'s **stake** in M Corp. from 20% to 30%.
- F 社は N 社の株を買い増しして**議決権株の保有比率**を 20% まで高めた．
  ① F Corp. bought「additional [more] shares of N Corp. and increased its **voting stake** to 20%.
  ② F Corp. added to its holding of N Corp. shares to bring its **voting stake** to 20%.
  ③ F Corp. increased its stake in N Corp. and acquired 20% of **the voting shares**.
- F 社は N 社の**市場に出ている株式**の 36%，**議決権のある株式**の 39% を取得したと発表した．　F Corp. announced that it had acquired 36% of N Corp.'s **outstanding shares** and 39% of its **voting shares**.

39-3-7　時価総額

- **時価総額**　① the market capitalization 《of a company》 ② the market cap ③ the aggregate market value　★（株価）×（発行済み株式数）または（株価）×（流通株式数）
- G 社の時価総額は 500 億ドルを超える．
  ① G Corp.'s market capitalization is over $50 billion.
  ② G Corp.'s market cap tops $50 billion.
  ③ G Corp. is worth more than $50 billion (in terms of market capitalization).
- ここ 1 か月で L 社の時価総額の 47% が消えた．　L Corp. has lost 47 percent of its market cap over the past month.
- 時価総額 40 億ドルを超える世界最大のメディア会社の一つ　one of the world's largest media companies, with a current market cap of over $4 billion

39-3-8 配当・利益

- 1 割の配当をする　pay a dividend of 10 percent
- 株主たちは 10 パーセントの**配当**を要求した．
  ① Shareholders demanded a 10 percent **dividend**.
  ② Shareholders demanded a 10 percent **return on their investments**.
- **1 株当たり配当金**　a dividend per share 《略 DPS》
- **配当率**　a dividend rate　★1 株当たりの年間配当金．2001 年の法改正で額面株が廃止されるまでは額面価格に対する割合で表わしていた．
- 1 株当たり 123 円の配当率　a dividend rate of 123 yen per share
- **配当性向**　a (dividend) payout ratio　★純利益に対する配当金の割合．
- **株主資本配当率**　the dividend rate for「stockholders'［shareholders'］equity　★資本に対する配当金の割合．
- **配当利回り［配当利率］**　a dividend yield　★1 株当たりの配当金を株価で割ったもの．
- **株価配当比率**　①a price-dividend ratio　②a P/D ratio 《略 PDR》　★株価を配当金で割ったもの．
- **1 株利益［1 株当たり利益］**　earnings per share 《略 EPS》
- **株価収益率**　①a P/E ratio　②a price-to-earnings ratio 《略 PER》　③the ratio of the price of a stock to its earnings　★株価を 1 株当たり利益の倍数で表わしたもの．
- P 社は **1 株利益**の予想を 143 円から 159 円に上方修正した．
  ① P Corp. increased its **earnings per share** estimate from ¥143 to ¥159.
  ② P Corp. now expects to **earn** ¥159 **per share**, up from its previous estimate of ¥143 per share.

39-3-9 発行

- **授権株式（数）**　authorized stock
- **発行済み株式（数）**　issued stock
- **自己株式［金庫株］**　treasury stock
- **流通株式［発行済み株式のうち自己株式を除いたもの，市場に出ている発行済み株式，社外株］**　①outstanding stock　②shares (issued and) outstanding
- **額面株式**　① stocks with par value　② (a) par value stock　③ a par value share　★額面は 50 円，500 円，5 万円があったが 2001 年から商法改正により額面株式は廃止．par は「等しい」が原義であるが，株式発行時に株主が会社に払い込んだ額に等しい価格が額面価格．
- **無額面株式**　① (a) stock without par value　② (a) no-par-value stock
- **額面価格で**　①〔証券など〕at face value　② at nominal value　③〔株など〕at par

- **株式発行価額**　the「issuing [issue] price of shares
- 1株10万円で発行された株　a stock issued at 100,000 yen per share
- 株価が額面を割って48円になった．　The stock fell below par to ¥48.
- **株式発行額**　① the《yen, dollar》amount of「stocks [shares] issued　② the size of a share issue

39-3-10　公開

- **株式公開**　① going public　② listing「stock [shares] (on a stock exchange)
- **新規株式公開**　an initial public offering《略 IPO》
- **公開株**　① a listed share　② stock listed on the stock exchange　③ a publicly offered「stock [share]
- **新規公開株**　① a new stock offer(ing)　② an initial offering of shares
- 新規公開株の長期収益率　the「long-run [long-term] performance of IPOs
- 新規株式公開する　① launch an IPO　② go public
- **未公開株**　① stocks [shares] that have not been (publicly) listed　② stocks [shares] offered privately to individuals before being publicly listed　③ a privately traded share　④ a prelisted share

39-3-11　株式分割

- **株式分割**　① a「stock [share] split　② stock [share] splitting　③〔分割した株〕a split share
- 1:3の株式分割[1対3の株式分割，3倍の株式分割，株式の3分割]　a 3-for-1 stock split
- 1:2の株式分割を発表する　announce a 2-for-1 stock split
- L社は株式を100分割した．　L Corp. split its「stock [shares] (at a ratio of) 100-for-1.
- **株式併合**　①《implement》a「reverse [negative] (stock) split　② a split-down　③ (a) (stock) consolidation

39-3-12　その他

- **一株株主**　a holder of a single share
- **一株運動**　① a movement to buy single shares of a company in order to acquire voting rights　② a campaign urging people to buy a single share in order to have a say at shareholders' meetings
- **単元株数**　the number of stock shares constituting a「trading unit [round lot]
- **端株**　① odd-lot stocks　② broken-lot stocks　③ an odd lot　④ a fractional lot　⑤ a broken lot

- **株式公開買い付け** ①a takeover offer ②a takeover bid《略 TOB》
- **株式交換** (an) exchange of「stock［shares］

■ 39-4　入札・オークション

- バッグを1500円で売りに出す　offer a bag for 1,500 yen
- ネットオークションに出す［出品する］　put《an item》up for sale through an online auction
- 700円で入札する　①bid 700 yen《for［on］an item》②enter a bid of 700 yen　③place a bid of 700 yen
- 現在の価格は1300円だ．　The current bid《on an item》is 1,300 yen.
- 落札する　①win《an item》②make a successful bid　③have *one's* tender accepted　④have《an item》knocked down to *one*　⑤〈物が主語〉be knocked down to《a person》
- 2500円で落札する　①win the auction with a 2,500-yen bid　②win《an item》at 2,500 yen
- 40ドルまで払う用意がある［最高入札額が40ドルの］入札者　①a bidder willing to pay up to $40《for an item》②a bidder with a maximum bid of $40
- あなたの最高入札額3000円より高い額でほかの人が入札しました．　A bid higher than your 3,000-yen maximum「amount［bid］was entered by another bidder.
- あなたが現在の最高額入札者です．　You are「the current［now the］highest bidder.
- 値をつける　①〔買い手が〕make an offer《of ¥3,000》for《an item》②name *one's* price　③〔売り手が〕price《an item at ¥5,000》④mark the price on《an item》⑤set the price《for an item at ¥10,000》
- よい値で売れる　①sell「at［for］a good price　②bring［fetch, command］a high price
- その絵が一番よい値がつきそうだ．　That picture promises to go for the highest price of all.
- その壺にはまだ値がつかない．　No one has「bid［put in a bid］yet for that pot.
- 堤防工事の発注で入札を行なう［を入札にかける］　put a contract for embankment construction work out to tender
- 応札する　①submit a「bid［tender］《for …》②put in a「bid［tender］《for …》③make a bid《for …》
- 応札額　the amount of the bid (tendered)
- 入札は20億円でB建設の手に落ち，次札はC不動産だった．　The bidding fell to the B Construction Company at 2 billion yen, with C Estate Agency as the next bidder.

- 落札価格　①a contract price　②a bid-winning price　③the amount of a successful tender　④a winning bid price　⑤a successful bid price
- 最低落札価格　①a minimum bid price　②〔競売の〕a reserve price
- 落札者［人］　a successful bidder
- （入札）予定価格　〔その額を超えた入札は無効となる〕a bid ceiling
- 落札率　①〔予定価格に対する実際の落札価格の割合〕a bid acceptance ratio　②the ratio of the winning bid to the bid ceiling　③〔特定の種類の落札者の割合〕the ratio of 《foreign companies》 among the winning bidders　④〔出品した品物のうち落札されるものの割合〕the ratio of successful auctions
- 落札率が90％を超えていた．〔落札額が予定価格の90％超〕The winning bid price was above 90% of the bid ceiling.

40. 料金・価格・収支

■ 40-1 料金

　料金を表わす語には charge, rate, fee, fare がある．charge, rate, fee は交換可能な場合もあるが，charge は課金一般，rate は料率によって決まる料金（電話料金，水道料金，ホテルの料金など），fee は専門的なサービスの対価（授業料，顧問料）や手数料，入場料，会費などに使うことが多い．fare は乗り物の料金．tuition（授業料），premium（保険料）など「料」にあたる語をつけない表現もある．実際に請求される料金は bill．

40-1-1 rate, charge を中心に訳す例

- ガス料金　① a gas rate　② a gas charge　③ a gas bill
- 水道料金　① a water rate　② a water charge　③ a water bill
- 水道料金がとても高い．
  ① The water rates are very high.
  ② The water bill is very high.
- 公共料金　〔水道・ガス・電気代など〕① public utility charges　② utility bills　③ utility rates
- 公共料金の引き上げ［引き下げ］　an increase [a decrease] in utility rates
  ★料率の意味では charge でなく rate を使うのが普通．
- 公共料金の改定　a revision of utility rates
- 広告料　① advertisement rates　② ad rates　③ advertising rates　④ advertising charges
- 国際電話料金　international (tele)phone「rates [charges]
- 電話料金　①〔1回の通話ごとの〕telephone「charges [rates]　② dialing「charges [rates]　③〔請求される〕a (tele)phone bill
- 通話料　a call rate 《of 10 yen per minute》
- 配達料　a delivery charge
- 平日料金　①〔電話など〕a weekday rate　②〔乗り物〕a weekday fare
- 均一料金　① a fixed charge　② a standard rate　③ a flat rate　④ a uniform rate
- 超過料金　①〔時間について〕an overtime charge　②〔上乗せ料金〕a surcharge　③ an excess fee
- 追加料金　① an extra charge　② an additional fee
- たいていのホテルは週末のほうが**料金が安い**．　At most hotels **lower rates are offered** on weekends.
- 一泊の料金はいくらですか．

① How much do you charge for an overnight stay?
② What is the charge for an overnight stay?

40-1-2 fee を中心に訳す例

- キャンセル料　a cancellation「charge [fee]
- キャディー料　〔ゴルフの〕① a caddie fee　② a caddying fee
- コンサルタント料　① a consultancy fee　② consultancy fees
- 受験料　① an examination fee　② the fee for (an) examination
- 授業料　① tuition fees　② tuition　③ a course fee
- 受講料　① a fee for (attendance at) a lecture　② a course fee　③ a tuition fee　④ tuition
- 空港使用料　①〔着陸料〕a landing「charge [fee]　② a navigation service fee　③〔駐機料〕a parking fee　④〔一般利用客の使用料〕an airport fee　⑤ an airport「service [facility] charge
- ターミナル使用料　〔空港などの〕① a terminal fee　② a terminal charge
- 手数料　① a commission　② (a) brokerage　③ a percentage　④ a fee　⑤ a charge
- 仲介手数料　① a brokerage fee　② an agency fee　③ (a) brokerage　④ a commission
- 駐車料金　① a parking fee　② a parking rate　③ a parking charge
- デザイン料　a design fee
- 登記料　a registration fee
- 特許料　①〔特許取得のための〕a patent fee　②〔特許使用料〕a royalty　③ a licensing fee
- 入場料　① an admission「fee [charge]　② an entrance「fee [charge]
- 振り込み手数料　a (money) transfer fee
- 弁護料　a lawyer's fee
- 放映権料　a (broadcasting [TV, television]) rights fee
- ライセンス料　① a license fee　②〔特許権・著作権使用料〕a royalty　③ royalties
- リサイクル料金　a recycling fee
- 利用料金　① a charge for use 《of the equipment》　② a charge　③ a rate　④ a fee　⑤〔オンラインサービスなどの〕a subscription fee
- レンタル料　a rental (fee)

40-1-3 fare を中心に訳す例

- タクシー料金　a taxi fare
- またバス料金が上がった．　Bus fares have「gone up [risen] again.

40. 料金・価格・収支 40-1-4

- 片道料金　① 《米》a one-way fare　② 《英》a single fare
- 往復料金　① 《米》a round-trip fare　② 《英》a return fare
- 特急料金　①〔乗車賃込み〕an express fare　②〔乗車賃に上乗せ〕an express charge
- 特急料金を払い戻す　refund the express charge
- 寝台料金　〔乗車賃に上乗せ〕a berth charge
- 通行料金　a toll

40-1-4　その他

- 郵便料金　① postage　② postal charges　③ postal fees
- 保険料　① a premium　② an insurance bill
- フランチャイズ料　royalties
- 岸壁使用料　① wharfage　② berthage　③ a wharfage charge　④ a berthage charge　⑤ quay dues
- ドック使用料　① dockage　② dock dues

■ 40-2　価格・値段

40-2-1　価格の表現

- この牛肉の**値段は** 100 グラム 2000 円だ.
  ① **The price** of this beef **is** ¥2000 per 100 grams.
  ② This beef **costs** ¥2000 per 100 grams.
  ③ This beef is priced at ¥2000 per 100 grams.
- **値段**は 1 個 500 円から 1000 円までいろいろです.　**Prices** range from ¥500 (up) to ¥1000 per item.
- **値段**は 100 グラム 500 円からある.　**Prices** start at ¥500 for 100 grams.
- 500 円の料金を取る　① charge ¥500 《for …》　② make a charge of ¥500 《for …》
- このタブレットは 5 万円で買った.　I bought this tablet for 50,000 yen.
- 350 円のグラスを 5 個買った.　I bought five glasses for 350 yen each.

40-2-2　価格の高低

- それらは同じ値段だ.　① They are the same price.　② They have the same price.　③ They cost the same.　④ Their prices are the same.　⑤ The price is the same for both of them.
- （値段が）高い　① expensive　② high in price　③ high-priced
- （値段が）安い　① inexpensive　② low in price　③ low-priced　④ cheap
- 高い値段で　① at a high price　② 《buy an article》dear

40. 料金・価格・収支 40-2-2

- 安い値段で　① at a low price　② 《buy an article》 cheap
- 手頃な値段の　① moderately priced　② reasonably priced　③ affordable
- マスクメロン1個**の値段で**スイカなら3個買える．　You can buy three watermelons **for the price of** a single muskmelon.
- このホテルでは8歳未満の子供の料金は半額になります．　This hotel offers a 50-percent discount for children under eight years of age.
- 若い人でも買える**価格**で発売される
  ① go on sale **at a price** within the reach of young people
  ② sell **for a price** that even young people can afford
- 初めてパソコンが売り出されたころは僕の月給の3倍くらいの**価格**だった．　When PCs first came onto the market, they **cost** about three times my monthly「salary [pay]」.
- もっと安い価格で手に入れる　① get … at a「lower [cheaper]」price　② get … more cheaply
- 元の値段より3割安く手に入れる　get … for 30 percent less than the original price
- その金貨は古銭市場で地金の価値よりもずっと高い**価格**がついている．　That gold coin fetches a much higher **price** in the old coin market than the value of the metal it contains.
- 価格が上がる　① the price rises　② the price goes up　③〈品物が主語〉rise in price　④ increase in price　⑤ go up in price
- 価格が下がる　① the price falls　②〈品物が主語〉fall in price　③ decrease in price　④ go down in price
- 価格を上げる　① raise a price　② put up a price　③《口》jack up a price
- 価格を下げる　① lower a price　② reduce a price　③ bring down a price　④ cut a price
- **価格**を2割引き上げる　raise **the price** by 20 percent
- **価格**を1000円から800円に引き下げる　lower **the price** from ¥1000 to ¥800
- **10年前の値段**に引き下げる　reduce the price to **what it was ten years ago**
- **価格**を据え置く　leave **a price** unchanged
- **価格**を低く抑える　① keep **a price** low　② hold down **prices**
- **価格**を1000円以下に抑える　hold [keep] **the price** at or below ¥1000
- 輸送費の値上げは商品の**価格**に跳ね返る．　Increases in shipping costs impact on commodity **prices**.
- 最近の天候不順のため**高値**が予想される．　After the recent bad weather, **high prices** are (to be) expected.
- この水彩画は今に**高値**がつく．　This watercolor will fetch **a「high [big]」price**.

- 最高級品になるとキロあたり1万円の**高値**がつくことも珍しくない． With top quality produce, it is not uncommon for prices to go as **high** as ¥10,000 a kilo.
- **破格の高値**で落札される　be「auctioned off [knocked down] at **an exorbitant price**
- この商品はプレミアがついて今では定価の50倍という**高値**で売買されている． There is a premium on this item, which is now being traded at 50 times its list price.
- 少雨高温のため野菜の**高値**に拍車がかかっている． Little rain and high temperatures have spurred on already **high** vegetable **prices**.
- （他の人よりも）安値で売る［をつける］　**undersell** [**underquote**] 《*one's* competitors*》*
- この教室は月謝が2万円かかる．
  ① This course「costs [will cost] ¥20,000 a month.
  ② The monthly fee for this course「is [will be] ¥20,000.
- メッセージを送るには5円かかります． It costs five yen to send a message.
- それはいくらかかったか．
  ① What did it cost (you)?
  ② How much did it cost (you)?
- 価格5万円は当時は**大金**だった． The price of 50,000 yen was then **a large sum**.
- 彼らは**当時の大金**を費やした． They spent **what was then a large sum**.
- 1億円と言えば**大金**だ． A hundred million yen is **quite a**「**sum** [《口》 **pile**] **of money**.

40-2-3　価格帯

- 価格帯　① a price range　② a price spectrum
- 最も売れている**価格帯**　the best-selling **price range**
- 10万から20万円の**価格帯**の商品　a commodity (selling) in the ¥100,000 to ¥200,000 **price range**
- どのくらいの**価格帯**をお考えでしょうか． What **price range** are you considering?

40-2-4　価格にまつわる術語

- 表示価格　①〔カタログ記載価格〕a list price　②〔店頭小売表示価格〕a displayed retail price　③ a sticker price
- 表示価格から割引をする　allow a discount from list prices［⇨ 40-4 割引］
- 表示価格で売る　sell at list price
- メーカー希望（小売）価格　①《米》the manufacturer's suggested retail price

40. 料金・価格・収支 40-2-4

《略 MSRP》 ② 《英》 the recommended retail price 《略 RRP》 ③ 〔自動車などの〕 the sticker price

- 推定小売価格　an estimated retail price
- オープン価格　〔メーカー希望価格が設定されず値付けが小売店の裁量に任される価格〕① a discretionary price ② a price that a retailer can fix at discretion ③ an open price ★英米ではカタログに「open price」などと表示するのではなく推定小売価格などが示されることが多い.
- それは日本でよくあるように「**オープン価格**」と表示されているが，実際の小売価格は3万円未満になると言われている.　It is listed as "**open price**" as is often done in Japan; the actual retail price is said to be less than 30,000 yen.
- 定価　① a marked price ② a labeled price ③ a list price ★メーカーが流通業者に「定価」などを示すことは再販売価格維持行為として独占禁止法に触れるとされている．書籍など再販売価格維持制度（再販制）のあるものには定価が表示されている.
- 再販売価格　a resale price
- 再販売価格維持　resale price maintenance 《略 RPM》 ★現在では英米とも特例品目以外は禁止されており，書籍なども再販制の対象とはなっていない.
- 税込み価格　① the posttax price 《of cigarettes》 ② the price「after [including] tax」③ the tax-inclusive price
- 税抜き価格　the tax-exclusive price
- 送料込みの価格　the price with「shipping [postage, freight charges] included」
- 生産者価格　a producer price
- 消費者価格　a consumer price
- 仕入れ価格　a cost price
- 市場価格　a market price
- 帳簿価格　a book value
- 公示価格　① a posted price ② a listed price
- 公示地価　① the official land value ② the government-declared [-assessed] land value ③ the「listed [posted] land price」[⇨第2部・ちか]
- 末端価格　〔小売価格〕① a retail price ② an end price 〔麻薬などの〕③ a street price ④ a street value
- その覚醒剤は末端価格で1グラム3万円する.
  ① The street price of the stimulant is ¥30,000 a gram.
  ② The stimulant is selling on the street for ¥30,000 a gram.
- 闇価格　a black-market price
- 現場渡し価格　an ex-factory price
- 倉庫渡し価格　an ex-warehouse price

40. 料金・価格・収支 40-2-5

- 本船渡し価格　①a free-on-board price　②an f.o.b. price
- 価格差　a price difference
- 内外価格差　the price difference between domestic and overseas markets
- 価格差補給金　①a price-support subsidy　②a subsidy to offset a price「differential [difference]

40-2-5 単価

- 単価　①a unit cost　②a unit price
- 商品の単価　the unit price of an item (of goods)
- 単価500円で　①at ¥500 per piece　②at ¥500 apiece　③at ¥500 each
- できるだけ単価を安く抑える　keep the unit price as low as possible
- 客単価　①(the) per-customer spending　②the (average) amount spent by each customer
- 小売単価　a unit retail price
- 生産単価　①a unit cost of production　②a production unit cost
- 診療報酬単価　a per-item fee for medical treatment

40-2-6 時価

- 時価　〔その時々の評価価格〕①the current price　②the market price　③the market value　④the prevailing price　⑤the going price　⑥the selling price prevailing at the time　⑦the price quoted 《for …》　⑧the current quotation 《for …》　★②③は「市場価格」の意．④以降は実勢価格の側面に着目した表現．
- 時価で販売する　sell at the current market price
- 時価100万円の花瓶　①a vase with a market value of a million yen　②a vase currently valued at a million yen
- 時価数十万円する浮世絵
  ①an ukiyoe print currently priced at several hundred thousand yen
  ②an ukiyoe print that currently goes for several hundred thousand yen
- それは**時価にする**といくらになりますか．　How much does that come to **at current market prices**?
- その品は**時価**より高く売れた．　The article was sold above **the current price**.
- これらの寿司ネタは**時価**です．　The prices for this sushi **depend on this morning's fish market prices**.　★sushiは不可算名詞なのでthese sushisなどとしない．
- **時価**で1000株購入できるストックオプション　a stock option to purchase 1000 shares **at market value**
- それらの株式の買い戻しには**時価**で50億ドル以上かかるだろう．　Repur-

chasing those shares will cost more than 5 billion dollars **at current prices**.
- 時価ベースで　on a market value basis
- 保有株式を時価で評価する　value shareholdings at market rates
- 時価発行の株　shares issued at「market［going］prices
- 時価発行増資　a capital increase by issuing new shares at the market price
- 時価総額　① the market capitalization　② the aggregate market value［⇨ 39-3-7 時価総額］
- 時価会計　① market-value accounting　② current-value accounting　③ current cost accounting《略 CCA》

40-2-7 物価

- 物価　(commodity) prices
- 消費者物価　consumer prices
- 消費者米価　the consumer price of rice
- 消費者物価調査　① a survey of consumer prices　② a consumer price survey
- 消費者物価上昇率　① the rate of increase in consumer prices　② the consumer price increase rate
- 物価指数　a price index
- 消費者物価指数　the consumer price index《略 CPI》
- 企業物価指数　the corporate goods price index《略 CGPI》★日本銀行による．以前は卸売物価指数と称した．
- 先月の**消費者物価指数**は前年同月比 3% の上昇となった．　Last month's **consumer price index** was three percent higher than for the same month last year.
- 小売り物価指数　《英》a retail price index《略 RPI》★日本やアメリカの消費者物価指数に相当．
- 卸売物価指数　a wholesale price index《略 WPI》
- 物価が高い［安い］．　Prices are「high［low］．
- 物価が上がった．　① Prices rose.　② Prices went up.
- 物価が下がった．　① Prices declined.　② Prices fell (off).　③ Prices came down.
- 物価は上昇傾向にある．　① Prices are tending upward(s).　② Prices are tending to rise.　③ Prices are showing an upward trend.
- 物価は上がるばかりだ．　① Prices continue to rise.　② Prices are steadily rising.
- 物価下落　① a (commodity) price fall　② a fall in (commodity) prices
- 物価下落率　the rate of a「price decline［decline in prices］
- 物価は為替相場の変動により変わります．　Prices are subject to fluctuations

in the exchange rate.
- 物価に連動させる　① link 《pension payments》 to a price index　② index [link] 《pension payments》 to prices
- 物価スライド制　① 《consumer price》 indexation　② indexing
- 物価スライド方式の　① indexed　② index-linked
- 物価スライド率　an indexing rate

40-2-8 その他

- 評価額1000万円の絵　a painting [valued [assessed] at ten million yen
- これは市価8万円する．
  ① This has a market value of ¥80,000.
  ② This is quoted at ¥80,000.
- 簿価ベースで　on a book value basis
- 1万円の価値がある　be worth ¥10,000
- 10万円の値打ちのある品　① an article worth ¥100,000　② an item valued at ¥100,000
- 1780年の1ペニー硬貨は現在どのくらいの値打ちがあるか．　How much is a penny from 1780 worth now?
- 1780年には1ペニーはどれくらいの値打ちがあったか．　How much was a penny worth in 1780?
- その時代の1ポンドは現在の20ポンドに相当すると言われている．　It is said that a pound in those days is equivalent to 20 pounds now.

■ 40-3 費用

- 費用　① (an) expense　② (an) expenditure　③ (a) cost　④ (an) outlay
  ★expenditure は「支出」，cost は「負担」の意味合いがある．
- 食費　food expenses
- 旅費　traveling expenses
- 教育費　educational expenses
- リサイクルの費用　the cost of recycling
- 家賃1か月分程度の費用で　① for about the cost of a month's rent　② for about the same amount as a month's rent
- わずかな費用で　① at [with] a small outlay　② without paying much
- 費用はどのぐらいだろうか．
  ① What will it cost?
  ② How much will it come to?
  ③ What will the [cost [expenditure] be?
- 費用は10万円ぐらいになるだろう．

① It will cost about ¥100,000.
② The cost will come to about ¥100,000.
- 費用は 5000 ドルを超える　① cost more than $5,000　② the cost exceeds $5,000　③ the cost is above $5,000
- 総コスト 3000 万円で　at a total cost of 30 million yen
- 費用を賄う　cover [meet] the cost(s) 《of equipment》
- 費用を負担する［出す］　① bear the expenses 《of …, for …》 ② defray the expenses 《of …, for …》 ③ pay 《for a job, for a trip》 ④《口》put up the money 《for …》 ⑤ foot the bill 《for …》 ⑥ pick up the tab 《for …》
- 費用を浮かせる　①(manage to) leave something over ② do not use (up) all 《the money》
- 500 万円未満まで費用を切り詰める　cut expenses below five million yen
- 費用をできるだけ低く保つ　keep the cost as low as possible
- 莫大な時間と費用をかけて　① at「an enormous [a huge] cost in time and money ② by spending an enormous amount of time and money
- 費用（対）効果　① (a) cost effect ②《improve》cost-effectiveness
- 費用（対）効果分析　cost-effectiveness analysis

■ 40-4 割引

- 割引　① (a) discount　② (an) allowance　③ price cutting
- 割引する　① discount　② give [allow, make] a discount　③ take [cut] off 《5%》
- 3 割引　〔表示〕① 30% Off　② Save 30%
- 5% 割引する　① give [allow] a 5-percent discount 《on [off] the price》 ② give [allow] a discount of 5 percent　③ make an allowance of 5 percent　④ reduce the price by 5 percent
- 全品 2 割引です．　All items are 20 percent off.
- 表示価格から割引をする　allow a discount from list prices
- 割引した値段で　① at a reduced price　② at a discount　③ at a cut rate
- 定価の 2 割引で買う　① buy at a discount of 20 percent「off [on] the list price　② buy for 20 percent off the list price　③ buy at a 20 percent discount
- 「少し割引できませんか」「5% まけましょう」　Can't you take off a little? — I can cut off 5 percent.
- 現金なら**いくらか割引してもらえますか**．　① Will you **allow any discount** for cash?　② Can you **make any allowance** for cash payment?
- この靴はバーゲン品ですので**割引はありません**．　These shoes are offered at specially reduced prices, so **we cannot give you a discount**.
- 大口の購入に対して**割引する**　**allow** [**make**] **a discount** for a bulk purchase

- 団体に対しては運賃を**割引してもらえる**．
  ① **A discount is allowed** on group tickets.
  ② **They will make special terms** for groups.
- 1週間の宿泊費を**割引してくれた**．　The hotel **gave us a reduction** for a week's stay.
- 学生には割引がある　《they》offer reductions for students
- まけてくれませんか．　Can't you「make [let me have] it cheaper?
- もう少しまけなさいよ．　① Come down a little more. ② Let me have a bit more off.
- 5,000円にまけてよ．　① Make it ¥5,000. ② Can't you come down to ¥5,000?
- もうこれ以上まけられません．　① I can go no lower. ② I can't take any more off.

■ 40-5 収入と支出

40-5-1 収支

- 収支　income [earnings, revenue] and「expenditure(s) [expenses]
- 歳入と歳出　revenue and expenditures
- 収支一覧表　① a statement of income and expenditure ② an income statement
- 収支決算　settlement of accounts [⇨ 41-2 決算の表現]
- 来年度の税収は53兆円と見込まれている．　Tax revenues for the next fiscal year are expected to be 53 trillion yen.

40-5-2 収入

- 収入　①(an) income ② earnings ③〔歳入〕revenue ④〔売り上げ〕proceeds ⑤〔入金〕receipts
- 安定した収入　a steady income
- 不安定な収入　a precarious income
- そこそこの収入　a modest income
- わずかな収入　a「scanty [meager] income
- 一人当たりの収入　(a) per capita income
- …の収入がある　have [earn, enjoy, draw] an income of 《four million yen》
- 収入が多い [少ない]　have [earn, draw] a「large [small] income
- 月収　① a monthly income ② a monthly salary ③ monthly wages ④ monthly earnings
- 20万円の月給で働く　work for a salary of ¥200,000 a month

40. 料金・価格・収支 40-5-2

- 20万円の月給を取る　① draw [receive, get] a salary of ¥200,000 a month　② draw a monthly salary of ¥200,000　③ make ¥200,000 a month
- 彼女の月給は2万円アップした．　① Her monthly salary was raised by ¥20,000.　② She got a raise of ¥20,000 per month.
- 初任給は月20万円だった．　I started with a salary of ¥200,000 a month.
- 初任給を20万円出せます．　We can start you out at ¥200,000 a month.
- 時給1000円でアルバイトを引き受ける　take a part-time job at ¥1,000 an hour
- 時給で働く　① work by the hour　② get paid by the hour
- 年収　① an annual income　② a yearly income
- 彼は年収500万円だ．
  ① He「draws [earns] an annual [a yearly] income of ¥5 million.
  ② His income is ¥5 million a year.
- 年収100万ドルの弁護士　① a lawyer who earns a million dollars a year　② a $1,000,000-a-year lawyer
- 平均年収　《earn》an average「annual [yearly] salary《of ¥8 million》
- 年俸　① an annual salary　② a yearly stipend
- 年俸10万ドルで　① at a salary of $100,000 a year　② at an annual salary of $100,000
- あの人は年俸800万円です．
  ① He draws a salary of ¥8 million a year.
  ② His salary is ¥8 million a year.
- 彼の俸給は年俸だ．　He is paid by the year.
- 年俸制　an annual「salary [wage] system
- 年俸制契約社員　an employee contracted under an annual salary system
- 手取り　① take-home pay　② take-home wages　③ spendable earnings
- 手取り年収　① one's「annual [yearly] take-home pay　② an annual [a yearly] take-home income《of …》
- 手取りで毎月50万ぐらいあればいいなあ．　I wish my take-home pay were around ¥500,000 a month.
- この仕事は税を引いて手取り月30万円になります．　This job「brings [fetches] me ¥300,000 per month after taxes.
- 月に手取り20万ではやっていけない．
  ① I can't make it on a net income of ¥200,000 a month.
  ② I can't survive taking home only ¥200,000 a month.
- 会計上の収益　(an) accounting profit
- 税務上の所得　① (a) taxable income　② (an) income for taxation purposes
- 税務と会計上の規則の違い　differences between tax and accounting rules
- 広告(料)収入　① advertising revenue(s)　② advertising income

- 保険料収入　①revenues from insurance premiums　②premium income
- ライセンス (料) 収入　licensing revenue(s)
- 高所得者　①a high-[large-]income earner　②a person in a high income bracket　③people with large incomes　④people in the higher income brackets
- 高所得者層　①a high income bracket　②a high-income group
- 高所得者層向けの　up-market
- 低所得国　a low-income「country [nation]
- 低所得者　①a low(er)-income earner　②a person with a low income
- 低所得者層　people in low income brackets
- 低所得者層向けの　down-market

関連項目 ⇨第2部・こうぎょうしゅうにゅう

40-5-3　支出

- 支出　①(an) expenditure　②(a) disbursement　③(an) outgo　④outgoings　⑤expenses　⑥(an) outlay
- 今月は出費が多かった．
  ①I've had a lot of expenses this month.
  ②I've spent a lot this month.
- 出費を抑える [切り詰める]　①cut down (on) [reduce,《文》curtail] expenses　②keep expenditure(s) down　③slash expenditure(s)
- その計画は巨額の**出費**を伴う [必要とする]．　The project「entails [requires] vast **expenditure**.
- 物価騰貴で**出費**はかさむばかりだ．　Owing to rising prices, our **expenses** keep「mounting [going up].
- そのほうが出費も少ないだろう．　That would be less expensive.
- 機関による30億円の年間支出を認める　authorize an annual expenditure by the agency of three billion yen
- 政府の負担は年額300万円だ．　The cost to the government is three million yen a year.
- 家賃9万円は彼の給料から支払われた．　The rent of ninety thousand yen was paid out of his salary.

40-6　日常的な各種表現

40-6-1　基本

- これはいくらですか．　How much is this?
- コーヒーは1杯220円です．　The coffee is ¥220 a cup.

40. 料金・価格・収支 40-6-2

- このTシャツは2枚で1000円です． These T-shirts are two for ¥1,000.
  ★TWO FOR $1（2個で1ドル）などは店頭表示でもよく見かける表現．
- その本を5000円で売った． I sold the book for ¥5,000.
- 1つ100円で売る sell「at [for]」one hundred yen「each [apiece]」
- 1ダース300円で買う buy《flowers》at ¥300 a dozen
- この自動券売機は2000円札は使えない． This ticket-vending machine does not take ¥2,000 bills.
- そのプロジェクトは10億円かかった． The project cost a billion yen.
- それで僕は1000円節約できる．
  ① That way I could save ¥1,000.
  ② That would save me a thousand yen.
- 牛肉を3000円分買う buy three thousand yen worth of beef

40-6-2 支払いに関係する表現

- お勘定お願いします．
  ①〔客が店員に〕The「bill [check]」, please.
  ② Could we have the「bill [check]」?
  ③〔店員が担当者に〕Could you get the bill ready?
  ④ The customer would like his bill.
- 1280円になります． ① That'll be 1280 yen. ② That comes to 1280 yen.
- 《食堂などで》二人一緒にお願いします．
  ① The same「bill [check]」, please.
  ② We'd like to pay together, please.
- 別々にお願いします．
  ① Separate「bills [checks]」, please.
  ② We'd like to pay separately.
- 割り勘でいこう．
  ① Let's split the bill.
  ②《口》Let's split the tab.
  ③《口》Let's go Dutch.
★ split the bill, split the tabは勘定を等分するが，go Dutch（名詞のDutch treatも）だと各自が自分の分を払うという意味になる．
- 勘定は私が払った．
  ① I paid (the bill).
  ②《口》I footed the bill.
  ③《口》I picked up the tab.
- 私に払わせてください． Let me pay the bill.
- 勘定は私のほうにつけておいてください．
  ① Charge the bill to me, please.
  ② Charge it to my account.
  ③ Put it on my「bill [account, check]」.

- 勘定は会社持ちになっている．
  ① My company will pay the bill.
  ② The account will be settled by the company.
- お勘定は月末で結構です．　You can「pay [settle up]」at the end of the month.
- 〔海外で〕この店は円が使えます．
  ① They accept yen at this shop.
  ② 〔掲示〕Yen accepted here.
- 円で払う　pay in yen

40-6-3 小銭

- 小銭　① change ② small change ③ loose change ④ loose money ⑤ loose cash
- 小銭で3000円ある．　I have three thousand yen「in (small) change [in coins]」.
- 小銭で払う　① pay with small change ② pay in coins
- 小銭をためて寄付する　save up small coins and make a donation
- 今小銭がない．　① I don't have any (small) change. ② I have no loose change.
- 小銭を切らす　① run out of (small) change ② do not have any (loose) change left
- 千円札をくずす　break [change] a ¥1,000 bill (into smaller money)
- この1万円札をくずしていただけませんか．　Would you (be able to)「break [change]」this ¥10,000 bill for me?
- これを20ドル札2枚と10ドル札6枚にしてください．　Could you change this to two twenties and six tens, please?
- 両替お断わり．〔掲示〕We cannot make change at this store. ★たとえば We do not exchange money. とすると「外貨両替は行なっておりません」の意味になってしまう．

40-6-4 おつり

- おつり　change
- 20円のおつりになります．　① Your change is twenty yen. ② That comes to twenty yen change.
- おつりに300円受け取った．　I「received [got]」300 yen (in) change.
- おつりは取っておいてください．　① Keep the change. ② You can keep the change. ③ Never mind the change.
- おつりが違うようなんですが．　I think you gave me the wrong change.
- 《小額紙幣がないので》50ドル札でおつりをいただけますか．　Can you give me change for a 50-dollar bill?

40. 料金・価格・収支 40-6-4

- つり銭のいらないようにお願いします．〔掲示〕Exact「change [fare] only, please.
- つり銭を数えて渡す　count out the change

> **トリビア　つり銭の渡し方**
>
> 英米では最初からおつりの額を計算して渡すのではなく，客が出した金額に等しくなるように順次おつりを渡す．たとえば2ドル44セントの商品を買って10ドル札を出した場合，2ドル44セントにおつりを足していって10ドルにするように考える．まず6セントを渡し（$2.44 + $0.06 = $2.50），次に50セントを渡し（$2.50 + $0.50 = $3.00），それから1ドル札2枚と5ドル札1枚を渡せば面倒な引き算なしに7ドル56セントのおつりを渡すことができる．そのとき，店員はおつりを渡しながら That'll be two-fifty, three, four, five, and ten. などと言う．

41. 英文会計

■ 41-1 用語

41-1-1 財務諸表

- 財務諸表　financial statements　★次の4つが代表的.
- 貸借対照表　a balance sheet
- 損益計算書　①an income statement　②a profit and loss statement　③a profit and loss account
- キャッシュフロー計算書　①a statement of cash flows　②a cash flow statement
- 利益剰余金計算書　a statement of retained earnings

41-1-2 貸借対照表

貸借対照表 (balance sheet) は左側に「資産」，右側に「負債」と「純資産」を表示する．以前は右側は「負債と資本」という分け方がされていたが，2005年の企業会計基準第5号「貸借対照表の純資産の部の表示に関する会計基準」で資産・負債以外のものは純資産とされた．このためかつては株主資本，自己資本，純資産は同義に使われていたが，狭義の株主資本と広義の純資産が異なるものと明確に規定された．自己資本は株主資本のほかに評価・換算差額等を含み，純資産はさらに新株予約権と非支配株主持分を含む．

- 借方　debit
- 貸方　credit
- 連結貸借対照表　a consolidated balance sheet
- **資産　assets**　★貸借対照表の左側
- 流動資産　total current assets
- 現金 [現預金]　cash
- 有価証券 [市場性のある有価証券]　marketable securities
- 売掛金 [売掛債権]　accounts receivable
- 未収収益　accrued revenue
- 棚卸資産　inventories
- 受取手形　notes receivable
- 貸倒引当金　allowance for doubtful accounts
- 消耗品　supplies

- 前払い費用　prepaid expenses
- 固定資産［非流動資産］　① noncurrent assets　② capital assets　③ fixed assets
- 有形固定資産　① (tangible) fixed assets　② property, plant, and equipment《略 PP&E》
- 無形（固定）資産　intangible (fixed) assets
- 投資有価証券　investments
- 特許権　patents
- 商標権　trademarks
- 営業権　goodwill
- **負債**　**liabilities**　★純資産とともに貸借対照表の右側
- 流動負債計　current liabilities
- 買入債務［買掛金］　accounts payable
- 支払手形　notes payable
- 未払費用　accrued expenses
- 短期借入金　short-term loans payable
- 非流動負債計　noncurrent liabilities
- 長期債務　long-term debt
- 社債　bonds payable
- **純資産**　**net assets**　★貸借対照表の右側．資産と負債の差に相当．
- 株主資本　① stockholders' equity　② shareholders' equity
- 資本金　① capital　②《米》capital stock
- 資本剰余金　(a) capital surplus
- 資本準備金　a capital reserve
- 利益剰余金　① earned surplus　② retained earnings
- 評価・換算差額等　valuation and translation adjustments
- その他有価証券評価差額金　valuation difference on (available-for-sale) securities
- 繰延ヘッジ損益　deferred gain(s) or loss(es) on hedges
- 土地再評価差額金　revaluation difference on land
- 為替換算調整勘定　a「foreign［currency］exchange adjustment account
- 新株予約権　subscription rights to shares
- 非支配株主持分［少数株主持分］〔子会社の資本のうち親会社に帰属しない部分〕　minority interests
- 自己資本　owned capital
- 払込資本　paid-in capital

- 配当　dividends
- 留保剰余金［留保利益］　retained earnings

41-1-3 損益計算書

- 連結損益計算書　a consolidated income statement
- 売上高［販売収益］　sales revenue
- 売上原価　cost of goods sold
- 粗利益［売上総利益］　①gross margin ②gross profit ★売上高－売上原価
- 営業経費　①operating expenses ②〔販管費〕selling, general, and administrative expenses《略 SG&A expenses》
- 販売費　①selling expenses ②sales expenses ③sales costs
- 広告費　advertising expenses
- 人件費　salaries
- 一般管理費　general and administrative expenses
- 家賃　rent
- 光熱費　utilities
- 減価償却　depreciation
- 営業利益　①operating income ②operating profit ★粗利益－営業経費
- 営業外利益　①nonoperating income ②other「income［gains］
- 営業外費用　①nonoperating expenses ②other expenses
- 経常利益　①ordinary income ②recurring income
- 特別利益　①extraordinary gains ②extraordinary income
- 特別損失　extraordinary losses
- 税引前（純）利益　(net) income before tax
- 税　taxes
- 純利益　net income

41-1-4 キャッシュフロー計算書

- 連結キャッシュフロー計算書　a consolidated cash flow statement
- 営業活動からのキャッシュフロー　①cash flow from operating activities ②operating cash flow《略 OCF》
- 投資活動からのキャッシュフロー　①cash flow from investing activities ②investing cash flow《略 ICF》
- 財務活動からのキャッシュフロー　①cash flow from financing activities ②financing cash flow《略 FCF》

41-1-5 収益性指標

- 売上高総利益率　① gross profit margin　② gross profit to net sales ratio
- 売上高営業利益率　① operating (profit) margin　② operating income to net sales ratio
- 売上高経常利益率　① ordinary (profit) margin　② ordinary income to net sales ratio
- 売上高純利益率　① net profit margin　② net income to net sales ratio
- 総資産利益率　return on assets《略 ROA》★純利益÷総資産
- 自己資本利益率［株主資本利益率］　return on equity《略 ROE》★純利益÷自己資本
- 資本利益率［投資収益率］　return on investment《略 ROI》★純利益÷投資資本
- キャッシュフローマージン　cash flow margin　★売上高営業利益率のキャッシュフロー版
- フリーキャッシュフロー　free cash flow《略 FCF》★経常的に必要な出費を引いたキャッシュフロー

41-1-6 安全性指標

- 自己資本比率　① capital adequacy ratio　② capital ratio　③ equity ratio　④ net worth ratio　★自己資本÷総資産
- 流動比率　① current ratio　② working capital ratio　★流動資産÷流動負債
- 当座比率　① acid test ratio　② quick ratio　③ liquidity ratio　★当座資産÷流動負債
- インタレストカバレッジレシオ　interest coverage ratio　★利益÷支払い利子額
- 負債比率［負債・自己資本比率］　① debt-to-equity ratio　② debt to net worth ratio

41-1-7 効率性指標・その他

- 総資産回転率　asset turnover　★売上高÷総資産
- 固定資産回転率　fixed asset turnover　★売上高÷固定資産
- 棚卸資産回転率　inventory turnover (ratio)　★売上原価÷棚卸資産額
- 在庫回転期間　average inventory investment period　★棚卸資産額÷1日当たりの売上原価
- 売上債権回転期間　① average collection period　② collection ratio　★売掛金÷1日当たりの売上

■ 41-2 決算の表現

41-2-1 決算報告の各種表現

- 決算　① settlement of accounts　② closing accounts　③ account settlement　④ (financial) results
- 決算する　① settle accounts　② balance accounts　③ square accounts　④ balance the books　⑤ close the books
- 2017年の通期決算を公表する　① publish full-year 2017 results　② publish 2017 full-year results　③〔「年度」と明示する場合〕publish financial results for the full fiscal year 2017
- 第2期決算を報告する　report second-quarter results

以下のように,英語では「決算」に対応する語を言わずに「利益」「損失」「報告」などを使って表現することも多い.

- B 社の第1期**決算**は赤字になる見込みである.　B Corp. is expected to report a loss for the first quarter.
- B 社の**決算**は5%の増益だった.
  ① B Corp.'s「profit [earnings]」rose 5 percent.
  ② B Corp. reported a 5% rise in profit.
- B 社の**決算**は大幅な減益だった.
  ① B Corp.'s profit dropped sharply.
  ② B Corp. reported sharply lower earnings.
- B 社の 2016 年**決算**は赤字だった.　B Corp. reported loss for 2016.
- B 社の**決算**は取引終了後に発表された.
  ① B Corp.'s report was released after the markets closed.
  ② B Corp.'s results were「reported [announced]」after the markets closed.
  ③ B Corp. reported its results after the close of trading.
- 上方修正　① (an) upward revision　② (an) upward adjustment　③ (a) revision upward(s)
- 収益予測を下方修正する　① revise an earnings forecast downward　② make a downward revision「of [in]」an earnings forecast　③ lower an earnings forecast
- P 社は 2018 年についての収益予測を従来の 700 億円から 800 億円に上方修正した.
  ① P Corp. raised its earnings「forecast [estimate]」for 2018 to ¥80 billion「from [versus]」its previous estimate of ¥70 billion.
  ② P Corp. projected earnings of ¥80 billion for 2018, up from its prior estimate of ¥70 billion.
- **増収増益**　① an increase in both income and profit(s)　② an increase in revenue and (an increase in) profit(s)　③ rising income and (rising) profit(s)
- **増収減益**　① an increase in revenue and a decrease in profit(s)　② rising

income and falling profit(s)
- **減収増益**　a decrease in income but a growth in profit(s)
- **減収減益**　① a decrease in both income and profit(s)　② a decrease in income and (a decrease in) profit(s)
- 2期連続の**増収増益**　an increase in both income and profits for two successive periods
- 約6割の企業が**増収増益**となった．　About 60 percent of the companies reported growth in both revenue and profits.
- 生産を抑制し，コストを削減することで**減収増益**となった．《The company》 increased its profits despite a drop in revenues by decreasing production and cutting costs.
- 2015年度は売上高で約3％，営業利益で約20％の**減収減益**となった．《The company》 reported a 3-percent「dip［decrease］in sales and a 20-percent fall in operating profit for the fiscal year 2015.

41-2-2　**用語**

- 中間決算　① an interim (budget) result　② a midterm settlement of accounts　③ interim closing
- 暫定決算　preliminary results
- 最終決算　final results
- 半期決算　a half-yearly settlement
- 連結決算　① consolidated accounts　② consolidated results　③ group accounts
- 決算期　① a term for the settlement of accounts　② a settlement term
- 決算日　① a settlement date　② a closing date
- 決算報告　a statement of accounts
- 決算報告をする　report on closing accounts
- 決算書　① a statement of accounts　② a balance statement
- 決算修正　① restatement of accounts　② restatement of results　③ restatement of earnings　④ earnings restatement

42. 大きさ・重さ

■ 42-1 長さ

⇨第2部・ながさ，きょり

- 長さ5メートルのケーブル　① a cable five meters long　② a five-meter-long cable　③ a cable of five meters
- 長さ5メートル，幅1メートルの布　① a cloth 5 meters long and 1 meter wide　② a cloth with a length of 5 meters and a width of 1 meter
- 256メートルの長さである　① be 256 meters long　② measure 256 meters (in length)
- このぐらいの長さの棒　① a stick about this long　② a stick (of) about this length
- 長さはどのぐらいですか．　① How long is it?　② What length is it?　③ What is its length?
- 長さは同じ（くらい）だ．
  ① They are (of) (about) the same length.
  ② They have (about) the same length.
- 縦方向の長さ　① (a) longitudinal length　②〔軸方向〕(an) axial length
- 移動方向の長さ　(a) length in the direction of「travel [movement]」
- 全長　① the total length　② the full length　③ the overall length
- (船が)全長約250メートルである　① be about 250 meters from stem to stern　② have「a total [an overall]」length of about 250 meters
- その道路の総延長は108,681マイルだ．　The total route mileage is 108,681.
- 5センチばかり長すぎる．
  ① It is about five centimeters too long.
  ② It is too long by about five centimeters.
- 3センチ長くする　lengthen … (by) three centimeters

■ 42-2 幅

- 幅　① width　② breadth
- 机の幅　the width of a desk
- 線の幅　the breadth of a line
- 幅は10メートルある．
  ① It is ten meters「wide [across]」.
  ② It is ten meters in width.
  ③ It has a width of ten meters.
- それは長さ20メートル幅15メートルだ．

① It is 20 meters long「by [and] 15 wide.
② It is 15 by 20 meters.
- 幅が足りない　① be not wide enough　② have insufficient breadth
- 幅の広い　① wide　② broad　★wide と broad は同義に使うことも多いが，wide が単に端から端までの距離が大きいことをいうのに対し，broad はゆとりに着目するニュアンスがある．
- 幅の狭い　narrow
- この川の幅はどれぐらいあるか．　How wide is this river?
- その道路の幅はどれくらいですか．　What is the width of the road?

■ 42-3　奥行き

- 奥行き　depth
- 幅 20 m，奥行き 8 m の舞台　a stage 20 meters wide and 8 meters deep
- その家は間口が 20 m，奥行きが 15 m だ．
  ① The house is 20 meters wide and 15 meters deep.
  ② The house has a frontage of 20 meters and a depth of 15 meters.
  ③ The house has a frontage of 20 meters and extends back 15 meters.
- 奥行き 100 メートルの地所　a plot of land 100 meters (long) from front to back
- この食器棚は横幅は狭いが奥行きがあるので結構はいる．　This cupboard is not very wide but it is deep enough to hold quite a bit.
- 奥行きの深い食器棚　a deep cupboard
- 奥行きのない食器棚　a shallow cupboard
- 奥行きの深い棚板　a「broad [wide, deep] shelf
- 奥行きの浅い棚板　a narrow shelf
- 両眼による奥行きの知覚　binocular depth perception

■ 42-4　深さ

- 深さ　depth
- そのプールは深さが 2 メートルある．　The pool is two meters「deep [in depth]．
- 足首までの深さである　be ankle-deep
- 深さ 2 メートルの溝　①a ditch two meters deep　②a two-meter-deep ditch
- 機雷は 50 メートルの深さで爆発した．　The mine exploded at a depth of 50 meters.
- 10 メートルの深さで水圧はどれくらいになりますか．　What is the water pressure at (a depth of) 10 meters?
- 深さ 20 メートルまで潜る　dive to a depth of 20 meters

- この池の深さはどれくらいですか.　How deep is this pond?
- 地下50メートルのところに　at 50 meters「underground [below ground]」
- 水面下50メートルのところに　at 50 meters「under the surface [under water]」
- 積雪は80センチに達した.
  ① Snow fell to a depth of eighty centimeters.
  ② The snow「was [lay]」eighty centimeters deep.
  ③ We had a snowfall of eighty centimeters.

■ 42-5 高さ

形ある物を「高い」というのはa「high [tall]」building, a「high [tall]」tree のように high, tall のどちらも使えるが，high は空間内における頂点の高さに，tall は地上などの基準面から続いている長さに重きをおく表現である．また，tall は縦が普通より長いという含みがある．また，人の背が高いのには tall を使う．基準面から離れたところまでの距離をいうときは high を使う（例：a high ceiling 高い天井).「高さ」についてはいずれも height が普通．［⇨第2部・たかさ，こうど【高度】，かいばつ］

- 高さ　①〔高いこと〕height　② tallness　③〔垂直方向の長さ〕(a) height　④〔高度〕(an) altitude　⑤ (an) elevation　⑥ a level
- 東京タワーの高さは333メートルだ．　Tokyo Tower is 333 meters「high [tall]」.
- あの山は高さが200メートルほどしかない．
  ① The hill is only about 200 meters high.
  ② The hill has a height of only about 200 meters.
- 高さ30メートルの煙突　① a chimney 30 meters tall　② a 30-meter(-tall) chimney
- 縦横20センチ，高さ30センチの箱　a box 20 by 20 cm at the base and 30 cm deep
- この部屋は天井までの高さが5メートルもある．
  ① The ceiling in this room is a full five meters high.
  ② The ceiling has a height of a full five meters.
- 地上2メートルぐらいの高さに　(at a height of) about two meters above the ground
- 10メートルの高さから飛び降りる　jump from a height of 10 meters
- 高さ5メートルの飛び込み台　① a five-meter-high diving board　② a diving board five meters「high [in height]」
- 当機はただ今シベリア上空1万メートルの高さを時速1000キロで飛行中です．　This aircraft is now flying over Siberia at an altitude of 10,000 meters at a speed of 1,000 kilometers per hour.

42. 大きさ・重さ 42-6

- 高さの順に並べる　arrange … in order of height
- 山の高さを計る　measure the height of a mountain
- そのビルは世界一の高さを誇る．
  ① The building boasts the greatest height in the world.
  ② The building boasts of being the world's tallest.
- いくつかの建物が市内一の高さを競っている．　Several buildings are vying to be the tallest in the city.
- 1年分の書類をすべて積み上げれば，その高さは富士山に匹敵する．　A year's documents, if piled on top of each other, would reach「the height of [as high as] Mt. Fuji.
- 高さ制限　〔陸橋の下などを通る車に対する〕a height limit
- 高さ制限2メートル　〔表示〕Clearance: 2 Meters
- 建築の高さ制限　a height limit for construction

■ 42-6　縦・横・高さ

42-6-1　二次元

- それは長さ20 m，幅15 m だ．
  ① It is 20 meters long「by [and] 15 wide.
  ② It is 15 by 20 meters.
- 縦2 m，横1 m の板
  ① a board (measuring) two meters by one (meter)
  ② a board two meters long and one (meter) broad
  ③〔立てて使う場合〕a board two meters「tall [high] and one (meter) wide
- 縦5 cm，横3 cm のカード　① a card 3 by 5 centimeters (in size)　② a 3-by-5-centimeter card
- 幅20 m，奥行き8 m の舞台　a stage 20 meters wide and 8 meters deep
- その家は間口が20 m，奥行きが15 m だ．
  ① The house is 20 meters wide and 15 meters deep.
  ② The house has a frontage of 20 meters and a depth of 15 meters.
  ③ The house has a frontage of 20 meters and extends back 15 meters.

42-6-2　三次元

- 縦20 cm，横30 cm，深さ15 cm の箱　① a box 20 cm long, 30 cm wide, and 15 cm deep
- 縦30 cm，横20 cm，高さ10 cm のブロック　a block 30 by 20 by 10 centimeters (in size)
- その箱の大きさは縦60 cm，横50 cm，高さ40 cm だった．　The box「was [measured] 60 centimeters long, 50 across, and 40 high.
- そのコンテナの大きさは幅2m, 高さ3m, 長さ6m である．

① The container measures 2 meters wide by 3 meters high by 6 meters long.
② The dimensions of the container are 2 (W) by 3 (H) by 6 (L) meters.
③ The container is 2 meters in width, 3 meters in height, and 6 meters in length.

■ 42-7 厚さ

- 厚さ　thickness
- 厚さ5mmである　① be 5 mm thick　② be 5 mm in thickness　③ have a thickness of 5 mm
- 厚さ20cmの壁　① a wall 20 cm thick　② a wall 20 cm in thickness
- 厚さはいくらありますか.
  ① How thick is it?
  ② What is its thickness?
- チーズを厚さ1センチに切る　① cut the cheese into one-centimeter-thick slices　② cut the cheese into slices one centimeter thick

■ 42-8 面積

- 面積　(an) area
- 面積が60平方メートルある　① be 60 square meters in area　② measure 60 square meters
- フロリダは面積が約14万平方キロの半島だ.　Florida is a peninsula with an area of about 140,000 square kilometers.
- アイスランドの面積は日本の約1/4だ.　The land area of Iceland is about a quarter that of Japan.
- 東京ドーム7つ分の広さ　seven times the area of Tokyo Dome
- その台形の面積を求めよ.　Find [Work out, Calculate] the area of the trapezoid.
- この土地の面積はどれくらいですか.　What is the area of this land?
- 側面積　lateral area
- 底面積　base area
- 円錐の底面積　the base area of a cone
- 床面積　① floor area　② floor space
- 面積要素　a surface element

広さ

- 庭の広さ　the size of the garden
- 広い　① large　② big　③ extensive　④ spacious　⑤ broad　⑥ 〔空間が〕open　⑦ commodious 《room》　⑧ roomy 《house》
- 広い部屋　① a large room　② a big room　③ a spacious room

- そのホールの広さはどのくらいですか. How big is the hall?
- 狭い ① small ②〔窮屈な〕cramped ③ tiny ④ close ⑤ tight
- 狭い部屋 a small room

■ 42-9 体積・容積

- 体積 volume
- 半径 r の球の体積は $(4/3)\pi r^3$ である. The volume of a sphere of radius r is $(4/3)\pi r^3$. ★式の部分は four thirds pi r cubed または four thirds times pi times r cubed などと読む. [⇨ 58-6 体積の公式]
- 容積 capacity
- 瓶の容積 the capacity of a bottle [⇨ 第2部・…いり]
- チャンバーの容積を量る measure the volume of a chamber
- このボトルは2リットルはいる. This bottle holds two liters.
- 1999年に世界で消費されたビールの量は東京ドーム約107杯分である. The amount of beer consumed around the world in 1999 was enough to fill Tokyo Dome roughly 107 times.

■ 42-10 重さと質量

日常語としては重さ・重量・質量は区別なく用いられるが，科学では物体の絶対的な量を表わすのは質量であり，重さ・重量は物体に及ぼされる重力をいう．したがって，宇宙空間では重さがなくなるが，質量は変わらない．質量の単位はキログラムなどでよいが，重さ・重量の単位は厳密にはニュートン，キログラム重などである．

- 重さ (a) weight
- 質量 (a) mass
- 10トンの岩 ① a rock weighing 10 tons ② a rock of 10 tons (in weight) ③ a rock 10 tons in weight ④ a 10-ton rock
- 5万トンの水 fifty thousand tons of water ★重さを使って水の量を表わしている．
- 重さが3キロある ① weigh 3 kilograms ② be 3 kilograms in weight ③ have a weight of 3 kilograms
- 4 kg の質量をもつ have a mass of 4 kg
- 1日当たり200ミリグラムのDHAサプリメントを摂取する take 200 milligrams per day of DHA supplement
- いろいろな魚を週に300グラム食べなさい. Eat 300 grams a week of a variety of fish.
- 重さが同じで大きさの違うボール balls that「weigh the same [have the same weight]」but「are (of) different sizes [differ in size]」

- はかりで重さを量る　① weigh … on a scale　② weigh … on a weighing machine
- 水1リットルの重さはいくらですか.
  ① What is the weight of a liter of water?
  ② How much does a liter of water weigh?
- (旅客機の)チェックイン時に預けられる荷物の重さは1人当たり20キロまでです.　Checked [Check-in] baggage should not exceed 20 kg (in weight) per person.
- 月では物体の重さは6分の1になる.　On the Moon, objects weigh one-sixth what they would on Earth.
- 送料は重さが10キロを超える場合，1キロにつき100円高くなります.
  ① If the weight exceeds 10 kg, the freight increases by ¥100 per kilogram.
  ② The transportation fee goes up by ¥100 for every kilogram「over [above] 10 kilograms.
- 肉を重さで売る　sell meat by (the) weight

43. 身体計測

43-1 身長

- 身長　① height　②《文》stature　③〔競泳〕a length
- 彼女は身長 168 センチだ.
  ① She is 168 centimeters (tall [in height]).
  ② She is one point six eight meters tall.
- 彼は身長 5 フィート 6 インチだ.　★英米では身長の単位にはフィート, インチを使うことが多い (⇨ 28. 伝統単位).
  ① He is five feet six inches (tall [in height]).
  ② He is five「foot [feet] six.　★数詞のあとでは複数形として feet, foot のどちらも用いられる.
  ③ He is five-six.　★口頭ではこのように数字のみをいうことが多い.
- 赤ん坊は身長 50 センチ, 体重 3800 グラムあった.　The baby was 50 centimeters long and weighed 3800 grams.
- 身長を測る　① take [measure]《a person's》height　② see [measure] how tall《a person》is
- 身長はいくらありますか.　How tall are you?
- 身長順に　in order of height
- 身長不足である　be under height
- 身長が増す[伸びる]　① get [become, grow] taller　② put on height　③《文》grow [increase] in stature
- 〔競泳〕2 身長…をリードする　be two lengths ahead of …
- 5 身長…に遅れてゴールインする　finish five lengths behind …
- 馬身　a horse's length
- 半馬身　a half length
- 3 馬身　three lengths
- 1 馬身の差で勝つ　win by a (horse's) length
- 半馬身の差で勝つ　win by a half

43-2 体重

- 体重　① *one's* weight　② *one's* body weight
- 体重が 60 キロある　weigh 60 kilograms
- ▶ 人の体重の単位としてはアメリカでは pound (約 454 g), イギリスでは stone (= 14 pounds ≒ 6.356 kg) がよく用いられる. stone の複数形は stone または stones. stone より細かい単位を表わすには 12 1/2 stone または 12 stone (and) 7 pounds (記号 12 st. 7 lbs.) などという (⇨ 28.

伝統単位 28-3).

- 身長 180 センチ体重 90 キロの男　a man 180 centimeters tall (and) weighing 90 kilograms
- 体重はどのぐらいですか.
  ① How much do you weigh?
  ② What is your weight?
- 体重を量る　①〔自分で〕weigh *one*self　②〔人に量ってもらう〕have *one's* weight「checked [measured]　③ have *one*self weighed
- 身長と体重のバランス　a balance between height and weight
- 出生時の体重　*one's* weight at birth
- 理想的な体重　*one's* ideal weight
- 体重オーバーである　be over a weight limit
- 体重制限に引っかかる　be unable to meet a weight limit

▶ **増減**

- 体重が増える　① put on weight　② gain weight
- 体重が 2 キロ増える　gain two kilograms
- 体重が減る　〈人が主語〉lose weight
- 体重が 2 キロ減る [体重を 2 キロ減らす]　lose two kilograms
- 体重の減少　〔個体の〕weight loss
- 体重の低下　〔集団の〕a「fall [drop] in《average》weight
- 90 キロあった体重が 70 キロを切った.　I went from 90 kilo(gram)s to under 70.
- 体重が 60 キロで変わらない.　My weight doesn't「move [change, budge, deviate] from 60 kilo(gram)s.
- 体重を減らす [落とす]　① lose weight　② reduce [lower] *one's* weight　③ shed weight　④ get「slimmer [trimmer]　⑤《口》〔減食などによって〕reduce　⑥ get *one's* weight down
- 私は 1 か月で 5 キロやせるという目標を立てた.　I set a「target [goal] of losing 5 kg in a month.
- 体重が 60 キロを超えないようにする　keep *one's* weight below 60 kg

▶ **その他**

- この恐竜はアフリカ象 10 頭分の体重があったと推定される.　This dinosaur is estimated to have weighed as much as ten African elephants.
- アリは自分の体重の何倍もあるえさを軽々と運ぶ.　An ant can easily carry food (that weighs) many times its own weight.
- 20 代の体重を維持する　maintain the weight *one* had in *one's* twenties

43-3 胸囲

- 胸囲　① *one's* chest measurement　② the measurement around the chest
- 胸囲が大きい　① be big around the chest　② have a big chest measurement
- 胸囲が小さい　① be small around the chest　② have a small chest measurement
- 胸囲が90センチある．　He measures 90 centimeters around the chest.
- 胸囲をはかる　① take 《his》 chest measurement　② measure (the girth of) 《his》 chest
- 胸囲はいくつですか．
  ① What's your chest measurement?
  ② How much [What] do you measure around the chest?
- バスト　① *one's* bust measurement　② the measurement around the bust
- バストが85センチある．
  ① Her bust measurement is 85 centimeters.
  ② Her bust measures 85 centimeters.
  ③ She has an 85-centimeter bust.
- アンダーバスト　an underbust measurement
- トップバスト　① an overbust measurement　② a full bust measurement

43-4 ウエスト

- ウエスト [胴囲, 胴回り]　① *one's* waist measurement　② the measurement around the waist　③ waist size　④ 〔ウエスト周囲径〕waist circumference
  ★メタボリックシンドロームの指標の「胴囲」はへそのところで測るもので，「ウエスト周囲径」「腹囲」ともいう．ファッションなどでいう「ウエスト」はそれより少し上の最も細い部分を指す．
- 腹囲　① (the) girth of the abdomen　② ventral girth　③ abdominal girth
  ★メタボリックシンドロームの指標としては上記「胴囲」を参照．
- 彼女のウエストは56センチだ．
  ① Her waist measures 56 centimeters around.
  ② She measures 56 centimeters around the waist.
  ③ Her waist measurement is 56 centimeters.
- ウエストの太い [細い] 人　a person with a「large [small, slim, slender] waist
- ウエストのゆったりとしたパンツ　slacks loose「around [at] the waist
- 若いころにはいていたジーンズは今ではウエストが合わなくなった．
  Jeans that I wore when I was young don't fit me around the waist anymore.
- ウエストを合わせると股下が足りない．　Those that fit me around the waist aren't long enough in the legs.
- 彼女はあと2cmウエストを絞れば理想の体型になると言っている．　She

says if she「can take [takes] two more centimeters off her「waistline [waist] she'll have the ideal figure.
- スラックスのウエストを絞ってもらう　have the waist of 《my》 slacks taken in 《three centimeters》
- ウエストの位置が高い　have a high waistline
- ウエストのサイズは？［ウエストはおいくつくらいになりますか．］　What's your waist size?

43-5 ヒップ

- ヒップ　① *one's* hip measurement ② the measurement around the hips
- ヒップを測る　measure the circumference of 《her》 hips

43-6 スリーサイズ

- 彼女のスリーサイズは 88, 60, 90 だ．
  ① Her「vital statistics [measurements] are 88 cm, 60 cm, and 90 cm.
  ② She measures 88-60-90.
  ③ Her bust measures 88, her waist 60, and her hips 90 centimeters.
- **スリーサイズ**はいくつですか．　What are your「measurements [vital statistics]?

43-7 股下

- 股下　①〔ズボンの筒の内側の，股から裾までの丈〕an inseam ②〔人の〕an inside leg measurement ③ *one's* inside leg
- 股下 80 センチのズボン　① trousers with an inside leg (measurement) of 80 cm ② trousers with an inseam (measurement) of 80 cm

43-8 指を表わす番号

手の指はそれぞれ固有の名前のほか，「第 4 指」のように数字で呼ぶこともあるが，数え方には 2 通りある．

親指　thumb　★通常 finger とは言わない．
人差し指　① forefinger ② first finger ③ second finger
中指　① middle finger ② second finger ③ third finger
薬指　① ring finger ② third finger ③ fourth finger
小指　① little finger ② fourth finger ③ fifth finger

ピアノなど鍵盤楽器の楽譜では親指を「1」と表示するが，ギター，バイオリンなど，普通親指を使わない楽器の楽譜では「1」は人差し指を指す．会話でも，third finger はピアニストどうしでは中指を，バイオリニストどうしでは薬指を指す．ある英英辞書が forefinger を first finger

43. 身体計測 43-8

と，ring finger を fourth finger と矛盾的に定義しているように，この 2 通りの数え方に気が付いていない英米人もいる．

足指では「第 1 指」は常に親指であり，次のようになる．
親指　①big toe　②first toe　★thumb とは言わない
人差し指　second toe　★first toe とは言わない
中指　①middle toe　②third toe
薬指　fourth toe
小指　①little toe　②fifth toe

関連項目⇨第 2 部・たいおん，けつあつ，しりょく

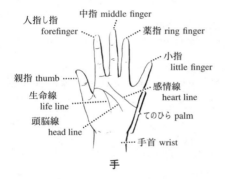

手

44. 服のサイズ

■ 44-1 靴のサイズ

世界の靴のサイズ表示は次のようにさまざまな相違点がある．

・単位…cm, mm のほかヨーロッパでは 2/3 cm (Paris point という), 英米では 1/3 インチ (barleycorn という) の単位が使われる．

・原点…英米ではある最小の長さを基準 (= 0) にしてそれよりどのくらい長いかで表示する．

・測定対象…足長を表示する方式と靴の木型 (last という) を表示する方式がある．木型は足長よりも通例 1.5〜2 cm 程度長い．日本は足長を使うが，英米・ヨーロッパでは木型長の表示が主流．

・形状…足長が同じでも幅などが異なることがある．JIS では足長ごとに，足幅，足囲 (足の甲を取り巻く長さ) に応じて細いほうから順に A, B, C, D, E, EE, EEE, EEEE, F, G を定めている．

44-1-1 日本

cm で測った足長を表示する．1983 年に規格が JIS S5037 に一本化されたときに，木型ではなく足長表示が決められた．

44-1-2 ISO9407

mm で測った足長を表示する．韓国も mm 表示を使っているが，日本よりも 1 cm ほど大きい数字が表示されると言われる．

44-1-3 ヨーロッパ

サイズのきざみ 1 は 2/3 cm に相当する．足長でなく木型長の表示なので，2/3 をかけたのちに 1 cm 程度差し引いたものが日本のサイズになる．

44-1-4 イギリス

サイズのきざみ 1 は 1/3 インチ (約 8.5 mm) に相当し，木型長を表示する．大人の場合，8 1/3 インチ (約 21 cm) を最小サイズ (= 0) としてそれを超える長さで表示する．子供用のサイズは 4 インチを最小サイズ (= 0) として表示し，子供サイズの 13 が大人サイズの 0 に一致するようになっている．

たとえば日本でいう足長 25 cm の場合，木型長が 27 cm とすると，21

cm を引いたものをインチに直して 3 倍することでイギリスサイズは 7 と求まる．この計算は $(x+2-21) \times 1.2 = 1.2(x-20) + 1.2$ を行なったことになるが（$3/2.54 ≒ 1.2$ 倍），木型長との対応でどうせ幅があるので，単純に「20 を引いて 1.5 を足す」程度の概算が行なわれることもある．

44-1-5 アメリカ

イギリス同様のシステムで，子供用のサイズ 1, 2, …, 13 に続いて大人用のサイズ 1, 2, … があることも同様だが，以下のような相違がある．

・最小サイズ（= 0）がイギリス式より 1/12 インチ（サイズでいうと 1/4）短い．よってイギリス式のサイズ表示に 1/2（1/4 のサイズはないので）を足したものがアメリカ式になる．ただし，実感としては + 1 の換算がよく使われる．

・女性用のサイズが男性用と異なる．女性用のサイズは同じ大きさの男性用サイズ表示に 1.5（慣用サイズ）または 1.0（FIA サイズ；FIA は Footwear Industries of America の略［現 AAFA］）を加えたものになる．一般には前者が使われる．

44-1-6 関連表現

- スニーカーは22センチから27センチまで**サイズ**がございます．　We have sneakers in **sizes** running from 22 to 27 centimeters.
- この靴は**ハーフサイズ**はありません．　These shoes don't come in **half sizes**.
- 君の靴のサイズは？［靴のサイズはおいくつですか．］
  ① What size shoes do you wear?
  ② What size do you take in shoes?

■ 44-2 ブラジャーのサイズ

ブラジャーのサイズを決めるのはベルトの長さ（アンダーバスト）とカップの大きさである．

44-2-1 日本

カップサイズはトップバストとアンダーバストの差で決まり，2.5 cm きざみでアルファベットで表示される．

AAA (5 cm), AA (7.5 cm), A (10 cm), B (12.5 cm), C (15 cm), D (17.5 cm), E (20 cm), F (22.5 cm), G (25 cm), H (27.5 cm), I (30 cm)

これにアンダーバスト (cm) を付記して A65, C70 などと表示される．

44-2-2 英米

英米ではブラジャーのサイズは 32C のようにベルト長（band size），カップサイズの順に表示される．

ベルト長はインチで測ったアンダーバストに 5 を加え，適当に丸めて偶数にしたものである．5 を加えるのは胴回りがアンダーバスト位置よりもブラジャーを装着する位置では大きくなることの補正である．

カップサイズはトップバストからこのベルト長を引いた差をもとに AA, A, B, C, D, DD, E, ... と表示される．具体的には，その差が 0.5 インチまでは AA，1 インチまでは A，2 インチまでは B，3 インチまでは C などとなる．

アメリカでは上記の差が 0.5 インチまでは AA，1.5 インチまでは A，2.5 インチまでは B などとすることもある．また，D より先の大きなカップについては表示が統一されておらず，DD の次に DDD を設けるなどさまざまである．ヨーロッパでは DD も使わず D の次が E となるのが普通．

■ 44-3 婦人服のサイズ

44-3-1 日本

しばしば標準的と言われる 9 号サイズはバスト 83 cm，ウエスト 64 cm，ヒップ 91 cm という体形として JIS（JIS L4005:1997）で定められている．他の号数はたとえば次のとおり設定されている（バストは 15 号までは 3 cm きざみだがそれから先は 4 cm きざみになる；ウエストは規格ではなく 20 代の参考値）．

サイズ	バスト	ウエスト	ヒップ
7 号	80	61	89
9 号	83	64	91
11 号	86	67	93
13 号	89	70	95
15 号	92	73	97
17 号	96	76	99

これは A 体型と呼ばれるいわゆる標準体型の場合であって，ウエストが 4 cm 大きい AB 体型，8 cm 大きい B 体型，標準より 4 cm 小さい Y 体型もある．さらに身長についても標準とされる R (regular)，長身とさ

れる T (tall)，標準より低い P (petite) が設定されている．いわゆる9号というのは9ARということになるが，JISにはこだわらずに独自表示をするメーカーも多い．

44-3-2 欧米

イギリスでは 8, 10, 12, 14 という偶数のサイズ表示が使われており，12号（ほぼバスト 88 cm，ウエスト 72 cm，ヒップ 96 cm）が標準といわれている．

アメリカも同じような偶数表示だが，1980 年代以降，店頭に並ぶ製品で同じサイズ表示の服の寸法が急速に大きくなり，規格は有名無実化している．1950 年代の 12 号が現在の 4 ないし 6 号と同じ大きさになっている．このような現象は size inflation（サイズ・インフレーション）または vanity sizing（体面向けサイズ表示）と呼ばれる．この根底にはアメリカ人の肥満傾向があるものと言われている．また，アメリカでは標準体型と言われる Misses のほか，低身長の Petite（平均的な日本人に合うサイズ），Women（ふくよかタイプ）などさまざまに区分されている．

ヨーロッパ大陸では 36, 38, 40, 44, ... といった表示が一般的だが，イギリスの 12 号サイズがフランスでは 40，ドイツでは 38，イタリアでは 44 など国によってまちまちである．婦人服に限らず統一的なサイズ表示として EN13402 シリーズの規格（EN は Euro Norm の略で欧州規格の意）が策定されたが普及には至っていない．

44-3-3 関連表現

- **9号**のドレス　a **size-9** dress
- このドレスのラベルは**9号**になっている．
  ① This dress is labeled **size 9**.
  ② The label says this dress is a **size 9**. ★a size 9 で「9号の服」の意．
- 自分の**号数**を知りたい．　I want to know **what size** I am.
- **8号**の人　① a person of **size 8**　② a **size 8** person　③ a **size 8**
- 私は普段**9号**を着ている．　I usually wear **a size 9**.
- 私は**8号**が着られる．　① I can wear **a size 8**. ② I can fit in **a size 8**. ③ I can fit into **a size 8**. ④ **A size 8** fits me.
- **1号分**やせる　drop one size　★drop は体重を落とすという感じの表現．
- セーターは普通 **M** を着ています．　I usually wear **a medium** in sweaters.
- サイズは **M** がよろしいですか．　Would **medium size** suit you?
- 私の**サイズ**はどれだろう．　I wonder what my **size** is.

44. 服のサイズ 44-3-3

- **サイズ**を計る　take 《a person's》 **size**
- サイズが合う［合わない］　① the size「fits［doesn't fit］　②《this shirt》「fits［doesn't fit］　③《this shirt》「fits［doesn't fit］《me》
- サイズが合うかどうか試着する　try 《it》 on for size
- このコート，**もっと小さい［大きい］サイズは**ありますか．　Do you have this coat **in a**「**smaller**［**larger**］**size**?
- フリーサイズ　one size fits all
- そのシャツはフリーサイズだ．
  ① The shirt is one-size-fits-all.
  ② One size of this shirt fits everyone.
- 一つ大きいサイズを買う　buy one size larger
- 袖を2センチほど詰める　take in the sleeves a couple of centimeters

45. 温度・気象・地震

■ 45-1 温度

45-1-1 温度の単位

- **セ氏 [摂氏]**　① Celsius《記号 C》　② centigrade《記号 C》　★科学技術文書では Celsius を用いるが，日常的には centigrade が使われることが多い．
- **カ氏 [華氏]**　Fahrenheit《記号 F》　★⇨ 28. 伝統単位 28-7
- **セ氏 8 度**　eight degrees「Celsius [centigrade]《記号 8°C》
- **カ氏 72 度**　72 degrees Fahrenheit《記号 72°F》
- **マイナス [プラス] 3 度**　three degrees「below [above] zero
- **セ氏 10 度はカ氏 50 度だ．**　Ten degrees centigrade is fifty degrees Fahrenheit.
- **セ氏で表わした温度**　① temperature in degrees Celsius　② Celsius temperature
- **セ氏目盛**　① the Celsius scale　② the centigrade scale
- **絶対温度**　absolute temperature
- **絶対零度**　absolute zero［⇨第 2 部・ぜったいれいど］
- **ケルビン温度目盛**　the Kelvin temperature scale
- **ケルビン (で表わした) 温度**　① Kelvin temperature　② temperature in Kelvin　③ temperature in kelvins
- **77 ケルビン**　77 kelvins　★かつては Fahrenheit などと同じように 77 degrees Kelvin の形で使っていたが，1967 年に degree は付けず，記号も °K ではなく K とすることになった．しかし，かつての名残りか複数形にせず 77 kelvin と書くこともしばしばある．文書では 77 K が普通．

45-1-2 温度の表現

- **屋内の温度はセ氏 18 度です．**
  ① The temperature「indoors [inside] is 18°C.　★ 18°C は eighteen degrees Celsius と読む．
  ② The indoor temperature is 18°C.
- **寒暖計は氷点下 5 度を示していた．**　① The thermometer showed 5 degrees below「freezing [zero].　② The mercury stood at 5 degrees below「freezing [zero].
- **セ氏 4 度の水**　water at 4°C
- **冷凍庫の中の温度は何度ですか．**　**What's the temperature** inside a freezer?
- **室温はセ氏で今何度ですか．**　**What is the room temperature** in (degrees)

45. 温度・気象・地震 45-1-2

「Celsius [centigrade]」?
- 水の沸点はカ氏で**何度**ですか．
  ① **What** is the boiling point of water in Fahrenheit?
  ② **At how many degrees** Fahrenheit does water boil?
- その金属は何度で溶けますか． **At what temperature** does the metal melt?
- 温度が60度にも**達した**． The temperature **reached** as high as 60°C.
- **35 K で超伝導になる**　become superconducting **at 35 K**
- **90°C までの温度に耐える**　withstand temperatures **up to 90°C**
- 10,000 K のオーダーの温度　a temperature **of the order** 10,000 K
- 数十 K 以上の温度では　at temperatures above a few tens of kelvins
- 水が沸騰する温度　the temperature at which water boils
- 融点よりわずかに低い温度　(a) temperature slightly below the melting point
- 室温で　at room temperature
- 液体窒素温度で　at liquid nitrogen temperature
- 鉄の bcc 構造はセ氏約 910 度で fcc に変わり，セ氏約 1400 度で再び bcc に戻る． The bcc form of iron changes to fcc at about 910 degrees Celsius and reverts to bcc again at about 1400 degrees Celsius.
- (十分に) 低温では　at (sufficiently) low temperatures
- ごく低温にまで冷却された検出器　detectors cooled to very low temperatures
- 高温によって起こる電離　ionization caused by high temperatures
- この反応は，**あらゆる温度において**自発的に起こる． This reaction is spontaneous **at all temperatures**.
- 2つの接点は**異なる温度である**． The two junctions **are at different temperatures**.
- 温度の上昇 [低下]　a「rise [fall, drop] in temperature
- 1 パーセントの温度上昇　one percent increase in temperature
- 温度が上がる． The temperature「rises [goes up, climbs].
- 温度が下がる． The temperature「falls [goes down].
- 温度を上げる　raise the temperature
- 温度を下げる　lower the temperature
- 温度の激変　a sudden [an extreme, a violent] change in (the) temperature
- 温度を調節する　adjust [control, regulate] the 《room》 temperature
- …を一定温度に保つ　keep … at a constant temperature
- 温度がちょうどいい． The temperature is just right.
- **設定温度**　〔エアコンなどの〕the temperature setting

- 冷房の温度を 26 度に設定する　set the air conditioning temperature at 26 degrees
- 推奨設定温度は 28℃ だ．　The recommended temperature setting is 28℃.
- エアコンの設定温度を **2 度上げる**
  ① **raise** the temperature setting of the air conditioner (**by**) **two degrees**
  ② **raise** the thermostat setting on the air conditioner (**by**) **two degrees**
  ③ **turn** the air conditioner's thermostat **up** (**by**) **two degrees**
- エアコンの設定温度を **1 度上げる**ごとに冷房費を数パーセント節約できる．　**For every degree you raise** the thermostat setting on your air conditioner, you can cut your cooling costs by several percent.
- 気体の溶質に対しては溶解度は**温度とともに減少する**．　Solubility **decreases with temperature** for gaseous solutes.
- 冷却速度は物体と環境との**温度差**に比例する．　The cooling rate is proportional to **the temperature difference** between the substance and its environment.
- 温度には関係ない　be independent of temperature
- **体感温度**　sensible temperature
- **表面温度**　surface temperature
- **温度管理[制御]**　temperature control
- **温度係数**　a temperature coefficient
- **温度勾配**　a temperature gradient
- **温度分布**　a temperature distribution

45-1-3　気温

- **気温**　(atmospheric) temperature
-〔天気概況で〕気温 16 度．　The temperature is sixteen degrees (Celsius).
- 氷点下 10 度　① ten degrees below zero ② ten degrees below「freezing [the freezing point] ③ ten degrees of frost
- 気温が 30 度に**上昇した**．　The「temperature [mercury] **rose [went up, climbed]** to 30℃.
- 気温が 30 度を**超した**．　The「temperature [mercury] **went [climbed] above** thirty.
- ここでは日中の気温はしばしば 40 度を**超える**．　The daytime temperatures here often **exceed** 40℃.
- 気温がセ氏 10 度に**低下した**．　The「temperature [mercury] **went down [fell, dropped]** to ten degrees Celsius.
- 昼になっても気温が 0 度を**下回ったままだった**．　Even the daytime temperature **stayed below zero**.
- 明日気温は少し**下がる**見込みである．　Tomorrow the temperature is expect-

ed to「**fall** slightly [**be** slightly **lower**].
- 今日は大変暖かく，3月下旬ごろの気温です．　It's very warm today, on a level with average temperatures for late March.
- **最高気温**　① the maximum temperature　②〔天気予報で〕today's high
- 昨日の最高気温は何度でしたか．　What was the high (temperature) yesterday?
- **最低気温**　① the minimum temperature　②〔天気予報で〕today's low
- 最低気温が零度を割った．　The low temperature fell below zero.

★ 1日の最低気温は lowest などといわずに単に the low temperature または the low というのが普通．

45-1-4 体温

- 体温が39度2分ある．
  ① My temperature is 39.2 degrees (Celsius).
  ② I have a temperature of 39.2 degrees (Celsius).
  ③ I have a fever of 39.2 degrees (Celsius).

★ 39.2 は thirty-nine point two と読む（⇨ 52. 小数）．

- 昨夜は(熱が)何度ありましたか．　What was your temperature last night?
- 体温を計る　take *one's* temperature
- 体温が高い[低い]　have a「high [low] temperature
- 体温が平熱よりやや高い[低い]．　My temperature is a little「above [below] normal.
- 体温が平熱まで上がった[下がった]．　His temperature has「risen [fallen] to normal.
- 体温が36度5分に下がった．　His temperature「went down [dropped] to 36.5.
- 外気温に応じて体温が変化する動物[変温動物]　① animals whose body temperatures vary with the atmospheric temperature　② cold-blooded animals
- 体温を一定に保つ生理機能　the physiological function of maintaining a stable body temperature
- 低体温(症)　hypothermia
- 体温計　a (clinical) thermometer
- 脇の下に体温計をはさむ　place a thermometer in *one's* armpit
- 体温計をくわえる　put [keep] a thermometer「under *one's* tongue [in *one's* mouth]
- 体温計を振って水銀を下げた．　He shook the thermometer to lower the mercury.
- **体温**でチョコレートが溶けてしまった．

① The chocolate melted **with the heat of my body**.
② **My body heat** melted the chocolate.
★英語はチョコレートを溶かすのは「温度」ではなく「熱」であることを反映した表現になっている.

■ 45-2 気圧

- **気圧** ① atmospheric pressure ② air pressure
- 昨日の気圧は 980hPa を示した.　The barometer「registered [stood at] 980 hectopascals yesterday. ★hPa（ヘクトパスカル）は気圧の SI 単位.
- 中心気圧 940hPa の台風　a typhoon with a central pressure of 940 hectopascals.
- 高度が増すと気圧は低下する.　The atmospheric pressure decreases「with altitude [with height, as you go higher].
- **標準気圧**　the standard pressure
- **気圧傾度**　a pressure gradient
- **気圧の尾根 [峰]**　a (pressure) ridge
- **気圧の谷**　a (low pressure) trough
- **気圧配置**　a pressure pattern
- **高気圧**　① high「atmospheric [air] pressure　②〔領域〕a high pressure area　③ a high pressure system　④ a high
- **低気圧**　① low「atmospheric [air] pressure　②〔領域〕a low pressure area　③ a low pressure system　④ a low

■ 45-3 湿度

- **湿度**　humidity
- **高い [低い] 湿度**　high [low] humidity
- 今日は湿度がとても高い.　It is very「humid [damp] today.
- 湿度は現在 80% です.　The humidity is 80 (percent) now.
- **絶対湿度**　absolute humidity
- **相対湿度**　relative humidity
- その部屋の湿度はどのくらいですか.
  ① How high is the humidity in the room?
  ② What is the room's humidity?
  ③ How humid is the room?

■ 45-4 降水・積雪

- **雨量**　① (an amount of) rainfall　② (an amount of) rain
- **時間雨量**　① the hourly rainfall　② the hourly precipitation

45. 温度・気象・地震 45-5

- 積算［累積，総］雨量　the total rainfall 《over [during] a 24-hour period》
- 年間雨量　an annual rainfall 《of about 1,000 millimeters》
- 予想雨量　an expected amount of rainfall
- 昨日の雨量は 30 ミリであった．　We had thirty millimeters of rain yesterday.
- 降り始めからの総雨量が 900 ミリに達した．　The total rainfall 「was [came to] 900 millimeters.
- 1 時間に 110 ミリという記録的な雨量を観測した．　A record rainfall of 110 millimeters an hour was recorded.
- 屋久島は年間を通じて雨量が多い．　Yakushima has a lot of rainfall throughout the year.
- **降水量**　〔雨のほか雪なども含めて〕(a quantity [an amount] of) precipitation
- 月間降水量　monthly precipitation
- この地域の年間降水量はわずか 200 ミリだ．　Annual precipitation in this region is only 200 mm.
- **積雪**は 80 センチに達した．　① Snow fell to a depth of eighty centimeters. ② The snow 「was [lay] eighty centimeters deep. ③ We had a snowfall of eighty centimeters. ④ Eighty centimeters of snow fell.
- 雪が 10 センチ積もっている．　The snow lies ten centimeters deep.
- 地面には雪がまだ 1 メートルも積もっていた．　There was still one meter of snow (remaining) on the ground.
- **降水確率**　① a probability of precipitation　② a chance of 「precipitation [rain, rainfall]　③ a likelihood of rain　④ a precipitation percentage
- 今夜の降水確率は 30 パーセントです．
  ① The chance of rain tonight is 30 percent.
  ② There is a 30 percent 「likelihood [probability, chance] of 「rain [precipitation, rainfall] tonight.

■ 45-5 風速

- **風速**　① wind speed　② wind velocity
- 最大風速 40 メートルの台風　① a typhoon with a maximum wind 「speed [velocity] of 40 meters per second　② a typhoon with (sustained) winds of 40 m/s
- ▶ 日本では風速は秒速 (m/s) で測るが，海外では kt（ノット），mph（マイル毎時），km/h（キロメートル毎時）もよく使われる．1 m/s＝3.6 km/h≒2.2 mph≒1.9 kt である．
- ▶ 日本も含め国際的には風速は 10 分間の平均値をとるが，アメリカでは 1 分間の平均値とする．このためアメリカの測定値のほうが大

きな値が出やすい．いずれにせよこのように平均として定義した風速を sustained wind speed という．

- 現在の風速は3メートルです． The wind is blowing (at) three meters per second.
- 風速30メートルに達した． The wind has attained a velocity of 30 meters per second.
- **瞬間最大風速**　① the maximum「instantaneous [momentary] wind「speed [velocity] ② the maximum wind gust　★英語では「突風」の意の gust を使って後者のようにいうことが多い．
- **風速計**　① an anemometer ② a wind gauge

■ 45-6 震度とマグニチュード

45-6-1 震度

- **震度**　seismic intensity
▶ 震度は日本独自の表示法であり，seismic intensity「according to [on] the Japanese scale of 0 to 7 のように説明するとよい．震度5と震度6は1996年以来「5弱」「5強」「6弱」「6強」に細分され，全部で10段階となっている．
- **震度4**　(seismic intensity of) 4 on the Japanese scale
- **震度5弱**　(seismic intensity of)「5-weak [5-minus, 5-lower] on the Japanese scale
- **震度5強**　(seismic intensity of)「5-strong [5-plus, 5-upper] on the Japanese scale
- **震度4の地震**　① an earthquake registering 4 on the Japanese scale ② an earthquake measuring 4 on the Japanese scale ③ an earthquake with an intensity of 4 on the Japanese scale ④ an earthquake of intensity 4 on the Japanese scale ⑤ an intensity-4 (earth)quake ⑥ an earthquake of 4 on the Japanese scale ⑦ a 4 on the Japanese scale

★ an earthquake registering a 4 on the Japanese scale のように数値に不定冠詞をつけることがあるが，これは読者が震度になじみのない表示法の数値であることを含意している．また，⑦のように「震度4の地震」を略式に a four ということもある．

- 新潟では**震度3**だった． In Niigata, the earthquake「**measured [registered, was] 3 on the Japanese scale**.
▶ 地震はかつては震度ごとに次のような呼び方がされていた（英語は参考訳）．

| 0 | 無感 (imperceptible) | 2 | 軽震 (light) |
| 1 | 微震 (slight) | 3 | 弱震 (weak) |

4	中震 (moderate)	6	烈震 (severe)
5	強震 (strong)	7	激震 (disastrous)

1996年10月の震度階級改訂で震度5と震度6が強と弱に2分された際にこれらの呼び方は廃止されたが，今でも英字新聞などでは a moderately strong earthquake（震度5弱の地震），a very strong earthquake（震度5強の地震），a moderately severe earthquake（震度6弱の地震），a very severe earthquake（震度6強の地震）のような表現を使うことがある．

▶ なお，震度（震度階級）は震度計により測定される計測震度を丸めて整数値にしたもの．かつては体感や周囲への影響から人が決めていたが，1996年4月に測定方法が震度計に基づく方式に変更された．

▶ それぞれの震度の揺れ具合の目安の一例は次のとおり．

震度0： 人間には感じられない．

震度1： 屋内にいる一部の人が感じる．

震度2： 屋内にいる多くの人が感じる．吊り下げた電灯などが揺れる．

震度3： 屋内にいるほとんどの人が感じる．重ねた皿などが音を立てる．

震度4： 眠っていても目を覚ますほどで，恐怖感があり，机の下にはいるなど身の安全を図る人も出る．自動車を運転していても気づくことがある．

震度5弱： 多くの人が身の安全を図る．歩くのにも支障を感じる人も出る．棚のものが落ちる．

震度5強： 歩くのにも支障が出る．棚のものの多くが落ちる．家具が倒れることもある．

震度6弱： 立っているのも困難．多くの家具が移動・転倒する．耐震性の低い木造住宅では倒壊するものもある．

震度6強： 立っていることもできない．ほとんどの家具が移動・転倒する．多くの窓ガラス・壁面タイルが破損・落下する．耐震性の低い鉄筋コンクリートのビルには倒壊するものもある．

震度7： 家具が飛ぶこともある．耐震性の高い建物でも傾いたり，大きく破壊されるものもある．

▶ 他の震度表示の一つにI〜XIIの12階級に分けるメルカリ震度階級（Mercalli intensity scale）がある．

45. 温度・気象・地震 45-6-2

> **トリビア** 地震を知らない人々
>
> 　英米ではアメリカの西海岸などを別にすれば地震がほとんどないので，英米人には大人になっても地震を経験したことのない人が多い．来日中に初めて地震を経験したりすると，ちょっとした地震でもたいへん驚くのも無理はない．
>
> 　地震はその土地の建築構造にも関わってくる．明治時代の日本では耐火性にすぐれた欧米式のれんが造りや石造りの建築が取り入れられたが，1891年の濃尾地震でそうした建物に大きな被害が出たことで耐震性が考慮されるようになった．

45-6-2　マグニチュード

- M6［マグニチュード6］の地震　a magnitude 6 earthquake　★「マグニチュード6」を「M6」と書くのは英語では日本語ほど一般的でない．

- その地震は**マグニチュード6**だった．
  ① The quake **was 6 on the Richter scale**.
  ② The quake **measured 6 on the Richter scale**.
  ③ The quake **registered (a magnitude of) 6 on the Richter scale**.

★ Richter scale は「リクター・スケール」と読み，地震波の振幅を初期微動継続時間（震源までの距離に関係）により一定距離に換算する地震規模尺度を考案した米国の地震学者 Charles F. Richter に由来する．

45-6-3　耐震強度

- そのビルは**震度5強の地震で倒壊する**かもしれない．
  ① The building might **collapse if struck by an earthquake of 5-strong on the Japanese scale**.
  ② The building is susceptible to **collapse in an earthquake of intensity 5-strong**.

- このビルは**震度7にも耐えられる**よう設計されています．　This building is designed to **withstand earthquakes of intensity 7 on the Japanese scale**.

- そのマンションは**必要な耐震強度**［基準］の7割しかない［**耐震強度**が0.7だ］．
  ① That condominium has only 70 percent of **the required strength to withstand earthquakes**.
  ② That condominium's 「**strength [seismic resistance]**」stands at only 70 percent of the standard.
  ③ That condominium has 「**a strength rating [seismic resistance]**」of 0.7.
  ④ That condominium is rated at 0.7 in **seismic resistance**.

46. 住所と電話番号

■ 46-1 住所

欧米では 36 Craven St.（クレーヴン通り 36 番地）のように通りの名と番地を組み合わせて住所を表示する．また，番地，通り，都市，州など小さい単位から順に記される点で日本とは逆になっている．日本の住所を欧米式に表記するとたとえば次のようになる．

- 東京都千代田区富士見 2 丁目 11 番 3 号
  ① 11-3, 2-chome, Fujimi, Chiyoda-ku, Tokyo
  ② 2-11-3, Fujimi, Chiyoda Ward, Tokyo
  ③ Fujimi 2-11-3, Chiyoda-ku, Tokyo
- ★ 2-11-3 のハイフンは dash と読む．

ニューヨーク市では南北方向の通りを Avenue，東西方向の通りを Street という．

- Fifth Avenue　五番街《略 5th Ave.》
- 34th Street　34 丁目《略 34th St.》
- 1st Avenue at 46th Street［46th Street and 1st Avenue, 1st Avenue and 46th Street］　一番街 46 丁目
- 131 East 10th Street［131 E. 10th Street］　10 丁目東 131 番地　★ Street に面した地番は五番街を境に東と西に分かれ，五番街から離れるほど番地が大きくなる．

■ 46-2 郵便番号

- **郵便番号**　①《米》the「zip［ZIP］code　②《英》the postcode　③ the postal code　★ zip［ZIP］は zone improvement program に由来．
- 7 桁の数字の郵便番号　a seven-digit zip code

トリビア　テレビドラマ「90210」

テレビドラマに関する文章でいきなり 90210 という数字が出てくることがある．実はこれは Beverly Hills 90210 というアメリカのテレビドラマのことで，日本では「ビバリーヒルズ青春白書」などとして知られている．この 90210 というのがビバリーヒルズの郵便番号である．

> **トリビア**　市外局番と郵便番号の地理的分布
>
> 　日本の市外局番は札幌が011，東京23区が03，大阪が06，鹿児島が099（沖縄は098）と北から南に番号が振られている．（厳密には先頭の0は市外発信用のプレフィックスで，市外局番には含まれない．）郵便番号は皇居のある東京都千代田区に100xxxxがあり，東京から離れるにつれほぼ大きくなっていく．北海道などは0で始まるが，これは0を1の前でなく9の次と考えて割り振っていたためだという．アメリカの郵便番号の地理的分布を見ると，0で始まるのはニューイングランド地方などで，西部に向かって大きくなっていき9で始まるのは西海岸，999はアラスカとなる．
>
> 　イギリスの郵便番号はSW1A 1AAのように英数字の入り交じった形になっている．前半は地域を表わす英字（1～2字）と地区を表わす英数字（「数字」「数字2桁」「数字＋英字」のいずれか）からなる．後半は数字＋英字2字からなり，通りまで，時にはさらに細かく住所を指定できるようになっている．ロンドンの場合，地域を表わす部分は中心部がWC, ECで，あとはN, NW, W, SW, SE, Eがある．

■ 46-3 **住居**

[⇨第2部・…かい【…階】]

- 2号棟の403号室　① Room 403 in Building 2　② Room 403, Building 2　③ Rm. 403, Bldg. 2
- 705号室　① Room 705　② Apartment 705
- **2DK**
  ① (an apartment with) two rooms and「a kitchen with a dining area［《米》an eat-in kitchen, 《英》a dining-room-cum-kitchen］
  ② a two-bedroom apartment with kitchen
- ★DKは和製英語「ダイニングキッチン」の略．②はDを省いて簡潔にいう例．
- **3LDK**　three bedrooms with a living room plus kitchen
- **四畳半**　a four-and-a-half-mat (tatami) room
- **八畳間**　an eight-mat (tatami) room
- あなたの部屋は**何畳**ですか．
  ① **How many mats** does your room have?
  ② **How big** is your room?
- ワンルームマンション　① a one-room apartment　② a one-room condo　③《米》a studio apartment　④《英》a studio flat　⑤《英》a bedsit　⑥ a

- bedsitter ⑦ a bedsitting room
- **一戸建て**　a detached house
- **二世帯住宅**　① a two-family house ② a house for a two-generation family ③ a duplex (house)
- **容積率**　① a floor-area ratio 《略 FAR》 ② the ratio of total floor area to site area
- **建蔽率**　① a building-coverage ratio ② a building-to-land ratio ③ land coverage ④ site coverage
- この敷地の建蔽率は5割です．　The zoning law permits 50-percent building coverage of the lot.

■ 46-4　電話番号

- **電話番号**　① a telephone number ② a phone number
- 電話帳に載っていない**電話番号**　①《米》an unlisted **number** ②《英》an ex-directory **number**
- 電話帳で市役所の**電話番号**を探す［調べる］　look up［check］**the phone number** of the city office in the「telephone directory［《口》phone book］
- **電話番号**を教えてくれればあとで電話するよ．　If you give me your (**phone**) **number**, I'll call you later.
- この**電話番号**は社長室直通です．　This is the direct **phone number** for the president's office.
- **電話番号案内**　① directory assistance ② a directory inquiry service ③《英》directory enquiries
- **電話番号表示機能**　a caller ID function　★caller ID は発信者 ID の意．

46-4-1　電話番号の読み方

03-3288-7711

oh three, three two eight eight, seven seven one one

oh three, three two double eight, double seven double one

▶ 1桁ずつ分けて読むのが基本だが，区分の中に同じ数字があれば eight eight とせずに double を使うことが多い．3288 を three two double eight, 3882 を three double eight two のように読むのである．

▶ oh は zero と読んでもよい．

▶ 日本語ではしばしば「-」を「の」と読むが，英語では電話番号の「-」は読まず，間をとるだけである．

46-4-2 局番

- **局番**　a telephone exchange number
- **市内局番**　① a local exchange number　② a local exchange prefix
- **市外局番**　① an area code　②《英》an STD code　★STD は Subscriber Trunk Dialling（文字通りには「加入者基幹線ダイヤル通話」の意）に由来.
- **国番号**　an international call prefix

46-4-3 海外向けの番号表記

　海外から日本に電話をかけるには日本の国番号 81 を付け，市外局番の最初の 0 は付けない．そこで，海外向けにはたとえば次のように書く．先頭の＋は国際電話のアクセス番号のあとに続けることを示唆している．
　＋81-3-3288-7711
　＋81-(0)3-3288-7711

46-4-4 アメリカの特殊な電話番号

　911…緊急番号（警察・消防・救急）（イギリスでは 999，また EU 諸国共通番号として 112 がある）

　411…電話番号案内　▶ 米俗語では 411（four one one と読む）を「情報」の意味に使い，たとえば for your information の代わりに for your 411 と言うなどする.

　このほか，地域にもよるが 211（健康・生活相談），311（役所），511（交通情報），611（電話故障時の窓口），711（聾唖者支援），811（電話会社の手続き窓口）がある．また局番として次のものがある.

　800…フリーダイヤル（ほかに 888，877，866 なども追加されたがまとめて 800 numbers という）

　900…有料情報番号

トリビア　映画に出てくる電話番号

　日本のドラマや映画では電話番号の全部の桁は出さないよう配慮することが多いが，アメリカ映画を見ているとせりふや画面で完全な電話番号が示されることがよくある．実はそうしたシーンはたいてい 555-2368 のように市内局番が 555 になっている．これは 555 が実際の電話番号に割り当てられていなかったためで，フィクションのほか電話番号の記入例などでもよく使われる．1994 年からは 555 の市内局番にも電話番号の割り当てが行なわれるようになった

が，555-0100 から 555-0199 まではフィクションでの使用のために残されている．555 は普通に five five five と読む．

46-4-5 電話の関連表現

- もしもし． ① Hello! ②〔相手の声が途絶えたとき〕Are you there?
- もしもし，小川さんですか． Hello! Is「this [that] Ms. Ogawa?
- ファクスは何番ですか． What is your fax number?
- 何番におかけですか． What number are you trying to reach?
- 番号を間違ったらしい． I must have dialed the wrong number.
- 間違い電話ですよ． I think you must have the wrong number.
- 急いで受話器を取ったが間違い電話だった． I rushed to pick the phone up, but it was a wrong number.
- 私の番号 123-4567 に電話してください． Please call me at 123-4567.
- 内線 105 で呼び出してください． Please call me「at [on] extension 105.
- 内線 105 をお願いします． ① Give me extension 105, please. ② Put me through to extension 105, please. ③ Extension 105, please.

トリビア 電話とテンキーの配列の違い [⇨次ページ・イラスト]

電話では 1, 2, 3 のキーが上にあるが，電卓やパソコンのテンキーでは 1, 2, 3 がいちばん下にある．プッシュホン電話とテンキー式電卓が独立して開発されたため，早いうちからそれぞれの慣習が固定し，今では電話は ITU-T，電卓は ISO で規格化されている．電卓についてはよく使う 0, 1 が手前にあるほうが使いやすいための配列と言われている．電話については公衆電話のような縦の面にキーを配列するときには 1 を上にするというのは自然な発想だったのだろう．

銀行の ATM では手の動きから暗証番号の入力を読み取られないよう，使うたびに画面上の数字の配列が変わることもある．

46. 住所と電話番号 46-4-5

電卓と電話の数字キー

47. 学校

47-1 学年

- **学年**　① a year　②《米》(小・中・高) a grade　③ 〔修学期間〕a school year
- 1 **学年**に 360 人の生徒がいる．　There are 360 students in each「**grade** [**year**]」．
- **学年**平均　the average score for all (the) students in **a particular**「**year** [**grade**]」
- 私たちのクラスの平均点は**学年**の平均点より高かった．　Our class average was higher than the average for students of **our year as a whole**.
- **学年**が上がるにつれて「はい」の答えが多くなった．〔アンケートで〕More children answered "yes" in higher **grades**.
- 3 年に編入される　① be enrolled in the third year　②《米》(小) be enrolled in the third grade
- 同学年である　① be in the same year《as…》　②《米》(小・中・高) be in the same grade《as …》
- 2 級下［上］である　① be two years「below [above]」《me》　②《米》(小・中・高) be two grades「below [above]」《me》
- 彼とは同じ大学でしたが，私のほうが 2 年下です．　We went to the same university, but I was two years behind him.
- 低学年　① the lower「years [grades]」at school　② the first and second grades「at [of]」elementary school
- 中学年　① the middle「years [grades]」at school　② the third and fourth grades「at [of]」elementary school
- 高学年　① the higher「years [grades]」at school　② the fifth and sixth grades「at [of]」elementary school
- ★ 1～3 年を低学年，4～6 年を高学年と 2 分することもある．
- 2000 年 (卒業) 組　the class of 2000　★主にアメリカの表現．
- 1985 年の本学卒業生　① a graduate of this university in 1985　②《主に米》a member of the (graduating) class of 1985 of this university
- **6-3-3 制**　the 6-3-3 school system

47-2 …年生

- 何年生ですか．
  ① What year are you (in)?
  ②《米》〔小中高生に〕What grade are you (in)?
- 小学 4 年生です．
  ①《米》I am in the fourth grade.

② 《米》I am a fourth grader.
③ 《英》I am in the fourth year (class).
- 僕らはみな中学1年だった．
  ① 《米》We were all in our first year of junior high school.
  ② 《米》We were all seventh graders.　★grade は小学校から通して数える．
  ③ 《英》We were all in our first year at secondary school.

▶ アメリカの教育制度は school district 単位で決まるのが普通で，州や市によって異なる．小学校・中学校・高校にあたる教育は，日本の 6-3-3 制に対して 6-3-3 制，6-2-4 制，8-4 制，6-6 制があり，ほかに 5-3-4 制，4-4-4 制もあるが，12 年間であることはみな同じ．義務教育は日本と同じ 9 年とする州が多い．6-6 制では日本の中学（junior high school）・高校（high school）に当たる学校が high school であり，4-4-4 制や 5-3-4 制などでは真ん中の学校が middle school と呼ばれる．

- 4年制の大学　a four-year college
- 4年制のハイスクール　〔アメリカの8-4制や5-3-4制の地域の〕a four-year high school
- 大学1年生　① 《米》a freshman　② 《英》a first-year student
- 大学2年生　① 《米》a sophomore　② 《英》a second-year student
- 大学3年生　① 《米》a junior　② 《英》a third-year student
- 大学4年生　① 《米》a senior　② 《英》a fourth-year student

▶ 制度の違いのため，日本の「高校…年生」に当たる学年の英語表現は注意を要する（ここでは米国式を扱う）．数字で表わす場合，最終学年が twelfth grader になるのは共通だが，これは 4 年制なら 4 年目，3 年制なら 3 年目となる．3 年制高校の 1 年生は sophomore という場合と freshman という場合がある．

- 高校1年生　① a tenth grader　② 《4年制高校の》a sophomore　③ 《3年制高校の》a「sophomore [freshman]
- 高校2年生　① an eleventh grader　② a junior
- 高校3年生　① a twelfth grader　② a senior

47-3 学級

- 40人学級　a class of forty students
- 1学年8組まである．
  ① There are eight classes in each year.
  ② Each year is divided into eight classes.
- 3年A組　① 3A　② the 3A class

- 2年8組　① class 8, year 2　② the 2-8 class
- 今度はC組になった．　This time I'm in the C class.
▶ アメリカの小学校ではクラスは Mr. Hamilton's class, Ms. Wong's class などのように担任の名前で呼ぶのが普通．
- 5・6年生は3クラスだが4年生以下は2クラスです．　The fifth and sixth graders are divided into three classes each, with two classes for fourth graders and「below [under]．

47-4　学期

- 学期　① a term　② a school term　③ an academic term　④ a session　⑤〔2学期制の〕a semester　⑥〔3学期制の〕《米》a trimester　⑦〔4学期制の〕《米》a quarter　★semester は語源的にはラテン語の sex (6)，mensis (月) がもとになっている．
- 1学期　the first term
- 2学期　the second term
- 3学期　the third term
- 前期　〔2学期制の〕the first semester
- 後期　〔2学期制の〕the second semester
- 3学期制　① a three-term system　② a three-term school year　③《米》a trimester system
- 2学期制　a semester system
- 3学期の期末テストの結果　① the results of the「exam [test] at the end of the third term　② the results of the third-term final exam
- 1学期のまとめをしましょう．　Let's summarize what we've done during the first「term [semester]．
- 期末試験　① an end-of-term「exam [test]　② a final「test [exam]　③ a test [an exam] at the end of a semester

関連項目⇨ 25-6 平均点, 第2部・てん, へんさち, じかん, たんい4

48. 法律・条約

48-1 法令番号

- 著作権法（昭和四十五年法律第四十八号）　① the Copyright Law (Law No. 48 of 1970)　② the Copyright Act (Act No. 48 of 1970)
- 性同一性障害者の性別の取扱いの特例に関する法律（平成十五年法律第百十一号）　the「Law［Act］Concerning Special Cases in Handling Gender for People with Gender Identity Disorder (Law［Act］No. 111 of 2003)

48-2 条項

政府の『法令用語日英標準対訳辞書』（2015年3月改訂版）は日本の法令の外国語訳に使う標準的な訳語として下記を挙げている．

- **編**　Part
- **章**　Chapter
- **節**　Section
- **款**（か ん）　Subsection
- **目**　Division
- **条**　Article《略 Art.》
- **項**　paragraph《略 para.》★見出しとして用いる場合は (1) (2) (3) などとする．
- **号**　item ★見出しとして用いる場合は (i) (ii) (iii) などとする．
- **イロハ**　(a) (b) (c)
- (1) (2) (3)　1. 2. 3.
- (i) (ii) (iii)　i. ii. iii.
- の1, の2, の3　〔枝番〕-1, -2, -3

48-3　article と section

「条」に当たる英語には article のほか section が用いられることもある．
国連憲章や各種条約の「条」は article が多いが，英米の議会法では「条」は section が普通．アメリカ合衆国憲法は全体が Article I～VII に，各 Article が Section に分かれており，Article は「条」，Section は「節」と訳すのが通例だが，日本的な感覚では Article は「章」，Section が「条」に該当する．「修正第 13 条」は Amendment XIII または the Thirteenth Amendment であり，その下に Section（節）がある．

日本の節（section）や款（subsection）はたとえば著作権法にあるが，これは条（article）より大きな区分となっている．条文は通し番号なので引

用の際には節や款を示す必要はない．

アメリカの議会法は章ごとに条文に番号を付けるために番号に飛びがある場合がある．たとえば著作権法の Chapter 1 は Section 101 から始まって Section 122 まであり，次の Chapter 2 は Section 201 から始まる．

48-4 条［節］・項・号

アメリカの法律ではSectionの下は (a) (b) (c) … であり，これは subsection と呼ばれる．その下が (1) (2) (3) … でこれは paragraph [clause] と呼ばれる（文法的に完全に独立しているときがparagraph，主文の一部が (1) (2) (3) … と分けられているときには clause）．その下は (A) (B) (C) となりこれは subparagraph である（合衆国憲法ではSectionの下がparagraph）．その下には (i) (ii) (iii) … がきてこれも clause という．引用するときには subsection (a) of section 123，subparagraph (B) of paragraph (3) のようにもいえるが，単に section 123(a)，paragraph (3)(B) でもよい（上の階層の名称を使うことに注意）．特に階層が深い場合は section 123(a)(3)(B) のように簡潔に表わすことが好ましい．

なお，日本の法律では「第1項」には特に表示はなく，第2項以降に2などと番号が振られているだけであるが，他の条文で言及するときには「第1項」という言い方がされる．

48-5 枝番

法律の改正で「29条」と「30条」の間に新しく条項が追加されると，それは「29条の2」となる（29条第2項とは別物である）．1章がごそっと追加されたりすると「184条の20」などというものも出てくる．英訳の際には単に Article 29-2 などとするのが一般的だが，Article 29 bis などという言い方もある．以下にそのような枝番のラテン語表示（「…回」「…倍」という意味の副詞）を示す．

2	bis	9	novies	16	sexdecies
3	ter	10	decies	17	septdecies
4	quater	11	undecies	18	octodecies
5	quinquies	12	duodecies	19	novodecies
6	sexies	13	terdecies	20	vicies
7	septies	14	quaterdecies	21	unvicies
8	octies	15	quindecies	22	duovicies

「99条の2」と「99条の3」の間に「99条の2の2」があるような場合もある．これも Article 99-2-2 と訳せばいいのだが，ラテン語形を使うとすると Article 99 bis bis と訳せる．法律以外では規格文書で V.32 bis のように使われるが，これは日本語でもそのまま V.32 bis と書くことが多い．

上記の語形は4を過ぎると英語としてはなじみのない形であり，海外の法律でもラテン語ではなく Section 288n だとか Section 53A, Section 53AA といった表記が使われている．

48-6 訳例

- 第10条　① Article 10《略 Art. 10》② 〔米国風〕Section 10《Sect. 10》
- 第29条の2　① Article 29-2　② Article 29 bis
- 第29条第2項　① Article 29, paragraph 2　② Article 29(2)　③ Paragraph [Para.] 2 of Article 29
- 第24条1項1号　① Article 24, paragraph (1), item (i)　② 〔米国風〕Paragraph 1 of Subsection 1 of Section 24　③ Section 24(1)1
- 前条　the preceding article
- 右の条　the above articles
- 第17条の規定に基づく措置　measures pursuant to Art. 17
- 前項に規定する場合において　in the case prescribed in the preceding paragraph
- 前項の規定により　pursuant to the provisions of the preceding paragraph
- 第108条第1項に規定する期間　the period provided for in Article 108(1)
- 前項ただし書に規定する30日の期間　the 30-day period as provided in the proviso to the preceding paragraph
- 第195条の規定により納付すべき手数料　the fees payable under Article 195
- 第37条の規定に違反している［第37条に規定する要件を満たしていない］　① do not comply with Article 37　② do not comply with the requirements of Article 37
- 第17条の2第1項第3号に掲げる場合　in cases referred to in Article 17-2(1)(iii)
- 次の各号に該当する者　a person who falls under any of the following items
- 第67条第2項の政令で定める処分　the disposition designated by the Cabinet Order under Article 67(2)
- 第41条第1項の優先権の主張　a priority claim under Article 41(1)
- 民法958条の期間内に　within the time limit designated in Article 958 of

the Civil Code
- 第126条第5項の規定は前項第2号の場合に準用する． Article 126(5) shall apply mutatis mutandis to cases under item (ii) of the preceding paragraph.
- 第50条（第159条において準用する場合を含む） Article 50 (including the cases where it is applied mutatis mutandis pursuant to Article 159)

49. 野球の数字表現

49-1 回／イニング

- 回 [イニング]　an inning
★ inning は野球では an inning/innings と通常の単複の変化をするが，イギリスのクリケットでは innings の形を単複同形に使う．すなわち，単数形で a long innings のようにいい，複数形も two innings となる（口語ではさらに two inningses の形もある）．

- 7回の**表**に　in **the top** of the seventh inning
- 7回の**裏**に　in **the bottom** of the seventh inning
- その回の裏に　in **the bottom (half)** of the inning
- ジャイアンツは**6回**に点を入れて4対1としたが，**7回**にタイガースは4点上積みして点差を広げた．　The Giants scored to make it 4-1 **in the sixth**, but the Tigers「boosted their lead [pulled away]**in the seventh** with four more runs.
- **5回**まで行ったところで雨がひどくなり，試合は中止になった．
  ① The game had just got to **the fifth inning** when the rain became so heavy that it had to be called off.
  ② The game was rained out at the start of **the fifth inning**.
- 両軍無得点のまま**最終回**を迎えた．　They entered **the last inning** with neither team having scored a run.
- 試合も大詰めで**9回裏**を迎えました．　The game is drawing to「a close [an end] and we are in **the bottom of the ninth inning**.
- **毎回**出塁はしたが，残塁で終わった．
  ① Batters got on base **every inning**, but none of them scored.
  ② Runners were left on base **in every inning** with none scoring.
- ピッチャーは**そのイニング**を無失点で切り抜けた．　The pitcher got through **the inning** without giving up a run.
- 彼は3イニング投げて失点1だった．　He pitched three innings and gave up one run.
- ピッチャーは3回以降現在までの3イニングをパーフェクトに抑えている．
  ① The pitcher has, beginning with the third inning, pitched three innings of perfect baseball.
  ② The pitcher has thrown three perfect innings since the third.
- その救援投手は**3分の2イニング**投げただけで降板した．　The relief pitcher was「taken out of the game [replaced] after pitching only **two-thirds of an inning**.
- **8回**終了時点でコールドゲームとなった．　The game was called at the end of **the eighth inning**.

- ジャガーズはパイレーツに15対0で**7回**コールド勝ちした． The Jaguars defeated the Pirates 15 to 0 in a game called **in the seventh inning**.
- アルファ付きで勝つ　win a game with (part of) the last inning left
- ★最終回の裏で後攻チームの勝ちが決まっていればその時点で試合終了にすること．スコアボードにXと書いたのをαと見誤ったことに由来する日本独自の表現だったが，今ではほとんど使われない．俗に「X(エックス)ゲーム」と表記され，これがさらに「×(バツ)ゲーム」と解されることもある．

49-2 延長

- 試合は延長戦に持ち込まれた．　The game went into extra innings.
- 試合は延長10回に突入した．　The game went into the tenth inning.
- 試合は延長12回まで行った．　The game went twelve innings.
- 試合は延長13回で決着がついた．　The game went four extra innings before being decided.
- 両チームは3対3のまま延長15回で引き分けた．　The teams went into extra innings but the game ended in the 15th with the score still tied at 3 to 3.

49-3 ゲーム差

- ゲーム差　①〔2位以下から見て〕game(s) behind the「leading team [team (immediately) ahead]　② game(s) back　③〔首位から見て〕game(s) ahead 《of the next team》
- 3ゲーム差　three games「behind [back, ahead, apart]
- 開幕早々ジャイアンツは首位に2ゲーム差をつけられている．　Early in the season the Giants are two games behind first place.
- ファイターズは2位に6ゲーム差をつけて首位を独走中だ．　The Fighters are running away with the lead, six games ahead of the second-place team.
- ゲーム差を広げる　widen [increase] one's lead 《over another team》
- マジック(ナンバー)〔優勝マジック〕　a magic number　★米国で使われるmagic numberは日本の「マジックナンバー」とは定義が異なり，点灯（他のチームの勝敗に関わらず首位チームがその数だけ勝てば優勝できる状態）の概念はない．

49-4 点〔⇨ 49-14 打点，第2部・てん〕

- **点**を取る［入れる］　score **a run**
- 7回に3点入れる　score three runs in the seventh inning
- 3点取られる　give「away [up] three runs
- バッファローズを**2点に**抑える　**hold** the Buffaloes **to two runs**
- 彼はジャイアンツを**0点に**抑えた．

49. 野球の数字表現 49-5

① He **held** the Giants **scoreless**.
② He **blanked** the Giants 《2-0》.

- 点は 5 対 1 だ．　① The score is 5 to 1.　② The score stands at 5 to 1.
- 今タイガース何点？
  ① **What**'s the Tigers' **score**?
  ② **How many runs** do the Tigers have?
- 今，何対何？　① Now it's **what to what**?　② **What's the score** now?

49-5 点差

- ブレーブスは 1 回が終わった時点では **4 対 0** でリードしていた．　The Braves were leading **4-0** after the first inning. ★「…対…の得点で」というとき，by (a score of) などを付けずにこのように単に 4-0 のようにいうことが多い．得点 4-0 の読み方は four to nothing, four nothing, four zero, four oh など．
- **8 対 5** とリードする　have [roll up] an「**8 to 5** [**8-5**]」lead
- **2 点リード**で 7 回を迎える　go into the seventh inning with **a two-run lead**
- 巨人は **3 点リード**されたまま最終回を迎えた．　The Giants entered the final inning **three runs**「**behind** [**down**]」．
- 3 対 2 でこっちが勝っています．　We're「ahead [up]」3-2.
- 3 対 2 で向こうが勝っています．　① They're「ahead [up]」3-2.　② We're down 3-2.
- 3 対 2 でホークスが勝っています．
  ① It's 3-2, Hawks.
  ② It's 3-2 in favor of the Hawks.
- 7 回に彼がホームランを打って **3 対 1** にした．
  ① He hit a home run to **make it 3-1** in the seventh.
  ② His home run in the seventh **made it 3-1**.
- 3 対 3 の**同点にする**　① **tie** 《the game》 at three all　② **tie** 《the game》 3-3
  ③ **even the score** at three all
- 1 点あげて同点に追いつく［こぎつける］　score [put in] the tying run
- **得点差**が**開く**［**縮まる**］　the difference in scores「**widens** [**diminishes**]」
- **点差**を 5 対 2 まで広げる　① widen **the lead** to 5-2　② boost **the lead** to 5-2
- そのホームランのあと回を追うにつれて**点差**が開いていった．　After that home run **the gap in the scores** grew with each inning.
- **点差**を縮めて 3 対 2 にする　cut **the deficit** to 3-2　★deficit は負けているときの点差．
- タイガースは **6 点差**をひっくり返してジャイアンツに勝った．　The Tigers turned around **a six-run deficit** and beat the Giants.
- **2 対 1（の得点）**で勝つ　win (a game) **by** (**a score of**) **2 to 1**

282

- 12対0という**大きな得点差**をつけて勝つ　win by the **lopsided** score of 12 to 0
- **3対4**で私たちの勝ち[負け]です． We「won [lost], **three (points) to four**.
- **0対7の大差**で負ける　lose **by the huge margin of zero to seven**
- **5点差**で勝った． We won **by a margin of five runs**.
- **わずかの差**で勝つ　win **by a narrow margin**
- **3対3**の引き分けに終わった．
  ① The game ended in a「tie [draw], **three to three**.
  ② They played to a「**three-all** draw [**three-to-three** tie].
  ③ They drew **3-3**.
- **ダブルスコア**で勝つ　win with **double the score** of the other team
- **ダブルスコア**で負ける　lose with **half the score** of the other team

49-6　打順

- 1番**打者**　the leadoff batter
- 2 [3, etc.] 番打者　the player who bats「second [third, etc.] in the lineup
- 2 [3, etc.] 番を打つ　① bat in the「two [three, etc.] hole　② bat「second [third, etc.] in the lineup
- 4番打者　the cleanup batter
- 4番を打つ　bat cleanup
- **打順**　the batting order
- 次の回は打順よく1番からだ． The top of the batting order will come to the plate in the inning coming up.
- 7回に本塁打2本を含む**打者一巡**の猛攻で我がチームは一気に逆転した． Our team took the lead in the seventh inning when「the whole lineup came to bat [we batted around] in a run-scoring spree that included two home runs.

49-7　カウント

- (ボール) カウント　① the count　② the balls-and-strikes count　③ the count on the batter
- カウントは**ツーボール，ワンストライク**． The (batter's) count is **two balls and one strike**. ★日本では審判のコールも球場の表示も長らくストライク→ボールの順 (SBO式) だったが，最近では英語と同じくボール→ストライクの順 (BSO式) に言う．以前から大リーグ中継ではBSO式も使われ，高校野球では1997年から審判のコールはBSO式になっていたが，2010～2011年ごろからは球場でも放送でもBSO式が一般的になった．中継のアナウンサーは誤解のないよう「ツーワン」のように略さず「ツーボールワンストライク」「ワンボールノーストライク」のような言い方をすることもある．

- カウントは**スリーワン**［**スリーボール，ワンストライク**］だ．
  ① The count is **three balls, one strike**.
  ② The count is **three and one**.
  ③ The count is **3-1**. ★3-1 は普通 three and one と読むが，three to one と読むこともある．
- カウントは**スリーボールノーストライク**［**ノースリー**］だ．★「ノースリー」は以前の SBO 式の表現．
  ① The count is **three balls and no strikes**.
  ② The count is **three and「nothing[zero]**.
  ③ The count is **3-0**. ★3-0 は three and oh と読む．
- **ツーツー**のカウント　a **two and two** count
- カウントは**ツーナッシング**．〔以前の SBO 式の表現〕The count is **nothing[zero] and two**.
- 彼はカウント **3-0** までいったがゴロに倒れた．　He got ahead (in the count) **3-0** but grounded out.
- 彼はカウント **0-2** まで追い込まれた．　He fell behind **0-2** (in the count).
▶ get ahead は「有利なカウントを得る」，fall behind は「不利なカウントを得る」の意で，次のように投手の観点から使うこともできる．
- 松坂《投手》はイチロー《打者》を **0-2** に追い込んだ．　Matsuzaka got ahead of Ichiro **0-2**.
- 松坂はイチローに **3-0** まで粘られた．
  ① Matsuzaka fell behind against Ichiro **3-0**.
  ② Matsuzaka fell behind **3-0** to Ichiro.
- 彼は**スリーワン**で松坂の球を打ってツーランホームランにした．　He hit a **3-1** pitch from Matsuzaka for a two-run homer.
- **フルカウント**　**a full count** 《of 3 and 2》
- 彼は**フルカウント**まで粘って二塁打を放ち，同点の１点を上げた．　He worked **a full count** and then doubled to tie the score.
- カウントを取りにいく　go for a strike
- **スリーバント**　① a bunt on the third strike　② a bunt with two strikes　③ a two-strike bunt
- **スリーバントする**　① bunt「after[with]」two strikes　② lay down a two-strike bunt
- **スリーバントを決める**［失敗する］　make [miss,《口》blow] a two-strike bunt
- **スリーバント失敗**　a foul bunt on the third strike

49-8 アウト

- **アウト**　① (an) out　② a putout 《略 PO》

- アウトになる ① be put out ② be「thrown [tagged, called, etc.] out ③ go down
- タイガースは**ノーアウト**でランナー二塁,三塁だった.
  ① The Tigers had「men [runners] on second and third **with none out**.
  ② There were Tigers on second and third **with nobody out**.
- **ツーアウト**満塁だった.
  ① The bases were loaded **with two out(s)**.　★文法的には with two outs なら「2つのアウトで」, with two out「2人がアウトになって」の意.
  ② The bases were full **with two gone**.
  ③ There were three runners on base **with two away**.
  ④ The bases were loaded **with two down**.
  ⑤ There were **two**「**out(s)** [**down**] and the bases were loaded.
- **ツーアウト**,ランナーはありません.カウントはスリーワン. There are **two down**, nobody's on base, and the count is three and one.
- まだ**ワンアウト**だ.
  ① It's [There's] still **one out**.
  ② It's [There's] **one away**.
- **ツーアウト**から3点を奪う　collect three runs「on [after] **two outs**
- 9回**ツーアウトまで来ました**.あとアウトひとつで完投勝ちです.　**We've come to the final out** of the game; one more and the pitcher has a complete-game victory.
- **アウトカウント**　① the number of outs ② the number of batters out
- **今何アウト**？　How many outs?

49-9　三振・三者凡退

- **三振**　a strikeout
- 三振する　① strike out ②《口》be fanned ③ fan ④ whiff
- 三振させる　① strike《a batter》out ②《口》fan ③ whiff
- 三振14を奪う　strike out 14
- 三振に倒れる　go down on strikes
- 三振の山を築く　pile up strikeouts
- 7回裏は**三者凡退**に倒れた.
  ① It was three up and three down in the bottom of the seventh (inning).
  ② They went three up and three down in the bottom of the seventh (inning).
- またもや三者凡退に終わった.　It was another three up and three down《for the Dragons》.
- 三者凡退のイニング　① a three up and three down inning ② a 1-2-3 inning
- 三者凡退に打ち取る　① retire the side ② retire the side 1-2-3 ③ pitch a 1-2-3 inning
- 彼はまたもや三者凡退に打ち取った.　He pitched another 1-2-3 inning.

49-10 四球

- 四球　① a base on balls　② a walk
- フォアボールで一塁に出る　① get a base on balls　② get a walk　③ go to first (base) on a walk　④ walk to first (base)　⑤《口》get free ticket to first

49-11 塁

- 本塁　① home plate　② home
- 一［二，三］塁　first [second, third] base　★無冠詞
- ノーアウト，**ランナー一塁**．　They have **a runner on first** with no outs.
- 9回表**二死一塁**で代打が登場した．　With two out(s) and a runner on first in the top of the ninth, a pinch hitter came to「bat [the plate].
- 二塁に達する　① get to second　② reach second
- ランナー，一塁を回って二塁へ向かいます．　The runner has turned first base and is「running to [heading for] second.
- 一［二，三］塁ランナー　a runner on「first [second, third] (base)
- ランナー二塁，三塁で　with runners on second and third
- 一［二，三］塁手　① the「first [second, third] baseman　②《口》the「first [second, third] sacker
- 一塁を守る　play first base
- 一塁へ牽制球を投げる　make a pickoff throw to first base
- 一塁ゴロ　a grounder to first (base)
- 一塁打　① a one-base hit　② a single　③《口》a one-bagger
- 二塁打　① a two-base hit　② a double　③《口》a two-bagger
- 三塁打　① a three-base hit　② a triple　③《口》a three-bagger
- 一塁打を打つ　① hit a single　② single《to left field》
- レフトへ二塁打を打つ　① double to left　② bang out a double to left　③ hit a two-bagger to left
- 中堅深く二塁打を放つ　blast a long double to center
- 右中間に強烈な二塁打を放つ　send a mighty double between center and right
- 三塁打をかっ飛ばす　① swat [slam, bang out] a triple　② triple
- 鈴木はセンターオーバーの三塁打を放った．　Suzuki hit a「triple [three-bagger] over the center fielder's head.
- 彼は 3 塁打では 7 本で 9 位タイだった．　He was tied for ninth in triples with seven.
- **出塁率**　① an on-base percentage《略 OBP》② an on-base average《略 OBA》

- 彼は出塁率0.414で2位だった． He was second with a .414 on-base percentage. ★.414 は four fourteen と読む．
- 一［三］塁側 《sit on》the「first [third] base side
- 一塁側スタンド ①the right-field stands ②the right wing of the bleachers
- 三塁側スタンド ①the left-field stands ②the left wing of the bleachers
- 一［三］塁側ダッグアウト ①the「first [third] base dugout ②the dugout on the「first [third] base side
- 一［三］塁線 the「first [third] base line

49-12 打率

- 打率 a batting average《略 BA》
- 彼女の**打率は**3割2分5厘である． She **has a batting average of** .325. ★.325 は three twenty-five と読む．
- 彼の**打率は**今3割である． He **is** now「**hitting**［**batting**］.300. ★.300 は three hundred と読む．
- シーズン3週目に入ったところで彼の**打率は**3割4分9厘，ホームラン5本である． Three weeks into the season, he **is batting** .349 and has 5 home runs.
- 昨シーズンの彼は**打率**3割1厘，打点87，ホームラン31本だった． Last season he **batted** .301 with 87 RBIs and 31 home runs. ★.301 は three oh one と読む．
- **通算打率** *one's* career batting average
- **生涯［終身］打率，生涯［終身］通算打率** a「lifetime [career] batting average《of .367》

49-13 打数・安打

- 打席数4 ①four times at the plate ②four trips to the plate ③four plate appearances
- 打数4 ①four at bats《略 4 ab.》②four times at bat ★打数は打席数のうち四球，死球などを除いたもの．
- 5打数3安打である ①have three hits in five at bats ②be「three for five [3-for-5]
- 5打数3安打になる go「three for five [3-for-5]
- 彼は4回の打席のうち四球が1回あって3打数1安打だった． He was 1-for-3 with a walk in four plate appearances.
- （投手が）敵を3安打に抑える hold [limit] the other team to three hits
- 散発の4安打に終わった． They made only four scattered hits.
- 5打席目に in his fifth trip to the plate
- 彼は安打数で10位，打数で5位だ． He ranks tenth in hits and fifth in at

bats.

49-14 打点

- 打点　a run batted in 《略 rbi, RBI》 ★複数形は runs batted in.
- 彼は 2 打点入れた．　He「batted [drove] in two「runs [runners].
- 彼は打点でトップだ．　① He's the leader in RBIs. ② He has the most RBIs.
- 打点王　① the RBI leader ② the top RBI hitter
- 打点記録　① the RBI record ② the record for runs batted in

49-15 防御率

- 防御率　an earned run average 《略 ERA》
- 彼の防御率は 3.14 である．　His earned run average is 3.14.

49-16 記録

- 通算 735 号目のホームラン　his 735th career home run
- 彼は通算で 560 ホーマーを放った．
  ① He hit 560 home runs in all (during his career).
  ② He hit a total of 560 home runs (during his career).
- 彼は今日通算 3000 安打を達成した．　He reached the 3,000-hit mark today.
- プロ通算 200 勝　① 200 professional victories ② 200 wins as a pro
- 日米通算 200 勝 [2500 安打]　a total of「200 victories [2,500 hits] in Japan and the major leagues
- 彼は通算出場試合数で (歴代) 4 位だ．　He ranks fourth (all-time) in career games played. ★career が通算，all-time は史上通した歴代記録の意．
- 4 打席連続ヒット　four consecutive hits
- 彼は現在 10 試合連続安打を記録している．　He has hit safely in 10 successive games now.
- 読売ジャイアンツは今日の試合で毎回安打を記録した．　The Yomiuri Giants recorded a hit in every inning today.
- 3 連続安打を連ねる [許す]　string together [give up] three consecutive hits
- 連続試合出場記録　a record for the number of consecutive games played
- 連続試合フルイニング出場　《a player's》 full-game appearances in consecutive games
- 連続出塁　an on-base streak
- 32 試合連続出塁を達成する　① extend *one's* consecutive on-base streak to 32 games ② get on base in 32 straight games
- 6 回を被安打 1, 奪三振 7 の好投で乗り切る
  ① pitch well through six innings with one hit given up and seven strikeouts

② pitch well through six innings giving up one hit and striking out seven
- 6回表で球数がすでに100球を超えていた．　By the bottom of the sixth inning he had already thrown more than 100 pitches.
- 42セーブを挙げて新人セーブ記録を達成する　set a season record as a rookie relief pitcher with 42 saves
- 彼は得点数でトップだ．　He ranks first in runs scored.
- ヘンダーソンの得点数146は1950年のテッド・ウィリアムズの記録150以来最多だった．　Henderson's 146 runs scored were the most since Ted Williams' 150 in 1950.
- 彼は盗塁数で2位だ．　He ranks second in stolen bases.
- ヘンダーソンの通算最多四球記録2190はボンズに破られた．　Henderson's record of 2,190 for most career walks was broken by Barry Bonds.
- **最多本塁打**　the most home runs
- 最多本塁打者　① the batter with the most home runs　② the leading home-run hitter
- 最多本塁打記録　① a record number of home runs　② the home-run record　③ 《set》 a record for most home runs (in a season)
- 最多本塁打記録をもつ　have the record for most home runs
- **最多安打**　the most hits
- **最多四球**　① the most walks　② the most bases on balls
- **最多与四球**　the most walks (given up)
- **最多出場**　① the most appearances　② the most games played
- **最多勝利**　① the most victories　② the most wins
- 最多勝利記録　a record number of winning games
- 最多勝利投手　the pitcher with the most wins
- **最多セーブ**　the most saves
- 最多セーブポイント　most relief wins plus saves
- 最多セーブ投手賞　the prize for the pitcher with the most saves
- **最多奪三振**　the most strikeouts
- 最多奪三振投手　the pitcher with the most strikeouts
- **最多盗塁**　the most stolen bases

49-17　背番号

- 背番号　① a player's number　② a uniform number
- 背番号55番の選手　① the player with number 55 on the back of his uniform　② the player wearing number 55　③ (player) number 55
- 長嶋の背番号は何番ですか．　What's Nagashima's number?

49. 野球の数字表現 49-18

- 永久欠番　① a retired (uniform) number　② a number retired forever
- 3番，ファースト，王，背番号1．〔野球場のアナウンス〕Batting third and wearing number one, first baseman Sadaharu Oh.
- 背番号 16 は読売ジャイアンツの永久欠番である．
  ① Number 16 is a retired number on the Yomiuri Giants' team.
  ② Number 16 has been retired by the Yomiuri Giants.

49-18　守備位置

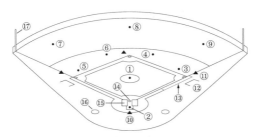

① ピッチャー(投手) pitcher
② キャッチャー(捕手) catcher
③ ファースト(一塁手) first baseman
④ セカンド(二塁手) second baseman
⑤ サード(三塁手) third baseman
⑥ ショート(遊撃手) shortstop
⑦ レフト(左翼手) left fielder
⑧ センター(中堅手) center fielder
⑨ ライト(右翼手) right fielder
⑩ 主審 home-plate umpire
⑪ 塁審 base umpire (一塁塁審 umpire at first base)
⑫ (一塁)コーチャーズボックス coach's box (at first base)
⑬ スリーフィートライン three-foot line
⑭ ホームプレート home plate
⑮ バッターボックス batter's box
⑯ ネクストバッターズサークル on-deck circle
⑰ ファウルポール foul pole

　9人の守備位置（fielding positions）には次頁の表のような番号が振られており，記録の簡略化などに利用される．たとえばサードがファーストに送球してアウトになればスコアブックには 5-3 と記載される．a 4-6-3 double play（4-6-3 のダブルプレイ）といえばセカンドが捕球して（二塁に入った）ショートが封殺後ファーストに送球したことがわかる．野球場のスコアボードでも選手名の守備位置が守備番号で示される．背番号が 1930 年代に日本の野球に導入されたときには守備位置の順番に番号が与えられた．高校野球では今でも守備位置を背番号にするのが普通になっている．

1	ピッチャー（投手）	pitcher	投（P）
2	キャッチャー（捕手）	catcher	捕（C）
3	ファースト（一塁手）	first baseman	一（1B）
4	セカンド（二塁手）	second baseman	二（2B）
5	サード（三塁手）	third baseman	三（3B）
6	ショート（遊撃手）	shortstop	遊（SS）
7	レフト（左翼手）	left fielder	左（LF）
8	センター（中堅手）	center fielder	中（CF）
9	ライト（右翼手）	right fielder	右（RF）

50. その他の競技・勝敗の数字表現

■ 50-1 **勝敗**

50-1-1 …勝…敗

- 3勝1敗 ① three victories「and [against] one defeat ② three wins「and [against] one defeat ③ three wins and one loss ④ a three-one record
- 3勝1敗だった. ①《We》won three games and lost one. ②《We》won three games out of four.
- 3敗1分けだった. 《We》lost three games and「tied [drew] one.
- 春場所は**13勝2敗の成績で**竜田川が優勝した. Tatsutagawa walked off with the spring Grand Sumo championship「**with thirteen wins and two defeats [with a 13-2 win-loss record]**.
- 日本シリーズは7戦で先に4勝したほうが優勝だ.
  ① The Japan Series goes to the team that wins four out of seven games.
  ② The Japan Series is a best-of-seven championship.

50-1-2 連勝・連敗

- **連勝** ① straight「victories [wins] ② consecutive「victories [wins] ③ successive「victories [wins] ④ a series of「victories [wins] ⑤ victory after victory ⑥ win after win ★《米》では1980年代末からrepeatのre-(再)をもじってthree-peat(3連勝)などの表現が使われるが, 2016年現在Three-Peatは米国では登録商標.
- 10連勝 a 10-game winning streak
- 連勝する ① gain [win]《two》「consecutive [successive] victories ② win game after game ③ win match after match ④ win victory after victory ⑤ have an unbroken series of victories ⑥ have a winning streak
- AチームはBチームに連勝した.
  ① The A team won two games in a row「against [over] the B team.
  ② The A team defeated the B team two games in a row.
  ③ The A team took two in a row from the B team.
- 5連勝する ① win five「consecutive [successive, straight] victories《over …》 ② win five games successively ③ win five games in a row
- 引き分けを挟んで**8連勝する** **have eight consecutive wins** interrupted by one tie
- 5連敗する ① lose five games「straight [in a row, in succession] ② lose five consecutive games

- 柔道の世界選手権大会**5連覇** **five consecutive victories** in the world judo championship
- 3連覇する　win the championship (for) three years running
- タイガースの**V2**はならなかった．　The Tigers didn't win **a second consecutive championship**.
- **連勝記録**を作る　set **a record for consecutive wins**
- 彼は自分の**連勝記録**を 30 に伸ばした．
  ① He set a new personal **record of** 30 **consecutive wins**.
  ② He extended his「**successive** [**consecutive**] **victory record** to 30.

■ 50-2　サッカー

- 日本・イラン戦は日曜日の午後1時に**キックオフ**だ．　The Japan-Iran match **kicks off** at 1:00 p.m. on Sunday.
- 点を入れる [ゴールする]　① score　② score [get, win, make] a goal
- 点を入れられる [点を許す]　① give up a goal　② leak a goal
- 前半に2点入れる　score two goals in the first half
- **後半5分に**彼女は2度目のゴールを決めた．　**In the fifth minute of the second half**, she scored a second goal.
- **シュート数**はうちのチームのほうが勝っていたのに試合には負けてしまった．　Our team was ahead on **the number of shots on goal**, but we ended up losing the game.
- **ハットトリック**は一人の選手が1ゲーム中に3回ゴールを決めることです．　**A hat trick** is three goals scored by one player in a single game.
- ハットトリックを決める [達成する，記録する]　score [make, achieve, record] a hat trick
- **2対1**の得点で勝つ　win (a game) by (a score of) **2 to 1** [⇨ 49-4点, 49-5点差]
- **3対3**の引き分けに終わった．　① The game ended in a「tie [draw], **three to three**. ② They played to a「**three-all** draw [**three-to-three** tie]. ③ They drew **3-3**.
- ハーフタイムでの得点は**3対1**だった．　The score at halftime was **3-1**.
- 日本は前半が終わった時点では**1対0**でリードしていた．　Japan was leading **1-0** at the end of the first half.
- ドイツが2点**リードしている**．
  ① Germany is **leading** by two goals.
  ② Germany is two goals **in the lead**.
  ③ Germany is two goals **ahead**.
  ④ Germany is two goals **up**.
- FIFA ワールドカップの一大会での**最多得点**は1954年にハンガリー・チームが記録した 27 だ．　**The most goals** scored in one tournament of a FIFA

World Cup were the 27 recorded by the Hungarian team in 1954.
- **残り5分に**ゴールキーパーはベッカムからのヘディングシュートを浴びたがセーブした. **With five minutes remaining**, the goalkeeper was called into action to save a header from Beckham.
- **最後の1分に**同点に持ち込んだ. They tied the score **in the final minute**.
- 彼がレッドカードで退場になったことで選手は**10人**に減った. They were reduced to **ten men** when he was sent off with a red card.
- FIFA 世界ランキング**3位である** **be ranked third** in the FIFA world rankings
- **得点王** the top scorer

■ 50-3 **ゴルフ**

50-3-1 **ホール**

- 6番ホール ① the sixth (hole) ② hole 6
- ロングホール a par-five hole
- ミドルホール a par-four hole
- ショートホール a par-three hole
- アウト the front nine
- イン the back nine
- 彼女は3打でグリーンにオンした. She [reached [was on]] the green in three strokes.
- ボールを4回打ちでホールに入れる ① hole out in four ② make a hole in four
- 4番ホールをパーで回った. I finished the fourth hole at par.
- 18番ホールでパーを出す par the 18th (hole)
- 連続8つのパーを取る card eight straight pars
- 15アンダーで優勝した. She won (the tournament) with 15 under par.
- 通算18アンダー, 270で優勝した. He won the tournament with an 18-under-par 270.
- 彼女だけがその日アンダーパーの71で回った. She was the only one to finish under par that day with a 71.
- 5番ホールでボギーをたたいた.
  ① He bogeyed (out on) the fifth hole.
  ② He scored a bogey on the fifth hole.
- 5番ホールでダブルボギーをたたいた. She double-bogeyed the fifth hole.
- 18番ホールでバーディーを奪う ① make a birdie on the 18th hole ② birdie the 18th hole
- ホールインワンをやってのける ① make a hole in one ② hole in one ③ hit

an ace
- ボールが一直線に飛んでホールインワンになった．　The ball「flew［sailed］directly into the cup for a hole in one.

50-3-2 ハンデ

- ハンデ 20 のゴルファー　① a 20-handicap player　② a 20-handicapper
- 私はハンデ 2 だ．　I have a two handicap.
- ハンデ 3 でプレーした．　I played off three.
- ハンデはいくつですか．　What is your handicap?
- ハンデの多い人　① a high-handicapped player　② a high-handicapper
- ハンデの少ない人　① a low-handicapped player　② a low-handicapper

50-3-3 その他

- 1 日に 2 ラウンドする　play two rounds a day
- ツーサム　a twosome
- フォーサム　a foursome
- ゴルフクラブ　a golf club
▶ ゴルフクラブはウッド（wood）（ヘッドが元来木製だった）とアイアン（iron）（ヘッドが金属）に大別でき，それぞれロフト（クラブフェースの傾斜角）の小さい順にさまざまな番手があって，目指す飛距離などに応じて使い分ける．
▶ 1 番ウッドから 5 番ウッドまでは次のような名称がある：(1W) ドライバー (driver)，(2W) ブラッシー (brassie)，(3W) スプーン (spoon)，(4W) バッフィー (baffy)，(5W) クリーク (cleek)．ただし，4 番ウッド，5 番ウッドの名称には歴史的に混乱があり，上記の名称は日本では知られているが，英語では a four-wood または a No. 4 wood のように数字で呼ぶのが普通．
▶ 1 番アイアンから 9 番アイアンまでは次のような名称がある：(1I) ドライビングアイアン (driving iron) またはクリーク (cleek)，(2I) ミッドアイアン (midiron)，(3I) ミッドマッシー (mid-mashie)，(4I) マッシーアイアン (mashie iron)，(5I) マッシー (mashie)，(6I) スペードマッシー (spade mashie) またはマッシーニブリック (mashie niblick)，(7I) ピッチャー (pitcher) またはマッシーニブリック (mashie niblick)，(8I) ピッチングニブリック (pitching niblick)，(9I) ニブリック (niblick)．ただし，これらのアイアンは日本語でも英語でも a five iron のように数字で呼ぶのが普通．

なお，1, 2, 3番アイアンを a long iron, 4, 5, 6番アイアンを a middle iron, 7, 8, 9番アイアンを a short iron と呼ぶ．

- 3番ウッドではクラブが大きすぎた［小さすぎた］．　A 3-wood was too "much [little] club.　★クラブが大きすぎるというのは飛びすぎる，つまり番手が小さすぎる意．
- 大きすぎる［小さすぎる］クラブを使う　over-club [under-club]
- もっと上のクラブが必要だ．　I need more club.

■ 50-4 トランプ

- スペードの 10　the ten of spades
- ハートのエース　the ace of hearts
- ▶ 11, 12, 13に相当するのは the jack（ジャック），the queen（クイーン），the king（キング）．
- ▶ スペード（spades），クラブ（clubs），ハート（hearts），ダイヤ（diamonds）のマークは複数形でいう．単数形で a spade というと「スペードの札（1枚）」の意になる．各マークの 13 枚の揃いを英語で suit といい，トランプ 52 枚の組を a pack of cards,《米》a deck of cards という．なお，trump は英語では「切り札」の意味で，日本語の「トランプ」に当たる英語は cards, playing cards, a card game などである．

> **トリビア　クラブ vs. クローバー**
>
> 日本語ではクラブをクローバーともいうが，英語の club は「棍棒」の意である．トランプのマークは中世には国によってさまざまだった．クローバーの葉のようなおなじみのマークは中世にフランスなどで使われていたものに由来するが（フランス語では今でもクローバーの意の trèfles の語を使っている），その一方，「棍棒」という名称はイタリアなどで使われていたものが取り入れられた．

- 私は 5 が 2 枚配られた．　I was dealt two "fives [5s].
- ワンペア　〔ポーカーの〕one pair
- ツーペア　〔ポーカーの〕two pairs
- スリーカード　〔ポーカーの〕three of a kind
- フォーカード　〔ポーカーの〕four of a kind

51. 電池・テレビ

51-1 電池

- **単一電池**　① a D-size battery　② a size-D battery　③ a D battery　④〔国際記号〕R20　⑤〔旧 JIS〕UM-1
- **単二電池**　① a C-size battery　② a size-C battery　③ a C battery　④〔国際記号〕R14　⑤〔旧 JIS〕UM-2
- **単三電池**　① an AA-size battery　② a size-AA battery　③ an AA battery　④〔国際記号〕R6　⑤〔旧 JIS〕UM-3
- **単四電池**　① an AAA-size battery　② a size-AAA battery　③ an AAA battery　④〔国際記号〕R03　⑤〔旧 JIS〕UM-4
- **単五電池**　① an N-size battery　② a size-N battery　③ an N battery　④〔国際記号〕R1　⑤〔旧 JIS〕UM-5
- ▶ 単三の AA は double A, 単四の AAA は triple A とも読み，その場合は a AA-size battery のように冠詞は a になる．

　国際記号は IEC（国際電気標準会議）が定めているもので，アルカリ電池なら L を付けて LR20, LR14… とするなど，サイズ・構造の両面から命名されるようになっている．リチウム電池は CR で始まる記号になる．

51-2 バッテリー・充電・放電

- **充電時間は** 60～80 分です．
  ① **Charging time is** 60 to 80 minutes.
  ② **Charging takes** 60 to 80 minutes.
  ③ It takes 60 to 80 minutes to charge 《the battery》.
- バッテリーはフル充電で**90分もちます**．　The battery **lasts 90 minutes** on a full charge.
- フル充電で 50 分まで使用可能．〔表示〕Up to 50 minutes of use on a full charge.
- **バッテリー寿命**はフル充電で7時間です．　**Battery life** is 7 hours on a full charge.
- **バッテリー残量**[**充電レベル**]が 80% 以下になると要充電ランプが点灯します．　When **the battery**「**level**［**charge**］has dropped below 80% (of full charge), the low-charge light comes on.
- 完全充電［容量］の 40% **以下にまで放電される**　**be discharged to less than** 40 percent of full「charge［capacity］
- 鉛蓄電池は 80% **以下まで放電する**べきではない．　Lead acid batteries should not **be discharged to below** 80 percent.

- **60％の放電深度まで放電する**　**discharge to** 60 percent「depth-of-discharge [DOD]」
- **放電深度**20％というのはバッテリー容量の80％を消費して20％しか残っていないことを意味する．　A **depth-of-charge** of 20% means that you have consumed 80% of the battery's capacity and only 20% is left.
- 完全放電したバッテリーを全容量の95％**にまで再充電する**には約4時間かかります．
  ① **Recharging** a fully discharged battery **to** 95 percent of full capacity takes about four hours.
  ② **Recharging** a battery from a fully discharged condition **to** 95 percent of full capacity takes about four hours.
- バッテリーが切れかかっている．　The battery is running out.
- バッテリーが切れた［上がった］．　The battery is dead.
- 切れたバッテリー　① a dead battery　②《英》a flat battery

51-3　テレビ・ディスプレイ

- 20型のテレビ　① a 20-inch TV　② a 20″ TV　③ a 20-inch diagonal TV
  ★数値は画面の対角線の長さを表わす．

51-4　チャンネル

- 1チャンネルをつける　turn on Channel 1
- 3チャンネルにする　① turn to Channel 3　② switch to Channel 3
- 6チャンネルを見る　watch Channel 6
- 8チャンネルで今何やってる？
  ① What is Channel 8 showing now?
  ② What's showing on Channel 8 right now?
  ③ What's on Channel 8 right now?
  ④ What's on on Channel 8 right now?
- 10チャンネルで今晩9時から好きなドラマがある．　A drama I like is (showing) on Channel 10 at nine this evening.
- それは何チャンネルでやっていますか．
  ① What channel is it on?
  ② What channel can you see it on?
  ③ On what channel is it aired?
  ④ What's the channel for it?
- 何チャンネルで何時から何がやっているかを載せた雑誌　a magazine showing what programs are on what channel at what time

51-5　録画

- タイマーを6時にセットした．　I set the timer for six o'clock.

51. 電池・テレビ 51-6

- このディスクは標準モード (SP) で2時間はいる．This disc can hold two hours at standard play (SP).
- このディスクに何分はいりますか．
  ① How many minutes (of video) can I record on this disc?
  ② How many minutes (of video) can be stored on this disc?
- このディスクは何回書き換えできますか．How many times can you rewrite this disc?
- 録画開始から30分たったところでディスクがいっぱいになった．The disk was full thirty minutes after recording was begun.
- メーカーによれば, DVDのディスクは適切に扱えば100年はもつと思われる．According to manufacturers, DVD discs can be expected to last for at least 100 years if handled properly.

51-6 その他

- クリップを使ってリセットボタンを**3秒以上**押してください．Use a paper clip to push the reset button **for at least 3 seconds**.
- そのドラマの放送時間は月曜から金曜までの午後5:30から6:00までだ．
  ① The drama is aired from 5:30 p.m. to 6:00 p.m. Monday to Friday.
  ② The drama is aired from Monday to Friday from 5:30 p.m. to 6:00 p.m.
  ③ The air time of the drama is from 5:30 p.m. to 6:00 p.m. Monday to Friday.
  ④ The time slot of the drama is from 5:30 p.m. to 6:00 p.m. Monday to Friday.

関連項目⇨第2部・しちょうりつ

52. 小数

52-1 小数の読み方
小数点以下は1桁ずつ読むのが基本.

2.78	two point seven eight
2.5	① two point five ② two and a half
0.1405	zero point one four「oh [zero] five
273.15	two hundred and seventy-three point one five
0.3̇	zero point three recurring
0.2̇4̇	zero point twenty-four recurring
0.122̇4̇	zero point one two twenty-four recurring

野球の打率をいう.342（3割4分2厘）は three forty-two と読む.
[⇨ 49-12 打率]

52-2 小数点 vs. コンマ
イギリスでは小数点をやや上に打つ.

フランスやドイツなどイギリス以外のヨーロッパ各国では桁区切りのコンマと小数点の使用が英米とは逆で，円周率は3,14,「一万五千」は15.000となる（そうした国では小数点のことを decimal point ではなく decimal comma という）. このヨーロッパ式慣用が英語への翻訳でそのままにされる場合があり，一部の国際機関は公式文書でも用いているという. たとえば4,5 or 6 liters は英語のコンマの用法に従って解釈すると「4リットルまたは5リットルまたは6リットル」だが，実は「4.5リットルまたは6リットル」を表わしていたりするのである. 誤解を減らすためヨーロッパでは桁区切りにはピリオドもコンマも使用せず空白を空けることが行なわれているが，小数点の問題は国際度量衡委員会で議論されたものの決着がついていない.

1より小さな小数の場合，欧米では1の位の0を表記しないことがしばしばある. 1より大きな小数と混在するときには0を書くのが普通だが，統計数字などで1の位が常に0のときは0が省かれることが多い. 野球の打率と銃の口径については常に0は省略される.

52-3 小数点と複数形

1未満の小数に対しては後続の名詞は単数形，1を超える小数に対しては後続の名詞は複数形とするのが原則．ただし，口語では1未満の小数について複数形を使うことも少なくない．

- 0.5 グラム　①0.5 gram　②《口》0.5 grams
- 1.1 グラム　1.1 grams

52-4 小数と分数

スポーツの記録は，日本語では0.1秒，0.02秒のように小数を使うが，英語では one tenth, two hundredths のように分数でいうことが多い．

- 彼は自己ベストを0.03秒更新して10.69秒でゴールした．　He broke his own record by three hundredths of a second, finishing in 10.69.

52-5 各種表現

- **小数**　①a decimal fraction　②a decimal　★単にfractionというと分数の意味になる．fractionの基本的な意味は「端数」で，decimal fraction は「十進法の端数」の意.
- **小数第1位**　①the first decimal place　②the tenths place　★後者は「10分の1の位」の意．[⇨ 10-1 位取り]
- **小数第2位**　①the second decimal place　②the hundredths place
- 小数第2位の数字　①the second digit to the right of the decimal point　②the digit at the second decimal place
- 小数点以下第3位まで計算する　①calculate down to three decimal places　②calculate down to the third decimal place　★three decimal places は「小数点以下3桁」の意なので複数形.
- 小数第2位まで正しい　correct to two decimal places
- 円周率を小数点以下15桁まで暗記する　①memorize pi to 15 decimal places　②memorize pi to 15 places of decimals　③memorize pi to the fifteenth decimal place
- 小数点以下2桁の精度で表わす　①express … with two decimal place precision　②show to (a precision of) two decimals
- **小数点**　a decimal point
- 小数点をn桁右に動かす　move the decimal point n digits to the right
- 小数点の位置が固定されている記数法　①a notation in which the decimal point is fixed　②fixed-point notation
- **有限小数**　①a terminating decimal　②a finite decimal
- **無限小数**　①a nonterminating decimal　②an infinite decimal
- **循環小数**　a「recurring [circulating, repeating] decimal

53. 分数

53-1 基本

「…分の 1」は序数 (⇨ 4. 序数) を使って表現する．たとえば「3 分の 1」なら「one third」または「a third」となる．「3 分の 2」は「2 つの『3 分の 1』」と考え，two thirds という．

1/2	one half
3/2	three halves
1/3	one third
2/3	two thirds [⇨ 16-4 3 分の 2 の多数]
1/4	① one fourth　② one quarter
1/5	one fifth
1/10	one tenth
1/20	one twentieth
1/21	one twenty-first
2/21	two twenty-firsts
1/22	one twenty-second
7/22	seven twenty-seconds
1/100	① one one-hundredth　② one hundredth
1/365	one three-hundred(-and-)sixty-fifth
1/1000	① one one-thousandth　② one thousandth
1/10000	one ten-thousandth
1/1000000	① one one-millionth　② one millionth

帯分数は次のように言える．

2 2/5　two and two fifths

53-2 分数の読み方

1 より小さい分数が名詞の前につくときには of a を入れて読むのが普通．「…の (うちの) 3 分の 2」などという発想である．

2/3 liter	two thirds (of a) liter
1/12 shilling	one twelfth (of a) shilling
1/72 inch	one seventy-second (of an) inch
1/7000 pound	one seven-thousandth (of a) pound

整数 + 分数 (帯分数) の形の場合には of は入れないのが普通．これは

整数だけの場合と同じ扱いである．

 8 2/3 liters eight and two-third(s) liters
 11 3/8 inches eleven and three-eighth(s) inches

 分母，分子が複雑な場合や変数を含む場合は，次のように「分子 + over + 分母」の形が好まれる．式の読み方については⇨ **55. 式の読み方**

 123/456 one hundred and twenty-three over four hundred and fifty-six
 1/x one over x

- 1/60 秒 one sixtieth (of a) second
- 1/24 秒ごとに映像が表示される． A picture is displayed every 1/24 second. ★every 1/24 second は every (one-)twenty-fourth of a second または every (one-)twenty-fourth second と読む．
- 1/30 秒の周期 a 1/30 second period ★a one-thirtieth second period または a one-thirtieth of a second period と読む．
- フレームレートは 1000/1001 に下げられた． ①The frame rate was reduced by a factor of 1000/1001. ②The frame rate was reduced at a ratio of one thousand to one thousand and one. ★1000/1001 は one thousand over one thousand one などと読めるが，このような用例中ではわかりにくいので，口頭ではたとえば②の訳例のようにパラフレーズすることもできる．

53-3 「…分の…拍子」の言い方

- 4 分の 2 拍子 〚音楽〛①《in》 two-four time ②《米》 two-four meter
- 4 分の 3 拍子 〚音楽〛①《in》 three-four time ② three-quarter time ③《米》 three-four meter ④ waltz time

53-4 ハイフンの使用

 分数は two-thirds, one-fifth のようにハイフンを入れて書くことも多い．特に形容詞用法ではハイフンを入れるのが原則．名詞用法ではハイフンは不要だが，名詞用法も含めて常にハイフンを入れるという立場もある．

 分母や分子が大きくなると事情は複雑になる．まず，分母はすべてハイフンでつなぐのがよい．一方，分母か分子がすでにハイフンを含んでいるときには分母と分子の間にはハイフンを入れないほうがすっきりする．

53-5 分数の用法

(i) 名詞としての用法

two thirds of the members メンバーの 3 分の 2
a quarter of a century 1 世紀の 4 分の 1

53. 分数 53-6

one twelfth of a shilling　1 シリングの 12 分の 1《ペニー》
one sixteenth of a pound　1 ポンドの 16 分の 1《オンス》
be reduced by one third　3 分の 1 削減される

(ii) 名詞の前につける用法
a quarter mile　4 分の 1 マイル
2/3 liter　3 分の 2 リットル　★読み方については⇨ 53-2
a one-half owner　1/2 の所有者（= an owner of one half）
a one-third share　1/3 の分け前（= a share of one third）
a two-thirds majority　3 分の 2 の多数（= a majority of two thirds）

(iii) 倍数形容詞としての用法．double the price（その 2 倍の価格）の double に相当する用法であり，名詞用法の of が省略されたものに由来する．

one third the total number of schools　学校の総数の 3 分の 1
two thirds the height　その高さの 3 分の 2
quarter the price　その値段の 4 分の 1

Image A has only one quarter the number of pixels as does image B.　画像 A は画像 B の 4 分の 1 のピクセル数しかない．★下記 (iv) の用法で Image A has only one quarter as many pixels as image B ともいえる．

A nucleus is a mere ten-thousandth the size of an atom.　原子核は原子のほんの 1 万分の 1 の大きさだ．★a ten-thousandth（1 万分の 1）の間に mere がはいりこんだ例．

(iv) 副詞としての用法．twice as much as...（…の 2 倍で）の twice に相当する表現である．

one third as long as...　…の 3 分の 1 の長さで
two fifths higher than...　…よりも 5 分の 2 高い　★twice higher than は「2 倍の高さ」の意味が普通だが，このような分数の場合，「5 分の 2 の高さ」の意味にはならずに「5 分の 2 の高さだけプラスされた高さ」を表わす．

She is one-quarter English and three-quarters German.　彼女（の血筋）は 1/4 はイギリス人，3/4 はドイツ人である．
The bottle is two-thirds full.　びんは 3 分の 2 まで入っている

53-6　いろいろな分数

・普通の分数　① a common fraction　② a vulgar fraction

- 真分数　a proper fraction
- 仮分数　an improper fraction
- 帯分数　a mixed number
- 繁分数　① a compound fraction　② a complex fraction
- 仮分数は分子が分母より大きい分数である．　An improper fraction is a fraction in which the numerator is greater than the denominator.
- 帯分数の分数部分　the fractional part of a mixed number
- 22/7 を帯分数に直しなさい．　Convert [Change] 22/7 to a mixed number.
- 帯分数は整数と真分数の組み合わせだ．　A mixed number is a combination of a whole number and a proper fraction.
- 部分分数　partial fractions
- 連分数　a continued fraction

53-7 分母と分子

- 分母　a denominator
- 分子　a numerator
- それらの分数を共通の分母で表わす《通分する》　write those fractions with a common denominator
- 分母を払うには，分母の最小公倍数をかけなさい．　To clear fractions, multiply by the lowest common multiple of the denominators.
- …の分母を有理化する　① rationalize the denominator of …　② write … with a rational denominator

> **トリビア　分母と分子**
>
> 英語では分母は denominator, 分子は numerator という．英語の分数の呼称はたとえば3/5ならまず分母で基本となる称 fifth を決めて，それが1つ，2つ，3つという意味で one fifth (1/5), two fifths (2/5), three fifths (3/5) のように表現する．denominator というのは文字通りには「名称を決めるもの」の意で，numerator は「数えるもの」という意味からきている．
>
> また，分数を普通に縦に書く場合，通例，日本人は発音通り分母を先に書くが，英米人はやはり英語の発音の順番で分子を先に書く．

53-8 通分

- 通分　reduction to a common denominator
- 通分する　① reduce [change, convert] 《fractions》 to a common denominator　② write 《fractions》 with a common denominator

- 3/4 と 1/3 を足すにはまず通分する必要がある． To add 3/4 and 1/3 you need first to change the fractions to a common denominator.

53-9 約分

- 約分　reduction
- 約分する　① reduce ② cancel
- 最も簡単な分数に約分する　① reduce to a fraction in its lowest terms ② reduce to the lowest terms
- 約分できる　reducible
- 約分できない　irreducible

53-10 各種表現

- ナノ秒は10億分の1秒だ． A nanosecond is a billionth of a second.
- 奇数の目が出る確率は2分の1である． There is a one-in-two「probability [chance, likelihood]」of an odd number (turning up).
- 10分の数ミリ［零コンマ数ミリ］　a few [several] tenths of a millimeter
- 原子を絶対温度で100万分の数度以内まで冷却する　cool atoms to within a few millionths of a degree above absolute zero
- 整数分の一　an integral submultiple of …
▶「数百分の一」などは「百分の一より（ずっと）小さい」「数百倍（小さい）」「ごく一部分」などと発想して訳せる．
- 数百分の一　① (far) less than a hundredth《as「many [much]」》② several hundred times《smaller》③〔割合など〕(far)「fewer [less]」than「one in a hundred [one percent]」④〔定性的に〕a (small [tiny, minute]) fraction《of …》
- これらの農地にかかる固定資産税は宅地の数十分の一にすぎない． The local government tax on these farming plots「is less than [doesn't come to]」a tenth what it is for residential land.
- 髪の毛の数百分の一ほどの太さの繊維　a fiber (much) less than a hundredth the width of a hair
- その病気が生まれてくる子供に感染する確率は数百万分の一である． The likelihood of a newborn child getting infected with this disease is「less than one in a million [one in several million]」.
- チャンネル数分の一に減る　decrease [be reduced] by a factor of the number of channels
- 分数の　① fractional ② fractionary
- 分数の足し算　① addition of fractions ② adding fractions
- それぞれの分数を共通の分母をもつ等価な分数に直す　convert [change] each fraction to an equivalent fraction with a common denominator

- 分数で割るには，単にその分数の逆数をかければよい．　To divide by a fraction, just multiply by the reciprocal of that fraction.
- 縦に組んだ［書いた］分数　a built-up fraction
- 既約分数　①an irreducible fraction　②a fraction reduced to its lowest terms
- 分数関数　a fractional function
- 分数式　a fractional expression
- 分数方程式　a fractional equation
- 三分の一ルール　〔分野により内容はさまざま〕the one-third rule
- 四分の一波長板　〚光学〛a quarter-wave plate
- 十分の一税　〚西洋史〛a tithe

⇨ 第2部・こうばい，しゅくしゃく

53-11 何分の一

- 1分は1時間の何分の一か．　What fraction of an hour is one minute?
- 距離が10倍になると明るさは何分の一になるか．
  ① By what factor does the luminosity decrease if you multiply the distance by 10?
  ② How many times dimmer does the luminosity get if the distance increases ten times?
- この文章は何分の一かに短縮したほうがいい．　You should shorten this text 「to less than half the original length〔by more than half〕．
- 電子を光速の何分の一というところまで加速する　accelerate electrons to a sizeable fraction of the speed of light
- ネットワークの反応速度が急に何分の一かに低下した．　Network response time suddenly slowed down by a very large factor.

54. 加減乗除

■ 54-1 足し算

54-1-1 足し算

- 足し算 [加法]　① addition　② adding up
- 足す　① add　② 〔合計する〕add up　③ do addition　④ do a sum
- 2 足す 4 は 6.《(2 + 4 = 6)》　① Two and four「make [are] six.　② Two plus four「is [equals] six.
- 5 に 9 を足す　add 9 to 5
- 5 と 9 を足す　① add 5 and 9 together　② take the sum of 5 and 9
- その 3 つの数を**足すと** 100 **になる**.　The three numbers will **add up to** 100.
- きょうの出費を**全部足す**　**add up** today's expenses
- 400 円**足して**ちょうど 1 万円にした.　I **added** ¥400 to make it exactly ¥10,000
- 16 に**何を足すと** 35 になりますか.　What number added to 16 gives 35?
- 4 桁の足し算　four-digit addition
- 足し算をする　① do a sum　② add《figures》up　③〔合計する〕total (up)
- 簡単な足し算をする　do (a) simple addition

関連表現

- 足して 2 で割る　① add [put]《the two numbers》together and divide (the sum) by two　②〔中間を取る〕split the difference
- 両方の提案を足して 2 で割ればよいと思う.　I think we should「split the difference [strike a balance]」between the two proposals.
- クレオパトラと楊貴妃を足して 2 で割ったような美女　a beauty who seems to possess the best features of Cleopatra and Yang Kuei-fei

54-1-2 加算

- 加算　① addition　② adding
- 加算する　add
- 元金に利子を**加算する**　**add** interest to the principal
- 加算額　① an addition　② an additional「amount [sum]

54-1-3 和

- 和　① the sum　②〔合計〕the sum total　③ the total (amount)
- 2 数の和　the sum of two numbers

- 2と3の和は5だ．　The sum of two and three is five.
- **三角形の内角の和**は二直角である．
  ① **The sum of the internal angles of a triangle** is equal to two right angles.
  ② **The internal angles of a triangle** [**added** [**put**] **together**] make two right angles.
- 魔方陣では縦・横・斜めのどの方向の数の和も同じになる［あらゆる行，列，主対角線の数の和が同じになる］．
  ① In a magic square, the sum of the numbers in any vertical, horizontal, or main diagonal line is the same.
  ② In a magic square, the sum of the numbers in any row, column, or main diagonal is the same.
- 行列 A の行の要素と行列 B の列の要素との積の**和**　**the sum** of the products of the elements in a row of matrix A and a column of matrix B
- 和は i と j のすべての値について取る．　The sum is (taken) over all values of i and j.

54-1-4 術語

- 加法性　additivity
- 加法群　an additive group
- 加法の逆元　an additive inverse
- 加法の単位元　an additive identity
- 加法の結合則　additive associativity
- 加法定理　①〔一般の関数の〕an addition theorem　②〔三角関数の〕addition formulae
- 加法混色　(an) additive color mixture

54-2 引き算

54-2-1 引き算

- 引き算［減法，減算］　subtraction
- 引く　subtract 《from …》
- 10から3を引く　① subtract 3 from 10　③ take away 3 from 10
- 13引く8は5．《13 − 8 = 5》　13 minus 8 is 5.
- 引く数［減数］　a subtrahend　★subtrahend は語源的には「subtract されるもの」の意．
- 引かれる数［被減数］　a minuend　★minuend は語源的には「diminish されるもの（減らされるもの）」の意．
- **引く数**が**引かれる数**より大きい場合には引かれる数に10を足しなさい．
  When **the subtrahend** is greater than **the minuend**, add 10 to the latter.

- 総利益率は純売上高から売上原価**を引いた**ものを純売上高で割ったものだ。　Gross profit margin is net sales「**minus**［**less**］cost of goods sold divided by net sales.
- 差し引く　① take away　② take off　③ deduct　④ subtract

54-2-2　差［⇨ 13. 比較・差・増減 13-2-1］

- 差　(a) difference
- A と B の差　the difference between A and B
- 新旧ファイルのサイズの差　① the difference between the sizes of the new and old files　② the difference in size between the new and old files
- 測定値と参照信号の差　the difference between the measured value and the reference signal
- ある値と平均値との差を標準偏差で割る　divide the difference between a value and the average by the standard deviation
- その 2 数の差　the difference「of［between］these two numbers
- 数ドルの差　a difference of a few dollars
- 価格の差　① a difference in price　② a price difference
- 年齢の差　① a difference「in［of］age　② (an) age difference　③ a disparity「in［of］age
- 夫婦の年齢の差
  ① the age difference between a married couple
  ② the difference in age(s) between a man and wife
- 男女の平均寿命の差　the difference in average life expectancy between men and women
- 輸出入の差　the balance of trade
- 原子量の**差が 2 未満の**イオンを区別する　differentiate ions with an atomic weight difference (of) less than 2
- 最大放射電力との**差が 3dB 以下の**すべての方向　all directions in which radiation power is different (by) up to 3 dB from the maximum radiation power

54-2-3　術語

- 減法混色　(a) subtractive color mixture

■ 54-3　かけ算

54-3-1　かけ算

- かけ算［乗法，乗算］　multiplication
- かける　multiply

54. 加減乗除 54-3-2

- 5 に 3 をかける   multiply 5 by 3
- 2 に 2 をかければ 4 になる. 《$2 \times 2 = 4$》
  ① Two (multiplied) by two「makes [is]」four.
  ② Two times two「makes [is]」four.
- 方程式の両辺に -1 をかける   multiply both sides of the equation by -1
- …に y を右からかける   multiply … by y from the right
- 2 つの指数をかけ合わせる   multiply (together) the two exponents
- x を求めるには，方程式の両辺にどんな数をかけたらいいですか. **By what number would you multiply** both sides of the equation to find the value of x?
- x にかける係数   ① a coefficient to be multiplied by x ② a coefficient by which x is multiplied ★① は multiply … by x, ② は multiply x by … がベースの表現.
- **かけると 70 になり**［積が 70 で］差が 3 の 2 つの数   two numbers that **multiply to** 70 and differ by 3
- 2 桁の数どうしのかけ算   ① multiplication of two-digit numbers ② multiplication of a two-digit number by a two-digit number
- 分数のかけ算   multiplication of fractions
- かけ算をする   ① multiply ② do multiplication ③〔装置などが〕perform multiplication
- 反復毎の乗算の回数   the number of multiplications per iteration
- **九九**（の表）   ① a multiplication table ② a times table ★the nine times table というと nine times…（9 かける…）の表，つまり九の段になる.

トリビア **英語の九九**

英語でもたとえば Six times seven is forty-two.（6 かける 7 は 42）などをふしをつけて唱えて暗唱することはある（たとえば映画『ライアンの娘』『戦場の小さな天使たち』でそのようなシーンが見られる）．ただし，日本の「ににんがし（$2 \times 2 = 4$）」のような特別な言い方があるわけではなく，また全国的に行なわれているわけでもない．また，英米の九九はしばしば 12×12 まであるが，かつてイギリスで 12 ペンスで 1 シリングという貨幣単位が使われていた（⇨ 39-1-4 ポンド）ときには日常生活上も必須だったものと思われる．

54-3-2 積

- 積   a product
- 力と時間の積   ① the product of force and time ② force times time ③ force multiplied by time

54. 加減乗除 54-3-3

- 運動エネルギーは質量と速度の2乗との積の1/2である． Kinetic energy is one half of the product of mass and velocity squared.
- X と Y の積に C を足す．
  ① The product of X and Y is added to C.
  ② X multiplied by Y is added to C.

54-3-3 術語

- 乗法群　a multiplicative group
- 乗法の逆元　a multiplicative inverse
- 乗法の単位元　a multiplicative identity
- 乗法の交換則　multiplicative commutativity

■ 54-4 割り算

54-4-1 割り算

- 割り算〔除法，除算〕　division
- 割り算をする　① divide　② do division　③〔装置などが〕perform division
- 割る数〔除数〕　① a divisor　②〔計算の途中で〕the number 《you are》 dividing by
- 割られる数〔被除数〕　① a dividend　② the number to be divided　③〔計算の途中で〕the number being divided
- x を割る因子　a factor by which x is divided
- 6 割る 2 は 3．《$6 \div 2 = 3$》
  ① 6 divided by 2 gives 3.
  ② Divide 6 by 2 and you get 3.
  ③ 2 goes into 6 three times.
- 13 を 6 で割ると 2 が立って 1 余る．
  ① 6 goes twice into 13, leaving 1 over.
  ② 6 goes into 13 twice with 1 left over.
  ③ 13 divided by 6 gives 2「with〔and〕a remainder of 1.
- (5125 割る 18 という筆算で) 51 を 18 で割ってみると，商にまず 2 が立つことがわかります．　Divide 51 by 18 and you'll see that the whole number answer 2 is the first digit of the quotient.
- 有理数の集合では 0 で割る場合を除いて常に割り算ができる．　In the set of rational numbers, division is always possible except for division by zero.
- 0 による除算　division by zero

54-4-2 商

- 64 を 17 で割ると，商は 3 で余りは 13 だ．　When you divide 64 by 17, the quotient is 3 and the remainder is 13.

- その額を単価で割った商　the quotient of the sum divided by the unit price

54-4-3 余り

- 余り　① a remainder　② a residue
- 余りのある割り算　division with remainders
- 5割る2は2**余り1**．
  ① 5 divided by 2 is 2 **with a remainder of 1**.
  ② 5 divided by 2「is [yields, gives] 2 **with 1 left over**.
- その数は, …で割ると r **余る**．
  ① The number「**leaves** [**gives**] **a remainder of** r「when divided [on division] by ….
  ② The number is divisible by … **with** r **left over**.
- 合計を A で割ったときの**余り**　the **remainder** left (over) when the total is divided by A

▶ 日本では余りを $5 \div 2 = 2$ 余り1 または $5 \div 2 = 2 ... 1$ のように書くが，英語では $5 \div 2 = 2$, remainder 1 または $5 \div 2 = 2$ R 1 などと書く．

54-4-4 整除

- 割り切れる　① can be (evenly [exactly]) divided 《by …》　② be (evenly [exactly]) divisible 《by …》
- 割り切れない　① be indivisible 《by …》　② cannot be (evenly [exactly]) divided 《by …》
- 30は6で割り切れる．
  ① 30 can be divided by 6 (without a remainder).
  ② 30 is (exactly) divisible by 6.
  ③ 6 divides 30.
  ④ 6 will go into 30.
  ⑤ 6 is an aliquot part of 30.
- 12は2でも3でも4でも6でも割れる．　12 can be divided by 2, 3, 4, and 6.
- 16は5では割り切れない．
  ① 16 cannot be divided by 5 without a remainder.
  ② 5 does not divide 16.
  ③ 5 will not go into 16 (exactly).
  ④ 5 is an aliquant part of 16.
- 9は4で割れない．　9 cannot be divided by 4.
- 7で割り切れる数　a number that「can be divided [is divisible] by 7
- 7で割り切れない数　a number that「cannot be divided [is not divisible] by 7
- 割り切る　divide

54. 加減乗除 54-5

- $p-1$ を割り切る整数　an integer which divides $p-1$
- 整数はすべての桁の数字の和が3で割り切れれば3で割り切れる．　A whole number is divisible by 3 if the sum of all its digits is divisible by 3.
- 4で割り切れる年はうるう年だが，00で終わる年は400で割り切れる場合のみうるう年になる．　A year divisible by four is normally a leap year, but years ending in 00 are leap years only if divisible by 400.

■ 54-5　累乗

54-5-1　2乗

- 2乗〔自乗〕　a square
- 2乗する　① square ⟪a number⟫ ② multiply ⟪a number⟫ by itself
- 9の2乗は81．⟪$9^2 = 81$⟫　① The square of 9 is 81. ② 9 squared is 81.
- BMIは体重を**身長の2乗**で割った値である．　One's BMI is the value obtained by dividing one's weight by **the square of one's height**. ★BMI は body mass index（肥満度指数）．
- 距離の2乗で〔に比例して〕増加する　① increase **by the square of** the distance　② increase **in proportion to the square of** the distance
- 容器の大きさが大きくなると，表面積は**その2乗**で大きくなる．　As the size of a vessel increases, its surface area increases **by a power of 2**.
- **2乗可積分**な　square-integrable
- **二乗平均（平方根）**　a root mean square ⟪略 RMS⟫
- **平均二乗誤差**　a mean square error ⟪略 MSE⟫

54-5-2　3乗

- 3乗　a cube
- 3乗する　① cube ⟪a number⟫ ② multiply ⟪a number⟫ twice by itself
- 2の3乗は8．⟪$2^3 = 8$⟫　① The cube of 2 is 8. ② 2 cubed is 8.

54-5-3　…乗

- 累乗　①〔演算〕exponentiation ②〔結果〕a power
- 4乗する　① raise to the fourth (power) ② raise to the power (of) 4
- n乗する　① raise to the nth (power) ② raise to the power (of) n
- xの整数乗　an integer power of x
- 正の整数乗する　raise … to a positive integer power
- 10を何乗かしたもの　ten raised to some power
- 2の何乗かで割る　divide by some power of 2
- 10の2乗（10^2）　10 squared

- 10 の 3 乗 (10^3)　10 cubed
- 10 の 4 乗 (10^4)　① 10 (raised) to the power (of) four　② 10 (raised) to the fourth　③ 10 (raised) to the fourth power　④ the fourth power of 10
- 10 の 20 乗 (10^{20})　① 10 (raised) to the power of twenty　② 10 (raised) to the twentieth
- a の n 乗　① a (raised) to the power of n　② a (raised) to the n(th) power　③ a to the n(th)
- r の $n-1$ 乗　① r (raised) to the power of n minus one　② r (raised) to the n minus one (power)
- x の $-1/2$ 乗　① x (raised) to the power of minus one-half　② x (raised) to the minus one-half (power)
- x の 2/3 乗　① x (raised) to the power of two thirds　② x (raised) to the two thirds (power)
- x の $1/n$ 乗　① x (raised) to the power of one over n　② x (raised) to the one over n (power)
- 電圧の 2.5 乗　the voltage raised to the power 2.5
- 時間の 1/2 乗　① time (raised) to the power of one-half　② the one-half power of time
- すべての数の 0 乗は 1 になる．　Any number to the power of zero equals 1.
- 10 の 5 乗とは 10 を 5 回かけることだ
  ① Raising 10 to「the power of five [the fifth power]」means multiplying together five 10s.
  ② Raising 10 to「the power of five [the fifth power]」means multiplying 10 by itself four times.

54-5-4　累乗・冪乗

- x の累乗　① x raised to some power　② powers of x
- 2 の冪乗でなければならない．　It must be a power of two.
- **冪乗則**に従う　① follow [obey] **a power law**　② follow [obey] **a power law relationship**
- z の冪で展開する　expand … **in powers of** z
- 科学的記数法では値は 1 から 10 の間の数と 10 の**冪**との積で表わされる．
  In scientific notation, a value is expressed as a number between 1 and 10 times some **power** of 10.
- **冪級数**　**a power series**
- x の冪級数　a power series in x
- 冪級数展開　expansion into a power series
- x の**降冪の順**で　**in descending powers** of x
- x の**昇冪の順**で　**in ascending powers** of x

- **冪指数**　an exponent
  - 多項式の次数は x の最も高い**冪指数**である．　The degree of a polynomial is the highest 「**power** [**exponent**] of x.
  - そのような点では，その関数の冪級数展開で z の**冪指数**が負の項は有限個のみとなる．　At such a point, the power series expansion of the function has a finite number of terms with negative **powers** of z.

54-5-5　何乗

- 2 を何乗すれば 1024 になりますか．
  ① To what power must 2 be raised to get 1024?
  ② 2 raised to what power gives 1024?
- 10 を何乗かしたもの　10 raised to some power
- 2 の何乗かで割る　divide by some power of 2

■ 54-6　累乗根

54-6-1　平方根

- 平方根　a square root
- 平方根をとる　take the square root 《of …》.
- 4 の平方根は 2 である．《$\sqrt{4}=2$》　① The (square) root of 4 is 2.　② Root 4 is 2.

54-6-2　立方根

- 立方根　a cube root
- 125 の立方根は 5 だ．　The cube root of 125 is 5.

54-6-3　累乗根

- 累乗根　a (power) root
- 四則計算と**累乗根を取る操作**の有限の組み合わせからなる公式　a finite formula involving only the four arithmetic operations and **the extraction of roots**

54-6-4　…乗根

- x の n 乗根　the nth root of x
- n 乗根をとる　take the nth root
- 16 の 4 乗根は 2．《$\sqrt[4]{16}=2$》　The fourth root of 16 is 2.
- a の n 乗根を求める　extract [find] the nth root of a
- 1 の原始 n 乗根　a primitive nth root of 「one [unity]

55. 式の読み方

55-1 式の読み方の原則

日本語では「=」を「イコール」,「≦」を「小なりイコール」と読むような特別な読み方があるが,英語では式の表わす内容を文法に則って表現するのが基本で,読み方にも幅がある. $x=2$ の場合, x equals two; x is equal to two; x is two などの読み方が可能である. 式は文法上の節として機能することもでき, if $x=2$ ($x=2$ であれば), unless $x=2$ ($x=2$ でない限り) のような書き方もできる. Let $n=2k+1$. なら let n 「equal [be equal to] two times k plus one となり, 式の文法的役割に合わせて読み方も変わってくることになる. if $x>2$ ($x>2$ であれば) は if x is greater than 2 と読むが, for $x>2$ ($x>2$ については) の場合は for x greater than 2 となり, $F(t)$ is constant for $a<t<b$. なら F (of) t is constant for t larger than a and smaller than b のように言えばいい.

以下では式を独立して読む場合について読み方の例を示す.

55-2 大文字と小文字

「M は太陽の質量, m は地球の質量である」のような文で M と m を区別して読む必要がある場合, 日本語ではしばしば「ラージ・エム」「スモール・エム」といった読み方がされるが, 英語の場合, 大文字は large M, big M, capital M, uppercase M, 小文字は small m, little m, lowercase m などと読む.

55-3 添え字

a_n ① a sub n ② a subscript n

$_na$ ① a pre-sub n ② a pre-subscript n

a^n ① a super n ② a superscript n [⇨ 54-5 累乗]

^na a pre-superscript n

55-4 四則演算, 累乗根

$3+4=7$ ① three plus four equals seven   ② three plus four is equal to seven   ③ three plus four is seven   ④ three plus four makes seven

$5-3$ five minus three

4×5 ① four times five   ② four multiplied by five

55. 式の読み方 55-5

$12 \div 4$	twelve divided by four
a^2	a squared
a^3	a cubed
a^4	① a (raised) to the fourth power ② a raised to the power of four ③ a to the fourth ④ the fourth power of a
$\sqrt{2}$	the square root of two
$\sqrt[3]{2}$	the cube root of two
$\sqrt[n]{a}$	the nth root of a
$n!$	① n factorial ② factorial n ③ the factorial of n

55-5 関数

$f(x)$	(the function) f of x
$f(x,y)$	① (the function) f of x y ② (the function) f of x comma y
e^x, $\exp(x)$	① e to the x ② the exponential of x
$\log x$	① log x ② the log of x ③ the logarithm of x
$\log_a x$	the log of x to the base a
$\ln x$	the natural logarithm of x
$\log_{10} x$	the common logarithm of x
$\sin x$	① sine x ② the sine of x
$\cos x$	① cosine x ② the cosine of x
$\tan x$	① tangent x ② the tangent of x
$\cot x$	① cotangent x ② the cotangent of x
$\sec x$	① secant x ② the secant of x
$\csc x$	① cosecant x ② the cosecant of x

55-6 関係

$a = b$	① a equals b ② a is equal to b
$a < b$	a is less than b
$a > b$	a is greater than b
$a \leq b$	a is less than or equal to b
$a \geq b$	a is greater than or equal to b
$a \in A$	a is a member of A
$A \subset B$	① A is contained in B ② A is a subset of B
$A \supset B$	① A contains B ② A is a superset of B

55-7 応用例

$-1+2\sqrt{5}$ minus one plus two times the square root of five

$2ab$ ① two a b ② twice a b

ar^{n-1} ① a times r (raised) to the n minus one (power)
      ② a times r (raised) to the power of n minus one

$x^{-1/2}$ ① x (raised) to the minus one-half (power)
      ② x (raised) to the power of minus one-half

$(x^2+1)^{2/3}$ ① x squared plus one (raised) to the two-thirds (power)   ② x squared plus one (raised) to the power of two-thirds

$a^{1/n}$ ① a (raised) to the one over n (power)   ② a (raised) to the power of one over n

$\sin^2\theta + \cos^2\theta = 1$ the square of the sine of theta plus the square of the cosine of theta equals「one [unity]

$y'' + a_1(x)y' + a_2(x)y = \phi(x)$ y double prime plus a sub one of x times y prime plus a sub two of x times y equals phi of x

$(2/3)[\{a+k(1-e)\}+c]$ two thirds open bracket open brace a plus k open parenthesis one minus e close parenthesis close brace plus c close bracket ▶ 複雑な式を口頭だけで間違いなく伝えるにはこのように括弧を一つずつ読むしかないが，実用上は以下のような読み方でさしつかえないことが多い．

$(a+b)^2$ a plus b squared

$(a+b)(a-b)$ ① a plus b times a minus b ② the quantity a plus b times the quantity a minus b ③ parenthesis a plus b times parenthesis a minus b

$(a+b)c$ ① a plus b in parenthesis times c ② the quantity a plus b times c

$(n-r)!$ n minus r factorial

$\sin(A+B)/2$ the sine of one-half of A plus B

$(a-b)/(c-d)$ a minus b over c minus d

$(a+2b-c)/a$ a plus two b minus c, all divided by a

$\dfrac{-b \pm \sqrt{b^2-4ac}}{2a}$ minus b plus or minus the square root of b squared minus four a c「divided by [all over] two a

$\sqrt{x+y}$ the square root of the quantity x plus y

55-8 極限・微積分

$\sum_{i=1}^{n} a_i$ ① the sum of a sub i, i running from one to n ② the sum of a sub i for i from one to n

$\prod_{i=1}^{n} a_i$ ① the product of a sub i, i running from one to n ② the product of a sub i for i from one to n

$\lim_{n \to \infty} \frac{1}{n} \sum_{i=1}^{n} a_i$ the limit as n tends to infinity of one over n times the sum of the a's from sub one to sub n

dy/dx ① the derivative of y with respect to x ② d y (over) d x

∂y/∂x ① the partial derivative of y with respect to x ② d y (over) d x ③ partial y partial x ▶ 日本語では∂を「デル」「ラウンド」「ラウンドディー」「ディー」「パーシャル」などと読むが，英語ではd, rounded d, curly d, partial などと読む．英語の del は普通ベクトル微分の∇を指す．

- ∂²y/∂x² ① the second(-order) partial derivative of y with respect to x ② d squared y (over) d x squared ③ partial squared y (over) partial x squared

∫fdx ① the integral f d x ② the integral of f with respect to x

∬zdxdy ① the double integral of z with respect to x and y ② the integral of z d x times d y

$\int_0^{\pi/2}(1+\cos x)\mathrm{d}x$ the integral from zero to pi over two of the quantity one plus the cosine of x with respect to x

$-i\hbar\partial\psi/\partial t = -\partial^2\psi/\partial x^2 + V(x)$ minus i h bar D psi D t equals minus D squared psi D x squared plus V of x

56. 式の書き方

56-1 記号と複数形

一般に記号の複数形には -s または -'s を使う．

- according to Refs. (2) and (3)　文献 (2), (3) によれば
- from Eqs. (4) and (6)　式 (4), (6) から
- in Figs. 2 and 3　図 2, 3 において
- This code has an equal number of「1s and 0s [1's and 0's, ones and zeros].　この符号は同数の 1 と 0 をもつ．
- More than 1000「TNOs [TNO's] have been discovered.　1000 を超える TNO が発見されている．

もとの名詞が -s 以外の複数語尾をもつ場合，略語の複数形にも踏襲されることがある．

- SNe 1968V and 1968W　SN1968V と SN1968W　★supernova（超新星）の複数形は supernovae または supernovas.

文字を重ねることで複数を示すことが慣習になっているものもある．

- pp. = pages
- ll. = lines
- ff. = (and the) following pages
- MSS = manuscripts

56-2 変数記号と複数形

a_i (i = 1, 2, 3, ...) のような変数記号も複数形にできる．

- The x_i's are the coordinates of the particle. = The x's are the coordinates of the particle.　x_iは[xは]粒子の座標である．★簡単のため明らかな場合には添え字 i を省くこともある．
- All of the a_i's are zero.　a_i はすべて 0 である．
- values of f for various x_i = values of f for various x_i's　さまざまな x_i についての f の値　★簡単のため 's を省いてもよい．
- The variables x_i are coordinates of the particle.　変数 x_i は粒子の座標である．★複数形の名詞に同格として付記するときには 's はつけない．動詞は variables に合わせて複数になっている．（なお，名詞の直後に記号をつける場合はコンマで区切る必要はない．）

56-3 記号と冠詞

名詞に記号を付すときにも冠詞をつけられる．不定冠詞，定冠詞の使

い分けは記号がない場合と同じで，受け手にとって未知のものには不定冠詞，既知のものや了解されると期待されるものには定冠詞をつける．

- at a given point P　（ある）所与の点 P において
- have a length L　（ある）長さ L をもつ
- The wave is reflected at a boundary P.　その波は（ある）境界 P で反射される．
- The points G and B lie on the line l.　（その）点 G および B は直線 l 上にある．
- The length is twice the distance XY.　（その）長さは距離 XY の 2 倍である．
- double the length L　長さ L を 2 倍にする
- If the distance $AP = 8$ cm, ⋯　距離 $AP = 8$ cm であれば⋯
- each point on the wavefront XY　波面 XY 上の各点

番号のついた式や図表への言及は無冠詞が好まれる．

- Equation (1) holds.　式 (1) が成り立つ．
- Figure 5 shows ⋯　図 5 は⋯を示している．
- See Table 2A.　表 2A を参照．

その他，記号と併記する名詞はしばしば無冠詞でよい．

- Point P represents the position of the observer.　点 P は観測者の位置を表わす．★図などに既出のものであれば The point P としてもよい．
- Consider point P on the screen.　画面上の点 P を考える．★初出であれば a point P としてもよい．
- a sphere of radius r　半径 r の球

56-4 所有格と冠詞

my, Albert's のような所有格がついている名詞には a, the, this などがつかないので，「ある⋯」「その⋯」の意味を出すには工夫が必要になる．

- my friend　私の友人
- a friend of mine　私のある友人
- that friend of mine　私のその友人
- a friend of John's　ジョンのある友人

人名を冠する術語でも人名が所有格の場合には冠詞がつかないことに注意．

- the Hubble constant = Hubble's constant　ハッブル定数
- Assuming a Hubble constant of 70 km/sec/Mpc, ⋯　ハッブル定数を 70 km/sec/Mpc とすると⋯

ただし,所有格を冠した語が普通名詞化しているととらえられる場合には冠詞がつくこともある.

- in a standard Young's double slit experiment　標準的なヤングの二重スリット実験では

56-5　複数行にわたる式

英語でも日本語でも共通の目安がある.

改行して書く独立した数式が 2 行にわたるときには,＝や＋が 2 行目以降の行頭にくるように区切る.積の途中で切る場合,積記号×を行頭に省かずに書く.複数の数式は＝をそろえて書くのがよい.

$$\xi'' = X'\cos\theta - Y''\sin\theta - 2nX'\sin\theta - 2nY'\cos\theta - n^2X\cos\theta \\ + n^2Y\sin\theta$$
$$2\eta'' = X''\sin\theta + Y''\cos\theta + 2nX'\cos\theta - 2nY'\sin\theta - n^2X\cos\theta \\ - n^2Y\cos\theta$$

テキスト中の数式では＝や＋を行末として切るのがよい(単語の途中で切るときに行末にハイフンを残して次に続くことを示すのと同様である).

The generating polynomial used in this error correction system is $x^{16} + x^{15} + x^2 + 1$.

56-6　式と句読点

改行して書く式であっても,文の一部であり,適宜句読点をつける(次章の例を参照).英語の語順の性質上,式が文末にくるケースが多い.

57. 式変形の英語

57-1 変数の定義

- I が電流，V が電圧を**表わすとする**． ① **Let** I **denote** the current and V the voltage. ② **We denote** the current as I and the voltage as V. [⇨第2部・あらわす]

- $d(n)$ を n を割り切る正の整数の数とする． Let $d(n)$「**denote** [**be**] the number of positive integers that divide n.

- k は素数である**とする**． ① **Let** k **be** prime. ② **Assume** that k is prime. ③ **Let it be assumed** that k is prime.

- i を現在のピクセルの添え字**とする**． Let i **be** the index of the current pixel.

- $n = 2k + 1$ **とする**． Let $n = 2k + 1$. ★ Let n「**equal** [**be**] $2k + 1$. と等価．

- ボルツマン定数は k で**表わされる**． The Boltzmann constant **is denoted** (**by** [**as**]) k.

- 距離 $1.4a$ が得られた．**ここで** a はボーア半径である． A distance of $1.4a$ was obtained, **where** a is the Bohr radius.

- 太陽質量を M と**表わすことにしよう**．
  ① **Let us denote** the solar mass by M.
  ② **Let** the solar mass **be denoted** (**as**) M.

- ボーア半径を a で**表わすとすると**，その距離は $1.4a$ で与えられる． **If we denote** the Bohr radius by a, the distance is given by $1.4a$.

- 横軸は時間を，縦軸は粒子の速度を**表わしている**． The abscissa **represents** time and the ordinate **represents** the velocity of the particle.

- 位置 i における温度 T_i the temperature T_i at position i

57-2 式の呈示

- シュヴァルツシルト半径は：
  $R = 2GM/c^2$
  として定義される．ここで，M はブラックホールの質量，G は重力定数，c は光速度である．
  The Schwarzschild radius **is defined as**:
  $R = 2GM/c^2$,
  where M is the mass of a black hole, G is the gravitational constant, and c is the velocity of light.

- 式 (52.3) からブラックホール半径に対する**式**
  $R = 2GM/c^2$
  が得られる．
  From Eq. (52.3), we obtain **the expression**

$R = 2GM/c^2$
for the black hole radius.

- 断面積は $\sigma = \pi b^2$ **で与えられる**．　The cross section **is given**「**by**［**as**］$\sigma = \pi b^2$.
- 断面積は $\sigma = \pi b^2$ **と表わせる**．　The cross section **can be expressed as** $\sigma = \pi b^2$.
- 断面積は $\sigma = \pi b^2$ **として計算される**．　The cross section **is computed as** $\sigma = \pi b^2$.
- 断面積は容易に $\sigma = \pi b^2$ **となることがわかる**．　The cross section **is** readily **found to be** $\sigma = \pi b^2$.
- 断面積は**次の形をとる**：
  $\sigma = \pi b^2$.
  The cross section **takes the following form**:
  $\sigma = \pi b^2$.
- 次の不等式が**成り立つ**：　The following inequality **holds**:

57-3 式の導出

- $k = 0$ については $S = 1$ となる．　For $k = 0$, **we**「**obtain**［**get**］$S = 1$.
- 式 (1) は $H = U + pV$ と**書き直すことができる**．　Eq. (1) **can be rewritten** as $H = U + pV$.
- 式 (1) は次の形に**書き直すことができる**：　Eq. (1) **can be rewritten** into the following form:
- 両辺を電子の数で割ると…**となる**．　Dividing both sides by the number of electrons「**yields**［**gives**, **results in**］….
- 時間で微分すると…**が得られる**．　Differentiating with respect to time **yields** ….
- この式を式 (1) に代入して整理すると…**が得られる**．　Substituting this expression in Eq. (1) and rearranging **yields** ….
- パラメータ k は 0 でもよく，その場合，式 (1) は…と**簡単になる**．　The parameter k may be zero, in which case Eq. (1)「**simplifies**［**can be simplified**］**to** ….

57-4 論理

- そのことは $m_G = m_I$ ということを示している．　It **shows that** $m_G = m_I$.
- 式 (1.13) は $a \sim 10^{-6}$ **ということを意味している**．　Equation (1.13) **implies that** $a \sim 10^{-6}$.
- $k = 2p + 1$ とおくと，式 (5) から…**であることがわかる**．　If we「**set**［**let**］$k = 2p + 1$, **we find** from Eq. (5) **that** ….
- $m_G = m_I$ であれば…　If $m_G = m_I$, …

- $m_G = m_I$ とすると… **Assuming (that)** $m_G = m_I$, 《we can …》
- $x > k$ については… **For** $x > k$, …

57-5 その他文中の式

- 原子核の半径は $r \sim 1.2 \times A^{1/3}$ という簡単な公式に従う． The radius of a nucleus follows the simple formula $r \sim 1.2 \times A^{1/3}$.
- 磁場 B 内にある陽子は半径 $R = mv/eB$ の軌道を描く． A proton in a magnetic field B describes an orbit with radius $R = mv/eB$.
- これは $\Delta x = \hbar c/E$ のオーダーの空間解像度を達成できる． This can achieve a spatial resolution of order $\Delta x = \hbar c/E$.

57-6 懸垂分詞

式変形も含めしばしば直面する問題に懸垂分詞（dangling participle）がある．分詞構文の分詞には主語が表わされないが，主節の主語と同じであることが前提となっている．これに反して主節の主語と異なる主語を想定した分詞は懸垂分詞などと呼ばれている．ただし，次のような慣用表現は主節の主語にかかわりなく容認されている．

Generally speaking,（一般的にいうと）

Judging 「from [by] …,（…から[によって]判断すれば）

Speaking [Talking] of …,（…といえば）

さらに，意味が明確であれば容認するという立場もあり，実際，ネイティブの英語でも非常に多く見られるものであるが，論文などでは避けるべきとされることが多い．

- 式 (3) を式 (1) に代入すると，光度は $4\pi R^2 \sigma T^4$ となる．
  ① Substituting Eq. (3) in Eq. (1), the luminosity becomes $4\pi R^2 \sigma T^4$.（懸垂分詞）★substitute の主語が luminosity になるので避けるべきとされる．
  ② Substituting Eq. (3) in Eq. (1), we obtain $4\pi R^2 \sigma T^4$ for the luminosity.
  ③ Substituting Eq. (3) in Eq. (1) gives $4\pi R^2 \sigma T^4$ for the luminosity.

動名詞を使った前置詞句も同様．

  ④ By substituting Eq. (3) in Eq. (1), the luminosity becomes $4\pi R^2 \sigma T^4$. ★避けるべき構文とされる．
  ⑤ By substituting Eq. (3) in Eq. (1), we obtain $4\pi R^2 \sigma T^4$ for the luminosity.

次のような省略構文も同様．

- 直交座標系で考えると，距離 Δ は $\Delta^2 = dx^2 + dy^2 + dz^2$ で与えられる．
  ① When working in cartesian coordinates, the distance Δ is given by $\Delta^2 = dx^2 + dy^2 + dz^2$. ★避けるべき構文とされる．
  ② When we are working in cartesian coordinates, the distance Δ is given by $\Delta^2 = dx^2 + dy^2 + dz^2$.

58. 図形の基本表現

58-1 基本用語

点　a point
線　a line
曲線　a curve
直線　a (straight) line
線分　a segment
垂線　a perpendicular (line)
垂直二等分線　a perpendicular bisector
角　an angle
直角　a right angle
鋭角　an acute angle
鈍角　an obtuse angle
補角　a supplementary angle
余角　a complementary angle
対頂角　vertical angles
同位角　corresponding angles
錯角　alternate angles
内角　an interior angle
外角　an exterior angle
頂点　a vertex
辺　a side
底辺　a base
斜辺　a hypotenuse
対角線　a diagonal
多角形　a polygon
三角形　a triangle
四角形　a quadrilateral
五角形　a pentagon ［⇨ 58-2 …角形］
正多角形　a regular polygon
正三角形　an equilateral triangle
二等辺三角形　an isosceles triangle
直角三角形　a right(-angled) triangle

58. 図形の基本表現 58-1

直角二等辺三角形　an isosceles right triangle
鋭角三角形　an acute triangle
鈍角三角形　an obtuse triangle
不等辺三角形　a scalene (triangle)
内心　an incenter
外心　a circumcenter
重心　a centroid
垂心　an orthocenter
正方形　a square
長方形　a rectangle
菱形　a rhombus
平行四辺形　a parallelogram
等脚台形　an isosceles trapezoid
台形　①《米》a trapezoid　②《英》a trapezium
不等辺四角形　①《米》a trapezium　②《英》a trapezoid
円　a circle
円板　a disk
中心　a center
半径　a radius
直径　a diameter
円周　a circumference
円弧　an arc
弦　①a chord　②a subtense
弓形　a segment
扇形　a sector
接線　a tangent
法線　a normal
内接円　an inscribed circle
外接円　a circumscribed circle
二次曲線　a quadratic curve
楕円　an ellipse
放物線　a parabola
双曲線　a hyperbola
直角双曲線　a rectangular hyperbola
焦点　a focus

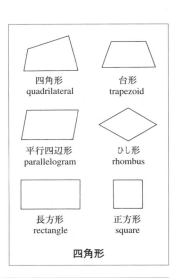

四角形 quadrilateral　　台形 trapezoid
平行四辺形 parallelogram　　ひし形 rhombus
長方形 rectangle　　正方形 square

四角形

漸近線　an asymptote

58-2 …角形

triangle（三角形），quadrilateral, quadrangle, tetragon（四角形），pentagon（五角形），hexagon（六角形），heptagon（七角形），octagon（八角形），nonagon, enneagon（九角形），decagon（十角形），hendecagon, undecagon（十一角形），dodecagon, duodecagon（十二角形），tridecagon, triskaidecagon（十三角形），tetradecagon, tetrakaidecagon（十四角形），n-gon（n 角形），polygon（多角形）

▶ 形容詞形は次の通り．これを使って quadrangular prism（四角柱），quadrangular pyramid（四角錐），pentagonal prism（五角柱），pentagonal pyramid（五角錐）などの表現もできる．
triangular, trigonal（三角形），quadrilateral, quadrangular, tetragonal（四角形），pentagonal（五角形），hexagonal（六角形），heptagonal（七角形），octagonal（八角形），nonagonal, enneagonal（九角形），decagonal（十角形），hendecagonal, undecagonal（十一角形），dodecagonal, duodecagonal（十二角形），polygonal（多角形）

▶ pentagon（五角形），hexagon（六角形）のように原則としてギリシア語系の接頭辞を使っているが，九角形についてはギリシア語系の enneagon よりもラテン語系の nonagon のほうがなじみやすい．

▶「十…角形」は使用頻度が少ないので語形が一定しない．たとえば十五角形は pentadecagon のほか pentakaidecagon（-kai- は英語の and に当たるギリシア語から），quindecagon といった表現もある．また，説明的に 15-sided polygon と言ってもよいし，大きな数なら 15-gon のような便法もある．

58-3 …面体

tetrahedron（四面体），pentahedron（五面体），hexahedron（六面体），heptahedron（七面体），octahedron（八面体），enneahedron（九面体），decahedron（十面体），hendecahedron（十一面体），dodecahedron（十二面体），icosahedron（二十面体），polyhedron（多面体）

このほか派生的な多面体は接頭辞を組み合わせて命名する．たとえば hexoctahedron は正八面体（"octahedron"）の三角形の各面を6つ（"hex-"）の三角形に分割したような多面体で，結果的に 6×8＝48 面体になる．この種の多面体には次のようなものがある．

hexoctahedron（六八面体，六方八面体），tetrahexahedron（四六面体，四方六面体），trisoctahedron（三八面体，三方八面体），tristetrahedron（三四面体，三方四面体）

また，icosidodecahedron（二十面十二面体）は三角形の面 20 ("icosi-")，五角形の面 12 ("dodeca-") をもつ準正多面体の名である．ちなみに六角形 20，五角形 12 の準正多面体は古典的な「サッカーボール形」であるが，これは truncated icosahedron（切頂二十面体）という．

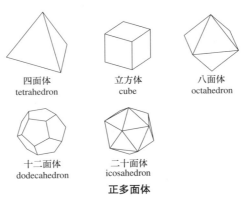

正多面体

58-4 基本的な図形の性質

- 鋭角三角形は 3 つの角が鋭角である三角形である．
  ① An acute triangle is a triangle that has three acute angles.
  ② An acute triangle is a triangle all (of) the angles of which are acute.
- 鈍角三角形は鈍角をもつ三角形である．
  An obtuse triangle is a triangle that has an obtuse angle.
- 直角三角形は直角をもつ三角形である．
  A right triangle is a triangle that has a right angle.
- 二等辺三角形は 2 辺が等しい三角形である．
  An isosceles triangle is a triangle that has two equal sides.
- 正三角形は 3 辺が等しい三角形である．
  An equilateral triangle is a triangle that has three equal sides.
- 3 辺が等しい三角形は合同である．
  ① Two triangles with equal corresponding sides are congruent.
  ② Two triangles are congruent if all three corresponding sides are equal.
- 2 辺とそのはさむ角が等しい三角形は合同である．
  Two triangles are congruent if two sides and the included angle are equal.
- 1 辺とその両端の角が等しい三角形は合同である．

Two triangles are congruent if two angles and the included side are equal.
★英語圏では三角形の合同条件を SSS (Side-Side-Side) (三辺), SAS (Side-Angle-Side) (二辺とはさむ角), ASA (Angle-Side-Angle) (一辺とその両端の角) のように覚える.
- 三角形の内角の和は 180° である.
  ① The sum of the angles of a triangle is 180°.
  ② The three (interior) angles of a triangle add up to 180 degrees.
- 平行四辺形は 2 組の平行な辺をもつ四角形である.
  A parallelogram is a quadrilateral「that has two sets of opposite parallel sides [with two pairs of parallel sides].
- 平行四辺形の向かい合う辺は等しい.
  ① In a parallelogram, the opposite sides are equal in length.
  ② The opposite sides of a parallelogram are equal in length.
- 平行四辺形の向かい合う角は等しい.
  In a parallelogram, the opposite angles [The opposite angles of a parallelogram] are congruent [have the same measure].
- 平行四辺形の対角線は互いに他を二等分する.
  The diagonals in a parallelogram bisect each other.
- 一組の向かい合う辺が平行で等しい四角形は平行四辺形である.
  A quadrilateral is a parallelogram if one pair of opposite sides「are [is] parallel and equal in length.
- 菱形は 4 辺が等しい平行四辺形である.
  ① A rhombus is a parallelogram in which all four sides are of equal length.
  ② A rhombus is a parallelogram with equal sides.
- 長方形は 4 つの角が直角である平行四辺形である.
  ① A rectangle is a parallelogram whose angles are all right angles.
  ② A rectangle is a parallelogram with all right angles.
- 合同な [相似な] 図形の対応する角は等しい.　Corresponding angles of「congruent [similar] figures「are congruent [have the same measure].
- 合同な図形の対応する辺は等しい.
  Corresponding sides of congruent figures are equal in length.
- 相似な図形の対応する辺の比は等しい.
  ① The ratios of (the lengths of) corresponding sides of similar figures are「constant [equal].
  ② Corresponding sides of similar figures are「in proportion [proportional].
- ★② は対応する辺は比例関係にあるという発想の表現.
- 直角三角形の直角をはさむ 2 辺の平方の和は斜辺の平方に等しい. (ピタゴラスの定理, Pythagorean theorem)
  ① In a right triangle, the sum of the squares of the sides「forming [adjacent to] the right angle is equal to the square of the hypotenuse.
  ② The sum of the squares of the legs of a right triangle is equal to the square of the hypotenuse. ★leg は直角の隣の辺

③ The square of the hypotenuse of a right triangle is equal to the sum of the squares of the other two sides.
- 楕円は2つの焦点からの距離の和が一定である点の軌跡である． An ellipse is a locus of points such that the sum of the distances from the two foci is constant.
- 楕円上の任意の点から2つの焦点までの距離の和は一定である． The sum of the distances from any point on an ellipse to the two foci is constant.

58-5 面積の公式

- 三角形の面積は底辺かける高さ割る2である．
  ① The area of a triangle is the base times the height divided by two.
  ② The area of a triangle is half the base times the height.
  ③ The area of a triangle is one half of the product of the altitude and the base.

▶ is のほかに is equal to, equals, is calculated as などを使うことができる．以下も同様．

- 平行四辺形の面積は底辺かける高さである．
  ① The area of a parallelogram is the product of its base and height.
  ② The area of a parallelogram is its base times its height.
- 台形の面積は上底足す下底かける高さ割る2である．
  ① The area of a trapezoid is found by multiplying the「height [altitude]」by the sum of the two bases and dividing by two.
  ② The area of a trapezoid is half the product of its height and the sum of the (lengths of the two) bases.
  ③ The area of a trapezoid is the average of the parallel sides times the height.
- 半径 r の球の表面積は $4\pi r^2$ である．
  The surface area of a sphere of radius r is $4\pi r^2$. ★$4\pi r^2$ は four pi r squared または four times pi times r squared などと読む．

58-6 体積の公式

- 円錐の体積は底面積かける高さかける 1/3 である． The volume of a cone is one third the product of the area of its base and the height.
- 角錐の体積は底面積かける高さかける 1/3 である． The volume of a pyramid is one third the product of the area of its base and the height.
- 角柱の体積は底面積かける高さである．
  The volume of a prism is the product of the area of its base and the height.
- 半径 r の球の体積は $(4/3)\pi r^3$ である．
  The volume of a sphere of radius r is $(4/3)\pi r^3$. ★式の部分は four thirds pi r cubed または four thirds times pi times r cubed などと読む．

59. 方向・向き

■ 59-1 左右

59-1-1 基本

- 右　the right
- 左　the left
- 右側にいる人　a person on *one's* right
- 右側に　① on [at] the right 《of …》 ② at [on, to] *one's* right hand ③ 〔道路などで〕on the right(-hand) side 《of …》
- 彼女はその車の左前方 3 メートルの所に立っていた．　She was standing three meters to the front and left of the car.
- 右側通行．〔掲示〕Keep to the right.
- 日本では車は左側通行だ．
  ① In Japan, cars are driven on the left-hand side of the road.
  ② We [They, Cars] drive on the left in Japan.

59-1-2 向かって右，向かって左

- 向かって右に　① on the right facing 《it》 ② on the right as *one* faces 《it》
- 向かって右の　《the door》 on the right as *one* faces 《the building》
- 海に向かって右に　on the right facing the sea
- 私は列車の進行方向に向かって左側のドアの近くに立っていた．　I was standing by the door on the left side in the direction the train was moving.
- 《写真で》前列の向かって左から 3 人目が私です．　① I'm in the front row, third from the left. ② The one (the) third from the left in the front row is me.

59-1-3 上下左右

- 右から左に　from right to left
- 上から下に　① from top to bottom ② downwards
- 右上の [に]　① above to the right ② at the upper right ③ at the top right
- 右下の [に]　① below to the right ② at the lower right ③ at the bottom right
- 左上の [に]　① above to the left ② at the upper left ③ at the top left
- 左下の [に]　① below to the left ② at the lower left ③ at the bottom left
- 33 ページの右上に　at the upper right of page 33
- 右下の写真　① the picture below to the right ② the picture at the lower right
- さし絵の左下に　to the lower left of the illustration

- …のもっと左に further to the left of …
- 右過ぎる be too far to the right
- いちばん右 ① the rightmost … ② 《be》 at the right end ③ 《be》 farthest to the right ④ 《be》 on the far right
- 彼はその写真のいちばん左に写っている． He appears at the extreme left of the picture.
- いちばん上の ① uppermost ② highest ③ topmost ④ top
- いちばん下の ① lowest ② bottom
- 横から見た図 ① a view from the side ② a side view
- その図は車を上から見たところだ． The figure shows the car as seen from above.

59-1-4 前後

- …の前に in front of …
- …の後に ① behind … ② at the back of … ③ in the rear of … ④ 《米》 in back of … ⑤ after …
- 前から3番目にすわっている be sitting in the third seat from the front
- 後から2両目 the second car from the rear
- 前に5人，後ろに50人並んでいた． There were five people ahead of 《her》 and fifty behind in the line.
- 列の先頭にいる ① be first in「line [《英》 a queue]」② be at the「front [head]」of a「line [《英》 queue]」
- 5台編成のトラック隊の先頭の車 the lead truck of a five-truck convoy
- 100メートル前方に線路がある． There are tracks 100 meters ahead.
- 前方に (向かって) ① forward(s) ② in a forward direction ③ frontward(s)
- 後方に (向かって) ① backward(s) ② in a backward direction ③ rearward(s)
- 斜め前の席 a seat in front and to the side
- 斜め後ろの席 a seat diagonally to the rear
- 右斜め後ろの席 a seat behind and to the right

■ 59-2 縦・横

[⇨ 42-6 縦・横・高さ]

- 縦の ① longitudinal ② lengthwise ③〔鉛直な〕vertical
- 横の ① horizontal ② lateral ③ transverse
- 縦波 a longitudinal wave
- 横波 a transverse wave

- 《表などの》行　a row
- 《表などの》列　a column
- m 行 n 列の行列　① an $m \times n$ matrix　② an m-by-n matrix　③ a matrix「with [having, of] m rows and n columns
- 縦3，横3の9個のマスを描きなさい．　① Draw nine squares, three across and three down.　② Draw a 3-by-3 matrix of nine squares.
- 《クロスワードの》縦の5番　five down
- 《クロスワードの》横の12番　twelve across
- 《チェス盤の》縦の筋と横の筋　ranks and files　★軍隊の縦列 (file), 横列 (rank) に由来.
- 縦長の　① vertically oriented　② longer [taller] than 《it》 is wide　③ 《用紙・写真など》 portrait
- 横長の　① horizontally oriented　② wider than 《it》 is「long [tall]」　③ 《用紙・写真など》 landscape
- 縦長［横長］で撮影した動画　video taken in「portrait [landscape] orientation
- 用紙を縦長に置く　① place a sheet longitudinally　② place a sheet with the shorter side at the top
- 縦置きの　〔印刷用紙が〕portrait 《orientation, format》
- 横置きの　〔印刷用紙が〕landscape 《orientation, format》
- 横断面　a cross section
- 縦断面　① a longitudinal section　② a longitudinal cross section　③ a vertical section
- 水平断面　a horizontal section
- 縦横比　① an aspect ratio　② a length-to-width ratio
- 魔方陣では縦・横・斜めのどの方向の数の和も同じになる［あらゆる行，列，主対角線の数の和が同じになる］．
   ① In a magic square, the sum of the numbers in any vertical, horizontal, or main diagonal line is the same.
   ② In a magic square, the sum of the numbers in any row, column, or main diagonal is the same.

■ 59-3 道順

59-3-1 基本動作

- まっすぐ進む　go straight
- 道を渡る　① cross a street　② 《英》go over a road
- 交差点を渡る　① go through a crossing　② cross an intersection　③ cross at an intersection　④ cross through an intersection

- 信号を渡る　cross at a light
- 道なりに行けば駅に出ます．　If you just follow the road, you'll end up at the station.

59-3-2 曲がる

- 右に曲がる　① turn right　② turn to the right　③ make a right turn
- 左に曲がる　① turn left　② turn to the left　③ make a left turn
- この角を左に曲がってまっすぐですよ．　Turn this street corner to the left and go straight on.
- 最初の角を左に曲がってください．　① Turn to the left at the first corner. ② Take the first「turn [《英》turning] to the left.
- 次の信号を右折すると学校が見えてきます．　Turn right at the next traffic「signal [lights] and you'll see the school.
- 信号の1つ手前の角を右に曲がる　turn right at the first corner「this side of [before] the (traffic) lights
- たばこ屋の角を右に折れた．　We turned right at the corner where the tobacco store stood.
- 交番はあの突き当たりを右に曲がったところです．　Turn right at the end there and you'll find the police box.
- その家は角を曲がった所だ．　The house「is [stands] around [round] the corner.
- その角を曲がった所で降ろしてください．　Please drop me off just after you turn that corner.
- そこの角で降ろしてください．　Let me off「on [at] the next corner, please.

59-3-3 位置

- それは2ブロック先です．　It's two blocks away. ★block はアメリカの一街区のこと．
- 50メートルほどまっすぐ行くと右手に郵便局があります．
  ① There's a post office about fifty meters straight ahead on the right.
  ② Go straight about fifty meters and you will see a post office on the right.
- 交番はその出口を出てすぐ左にあります．　The police box is right there on your left as you come out of the exit.
- 入口をはいってすぐ右に　immediately to the right as you go in the entrance
- 「ネクタイの売り場はどこですか」「正面右手です」　Where is the necktie section? — Straight ahead on the right.
- その店ならこの道の突き当たりにあります．　You'll find the store at the end of the street.
- 郵便局の向かいに　① opposite (to) the post office　② across from the post

office
- 我々は目的地の手前 500 メートルの所にいた. We were 500 meters short of our destination.

■ 59-4　将棋の駒の動き

- 3 マス前に進む　move forward (by) three squares
- 王はどの方向にも 1 つ動ける. The King can move one square in any direction (per move [at a time]).
- 金は前後，横，斜め前に 1 つ動ける. The Gold General can move one square forward, backward, sideways, or diagonally forward.
- 金は斜め後ろ以外どの方向にも 1 つ動ける. The Gold General can move one square in any direction except diagonally「backward [rearward].
- 銀は前と斜め前，斜め後ろに動ける. The Silver General can move one square straight forward or diagonally in any direction.
- 銀は横と真後ろを除いてどの方向にも 1 つ動ける. The Silver General can move one square in any direction except sideways or straight rearward.
- 桂馬は途中［他の駒］を飛び越して 1 つ右または左の 2 マス前方に動ける. The Knight can move one square to the left or right and two squares forward,「leaping [jumping]」over any「occupied squares [other pieces].
- 桂馬は西洋のチェスのナイトと同じように動けるが，前だけで，横や後ろには進めない. The Knight can move like the Knight in Western chess, but only forward, not to the side or back.
- 飛車は縦または横にいくらでも［何マスでも］進める. The Rook can move forward, backward, or sideways「any distance [any number of squares].
- 角は斜めにいくらでも［何マスでも］進める. The Bishop can move diagonally「any distance [any number of squares].
- 香車は前にいくらでも進める. The Lance can move forward any distance.
- 歩は前に 1 つ進める. The Pawn can move one square (straight) forward.

■ 59-5　東西南北

59-5-1　基本方位

- 東西南北　①north, south, east, and west　②the (four) cardinal points (of the compass)
▶ 日本語では「東西南北」の順にいうが，英語は「北南東西」の順になる（中国語では「東南西北」である）．また日本語では北東／東北，南西／西南など 2 通りの言い方があるが，気象に関しては英語と同じ南北を先にいう北東，南西などが使われ，東北，西南など東西を先にいう言い方は地域名に主に見られる．

59. 方向・向き 59-5-1

- 北　north《略 N》
- 北北東　north-northeast《略 NNE》
- 北東　northeast《略 NE》
- 東北東　east-northeast《略 ENE》
- 東　east《略 E》
- 東南東　east-southeast《略 ESE》
- 南東［東南］　southeast《略 SE》
- 南南東　south-southeast《略 SSE》
- 南　south《略 S》
- 南南西　south-southwest《略 SSW》
- 南西［西南］　southwest《略 SW》
- 西南西　west-southwest《略 WSW》
- 西　west《略 W》
- 西北西　west-northwest《略 WNW》
- 北西［西北］　northwest《略 NW》
- 北北西　north-northwest《略 NNW》
- 北微東　north by east《略 NbE》★北よりやや (90/8° = 11°15′) 東寄り．北と北北東の中間．
- 北東微北　northeast by north《略 NEbN》★北東よりやや (90/8° = 11°15′) 北寄り．北東と北北東の中間．

北	N	north
北微東	NbE	north by east
北北東	NNE	north-northeast
北東微北	NEbN	northeast by north
北東	NE	northeast
北東微東	NEbE	northeast by east
東北東	ENE	east-northeast
東微北	EbN	east by north
東	E	east
東微南	EbS	east by south
東南東	ESE	east-southeast
南東微東	SEbE	southeast by east
南東	SE	southeast
南東微南	SEbS	southeast by south
南南東	SSE	south-southeast
南微東	SbE	south by east
南	S	south

トリビア　North by Northwest

1959年のヒッチコック映画『北北西に進路を取れ』の原題はNorth by Northwestで，北北西 (north-northwest) でも北西微北 (northwest by north) でもない．『ハムレット』のせりふ I am but mad north-north-west（狂気なのは北北西の風のときだけ）から取ったと言われるが，映画では主人公が西に向かう際に航空会社名 Northwest Airlines が見える場面がある．

59-5-2 基本例

- 東に　① [東部に] in the east 《of …》　② [東方に] to the east 《of …》　③ [境を接して東側に] on the east 《of …》
- …の東約30キロにある　lie [be (located)] about 30 kilometers east of …
- 東は山に面する　face the mountains on the east
- 太陽は東から出て西に沈む．　The sun rises in the east and sets in the west.
- 風が北から吹いている．
  ① The wind is (blowing) from the north.
  ② There is a north wind.
- 南東の風　① a southeast wind　② a southeasterly wind
- 東南アジア　Southeast Asia
- 中北部　the north central region
- 中西部　① the west central region　② [米国の] the Middle West　③ the Midwest
- イングランド中東部にある町　a town in east-central England
- ドイツ中南部を流れる川　a river flowing through south-central Germany

■ 59-6 内外

- 内側の　① inner　② inside　③ interior　④ internal
- 外側の　① outer　② outside　③ exterior　④ external

■ 59-7 各分野での方向・向きの表現

59-7-1 日常

- その方向に　in that direction
- 反対方向に　① in an opposite direction　② in a contrary direction
- 音のする方向に動く　① move in the direction from which the sound is coming　② move toward the sound
- 後ろ前に着る　① put … on back to front　② wear … backwards　③ wear … (with the) front side back
- 裏表に着る　put … on inside out
- さかさにする　turn … upside down

59. 方向・向き 59-7-2

- 上下の向きを正しく置く　put … right side up

59-7-2　乗り物・機械

- 7時の方向に敵機．　There's an enemy plane at seven o'clock.［⇨第2部・…じ【…時】］
- 長手軸［前後軸，縦軸］　① a longitudinal axis　②〔飛翔体や船のロール軸〕a roll axis
- 左右軸［横軸］　① a transverse axis　② a lateral axis　③〔飛翔体や船のピッチ軸〕a pitch axis
- 鉛直軸［上下軸］　① a vertical axis　②〔飛翔体や船のヨー軸〕a yaw axis
- ピッチは横方向の軸のまわりの回転である．　Pitch is rotation around the 「side-to-side axis [lateral axis, transverse axis].　★機首などを上下させる回転．
- ロールは前後方向の軸のまわりの回転である．　Roll is rotation around the 「front-to-back [longitudinal] axis.　★機体などを左右に傾ける回転．
- ヨーは鉛直軸のまわりの回転である．　Yaw is rotation around the vertical axis.　★機首などを左右に振る回転．
- 右舷　the starboard
- 左舷　the port
- 船首　the bow
- 船尾　the stern
- 右舷前方に　on the starboard bow
- 右舷後方に　on the starboard quarter
- 右ハンドル車　① a right-hand drive car　② a right-hand drive vehicle
- 左ハンドル車　① a left-hand drive car　② a left-hand drive vehicle

> **トリビア**　内側車線と外側車線
>
> 　日本で内側車線といえば中央分離帯に近い側の車線を指し，これはアメリカの inside lane も同じである（ただし，アメリカでは車は右側通行なので日本の内側車線は右車線だが，アメリカの inside lane は左車線ということになる）．外側車線 (outside lane) はその逆で路肩側の車線となる．
>
> 　これに対し，イギリスでは inside lane は歩道に近い側をいい，outside lane が歩道から遠い追い越し車線を表わす．イギリス英語では歩道に近い側の車線を nearside，遠い側の車線を offside ともいう．

59-7-3 **物理**

- 時計回りの[に]　clockwise
- 反時計回りの[に]　counterclockwise [⇨第２部・かく]
- 回転の向きは右ねじを進める向きである．　The sense of rotation is to advance a right-handed screw.
- 右手を握って親指を導線を流れる電流の向きにすると，残りの指の方向が磁場の向きになる．
  ① If you curl the fingers of your right hand with your thumb in the direction of the current flowing through a wire, the magnetic field will be in the direction of the fingers.
  ② Grasp a wire with the right hand with the thumb in the direction of the current through the wire. The direction of the fingers indicates the direction of the magnetic field.
- 右手座標系　a right-handed coordinate system
- 左手座標系　a left-handed coordinate system
- 右偏光［右偏波］　right-hand polarization
- 左偏光［左偏波］　left-hand polarization
- 右偏光では伝搬方向に向かって［送信側から］見たときに電場ベクトルが時計回りに回転する．　With right-hand polarization, the electric field vector rotates in a clockwise direction「when you look in the direction of propagation [as seen from the transmitter]．★歴史的な慣行により，電気工学では伝搬方向に向かって見たときの回転で定義するが，光学・天文学では光源に向かって見たときにの回転に着目する．
- z 軸方向の単位ベクトル　the unit vector in the direction of the z-axis
- ベクトル **B** は **z 軸の正方向**を向いている．
  ① The vector **B** points in **the positive z direction**.
  ② The vector **B** points in **the direction of the positive z-axis**.
  ③ The vector **B** points in **the positive direction of the z-axis**.
- 紙面を手前に貫く向きのベクトル　① a vector pointing out of the page　② a vector directed out of the page　③ a vector coming out of the page
- 紙面を向こうに貫く向きのベクトル　① a vector pointing into the page　② a vector directed into the page　③ a vector going into the page
- 真ん中に点のある丸は紙面から出てくる向きの磁場を表わしている．　The circle with a dot in the「center [middle] represents [indicates] a magnetic field coming out of the page. ★矢の先端のイメージから慣習的に用いられる記号（⊙）．
- × のついた丸は紙面に向かう磁場を表わしている．　The circle with an X「represents [indicates] a magnetic field going into the page. ★矢の末尾のイメージから慣習的に用いられる記号（⊗）．
- 電池を正しい向きで入れる　① insert the battery with the correct orientation

② insert the battery in the proper direction
- プラスが上［手前］になるようにして電池を入れなさい.
  ① Put a battery in with the positive side facing「up [you].
  ② Put a battery in, making sure that the positive side is facing「up [you].
- 接線方向　the tangential direction
- 法線方向　the normal direction
- 接線方向の加速度　tangential acceleration
- 動径方向　the radial direction
- 視線方向　the line-of-sight direction
- 水平面　a horizontal plane
- 鉛直面　a vertical plane
- 軸に垂直な面　a plane perpendicular to the axis
- 表面に垂直な方向　the direction「normal [perpendicular] to the surface
- 水平解像度　horizontal resolution
- 垂直解像度　vertical resolution
- 赤道面　an equatorial plane
- 子午面　a meridional plane
- 赤道軌道　an equatorial orbit
- 極軌道　a polar orbit
- トロイダル方向　the toroidal direction
- ポロイダル方向　the poloidal direction
- 一方向にのみ流れる　flow only in one direction
- 一方向の　① unidirectional ② one-way
- 双方向の　① bidirectional ② two-way ③〔テレビなど〕interactive
- 全方向の　① omnidirectional ② all-direction
- 向き付け不能な面　a non-orientable surface

59-7-4 医学

- 前後方向［腹背方向，AP方向］　① the anterior-posterior direction ② the anteroposterior direction ③ the AP direction ④〔一般に〕the front-to-back direction
- 左右方向［LR方向］　① the left-right direction ② the LR direction
- 頭尾方向［SI方向］　① the superior-inferior direction ② the SI direction
- 後前方向［背腹方向，PA方向］　① the posterior-anterior direction ② the posteroanterior direction ③ the PA direction ★X線照射などでは前後方向と後前方向を区別する.
- 右左方向［RL方向］　① the right-left direction ② the RL direction

- 尾頭方向［IS 方向］ ① the inferior-superior direction ② the IS direction
- 水平面［アキシャル面］〔体の長軸に垂直な面〕① a horizontal plane ② an axial plane ③ a transaxial plane
- 冠状面［前額面，コロナル面］〔体を前後に分ける面〕① a coronal plane ② a frontal plane ★① は冠状縫合（coronal suture: 頭蓋骨頂部を前後に分けるような縫合部）に，② は額に平行であることに由来する称．
- 矢状(しじょう)面［サジタル面］〔体を左右に分ける面〕a sagittal plane
- 正中矢状面 〔体を真ん中で左右に分ける面〕① a median plane ② a mid-sagittal plane

59-7-5 舞台

- 上手 ① the left stage ② the stage left ★観客席から見て舞台右側であるが，英語では舞台から観客席に向かって左 (left) と発想する．the right of the stage などの表現は観客から見た右か舞台から見た右かは文脈次第となる．
- 下手 ① the right stage ② the stage right
- 上手に［で］ stage left
- 下手に［で］ stage right
- 主役が上手から登場した．
  ① The main character entered stage left.
  ②〔舞台から見た場合〕The main character entered the stage from the left.
  ③〔客席から見た場合〕The main character entered the stage from the right.
- その歌手は上手へ退場した．
  ① The singer exited stage left.
  ②〔舞台から見た場合〕The singer left the stage from the left.
  ③〔客席から見た場合〕The singer left the stage from the right.
- 舞台の袖 ① the wings of a stage ② the coulisses of a stage
- 舞台前方で［に］ downstage ★観客からみて手前側．
- 舞台後方で［に］ upstage
- 上手前で［に］ left down
- 上手奥で［に］ left up

60. 有名な科学の法則

60-1 ニュートンの運動の法則 Newton's laws of motion

第一法則 (the first law of motion):

- 外力がはたらかなければ物体は静止し続けるか,一定の速さで直線上を運動し続ける.
  In the absence of external forces [Unless acted upon by external forces], a body remains at rest or continues to move with constant speed in a straight line.

第二法則 (the second law of motion):

- 物体の加速度はそれにはたらく外力に比例し,その質量に反比例する.
  The acceleration of a body is directly proportional to the external force acting upon it and is inversely proportional to its mass.

第三法則 (the third law of motion):

- 物体が他の物体に力を及ぼすとき,第2の物体は大きさが同じで向きが反対の力を第1の物体に及ぼす.
  When one body exerts a force on another, the second body exerts an equal and opposite force on the first body.

60-2 万有引力の法則 the law of gravitation

- いかなる2つの物体も,両者の質量の積に比例し,両者の間の距離の2乗に反比例する力で引きつけ合う.
  Any two bodies attract each other with a force that is proportional to the product of their masses and inversely proportional to the square of the distance between them.

60-3 ケプラーの法則 Kepler's laws

楕円軌道の法則 (the law of ellipses):

- 太陽のまわりを回る惑星の軌道は太陽をその焦点の一つにもつ楕円である.
  The orbit of a planet about the Sun is an ellipse with the Sun at one focus.

面積速度一定の法則 (the law of equal areas):

- 惑星と太陽を結ぶ線分が一定時間に掃く面積は一定である.
  A line joining a planet and the Sun sweeps out equal areas during equal intervals of time.

調和の法則 (the harmonic law):

- 惑星の公転周期の2乗は太陽からの平均距離[軌道長半径]の3乗に比例

する．
The squares of the orbital periods of planets are proportional to the cubes of ⌈their average distances from the Sun ⌊their semimajor axes⌋.

60-4 電荷の法則 the law of charges

- 同符号の電荷は反発する．異符号の電荷は引きつけ合う．
  Like charges repel each other. Unlike charges attract each other.

60-5 フックの法則 Hooke's law

- ばねの伸びは加えられる力に比例する．
  ① The stretch of a spring is proportional to the applied force.
  ② The amount by which a spring is stretched is proportional to the applied force.

60-6 熱力学の法則

熱力学の第一法則 (the first law of thermodynamics)：

- 系に加えられた熱量は系の内部エネルギーの増加と系によってなされる仕事の和に等しい．　The heat supplied to a system is equal to the increase in internal energy of the system plus the work done by the system.

熱力学の第二法則 (the second law of thermodynamics)：

- 外から仕事を加えない限り熱を低温の物体から高温の物体に移動させることはできない．　Heat cannot be transferred from a cold body to a hot body unless external work is done.
- 閉じた系のエントロピーは時間とともに増加する．　The entropy of a closed system increases with time.

熱力学の第三法則 (the third law of thermodynamics)：

- 純粋な結晶のエントロピーは絶対零度では一定（定義により0）である．
  The entropy of all pure crystalline substances is constant (zero by definition) at absolute zero temperature.

60-7 メンデルの法則 Mendel's laws

優性の法則 (the law of dominance) ▶ メンデル以後多様な遺伝現象が明らかになったこともあり，英語では含めないことが多い．

- 雑種第一代では対立形質の一方のみが現われる．
  In the first filial generation, only one of the contrasting ⌈traits ⌊characters⌋ expresses itself.

分離の法則 (the law of segregation)：

- 遺伝形質を支配している2つの遺伝子は分離して別々の配偶子に移行す

る. Two genes controlling a hereditary characteristic segregate and pass into separate gametes.

独立の法則 (the law of independent assortment):

- 2組以上の対立遺伝子は配偶子が形成されるときに互いに独立に分離する.
  Two or more pairs of alleles segregate independently of one another when gametes are formed.

60-8 ボイルの法則 Boyle's law

- 一定温度のもとで気体の体積はその圧力に反比例する.
  At a「fixed [constant]」temperature, the volume of a gas is inversely proportional to its pressure.

60-9 シャルルの法則 Charles' law

- 一定圧力のもとで気体の体積はその絶対温度に比例する.
  At a「fixed [constant]」pressure, the volume of a gas is directly proportional to the absolute temperature.

60-10 気体反応の法則 the law of combining volumes

- 気体の化学反応では,反応物と生成物の体積は簡単な整数比をなす.
  In a chemical reaction of gases, the relative volumes of reactants and products are in a ratio of small integers.

61. ギリシア語／ラテン語系の数を表わす接頭辞

　英語では数を含む単語をつくるのにギリシア語，ラテン語に由来する接頭辞を使ったものが多数ある．「二項定理」(binomial theorem)，「四足歩行」(quadrupedalism)，「オクターブ」(octave)，「10年」(decade)，「13恐怖症」(triskaidekaphobia)，「十六進」(hexadecimal)など枚挙にいとまがない．こうした数を表わす接頭辞は次のようにギリシア語系とラテン語系の2系統のものがある．

■ 61-1 基本的な数を表わす接頭辞

	ギリシア語系	ラテン語系
1	mono-（モノ）	uni-（ユニ）
2	di-（ジ）	bi-（ビ）
3	tri-（トリ）	ter-（テル）
4	tetra-（テトラ）	quater-（クァテル）
5	penta-（ペンタ）	quinque-（キンク）
6	hexa-（ヘキサ）	sexi-（セクシ）
7	hepta-（ヘプタ）	septi-（セプチ）
8	octa-（オクタ）	octi-（オクチ）
9	ennea-（エンネア）	nona-（ノナ）
10	deca-（デカ）	deci-（デシ）
11	hendeca-（ヘンデカ）	undeca-（ウンデカ）

　元来はギリシア語系の接頭辞はギリシア語系の語根と，ラテン語系の接頭辞はラテン語系の語根と組み合わされていた．ギリシア語系のmono-が含まれるmonogamy（単婚），monogram（モノグラム），monologue（独白），monopoly（独占）は後半の語根もギリシア語系になっているし，ラテン語系のuni-が含まれるunanimous（満場一致の），unicorn（一角獣），uniform（一様な）はみなラテン語系の語根を含んでいる．しかし，使用範囲が広がるにつれ語根の出自には関係なく比較的自由に組み合わされるようになった．近代以降は科学の諸分野で接頭辞を系統的に使って造語がされるが，その傾向が特に顕著なのが化合物命名法である．健康関

連で話題の魚油成分 DHA は「ドコサヘキサエン酸」の略であるが，化学者はこの名前を見れば炭素原子が 22 個 (= ドコサ)，二重結合 (= エン) が 6 個 (= ヘキサ) 含まれている酸であることがすぐにわかる．そのような化合物命名法で使われる接頭辞を次に示す．

■ 61-2 化合物名の倍数接頭辞

1	mono- (モノ)
2	di- (ジ)
3	tri- (トリ)
4	tetra- (テトラ)
5	penta- (ペンタ)
6	hexa- (ヘキサ)
7	hepta- (ヘプタ)
8	octa- (オクタ)
9	nona- (ノナ)
10	deca- (デカ)
11	undeca- (ウンデカ)
12	dodeca- (ドデカ)
13	trideca- (トリデカ)
14	tetradeca- (テトラデカ)
15	pentadeca- (ペンタデカ)
16	hexadeca- (ヘキサデカ)
17	heptadeca- (ヘプタデカ)
18	octadeca- (オクタデカ)
19	nonadeca- (ノナデカ)
20	icosa- [eicosa-] (イコサ [エイコサ])
21	henicosa- [heneicosa-] (ヘンイコサ [ヘンエイコサ])
22	docosa- (ドコサ)
23	tricosa- (トリコサ)
24	tetracosa- (テトラコサ)
25	pentacosa- (ペンタコサ)
26	hexacosa- (ヘキサコサ)
27	heptacosa- (ヘプタコサ)
28	octacosa- (オクタコサ)

29	nonacosa-（ノナコサ）
30	triaconta-（トリアコンタ）
31	hentriaconta-（ヘントリアコンタ）
32	dotriaconta-（ドトリアコンタ）
33	tritriaconta-（トリトリアコンタ）
34	tetratriaconta-（テトラトリアコンタ）
35	pentatriaconta-（ペンタトリアコンタ）
36	hexatriaconta-（ヘキサトリアコンタ）
37	heptatriaconta-（ヘプタトリアコンタ）
38	octatriaconta-（オクタトリアコンタ）
39	nonatriaconta-（ノナトリアコンタ）
40	tetraconta-（テトラコンタ）
41	hentetraconta-（ヘンテトラコンタ）
42	dotetraconta-（ドテトラコンタ）
50	pentaconta-（ペンタコンタ）
60	hexaconta-（ヘキサコンタ）

　大半はギリシア語系の接頭辞をそのまま使っており，化合物以外の造語要素としてもそのまま使えることがある．9のnona-や11のundeca-では変則的にラテン語系の語形を採用しているが，9についてennea-よりnona-が好まれる慣用は他分野でも見られる（九角形はenneagonよりもnonagonのほうが通じやすい）．

　20についてはIUPAC（国際純正応用化学連合）は1993年にeicosa-からicosa-に切り換えたが，CAS（化学情報検索サービス機関）ではその後もeicosa-を使っている．

■ 61-3 重複を表わす倍数接頭辞

　化学ではたとえば「トリメチルフェニル」基が3つあることを表わすとき，その「3つ」は「トリ」ではなく「トリス」という別の形を使って「トリス（トリメチルフェニル）」のようにいう．次に示すのはこのような構造の重複を表わす倍数接頭辞である．4以降で使われている-kis-はギリシア語の「…回」「…倍」を意味する語に由来する．化合物以外では，結晶学でのtetrahexahedron（⇨ 58-3 …面体）の同義語としてtetrakis-hexahedronのように使うこともある．

2	bis-	ビス
3	tris-	トリス
4	tetrakis-	テトラキス
5	pentakis-	ペンタキス
6	hexakis-	ヘキサキス
7	heptakis-	ヘプタキス
8	octakis-	オクタキス
9	nonakis-	ノナキス
10	decakis-	デカキス

■ 61-4 新元素名

元素は110余りの名前が決まっているが，名前が未決定の新元素については原子番号の数字を次の造語要素で置き換えて体系的な名称を作ることができる．もちろんこうした名称を使わず，element-114（114番元素）のようにいうこともできる．

0	nil	ニル
1	un	ウン
2	bi	ビ
3	tri	トリ
4	quad	クァド
5	pent	ペント
6	hex	ヘキサ
7	sept	セプト
8	oct	オクト
9	enn	エン

例）

106番元素	unnilhexium	ウンニルヘキシウム
113番元素	ununtrium	ウンウントリウム
115番元素	ununpentium	ウンウンペンチウム
116番元素	ununhexium	ウンウンヘキシウム
117番元素	ununseptium	ウンウンセプチウム
118番元素	ununoctium	ウンウンオクチウム

119番元素	ununennium	ウンウンエンニウム
120番元素	unbinilium	ウンビニリウム
128番元素	unbioctium	ウンビオクチウム
130番元素	untrinilium	ウントリニリウム

■ 61-5 数字を造語要素として含む単語のいろいろ

61-5-1 …年ごとの
annual（1年），biennial（2年），triennial（3年），... [⇨ 36-4 …年ごとの]

61-5-2 …周年
centenary（100年），bicentenary（200年），... [⇨ 36-5 …周年]

61-5-3 …角形
triangle（三角形），quadrilateral [quadrangle, tetragon]（四角形），pentagon（五角形），... [⇨ 58-2 …角形]

61-5-4 …面体
tetrahedron（四面体），pentahedron（五面体），... [⇨ 58-3 …面体]

61-5-5 …次 [⇨ 第2部・…じ【…次】]
（数学）linear（一次），quadratic（二次），cubic（三次），quartic（四次），quintic（五次）

（その他）primary（一次），secondary（二次），tertiary（三次），quaternary（四次）

61-5-6 …つ子
twin（双子），triplet（三つ子），quadruplet [quad]（四つ子），quintuplet [quin, quint]（五つ子），sextuplet（六つ子），septuplet（七つ子），octuplet（八つ子），nonuplet（九つ子）

61-5-7 …重奏，…重唱
solo（独奏），duet [duo]（二重奏），trio（三重奏），quartet（四重奏），quintet（五重奏），sextet（六重奏），septet（七重奏），octet（八重奏），nonet（九重奏）

61. ギリシア語／ラテン語系の数を表わす接頭辞 61-5-8

61-5-8　…倍
single (単一), double (2倍), triple (3倍), quadruple (4倍), quintuple (5倍), sextuple (6倍), septuple (7倍), octuple (8倍), nonuple (9倍), decuple (10倍), multiple (倍数) [⇨第2部・ばい]

61-5-9　…重項
singlet (一重項), doublet (二重項), triplet (三重項), quartet (四重項), quintet (五重項), sextet (六重項), septet (七重項), octet (八重項), nonet (九重項), decuplet (十重項), multiplet (多重項)

分光学や素粒子物理学での用語で、原義は「…重のもの」.

61-5-10　…重極，…極子
monopole (単極子), dipole (双極子), quadrupole (四極子), octupole (八極子), multipole (多重極子)

61-5-11　…個組
unary (1), binary (2), ternary (3), quaternary (4), quinary (5), senary (6), septenary (7), octonary (8), nonary (9), denary (10), undenary (11), duodenary (12)

「…個からなる」の意味が基本であり，binary system といえば「二進法」「連星系」「二成分系」などの意味にもなる.

61-5-12　…進法
binary (二進法), ternary (三進法), quaternary (四進法), quinary (五進法), senary (六進法), septenary (七進法), octal (八進法), nonary (九進法), decimal (十進法), duodecimal (十二進法), hexadecimal (十六進法), vigesimal (二十進法), sexagesimal (60進法), n-ary (n進法)

数字の小さな部分は 61-5-11 の「…個組」が基本になっているが，慣用のため一部異なる形が好まれる.「…進法」の「…」の数字のことを基数 (base) といい，たとえば vigesimal は a base-20 numeral system と説明できる.

61-5-13　経妊婦 [⇨ 38-5 妊娠・出産]
nulligravida (未妊婦), primigravida (初妊婦), secundigravida (2回経妊婦), tertigravida (3回経妊婦), multigravida (経妊婦)

61-5-14 同姓同名の区別

primus（その 1），secundus（その 2），tertius（その 3），quartus（その 4），quintus（その 5），sextus（その 6），septimus（その 7），octavus（その 8），nonus（その 9），decimus（その 10）

イギリスのパブリックスクールで同姓の生徒の姓に付けて Smith primus（スミス 1）のように区別する．ラテン語の序数詞である．

61-5-15 …折判

folio（二折判），quarto（四折判），sixmo [sexto, 6to, 6mo]（六折判），octavo [8vo]（八折判），twelvemo [duodecimo, 12mo]（十二折判），sixteenmo [sextodecimo, 16mo]（十六折判），eighteenmo [octodecimo, 18mo]（十八折判）

もとはラテン語の序数，たとえば sextus（第 6 の，6 回目の）の奪格形 sexto（6 回）や duodecimus（第 12 の，12 回目の）の奪格形 duodecimo（12 回）を使っていたが，今では quarto, octavo のような人口に膾炙したものを除いて英語の数詞に語尾 -mo を付けることが多い．

61-5-16 法律・規格文書の枝番 [⇨ 48. 法律・条約 48-5]

bis (2), ter (3), quater (4), quinquies (5), sexies (6), septies (7), octies (8), novies (9), decies (10)

61-5-17 トランプやさいころ

ace (1), deuce (2), trey (3), cater (4), cinq(ue) (5), sice (6)　▶ deuce 以下は古フランス語に由来する語形で（⇨ 61-6 各国語の数詞），今ではトランプの ace と deuce 以外はほとんど使われない．

61-5-18 その他

biathlon（バイアスロン，二種競技），triathlon（トライアスロン，三種競技）

bicameral（二院制の）

biconvex（両凸の）

bicorne（二角帽），tricorne（三角帽）

bifocal（二焦点の）

bilinear（双線形の）

bimonthly（隔月の／月 2 回の）

61. ギリシア語／ラテン語系の数を表わす接頭辞 61-5-18

bipedalism（二足歩行），quadrupedalism（四足歩行）
bistable（双安定な）
biweekly（隔週の／週2回の）
centipede（ムカデ），millipede（ヤスデ）
century（世紀），millennium（千年紀）
decade（10年），score（20年）
deci-（デシ＝10分の1），centi-（センチ＝100分の1），milli-（ミリ＝1000分の1）
digraph（二連字），trigraph（三連字）
diphthong（二重母音），triphthong（三重母音）
hexaemeron（天地創造の6日間）
monocle（片眼鏡），binoculars（双眼鏡）
monogamy（単婚，一夫一婦制），bigamy（重婚），polygamy（複婚，一夫多妻制）▶digamyは再婚
monolingual（単言語使用の），bilingual（二言語使用の），trilingual（三言語使用の），quadrilingual（四言語使用の），multilingual（多言語使用の）
monomial（単項式），binomial（二項式），trinomial（三項式），quadrinomial（四項式），polynomial（多項式）
monoploid（一倍体）＝haploid（半数体），diploid（二倍体），triploid（三倍体），tetraploid（四倍体），pentaploid（五倍体）
monosyllable（単音節語），disyllable（二音節語），trisyllable（三音節語），tetrasyllable［quadrisyllable］（四音節語），pentasyllable（五音節語），hexasyllable［sexisyllable］（六音節語），heptasyllable［septisyllable］（七音節語），octosyllable（八音節語），enneasyllable（九音節語），dodecasyllable（十音節語），plurisyllable（2音節以上の多音節語），polysyllable［multisyllable］（3音節以上の多音節語）
monovalent（一価の），divalent（二価の），trivalent（三価の），tetravalent（四価の）［⇨第2部・いっか］
octave（オクターブ＝8度）
quadrant（四分儀；象限），sextant（六分儀），octant（八分儀）
quadrugenarian（40代），quinquagenarian（50代），sexagenarian（60代），septuagenarian（70代），octogenarian（80代），nonagenarian（90代），centenarian（100歳以上），supercentenarian（110歳以上）
uniaxial（一軸の），biaxial（二軸の），triaxial（三軸の）
unicycle（一輪車），bicycle（二輪車），tricycle（三輪車）

unigram（単字），bigram（二字連接），trigram（三字連接），N-gram（N字連接）

unilateral（一方向的な），bilateral（相互的な），trilateral（三者間の），multilateral（多角的な，多国間の）

univalent（一価の），bivalent（二価の），tervalent（三価の），quadrivalent（四価の）[⇨第2部・いっか]

■ 61-6 付録：各国語の数詞

	イタリア語	スペイン語	フランス語	オランダ語	ドイツ語	ロシア語
1	uno, una	uno, una	un, une	één	eins	один
2	due	dos	deux	twee	zwei	два
3	tre	tres	trois	drie	drei	три
4	quattro	cuatro	quatre	vier	vier	четыре
5	cinque	cinco	cinq	vijf	fünf	пять
6	sei	seis	six	zes	sechs	шесть
7	sette	siete	sept	zeven	sieben	семь
8	otto	ocho	huit	acht	acht	восемь
9	nove	nueve	neuf	negen	neun	девять
10	dieci	diez	dix	tien	zehn	десять
11	undici	once	onze	elf	elf	одиннадцать
12	dodici	doce	douze	twaalf	zwölf	двенадцать
13	tredici	trece	treize	dertien	dreizehn	тринадцать
14	quattordici	catorce	quatorze	veertien	vierzehn	четырнадцать
15	quindici	quince	quinze	vijftien	fünfzehn	пятнадцать
16	sedici	dieciséis	seize	zestien	sechzehn	шестнадцать
17	diciassette	diecisiete	dix-sept	zeventien	siebzehn	семнадцать
18	diciotto	dieciocho	dix-huit	achttien	achtzehn	восемнадцать
19	diciannove	diecinueve	dix-neuf	negentien	neunzehn	девятнадцать
20	venti	veinte	vingt	twintig	zwanzig	двадцать
21	ventuno	veintiuno	vingt-et-un	eenentwintig	einundzwanzig	двадцать один

▶ ラテン系の言語（イタリア語，スペイン語，フランス語）で20を表わす語が2を表わす語とは別の語根になっている．

▶ フランス語では80を quatre-vingts（4つの20），90を quatre-vingt-dix（4つの20＋10），また70を soixante-dix（60＋10）と表現するという特徴がある．ただし，ベルギーやスイスのフランス語では septante, octante (huitante), nonante という規則的な数詞が使われる.

▶ ゲルマン系のドイツ語,オランダ語では 20 以上の 2 桁の数の表現で 1 の位を先にいう特徴がある.たとえばドイツ語で 21 は einundzwanzig (1 と 20) という.

▶ 外国語の数詞が特にその国の事物を表わすときにそのまま英語の語彙になっているケースがある.特にフランス語が顕著で,pas de deux (パドドゥ,二人舞踏),ménage à trois (愛人を含めた三人所帯),Louis Quatorze (ルイ 14 世時代風の),Quatorze Juillet (7 月 14 日＝フランス革命記念日) などがよく知られている.日本でも「25ans」(ヴァンサンカン vingt cinq ans＝25 歳の意) のような雑誌名でおなじみである.イタリア語の seicento (600 の意) は英語では 17 世紀イタリアの芸術を指して使われる.

▶ 中国語では一・二・三・四…という表記 (小写) のほかに壹 (1)・貳 (2)・叁 (3)・肆 (4)・伍 (5)・陆 (6)・柒 (7)・捌 (8)・玖 (9)・拾 (10)・佰 (100)・阡 (1000) の表記 (大写) があって金額表記などに使われている.日本でも壱 (1)・弐 (2)・参 (3)・拾 (10) は使われている (大字という).

▶ 朝鮮語 (韓国語) は日本語の大和言葉と漢語に相当する 2 つの系統の語彙がある.数詞についても中国由来の一・二・三・四…と並んで日本語の「一つ」「二つ」に相当する固有語の系統があるのだが,10 までしかない日本語の場合と違って 99 まである.

トリビア　数字を英語読みする日本語の名称

アイドルグループ「AKB48」は「エーケービー フォーティエイト」と読む.「…よんじゅうはち」と読む人がいるとそのことが話題になったりする.このような大きな数の英語読みが日本語の名称の一部として流布することはめずらしい.CO_2 (シーオーツー) やビタミン B_1 (ビタミンビーワン) くらいならともかく,ビタミン B_{12} など数字が大きくなると,「ビタミンビーじゅうに」と読む人が多いのではないだろうか.

62. 数の一致

動詞は主語の単数・複数に合わせた形をとる．

- The **difference** between the two values **is** divided by two.　その2つの値の差を2で割る．
- All the **numbers** in the set **are** even.　その集合中の数はすべて偶数である．

単複について注意すべき名詞に以下のようなものがある．

(1) 単数語形なのに複数扱いする名詞（集合名詞）

▶ **people 人々**
- **Ten people were** injured.　10人の人が負傷した．
- **A lot of people were** injured.　大勢の人が負傷した．

★「民族」の意味では a people/peoples と普通の単数／複数の区別をする．

▶ **police 警察**
- **The police are** investigating the case.　警察がその件を調べている．
- **Two police were** hurt.　警官2人が負傷した．★two police は two policemen または two police officers と言い換えることができる．

▶ **cattle 家畜**
- **Five cattle were** stolen.　5頭の家畜が盗まれた．

(2) the＋形容詞の形の集合名詞

- **The rich are** not always happy.　金持ちが幸福とは限らない．
- **The wounded were** transported to a hospital.　負傷者は病院に運び込まれた．

(3) 単複両様の扱いがある集合名詞

イギリス英語では一つの単位と見なすときには単数扱い，複数の構成員の集合と見なすときには複数扱いする．アメリカ英語では意味が複数でも語形が単数のものは単数扱いする傾向がある．

▶ **family 家族**
- How「**is**〔**are**〕your family？　ご家族はお元気ですか．
- **My family are** all very well.　家族一同元気です．

▶ **class クラス**
- **The class**「**were**〔**was**〕all cheerful.　クラスの者はみな陽気だった．

62. 数の一致

▶ team チーム
- **The team has** twenty members.　そのチームには20人のメンバーがいる.
- **Our team** [**were** [**was**] in the best of spirits.　我がチームの士気は最高だった.

▶ committee 委員会
- **The committee** [**are** [**is**]] all against the bill.　委員会はその法案に反対で一致している.
- **The committee (members) differ** as to the details.　細部については委員たちの意見は分かれている.

▶ government 政府
- **The government** [**was** [**were**]] divided.　政府は割れていた.
- **The government** [**has** [**have**]] decided to accept the peace proposal.　政府はその和平提案を受け入れることを決めた.

▶ nation 国民
- **The whole nation** [**supports** [**support**]] him.　全国民が彼を支持している.

▶ public 大衆
- **The public** [**is** the best judge [**are** the best judges]].　世間は最良の判断者である.

▶ staff スタッフ
- a fifteen-person staff [a staff of fifteen (people)]　15名の職員　★staff の一員は a staff member という.
- **The staff** [**are** [**is**]] concerned about the matter.　スタッフはその問題を懸念している.

▶ audience 聴衆
- **The audience** [**were** [**was**]] mostly young people.　聴衆は大部分若者だった.

(4) 複数語形なのに単数扱いするもの

(4.1) 一般語

news ニュース

- The news was a shock to us all. その知らせは我々みなにとってショックだった.

measles はしか(病名)　▶はしかの発疹を指すときには複数扱い.

(4.2) 学問名

physics 物理学

mathematics 数学
　以下は学問名・科目名としては単数扱いでよいが，意味によって複数扱いすることもあるもの．
　politics 政治学　▶「政治的意見」の意味では複数扱い，「政治活動」の意味では単複両様の扱いをする．
　statistics 統計学　▶「統計データ」の意味では複数扱い．
　athletics 体育　▶「運動競技」の意味では複数扱い．
　gymnastics 体操　▶「体操競技」の意味では複数扱い．

(4.3) 固有名詞
the United States アメリカ合衆国
the Netherlands オランダ
Gemini ふたご座　▶ラテン語の複数形であるが単数扱い．Pisces（うお座）も同様．
ただし，複数のイメージがあるものは複数扱いする．
the Canaries カナリア諸島
the Alps アルプス山脈
the Pleiades プレアデス星団

(4.4) タイトル
The Times タイムズ
ただし，内容が物語集などの場合には複数扱いされることもある．
The Canterbury Tales カンタベリー物語

(4.5) 普通の単語の複数形も，全体を一まとまりのデータとみなす場合には単数扱いする．

- Ten dollars is enough.　10 ドルで十分だ．
- At least four hours is recommended.　少なくとも 4 時間が推奨される．
- A million years is only an instant in the history of the universe.　100 万年は宇宙の歴史の中では一瞬でしかない．
- An additional two gigabytes is required.　追加の 2 ギガバイトが必要とされる．
- An extra 100 dollars was added.　追加で 100 ドルが加えられた．
- Another three months was wasted.　さらに 3 か月が無駄にされた．
- The sixties was a period of transition.　60 年代は移行の時期だった．

(5) グループ名について

(5.1) スポーツチーム

スポーツチーム名は the + 複数形をとることが多い.

the Tigers タイガース

the Carp カープ　★carp は単複同形の名詞.

the Mets メッツ

これは語形通り複数扱いするのが通例である.

- **The Tigers were** in first place in the initial stages of the pennant race.　タイガースはペナントレースの序盤戦では首位だった.

また, そのチームに属する一人の選手を a + 単数形で表わすことができる. それをさらに複数にすることもできる.

- When he was **a Met**, ...　彼がメッツの選手だったとき…
- With nobody out and **two Mets** on base in the ninth inning, the batter hit into a triple play.　メッツが9回にノーアウトで2人出塁していたとき, バッターがトリプルプレーを出した.

ただし, Red Sox (レッドソックス) の場合, sox は sock の複数形だが, a Red Sock の形は使わず, 選手のことも a Red Sox といっている. 複数の選手はもちろん two Red Sox などでよい.

一方, チームを地名で呼ぶ場合には単数形である. また, 近年はチーム名に伝統的な the + 複数形ではなく, 単数形の名詞を使うことも増えてきている. そのような場合, アメリカ英語では単数扱い, イギリス英語では複数扱いが普通.

- **Portsmouth** ﹁**is**〔**are**〕 unbeaten in their last six games.　ポーツマスは過去6試合で無敗である.
- **Chelsea** ﹁**has**〔**have**〕 won three, drawn one, and lost one of five games this season.　チェルシーは今季の5ゲームのうち3勝1敗1引き分けである.

なお, 最近のユニークな名称の場合には, a Met のような選手を指す用法では使わなかったり, 使っても単数形のみだったりすることもある. そのような場合は「a 〜 player」「〜 players」と言い換えることができる.

(5.2) バンド名

複数形のバンド名は複数扱いが普通. 単数形をそのメンバーに使うこともできる.

- The Beatles are a well-known band.　ビートルズは有名なバンドだ.

• When he was a Beatle …　彼がビートルズのメンバーだったとき…

　単数形のバンド名についてはアメリカ英語では単数扱い,イギリス英語では複数扱いが普通.

(6) 通例複数形でのみ使うもの (絶対複数)

　複数語形で複数扱いという意味では普通の名詞だが,日本語の感覚からすると単数のものを複数で使うものも多い.socks のたぐいについては⇨ 2. 数え方.単数扱いする例については⇨ (4).

　customs　税関
　odds　可能性

(7) 単数形と複数形がまぎらわしいもの

　次のような名詞は単複同形である.動物名の個体でなく種類を指すときには -s のつく複数形をつくれるものもあるが,-s の形が許容される度合いはまちまちで一定の規則はない.また,分類上,集合名詞に近いものもある.

　動物名: sheep (羊),deer (鹿),fish (魚),carp (鯉)
　国民名: Japanese (日本人),Portuguese (ポルトガル人),Swiss (スイス人)
　その他: series (シリーズ),species (種)
　外来語: yen (円)
　綴り字のみの単複同形: corps (軍団),rendezvous (会合)　★発音では複数形は [-z] の音が加わる.

▶「手段」の意味の means は歴史的には「真ん中」の意味の mean の複数形であったが,現在は means の形で単数 (a means) にも複数 (means) にも使う.

▶ inning は野球では an inning/innings と通常の単複の変化をするが,イギリスのクリケットでは innings の形を単複同形に使う.すなわち,単数形で a long innings のようにいい,複数形も two innings となる (口語ではさらに two inningses の形もある).

▶ その他,外来語では元来複数形であるものが単数形として使われることもしばしばある (例: agenda, data, media).

▶ summons (召喚 (状)) は s がついているが完全に単数名詞で,複数は summonses.

63. 不定代名詞と単数／複数

■ 63-1 数詞

「2つ」などの意味では複数扱い．

- Two of the members were women.　メンバーのうち2人は女性だった．
- There are two hundred.　200個ある．

数字の「2」などの意味では単数扱い．

- Thirteen is a prime.　13は素数である．
- Seven is my lucky number.　7は私のラッキーナンバーだ．
- Forty is the number of trials and tests in the Bible.　40は聖書では苦難と試練の数字だ．

■ 63-2 all

63-2-1 形容詞の all

複数名詞にも単数名詞にもかかる．動詞は名詞の単複に一致する．

- **all people**　あらゆる人
- **all his money**　彼の金全部
- **all (the) students** in the school　学校にいる**生徒全員**　★the をつけないと漠然と「あらゆる生徒」という感じ．the があると学籍をもつ全校生徒が確定した集合であることを意識する感じ．
- **all (the) files** on the disk　ディスク上の**すべてのファイル**　★the をつけないと漠然と「あらゆるファイル」という感じ．the があるとディスク上にあるファイルが有限個の確定した集合であることを意識する感じ．
- **All these books were** published prior to 1957.　**これらの本はすべて** 1957年より前に出版された．

63-2-2 代名詞の all

全体をひとまとまりとして all というときには単数扱い．人を表わす場合の all（全員）や「all of + 複数名詞」の形は複数扱い．

- **All is** lost.　**すべては**だめになった．
- **All** I want **is** to sleep.　眠りたい**だけだ**．
- **All were** present.　**全員**出席していた．
- **All of** these books **were** published prior to 1957.　これらの本は**すべて** 1957年より前に出版された．

63-2-3 副詞の all

副詞の all は単複には影響しない．

- These **methods** all **give** the same result.　これらの**方法は**みな同じ結果を与える．
- These **books were** all published prior to 1957.　これらの**本は**すべて 1957 年より前に出版された．

■ 63-3 **each**

63-3-1 形容詞の each

形容詞の each は単数名詞にかかる．

- **Each user** is assigned a unique user ID.　**各ユーザー**は一意的なユーザー ID を割り当てられる．

63-3-2 代名詞の each

代名詞の each は単数扱い．

- **Each** of the eight sections **is** divided into three subsections.　8つのセクションの**それぞれは** 3 つのサブセクションに分割される．

63-3-3 副詞の each

副詞の each は単複には影響しない．

- **Users are** each assigned a unique user ID.　**ユーザーは**それぞれ一意的なユーザー ID を割り当てられる．
- These **functions** each **output** an 8-bit value.　これらの**関数は**それぞれ 8 ビットの値を出力する．

■ 63-4 **either / neither**

63-4-1 形容詞の either / neither

形容詞の either, neither は単数名詞にかかる．

- This allows the panel to move in **either direction**.　これによりパネルは**どちらの方向にも**動くことができる．
- **Neither side** shows signs of giving up.　**どちらの側も**あきらめる気配を見せてい**ない**．

63-4-2 代名詞の either / neither

単数扱いが本来だが，「either of + 複数名詞」「neither of + 複数名詞」の場合，口語ではしばしば複数扱いする．

- **Either of them** [is [are] good enough.　**どちらも**結構です．

- **Neither of these variables** 「**was**〔**were**〕above the threshold. **これらの変数のどちらも閾値を超えていなかった**.

63-4-3 副詞の either / neither
⇨ 64. 各種構文と単数／複数 64-4

■ 63-5 **both**

63-5-1 形容詞の both
形容詞の both は複数の名詞にかかる.

- **Both theories were** formulated by Einstein. **両方の理論は**アインシュタインによって定式化された. ★限定詞がつく場合は both the theories, both these theories, both his theories などの語順になる.
- **Both special relativity and general relativity were** formulated by Einstein. **特殊相対論と一般相対論は両方とも**アインシュタインによって定式化された.

63-5-2 代名詞の both
代名詞の both は複数扱い.

- **Both were** formulated by Einstein. **両方とも**アインシュタインによって定式化された. ★なお,《米》では the both と定冠詞をつけることがあるが, 非標準的.

63-5-3 副詞の both
副詞の both は単複には影響しない.

- These **theories were** both formulated by Einstein. **これらの理論は両方とも**アインシュタインによって定式化された.

■ 63-6 **every**
単数形の名詞にかかる形容詞である.

- **Every** pixel is assigned a grayscale value. **すべての**ピクセルに中間階調値が割り当てられる.

「…ごとに」というときには反復の単位となる「…」の部分は複数形でもよい.

- **every** three weeks 3 週間ごとに
- **every** few days 数日ごとに
- **every** hundred meters 100 メートルごとに

■ 63-7 everybody / everything / everyone / anybody / anything / anyone / nobody / nothing / no one

これらの代名詞は単数扱いである.

- **Everybody was** satisfied. **全員が**満足した.
- **Everything depends** on the size of the cluster. **すべては**クラスターのサイズに**依存する**.
- **Nothing comes** of nothing. 《諺》無から**有は生じない**.
- If **anyone is** interested, I will make it available on my website. **誰か**興味がある人がいれば私のウェブサイトに載せます.

■ 63-8 any

63-8-1 形容詞の any

［**肯定文-1**］「任意の」「どんな…でも」の意味では通例単数名詞につける.

- **Any form** of government is better than none (at all). **どんな形**の政府でも全くないよりはいい.
- This system is scalable to **any number** of users. このシステムはユーザー数が**何人にでも**拡張できます.

［**肯定文-2**］「もしあればすべての…」のニュアンスでは可算名詞の複数形,不可算名詞につける.

- It will delete **any files** on the disk. ディスク上の**ファイルを(もしあれば)すべて**消去します.

［**疑問文・条件節-1**］「いくらかの」の意味で可算名詞の複数形,不可算名詞につける.肯定文の some books (何冊かの本),some money (若干の金)などの用法に対応する.

- Do you have **any questions**? **何か質問**はありますか.
- Do you have **any information** about the case? その件について**何か情報**はありますか.

［**疑問文・条件節-2**］「何らかの」の意味で単数名詞につける.肯定文の some book (何らかの本)などの用法に対応する.

- If **any signal** is detected, … もし**何らかの信号**が検出されたら…

［**否定文-1**］「少しも(…ない)」の意味で可算名詞の複数形,不可算名詞につける.

- I don't have **any questions**. 質問は全然ない.
- I don't have **any information**. 情報は全然ない.

[**否定文-2**]「どの一つとして（…ない）」の意味で単数名詞につける.

- It has not been explained by **any theoretical model** up to now. それは今に至るまで**いかなる理論モデルによっても**説明されて**いない**.

63-8-2　代名詞の any

「任意のもの」という意味では単数扱いが普通（上記［肯定文-1］と同様）. 疑問文・条件節で「いくらか」「どれか」という意味では複数扱いと単数扱いがある（上記［疑問文・条件節-1］［疑問文・条件節-2］と同様）.

- **Any** of them **is** better than none. それらのどれでもないよりはいい.
- If **any** of these lights「**are**［**is**］on, let me know. これらのランプのどれかが点灯していたら知らせてください.

■ 63-9　none

「none of ＋ 名詞」で「…のうちのどれも…ない」の意味になる場合，単数扱いが本来だが，名詞が複数形であれば特に口語で複数扱いすることも多い.「of ＋ 名詞」が省略された none 単独の場合もそれに準じる.

- **None of these approaches**「**has**［**have**］proved successful. **これらのアプローチのいずれも**成功に至って**いない**.
- **None of the money was** recovered. **その金は一銭も**取り戻せ**なかった**.
- "Is there any milk left?" — "No, **there's none** left." 「牛乳はいくらか残っていますか」「いいえ，**全然残ってません**」

一方，省略ではなく no one や nobody のより形式張った表現として使われる none の場合，現在では複数扱いが一般的とされる.

- **There were none** present. **誰も**出席してい**なかった**.

■ 63-10　no

単数名詞にも複数名詞にもかかる.

- I have **no**「**brothers**［**brother**］. 私には兄弟はいない. ★I don't have any brothers. または I don't have a brother. と同義. 単数形か複数形かの違いはニュアンスの相違になる.

ちなみに，zero を単位につけるときには複数形を使う（⇨第２部・れい）.

- zero degrees　0 度

■ 63-11　most of 〜 / half of 〜 / part of 〜 / the rest of 〜

of のあとの名詞の単複により単数扱いと複数扱いがある．

- **Most of** the planet **is** composed of hydrogen and helium.　その惑星**の大半**は水素とヘリウムでできている．
- **Most of** the planets **have** moons orbiting them.　惑星**の大半は**そのまわりを回る衛星をもつ．
- ★英語の most of the…は「…のうち最大の部分」の意味であり，50 数パーセントの場合に使うこともめずらしくない．特に書き言葉の場合，日本語では「…のほとんど」よりも「…の過半数」「…の大半」と訳したほうが適切なことが多い．
- **Half of** the country **is** uninhabitable.　国**の半分は**居住に適さない．
- **Half of** the countries studied were faced with this problem.　調査した国**の半数が**この問題に直面していた．
- **Part of** the solvent **evaporates** during the process.　その過程で溶媒**の一部**が蒸発する．
- **Part of** these solvents **are** toxic.　これらの溶媒**の一部は**毒性がある．★複数名詞を従えるときには some of のほうがよいとされる．
- **The rest of** the signal **is** discarded.　その信号**の残りの部分は**破棄される．
- **The rest of** the signals **are** discarded.　**残りの信号は**破棄される．

■ 63-12　another と other

63-12-1　形容詞の another と other

another は「an + other」と不定冠詞の an を含んでいることからわかるように可算名詞の単数形について「もう一つの」「別の」の意味になる．ただし，2 つのうちの「もう一方の」の意味，3 つ以上のうちの「残り一つの」の意味では特定の一つに決まっているので another は使えず，the other という．

- if another card is selected　もう 1 枚のカードが選ばれる場合には　★その 1 枚のほかにもカードはある．
- if the other card is selected　(2 枚のうち)もう一方の[(3 枚以上のうちの)残りの 1 枚の]カードが選ばれる場合には　★その 1 枚のほかにカードは残っていない．

「other + 単数形」に an, the 以外がつくこともある．

- if some other card is selected　他の何らかのカードが (1 枚) 選ばれる場合

には
- if no other card is selected = if no other cards are selected　他のカードが何も選ばれない場合には
- Any other card may be selected.　他のどのカードを選んでもよい．

other は複数形にもつくことができ，「他の」を表わす．ただし，残り全部を指す場合はやはり特定の集合に決まっているので the other という．

- Other cards may also be used.　他のカードを使ってもよい．
- The other cards are discarded.　残りのカードは（すべて）捨てられる．

複数形をひとまとまりの単位と見なすときには another を付けることができる．

- Another 16 gigabytes costs ¥5000.　もう 16 ギガバイト追加するには 5000 円かかる．

other は不可算名詞（単数形）にもつくことができる．

- Refer to [See] the next section for other information.　その他の情報については次節参照．

63-12-2　代名詞の another と other

使い分けは形容詞の場合に準じる．

- Keep one and discard the other.　一方を残してもう一方は捨てなさい．
- Keep one and discard the others.　一つ残して残りは（全部）捨てなさい．
- Take one and give me another.　一つ取って私にも一つください．

■ 63-13　「それぞれ」の用法

- それぞれの　① each　② respective　③ several
- それぞれ（に）　① each　② respectively　③ severally
- **各**ブロックは 64 ビットの長さである．　**Each** block is 64 bits long.
- 《オーディオデータにおいて》**それぞれ** 1536 サンプルの［からなる］10 フレーム　10 frames「of［with, having, consisting of］1536 samples **each**
- 5 人の当選者は**それぞれ** 10 万円ずつ受け取った．
  ① The five winners received 100,000 yen **each**.
  ② The five winners **each** received 100,000 yen.
  ③ **Each of** the five winners received 100,000 yen.
- 下院は**各**州の人民によって 2 年目ごとに選出される議員によって構成される．　The House of Representatives shall be composed of members chosen every second year by the people of the **several** states.　★アメリカ合衆国憲

63. 不定代名詞と単数／複数

法の一節.

- 記号 p, V, T は**それぞれ**圧力，体積，温度を表わす．　The symbols p, V, and T denote pressure, volume, and temperature, **respectively**.
- ラベル**それぞれ**に異なるパターンを印刷する
  ① print a different pattern on **each** label
  ② print different patterns on **individual** labels
- 代表たちはその問題を**それぞれの**政府に照会した．　The delegates referred the matter to their **respective** governments.
- 信号 A および B は**それぞれ**装置 X および Y によって処理される．　The signals A and B are processed by the devices X and Y, **respectively**.
- 信号 A および信号 B は**それぞれ**中央処理装置によって処理される．
  ① The signals A and B are **each** processed by a central processing unit.
  ② **Each** of the signals A and B is processed by a central processing unit.
- 案 A, 案 B **それぞれ**に 20 代，30 代から反対が寄せられた．（＝案 A と案 B はいずれも 20 代，30 代からの反対が寄せられた）
  ① **Each of** plan A and plan B drew opposition from people in their twenties and thirties.
  ② Plan A and plan B **each** drew opposition from people in their twenties and thirties.
- 案 A, 案 B は**それぞれ** 20 代，30 代の反対が強かった．（＝案 A は 20 代，案 B は 30 代の反対が強かった）　Plan A and Plan B received strong opposition from people in their twenties and thirties, **respectively**.
- 表には**それぞれの**企業について**一つずつ**で（合計）5 つの列がある．　There are (a total of) five columns in the table, **one for each** company.

64. 各種構文と単数／複数

64-1 修飾句

修飾句は述語動詞の単複には影響しない

- **A computer** with multiple processors **is** desirable.　複数プロセッサーをもつ**コンピューター**が望ましい．
- **The present experiment** together with previous studies strongly **supports** the hypothesis.　**本実験**は以前の研究と相俟ってその仮説を強く支持するものである．
- **Programs** like this **are** capable of sorting any length of list.　このような**プログラム**はどんな長さのリストでもソートできる．
- **All amino acids** except glycine **occur** in two possible optical isomers.　グリシン以外の**すべてのアミノ酸**は 2 通りの光学異性体が存在する．
- **All patients** but one **were** able to return to work in one week.　一人を除いて**すべての患者**は 1 週間で仕事に戻ることができた．
- **All** but one **are** wrong.　一つを除いて**全部**が間違っている．
- **Economists** no less than other human beings **have** a desire to raise their status and income.　**経済学者**とて他の人間に劣らず地位と収入を向上させたいとの欲求がある．

64-2 A and B

複数扱いするのが原則．

- **One multiplier and one adder are** sufficient for this implementation.　この実装には**乗算器 1 つと加算器 1 つで**十分だ．

次のような場合には単数扱いとなる．

▶ every や each がかかる場合．

- **Every boy and (every) girl has** the right to a basic education.　**男の子も女の子もみな**何らかの基礎教育を受ける権利がある．

▶ A と B が同一の人・物を指す場合．このような場合，B の前には冠詞をつけないが，同一の人・物でなくても B に冠詞をつけないことはあるので冠詞の有無だけで判断することはできない．

- **The novelist and poet was** born in 1840.　**その小説家にして詩人は** 1840 年に生まれた．

▶ A and B で一つの単位になっている場合．

- **Bread and butter was** all I had that morning.　その朝食べたのは**バターを塗ったパン**だけだった．

▶ 口語では there is が固定した形式とみなされて複数のものを列挙するときにもしばしば there are に代わって用いられる．
- **There's** a bed, a table, and two chairs in this room.　この部屋にはベッドとテーブルといすが2つ**ある**．

64-3　A as well as B

as well as B は修飾句とみなして A の単複に一致するのが本来だが，今では A and B と同じように複数扱いすることもある．これは A as well as B の「B と同様に A も」という原義が薄れて今日では「A のほかに B も」「A も B も」の意味で普通に使われるようになったことも関係していると思われる．A, as well as B, とコンマを使って挿入句であることを明示する場合には原則通り A の単複に一致する．

- The taxpayers are beginning to realize that the interest, **as well as** the principal, **has** to be paid back somewhere down the road.　納税者は元本**のみならず**金利**も**いつの日か返済しなければならないということを認識し始めています．
- The prevalent Windows operating system **as well as** less common operating systems「is [are] supported.　主要OSであるウィンドウズ**のほか**それほど一般的でない OS **も**サポートされている．

64-4　A or B / either A or B / neither A nor B

B の単複に合わせるのが本則．たとえば「A と B が走る」と異なり，「A または B が走る」の場合，走るのは A か B の一方だけである．このため A and B はまとめて複数扱いするのに対し，A or B などは動詞に近いほうをとって B の単複に合わせる．ただし，口語では複数扱いすることもある．

- **Either** local devices **or** the central server **is** responsible for the storage of this data.　ローカルデバイス**または**中央サーバーのどちらかがこのデータの記憶を担う．
- **Neither** gold **nor** silver **is** used.　金も銀も使われていない．
- One **or** two errors **were** found.　一つ二つの誤りが見つかった．

64-5　one or more

上記の A or B と同じ原則により more に合わせるので，後続の名詞は複数形になる．

- **One or more clients** are connected.　**一つまたは複数のクライアント**が接続されている．
- There are **one or more errors**.　**一つ以上の誤り**がある．

64-6 at least one

文法的には one と同じ扱いで，後続の名詞は単数形になる．

- **At least one disk** is held in reserve.　**少なくとも1つのディスクが**予備として保持される．
- There is **at least one supporter**.　**少なくとも1人の支持者**がいる．

64-7 more than one

内容的には完全に複数を表わしているにもかかわらず，最後の one に合わせて単数扱いされることもある．

- **More than one point**「**is**〔**are**〕contained in the set.　**複数の点が**その集合に含まれる．
- **More than one**「**was**〔**were**〕present.　**複数が**出席していた．
- **More than one of the options**「**was**〔**were**〕specified.　**そのオプションのうち2つ以上が**指定された．

64-8 half of … / more than half of …

…の部分の単複に合わせる．

- リンゴの半分が腐っていた．
  ①〔半分の個数〕Half (of) the apples were rotten.
  ②〔1個の半分〕Half (of) the apple was rotten.
- リンゴの半分以上が腐っていた．
  ①〔半分以上の個数〕More than half (of) the apples were rotten.
  ②〔1個の半分以上〕More than half (of) the apple was rotten.

64-9 one of + 複数名詞

one に合わせて単数扱いする．なお，one of のあとの名詞を複数にし忘れる誤りも多いので注意．

- **One of** the environmentally friendly aspects of Linux **is** its ability to breathe new life into supposedly obsolete hardware.　リナックスの環境にやさしい側面**の一つは**古くなったとされるハードウェアに新しい命を吹き込めることだ．

64-10 a + 名詞 + of + 複数名詞

この形の扱いはさまざまである．たとえば次の例では動詞は単数になる．

- **A committee** of six members **was** set up.　6名の**委員会が**設置された．

前置詞句 of six members はあくまでも修飾句であって，動詞の単複を

決めるのは a committee となっている．一方，次のような場合には同じ形にもかかわらず動詞は通例複数形になる．

- A lot of **websites were** affected.　多くの**ウェブサイトが**影響を受けた．
- A number of **websites were** affected.　いくつかの［いくつもの］**ウェブサイトが**影響を受けた．
- A small number of **websites were** affected.　少数の**ウェブサイトが**影響を受けた．
- A couple of **websites were** affected.　2～3の**ウェブサイトが**影響を受けた．

これらの場合，a lot of, a number of, a couple of のほうが修飾句で，主語の主要部は of の後の websites のほうであると意識されるためである．

以上は比較的はっきりしているが，次のように多数ある類例では判断が分かれるケースも多い．

a group of
a series of
a total of
a sum of
a variety of
a plurality of
a multitude of
a majority of
a minority of

原則は単数扱いとされるが，アメリカでは特に複数扱いが好まれる傾向が強い．たとえば米国化学会のスタイルマニュアルは次の例を掲げている．

- A series of **compounds were** tested.　一連の化合物が試験された．
- A variety of **materials are** being tested for selective removal of ^{90}Sr from nuclear waste solutions.　核廃棄物の溶液から ^{90}Sr を選択的に除去する目的で多様な材料が試験中である．

64-11　複数名詞 + of + 単数名詞

「of + 単数名詞」は修飾句ととらえて複数扱いするのが原則であるが，複数名詞の部分が物質の量を表わすような場合，やはり「複数名詞 + of」の部分は修飾句ととらえて単数扱いすることがある．

- **Five grams of salt**「**were**［**was**］added to the solution.　**5グラムの塩が**溶液に加えられた．

これもアメリカでは of の後を主要部ととらえることが許容される傾向がある．米国化学会は「複数名詞＋of」が物質の量を表わす場合には単数扱いを推奨しており，次の例を掲げている．

- The mixture was stirred, and 5 mL of **diluent was** added.　混合物が撹拌され，5 mL の**希釈液**が加えられた．
- Under high pressure, 5 volumes of **solution A was** added.　高圧下で5体積の**溶液 A** が加えられた．

一方，次のような例ではモル数比が文の主題なので原則通り動詞は two moles に一致して複数語形になっている．

- **Two moles** of hydrogen **react** with one mole of oxygen and produce two moles of water.　水素**2 モル**は酸素1モルと反応して2モルの水を生じる．

逆に，単位の部分が単数となる「単数名詞＋of＋複数名詞」の場合には次のような例が見られる．

- **One gram** of carbohydrates **contains** four calories.　炭水化物**1 グラム**は4カロリーになる．
- **One kilo** of apples **costs** 40 soms (about $1.00).　りんご**1 キロ**が 40 ソム（約 1 ドル）する．

64-12　仮定法

仮定法過去では be 動詞は主語の数によらず were を使うので，一見，不一致のように見える．

- If **she were** president now, she would make a peace proposal.　今もし**彼女が**大統領**だったら**和平提案をするだろう．★口語では単数主語に対しては was を使うこともある．
- **Were it not for** the Sun's gravity, Earth would fly off through space in a straight line at constant speed.　太陽の重力が**なかったとしたら**，地球は宇宙空間の中を等速直線運動して飛び去るだろう．★were it not for … は決まり文句になっている．

第２部

和英編

あ行

アール 〔面積の単位〕an are 《= 100 m²；記号 a》
- 10 アール当たりの米の収穫量　the harvest of rice per 10 ares
- 10 アールの農地　ten ares of farmland

アイエスビーエヌ【ISBN】　〔国際標準図書番号〕(an) ISBN ★International Standard Book Number の略．
- 2007 年 1 月 1 日から ISBN は 13 桁の長さだ．　Since January 1, 2007, ISBNs are thirteen digits long.
- ISBN 番号の最後の数字はチェック数字だ．　The last digit of the ISBN number is a check digit.
- ★日本の書籍のバーコードは 2 段になっているが，これは 1990 年に制定された日本独自の書籍 JAN というもので，上段は国際的な ISBN コード (978 で始まる 13 桁)，下段は C コードという分類コードに価格表示を組み合わせたものとなっている．

アウト　① (an) out ② a putout［⇨第 1 部・49. 野球の数字表現 49-8］
- ツーアウト満塁だった．
  ① The bases were loaded **with two out(s)**.
  ② The bases were loaded **with two gone**.

あげどまる【上げ止まる】　① stop rising ② stop increasing ③ top out ④ hit a ceiling［⇨第 1 部・14-4 頭打ち］

あさって【明後日】　the day after tomorrow［⇨第 1 部・31-5-1「来…」］
- あさっての朝　① the morning of the day after tomorrow ② the day after tomorrow in the morning ③ the morning after next

あしかけ【足かけ】　〔前後の端数も数える年月の数え方〕
- 足かけ 10 年にわたる研究
  ① nearly ten years of research
  ② research over eight full years and some months
  ③ research over ten years, counting the odd months of the first and last years as full years
  ④ research spanning ten calendar years

あした【明日】　tomorrow［⇨第 1 部・31-5-1「来…」］
- あしたの朝　tomorrow morning
- 関東地方のあしたの天気は，くもりのち晴れでしょう．　Tomorrow's weather for the Kanto region will be cloudy at first, then「clear [fair, fine]．
- あしたの予定は？　What're your plans for tomorrow?
- あしたの今ごろは僕はもう北京に着いてるはずだ．　About this time tomorrow I should already be in Beijing.

あす【明日】 tomorrow［⇨あした］

あたい【値】 a value
- …の典型的な**値**は 30 km/s 程度である． Typical **values** for … are around 30 km/s.
- A と B は同じ**値**だ． A and B have the same **value**.
- 連続的な範囲内の任意の**値**をとる take (on) any **value** over a continuous range
- -1 と 1 の間の**値**をとる take values between -1 and 1
- x の実数値に対して y のとるべき**値**の集合 the set of **values** which y must take for real values of x
- 下記の方程式を満たす x の**値**を求めよ． Find **the value** of x which satisfies the following equation.
- グラフから**値**を読み取る read off **a value** from the graph
- 0.85 という**値**が得られた．
  ① **A value** of 0.85 was obtained.
  ② We obtained **a value** of 0.85.
- 圧力が一定の**値**を超えると機械は自動的に止まることになっています． If the pressure rises above a certain **value**, the machine is set to shut off automatically.
- n の現実的な**値**については f_n は 1 よりずっと大きい． For practical values of n, f_n is much greater than 1.

あたまうち【頭打ち】 ［⇨第 1 部・14-4 頭打ち］
- 頭打ちになる ① reach [come to] a limit [an upper limit] ② reach a ceiling ③ hit a ceiling ④ reach a maximum ⑤ peak ⑥ level off

…あたり【…当たり】 ① per … ② a [an] … ③ … each ★ per のあとは無冠詞．［⇨第 1 部・22-2 単位量当たりの割合］
- 1 人当たり ① each ② a head ③ per head ④ per capita ★ per capita はラテン語で by heads の意から．
- 人口 1 人当たり ① per head of the population ② per capita ③ per person
- 1 日当たり ① a day ② per day ③《文》per diem
- 1 年当たり ① a year ② per year ③《文》per annum
- 1 日当たり 1,000 円 1,000 yen「a [per] day
- 1 人 1 日当たりの米の消費量 ① (the) per capita daily consumption of rice ② rice consumption per person per day
- 1 人当たり 1 年に消費するコーヒーの量 the amount of coffee consumed per capita each year
- 国民 1 人当たりの国内総生産（GDP） ① (the) per capita gross domestic product ③ (the) gross domestic product per capita

あつさ

- トン当たり ①a ton ②per ton
- 1キロメートル当たり5分 ①five minutes「a [per] kilometer ②five minutes to the kilometer
- 1平方キロ当たり200人の人口密度 a population density of 200「inhabitants [people] to the square kilometer
- ページ当たりの語数 the number of words per page
- 人口1,000人当たりの公園面積 ①the park area per one thousand (of the) population ②the park area per one thousand people
- 代金1万円当たり500円の手数料 a fee of ¥500 per ¥10,000 (of the price)
- 燃焼されるその燃料1キロ当たり約3キロの二酸化炭素が排出される. For every kilogram of the fuel burned, about three kilograms of carbon dioxide is 「released [emitted].
- 単位時間・単位面積当たりの熱の移動 ①heat transfer per unit time per unit area ②heat transfer「through [crossing] a unit area per unit time
- 生産コストは1個当たり100円下がった.
  ① The production cost declined by 100 yen per piece.
  ② The per-unit production cost declined by 100 yen.

あつさ【厚さ】 thickness [⇨第1部・42. 大きさ・重さ]

- 厚さ5mmである ①be 5 mm thick ②be 5 mm in thickness ③have a thickness of 5 mm
- 厚さ20cmの壁 ①a wall 20 cm thick ②a wall 20 cm in thickness
- 厚さはいくらありますか.
  ① How thick is it?
  ② What is its thickness?
- チーズを厚さ1センチに切る ①cut the cheese into one-centimeter-thick slices ②cut the cheese into slices one centimeter thick
- その膜はたった3原子層の厚さだ. The film is only three「atomic layers [atoms] thick.
- 一様な厚さの板 a board of uniform thickness

あっしゅくひ【圧縮比】 〔圧縮後の容量の圧縮前に対する比〕a compression ratio

- 8:1の**圧縮比**なら8の体積を1に圧縮することになる. An 8-to-1 **compression ratio** would compress a volume of 8 into a volume of 1.
- このエンジンの**圧縮比**は下は7:1から最高9:1にまでなりうる. **The compression ratio** in this engine can be from as low as 7 to 1 to a high of 9 to 1.

あっしゅくりつ【圧縮率】

1 〔加圧による物質の体積減の割合〕compressibility

- 液体や固体の**圧縮率**は気体よりずっと小さい. **The compressibility** of

liquids and solids is much smaller than that of gases.

2 〔圧縮後のデータ量の圧縮前に対する比〕a (data) compression ratio
- 10:1 の**圧縮率**で　at [with] **a compression ratio** of 10:1　★10:1 は ten to one と読む．
- 動き補償技術により MPEG-2 は画質を維持しながら高い**圧縮率**を実現している．　By utilizing motion compensation techniques, MPEG-2 achieves high **compression ratios** while maintaining video quality.

あつりょく【圧力】　pressure　〔⇨第 1 部・45-2 気圧〕

- 約 5 Pa の圧力で　at a pressure of about 5 Pa
- 1 GPa より高い［より低い，までの］圧力で　at pressures「above [below, up to] 1 GPa
- 1 MPa の圧力下にある　be under a pressure of 1 MPa
- 1 気圧は 1 平方メートル当たり約 1 万キログラム重の**圧力**に相当する．　One atmosphere corresponds to **a pressure** of about ten thousand kilograms-force per square meter.
- 1 MPa, 1.5 MPa, 2 MPa **の圧力について**作成した図　diagrams constructed **for pressures of** 1 MPa, 1.5 MPa, and 2 MPa
- この構造は**あらゆる圧力において**不安定である．　This structure is unstable **at all pressures**.
- 圧力を加える［かける］　① apply pressure 《to …》 ② subject … to pressure ③ pressurize
- 壁に 1.5 気圧の圧力を及ぼす　exert a pressure of 1.5 atm on the wall
- **圧力**は気圧の単位で与えられている．　**Pressure** is given in atmospheres.
- ミリバール単位の**圧力**をパスカルに換算する　convert **pressure** in millibars to pascals
- 圧力が高い［低い］．　The pressure is「high [low].
- 圧力が上がった．　The pressure rose.
- 圧力が下がった．　The pressure「fell [dropped].
- 圧力の変動　variation in pressure

関連表現

- 定圧下で　at constant pressure
- 高圧で　at high pressure(s)
- 多くの気体は**十分低圧では**理想気体の法則に非常に近いふるまいをする．　Many gases follow the ideal gas law very closely **at sufficiently low pressures**.
- 気体の混合物の示す**全圧**は個々の気体の**分圧**の和に等しい．　**The total pressure** exerted by a mixture of gases is equal to the sum of **the partial pressures** of the individual gases.

あと【後】

1 〔後方〕① the back ② the rear

2 〔時間的に未来〕[⇨第 1 部・31-7-2「…後」]

- あとに［で］　① after ② afterward(s) ③ later ④ subsequently ⑤〔のちほど〕later on ⑥ in a while
- 何日かあとに　① a few days later ② a few days after ③ after a few days

3 〔残り〕① the rest ② the remainder ③ the others [⇨第 1 部・35-2-2 期日まであと…]

- 正午まであと 5 分．
  ① There's five minutes to go to 12 noon.
  ② It'll be 12 noon in five minutes.
- 《クイズなどで》あと 3 問です．
  ① You have three questions to go.
  ② You have three more questions.
- 彼はあと何か月生きられますか．　How many months does he have (to live)?
- 試合まであと 2 日しかない．
  ① The「game [match] is only two days「off [away].
  ② We have only two days left before the「game [match].
- 大学を卒業するまであとまだ 2 年あります．　I still have two more years to go before I graduate from college.
- あと 5 年たてば　① in five years ② five years from now ③《文》five years hence
- あと数日は雨は降らないだろう．　There will be no rain for a few more days.
- あと 6 個あると 100 になる．　I only need six more to have a full hundred.

アト…　[10^{-18}] atto- [⇨第 1 部・27-4 SI 接頭語]

あまり【余り】　〔割り算の〕① a remainder ② a residue [⇨第 1 部・54-4 割り算 54-4-3]

…あまり【…余り】　① -odd ② -plus ③ -some [and some] ④ -something ⑤ something over ⑥ just over [⇨第 1 部・9-2「…何」「…数」「…余り」など]

あらりえき【粗利益】　① a gross profit ② a gross margin [⇨第 1 部・41-1-3 損益計算書]

あらわす【表わす】　①〔表現する〕express ②〔記号などで示す〕denote ③〔ある内容を表現している〕represent ④ stand for … [⇨第 1 部・57. 式変形の英語 57-1]

- y を x を用いて表わす　give [express] y in terms of x
- 地震の規模を表わす単位　a unit that「represents [shows] the magnitude of an

earthquake
- この記号は何を表わすのですか. What does this symbol stand for?
- 点は内積を表わす. The dot denotes the inner product.
- I は恒等置換を表わすものとする. Let us denote by I the identity permutation.
- 商群は G/H で表わされる. The quotient group is denoted (by) G/H.

あんだ【安打】 ① a (safe) hit ② a base hit ③ a safety [⇨第 1 部・49. 野球の数字表現 49-13, 49-16]
- 5 打数 3 安打である ① have three hits in five at bats ② be「three for five [3-for-5]

あんていたすう【安定多数】 ⇨たすう

アンペア 〔電流の大きさの単位〕an ampere《記号 A》[⇨でんりゅう, 第 1 部・27-2 SI 基本単位]
- 1.2 アンペアの電流 a current of 1.2 amperes
- その抵抗を流れる電流は何アンペアか. How many amperes flow through the resistor?
- アンペア数 amperage
- アンペア時 an ampere-hour
- アンペアターン an ampere-turn《記号 At》
- アンペア毎平方メートル 〔電流密度の単位〕an ampere per square meter《記号 A/m^2》
- アンペア毎メートル 〔磁界強度の単位〕an ampere per meter《記号 A/m》

あんもくてき【暗黙的】
- 暗黙的な implicit
- 温度の時間依存性を通じて暗黙的に時間に依存する depend on time implicitly through the time dependence of temperature

…い【…位】

1 〔等級・順位〕① place ② rank [⇨第 1 部・15-2 順位]
- 1 位である ① occupy (the) first place ② come [be, rank, stand, be ranked] first ③ be in the first rank ④ be at the top of《a class》⑤ head [top] the list《of …》⑥ lead ⑦ be No. 1
- 2 位である ① rank [be, stand, be ranked, be placed] second ② hold (the) second place ③ be (the) runner-up ④ be No. 2
- 20 人中 3 位である rank [be, etc.] (the) third out of twenty

2 〔位取り〕a place [⇨第 1 部・52. 小数 52-5, 10-1 位取り]
- 答えは小数第 2 位まで出しなさい. Give the answers up to 2 decimal places.

いか【以下】

①… or less ②… or fewer ③not more than … ④not exceeding … ⑤no more than … ⑥less than or equal to … ⑦equal to or less than … ⑧〔高々〕at most …［⇨第1部・12.「以上」「以下」等の表現，11. 数値範囲の表現］

- 100 以下の整数　①an integer less than or equal to 100　②an integer equal to or less than 100　③an integer not more than 100
- 原価以下で売る　sell at or below cost
- 500 万円以下では売るまい．　He wouldn't sell it for under five million yen.
- 訪問者数 1000 人以下のブログ　blogs with 1,000 or「fewer［《口》less］visitors

いくつ

1〔数量の疑問〕how many［⇨第1部・26. 数量に関する疑問文 26-1］

- テーブルの上にコップは**いくつ**ありますか．　**How many** glasses are there on the table?

2〔年齢の疑問〕how old［⇨第1部・26. 数量に関する疑問文 26-6］

3〔不定の数〕

- この会社には関連会社が 40 **いくつ**あります．　This corporation has「forty-**plus**［forty-**odd**, forty-**some**, forty-**something**］related firms.［⇨第1部・9-2「…何」「…数」「…余り」など］
- **いくつかの**　①some　②a few　③a number of　④several［⇨第1部・9-6「数個」「いくつか」］
- クラスを**いくつかの**グループに分ける　divide the class into several groups
- **いくつでも**　①any number《of …》　②as many as *one* likes　③ever so many
- **いくつでも**欲しいだけ持っていっていいですよ．　You can take **as many as** you「like［want］．
- 増幅器は**いくつ**あってもよい．　There may be **any number of** amplifiers.
- **いくつもの**　〔多数の〕①any number of …　②a large number of …　③a great number of …　④a lot of …　⑤masses of …　⑥《口》piles of …　⑦heaps of …　⑧many［⇨第1部・19-1 多数］
- 調べてみると同じような間違いが**いくつも**出てきた．　When we looked into it, we found **a huge number of** similar mistakes.
- リンゴはもう**いくつも**残って**ない**．　There are **hardly any** apples left now.

4〔不定の年齢差〕

- 彼のほうが僕より**いくつか**年上です．
  ①He is「**some**［**a few**］**years** older than me.
  ②He is「**some**［**a few**］**years** my senior.
- 彼は僕とは**いくつも**違わ**ない**のにずいぶん老けて見える．　There's **hardly any** difference in our ages, but he looks a lot older than me.

いくら

1 〔疑問〕how much〔⇨第1部・26. 数量に関する疑問文 26-7, 26-2〕

- これは**いくら**ですか. **How much** is this?

2 〔不定の値段・数量〕

- この万年筆は**1万いくら**で買った. I paid **something over ¥10,000** for this fountain pen.〔⇨第1部・9-2「…何」「…数」「…余り」など〕
- 米国では今でも果物を**1ポンドいくら**で売っているが，英国では**1キロいくら**が普通になっている. In the United States they still sell fruit **by the pound**, but in Britain it has become common to sell「**at so much per kilogram**〔**by the kilogram**〕.
- **時給いくらの**パートの身じゃ，あまりわがままも言えない. As a part-timer, **working for so much an hour**, I'm not in a position to「lay down conditions〔make demands〕.
- バス代が**いくら**，宿泊代が**いくら**，お土産代が**いくら**と書いてごらんなさい. Write down your expenses: **so much** for bus fares, **so much** for board and lodging, **so much** for presents, and so on.
- 子供の遠足の小遣いは**いくら以内**と決まっていることが多い. When children go on a school trip, we're often told that they should be given **no more than**「**such-and-such a sum**〔**some specific figure**〕as pocket money.
- 金はもう**いくらも**残って**いない**. I have **hardly any** money left.
- 出発の時間まであと**いくらもない**. There's **hardly any** time left before we leave.
- そんなふうに考える人は**いくらもいない**.
  ① **Hardly anybody** thinks that way.
  ② **Very few people** think that way.
- 駅までは**いくらもない**.
  ① The station is **no distance** (away).
  ② The station is **not far off**.
- 彼が結婚して**からまだいくらにもならない**.
  ① **It is only very recently that** he got married.
  ② **It is almost no time since** he got married.
- 内職は手間賃が安くてひと月働いても**いくらにもならない**. The rates for piecework done at home are so low that you can work for a month and「**earn**〔**it comes to**〕**hardly anything**〔**almost nothing**〕.
- **いくらでも** ①〔数・量について〕as「many〔much〕as *one* likes ② any「number〔amount〕of … ③〔金額〕any sum ④ any price ⑤〔程度〕to any degree ⑥ to any extent
- そのような本は世の中に**いくらでもある**.
  ① **You can find** that sort of book **anywhere**.
  ② **There are any number of** books of that sort around.

いご

- お金さえ払えば欲しいものは**何でもいくらでも**得られる世の中だ．　In the world today you can have **as much as you want of anything** you want if you're willing to pay for it.
- **いくら…でも**　① however 《good, expensive》 ② no matter how ③ however much 《*one* does …》
- その本なら**いくら高くても**欲しい．
  ① I want that book, **however expensive it is**.
  ② **I will pay any price** to obtain that book.
- **いくら遅くても**5時には向こうに着くだろう．　We should be there by 5 o'clock **at the latest**.

いご【以後】

1 〔今後〕① after this ② from now on ③ from this time (on [forward, onward]) ④ hereafter ⑤ henceforth ⑥ henceforward ⑦〔将来は〕in the future ⑧ in future

2 〔その後〕① after that (time) ② thereafter ③ since (then) ④ afterward(s) ⑤ from that time「on [onward] ⑥ thenceforth ⑦ thenceforward

- その日以後今日に至るまで　from that day down to this

いこう【以降】

- それ以降　① (ever) since that time ② (ever) since then ③ after that ④ from that point forward
- 今月の10日以降は　① on and after the 10th of this month ② from the 10th of this month
- 《求人広告で》募集対象，1989年**以降に**生まれた人．　Applications will be accepted from those born「**in and after** 1989 [**in** 1989 **or later**].
- 1930年**以降の**米相場を示すグラフ　a graph that shows the market price of rice **from** 1930 **onward**
- 住宅ローンの返済は返済開始6年目**以降**利息が高くなります．　The interest rate on「mortgages [home loans, housing loans] rises **beginning with** the sixth year after payments start.
- 夜8時**以降**は外出禁止です．　There is a curfew in effect **beginning at** 8 p.m.
- 明治時代**以降は**　beginning「**in** [**with**] the Meiji period
- 50番**以降の**番号札をお持ちの方はこちらにお並びください．　Those of you holding numbers 50 **and above** please「form a line [stand in line] here.

いこう【移項】

- 移項する　① transpose ② move ③ shift
- その項を等号の反対側に**移項する**　**move** the term across the equals sign
- **移項する**ときにはその項の符号を変えなさい．　When **moving terms from one side to the other**, change the sign of the term.

- x を含む項が全部一方に，数字の項が他方にくるように**移項しなさい．** **Move terms** so that all the *x*-terms are on one side and the number terms are on the other side.

イコール 〔＝の記号〕an equal(s) sign〔⇨とうごう，第1部・55. 式の読み方〕
- …とイコールになる　equal …
- 3足す5イコール8．　3 plus 5 equals 8. ★3＋5＝8
- x イコール2．　x equals 2. ★$x=2$

いじょう【以上】　①… or more ②… or greater ③… or above ④… or over ⑤… or up ⑥not less than … ⑦no fewer than … ⑧greater than or equal to … ⑨equal to or greater than … ⑩〔少なくとも〕at least … ⑪at least equal to …〔⇨第1部・12.「以上」「以下」等の表現，11. 数値範囲の表現〕
- 100以上の整数　①an integer greater than or equal to 100　②an integer equal to or greater than 100　③an integer not less than 100
- 100ボルト以上の電圧　a voltage of 100 volts or「more［higher］

いすう【位数】〔集合や群の元の〕an order
- 位数 $p-1$ の元　an element of order $(p-1)$

いぜん【以前】

1〔今より前〕
- 以前（に）　①before ②earlier ③previously
- 以前は　〔昔は〕①before ②formerly ③in「earlier［former］times ④in the past ⑤in the old days ⑥long ago ⑦a long time ago ⑧in days gone by ⑨《文》long since
- ずっと以前から　①from［since］long ago ②from［since］the distant past ③《文》long since ④《口》from［since］way back ⑤from［since］ages ago
- この村も以前はとても静かだった．
  ①This village used to be「very quiet［much quieter］．
  ②In the old days this village was very quiet.
- パソコンは以前に比べると非常によくなった．　Personal computers are far better than they used to be.

2〔ある時より前〕before …
- それより以前　①before「then［that］②prior to「then［that］③before that time
- ずっと以前から　①from［since］long before ②from［since］much earlier ③from［since］the distant past ④《口》from［since］way before ⑥from［since］ages before
- その話はお前が生まれるずっと以前のことだ．　That happened long before you were born.
- 光ファイバーの出現以前は　①before the emergence of optical fiber ②in the

いそう

days before the emergence of optical fiber ③ before optical fiber emerged
- 境界線を1914年以前の状態に戻す運動　a campaign to restore boundaries to 「the way [where] they had been before 1914

いそう【位相】

1 〔周期現象のある段階〕a phase
- …と位相が合っている　be in phase with …
- …と位相が合っていない　be out of phase with …
- 位相が90°ずれている　① be 90 degrees apart in phase ② be 90 degrees out of phase
- 位相は入力信号より90°遅れている．
  ① The phase lags (behind) the input signal by 90°.
  ② The phase lags 90° behind the input signal.
- 出力信号は入力信号より（位相が）90°進んでいる．
  ① The output signal 「is ahead of [leads] the input signal by 90°.
  ② The output signal is 90° ahead of the input signal.
- 位相の遅れ　① (a) phase lag ② (a) phase delay
- 位相の進み　① (a) phase lead ② (a) phase advance
- その信号と参照信号との間の位相差　the phase difference between that signal and the reference signal
- AとBの間の相対位相を維持する　maintain the relative phase between A and B
- 光線は反射のため位相反転を受ける．　The beam undergoes phase reversal due to reflection.
- 位相だけ異なる2つの波動関数は同じ物理を記述する．　Two wave functions which differ only by a phase describe the same physics.
- 月の位相　a phase of the moon [⇨げつれい]

2 〔位相空間の〕
- 位相空間での時間発展　time [temporal] evolution [development] in phase space
- 位相空間での体積を保存する　preserve phase space volume
- 位相空間での特定の点は系を完全に指定する．　A particular point in phase space specifies the system completely.
- 運動の定数とは，ある軌道上のすべての点で同じ値を取る位相空間上の関数である．　A constant of motion is a function on phase space which takes the same value at all points on an orbit.

3 〔位相幾何学の〕topology
- 位相をもつ集合　a set that has a topology
- 環Z［整数の集合］に位相を定義する　define a topology 「on the ring Z [on the

set of integers]

いそん, いぞん【依存】　① dependence　② reliance

- 依存する　① depend 《on …》　② rely 《on …》　③ be dependent 《on …》
- …の z (への) 依存性　the z-dependence of …
- 伝導度の温度, 圧力, 周波数への依存性　the dependence of the conductivity on the temperature, pressure, and frequency
- …に強く依存する　strongly depend on …
- 振り子の周期はおもりの重さに依存しない.
  ① The period of a pendulum does not depend on the weight of the bob.
  ② The period of a pendulum is independent of the weight of the bob.
- このポテンシャルは明示的には時間に依存しない.　This potential does not depend on time explicitly.
- 温度の時間依存性を通じて暗黙的に時間に依存する　depend on time implicitly through the time dependence of temperature

いたるところ【至る所】

- ほとんどいたるところで収束する　converge almost everywhere
- いたるところ微分不可能な連続関数　a continuous function which is nowhere differentiable
- いたるところで疎な集合　a nowhere-dense set

いち【一】　① one　② unity

- x^3 の係数が 1 の 3 次式　a cubic in which the coefficient of x^3 is「one [unity]」
- これらの関数は 1 に規格化されている.　These functions are normalized to「one [unity]」.
- 1 の位　⇨第 1 部・10-1 位取り
- 1 の対数は 0 である.　The logarithm of「one [unity]」is zero.
- 1 の原始 n 乗根　a primitive nth root of「one [unity]」
- 1 の分割　(a) partition of unity
- 絶対値が 1 より大きい定数　a constant of absolute value greater than one
- 絶対値 1 の複素数　a complex number of unit「magnitude [modulus]」
- 半径 1 の球　a sphere of unit radius
- 水素原子の結合力を 1 としてある.　The combining capacity of a hydrogen atom is taken as unity.
- その変数は 0 か 1 の値をとる.　The variable「has [assumes]」a value of either zero or one.
- すべての情報は 1 と 0 として保存されている.　All information is stored as ones and zeros.
- 二進法では 1 と 0 の 2 つの数字しか使わない.　Binary notation employs only

いちい

two digits, 1 and 0.
- 1のビットの数と0のビットの数の差　the difference between the number of one-bits and the number of zero-bits
- $n \times n$ の単位行列は対角線上に1があるほかはすべて0である．　An n-by-n identity matrix has zeros everywhere ⌈except along its main diagonal, where lie ones [except for ones along its main diagonal]．
- 現実の世界では1足す1は2というわけにはいかない．
  ① In the real world one plus one does not always equal two.
  ② In the real world, two plus two doesn't always ⌈make [add up to] four.
  ★② はオーウェルの『1984年』で two plus two make five（2＋2＝5）が不条理なこととして言及されたのが慣用表現となったもの．
- ハートの1　《トランプ》the ace of hearts
- （さいころなどの）1の目　① the one (on a dice, etc.)　② the snake's eye
- 1が出たら負けだ．
  ①〔トランプで〕If you ⌈pick [draw] an ace, you've lost.
  ②〔さいころで〕If you ⌈shake [throw] a one, you're out.
- 一, 二の三で始めよう．一, 二, 三！　Let's start on a count of three: one, two, three!

いちい【一位】　[⇨第1部・15-2 順位]
- 1位である　① occupy (the) first place　② come [be, rank, stand, be ranked] first　③ be in the first rank　④ be at the top of《a class》　⑤ head [top] the list 《of …》　⑥ lead　⑦ be No. 1

いちいせい【一意性】　uniqueness

いちいてき【一意的】
- 一意的な　unique
- 一意的に決められる　can be determined uniquely
- 個々のデバイスを一意的に指定するアドレス　an address which uniquely specifies individual devices

いちげん【一元】
- 一元一次方程式　a linear equation ⌈with [in] one ⌈unknown [variable]

いちじ【一次】　①〔一つ目の・主要な〕first　② primary　③〔1乗冪に関する〕 linear　④ first-degree　⑤〔一般に次数に関する〕first-order　[⇨…じ【…次】]
▶ first を使うもの
- 第一次世界大戦　① the First World War　② World War I
- 一次試験　① a first-stage examination　②〔予備試験〕a preliminary examination
▶ primary を使うもの

いちじげん

- 一次イオン化　primary ionization
- 一次宇宙線　primary cosmic rays
- 一次エネルギー　primary energy
- 一次感染　a primary infection
- 一次コイル　a primary coil
- 一次構造　〔タンパク質の〕a primary structure
- 一次産業　a primary industry
- 一次産品　① a primary commodity　② a product of a primary industry
- 一次消費者　《生態》a primary consumer
- 一次資料　① primary sources　② original sources
- 一次史料　primary historical「materials [resources]
- 一次性徴　① a primary sex character　② a primary sexual characteristic
- 一次電池　① a primary battery　② a primary cell

▶ linear, first degree を使うもの

- 一次関数　a linear function
- 一次式　a linear expression
- 一次不等式　① a linear inequality　② an inequality of the first degree
- 一次変換　a linear transformation
- 一次方程式　① a linear equation　② an equation of the first degree
- 一次従属な　linearly dependent
- 一次独立な　linearly independent
- 一次独立なベクトルの集合　a set of linearly independent vectors

▶ first order を使うもの

- 級数の一次と二次の項　the first and second order terms「in [of] a series
- 一次相転移　(a) first-order phase transition
- 一次反応　a first-order reaction
- 2つの値の間の線形関係が，その変換が一次の反応であることを示している．The linear relation between the two values indicates that the conversion is a first-order reaction.

いちじげん【一次元】　one dimension [⇨じげん]

- 一次元の　one-dimensional
- 一次元の流れ　(a) one-dimensional flow
- 一次元結晶　a one-dimensional crystal
- 擬一次元結晶　a pseudo-one-dimensional crystal
- 一次元での運動　motion in one dimension
- 一次元的に動く　move one-dimensionally

いちど

いちど【一度】

1 〔単位〕a degree 〔⇨ど〕

2 〔1回〕① once ② one time 〔⇨いっかい，第1部・36. 回数・頻度の表現〕

- 5年に1度　① once in five years　② (once) every five years
- 3度に1度は麺類を食べる　have noodles once (in) every three meals
- ただ一度　① only once　② once only
- もう一度　① once again　② once more　③ one more time
- もう一度だけチャンスをやろう．　I'll give you just one more chance.
- 一度行なうだけでよい．　You need to do it only once.
- 一度ぐらい私の言うことを聞いてくれたっていいでしょ？　Can't you listen to me just for once?
- 一度ならず　① more than once　② once and again　③ again and again　④ several times　⑤ repeatedly
- 一度に　①〔一時に〕(all) at once　② at「a [one] time　③〔一挙に〕at a「stretch [sitting, stroke]　④ in「one [a single] sitting　⑤ in one go　⑥〔みな一緒に〕all together　⑦〔同時に〕at the same time　⑧ simultaneously
- 一度に2つのことをするな．　Don't try to do two things at「once [a time].
- 一度にいろんなことが起きた．　All sorts of things happened at once.
- 一度に返すのは無理なので，分割にしてもらった．　As I couldn't pay it all back「at once [《英》in one go], I arranged to do it in installments.
- 一度言いだしたらなかなかきかない男だ．　Once he has said something, he never goes back on it.
- こんな機会は二度とない，一度きりだ．
  ① There'll never be another chance; it's now or never.
  ② This is your one and only chance. If you don't take it, that's it.

いちばん【一番】

1 〔1位〕① the first　② No. 1　③ the first place

- 一番になる　reach [attain, win, take, get, secure] (the) first place 〔⇨第1部・15. 順位・順番の表現 15-2-1〕
- 体力・技術ともに彼が一番だ．　He is number one in both strength and skill.
- 疲労回復には睡眠が一番だ．　Sleep is the best thing for recovering from exhaustion.
- 一番の問題は資金不足だ．　The「big [main] problem is lack of「capital [funds].
- 弁護士になった一番の理由は…　The「main [primary] reason I became a lawyer is that …
- この店での一番人気はビーフシチューだ．　The most popular dish at this restaurant is beef stew.

2 [最も…]

- いちばん重い　heaviest
- いちばんよい　best
- いちばん悪い　worst
- いちばん左の　leftmost [⇨第 1 部・59-1 左右]
- 私はこれがいちばん好きだ．　①I like this best (of all). ②I like this better than the others. ③I prefer this over the others.
- 彼がいちばんあとに着いた．　①He was the (very) last to arrive. ②He arrived last.

3 [勝負の 1 回] ①a game ②a round ③a bout

- 優勝をかけた一番　the bout for the championship
- 《碁・将棋で》もう一番お相手願います．　Would you mind playing one more game?

いちよう【一様】

- 一様な　①uniform ②homogeneous
- 一様性　uniformity
- 一様運動　uniform motion
- 一様収束　uniform convergence
- 一様収束する　①converge uniformly ②be uniformly convergent
- 一様等方な時空　a homogeneous and isotropic space-time
- 一様分布　(a) uniform distribution
- 一様流　(a) uniform flow

いつ　when [⇨第 1 部・26. 数量に関する疑問文 26-5-3, 26-5-4, 26-5-5]

いっか【一価】

1 [関数]　single-valued　★対語は多価 (multivalued, multiple-valued).

- 一価関数　a single-valued function

2 [原子価]　univalent　★以下，bivalent, tervalent, quadrivalent と続く．このようにラテン語系の数詞接頭辞を使うのが本来だったが，ギリシア語系の monovalent, divalent, trivalent, tetravalent もよく使われる．

3 [官能基の数]

- 一価アルコール　[一水酸基アルコール] monohydric alcohol

4 [染色体]

- 一価染色体　a univalent chromosome　★二価，三価，四価は bivalent, trivalent, quadrivalent [tetravalent] の組み合わせが多い．

いっかい【一回】　①once ②one time [⇨…かい【…回】, いちど, 第 1 部・36.

回数・頻度の表現〕
- 週に 1 回　once a week
- もう 1 回　① once more　② one more time　③ once again
- 1 回だけ　① only once　② just once
- 1 回だけの催し物　a「one-time [one-off] event
- 1 回 100 円　a hundred yen a time
- 1 回で試験に合格する　① pass an examination「the first time [on the first attempt,《口》straight off,《英》(at the) first go]
- 1 回で払いこむ　① pay《the tuition fees》as a lump sum　② make a single payment《for the tuition fees》
- 1 回払い　〔クレジットの〕(a) single-installment payment
- 支払いはカードでお願いします．1 回払いです．I'd like to pay with my card—in full.
- 1 回分　①〔薬の〕a [one] dose　②〔月賦などの〕an [one] installment

いっきゅう【一級】

1 〔最上の等級〕⇨ きゅう【級】

2 〔最高〕① first-class　② first-rate　③ of the「highest [best] quality　④ of the first order　⑤ top-quality　⑥《口》topflight　⑦《口》top-notch　⑧《米》ranking

- この写真は第一級の史料だ．This handwritten copy is a historical source of the highest value.
- 彼は世界的にも第一級の指揮者だ．
  ① He is a conductor of world class.
  ② He is a world-class conductor.
  ③ On the international stage, too, he is a top conductor.

いっこだて【一戸建て】　a detached house [⇨第 1 部・46-3 住居]

いっさくげつ【一昨月】　① the month before last　② two months ago [⇨第 1 部・31-5-2「先…」]

いっさくさくじつ【一昨昨日】　three days ago [⇨第 1 部・31-5-2「先…」]

いっさくさくねん【一昨昨年】　three years ago [⇨第 1 部・31-5-2「先…」]

いっさくじつ【一昨日】　the day before yesterday [＝おととい] [⇨第 1 部・31-5-2「先…」]

いっさくねん【一昨年】　the year before last [＝おととし] [⇨第 1 部・31-5-2「先…」]

いったいいち【一対一】

- 一対一対応　a one-to-one correspondence《between …》
- 文字と発音は必ずしも一対一に対応しない．

① Characters and pronunciations do not always correspond one-to-one.
② There is not always a one-to-one correspondence between characters and pronunciations.

いったいた【一対多】 one-to-many 《relationship, mapping, correspondence》

いってい【一定】

1 〔数値が変化しない〕
- 一定の ① constant ② fixed
- 約2倍の範囲内で一定である　be constant to within a factor of about 2
- H は流線に沿って一定である　H is constant along streamlines.
- 密度は半径に関して一定である．　The density is constant with radius.
- 時間的に一定である　be constant「with [over] time
- 信号の振幅はその期間比較的一定している．　The signal amplitude is relatively constant over the period.
- その関数は $a<t<b$（の区間）に対して一定である．　The function is constant for (the interval) $a<t<b$.
- 一定速度で運動する　move with constant velocity
- その体積にわたって電場をできるだけ一定にする　make the electric field as constant as possible over the volume
- …を一定に保つ　keep … constant

2 〔ある決まった〕
- 一定の書式　a「prescribed [set] form
- 一定の期間内に　within a given period
- 水がある一定の量たまるとブザーが鳴る．　When the water level rises to a 「certain [fixed] point a buzzer sounds.

いっとう【一等】

1 〔分類等級〕① (the) first class ② (the) first rank ③ (the) first grade ④ A1 [⇨…とう]

2 〔第1位〕① (the) first place ② (the) first prize [⇨…とう]

3 〔段階〕a degree
- 罪一等を減ずる　① reduce the penalty by one degree ② commute the sentence by one degree
- 死一等を減ずる　commute a death sentence

いっぱく【一泊】　an overnight stay [⇨第1部・31-4-3　1泊2日]

いっぱん【一般】
- 一般解　a general solution

- 一般角 ① 《the trigonometric function of》 the general angle ② angles of any size
- 一般項　a general term［⇨すうれつ］
- 一般式　a general expression
- 一般性を失うことなく $a=1$ とすることができる．　Without loss of generality, we can assume $a=1$.

いっぱんか【一般化】

- 高次元への一般化　(a) generalization to higher dimensions
- ここで述べた考え方の一部はより高次の方程式に一般化できる．　Some of the ideas described here can be generalized to equations of higher degree.
- この結果は外場の影響を取り込めるように一般化することができる．　This result can be generalized to include the effects of external fields.
- 相対論の要請を満たすように運動量の概念を一般化する　generalize the notion of momentum to satisfy the requirements of relativity
- リーマン面は複素平面の一般化である．　A Riemann surface is a generalization of the complex plane.

いど【緯度】 latitude

★緯度は北緯 (north latitude) または南緯 (south latitude) を使って次のように表わす．［⇨けいど］

- **北緯** 65 度 38 分に　at 65°38′N.　★at sixty-five degrees thirty-eight minutes north (latitude) と読む．
- 東京は**北緯** 35 度 45 分・東経 140 度にある．　Tokyo is located at **lat.** 35°45′ **N.** and long. 140°E.
- かつてベトナムは**北緯 17 度線**で分割されていた．　Vietnam used to be divided at **the 17th parallel north**.
- その地方は北海道と同**緯度**だ．　That area is「in [at] the same **latitude** as Hokkaido.
- その国は**緯度**が低い［高い］．　That country lies at a「low [high] **latitude**.
- 高［低］**緯度**では　at「high [low] **latitudes**
- イギリスは**緯度**から思うほど寒くない．　Britain is not as cold as its **latitude** might lead you to think.

いない【以内】

1〔期間内〕within

- 1 週間**以内**に　① **within** a week　② **inside of** a week　③ **in** a week **or less**
- 1 年**以内**に返済しなければならない負債　liabilities due to be repaid **within** one year
- 購入から 1 週間**以内**に　**within** a week「**after** [**from, of**] purchase
- 本条約の批准書の交換**の日から** 3 か月**以内**に

① **within** three months **from the date of** the exchange of the ratifications of this treaty
② **within** three months **from the date** ⌈**when** [**that**] the instruments of ratification of this treaty are exchanged

- (過去) 6 か月**以内に**撮影された写真　a photograph taken **within the** ⌈**last** [**past**] six months

2 〔空間的範囲内〕within

- 駅**から** 2 キロ**以内に**デパートが 3 軒ある．　There are three department stores **within** two kilometers **of** the station.
- 一連の放火事件はすべて**半径** 2 キロ**以内で**発生している．　The spate of arson cases have all occurred **within a** two-kilometer **radius**.
- 境界線**以内に**位置する建物　buildings located **within** the boundary line

3 〔数値の上限〕① within … ② up to (and including) … ③ not in excess of … ④ not exceeding … [⇨いか]

- 1 時間**以内の**外出　① going out for **up to** an hour　② absence for **up to** an hour or less
- 500 円**以内の**金額　a sum **not exceeding** 500 yen
- 論文の長さは 400 字詰め原稿用紙で 40 枚**以内とする**．　The length of the thesis **should not exceed** forty manuscript pages of 400 characters each.
- 招待客は 50 名**以内に**抑えたい．　I want to keep the guest list to **within** fifty.
- 駅から車で 10 分**以内の**距離にあるホテル　hotels **no more than** ten minutes from the station by car
- 彼の成績はクラスで**上位 3 分の 1 以内**である．　His grade average is **in the upper third** of his class.

イニング　an inning [⇨第 1 部・49. 野球の数字表現 49-1]

いらい【以来】

1 〔継続期間の起点〕since …

- それ以来 [その時以来]　① since then　② from that time ⌈on [onward(s)]　③ after that　④ afterward(s)　⑤ 〔それからずっと〕ever since (then)　⑥ ever afterwards
- 彼は 5 年前に渡米して**以来**ずっとアメリカに住んでいる．　He has lived in America ever **since** ⌈he went [moving, his move] there five years ago.

2 〔考慮対象期間の起点〕《first [biggest, etc.]》since …

- 利上げがされたのは 1995 年**以来のこと**だった．　It was **the first time since** 1995 that the interest rates were raised.
- 測候所開設**以来の**大雪が降った．　It was **the heaviest** snowfall **since** the meteorological station was set up.
- 今回の我が校の優勝は 99 年**以来のこと**だ．　This win for our school is **the**

first since '99.

…いり【…入り】

- 1.8 リットル入りの瓶　① 〔空の〕 a 1.8 liter bottle　② a bottle with a capacity of 1.8 liters　③ 〔中味が入っている〕 a bottle containing 1.8 liters　④ a bottle 「with [that has] 1.8 liters in it
- 500 ミリリットル入りのペットボトル飲料　beverages in 500 ml 「PET [plastic] bottles
- 一瓶 30 錠入りが 500 円，45 錠入りで 700 円です．
  ① A bottle 「of [with, containing] thirty pills costs ¥500 and one 「of [with, containing] forty-five costs ¥700.
  ② A thirty-pill bottle is ¥500 and a forty-five-pill bottle is ¥700.
- そのたばこは一箱何本入りですか．
  ① How many of those cigarettes come in one pack?
  ② How many of those cigarettes does one pack contain?
- そのワイン（のボトル）は何ミリリットル入りですか．
  ① How many milliliters of wine does that bottle contain?
  ② What is the size (in milliliters) of that bottle of wine?

いれる【入れる】　⇨さんにゅう 関連表現，…こみ

いんがかんけい【因果関係】　① a relation(ship) of cause and effect　② a cause-and-effect relation(ship)　③ cause and effect　④ a causal relation(ship)　⑤ a causal link

- A と B の因果関係　a cause-and-effect relation(ship) between A and B
- エルニーニョ現象と異常気象の間には**因果関係**がある．
  ① There is **a cause-and-effect relation(ship)** between El Niño and abnormal weather.
  ② **A (causal) relation(ship)** has been established between El Niño and abnormal weather conditions.
- これらの出来事の間の**因果関係**の有無は明らかではない．　It is not clear whether there is any **cause-and-effect relation(ship)** among these events.
- 彼らは，車の欠陥と事故との**因果関係**を実験によって証明した．
  ① They demonstrated experimentally that there was **a cause-and-effect relation(ship)** between the car's design defects and these accidents.
  ② They showed through these experiments that the faulty design of the car was **involved in causing** the accidents.
- 手術結果に関する損害賠償請求権が認められるか否かは最終的には**因果関係の問題**である．　Whether or not a right is recognized to seek damages for the results of surgery is ultimately **an issue of cause and effect**.
- 相関関係があっても**因果関係**があるとは限らない．　Correlation does not imply **causation**.　[⇨そうかん]

いんかんすう【陰関数】　an implicit function

- x と y の方程式が与えられれば，y を x の陰関数だと考えられる． Given an equation in x and y, we can think of y as an implicit function of x.

いんし【因子】 a factor
- p と共通因子をもたない整数 an integer that has no common factor with p
- 1 のオーダーの数因子だけ異なる differ by a numerical factor of order「one [unity]
- 共通因子をくくりだす take out a common factor

いんすう【因数】 a factor [⇨そいんすう]
- 因数に分解する ① decompose [resolve, break down, break up] into factors ② factor ③ factorize
- 因数分解 ① resolution into factors ② factorizing ③ factorization
- 因数分解する ① factor ② factorize
- a は $b \times c$ に因数分解される． a「factors [factorizes] into $b \times c$.
- 低次の多項式に因数分解できる 5 次式 a quintic that「factors [factorizes] into lower degree polynomials
- その整数は 2005 年に 2 つの 97 桁の数に因数分解された． The integer was factored into two 97-digit numbers in 2005.

インチ an inch 《= 2.54 cm；記号 in. または ″》[⇨第 1 部・28. 伝統単位 28-1]
- 3 フィート 5 インチ ① three feet five inches ② 3 ft. 5 in. ③ 3′5″
- 平方インチ a square inch《記号 sq. in.》
- 立方インチ a cubic inch《記号 cu. in.》
- 20 インチのテレビ ① a 20-inch TV ② a 20″ TV ③ a 20-inch diagonal TV ★数値は画面の対角線の長さを表わす．
- 26 インチの自転車 a bicycle with 26-inch wheels ★数値は車輪の直径を表わす．

ウェーバー 〔磁束の単位〕a weber《記号 Wb》

ウエスト ① *one's* waist measurement ② the measurement around the waist [⇨第 1 部・43-4 ウエスト]

ウォン a won ★単複同形 [⇨第 1 部・39-1 通貨単位 39-1-5]

うちのり【内法】

① 〔容器や管の〕the「internal [inside, interior] dimensions [measurement(s)]
② 〔建物の〕the internal dimensions《of a room》
- この箱の幅は**内法**で 10 センチある．
  ① This box is 10 centimeters wide **on the inside**.
  ② The **internal** width of this box is 10 centimeters.

うへん【右辺】 the right(-hand) side《of an equation》《略 RHS, r.h.s.》

うりあげ(だか)【売り上げ(高)】 ①sales ②the sales figures ③(a) turnover ④proceeds ⑤takings [⇨第1部・41-1-3 損益計算書]

- **売り上げ**は2,550億円で，昨年の2,500億円より2%増だった． **Sales** were [**Revenue** was] ¥255 billion, up 2% from ¥250 billion a year ago.
- その遊園地は最初の1年で10億円の**売上高**を記録した． That amusement park recorded 「**sales** [**a turnover**]」 of 1 billion yen in its first year.
- 新店舗の初年度**売上高**は約8億円を見込んでいる． They are expecting a **turnover** of about 800 million yen in the first year of their new outlet.
- 我が社の**売り上げ**は最近急激に伸びて年総額100億円に達した． **The sales figures** of our firm recently soared to an annual total of ten billion yen.
- この商店街全体の**売り上げ**は前年に比べ20%近く減った． Total **sales figures** of this shopping district are down almost 20% on the previous year.
- (劇場などの)チケットの**売り上げ**　box-office **receipts**
- その日の**売り上げ**　the day's **takings**
- **総売上高**　gross 「sales [proceeds]」
- **純売上高**　net 「sales [proceeds]」
- **年間売上高**　①annual 「sales [proceeds]」 ②yearly turnover [⇨ねんしょう]
- **海外売上高**　①overseas sales volume ②overseas sales turnover
- **海外売上高比率**　〔売上総額に占める〕the overseas sales ratio

うりょう【雨量】 ①(amount of) rainfall ②(amount of) rain ③precipitation [⇨第1部・45-4 降水・積雪]

うれゆき【売れ行き】 ①sales ②sales performance ③market performance ④demand

- 過去最高[空前]の売れ行き　①unprecedented sales ②unparalleled sales
- 100万部を超す売れ行き　①sales in excess of a million copies ②sales exceeding a million copies ③sales of over a million copies
- 売れ行きがよい　①sell well ②sell briskly ③find a large market ④encounter great demand ⑤〔堅調〕sell steadily
- 売れ行きが悪い　①sell poorly ②find a small market ③encounter little demand
- 売れ行きが伸びている[好調だ，上々だ]． Sales are 「rising [healthy, strong]」．
- 売れ行きが伸びている商品　①a product showing increasing sales ②a product whose sales are on the rise
- 売れ行きが落ち込んでいる． Sales are falling off.
- 売れ行きに響く　①affect sales adversely ②have a bad effect on sales ③dampen sales
- 彼の新著はすばらしい売れ行きを見た． His new book has seen tremendous sales.

関連表現
- 彼らのデビュー CD は 20 万枚売れた.
  ① Two hundred thousand copies of their debut CD were sold.
  ② Their debut CD sold two hundred thousand copies.
- 同社は昨年の発売以来そのモデルを 5 万台売った.　The company has sold 50,000 units of the model since introducing it last year.

うわまわる【上回る】　① exceed　② surpass　③ be「more [better]」than …　④ be above …　[⇨第 1 部・13. 比較・差・増減 13-1-3]

うんじゅう【うん十】　[⇨第 1 部・8-3「うん十」など]
- うん十万円　some hundreds of thousand yen

うんどうりょう【運動量】　momentum
- 運動量の保存　conservation of momentum
- 光子はドブロイの関係式で与えられる**運動量をもっている**.　A photon **has a momentum** given by the de Broglie relationship.
- 重心系ではその 2 つの粒子は**大きさが同じで逆向きの運動量をもつ**.　In the center-of-mass system, the two particles have **equal but opposite momenta**.
- 角運動量　an angular momentum

えいかく【鋭角】　an acute angle
- …と鋭角をなす　make an acute angle with …
- 鋭角三角形　an「acute [acute-angled]」triangle

えいぎょうび【営業日】　① a business day　② a trading day
- ご注文の商品は注文受付後 5 営業日以内に発送いたします.　We will「ship [dispatch]」your order within five business days (of receiving it).

エクサ…　[10^{18}] exa-　[⇨第 1 部・27-4 SI 接頭語]

えだばん【枝番】　⇨第 1 部・48-5 枝番

エックス・ワイへいめん【xy 平面】　the xy-plane

エヌじ【n 次】　① nth-degree　② nth-order　③ of degree n　④ of order n

エネルギー　energy
- 核反応で解放されるエネルギー　energy released「in [by]」nuclear reactions
- 単位面積当たりに放出される全エネルギー　the total energy emitted per unit area
- その原子をイオン化するのに必要なエネルギー　the energy required to ionize the atom
- γ 線は X 線より 100 倍程度エネルギーが高い.　Gamma rays are about 100 times more energetic than X rays.
- ほとんどエネルギーの消費なしに　① with almost no「consumption of energy

エルグ

[energy consumption] ② consuming almost no energy
- 電波の形でエネルギーを失う　lose energy in the form of radio waves
- 光子の失ったエネルギーに等しい運動エネルギーをもつ電子　an electron with a kinetic energy equal to the energy lost by the photon
- その系では運動エネルギーが0になる　have zero kinetic energy in that frame
- 各原子の運動エネルギーの和　the sum of the kinetic energies of the atoms
- 運動エネルギーとポテンシャルエネルギーの和　① the sum of the kinetic and potential energies　② the sum of the kinetic energy and the potential energy
- 低エネルギーでの断面積　a cross section at low energies
- …以上のエネルギーの陽子　protons with energies above …

エルグ　〔エネルギーの CGS 単位〕an erg 《= 10^{-7} ジュール；記号 erg》

エルステッド　〔磁界の強さの CGS 単位〕an oersted 《記号 Oe》

エルディーケー【LDK】　⇨第 1 部・46-3 住居

えん【円】

1　〔図形〕a circle
- 点 A, B, C を通る円　the circle which passes through the points A, B, and C
- この円の面積を求めよ．　Find the area of this circle.
- 円の面積は πr^2 で表わされる．　The area of a circle is expressed as πr^2.
★ πr^2 は pi r squared と読む．
- コンパスで円を描く　draw a circle with「a compass [a pair of compasses]
- 大きく円を描くように腕を回してください．　Turn your arms around in big circles.
- 円運動　circular motion
- 円軌道　a circular orbit
- 円軌道を描く　describe a circular orbit
- 円偏光　circular polarization

2　〔日本の通貨単位〕a yen 《記号 ¥》　★yen は単複同形．〔⇨第 1 部・39-1-1 円, 40-2 価格・値段〕
- 100 円硬貨　a 100-yen coin
- 1 万円紙幣 [札]　①《米》a 10,000-yen bill　②《英》a 10,000-yen note
- 500 円分の切手　five hundred yen('s) worth of stamps
- 「これはいくらですか」「500 円です」　How much is this? — 500 yen.
- 円で払う　pay in yen
- 円建ての　① yen-based　② yen-denominated　③ yen-priced
- 円建て借款　① a yen-denominated loan　② a yen-based loan

- 円建て輸出　yen-denominated exports
- 円記号［円マーク］　① a [the] yen symbol　② a [the] yen sign (¥)　★中国などで元 (yuan) の記号として使うことが増えてきている．★JIS で円記号に割り当てられたコード 5C は ASCII ではバックスラッシュを表わすので，システムによっては文字化けが起こる．

えんこ【円弧】　① a circular arc　②〔円周の一部〕an arc of a circle

えんざん【演算】　① an operation　② a mathematical operation

えんざんし【演算子】　an operator
- 逆演算子　an inverse operator

えんしゅう【円周】　the circumference of a circle
- この円の円周を求めなさい．　Find the circumference of this circle.
- 円周は $2\pi r$ で表わされる．　The circumference of a circle is expressed as「πd [$2\pi r$]．★英語では $2\pi r$ (r は radius) のほか πd (d は diameter) とも言う．

えんしゅうかく【円周角】　① an inscribed angle　② an angle at the circumference　★inscribed は「内接している」の意．
- 円周角の大きさは同じ弧に対する中心角の大きさの半分である．
① The measure of **an inscribed angle** is half the measure of the central angle with the same intercepted arc.
② The measure of **an inscribed angle** is half the measure of its intercepted arc.　★単位円上では弧長がラジアンで表わした中心角と等しいことを前提としている．
- 同じ弧に対する**円周角**は等しい．
① **Inscribed angles** that intercept the same arc are「congruent [equal to each other]．
② **Inscribed angles** that sit on the same arc are「congruent [equal to each other]．
③ **Inscribed angles** subtended by the same arc are「congruent [equal to each other]．

えんしゅうりつ【円周率】　π [pi]
- **円周率**は円周のその直径に対する比である．　**Pi** is the ratio of the circumference of a circle to its diameter.
- **円周率**を小数点以下 100 桁まで計算する　① calculate **pi** to 100 decimal places　② calculate the first 100 decimals of **pi**　③ calculate the first 100 digits of the decimal expansion of **pi**

えんすい【円錐】　a (circular) cone
- **円錐**の体積は底面積かける高さかける 1/3 である．　The volume of **a cone** is one third the product of the area of its base and the height.
- 底面の半径が 2 cm，高さが 12 cm の**円錐**　**a cone** with base radius 2 cm and height 12 cm

- r はその**円錐**の底面の半径である． r is the radius of the base of the **cone**.
- **円錐**の展開図は底面になる円と側面になる扇形からなる． The net of **a cone** consists of a circle that gives the base and a sector that gives the lateral surface.
- 楕円錐　an elliptic(al) cone
- 直円錐　a right (circular) cone
- 斜円錐　an oblique (circular) cone
- 円錐曲線　⇨えんすいきょくせん
- 円錐台　① a truncated cone ② a frustum of a cone

えんすいきょくせん【円錐曲線】　a conic (section)

- 円錐曲線の離心率　the eccentricity of a conic
- 円錐曲線の幾何学的な作図　geometrical construction of a conic
- 双曲線は楕円と同じく**円錐曲線**である． A hyperbola is, like an ellipse, **a conic section**.
- **円錐曲線**とは楕円，放物線，双曲線のことです． **The conic sections** are the ellipse, the parabola, and the hyperbola.
- 太陽のような中心天体のまわりの物体の軌道は常に**円錐曲線**と呼ばれる種類の曲線のどれかになります． The orbit of a body around a central body like the Sun is always one of the class of curves called **conic sections**.
- これらの曲線は，平面が円錐を切るときにできることから**円錐曲線**と呼ばれる． These curves are called **conic sections** because they are formed「when a plane passes through a cone［as the intersection of a plane with a cone］.

えんだか【円高】　①〔高いこと〕a strong(er) yen ②〔高くなること〕(an) appreciation of the yen《against the dollar》③ the yen's appreciation ④ a rise in (the value of) the yen［⇨第 1 部・39-2-4 円高］

- 5 円の円高　a 5-yen「appreciation [rise] against the dollar
- 円高になった． The yen「appreciated [rose] (against the dollar).
- 円高ドル安　① appreciation of the yen against the dollar ② a strong yen and (a) weak dollar
- 円高不況　a recession caused by the strong yen

えんちゅう【円柱】　a (circular) cylinder

- 斜円柱　an oblique (circular) cylinder
- 直円柱　a right (circular) cylinder

えんちょく【鉛直】

- 鉛直な　① vertical ② plumb
- 鉛直線　① a vertical line ② a plumb line
- 鉛直方向　a vertical direction

- 鉛直面　a vertical plane

えんとう【円筒】　a cylinder
- 円筒座標　cylindrical coordinates
- 円筒座標系　a cylindrical coordinate system

えんばん【円板】　a disk

えんやす【円安】　①〔安いこと〕a「weak [cheap, low] yen　②weakness of the yen　③a low (rate of exchange) for the yen　④〔安くなること〕(a) depreciation of the yen　⑤the yen's depreciation　⑥a「fall [drop, decline] in (the value of) the yen［⇨第1部・39-2-5 円安］
- 5円の円安　a 5-yen「depreciation [fall] against the dollar
- 円安になった．　The yen「depreciated [fell, dropped, weakened] (against the dollar).

おうぎがた【扇形】　a sector

おうごんひ【黄金比】　①the golden ratio　②the divine proportion

おうごんぶんかつ【黄金分割】　①the golden section　②the golden mean

おうさつ【応札】　bidding［⇨第1部・39-4 入札・オークション］

おうたかくけい【凹多角形】　①a concave polygon　②a reentrant polygon　③a reentering polygon

おおい【多い】　①〔多数〕many　②a large number of　③〔多量〕much　④a large amount of［⇨第1部・19. 多少の表現］

おおきさ【大きさ】　①(a) size　②〔寸法〕dimensions　③〔規模・絶対値〕magnitude　④〔体積〕volume　⑤〔かさ〕bulk　⑥〔ベクトルの〕magnitude［⇨第1部・42. 大きさ・重さ］
- そのコンテナの大きさは幅2m，高さ3m，長さ6mである．
　①The container measures 2 meters wide by 3 meters high by 6 meters long.
　②The dimensions of the container are 2 (W) by 3 (H) by 6 (L) meters.
　③The container is 2 meters in width, 3 meters in height, and 6 meters in length.
- 雄と雌とは大きさが違う．　The male and female differ in size.
- いろいろな大きさがある　①vary in size　②〔商品などが〕be of various sizes　③come in various sizes
- AとBは同じ大きさです．　A and B are the same size (as each other).
- …と同じくらいの大きさである　①be about the same size as …　②be as big as …
- (成長すると)…と同じくらいの大きさになる　reach [attain] about the size of …

オークション

- **親指くらいの大きさのネズミ**　a mouse about the size of「a [a person's, your] thumb
- **このくらいの大きさ**の箱が欲しいんですが．　I want a box **about this**「**big** [**size**].
- 新しい家は今の**半分 [2 倍] ほどの大きさ**だ．
  ① Our new house **will be about**「**half [twice] the size of** our present one.
  ② Our new house **will be about**「**half [twice] as big as** the one we have now.
- 胃にできた癌が先月調べたときの**倍くらいの大きさ**になっている．　The cancer in my stomach has grown to **about twice the size** it was when I was examined last month.
- この石は**大きさのわりには**重くない．　This stone is not very heavy **for its size**.
- 物体の特徴的な**大きさ**　〘物〙a characteristic (**linear**) **dimension** of an object
- **大きさはどのくらいにしましょうか．**　About「**what size [how big**] shall I make it?
- 速度はベクトル量であり，**大きさ**と方向をもつ．　Velocity is a vector quantity and has both **magnitude** and direction.
- 画面の**大きさ**は 1400×1050 だ．　The screen **size** is 1400×1050.
- その領域を覆うのに十分な**大きさ**である　be of sufficient **size** to cover the area
- 30 cm×50 cm の大きさに収まる　can fit within the dimensions of 30 cm by 50 cm

オークション　an auction [⇨第 1 部・39-4 入札・オークション]

おおくとも，おおくて【多くとも，多くて】　① at most ② at the most ③ at the outside ④ at the very most
- 立候補者は多くて 10 名だろう．　There will be no more than ten candidates.
- この事故による死者は多くとも 30 名を超えることはあるまい．　The number of deaths caused by this accident is very unlikely to exceed thirty.

オーダー　〔桁〕an order of magnitude
- …と同じオーダーである　be of [have] the same order of magnitude as …
- 数ナノメートルのオーダーの長さ　a length「of [on] the order of magnitude of a few nanometers
- オーダーエスティメート　an order-of-magnitude estimate
- 被害者の数は数万のオーダーだ．　The number of victims is on the order of tens of thousands.
- そのアルゴリズムの計算量は n のオーダーだ．　The computational complexity of the algorithm is「of the order n [of order n, of $O(n)$].

オープンかかく【オープン価格】　⇨第 1 部・40-2-4 価格にまつわる術語

オーム　〔電気抵抗の単位〕an ohm《記号　Ω》
- 50 Ω の抵抗　① a resistor of 50 ohms　② a 50-ohm resistor
- 全抵抗は何 Ω か．　What is the total resistance in ohms?
- 50 Ω の抵抗が 20 V のバッテリーにつながれている．　A resistor of 50 ohms is connected to a 20-volt battery.
- 100 Ω の抵抗 2 つを並列につないだものは 50 Ω の抵抗 1 つと同等である．　Two 100-ohm resistors in parallel are equivalent to one 50-ohm resistor.

おおよそ　⇨およそ

…おき　① every …　② at intervals of …
- 1 日おきに　① every other day　② every second day　③ on alternate days　④〔2 日に 1 度〕every two days
- 2 日おきに　① on every third day　② two days apart　③〔3 日に 1 度〕every three days
- (電車などが) 10 分おきに運行する　run every ten minutes
- この薬は 8 時間おきに飲むこと．〔服用方法の指示〕This medicine should be taken every eight hours.
- 5 メートルおきに木を植える　① plant trees five meters apart　② plant trees at intervals of five meters　③ plant trees at five-meter intervals　④ plant trees with a space of five meters in between
- 1 行おきに書く　① write on every other line　② write on alternate lines　③ skip every other line
- 行列の学生は 1 人おきに旗を持っていた．　Every second student in the parade carried a flag.

おく【億】　a [one] hundred million ［⇨第 1 部・1. 基数］
- 3 億円　three hundred million yen
- 1 億 2000 万　a [one] hundred and twenty million
- 10 億　a [one] billion
- 100 億　ten billion
- 何億もの　hundreds of millions of …　［⇨第 1 部・8. 漠然とした大きな数］
- 一億総懺悔　a national confession of (Japanese war) guilt
- 一億総中流　① Japan's pervasive middle-class mentality (in the 1980s)　② the middle-class mentality shared by the vast majority of Japanese
- 一億総白痴化　the transformation of the entire population of Japan into idiots

おくゆき【奥行き】　depth ［⇨第 1 部・42-3 奥行き］
- 幅 20 m，奥行き 8 m の舞台　a stage 20 meters wide and 8 meters deep

…おち【…落ち】
- 5 年落ちの車を 50 万円で買った．　I bought a five-year-old car for five hun-

dred thousand yen.

オッズ the odds ［⇨第1部・23. 確率と可能性］
- オッズとはある事象がどのくらい起こりそうかの数値表現である．　Odds are a numerical expression of「how likely an event is［the likelihood of an event］．
- さいころを振って6が出ることのオッズは1対5だ．　Odds for rolling six with a die are「1 to 5［1:5, 1-5］．★ある事象が起こる確率 (1/6) そのものではなく，その事象が起こらない確率との比で表わす．
- 5対1［5倍］のオッズは賭け手が100円の賭け金で勝った場合に500円の払い戻しを受けることを意味する．　Odds of「five to one［5:1, 5-1］mean the bettor will receive a payout of 500 yen on a 100-yen stake. ★上記の確率論での慣用とは逆にギャンブルでは最初の数字が大きいほどハイリターン（低確率）を表わす．
- 第3レースのオッズが確定した．　The odds for the third race have been set.
- 高いオッズがついた．　High odds were given.
- このオッズで当たったら，配当金はすごい額になるぞ．　If you win at these odds, the payout will be tremendous.

おつり【お釣り】 change ［⇨第1部・40-6-4 おつり］
- おつりに300円受け取った．　I「received［got］300 yen (in) change.

おととい【一昨日】 the day before yesterday ［⇨第1部・31-5-2「先…」］
- おとといの朝［午後］　the「morning［afternoon］of the day before yesterday
- おとといの夜　the night before last

おととし【一昨年】 the year before last ［⇨第1部・31-5-2「先…」］
- おととしの夏　the summer before last

おなじ【同じ】 ［⇨第1部・18. 同等・相当］
- …と同じである　① be the same as …　② be equal to …　③ equal …　④ be identical「to［with］…
- A と B は同じ値だ．　A and B have the same value.
- それらは同じ値段だ．
  ① They are the same price.
  ② They have the same price.
  ③ They cost the same.
  ④ Their prices are the same.
  ⑤ The price is the same for both of them.
- 線分 A と B は長さが同じだ．
  ① Line A is the same length as line B.
  ② Line A is of the same length as line B.
  ③ Line A has the same length as line B.
  ④ Lines A and B are equal in length.

- …と同じ数の… ①as many … as … ②the same number of … as … ③… equal in number to … ④… of the same number as …
- メッセージと同じビット数の鍵ストリーム a key stream having the same number of bits as the message

おもさ【重さ】 weight [⇨第1部・42-10 重さと質量]
- 重さが3キロある ①weigh 3 kilograms ②be 3 kilograms in weight ③have a weight of 3 kilograms

おもみ【重み】 weight
- 各質量は原点からの距離で**重みをかけてある**． Each mass **is weighted by** the distance from the origin.
- スピーカー信号にこれらの係数で**重みをかけたもの**を合計する sum [add] speaker signals **weighted** by these coefficients
- **重み関数** w について f を積分する integrate f with respect to **the weight function** w
- $f(x)$ を**重み**として正規直交系をなす ①form an orthonormal system with respect to **the weight** $f(x)$ ②be orthonormal with **weight** $f(x)$

およそ，おおよそ ①about ②approximately ③roughly ④around [⇨第1部・9. 概数]
- およそ100冊の本 ①about 100 books ②approximately 100 books ③roughly 100 books ④around 100 books

おりかえし【折り返し】 reflection
- 直線 $y=x$ に関する**折り返し** **a reflection** [across [about, over, in] the line $y=x$

関連表現
- そのグラフは，$f(x)$ のグラフを直線 $y=x$ **に関して折り返したもの**である． The graph is **the reflection** of the graph of $f(x)$ [**across** [**about**, **over**, **in**] the line $y=x$.
- グラフを x 軸**に関して対称に折り返す** **reflect** the graph [**across** [**about**, **over**, **in**] the x-axis

おわりね【終値】 ①the closing price ②the closing quotation ③the closing market price ④the close [⇨第1部・39-3 株]
- その株は急落して終値は890円，前日比130円安となった． The stock [ended [closed] sharply lower at 890 yen, down 130 yen from the day before.

オングストローム 〔長さの単位〕an angstrom （（= 10^{-10}m；記号 Å））

オンス an ounce （（常衡は 1/16 ポンド，28.35 g；金衡は 1/12 ポンド，31.103 g；記号 oz.）） [⇨第1部・28. 伝統単位 28-3]

おんそく【音速】 ①the speed of sound ②the velocity of sound ③sonic veloc-

ity ④ acoustic velocity ⑤ sound velocity ⑥ sonic speed [⇨マッハ]
- 音速で飛ぶ　fly at the speed of sound
- 音速の2倍で飛ぶ　① fly at twice the speed of sound ② fly at Mach 2
- 音速を超える　exceed the speed of sound

おんど【温度】　(a) temperature [⇨第1部・45-1 温度]
- 屋内の温度はセ氏18度です．　① The temperature「indoors [inside] is 18°C. ② The indoor temperature is 18°C. ★18°C は eighteen degrees Celsius と読む．

おんぷ【音符】　[⇨きゅうふ]
- 全音符　①《米》a whole note ②《英》a semibreve
- 二分音符　①《米》a half note ②《英》a minim
- 四分音符　①《米》a quarter note ②《英》a crotchet
- 八分音符　①《米》an eighth note ②《英》a quaver
- 十六分音符　①《米》a sixteenth note ②《英》a semiquaver
- 三十二分音符　①《米》a thirty-second note ②《英》a demisemiquaver
- 六十四分音符　①《米》a sixty-fourth note ②《英》a hemidemisemiquaver

か行

かい【解】 a solution
- 方程式の解　a solution「of [to] an equation
- 次の方程式の解を求めよ．　Solve the following equation.
- 一般に二次方程式は 2 つの**解**をもつ．　In general, a quadratic equation has two「**solutions**［**roots**］．
- フェルマー方程式は，$n > 2$ では，x, y, z に対する 0 でない整数**解**をもたない．
  ① The Fermat equation has no nonzero integer **solutions** for x, y, z when $n > 2$.
  ② The Fermat equation has no **solutions** in nonzero integers x, y, z with $n > 2$.
- その連立方程式の**解**は $x = 1$，$y = 2$ だ．　**The solution** of the simultaneous equations is $x = 1$, $y = 2$.
- 実数解　a real「solution [root]
- 整数解　an integer「solution [root]
- 有理数解　a rational「solution [root]
- 複素数解　a complex「solution [root]

かい【下位】　[⇨第 1 部・15. 順位・順番の表現 15-2-1]
- 下位にランクされる　be ranked low

…かい【…回】

1　[回数] a time [⇨第 1 部・36. 回数・頻度の表現]
- 1 回　① once ② one time [⇨いっかい，いちど]
- 2 回　① twice ② two times
- 3 回　three times
- 1, 2 回　once or twice
- 2, 3 回　two or three times
- 1 日 3 回　three times a day
- 2 回以上　① more than once ② two or more times ③ twice or more
- 何回も　① many times ② over and over again ③ again and again
- 何千回も，何千回となく　thousands of times
- 偶数回　⇨ぐうすう
- 奇数回　⇨きすう【奇数】

2　[繰り返しの番号] [⇨第 1 部・4. 序数]
- 初回の，第 1 回の　the first …
- 第 2 回の　the second …
- 最終回の　① the last … ② the final …

…かい

- 次回の会議は 10 月です．
 ① The next meeting will be in October.
 ② We will meet next in October.
- 1 回で成功する　succeed in ⌈*one's* [the]⌋ first ⌈attempt [try]⌋

3 〔競技の〕① a round　② a game　③〘野球〙an inning

- 7 回の表［裏］　〔野球の〕《in》the ⌈top [bottom]⌋ of the seventh inning ［⇨第 1 部・49. 野球の数字表現 49-1］
- 1 回戦　①〔第 1 試合〕the first game　②〔トーナメントの〕a [the] first round
- 10 回戦［試合］　〔ボクシングなどの〕① a ⌈bout [fight]⌋ of ten rounds　② a ten-rounder
- もう 1 回やろう．〔将棋など〕
 ① Let's ⌈have [play]⌋ another game.
 ② I'll play you another (game).

…かい【…階】

1 〔建物の〕① a ⌈story [《英》storey]⌋　② a floor　③ a level

- 1 階　① the ground floor　②《米》the first ⌈floor [story]⌋
- 2 階　①《米》the second ⌈story [floor]⌋　②《英》the first ⌈floor [storey, level]⌋
 ★《英》では日本でいう 1 階を ground floor といい，2 階を first floor, 3 階を second floor, … と数える．
- 地階　① a basement ⌈floor [story, level]⌋　② an underground floor
- 最上階　① the top ⌈floor [story, level]⌋　②〔最上階の高級室〕a penthouse
- 地下 3 階の倉庫　① a storage space three floors below ground level　② a depository on the third basement level
★日本では地下 3 階を「B3」と書くのは一般的だが，欧米のエレベーターの表示は一様ではない．欧米では地下 1 階はしばしば B (basement), P (parking), LL (lower level), −1 などと表示される．地下 2 階は SB (sub-basement), B2, P2, −2 などとなる．なお，1 階のボタンも G (ground), L (lobby), M (main) などと文字になっていることがある．イギリス式であればその上に「1」がくることになる．アメリカでは地下 1 階の駐車場を G (garage) と表示することもあって 1 階の「G」との混同に気をつける必要がある．
- 3 階に住んでいる．
 ① I live on the ⌈third [《英》second]⌋ floor.
 ② I live two flights up.
- その建物は 11 階建てだ．　The building has 11 floors.
- 10 階建てのビル　① a 10-story [-storied] building　② a building of ten stories　③ a building 10-stories high
- そのビルは地上 7 階地下 2 階だ．　The building has seven floors above ground and two below.
- 私の部屋は 8 階建ての 7 階です．　My apartment is on the ⌈7th [《英》6th]⌋

floor of an 8-story building.
- このエレベーターは各階に止まります．　This elevator「stops at [serves] every floor.
- このエレベーターは 30 階から 39 階に止まる．　This elevator serves floors 30「to [through] 39.
- このビルは何階建てですか．
  ① How many floors does this building have?
  ② How many stories (high) is this building?
- 事務所は何階にありますか．　What [Which] floor is the office on?
- 彼は 2 階上 [下] に住んでいる．
  ① He lives two floors「up [down].
  ② He lives two floors「above [below]《me》.
- 上の階の物音がうるさくてしょうがない．　The noise (from) upstairs gets on my nerves.
- 下の階の住人から苦情が来た．
  ① I got a complaint from the person「downstairs [in the room below mine].
  ② There were complaints from the people living downstairs.
- ★欧米では 13 は縁起の悪い数とされており，ホテルやアパートで 12 階の上の階が 14 階と表示されることがしばしばある．［⇨第 1 部・37-6 トリビア：縁起のいい数・悪い数］

2 ①〔微分方程式の〕an order　②〔テンソルの〕an order　③ a rank　④〔行列・群の〕a rank
- 2 階線形微分方程式　① a linear differential equation of「order two [the second order]　② a second-order linear differential equation
- 2 階テンソル　① a tensor of「order [rank] two　② a tensor of the second「order [rank]　③ a second-order[-rank] tensor
- 1 階偏微分　a first-order partial derivative

かいいんすう【会員数】　① the number of members　② (a) membership ［⇨にんずう］

がいかく【外角】　① an exterior angle　② an external angle　③〔壁・建物の〕a quoin

かいき【回帰】　regression
- 回帰係数　a regression coefficient
- 回帰分析　regression analysis

がいけい【外径】　① the external diameter　② the outside diameter　③ the outer diameter
- 水道管の外径を計測する　measure the outer diameter of a water pipe
- 配水管の外径に合わせて床に穴を開ける　cut holes in the floor to fit the

outer diameter of water pipes

かいさ【階差】 a difference
- 階差数列　① a progression of differences　② a sequence of differences

かいしゅうごう【開集合】 an open set
- 開集合を開集合に移す　map open sets to open sets
- **開集合上**で定義された連続関数　a continuous function defined **on an open set**

かいしゅうごう【解集合】 ① a set of solutions　② the solution set《to the equation》

かいじょう【階乗】 a factorial
- n の階乗　the factorial of n　★$n!$ と書き，n factorial, factorial n, the factorial of n と読む．

がいしん【外心】 a circumcenter
- 三角形の外接円の中心はその三角形の**外心**と呼ばれる．　The center of the circumcircle of a triangle is called **the circumcenter** of the triangle.
- 三角形の 3 辺の垂直二等分線は**外心**で交わる．　The three perpendicular bisectors of the sides of a triangle meet **at the circumcenter**.

かいすう【回数】 ① the number of times　②〔頻度〕(a) frequency
- 使うことのできる回数　the number of times it can be used
- 彼女はこのごろ遅刻の回数が増えた［減った］．　She has been late「more [less] often recently.
- 彼の無断欠勤の回数はどれほどですか．　How「often [many times] has he missed work without permission?
- シェイクスピアの最も上演回数の多い戯曲の一つ　one of Shakespeare's most often「performed [staged] plays

かいすう【階数】　[⇨…かい【…階】]

1〔建物の〕the number of floors《in the building》

2　①〔微分方程式の〕an order　②〔テンソルの〕an order　③ a rank　④〔行列・群の〕a rank

かいせき【解析】　(an) analysis
- 解析する　analyze
- 解析学　analysis
- 解析関数　an analytic function
- 解析接続　analytic continuation
- その関数は複素平面全体に解析接続することができる．　The function can be analytically continued over the whole complex plane.

がいせき【外積】 ① an exterior product ② an outer product

がいせつ【外接】
- 外接する　① circumscribe ② be circumscribed
- この円は五角形に外接している．　This circle「circumscribes [is circumscribed on] a pentagonal figure.
- 外接する2円の中心を通る直線　a line joining the centers of two circles which touch externally
- 外接円　① a circumcircle ② a circumscribed circle
- 外接多角形　a circumscribed polygon

かいてんりつ【回転率】　(a) turnover (rate) 《of capital, of merchandise》
- 客の回転率　(a) customer turnover
- 在庫回転率　(a) stock turnover

関連表現
- 客の回転をよくする方法　a way to increase customer turnover

かいばつ【海抜】　① a height above sea level ② an elevation (above sea level) ③ an altitude (above sea level)
- 海抜950メートルである　① be 950 meters above sea level ② be at an altitude of 950 meters (above sea level)
- 海抜ゼロメートル地帯　① a sea-level zone ② an area at sea level
- 富士山は海抜3,776メートルです．
 ① Mt. Fuji has an altitude of 3,776 meters.
 ② Mt. Fuji is 3,776 meters above sea level.
 ③ Mt. Fuji rises 3,776 meters above sea level.

かいひょうりつ【開票率】　the percentage of「votes [the vote] counted (so far) [⇨第1部・16-1 票数]

がいぶん【外分】　external division
- 外分する　divide externally
- 外分点　an externally dividing point

かいへい【開平】　① square root extraction ② extraction of a square root

かいり【海里】　①〔距離の単位〕a nautical mile ② a sea mile　★国際海里協定で1海里は1,852メートルと制定されている．これと区別して普通の陸上のマイルを land mile という．
- 200海里漁業水域　a 200(-nautical)-mile fishing zone
- 1時間に1海里進む速さを1ノットと言う．　A speed of one nautical mile per hour is called one knot.

ガウス　〔磁束密度のCGS単位〕a gauss《記号G》　★複数形は gauss と gausses がある．

カウント 〔数や秒数を数えること〕① a count ② counting
- カウントする ① count 《the score》 ② take the count
- カウントはツーボール，ワンストライク． The (batter's) count is two balls and one strike. [⇨第 1 部・49. 野球の数字表現 49-7]
- カウント 9 でようやく立ち上がった．〔ボクサーが〕
  ① He finally stood up at the count of nine.
  ② He took a count of nine before getting up.
- 今カウントはいくつ？ What's the「count [score]？
- （毎分）20 万カウントの放射能 radioactivity of 200,000 counts (per minute) ★counts per minute は cpm とも略す．SI 単位はベクレル（becquerel）．
- ノーカウント 〔数に入れないこと〕① not (to be)「counted [included] ② 《should [do]》 not「count [include]
- カウントダウンを開始する start a countdown

かかく【価格】 a price [⇨第 1 部・40-2 価格・値段]
- 牛肉の価格が 1 週間で 2 倍以上になった． The price of beef more than doubled within the space of one week.

かかん【可換】
- 可換な commutative
- A と B は可換である． A and B commute.
- A は B と可換である． A commutes with B.
- この演算子はハミルトニアンと可換である This operator commutes with the Hamiltonian.
- 群では積は可換である必要はない． In a group, multiplication does not have to be commutative.

かく【角】 an angle [⇨かくど]
- それらの 2 辺にはさまれる**角** **the angle** included by those two sides
- 辺 a に対する**角** **the angle** opposite the side a.
- その**角**に対する辺 〔三角形で〕① the side opposite **the angle** ② the side which subtends **the angle**
- **角** A, B, C に対する辺の長さをそれぞれ a, b, c とすると… If the lengths of the sides opposite **the angles** A, B, and C are a, b, and c, respectively, …
- 円弧が円の中心においてなす**角**
  ① **the angle** which an arc of a circle subtends at the center of the circle
  ② **the angle** subtended at the center of a circle by an arc
- 隣り合う**角** 〔多角形で〕consecutive **angles**
- 相接する**角** 〔頂点と一辺を共有する〕adjacent **angles**

- **角**の大きさ　the「measure [size] of **an angle**
- 45度の**角**をなす　form [make] **an angle** of 45°《with …》
- 実軸と**角** a をなしている　be at **an angle** a with the real axis
- 2角が等しい．
  ① Two angles are congruent.
  ② Two angles are equal (in measure).
  ③ Two angles have the same measure.
  ④ Two angles have equal measures.
- 反射角は入射角に等しい．
  ① The angle of reflection equals the angle of incidence.
  ② Light is reflected at an angle equal to the angle of incidence.

★angle には大きさとしての角度だけではなく，2つの線分が頂点で交わってなす図形という概念もある．そのため幾何学では角が等しいことを表わすのに congruent（合同の意）とか have the same measure のような言い方をする．純粋に角度としてとらえるときには equal でよい．

- 4センチ角のタイル　a tile four centimeters square
- 角運動量　(an) angular momentum
- 角速度　① (an) angular speed　② (an) angular velocity
- 角直径　an angular diameter
- 方位角30°，仰角70°のところに位置している．　It is (placed) at the azimuth of 30° and the elevation of 70°.
- 角は反時計回りに測る．　The angle is measured counterclockwise.
- x軸の正方向から反時計回りに測った角　an angle measured counterclockwise from the positive x-direction

…かくけい【…角形】　[⇨第1部・58. 図形の基本表現 58-2]

- 五角形　a pentagon

かくげつ【隔月】　[⇨第1部・36-3 頻度]

- 隔月で　① every two months　② every「other [second] month　③ in alternate months

かくしゅう【隔週】　[⇨第1部・36-3 頻度]

- 隔週で　① every two weeks　② every「other [second] week　③ in alternate weeks　④ biweekly　⑤《主に英》fortnightly

かくすい【角錐】　a pyramid

- **角錐**の体積は底面積かける高さかける1/3である．　The volume of **a pyramid** is one third the product of the area of its base and the height.
- 底面が正多角形の角錐　① a pyramid whose base is a regular polygon　② a pyramid having a regular polygon for its base
- 三角錐　a triangular pyramid

かくだいりつ

- 四角錐　a quadrangular pyramid
- 五角錐　a pentagonal pyramid ★以下は同様に「…角形」に準じて -gonal pyramid のようにいう．[⇨第 1 部・58-2 …角形]
- n 角錐　an n-gonal pyramid
- 正角錐　a regular pyramid
- 直角錐　a right pyramid
- 角錐台　① a prismoid　② a frustum of a pyramid　③ a truncated pyramid

かくだいりつ【拡大率】　① a degree of enlargement　② an enlargement《of 150%》　③ an enlargement ratio《of 1.5 [150%]》[⇨ばいりつ]

かくちゅう【角柱】　a prism
- **角柱**の体積は底面積かける高さである．　The volume of **a prism** is the product of the area of its base and the height.
- 三角柱　a triangular prism
- 四角柱　a quadrangular prism
- 五角柱　a pentagonal prism ★以下は同様に「…角形」に準じて -gonal prism のようにいう．[⇨第 1 部・58-2 …角形]

かくづけ【格付け】　rating [⇨第 1 部・15-3 格付けと星]
- 我が社は AA に格付けされています．
  ① Our company has been rated AA.
  ② We have been given an AA rating.

かくど【角度】　an angle [⇨かく，こうばい]
- 2 直線が交わる**角度**　**the angle** at which two lines「meet [intersect]
- 光が鏡に入射する**角度**　**the angle** at which light is incident on the mirror
- レンズの軸と結像可能な光線の最大許容角との間の**角度**　**the angle** subtended between the axis of a lens and the largest accepted angle of the image-forming rays
- その天体が観測者のところになす**角度**　**the angle** at the observer subtended by the celestial body
- 45 度の**角度**で [に]　at **an angle** of 45°
- 水平面に対して 20° の**角度**である　be inclined at **an angle** of 20°「from (the) horizontal [above (the) horizontal, to the horizontal, with respect to the horizontal, relative to the horizontal]
- 鉛直線に対する**角度**　**an angle** with respect to the vertical (line)
- 軸に対して 45° の**角度**に置かれている　be positioned at **an angle** of 45° to the axis
- 光線は表面の法線に対して**角度** A で入射する．　The light beam is incident on the surface at **an angle** A to the normal「of [on] the surface.
- 浅い**角度**で大気圏に再突入する　re-enter the atmosphere at a「shallow [low]

がくねん

angle
- この**角度**から見る富士山は妙に低く感じられる． Seen「from [at]」this **angle**, Mt. Fuji looks strangely low.
- あらゆる**角度**から検討する study [consider] … from「every **angle** [all **angles**, all **viewpoints**]
- 問題を別の**角度**から考える think about a problem from another **angle**

がくねん【学年】 ①《米》a grade ②《英》(小・中・高) a year ③《英》(中・高) a form [⇨第 1 部・47-1 学年]

がくめん【額面】
- 額面価格 ①〔証券など〕《at》face value ② nominal value ③〔株など〕《at》par [⇨第 1 部・39-3 株 39-3-9]
- 額面 100 円につき発行価額 94 円の公債 a bond with an issue price at 94 per ¥100 face value

かくりつ【確率】 ① (a) probability ② odds ③ chances ④〔見込み〕(a) likelihood [⇨第 1 部・23. 確率と可能性]
- 8 割の**確率**で ① with a probability of 80 percent ② with an eight-in-ten chance

かけざん【掛け算】 multiplication [⇨第 1 部・54-3 かけ算]

かける【掛ける】 multiply [⇨第 1 部・54-3 かけ算]
- 6 かける 7 は 42．
  ① Six (multiplied) by seven「makes [is]」forty-two.
  ② Six times seven「makes [is]」forty-two.

かげん【下限】 ① the lowest limit ② the minimum ③〚数〛the infimum ④ the greatest lower bound
- 予想範囲の**下限** **the lower end** of the forecast (range)
- 所要自己資本比率の**下限**を下回る fall short of **the minimum** capital requirements
- その人の生年の**下限**は 1544 年だ． **The latest possible** year for his birth is 1544.

かげんじょうじょ【加減乗除】 ① addition, subtraction, multiplication, and division ② the four arithmetic operations [⇨第 1 部・54. 加減乗除]

かこ【過去】 the past
- 過去 3 年間 for [during] the「past [last]」three years
- 過去 100 年間の人口統計 population statistics for the「past [last]」(one) hundred years
- 過去 10 年間の平均値 the mean (value) for the「last [past]」ten years
- 過去最高を記録する ① hit [set, mark] a record high ② hit [set, mark] an

all-time high ③ hit [set] an all-time record ④ hit [set] a new record ⑤ hit [set] a new high [⇨第 1 部・14-2 過去最高]
- 過去最低を記録する ①hit [set, mark] a record low ②hit [set, mark] an all-time low ③ hit [set] a new low [⇨第 1 部・14-6 過去最低]

かさん【可算】
- 可算な ① countable ② enumerable ③ denumerable
- 可算個の ① countably many ② a countable number of
- 可算集合 ① a countable set ② an enumerable set
- 可算性　countability
- 可算無限個の ① countably infinite ② a countably infinite number of
- 可算名詞 『文法』① a countable noun ② a count noun

かさん【加算】
① [上乗せすること] addition ② adding ③ [足し算] addition ④ adding [⇨第 1 部・54-1 足し算 54-1-2]

カし【華氏】
Fahrenheit《記号 F》[⇨第 1 部・45-1 温度, 28. 伝統単位 28-7]
- カ氏 72 度　72 degrees Fahrenheit《記号 72°F》

かしょう【過小】
- 過小な見積もり ① too low an estimate ② a quotation which is too low
- 過小評価　(an) underestimation
- 過小評価する ① underestimate ② underrate ③ undervalue ④ [みくびる] look down on …

かしょう【過少】
insufficiency [⇨第 1 部・21-1 不足]

かじょう【過剰】
① [数量] a surplus ② (an) overabundance ③ (a) superabundance ④ (a) redundancy ⑤ (a) superfluity ⑥ [程度] (an) excess [⇨第 1 部・21-2 過剰]

かず【数】
a number [⇨すう]
- 3 桁の数 ① a three-digit number ② a three-figure number ③ three figures
- 9 で割り切れる数 ① a number divisible by 9 ② a number that can be divided by 9
- 10 より大きい数　a number「larger [higher, greater, bigger] than 10
- 単語の数 ① the number of words ② a word count
- 駐車している車の数は 60 台に近い.
  ① The number of parked cars is close to 60.
  ② There are close to 60 parked cars.
  ③ The parked cars number nearly 60.
  ④ The parked cars are nearly 60 in number.
- 数はとても少ない.　The number is very「small [low].

- 参加者の数は予想より多かった［少なかった］.
  ① The number of participants was「higher [lower] than expected.
  ② The number of participants「rose beyond [fell short of] expectations.
  ③ There were「more [fewer,《口》less] participants than expected.
- 被害者の数は 1,300 万人に達した．日本の全人口の 1 割に等しい数である．
  The number of victims reached 13 million, a number equal to 10 percent of Japan's total population.
- 見逃す番組の数を減らす　① reduce the number of missed programs　② miss fewer programs　★②のように「数」にこだわらないほうが日常英語としては自然．
- 数に入れる　① count「in [among] the number《of …》　② include in the number　③ reckon《among …》　④〔勘定に入れる〕take into account
- 数で押し切る　① force through by (sheer) weight of numbers　② steamroller by (sheer) force of numbers

a number of とその変形

- いくつかの［いくつもの］　a number of　★a number of は「若干」と「多数」の両方の意味になるので注意．
- 非常に多数の　a very large number of
- 比較的多数の　a relatively large number of
- より多数の　① a larger number of　② a greater number of　③ more
- より多くの異なるタイプが入手可能である．　A greater number of different types are available.　★この場合 more different types だと「より多くの異なるタイプ」か「もっと異なるタイプ」かまぎらわしくなる．
- 出席者より多くの椅子があった．　① There were more chairs than participants.　② There were a greater number of chairs than participants.
- ますます多くの　an increasing number of
- かなりの数の　① a considerable number of　② a fairly large number of　③ a fair number of
- そこそこの数の　① a fair number of　② a reasonable number of　③ not too「many [few]
- 少数の　a small number of
- 任意の数の《いくつでも》　any number of
- 使える方法はいくらでもある．
  ① There are any number of methods that can be used.
  ② You can use one of any number of available methods.
- このプロセスを構成するステップは何ステップあってもよい．
  ① The process may consist of any number of steps.
  ② There may be any number of steps in the process.
- ある数の　a certain number of

かず

- 限られた数の　a limited number of
- 所定の数の　a predetermined number of
- 所定の秒数　《for》a predetermined number of seconds
- 偶数個の　an even number of
- 同数の　①an equal number of ②the same number of ［⇨第1部・18. 同等・相等］
- 対応する数の　the corresponding number of
- 車は限られた数しか用意できない．　Only a limited number of cars「can be provided [is available, are available]．
- クロックパルスごとにテープが読み取りヘッドに対して同じ数の位置ずつ移動する．　At every clock pulse, the tape moves the same number of positions with respect to the reading head.
- 読み出しポインターはパケットサイズに対応する数の位置だけ進められる．　The readout pointer is advanced by the number of positions corresponding to the size of a packet.

a number of と the number of

a number of computers は「たくさんのコンピューター」または「いくつかのコンピューター」の意味（複数扱い）だが，the number of computers は「コンピューターの数」の意味（単数扱い）になる．（ただし，特許では意味の違いによらず初出の場合には a, 2回目以降には the とする傾向がある．）［⇨第1部・64. 各種構文と単数／複数 64-10, 62. 数の一致］

- A number of computers are connected to the server.　サーバーには多数の［いくつかの］コンピューターが接続されている．
- The number of computers was reduced by half.　コンピューターの数は半分に減らされた．

a large number of などについても同様である．

- A large number of computers were affected by the virus.　多数のコンピューターがそのウイルスの影響を受けた．
- The large number of computers makes it difficult to distribute jobs among them.　コンピューターの数が多いことでコンピューター間でジョブを分配するのが困難になる．

ただし，the largest number of は the がついていても a large number of の最上級の意味になることも多い．

- The largest number of participants were Chinese.　最も多かった参加者は中国人だった．
- The largest number of participants was recorded in 1997.　最大の参加者数が記録されたのは1997年だった．
- the candidate who received the largest number of votes　得票数が最大だった

候補者

かぞえ【数え】　[⇨第1部・38-4 満年齢と数え年]

- 来月祖父は満で89，数えで90になる．　Next month my grandfather will be 89, or 90 by the traditional calculation that makes you one year old at birth.

かぞえる【数える】

1　[計数]　① count　② do [make, take] a count of …

- 人数を数える　① count the (number of) people　②〔賛成者・出席者などの〕《口》 count heads　③ do a head count
- 入場者数を数える　① count the audience　② count the house
- 年末までの日数を数える　count [figure out] the number of days [how many days are left (to go)] until the end of the year
- 漏れなく数える　count every single one
- 正の字を書いて票数を数える　use [draw] tally marks to count the votes　★英語圏では𝍲の記号を書く．まず縦棒を書いていって5つに達したら横棒を書く．
- 10ずつに分けて数える　① count … in tens　② count … in groups of ten　③ count … in sets of ten
- 紙幣を5枚ずつ数える　① count「bills [《英》notes]」in fives　② count off every five「bills [《英》notes]
- 指を折って数える　count (down, off)「on [with] *one's* fingers　★この英語表現に対応する動作は手を握った状態から人差し指，中指，薬指，小指，親指の順に立てていくもので指を「折る」のではない．
- 読み上げながら[声に出して]数える　count out loud
- 数えながらリンゴを箱に入れる[から取り出す]　count apples「into [out of]」a box
- 彼は紙幣を1枚1枚数えて彼女に渡した．　He counted the bills out to her one by one.
- 順番を数えたら前から48番目だった．　I worked out that I was forty-eighth (in line) from the front.
- 野生の鹿は最近数えたところでは500頭いる．　At [According to] the last count there are 500 wild deer.
- 今日は父が亡くなった日から数えて49日目です．　Today is the forty-ninth day (counting) from the day my father died.
- ざっと数えて2万になる　be roughly estimated at 20,000
- **数えるほど**　not many　[⇨第1部・19-3 少数]
- **数え切れない**　① countless　② uncountable　③ numberless　④ innumerable　[⇨第1部・19-1 多数]
- 小さすぎて数えられない　① so small as to be uncountable　② so small (that) they can't be counted　③ so small (that) it's impossible to count them

かそくど

2 〔数字を順に唱える〕
- 1 から 10 まで数える count from one to ten
- 10 から 1 まで逆に数える count「down [back, backwards] from ten to one
- 3 つ数える間に while I count (up to) three
- 10 数えたら目隠しを取っていいよ． After a count of ten, you can take off the blindfold.
- 《小さい子に》いくつまで数えられるの？ ① How many can you count (up to)? ② How「high [far] can you count? ★答えは I can count up to a hundred. など．

3 〔ある数に達する〕[⇨第 1 部・2-4 数値を呈示する各種表現]
- 強い地震がその日 1 日で 30 回を数えた． There were a total of 30 strong quakes on that single day.

4 〔算入〕
- 抱きかかえられる乳幼児は乗客数に数えません． Carried babies are not counted as fare-paying passengers.
- わが家の猫は生まれたばかりの子猫も数えると全部で 7 匹です． Counting [Including] the new-born kittens, there are altogether seven cats in our house.

かそくど【加速度】 (a rate of) acceleration
- 正の[負の]加速度 positive [negative] acceleration
- 水平，垂直方向の加速度 the accelerations in the horizontal and vertical directions
- 重力加速度 ① gravitational acceleration ② acceleration of gravity ③ free fall acceleration ④ acceleration of free fall ★地上での標準的な値（約 9.8 m/s^2）を記号 g で表わす．この値は航空学では加速度の単位として使われ，日本語では 1G，英語では 1 g, 1 G, one gravity などという．[⇨ジー]

かだい【過大】
- 過大な要求 ① an unreasonable demand ② an exorbitant demand
- 過大評価 ① overestimation ② overrating ③ overvaluation
- 過大評価する ① overestimate ② overrate ③ overvalue
- 観光リゾート地としてその町はあまりに過大評価されている． As a tourist resort, the town is vastly overrated.

かたむき【傾き】

1 〔傾斜〕① a slope ② an inclination ③ an incline ④ a gradient ⑤ a slant ⑥ a tilt ⑦ cant

関連表現
- ピサの斜塔は **4 度傾いている**． The Leaning Tower of Pisa **leans 4 degrees**.
- 地軸は地球の公転軌道面に**垂直な線に対して 23.5 度傾いている**． The earth's

axis **is tilted 23.5 degrees** ⌈**(away) from** [**with respect to**] **the perpendicular** to the plane of its orbit around the sun.

2 〔座標平面上で〕① a slope 《of a line》 ② a gradient 《of a line》

- **傾きが** m **で** y **切片が** c **の直線**　the line **with** ⌈**slope** [**gradient**] m and intercept c on the y-axis
- 曲線上のある点での接線の**傾き**はその点での微分係数である．　**The slope** of the tangent ⌈**at** [**to**] a point on a curve is the derivative at that point.
- 傾きの大きな直線　a line with a steep slope
- 傾きの小さな直線　a line with a small slope

かち【価値】　① value　② worth　③ merit
- 1万円の価値がある　be worth ¥10,000
- 大いに価値がある　be of ⌈great [much] value
- まったく価値がない　① be worth nothing　② be not worth anything　③ be completely worthless
- 読む価値がある　be worth reading

がっき【学期】　① a term　② a school term　③ an academic term　④ a session　⑤〔2期制の〕a semester ［⇨第 1 部・47-4 学期］
- 1 学期　the first term

…かっけい【…角形】　⇨…かくけい

かっこ【括弧】　①〔丸括弧〕parentheses 《★ 単数形は parenthesis》　② round brackets　③〔角括弧〕square brackets　④〔ブレース〕braces

　★ 数式で括弧が多重になるときには |[( )]| の順が普通．

- 括弧に入れる　① put [enclose] 《a word》in ⌈parentheses [brackets]　② put parentheses around …　③ bracket　④ parenthesize
- 英訳は日本語の後の**括弧に入れてある**．　English equivalents **are given in** ⌈**parentheses** [**brackets**] after Japanese words.
- **括弧内の数字**は前年度の売り上げです．　**The figures in parentheses** are sales for the previous year.
- **括弧でくくってある**足し算を先にして，その答えに 5 をかけなさい．
① First add (up) the figures **in brackets**, and then multiply the sum by five.
② First add (up) the **bracketed** figures, and then multiply the sum by five.
- 括弧をはずす　① remove the parentheses　②〔式変形で〕clear the brackets
- 左［開き］括弧　① a left parenthesis　② an open parenthesis
- 右［閉じ］括弧　① a right parenthesis　② a ⌈close [closing] parenthesis
- …を囲む括弧　the parentheses around …
- 対応のとれていない括弧　① unbalanced parentheses　② unmatched parentheses

がっさん【合算】 ① addition ② adding up ③ adding together ④ totaling
- 合算する　① add … up ② add [put] … together ③ total ④ aggregate
- 夫婦の月収を合算すると100万円を超える．
  ① Our combined husband-and-wife income comes to more than a million yen a month.
  ② If you add together what my「wife [husband] and I earn per month, the total「is [runs to, adds up to] over a million yen.
- 合算額　① a total (amount [sum]) ② a sum

がっぴ【月日】 ① the month and day ② the date [⇨第1部・30-2 月日]
- 生年月日　*one's* date of birth

かてん【加点】
- 加点する　①「add「a point [points] ②〔試験など で〕raise《a person's》score ③『野球』add「a run [runs]
- 出題ミスがわかったので全員に5点加点します．　Because an error was found in the examination questions, everyone's score will be raised five points.

かどうりつ【稼働率】 ① an operating rate ② a utilization rate ③ a rate of operation ④ a capacity utilization rate ⑤ capacity utilization ⑥ utilized capacity ⑦ capacity use ⑧ the working ratio
- **工場稼働率**　①a「plant [factory] utilization rate ② plant [factory] utilization ③ a「plant [factory] operating rate
- **設備稼働率**　① utilized capacity ② a capacity utilization rate
- 国内の**設備稼働率**は85%で前年の87%より下がった．　Domestic **capacity utilization** was 85%, down from 87% a year earlier.
- **設備稼働率**を改善する　improve **capacity utilization**
- **客室稼働率**　① an occupancy rate ② occupancy
- ホテルの**客室稼働率**が上がったおかげで　thanks to increased hotel **occupancy**
- **病床稼働率**　a hospital bed occupancy rate

かにゅうりつ【加入率】
- 非正規社員の厚生年金加入率　the enrollment rate of nonregular employees in employee pension insurance
- 労働組合加入率[組織率]　① the proportion of「workers [employees] who are trade union members ② the rate of trade union membership ③ the level of trade union membership ④ the ratio of organized labor (to the total labor force)

かのうせい【可能性】 ① (a) possibility ② (a) chance ③ (a) probability ④ (a) likelihood [⇨第1部・23. 確率と可能性]
- 50%の確率で吸収される可能性がある．　There is a 50-percent chance of

being absorbed.

かはんすう【過半数】 ① a majority ② a greater「part [number]」《of …》 ③ more than half [⇨第 1 部・16. 投票・選挙の表現 16-3]
- 合格者の過半数は女性であった.
① A majority of the successful candidates were women.
② More than half (of) the successful candidates were women.
③ Most of the successful candidates were women. ★英語の most of the … は「…のうち最大の部分」の意味であり，50 数パーセントの場合に使うこともめずらしくない．特に書き言葉の場合，「…のほとんど」よりも「…の過半数」「…の大半」に対応することが多い．

かぶ【株】 ① a stock ② a share [⇨第 1 部・39-3 株]

かぶか【株価】 ① the price of a「stock [share]」② a「stock [share] price [⇨第 1 部・39-3-1 株価]
- 平均株価は 13,000 円台を回復した． The average stock price index has「recovered to [regained, returned to] the ¥13,000 level.

かふそく【過不足】 ⇨第 1 部・21. 過不足の表現

かふばん【可付番】 〔可算〕
- 可付番集合 ① a countable set ② an enumerable set

かぶんすう【仮分数】 an improper fraction [⇨第 1 部・53. 分数]

かほう【加法】 addition [⇨第 1 部・54-1 足し算]

かほうしゅうせい【下方修正】 ①(a) downward revision ②(a) downward adjustment ③(a) revision downwards
- 下方修正する ① revise downward(s) ② adjust downward(s) ③ make a downward revision ④ make a downward adjustment
- 収益予測を下方修正する ① make a downward revision of an earnings forecast ② revise an earnings forecast downward

…から from [⇨第 1 部・33. 時間を表わす句・節 33-1-2]
- …から…まで ⇨第 1 部・11. 数値範囲の表現，12.「以上」「以下」等の表現

カラット

1 〔宝石類の重さの単位：200 mg〕a carat
- 5 カラットのダイヤモンド ① a 5-carat diamond ② a diamond of 5 carats
- そのダイヤ，何カラットあるの？ How many carats is that diamond?

2 〔金位〕⇨…きん

ガル 〔加速度の CGS 単位〕a gal《記号 Gal》
- 945 ガル 945 gals《記号 945 Gal》

カロリー

- 阪神大震災の際の最大加速度は818Galだった． The maximum acceleration during the Great Hanshin Earthquake was 818 Gal.

カロリー ①〔小カロリー〕a (small) calorie《略 cal》 ②〔大カロリー〕a「(large) calorie [Calorie]《略 Cal.》

★小カロリーは水1グラムを1℃昇温させる熱量．大カロリーは水1キロを1℃昇温させる熱量で栄養学で使われたが今日ではキロカロリーが使われる．1 large calorieは1 kilocalorieに等しい．1 calorieはSI単位では約4.19J．

- ご飯一杯は **80 キロカロリー**だ． A bowl of rice **has**「**80 kilocalories**[**80 kcal**]．
- カロリーが高い [低い] 〔食品が〕① contain「a lot of [few] calories ② be「high [low] in calorific value ③ have a「high [low] caloric value
- カロリーを抑えた食事 ① a meal with reduced calories ② a calorie-reduced meal
- 1日 2,000 カロリーの食事をとる ① be on a daily diet of 2,000 calories ② eat 2,000 calories per day

かわせそうば【為替相場】 ① the (foreign) exchange rate ② the rate of exchange ③ an exchange quotation [⇨第1部・39-2 外国為替]

- 1ドル100円の為替相場で at the (exchange) rate of 100 yen to the US dollar
- 為替相場の変動 exchange (rate) fluctuations

かんきゃくどういんすう【観客動員数】

①〔演劇などの〕audience「numbers [size] ② the size of an audience ③ box-office numbers

④〔スポーツなどの〕spectator numbers ⑤ the number of spectators ⑥ the gate

★box-office numbers と the gate は興行収入を意味することが多いので注意．

- その映画の観客動員数は 200 万人だった．
  ① The movie drew two million viewers.
  ② The movie drew an audience of two million viewers.
  ③ Two million people saw the movie.
- この映画は『タイタニック』を上回る観客動員数記録を打ち立てた． This movie has drawn a record number of viewers, exceeding that of *Titanic*.
- その映画は観客動員数では『スター・ウォーズ』を上回ったが，興行収入では及ばなかった． Though it turned out larger audience numbers, the film failed to「outdo [《口》best] *Star Wars* in box-office proceeds.
- 彼が出場する試合の観客動員数はすごい．
  ① The matches he's in attract fantastic numbers of spectators.
  ② When he's in a match, huge numbers of spectators come.
- 1試合平均の観客動員数は減少の一途をたどっている． The average number of spectators per match is going down steadily.

かんけい【関係】 ① a relation ② a relationship ③ a link

- 光子のエネルギーと振動数**の間の関係** **the relation between** a photon's energy **and** frequency
- 科学と産業**の関係** **the relationship between** science **and** industry
- 密接な関係 ① a strong relationship ② a close relationship
- 直接的な関係 a direct relationship
- 間接的な関係 an indirect relationship
- 相関関係 ⇨そうかん
- 因果関係 ⇨いんがかんけい
- …と関係がある ① be related to … ② have a relation to … ③ have a connection with … ④ be linked「to [with]」… ⑤ be associated with … ⑥〔主題として〕be concerned with … ⑦〔関わりがある〕have [be] something to do with … ⑧〔有意である〕be relevant to 《a subject》
- それらの座標系の間には**簡単な関係がある**. **There is a simple relationship** between those coordinate systems.
- ニュートンの第二法則により,物体に加えられる力と物体の加速度との**関係が確立された**. Newton's second law of motion **established a relationship** between the force applied to an object and the acceleration of the object.
- 酢酸はエタンに対して,ヘキサン酸がヘキサンに対するのと同じ関係にある.
① Acetic acid **bears to** ethane **the same relation that** hexanoic acid「**bears [does**]**to** hexane.
② Acetic acid **is to** ethane **what** hexanoic acid **is to** hexane.
③ **The relation between** acetic acid **and** ethane **is the same as that between** hexanoic acid **and** hexane.
- 金属では温度が高いほど抵抗も大きくなる. 半導体では**その関係は逆になる**. For metals, higher temperature corresponds to higher resistance. For semiconductors, **the relationship is reversed**.
- …についても同様の関係が成り立つ A similar relation holds for …
- …との間に線形関係を示す show a linear relation with …
- そのトルクが気体の圧力と**関係づけられる**. The torque **can be correlated with** gas pressure.
- **関係式** ① a relation ② a mathematical relation ③ a numerical relation ④〘電算〙〔関係演算子を含む式〕a relational expression
- エネルギーと振動数の間の関係式 a relation between energy and frequency
- 質量とエネルギーの関係式 the mass-energy relation ★$E=mc^2$ という特定の式なので定冠詞がつく.
- クラマース・クローニッヒの関係式 Kramers-Kronig relations ★2つの式で表わされるので複数形になっている.
- これらの関係式を満たす有理数をみつける find rational numbers that satisfy these relations

かんさん

かんさん【換算】 conversion
- 換算する　convert
- 尺をメートルに換算する　① convert *shaku* into「metric measurement [the metric system]　② convert *shaku* into meters [⇨第 1 部・28-8 日本の伝統単位]
- ドルを円に換算する　convert dollars into yen
- それを現在のお金に換算すると 1000 万円以上になる．
  ① If you convert that into today's money it comes to more than「10,000,000 [ten million] yen.
  ② That comes to more than「10,000,000 [ten million] yen in terms of today's money.
- 換算式　a conversion formula
- 換算表　a conversion table
- 換算率　① a conversion rate　② a rate of conversion
- 1 ドル 120 円の換算率で　at「the [a] conversion rate of ¥120 to the dollar
  ★conversion rate の冠詞は the だと実勢相場に即した感じ，a だと例示的な換算率という感じ．[⇨第 1 部・39-2 外国為替]
- 年換算で 0.4% の成長率　an annualized growth rate of 0.4%

かんじょう【勘定】

1 〔数えること〕counting [⇨かぞえる]
- 宿泊費は勘定に入れずに交通費だけで 5 万円だ．　Transportation expenses alone come to ¥50,000,「exclusive of [excluding, not including] accommodation.

2 ①〔支払うこと〕payment (of a bill)　② settlement (of an account)　③〔勘定書〕a [*one's*] bill　④ an account [⇨第 1 部・40-6-2 支払いに関係する表現]

かんすう【関数】　a function
- y は x の関数である．　y is a function「of [in] x.
- 温度のみの関数　① a function only of temperature　② a function of temperature alone
- そのグラフはアミノ酸濃度を時間の**関数**として表わしている．　The graph shows the amino acid concentration as **a function** of time.
- その信号の瞬間電圧は時間に対して正弦**関数**に従って変化する．
  ① The instantaneous voltage of the signal varies with time according to a sine **function**.
  ② The variation in the signal's instantaneous voltage over time forms a sine wave.
- k の増加関数　an increasing function of k
- 奇関数　an odd function

- 偶関数　an even function
- 逆関数　an inverse function
- 実数値関数　a real-valued function
- 初等関数　an elementary function
- 有理[無理]関数　a rational [an irrational] function.
- 三角関数　a trigonometric function
- 指数関数　an exponential function
- 連続[微分可能，なめらかな]関数　a「continuous [differentiable, smooth] function
- 線形[非線形]関数　a「linear [nonlinear] function
- 開集合 X 上の関数　a function on an open set X

カンデラ　〔光度単位〕a candela《記号 cd》〔⇨第 1 部・27-2 SI 基本単位〕

きあつ【気圧】　① atmospheric pressure ② air pressure 〔⇨第 1 部・45-2 気圧〕
- 昨日の気圧は 980 hPa を示した．　The barometer「registered [stood at] 980 hectopascals yesterday.
- 50 気圧に相当する圧力　a pressure of 50 atmospheres《記号 50 atm》

きおん【気温】　(atmospheric) temperature 〔⇨第 1 部・45-1-3 気温，37-7 気象用語〕
- 〔天気概況で〕気温 16 度．　The temperature is sixteen degrees (Celsius).

ギガ…　①〔10^9〕giga- ②〔ギガヘルツ〕a gigahertz ③〔ギガバイト〕a gigabyte 〔⇨第 1 部・27-4 SI 接頭語〕

きかくか【規格化】　normalization
- 規格化する　normalize
- 規格化因子　a normalization factor

きかん【期間】　① a term ② a period (of time) 〔⇨第 1 部・34. 期間の表現〕
- 3 年の期間　a period of three years

きかんすう【奇関数】　an odd function
- x についての奇関数　an odd function in x

きげん【紀元】　〔⇨第 1 部・29. 年・年度・元号・世紀 29-3〕
- 紀元 930 年　① AD 930 ② the year 930 of the Christian era ③ the year of「grace [our Lord] 930
- 紀元前 100 年　① 100 BC ② 100 (years) before Christ
- 神武天皇即位紀元 2600 年　the 2600th year after the accession of the Emperor Jinmu

きげん【期限】　① a time limit ② a deadline 〔⇨第 1 部・35. 期日・期限の表現，

きざみ

34-3 契約期間〕
- その契約は 1997 年に期限が切れた． The contract expired in 1997.

きざみ ①〔間隔〕an interval ②〔増分〕an increment
- 3 分きざみで発車する　depart at three-minute intervals
- 作業量に合わせて人員を 5 人きざみで増減員する　add or reduce workers in units of five depending on the amount of work
- その値は 0.5 きざみで変えられる． The value can be changed in「steps [increments, intervals] of 0.5.
- ロープに 50 センチきざみで印をつける　① mark (off) a rope in 50-centimeter segments　② mark (off) a rope every 50 centimeters
- 外国為替レートを 1 銭きざみで発表する　announce foreign exchange rates in denominations of one sen

きじつ【期日】　① an appointed day　② a due date［⇨第 1 部・35. 期日・期限の表現〕

きすう【奇数】　an odd number
- 奇数の　① odd　② odd-numbered
- 1 が**奇数個**あったら，パリティー数字は 1 である．
  ① If there are **an odd number of** ones, the parity digit is 1.
  ② If the number of ones is **odd**, the parity digit is 1.
- その直線と**奇数回**交わる　intersect the line **an odd number of times**
- 奇数根　〔方程式の〕an odd root
- 奇数乗根　〔累乗根〕an odd root
- 奇数の日　① an odd-numbered day　② a day bearing an odd number
- 奇数ページ　① an odd-numbered page　② an odd page　③〖製本〗a recto
- 下から奇数番目の桁　① digits in odd positions from the right　② odd-position digits from the right
- 奇数回目の試行　an odd-numbered trial

きすう【基数】

1　〔序数に対して〕a cardinal number［⇨第 1 部・1. 基数〕

2　〔位取り記数法の〕a radix　★複数形は radixes, radices．

きた【北】　north［⇨第 1 部・59-5 東西南北〕

きたいち【期待値】　① an expected value　② expectation　③〔量子力学の〕an expectation value
- 確率密度関数 $d(X)$ に対する変数 X の**期待値**　**the expected value** of variable X with respect to a probability density function $d(X)$
- この賭け方から得られる利益の**期待値**はいくつですか． What is **the expect-**

ed value** of profit resulting from this bet?
- 電子の原子核からの動径距離の**期待値**　**the expectation value** of the radial distance of the electron from the nucleus
- 基底状態での**期待値**　a ground-state **expectation value**
- **真空期待値**　a vacuum expectation value

きてい【基底】　① a base ② a basis ★basis の複数形は bases /béisi:z/ で，base の複数形 bases /béisəz/ とは発音が違う．
- 正規直交基底　an orthonormal basis

きど【輝度】　① brightness ② luminance ★②は測光で使われ，単位はニト（SI 単位系ではカンデラ毎平方メートル）．[⇨第1部・27. 単位]

きのう【昨日】　yesterday [⇨第1部・31-5-2「先…」]

きやく【既約】
- 既約な　irreducible
- 既約分数　an irreducible fraction
- 既約多項式　① an irreducible polynomial ② a prime polynomial

ぎゃく【逆】

1 ① the opposite ② the contrary ③ the reverse ④ the inverse
- 逆の符号　the opposite sign
- 需要は価格と**逆の**関係にある．　Demand **varies inversely with** the price.

2 〔逆行列・逆作用素など〕an inverse
- 各元が**逆をもつ**．　Each element **has an inverse**.
- 逆演算子［作用素］　an inverse operator
- 逆写像　(an) inverse mapping
- 逆変換　(an) inverse transformation

3 〔命題の〕the converse 《of a proposition》 ★論理学では「A ならば B」という命題に対し，「B ならば A」というのが逆 (converse)，「B でないなら A でない」というのが対偶 (contraposition)，「A でなければ B でない」というのが裏 (reverse) と区別する．
- **逆**は必ずしも真ではない．　The「**converse** [reverse, contrary, opposite] is not always true. ★論理学では converse が正式だが，科学技術以外の文脈では reverse, contrary, opposite も用いられる．

ぎゃくかんすう【逆関数】　an inverse function

ぎゃくぎょうれつ【逆行列】　an inverse (matrix)
- その行列は逆行列をもつ．　The matrix has an inverse.
- 逆行列の計算　① inversion of a matrix ② matrix inversion

ぎゃくげん【逆元】 an inverse (element)
- 乗法に関する逆元　a multiplicative inverse

ぎゃくじじょうそく【逆2乗則】 the inverse-square law
- 重力は**逆2乗則**に従う．　The gravitational force「follows [obeys] **the inverse-square law**.

ぎゃくすう【逆数】 ① a reciprocal ② an inverse (number)
- 5の逆数は1/5である．　The reciprocal of 5 is 1/5.
- 周波数の逆数　① the inverse of the frequency ② the inverse frequency

キャッシュフローけいさんしょ【キャッシュフロー計算書】 a statement of cash flows ② a cash flow statement [⇨第1部・41. 英文会計]

きゅう【球】 ① a sphere ② a globe ③ a ball
- 球状[球形]の　spherical

きゅう【級】

1 〔水準〕① a class ② a grade ③ a rank
- 1万トン級の船　a ship「in [of] the 10,000-ton class
- 3千メートル級の山々　①《a range of》3,000-meter mountains ② 10,000-footers《of the Japan Alps》
- 70キロ級　〔体重別競技の〕the 70-kg (weight)「class [category, division]
- 60キロ以下級　〖柔道〗① the under 60 kg (weight)「class [category, division] ② the −60 kg (weight)「class [category, division]
- 100キロ超級　〖柔道〗① the over 100 kg (weight)「class [category, division] ② the +100 kg (weight)「class [category, division]
- メガトン級の核爆発　a nuclear explosion in the megaton range
- 国宝級の重要文化財　an important cultural property of national treasure「rank [class]
- 大使級会談　① a conference on the level of ambassadors ② a conference at the ambassadorial level ③ an ambassadorial-level conference ④ an ambassador-level conference
- エジソン級の発明家　an inventor in a class with Edison
- オスカー級の演技　Oscar-caliber performance
- 第一級の　① first-class ② first-rate ③ top-quality [⇨いっきゅう]
- 最大[古]級　one of the「largest [oldest] [⇨ 15. 順位・順番の表現 15-2-1 (4)]

2 〔学年〕①《米》a grade ②《英》a form [⇨第1部・47. 学校 47-1]

3 〔資格の等級〕① a grade ② a class ③ a rank ★judo ranks というと級・段を含めた階級の意になることが多い．[⇨だん]

- 英検1級　EIKEN Grade 1
- 英検準1級　EIKEN Grade Pre-1
- 英検2級に合格する　pass Grade 2 of the EIKEN Test in Practical English Proficiency
- 私は英検3級です．
  ① I have EIKEN Grade 3.
  ② I have passed Grade 3 of the EIKEN Test in Practical English Proficiency.
- アマチュア無線技士試験の2級に受かった．　I passed the second grade exam for radio hams.
- 珠算3級　the third grade in abacus calculation
- 柔道3級　① a third kyū in judo ② a green belt in judo ★しばしば帯の色で級を表わすが，色の割当ては国や成年かジュニアかによって異なる．
- 一級［二級］建築士　a「first-class［second-class］registered architect
- 級が上がる　① be moved up to a higher「grade［class, rank］② be promoted to a higher rank
- 級に分ける　① divide into「grades［classes］② classify ③ grade ④ rank

4〖化〗

- 第一級アルコール　primary alcohol
- 第二級アルコール　secondary alcohol
- 第三級アルコール　tertiary alcohol
- 第一級アミン　primary amine
- 第二級アミン　secondary amine
- 第三級アミン　tertiary amine
- 第四級アンモニウム塩　quaternary ammonium salt

きゅうかくけい【九角形】　① a nonagon ② an enneagon［⇨第1部・58-2 …角形］

きゅうじょうしょう【急上昇】　① a sudden increase ② a rapid increase［⇨第1部・13-4-2 急増・急上昇］

きゅうじんばいりつ【求人倍率】　① the ratio of job「vacancies［openings］to job applicants ② the opening-to-application ratio ③ the ratio of job offers to job seekers ④ the job-offers-to-job-seekers ratio

▶ 新規求人倍率（前月からの繰り越し数を含まない当該月に新たに受け付けた求人数・求職者数の比）と区別するときは有効求人倍率という．訳し分ける必要があれば「有効求人倍率」は effective …，「新規求人倍率」は the ratio of new job vacancies to new job applicants などと訳せるが，いずれにせよ英米で一般的な指標ではない．

▶ 米国労働省の求人労働移動調査（JOLTS: Job Openings and Labor Turnover Survey）の発表する job openings rate（求人率）は仕事の空きの割合（求人数

を就業者数＋求人数で割ったもの）．hires rate（入職率）は就業者のうち新採用者の割合．［⇨りしょくりつ］

きゅうすう【級数】 a series ★複数形も series.
- **等差級数**とは等差数列の和である． **An arithmetic series** is the sum of an arithmetic progression.
- **級数の和**を求める公式 a formula to find **the sum of a series**
- この**級数**は S に収束する． This **series** converges to S.
- 公比を r として，$|r|<1$ の**幾何級数**は収束する． **A geometric series** with $|r|<1$ converges, where r is the common ratio.
- 公比の絶対値が1より大きい**幾何級数** ① **a geometric series** the absolute value of whose common ratio is greater than one ② **a geometric series** with a common ratio greater than one in absolute value
- 有限級数 a finite series
- 無限級数 an infinite series
- 収束級数 a convergent series
- 発散級数 a divergent series
- 冪級数 a power series
- フーリエ級数 a Fourier series
- 級数展開 (a) series expansion
- 等差級数［算術級数］ ① an arithmetic series ② an arithmetic progression
- 等比級数［幾何級数］ ① a geometric series ② a geometric progression
- **算術級数的に**増加する ① increase［grow (in number)］**in an arithmetic progression** ② increase［grow (in number)］**arithmetically**
- **幾何級数的に**増加する ① increase［grow (in number)］**in a geometric progression** ② increase［grow (in number)］**geometrically**
- マルサスによれば，人口は**幾何級数的に**増えるが，生活資財は**算術級数的**にしか増えない． According to Malthus, while the population increases **geometrically**, the means of subsistence increase only **arithmetically**.

きゅうぞう【急増】 ① a sudden increase ② a rapid increase［⇨第1部・13-4-2 急増・急上昇］

きゅうたいしょう【球対称】 spherical symmetry
- 球対称な ① spherically symmetric ② spherical
- 球対称な電荷の分布 a spherically symmetric charge distribution
- ポテンシャル V は球対称であるとする． We assume that potential V is spherically symmetric.
- 球対称の中心 the center of spherical symmetry

きゅうとう【急騰】 ① a jump ② a「sudden［sharp］rise ③ a surge ④ a sharp

upswing ［⇨第 1 部・13-4-2 急増・急上昇］
- 600 円に急騰する　jump ［soar, (sky)rocket］ to 600 yen

きゅうふ【休符】　［⇨おんぷ］
- 全休符　① 《米》 a whole rest　② 《英》 a semibreve rest
- 二分休符　① 《米》 a half rest　② 《英》 a minim rest
- 四分休符　① 《米》 a quarter rest　② 《英》 a crotchet rest
- 八分休符　① 《米》 an eighth rest　② 《英》 a quaver rest
- 十六分休符　① 《米》 a sixteenth rest　② 《英》 a semiquaver rest
- 三十二分休符　① 《米》 a thirty-second rest　② 《英》 a demisemiquaver rest
- 六十四分休符　① 《米》 a sixty-fourth rest　② 《英》 a hemidemisemiquaver rest

きゅうめん【球面】　a spherical surface
- 球面三角形　a spherical triangle
- 球面三角法　① spherical trigonometry　② spherics
- 球面調和関数　spherical harmonics
- 球面波　a spherical wave
- 球面鏡　a spherical mirror
- 球面収差　(a) spherical aberration

きゅうらく【急落】　① a ｢sudden ［sharp］ drop ［decline, fall, plunge］　② a steep decline　③ (a) free fall　④〔大量売りによる〕(a) sell-off ［⇨第 1 部・13-5-2 急減・急落］
- その株は**急落して**終値は 890 円，前日比 130 円安となった．　The stock ｢ended ［closed］ **sharply lower** at 890 yen, down 130 yen from the day before.

きゅうりょう【給料】　① pay　② wages　③ a salary　④ a stipend ［⇨第 1 部・40-5-2 収入］
- 給料として…円を受け取る　receive … yen in ｢salary ［wages］
- 月 40 万の給料をもらう　draw a monthly salary of ¥400,000 《from a firm》

きゅうれき【旧暦】　① the old calendar　②〔太陰暦〕the lunar calendar ［⇨第 1 部・37. 伝統暦］
- 旧暦 6 月 15 日に　on the 15th of June according to the ｢old ［lunar］ calendar
- この物語中の日付はすべて旧暦による．
  ① All the dates given in this story follow the old calendar.
  ② All the dates in this story are given in the old calendar.
- 旧暦の元旦　① New Year's Day according to the ｢old ［lunar］ calendar　② the lunar New Year's Day
- 地方によっては今でも伝統行事に旧暦を用いている．　In some parts of the country they still ｢use ［go by］ the old calendar for traditional events.

キュリー 〔放射能の単位〕a curie《記号 Ci》 ★SI 単位はベクレル.

きょう【今日】 ① today ② this day

- 今日現在　as of today
- 今日中に　①by the end of the day ②some time today ③in the course of this day ④before「this [the] day is out
- 今日から (ずっと)　①from this day「forth [forward, onward] ②from now on
- 今日から 1 週間　for a week beginning (from) today
- 今日の新聞　today's newspaper(s)
- 申し込みは今日までだ.
  ① Applications will be accepted through today.
  ② The application deadline is today.
- 今日は何日ですか.
  ① What day of the month is this?
  ② What's the date today?
  ③ What date is it today?
- 今日は 11 月 3 日です.
  ① Today is November (the) third.
  ② Today is the third of November.
- 今日は何曜日ですか.　What day of the week is it today?
- 今日は火曜日です.　① Today is Tuesday. ② It is Tuesday today.
- 今日は何の日ですか.　What is today?
- 今日は何の日だか覚えてますか.　①Do you know what today is? ②Do you remember what day it is today?
- 今日は憲法記念日です.　Today is Constitution Day.

…きょう【…強】

1 〔端数〕① a little over … ② more than … ［⇨第 1 部・9-2「…何」「…数」「…余り」など］

- 3 割**強**　**a little over** 30 percent
- 10 キロメートル**強**　① **a bit longer than** ten kilometers ② **a little over** ten kilometers
- 100 ヘクタール**強**　100**-plus** hectares
- 2 キログラム**強**　**a little over** two kilograms

2 〔並立する強者〕① a power(house) ② one of the「biggest [most powerful]《companies》［⇨…だい【…大】］

- ビール業界の**三強**時代　the era of **the Big Three** in the beer business
- 現在の水泳界はその二国による**二強**時代にある.　In today's swimming world those two countries reign as **the dual powerhouses**.

- 世界の二強を破った．We「defeated [beat] the two strongest teams in the world.

ぎょう【行】 ①a line ②a row ★row は表などの横に並んだ列をいい，縦に並んだ列は column という．
- 12 ページの 6 行目に　①on line 6 of page 12　②on page 12, line 6
- 12 ページの上［下］から 6 行目に　on the sixth line from the「top [bottom] on page twelve
- 15 ページ 19 行目から 16 ページ 5 行目まで　①page 15, line 19 to page 16, line 5　②from the 19th line of page 15 to the 5th line of page 16　③from line 19 on page 15 to line 5 on page 16
- 最上行　①the top「line [row]　②the first「line [row]
- 最下行　①the bottom「line [row]　②the last「line [row]
- 1 行おきに書く　①write on every other line　②write on alternate lines　③skip every other line
- この原稿用紙は 1 行 20 字詰めです．This「manuscript [writing] paper has twenty squares to the「line [column, row]．★square は正方形の意味で，ここでは原稿用紙のマスを指している．column は縦書きの場合，row は横書きの場合．
- 行数　①the number of lines　②〔印刷物の〕linage [lineage]
- 1 行で表示する　display《text》in one line
- 複数行に表示する　display《text》in「several [multiple] lines
- 《筆写などで》1 行飛ばす　skip a line
- 2 行 2 列の行列　〘数〙①a 2-by-2 matrix　②a 2×2 matrix　★2×2 は two by two と読む．
- 12 行 5 列の表　a table of 12 rows and 5 columns
- 表の第 5 列の 3 行目［第 3 行第 5 列］の数字　the figure「on the third line [in the third row] of the fifth column in the table
- その領域の左上のピクセルは第 13 行，第 34 列にある．The top left pixel of the region is at row 13 and column 34.
- 《表で》6 の行と 3 の列の交わるところの数字
①the number that stands at the intersection of the row headed by 6 and the column headed by 3
②the number that is found where the row of 6 and the column of 3 intersect
- X が位置しているのと同じ行に　①in the same row in which X is located　②in the same row as X
- 魔方陣ではあらゆる行，列，主対角線の数の和が同じになる．
①In a magic square, the sum of the numbers in any vertical, horizontal, or main diagonal line is the same.
②In a magic square, the sum of the numbers in any row, column, or main diagonal is the same.

きょうい【胸囲】 ① *one's* chest measurement ② the measurement around the chest [⇨第1部・43-3 胸囲]
- 胸囲が90センチある． He measures 90 centimeters around the chest.

きょうかい【境界】 ① a boundary ② a border ③ a limit ④ bounds
- 境界条件　a boundary condition
- 周期的境界条件　a periodic boundary condition
- 境界値　a boundary value

ぎょうかく【仰角】 ① elevation ② an angle of elevation ③〔送受信電波の〕a wave angle
- 45°の仰角で撃つ　fire at an elevation of 45 degrees
- 砲に仰角を与える　give elevation to a gun
- 仰角を増す　increase the elevation 《of …》

きょうど【強度】 ① intensity ② strength
★物理では光や電磁波などのエネルギーの単位時間・単位面積当たりの流れをいうときには intensity, 振幅や物理量の大きさをいうときには strength を使う傾向がある．抵抗力などの意味での強度は strength. [⇨つよさ]
- 光の強度　the intensity of light
- レーザー強度　laser intensity
- 電界強度　electric field strength
- 信号強度　signal strength
- 地震の強度　① the「intensity [strength] of an earthquake ② seismic intensity
- 耐震強度　⇨第1部・45-6-3 耐震強度
- 高温強度　① high-temperature strength ② strength at elevated temperature

きょうばい【競売】 an auction [⇨第1部・39-4 入札・オークション]

きょうへん【共変】 ①〔テンソルなどの共変性〕covariance ②〔二変数の相関した変動〕covariation
- 共変ベクトル　a covariant vector
- 共変テンソル　a covariant tensor
- 共変微分　① covariant differentiation ②〔結果〕a covariant derivative

きょうやく【共役】 ① conjugation ②〔共役なもの〕a conjugate
- **複素共役**　a complex conjugate
- 正方行列は逆行列が**その転置の複素共役**に等しければユニタリー行列である．A square matrix is unitary if its inverse is equal to **the complex conjugate of its transpose**.
- **共役複素数**　a complex conjugate ★複素数 z の共役複素数を z^* または $\bar{z}$ で表わす．

- アスタリスク［バー］のついた変数は**共役複素数**を表わす．　Variables with「an asterisk [a bar] denote **the complex conjugate**.
- **エルミート共役**　a [an] Hermitian conjugate
- **共役転置**　① a conjugate transpose　② an adjoint
- **共役点**　conjugate points

ぎょうれつ【行列】　a matrix　★複数形は matrices.
- 2×2の行列　① a 2-by-2 matrix　② a 2×2 matrix　★2×2 は two by two と読む．
- $n×m$ 行列　① an n-by-m matrix　② an $n×m$ matrix　③ an (n, m) matrix
- n 行 m 列の行列　a matrix with n rows and m columns
- 行列 A の成分［要素］a_{ij}　element a_{ij} of matrix A
- 6×4行列に4×2行列をかけると6×2行列になる．
  ① Multiplication of a 6×4 matrix by a 4×2 matrix「gives [results in]」a 6×2 matrix.
  ② When a 6×4 matrix is multiplied by a 4×2 matrix, a 6×2 matrix is obtained.
- 行列 A に右から P をかけたもの　① matrix A multiplied on the right「by [with]」 P　② matrix A right-multiplied「by [with]」P
- 零でない2つの行列の積が零行列になることもある．　The product of two nonzero matrices may be a null matrix.
- ユニタリー行列とは逆行列が転置の複素共役に等しい正方行列である．
  ① A unitary matrix is a square matrix whose inverse is equal to the complex conjugate of its transpose.
  ② A unitary matrix is a square matrix whose conjugate transpose is its own inverse.
- **正方行列**　a square matrix
- **単位行列**　an identity matrix
- **零行列**　① a null matrix　② a zero matrix
- **三角行列**　a triangular matrix
- **上［上半］三角行列**　an upper triangular matrix
- **下［下半］三角行列**　a lower triangular matrix
- **行列式**　a determinant　★$|A|$, $\det(A)$ などと書く．
- **逆行列**　an inverse matrix　★A^{-1} と書いて，the inverse of (matrix) A のほか A inverse などと読むこともある．
- 行列はその行列式が0でないときかつそのときにのみ逆行列をもつ．　A matrix has an inverse if and only if its determinant is not 0.
- **正則行列**　〔逆をもつ行列〕① a regular matrix　② a nonsingular matrix　③ an invertible matrix
- **転置行列**　① a transpose (of a matrix)　② a transposed matrix　★A^{T} などと書

く．
- **直交行列**　an orthogonal matrix
- **エルミート行列**　a [an] Hermitian matrix
- **ユニタリー行列**　a unitary matrix
- **行列力学**　matrix mechanics
- **行列要素**　〔遷移振幅を表わす〕a matrix element
- ある量の，状態 i から状態 f への遷移の [に対応する] **行列要素**　**a matrix element** of a quantity「for [corresponding to] the transition from state i to state f
- W 粒子生成の**行列要素**を計算する　calculate **the matrix elements** for W (particle) production
- 量 A が 0 でない**行列要素**をもつのはこれらの 2 つの遷移に対してのみである．　The quantity A has nonzero **matrix elements** only for these two transitions.

きょくげん【極限】　a limit
- n が無限大に近づくときの s_n の極限値　the limit of s_n as n「tends to [approaches] infinity
- x が 1 に近づくときの $f(x)$ の極限値　the limit of $f(x)$ as x approaches 1
- 右側極限値　a limit on the right
- 左側極限値　a limit on the left
- その数列は**極限値**をもつ．　The sequence has **a limit**.
- すべての n に対し有限の**極限値**が存在する．　A finite **limit** exists for every n.
- N が大きな極限では　①in the large N limit　②in the limit of large N　③if we take the limit of large N
- N が大きい**極限**ではその関数はガウス曲線に近づく．　The function approaches a gaussian in the **limit** of large N.
- レイノルズ数が大きな [無限大の] 極限で　in the limit of「large [infinite] Reynolds number
- 抵抗率が 0 になる極限で　in the limit of vanishing resistivity
- $v/c \to 0$ の極限で　in the limit $v/c \to 0$
- v が c よりはるかに小さい極限で　in the limit (that) v is much smaller than c
- 低速極限で　in the low velocity limit
- 小角度 [振動] 極限では運動は調和振動になる．　The motion is harmonic in the small「angle [oscillation] limit.
- 理想化された極限　an idealized limit
- 古典極限　〔量子力学の〕the classical limit
- 非相対論的極限　the nonrelativistic limit

- 極相対論的極限　the extreme relativistic limit
- 連続体極限　〔弾性体の〕the continuum limit

きょくざひょう【極座標】　polar coordinates
- 極座標系　the polar coordinate system

きょくしょう【極小】　① a minimum　② a local minimum　★minimum の複数形は minima または minimums．［⇨きょくだい］
- 極小の　① minimum　② minimal
- 極小値　a local minimum value
- 太陽活動の極小期　① a period of minimum solar activity　② the solar minimum
- 極小曲面　a「minimal [minimum] surface
- 極小元　a minimal element

きょくせん【曲線】　① a curved line　② a curve
- 曲線（状）の　① curvilinear　② curvilineal
- 曲線を描く　① draw [describe] a curve　② curve (a line)
- 連続曲線　a continuous curve

きょくだい【極大】　① a maximum　② a local maximum　★maximum の複数形は maxima または maximums．
- 極大値　a local maximum value
- 関数が x で極大になるのは，x における1階微分が0でありかつ2階微分が負の場合である．　A function has a local maximum at x if the first derivative is 0 and the second derivative is negative at x.
- この関数には極大が2つある．　This function has two local maxima.
- 極大元とは，順序集合において他のどの元よりも小さくない元である．　A maximal element is an element in an ordered set which is not smaller than any other element.　★全順序集合（totally ordered set）なら最大元と一致する．
- 太陽活動の極大期　① a period of maximum solar activity　② the solar maximum

きょくち【極値】　① an extreme value　② an extremum　★extremum の複数形は extrema または extremums．

きょくばん【局番】　a telephone exchange number ［⇨第1部・46-4 電話番号］

きょくりつ【曲率】　(a) curvature
- 曲率中心　the center of curvature
- 曲率半径　the radius of curvature
- 曲線のある点における**曲率半径**とはその点における接触円の半径である．　**The radius of curvature** of a curve at a point is the radius of the osculating

circle at that point.
- **曲率半径**が小さいほどカーブはきつい.
  ① The smaller **the radius of curvature** (is), the sharper the curve (is).
  ② Smaller **radii of curvature** mean sharper curves.
▶ 曲面の曲率
- ガウス曲率　(a) Gaussian curvature
- 主曲率　(a) principal curvature
- 主曲率方向　the direction of principal curvature
- 全曲率　① integral curvature　② total curvature
▶ 時空の曲率
- 時空の曲率　curvature of space-time
- 曲率テンソル　a curvature tensor

きょこん【虚根】　an imaginary root

きょじく【虚軸】　the imaginary axis

きょすう【虚数】　an imaginary number ［⇨せいすう 数の集合］
- 純虚数　a pure imaginary number
- i は**虚数単位**を表わす.　i denotes **the imaginary unit**. ★虚数単位は数学ではiで表わすが，電子工学では電流と区別するためにjで表わすことも多い.
- この理論では時間が虚数になる.　In this theory, time is imaginary.
- $v>c$ なら質量が虚数になる.　If $v>c$, the mass becomes imaginary.

きょねん【去年】　last year ［⇨第1部・31-5-2「先…」］
- 去年の今日　① this day (last) year　② a year ago today
- 去年の3月　①《in》March last year　②〔3月より前に言うとき〕last March ★last March は4月から6月ごろまでなら去年の3月の意に使えるが，それ以降に使うと去年の3月か今年の3月か曖昧になるので注意. ［⇨第1部・31-5-4 last … の使用例］
- 去年の8月25日に　① on August 25 (of) last year　②〔8月25日より前に言うとき〕last August 25

きょぶ【虚部】　the imaginary part 《of a complex number》

きょり【距離】　①(a) distance　②〔目標物までの〕(a) range　③〔間隔〕an interval
- 東京・大阪**間の距離**　① **the distance between** Tokyo **and** Osaka　② **the distance from** Tokyo **to** Osaka
- 3キロメートル**の距離**　**a distance of** three kilometers
- …から4キロメートル**の距離に**　(**at a distance of**) four kilometers **from** …
- 事務所は駅から200メートル**の距離にある**.　The office **is** 200 m from the station.

- 歩いて1時間の**距離** ① an hour's **distance** by foot ② an hour「on [by] foot ③ an hour('s) walk
- 彼女の事務所は**歩いて**15分の**距離**だ.
  ① Her office **is** fifteen minutes **away on foot**.
  ② Her office **is** fifteen minutes' **walk** 《from here》.
  ③ Her office **is a** fifteen-minute **walk** 《from here》.
- 私の家から半径500メートルの**距離内に within (a radius of)** 500 meters of my house
- その点**から等距離に at equal distances from** the point
- 横浜から東京までの**距離**はどのくらいですか.
  ① **How far is it** from Yokohama to Tokyo?
  ② **What is the distance** between Yokohama and Tokyo?
- 距離を測る measure the distance 《between [from, to] …》
- 10 メートルごとの**距離をおいて** ① **at intervals of** 10 meters ② 10 meters **apart** ③ 10 meters **from each other**
- 走行距離 ⇨そうこうきょり
- 明視の距離 the range of clear vision

関連表現

- その日は10キロ歩いた. We walked 10 kilometers that day.
- その店は500メートル離れたところにある. The store is 500 meters away.

きりあげる【切り上げる】 ① round (off) upwards ② round up [⇨第1部・10-3 切り上げ]
- 2.1を切り上げて3にする round 2.1 up to 3
- 切り上げて整数にする ① round up to whole numbers ② round up to the nearest「whole number [integer]

きりすてる【切り捨てる】 ① omit ② discard ③ drop ④ disregard ⑤ ignore ⑥〔切り捨てにより数値を丸める〕truncate ⑦ round down [⇨第1部・10-4 切り捨て]
- 切り捨て ① omission ② rounding down ③ truncation

キロ… ①〔10^3〕kilo- ②〔キロメートル〕a kilometer《略 km》③〔キログラム〕a kilogram《略 kg》[⇨第1部・27-4 SI 接頭語]
- キロ当たり2000円 2,000 yen a kilo ★英語でも《略式》では kilo を名詞として使う.
- 息子は21キロだ. My son weighs 21 kilos.

キログラム a kilogram《= 1000 g；記号 kg》[⇨第1部・27-2 SI 基本単位]
- キログラム重 〔力の単位〕a kilogram-force《≒9.8 ニュートン；記号 kgf, kg 重》 ★複数形は kilograms-force.

…きん【…金】 〔純金を 24 karats とする純金含有度の単位〕① 《米》a karat ② 《英》a carat
- 18 金　① gold 18 karats fine　② 18-karat gold

きんがく【金額】　① an amount (of money)　② a sum (of money)
- 大きな金額　① a large amount of money　② a large sum of money
- 金額にして 100 万円に達する　amount [come] to ¥1 million in value
- 金額にして 5 万円の賞品　① a prize worth ¥50,000　② 《英》a prize to the value of ¥50,000
- 金額にして 3,000 円ぐらいのものだ．
  ① It is valued at about ¥3,000.
  ② It is worth about ¥3,000.
- まだその**金額**には 1,000 円足りない．　We are still ¥1,000 short of that **amount**.
- 彼女は**金額の大小**にかかわらず，贈り物は一切受け取らない．　She never accepts gifts, regardless of **how much they「cost [are worth]**.
- この 1 年の輸入数量は 13,000 個，**金額**で 2,000 万円に近かった．　The number of imported items during the past year was 13,000, and they were **valued at** close to ¥20 million.
- 今年の売り上げは，**金額ベース**で 10% 増，台数ベースで 5% 増となった．　Sales this year resulted in a ten-percent increase **in value terms** and a five-percent increase in units.

きんこんしき【金婚式】　a golden wedding (anniversary) [⇨第 1 部・36-5 …周年]

ぎんこんしき【銀婚式】　a silver wedding (anniversary) [⇨第 1 部・36-5 …周年]

きんじ【近似】　(an) approximation
- 近似する　approximate
- 関数を多項式で近似する　approximate a function「by [with] a polynomial
- 近似的に　approximately
- 一次 [二次] 近似　(a [the]) first-[second-]order approximation
- 第ゼロ近似　(a [the]) zero-[zeroth-]order approximation
- 近似解　an approximate solution
- 近似公式　an approximate formula
- 近似値　① an approximate value　② an approximation

きんぼう【近傍】　a neighborhood
- …となるような開近傍が存在する．　There is an open neighborhood 《of x》 such that ….
- ε 近傍　an ε-neighborhood

きんり【金利】 ① interest (on money) ② 〔利率〕a rate of interest ③ an interest rate ④ a money rate [⇨ り し，り り つ]

- 金利は日歩 3 銭の割合だ． The interest is (at the rate of)「three sen [0.03 yen] a [per] day．
- 年 6 分の金利で at an annual interest rate of six percent
- 5% の金利での 1,000 万円の借り入れ a loan of 10 million yen at 5% interest

▶ 金利の高低

- 金利が高い［安い］． ① The interest rates are「high [low]． ② 〔調達〕Money is「tight [cheap]．
- 高金利 ① a high interest rate ② high interest
- 低金利 ① a low interest rate ② low interest
- 超低金利 ① an extremely low interest rate ② an extraordinarily low interest rate ③ a rock-bottom interest rate
- マイナス金利 a negative interest rate
- 低金利政策 ① a cheap money policy ② an easy money policy ③ a low-interest policy
- 低金利による貸し出し lending money at low rates
- 金利差 ① a difference in interest rates ② an interest (rate) differential ③ a gap in interest rates ④ an interest rate gap
- それにより日米金利差が縮小する［開く］．

① It「reduces [widens] the gap between Japanese and U.S. interest rates.

② It「reduces [widens] the interest rate gap between Japan and the United States.

▶ 金利の上げ下げ

- 金利を引き上げる raise [increase] the rate of interest
- 金利を引き下げる lower [decrease] the rate of interest
- 金利目標値を 0.25% 上げて 1.25% にする raise the target for the money rate「by a quarter point [by a quarter of a percentage point] to 1.25%
- 目標金利の 0.25% の上昇 a quarter-point increase in the target rate
- 金利が引き締まった［ゆるんだ］． Money rates have been「tightened [eased]．
- 金利を据え置く leave an interest rate「unchanged [as it is]
- 出資法による年 29.2% の**上限金利**を引き下げる lower **the maximum interest rate** of 29.2 percent under the Capital Subscription Law
- 利息制限法の上限金利を超えるが出資法の上限金利よりは低い**グレーゾーン金利**《2010 年の出資法の上限金利引き下げで解消》 **gray-area interest rates** that exceed the maximum rates permitted by the Interest Restriction Law but not the ceiling under the Capital Subscription Law

▶ 利払い

- **金利**の支払いを何千ドルも節約する　save thousands of dollars in **interest** payments
- 政府は 1,800 億ドルの**金利**を払った．　The government paid $180 billion in **interest**.
- 支払い**金利**は 2006 年の 2 億円から今年は 1.5 億円に減った．　The **interest**「expense [cost, burden] decreased from ¥200 million in 2006 to ¥150 million this year.
- ▶術語
- 短期金利　① a short-term rate of interest　② a short-term interest rate
- 中長期金利　① medium- and long-term interest rates　② medium- to long-term interest rates
- 長期金利　a long-term interest rate
- 固定金利　①a fixed (interest) rate　②a fixed rate of interest　③an interest rate (which has been) fixed《at 0.3%》
- 変動金利　①a「variable [floating, fluctuating] interest rate　② a variable rate of interest
- 変動金利住宅ローン　① an adjustable rate「mortgage [housing loan]　② a flexible rate「mortgage [housing loan]　③ a floating rate「mortgage [housing loan]　④ a variable rate「mortgage [housing loan]
- 調達金利　a borrowing rate
- 貸出金利　a lending rate
- 政策金利　a policy interest rate

くうかん【空間】　space
- **3 次元空間内**での剛体球の最密の配列　close-packed arrangements of rigid spheres **in three-dimensional space**
- 波動関数の 2 乗を**全空間にわたって**積分したもの　the square of the wave function integrated **over all space**
- **ユークリッド空間内**での剛体回転の群　the group of rigid motions **in Euclidean space**
- **宇宙空間**では爆発に続いて爆風は起こらない．　**In (outer) space**, an explosion is not followed by a blast.
- 3 次元より高次元の空間　spaces with more than three dimensions ★幾何学的考察の対象としての space は可算．
- 有限次元のベクトル空間　a finite-dimensional vector space

ぐうかんすう【偶関数】　an even function
- x についての偶関数　an even function in x

くうしゅうごう【空集合】　① an empty set　② a null set

ぐうすう【偶数】　an even number

- 偶数の　① even　② even-numbered
- 偶数回の置換　an even number of permutations
- 偶数根　〔方程式の〕an even root
- 偶数乗根　〔累乗根〕an even root
- 負の数の**偶数乗根**は実数では存在しない．　There is no real **even root** of a negative number.
- 偶数の日　① an even-numbered day　② a day bearing an even number
- 偶数の年　① an even-numbered year　② an even year
- 偶数ページ　① an even-numbered page　② an even page　③〖製本〗a verso
- その並びのうちの左から**偶数番目の**数字　① numbers **in even positions** from the left in the sequence　② **even-position** numbers from the left in the sequence
- **偶数番目のピン**　① an **even-numbered** pin　② an **even** pin
- フレームの**偶数番目の**走査線を含んでいるフィールド　a field containing the **even-numbered** lines of a frame
- **偶数回目の試行**　an **even-numbered** trial

クーロン　〔電荷の単位〕a coulomb《記号 C》

くかん【区間】　① an interval　②〔経路などの〕a section
- 開区間　an open interval　★ (a, b) のように丸括弧で表わす．
- 閉区間　a closed interval　★ [a, b] のように角括弧で表わす．
- **区間** [0, 1] 上で定義された関数　a function defined on **the interval** [0, 1]
- **区間** (0, 1) 上で連続である　be continuous on **the interval** (0, 1)

くく【九九】　a multiplication table ［⇨第 1 部・54-3-1 かけ算〕

くだる【下る】　〔⇨第 1 部・13-1-3 その他の比較表現〕
- 死者は 300 人を下らない．　No fewer than 300 were killed.

くち【口】　〔割り前〕a share 《in a business project, in a fund-raising effort》
- ひと口入る　① subscribe for [take] a share　② have a share 《in an enterprise》
- ひと口 5,000 円ですが，ふた口以上でお願いします．　One share is 5,000 yen, but we would like you to subscribe for two at least.

くつ【靴】　shoes ［⇨第 1 部・44-1 靴のサイズ〕

くっせつりつ【屈折率】　① a refractive index　② an index of refraction

くぶくりん【九分九厘】　① in ninety-nine cases out of a hundred　② ten to one　③ in nine cases out of ten　④ in all probability　⑤ in almost all cases　★ 日本語では文字通り「99%」という意識は薄いが，①②③の英語では「99%」「90%」という具体的な割合が感じられることもある．
- 我々の成功は九分九厘確実だ．　Our chances of success are「ninety-nine per-

くぶどおり【九分通り】 ①〔9 割方〕nine parts ②nine-tenths ③〔ほとんど・ほぼ〕almost [nearly, practically] ④all but ⑤〔ほとんどの〕almost [nearly, practically] all ⑥ all but a few

- 救援投手の失投で九分通り手中にしていた勝利が逃げていった．　The relief pitcher's bad pitching lost a game that was nine parts won.
- 家は九分通りできあがっていた．　The house was ⌈almost [nearly, practically, all but] finished.

くみあわせ【組み合わせ】 a combination

- 全部で 9 通りの可能な**組み合わせ**がある．　There are nine possible **combinations** ⌈altogether [in all].
- n 個のうちから r 個選ぶときの**組み合わせ**の数　the number of **combinations** of n things taken r at a time
- アルファベット 26 文字から 4 文字を取る**組み合わせ**の数　the number of **combinations** of four letters taken from the 26 letters of the alphabet
- **組み合わせ**の数は順列の数を並べ方の数で割ったものに等しい．　The number of **combinations** equals the number of permutations divided by the number of orderings.

くらい【位】 ①a place ②a position ③a column〔⇨第 1 部・10-1 位取り，52. 小数〕

- 10 の位　the tens place

…くらい，…ぐらい【…位】 ① about … ② around … ③ roughly ④ approximately ⑤ some … ⑥ something like … ⑦ … or so ⑧ … or thereabouts〔⇨第 1 部・9. 概数〕

- 10 時間くらい
  ① about [around, roughly, approximately, some] ten hours
  ② ten hours or ⌈so [thereabouts]
- 日本の人口は 1 億 2500 万人くらいだ．　The population of Japan is somewhere in the neighborhood of 125 million.
- 車で 1 時間くらいです．　It is an hour by car, more or less.
- 値段はこれと同じくらいです．　The price is about the same as this.
- その山の高さは富士山くらいある．　The height of the mountain is about the same as (that of) Mt. Fuji.
- 本はこれで全部じゃない．2 階にまだこのくらいある．　These are not all the books I have; there are just as many upstairs.

グラフ ① a graph ② a chart

- グラフにする　make a graph 《of …》
- 3 次関数のグラフの概形を描く　sketch the graph of a cubic function

- **円グラフ** a pie chart
- **帯グラフ** ①a segmented bar chart ②a component bar chart ③a band graph ④〔縦の〕stacked bar chart
- **折れ線グラフ** a line graph
- **棒グラフ** ①〔縦の〕a column「chart [graph] ②〔横の〕a bar「chart [graph]
- **グラフ用紙** 〔方眼紙〕① graph paper ② section paper

グラム a gram 《= 1/1000 kg；記号 g》[⇨キログラム，第 1 部・27-2 SI 基本単位]
- (100) グラム 1,000 円の牛肉　beef「at [costing, selling for]」¥1,000 per 100 gram　★食品業界では「100 g 当たり…」のことを「グラム…」ということがあるが，俗用であり，英語の gram にはこの用法はない.
- グラム重　〔力の単位〕a gram-force《記号 gf, g 重》　★複数形は grams-force.
- 2M の NaCl 溶液を 1.5 リットル作るには**何グラムの** NaCl が必要ですか. **How many grams of** NaCl「are [is] needed to make 1.5 liters of a 2M NaCl solution? [⇨第 1 部・64. 各種構文と単数／複数 64-11]

グラムとうりょう【グラム当量】　a gram equivalent
- 1 グラム当量の水酸化カリウムにより鹸化される油脂のグラム数　the number of grams of an oil or fat saponified by one gram equivalent of potassium hydroxide

くりあがり【繰り上がり】　a carry
- 繰り上がりが起こったら桁上げビットが 1 にされる．　If a carry occurs, the carry bit is set to one.
- 繰り上がりのない桁ごとの足し算　① digit-by-digit addition without carry ② non-carrying digit-by-digit addition

くりあがる【繰り上がる】

1〔期日が〕① move up ② be moved up ③ be advanced ④ be「brought [put] forward
- 1 時間繰り上がる　① move up [be moved up] an hour ② be advanced an hour ③ be「brought [put] forward an hour

2〔順番が〕① move up ② be moved up
- 次点の候補者が繰り上がった．　The runner-up candidate「moved [was moved]」up.
- 2 着の選手が繰り上がって 1 着になった．　The second-place finisher was moved up to first place.

3〔位取りが〕be carried (up)
- 1 繰り上がる　the one is carried

くりあげる【繰り上げる】

くりこし

1 〔期日を〕advance [bring forward, move forward, move up, move ahead] the date《from … to …》

★ move forward, move up, move ahead といった表現は「繰り上げる」の意味に使われるほか，反対の「繰り下げる」の意味にも使われる．文字通りには「前に持ってくる」ということで，これを「手前に動かす」と解すれば「繰り上げ」だが，「先に動かす」と解すれば「繰り下げ」になる．これらの表現は誤解を招かないような文脈で使うことが望ましい．

- 予定を繰り上げる　move「forward [up]《their》plans
- 2日繰り上げる　① move up《an event》two days earlier　② advance [move up]《the date》by two days
- 水曜日に予定した会議を月曜日に繰り上げる　move a meeting planned for Wednesday to Monday
- 繰り上げて開催する　hold《an exhibition》earlier than「planned [the scheduled date]

2 〔順番を〕move up [advance, raise] a step higher

- 大学は補欠の受験生を3人繰り上げて合格させた．　The university raised the status of three examinees from standby to pass.

3 〔位取りを〕carry (up)

くりこし【繰り越し】　① a transfer　②〔次期への〕a carryover　③ carrying「forward [over]　④〔前期からの〕bringing「forward [over]

- 前期より繰り越し　brought forward《略 BF》from the preceding period
- 次期へ繰り越し　carried forward《略 CF》to the next period
- 繰り越し勘定　①〔前期からの〕a「brought forward [BF] account　②〔次期への〕a「carried forward [CF] account
- 繰り越し金［額，残高］　①〔前期からの〕an amount of money [a balance] brought forward《from the previous period》　②〔次期への〕an amount of money [a balance] carried「forward [over]《to the next period》
- 繰り越し剰余金　①〔前期からの〕a reserve brought forward　②〔次期への〕a reserve carried forward
- 繰り越し欠損　① loss(es)「carried [brought] forward　② loss(es) carried over

くりさがり【繰り下がり】　a borrow

くりさがる【繰り下がる】

1 〔期日が〕be「put off [put back, postponed]《to a later date》

- 会合の日程が1日繰り下がった．　The date of the meeting has been「put back [postponed] one day.

2 〔順番が〕be「moved [put] back [down]《in the order》

- 私の順番が3番から4番に繰り下がった．　My turn has been moved down from third to fourth.

3 〔位取りが〕① be borrowed ② be carried down
- 引き算ではこの場合 1 繰り下がることになる． In subtraction, you borrow one in this case.

くりさげる【繰り下げる】

1 〔期日を〕① put off ② postpone ③ defer
- 6 日繰り下げる　① postpone for six days ② defer 《the date》 by six days
- 1 時間目の授業を 5 時間目に繰り下げる　move the first-hour[-period] lesson down to the fifth「hour [period]
- 日曜日に予定したことを月曜日に繰り下げる　postpone [put off] what was planned for Sunday till Monday

2 〔位取りを〕① borrow ② carry down
- 10 の位から 1 繰り下げて引き算をする　borrow one from the tens place and subtract

グレイ　〔吸収線量の単位〕a gray 《記号 Gy》

グロス　〔144（= 12 ダース）〕a gross
- 鉛筆 10 グロス　ten gross of pencils ★数詞などを伴う場合は単複同形．

けい【京】　《米》ten quadrillion ②《英》ten thousand billion [⇨第 1 部・7. 大きな数]

けいすう【係数】

1 〔多項式の〕a coefficient
- **整数係数**の多項式　a polynomial with **integer coefficients**
- x^3 の**係数**が 1 の 3 次式　a cubic in which **the coefficient** of x^3 is「one [unity]
- 数係数　a numerical coefficient
- 微分係数　a differential coefficient
- 相関係数　a coefficient of correlation

2 〔物性を表わす〕① a coefficient ② a modulus ③ a factor ★modulus の複数形は moduli.
- 温度係数　a temperature coefficient
- 収縮係数　a coefficient of contraction
- 膨張係数　a coefficient of expansion
- 摩擦係数　a coefficient of friction
- 弾性係数　a modulus of elasticity
- 反発係数　a coefficient of restitution

3 〔乗数因子〕
- 修正係数　a modifying factor

けいど

- 安全係数　a safety factor

4〔比率〕
- 分配係数　① a partition coefficient　② a distribution coefficient
- 分離係数　a separation factor

けいど【経度】　longitude

★経度は東経（east longitude）または西経（west longitude）を使って次のように表わす．[⇨いど]

- **東経** 20 度 15 分に　at 20°15′E.　★at twenty degrees fifteen minutes east (longitude) と読む．
- 東京は北緯 35 度 45 分・**東経** 140 度にある．　Tokyo is located at lat. 35°45′ N. and **long.** 140°**E.**
- トルデシリャス条約では**西経** 46 度 37 分の線より東の領土はポルトガルに，西の領土はスペインに属するものと合意された．　It was agreed in the Treaty of Tordesillas that territories lying east of (a line at) about (**longitude**)「46°37′ W.［46 degrees 37 minutes west］should belong to Portugal and the territories to the west should belong to Spain.
- 日付変更線はほぼ**経度 180° の線**［**子午線**］に一致する．
  ① The international date line「is located［lies, runs］approximately along **the 180° line of longitude**.
  ② The international date line approximately coincides with **the meridian of 180° longitude**.

けいばい【競売】　an auction［⇨第 1 部・39-4 入札・オークション］

ゲームさ【ゲーム差】　⇨第 1 部・49. 野球の数字表現 49-3

げじゅん【下旬】　① late《June》② the last ten days《of June》③ from the 21st to the end《of June》④ the last third《of June》[⇨第 1 部・33-2「初頭」「末」「旬」]

けた【桁】　①〔数字〕a digit　② a figure　③〔桁数（の差）〕an order of magnitude　④〔位置〕a place　⑤ a column［⇨くらい］

- 3 桁の数　① a three-digit number　② a three-figure number　③ three figures
- 日付を 4 桁の数字で入力してください．　Enter the month and day in four digits.
- 下 1 桁（の数字）　① the last digit　② the rightmost digit　③ the least significant digit
- 上 1 桁（の数字）　① the first digit　② the leftmost digit　③ the most significant digit
- 上位 2 桁の数字　① the first two digits　② the two most significant digits
- 西暦の上 2 桁を省略する　omit the first two digits of the year
- 下から 3 桁目の数字　the third digit from the right
- 整数はすべての桁の数字の和が 3 で割り切れれば 3 で割り切れる．　A whole number is divisible by 3 if the sum of all its digits is divisible by 3.

- 円周率を小数点以下15桁まで暗記する　① memorize pi to 15 decimal places　② memorize pi to the 15th decimal place
- 小数点を n 桁右に動かす　move the decimal point n digits to the right
- 市外局番が3桁になった．　The area code changed to three「digits [numbers]．
- 暗算で4桁の数どうしのかけ算をする　multiply「four figures by four figures [two four-digit numbers] mentally
- 昭和ひと桁生まれ　《a person》born in the first nine years of the Showa period
- 今月の交通事故件数はなんとかひと桁にとどまった．　We have managed to keep traffic accidents this month「within [down to] single figures．
- 彼女の支持率はかろうじて2桁だった．　Her support was barely in double「digits [figures]．
- 失業率がついに2桁に達した．　The unemployment rate has finally gone into double figures．
- 今季の売り上げは一気に2桁の伸びを示した．　There has been a sudden double-digit increase in this season's sales．
- 番組の視聴率は2桁を超えた．　The program had a rating in double figures．
- 番組の視聴率は2桁を割った．　The program's rating fell into single figures．
- ひと桁台の成績を狙います．　I want to come in the first nine (places)．
- 得点を2桁に乗せる　get at least 10 points
- 1桁の誤差　an error of an order of magnitude
- 桁を間違える　mistake a「zero [decimal place]
- 1万円なら安いと思ったらひと桁違った．　It seemed cheap at ¥10,000, but「there was one more zero [I was wrong by a factor of ten]．
- 新しいプロセッサーは現行のものより何桁も速い．　The new processor is several orders of magnitude faster than the current ones．
- 桁が違う　① differ widely《from …》　② be widely different《from …》　③ be poles apart《from …》　④ be on a different order of magnitude《from …》　⑤ make [stand] no comparison《with …》　⑥ be no match《for …》
- 桁違いに速い[強い，大きい]　an order of magnitude「faster [stronger, larger]
- 桁違いの集客力　unparalleled capacity to draw customers
- 桁外れの　① extraordinary　② extreme　③ exceptional　④ excessive
- 桁外れの大金持ち　an incredibly rich person
- 桁上げ　〘電算〙a carry
- 桁送り　〘電算〙a shift
- 桁数　the number of「digits [figures]《in a number》

けつあつ【血圧】　blood pressure
- 平均的な血圧は上が120で下が80だ．　The average blood pressure is 120/80．★120/80は120 over 80と読む．

- 血圧が 200 まで上がった．　My blood pressure「rose [increased] to 200.
- 血圧は加齢とともにだんだん上がる傾向がある．　Blood pressure tends to increase gradually with age.
- 血圧が正常値まで下がった．　My blood pressure「fell [dropped] to normal.
- 患者の血圧が急激に下がっている．　The patient's blood pressure is falling rapidly.
- 血圧が高い [低い]　have「high [low] blood pressure
- 高血圧　high blood pressure
- 低血圧　low blood pressure
- 血圧を計る　take [measure] 《his》 blood pressure
- 血圧を計ってもらう　have [get] *one's* blood pressure「taken [measured]
- 血圧計　① a sphygmomanometer　② a tonometer　③ a blood pressure gauge
- 血圧測定　① blood-pressure measurement　② sphygmomanometry　③ a blood-pressure check
- 最高血圧 [収縮期血圧]　① maximum (blood) pressure　② systolic (blood) pressure
- 最低血圧 [拡張期血圧]　① minimum (blood) pressure　② diastolic (blood) pressure
- 最高血圧も最低血圧も年齢とともに上がる．　Both systolic and diastolic blood pressures increase with age.

げっきゅう【月給】　① a monthly salary　② a monthly wage　③ monthly pay　④ monthly wages [⇨第 1 部・40-5-2 収入]

けっさん【決算】　① settlement of accounts　② closing accounts　③ account settlement　④ (financial) results [⇨第 1 部・41-2 決算の表現]
- B 社の**決算**は 5％ の増益だった．
 ① B Corp.'s「profit [earnings] rose 5 percent.
 ② B Corp. reported a 5% rise in profit.

げっしゅう【月収】　① a monthly income　② a monthly salary　③ monthly wages　④ monthly earnings [⇨第 1 部・40-5 収入と支出]

けっとうち【血糖値】　① a blood sugar level　② blood sugar
- 血糖値を測定する　① measure the level of sugar in the blood　② measure the blood sugar level
- 血糖値が上がる　the blood sugar level goes up
- 血糖値が下がる　the blood sugar level「goes down [falls]
- 彼は血糖値が標準をはるかに上 [下] 回っている．　His blood sugar level is far「above [below] normal.
- 血糖値を下げる [上げる]　lower [raise] the [*one's*] blood sugar level

- 血糖値を正常に保つ　keep *one's* blood sugar at a normal level
- 高［低］血糖値　① 《have》 a「high ［low］ blood sugar level　② 《have》「high ［low］ blood sugar

けつばん【欠番】　① a missing number　② an omitted number　③ ［縁起が悪いなどの理由で意図的に飛ばした番号］ a skipped number
- 13 は欠番になっている．　The number 13 is skipped.
- 永久欠番　［背番号の］ a retired number ［⇨第 1 部・49-17 背番号］

げつまつ【月末】　the end of the month ［⇨第 1 部・31-2-3 月末］

げつれい【月齢】

1 ［新月の日から経過した日数］ the age of the moon
- 月齢 5 日の月　① a moon 5 days old　② a 5-day-old moon

関連表現
- 十三夜の月　the moon on the thirteenth night of its cycle

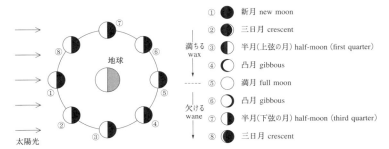

月の位相 (phases of the moon)

2 ［生後の月数］ ① the baby's age in months　② how many months it has been since the baby was born
- 月齢 3 か月の赤ちゃん　a three-month-old baby
- 月齢 18 か月のマウス 6 匹　six 18-month-old mice
- 月齢 20 か月以下の（子）牛　a calf twenty months old or「younger ［below, under］
- 月齢別のおもちゃ　toys for babies of different ages in months

げらく【下落】　① a「fall ［drop, decline］《in price》　② depreciation ［⇨第 1 部・13-5 減少・低下を表わす各種表現］
- 円相場はドルに対して半日で 3 円下落した．　The yen fell 3 yen against the dollar in half a day.

ケルビン　a kelvin《記号 K》 ［⇨第 1 部・45-1 温度］

げん

げん【元】

1 〔集合の要素〕① an element ② a member

2 〔代数方程式の未知数〕an unknown [⇨いちげん，にげん，さんげん]

3 〔中国の通貨単位〕a yuan ★単複同形 [⇨第 1 部・39-1 通貨単位 39-1-5]

げん【弦】 〔円の〕a chord

- その弧に対する弦　the chord which subtends the arc

…げん【…減】

- 2 割減になる　decrease (by) 20 percent [⇨第 1 部・13-2-2 増減の程度]

げんえき【減益】　① a「decrease [fall, drop] in profit(s)　② a profit decrease [⇨第 1 部・41-2 決算の表現]

げんか【原価】　① the cost price　② the prime cost　③ the first cost　④ cost [⇨第 1 部・41-1-3 損益計算書]

- 原価で売る　① sell at cost　② offer at cost
- 原価を切って，原価以下で　① for less than 《it》 costs　② 《sell》 below cost
- 売上原価　① the cost of goods sold 《略 COGS》　② the cost of sales　③ the sales cost
- 仕入れ原価　the purchasing cost
- 製造原価　① the cost of production　② the manufacturing cost　③ the production cost
- 原価率
  ① the cost of goods sold (as a percentage of net sales)
  ② the ratio of the cost of goods sold (to net sales)
  ③ the percentage of the cost of goods sold (relative to net sales)
  ④ the cost-of-sales「ratio [percentage]
  ⑤ the cost-to-sales「ratio [percentage]

げんごう【元号】　an (imperial) era name [⇨第 1 部・29-5 元号]

げんざん【減算】　subtraction [⇨第 1 部・54-2 引き算]

げんしか【原子価】　① (a) valence　② (a) valency

- その原子 [Si] の**原子価**は 4+ である．　**The valence** of「the atom [Si] is 4+.
- **原子価**が 4 より大きい [小さい] 原子　atoms that have **a valence**「greater [less] than four
- 酸素は常に**原子価** 2 であるが，硫黄は 2, 4, 6 と一定しない**原子価**を示す．　Oxygen always has **a valency** of two, while sulfur exhibits a variable **valency** of two, four, or six.
- 原子価が等しい　have the same valence

- 銅は2通りの原子価を示す．　Copper exhibits two valences.
- 遷移金属は一般に原子価が一定しない．　Transition metals generally have variable valence.
- 原子価の理論　the theory of valency
- 原子価の要請からは可能な化学式　a chemical formula possible according to the requirements of valency
- 元素の**原子価**は水素と結合する能力によって決定される．　**The valence** of elements is determined from their ability to combine with hydrogen.

げんしかんすう【原始関数】　a primitive function

げんししつりょうたんい【原子質量単位】　an atomic mass unit《記号 amu, u》

げんしばんごう【原子番号】　an atomic number

- 原子番号 Z の元素　an element of atomic number Z
- 原子番号が83より小さな［大きな］元素　elements with an atomic number「less［greater］than 83
- 原子番号の大きな物質　① a material with a high atomic number ② a material of high atomic number
- 原子番号が小さい［大きい］　have a「low［high］atomic number
- 原子番号が1増えること　(an) increase in atomic number by 1
- 元素を原子番号の（増加する）順番に並べる　arrange the elements in order of increasing atomic numbers
- 原子核中の中性子の割合は原子番号とともに増加する．　The proportion of neutrons in a nucleus increases with atomic number.

げんしゅう【減収】　a「decrease［drop, fall］in (the amount of)「income［revenue］

- 個人所得税の減収　a drop in the amount of individual income tax collected (by the government)
- 本年の市民税は約3000万円の減収の見込みだ．　It is estimated that revenue from this year's municipal tax will be down approximately 30 million yen.
- 減収減益　a decrease in income and (a decrease in) profit(s)［⇨第1部・41-2 決算の表現］

げんしょう【減少】　① (a) decrease ② (a) diminution ③ a decline ④ a fall ⑤ a drop ⑥ dropping off ⑦ a dip ⑧ (a) reduction［⇨第1部・13-4 増加・上昇を表わす各種表現，13-2-2 増減の程度］

- 減少する　① decrease ② diminish ③ lessen ④ be reduced ⑤ drop ⑥ fall ⑦ drop off ⑧ fall off ⑨ dip ⑩〔次第に〕dwindle
- 減少率　① a rate of「decline［decrease, reduction］② a「decline［reduction］rate

げんしょうかんすう【減少関数】　a decreasing function《of［in］x》

げんしりょう

- 単調減少関数　a「monotone [monotonic] decreasing function
- 狭義の [厳密な] 減少関数　a strictly decreasing function　★変化率が0にならず常に減少する関数．変化率が0または負のものは「非増加関数」．
- 非減少関数　a non-decreasing function　★変化率が0または正．

げんしりょう【原子量】　(an) atomic weight

- 水素の**原子量**は 1.00794 である．　Hydrogen has **an atomic weight** of 1.00794.
- 分子量は分子中のすべての原子の**原子量**の和である．　Molecular weight is the sum of **the atomic weights** of「all the atoms in a molecule [all the atoms making up a molecule].
- **原子量**の小さい物質中を通過させることで中性子を減速する　slow down neutrons by passing them through material of low **atomic weight**
- 半端な**原子量**をもつ元素は同位体の混合物である．　Elements which have fractional **atomic weights** are mixtures of isotopes.
- 原子量（の）表　a table of atomic weights

げんてん【減点】

- 減点する　① deduct points　② subtract points　③ take off points
- 減点される　have points taken off
- 《体操競技で》着地の失敗で 0.5 減点された．　Zero-point-five points were deducted for his poor landing.

げんど【限度】　① a limit　② limits　③ bounds　④ a boundary　⑤〔最高限度〕a ceiling [⇨…まで]

- この状況でダイバーが潜れるのは 60 メートルが限度だ．　Sixty meters is the limit for a diver under these conditions.
- 1 回のお引き出しは 100 万円が限度です．　① You are limited to one million yen per withdrawal.　② Single withdrawals are limited to one million yen.
- 5 万円を限度として　up to a limit of 50,000 yen
- 3 回を限度として予約の変更が認められる．　Reservations may be changed up to (a limit of) three times.
- 補助金は 10 万円を限度に購入価格の半額までとする．　The amount of the subsidy is limited to half the purchase price, up to a maximum of 100,000 yen.
- 限度に達する　reach the limit
- 最高限度価格　《set》a price ceiling 《on …》
- 最低限度価格　《set》a floor (price) 《on …》
- 限度額　① a limit　② the「highest [lowest] acceptable「sum [amount]　③ a「maximum [minimum] (sum)　④ the「most [least] 《*one* is prepared to accept》
- 借入限度額　① a borrowing limit　② the maximum one can borrow
- 非課税限度額　《up to》a tax-free limit 《of 25%》

けんぺいりつ【建蔽率】 ① a building-coverage ratio ② a building-to-land ratio ③ land coverage ④ site coverage [⇨第 1 部・46-3 住居]

げんぽう【減法】 subtraction [⇨第 1 部・54-2 引き算]

げんみつ【厳密】

- 厳密な ①〔境界がはっきりした〕strict ②〔近似を使わない〕exact ③〔精確さで妥協しない〕rigorous ④〔隙のない〕close
- 厳密な意味で　in the strict sense of the word
- 厳密に言えば ①strictly speaking ②technically (speaking) ③to be「precise [exact]
- 厳密に増加する《≧でなく＞》　strictly increase
- 厳密解　an exact solution 《of the Einstein equation》
- 厳密な証明　a rigorous proof 《of the theorem》
- 数学的に厳密な基礎　a mathematically rigorous basis
- 微積分に対する厳密な基礎づけ　rigorous foundations for the calculus
- 厳密な定量的比較　(a) rigorous quantitative comparison
- ガウスは，整数論の基本定理に対する初めての厳密な証明を与えた．　Gauss provided the first rigorous proof of the fundamental theorem of arithmetic.
- 彼が証明で用いた議論をより厳密にする　make the arguments he used in the proof more rigorous
- 厳密に調査する ①investigate [look into]《a matter》closely ②make a close investigation《of …》

こ【弧】　an arc

…こ【…戸】 ① a house ② a family ③ a household

- 被災地に **1 戸当たり** 5,000 円を支給する　pay ¥5,000 **to each family** in the disaster area
- 同国では **5 戸に** 1 台の割で自動車がある．　In this country there is one car **for every five families**.
- **50 戸の小村**　a hamlet of **fifty「families [houses]**
- 建売住宅が **10 戸**売り出される．　**Ten** prebuilt homes will be offered for sale.

…こ【…個】

- ナシ 3 個　three pears [⇨第 1 部・2. 数え方]

…ご【…後】 ① after ② later [⇨第 1 部・31-7-2「…後」]

こう【項】

1 〘数〙a term

- 単項式　a monomial (expression)
- 2 項式　a binomial (expression)

ごう

- 3項式　a trinomial (expression)
- 多項式　a polynomial (expression)［⇨たこうしき］
- 一般項が…である級数のはじめの n 項の和
  ① the sum of the first n terms of a series whose general term is …
  ② the sum to n terms of a series whose general term is …
- h の2次の項を無視する　ignore second-order terms in h
- 同類項をまとめる　collect like terms together［⇨どうるいこう］
- フィボナッチ数列は各項が直前の2つの項の和である数列である．
  ① The Fibonacci sequence is a sequence in which each term is the sum of the two previous terms.
  ② Each term in the Fibonacci sequence is determined by adding together the two previous terms.
- 右辺の第1項は体積エネルギー，第2項は表面エネルギー，第3項はクーロンエネルギーを表わす．　The first term on the right-hand side represents the volume energy, the second term the surface energy, and the third term the coulomb energy.

2 ①〔項目〕an item ②〔法律の〕a paragraph ③ a clause［⇨第1部・48. 法律・条約］

ごう【号】

1〔番号〕a number

- のぞみ10号　the「number ten［No. 10］Nozomi superexpress
- スプートニク1号　Sputnik 1
- パイオニア10号　Pioneer 10
- サンダーバード2号　Thunderbird 2
- 1号車　①〔列車の〕Car［Coach, Carriage］No. 1 ②〔バスの〕Bus No. 1 ③〔タクシーの〕Taxi No. 1
- 1号店　① the first store《opened by a company, franchise, etc.》② a company's premier store ③ store No. 1
- 200号ホームラン　① one's 200th home run ② home run「number 200［No. 200］［⇨第1部・49. 野球の数字表現］
- 国道1号線　① National Route 1 ②〔米国の〕US 1
- 伝馬町1丁目2番地3号　2-3, Tenmacho 1-chome［⇨第1部・46-1 住所］

2〔刊行物の〕① an issue ② a number

- 第1号　the first「number［issue］
- 次号　① the next「number［issue］② the following「number［issue］
- 『世界』の1月号　① the January「number［issue］of *Sekai* ② January's *Sekai* ③ the *Sekai* for January
- 『コスモポリタン』の2003年3月号　① the March 2003 issue of *Cosmo-*

politan ② the issue of *Cosmopolitan* for March 2003
- 『タイム』の 1972 年 5 月 8 日号　the May 8, 1972, issue of *Time*
- 古い号　① a back number ② a past issue

3 〔項目〕① an item ② a head ［⇨第 1 部・48. 法律・条約〕
- 第 1 号被保険者　① the insured of the first kind ② a person insured in the first category ③ a Class 1 insured person ④〔集合的〕the Class 1 insured　▶国民年金法第 7 条第 1 項第 1 号による「号」だが，普通は分類の一種として訳して差し支えない．
- 第 1 号被保険者として国民年金に加入する　register for the National Pension Insurance as Class 1 insured

4 〔服のサイズ表示〕a size
- 9 号のドレス　a size-9 dress ［⇨第 1 部・44-3 婦人服のサイズ〕
- 私は普段 9 号を着ている．　I usually wear a size 9.

5 〔キャンバスサイズ表示〕① a format ② a size
- 50 号の風景画　① a landscape of size 50 ② a landscape about 32 by 46 inches
- ▶キャンバスサイズは人物画（F: figure より），風景画（P: paysage より），海景画（M: marine より）があり，しばしば F50, P50 のように表示する．0 号から 120 号の間で 20 通りのサイズ（ほかに 500 までの若干の特殊サイズ）が規定されている．これはフランスのキャンバス型（formats des toiles）が明治時代に取り入れられたものである．

こうがく【高額】
- 高額小切手　① a check for a large sum ② a「large［big,《口》fat］check
- 高額紙幣　large denomination「bills［《英》notes］
- 高額商品　① an expensive item ② a high-priced commodity
- 高額所得　a「large［big, good, high,《口》fat］income
- 高額納税者　① a high(-income) taxpayer ② top(-income) taxpayers
- 高額療養費制度　a reimbursement system for high-cost medical care

こうかんかんけい【交換関係】　a commutation relation
- これらの行列は次の交換関係をみたす．　These matrices satisfy the following commutation relations.
- 反交換関係　an anticommutation relation

こうかんし【交換子】　a commutator
- 角運動量演算子の間の交換子　commutators between the angular momentum operators

こうかんど【好感度】　① how favorably … is viewed ② likableness ③ likability ④〔魅力〕charm ⑤〔人気〕popularity ⑥〔支持率〕support rating ⑦ approval

rating [⇨ひこうかんど]

- その候補者の好感度は49%だった． ① Positive views of the candidate were 49%. ② Forty-nine percent had a favorable「view [opinion] of the candidate. ③ Forty-nine percent viewed the candidate positively. ④ The proportion of people positively viewing the candidate was 49%.
- ドイツは好感度1位を維持した．　Germany kept its position as the most positively viewed country.
- その国の好感度は下がった．　Views of the country deteriorated.

こうき【後期】 ① the latter period ② the late period ③ the「latter [second] half year ④〔2学期制の〕the second semester ⑤〖生物〗〔細胞分裂の〕the anaphase
- 戦争の後期　the latter「period [stage] of a war
- 18世紀の後期　① the later eighteenth century ② the latter part of the eighteenth century

こうぎょうしゅうにゅう【興行収入】 ① box-office revenue(s) ② ticket proceeds ③ the gate [⇨かんきゃくどういんすう]
- その映画は公開後2日間で1億円の興行収入があった．　The movie took in ¥100 million in its first two days of release.
- 今年公開の新作映画興行収入ランキング表　a list of new films released this year, ranked according to their box-office figures
- 興行収入記録　a box-office record
- 歴代興行収入記録　an all-time box-office record
- 興行収入記録を打ち立てる　draw record box-office takings
- 総興行収入上位の映画　top grossing films

ごうけい【合計】 ① the total ② the total「amount [sum] ③ an aggregate ((of …)) [⇨第1部・24-1 合計・総計・総額]
- 合計12,000円　① 12,000 yen in total ② a total of 12,000 yen

こうさ【公差】

1 〔等差数列の〕a common difference
- 公差 −3 の減少数列　a decreasing progression with a common difference of −3

2 〔許容差〕① tolerance ② allowance
- 公差域 [範囲]　① a tolerance range ② a tolerance zone
- ±1% の**公差範囲内**で満たされる　be satisfied to **within a tolerance** of ±1%
- 規定の**公差範囲内**に維持する　maintain … **within a** specified **tolerance**
- 所望の長さに対して**公差範囲内**である　be [lie, come, fall] **within a tolerance**「of [relative to] the desired length
- ±0.003 mm の**公差**　**a tolerance** of ±0.003 mm

- 厳しい**公差** ① a close **tolerance** ② a tight **tolerance**
- 標準よりも厳しい［小さな］**公差** a **tolerance** closer than standard
- これによりメーカーは**公差**を緩和することができる． This allows a manufacturer to relax **tolerances**.
- **公差**を見込んでスロットはコネクターよりやや長くしなければならない． The slot must be made slightly longer than the connector to allow for **tolerances**.
- **検定公差** calibration tolerance
- **製造公差** manufacturing tolerance
- **寸法公差** ① tolerance ⌈in［of］size ② tolerance ⌈in［of］dimensions ③ size tolerance ④ dimensional tolerance ⑤ dimension tolerance
- **位置公差** tolerance ⌈in［of］position
- **形状公差** tolerance ⌈in［of］form

こうじ【高次】 higher-order
- 高次の項 higher-order terms
- 高次の補正 higher-order corrections
- 高次効果 higher-order effects
- 高次構造 higher-order structure
- 高次脳機能障害 (a) higher ⌈cortical［cerebral］dysfunction
- 高次反応 a higher-order reaction
- 高次方程式 a ⌈higher-degree［higher-order］equation

こうしき【公式】 a formula ★複数形は formulas, formulae.
- 球の体積**を求める公式** **a formula to find** the volume of a sphere
- 公式で表わす ① describe［express］… in a formula ② formulate
- その公式を t について解く ① solve the formula for t ② make t the subject of the formula
- 二次方程式の解の公式 the quadratic formula

こうじげん【高次元】 higher-dimensional
- 高次元多様体 a higher-dimensional manifold
- 高次元時空 higher-dimensional space-time
- 高次元で in higher dimensions

こうじゅん【降順】 descending order
- 数字［単語］を降順に並べる arrange ⌈figures［words］in descending order
- 降順になっている be in descending order

こうしょう【公称】
- 公称の ① nominal ② official ③ claimed ④ declared
- 公称応力 a nominal stress

- 公称寸法　a nominal dimension
- 公称電圧　a nominal voltage
- 公称馬力　a nominal horsepower 《略 NHP》
- 公称(発行)部数　〔雑誌・新聞などの〕① an official circulation ② a declared circulation
- 公称(発行)部数10万部の雑誌　a magazine with a declared circulation of 100,000

こうしん【更新】
- 世界記録を5秒更新した．　① She broke the world record by five seconds. ② She took five seconds off the world record.
- 平均株価は3日連続で最高値を更新した．　Average share prices reached record highs three days running.

こうすいかくりつ【降水確率】
① a probability of precipitation ② a chance of「precipitation [rain, rainfall]　③ a likelihood of rain ④ a precipitation percentage ［⇨第1部・45-4 降水・積雪］

こうすいりょう【降水量】
(a quantity [an amount] of) precipitation ［⇨第1部・45-4 降水・積雪］

こうせい【較正】　calibration
- ねじればかりを較正する　calibrate a torsion pendulum
- ばね定数の較正されたばね　a spring with a calibrated spring constant
- 陽子のエネルギースケールはよく知られた崩壊からの陽子を使って**較正された**．　The proton energy scale **was calibrated** using protons from a well-known decay.
- 絶対的なエネルギースケールはテストビームの**較正**データを使って設定された．　The absolute energy scale was set using test beam **calibration** data.

こうせん【交線】　a line of intersection

こうそく【光速】　① the speed of light ② the velocity of light ③ light speed ④ light velocity
- 物質中の光速は屈折率に依存する．　The speed of light in a material depends on the refractive index.
- 何も光速より速く進むことはできない．　Nothing can travel faster than (the speed of) light.
- 物体が光速に近づくにつれその質量が増加する．　As an object approaches the speed of light, its mass increases.

こうてん【交点】　① a point of intersection ② an intersection point
- その直線と x 軸との交点　① the point of intersection of the line with the x axis ② the point where the line「cuts [crosses, meets] the x axis

- 交点の座標　the coordinates「of [at]」the intersection《of the graph with the axis》
- これらの 2 直線の**交点を通る**直線　a line **through the intersection** of these two lines

こうど【光度】　① intensity of light　② brightness　③ luminous intensity　④ luminosity　★③は測光で使われ，単位はカンデラ．④は星の光度に使われ，単位はジュール毎秒またはワット．時に色の明るさにも使われる．［⇨第 1 部・27. 単位］

こうど【高度】　① (an) altitude　② (a) height　③ (an) elevation
- 5,000 メートルの高度を飛ぶ　fly at「an altitude [a height]」of 5,000 meters
- (飛行機が) 高度を上げる　① increase [raise]《its》altitude　② fly higher　③ rise　④ go up《to 10,000 meters》
- (飛行機が) 高度を下げる　① reduce [lower]《its》altitude　② fly lower　③ descend　④ go down《to 1,000 meters》
- 高度差　① (a) difference in「height [elevation, altitude]」　② (a) height [(an) altitude] difference
- 水平線から 30°の高度　an「altitude [elevation]」of 30 degrees above the horizon
- 高度測量　〚天〛altimetry

こうど【硬度】　hardness　★物体の機械的な硬さのほか，X 線の硬度や水の硬度にも使う．
- ダイヤモンドはモース硬度 10 だ．　Diamond has a Mohs hardness of 10.
- 水の硬度はカルシウムやマグネシウムイオンの濃度に依存する．　Water hardness depends on the concentration of calcium and magnesium ions.

こうとう【高騰】　① a「substantial [steep]」rise (in prices)　② a「substantial [major]」increase in prices　③ (a) strong appreciation《in share prices》［⇨第 1 部・13-4 増加・上昇を表わす各種表現］

ごうどう【合同】

1〔図形の〕congruence
- 三角形 ABC は三角形 PQR **と合同である**．　Triangle ABC **is congruent to** triangle PQR.
- 3 辺が等しい三角形は**合同である**．
① Two triangles with equal corresponding sides **are congruent**.
② Two triangles **are congruent** if all three corresponding sides are equal.

2〔整数の〕congruence
- 整数 7 と 17 は 10 を**法として合同である**．　★$7 \equiv 17 \pmod{10}$ と書く．
① Integers 7 and 17 **are congruent modulo** 10.

② 17 **is congruent to** 7 **modulo** 10.
- **合同式** a congruence equation

こうとうしき【恒等式】 ① an identical equation ② an identity
- ヤコビの恒等式　the Jacobi identity
- ビアンキの恒等式　the Bianchi identity

こうねん【光年】〔距離の単位〕a light-year《=約 10 兆 km》
- 地球から 450 光年のところにある星　a star 450 light-years from earth
- マゼラン雲はわれわれの銀河系からほぼ 17 万光年かなたにある．　The Magellanic Clouds are about 170,000 light-years「away [distant]」from our galaxy.

こうばい【勾配】

1〔傾斜〕① a slope ② an incline ③ an inclination ④ a fall ⑤〔道路や鉄道などの〕a grade ⑥ a gradient ⑦〔屋根・階段の〕a pitch
- 30 度の勾配で　① with [at] an incline of 30 degrees ② with [at] a gradient of 30 degrees ③ sloping at 30° ④ inclined at an angle of 30°
- 本線の最大勾配は 25/1000 だ．　The maximum「gradient [grade] on this railroad (line) is「25 in 1000 [25/1000].
- この道路は 30/1000 の登り勾配だ．　This road has an ascent of 30 in 1000.

2〚数〛a gradient
- 関数の勾配　the gradient of a function
- 温度勾配　the temperature gradient
- 圧力勾配に起因する力　the force due to pressure gradients
- 電子密度の勾配　the gradient(s) of the electron density ★空間の各方向を意識するときは複数形.
- 密度の勾配ベクトル　the gradient vectors of the density
- 力はポテンシャルの勾配に負号をつけたものである．　The force is the negative gradient of the potential.

こうばいすう【公倍数】　a common multiple
- 最小公倍数　the「least [lowest] common multiple《略 LCM, l.c.m.》

こうひ【公比】〔等比数列で〕① a common ratio ② a geometric ratio
- 公比が 1/2 の等比数列　a geometric progression with a common ratio of 1/2

こうべき【降冪】　descending powers
- x の降冪の順で　in descending powers of x

こうやくすう【公約数】　① a common divisor ② a common factor ③ a common measure

- 最大公約数　①the greatest common divisor《略 GCD, g.c.d.》 ②the greatest common measure《略 GCM, g.c.m.》

こえる【超える】　①exceed　②surpass　③be greater than …　④be more than …
- 40歳を超えている　①be over forty　②be more than forty　③《口》be on the「wrong [shady] side of forty
- 今日の気温は35度を超えるでしょう．
  ① Today's temperatures are likely to exceed 35 degrees.
  ② It will probably be over 35 degrees today.
- その事故による死者は100名を超えた．
  ① More than [Over] a hundred people were killed in the accident.
  ② The accident caused「more than [over] a hundred deaths.
  ③ The accident claimed「more than [over] a hundred lives.
- この台風による被害は10億円を超えたという．
  ① Damage from the typhoon is reported to exceed a billion yen.
  ② The typhoon is reported to have caused more than a billion yen in damage.
- 聴衆は1,000人を超えていた．　The audience「exceeded [was over] one thousand.
- 外国人労働者の数は数年で120万を超えるだろう．　The number of foreign workers will exceed 1.2 million in several years.
- 3名を超えぬ範囲で代表者を出すことができる．　We are permitted to have「up to [not more than] three representatives.
- 結果は予想を大きく超えるものだった．
  ① The result was far better than expected.
  ② The result greatly exceeded expectations.
- そのフェリーの乗客は定員を超えていた．　There were more than the (legally) permitted number of passengers on the ferry.
- 多摩川はすでに警戒水位を超えた．　The Tama River has already risen above the warning level.
- 計算された値が閾値を超えているかどうかを判定する　determine whether the calculated value exceeds a threshold
- ボリュームが閾値レベルを超える期間
  ① intervals in which the volume is above a threshold level
  ② intervals with volume above a threshold level
- あの候補者は世代を超えた圧倒的支持を集めている．
  ① The candidate is getting overwhelming support which is not limited to any「one age group [particular generation].
  ② The candidate's overwhelming support spans all age groups.

コード　a code
- 文字をコードで表わす　express a character in code
- プリンターの制御に使われるコード　① codes used to control the printer

ごかくけい

- ② printer control codes
- 20h から 7Eh までのコード　the codes from 20h through 7Eh
- ASCII では A の文字コードは 41h だ．　In ASCII, the character code for A is 41h.
- これらのコードは 2 バイトの長さだ．　These codes are two bytes long.
- これらのコードは 5 桁までの長さがある．　These codes can be up to 5 digits long.
- バーコード　①a bar code ②a barcode ③〔具体的な模様〕a bar code「symbol [pattern]〔⇨アイエスビーエヌ〕
- 分類コード　a classification code〔⇨としょぶんるいほう〕

関連用語

- 産業分類番号　an industrial classification code
- 国際特許分類　the International Patent Classification《略 IPC》
- 型番　a model number

ごかくけい【五角形】　a pentagon〔⇨第 1 部・58-2 …角形〕

ごご【午後】　the afternoon〔⇨第 1 部・32-1-2 午前と午後〕

- 午後 5:00　① 5:00 in the afternoon ② 5:00 p.m.

ごさ【誤差】　an error

- 計算値と測定値の間の誤差　the error between the calculated value and the measured value
- L の相対誤差は 2% だ．　The relative error in L is 2%.
- この農場の小麦の収穫予想量は 5,000 トン，誤差は ±100 トンだ．　The anticipated wheat harvest of this farm is 5,000 tons, allowing for an error margin of plus or minus 100 tons.
- 彼らはトップクォークの質量を 161 ± 17 (stat.) ± 10 (syst.) GeV/c^2 と決定した．　They determined the mass of the top quark to be 161 ± 17 (stat.) ± 10 (syst.) GeV/c^2.
- 報告された値は $X \pm r \pm s$ の形で，r は統計誤差，s は系統誤差である．　The reported value is in the form $X \pm r \pm s$, where r is the statistical error and s is the systematic error.
- 括弧内の誤差は最後の桁に適用される．　The error given in parentheses applies to the last figure. ★たとえば 1.728(4) で 1.728 ± 0.004 を表わす．$1.602176462(63) \times 10^{-19}$ のように有効数字の桁数が多い場合に誤差を簡潔に表わせる．
- …ここで誤差はそれぞれ統計，摂動論，電磁効果からくる．　… where the errors come from statistics, perturbation theory, and electromagnetic effects, respectively. ★170.123(11)(53)(7) のように要因ごとに誤差を並記するときの説明．

- 0.1% 以下の誤差で測定可能である． It can be measured with an error less than 0.1%.
- 実験誤差として説明する　explain … as experimental error(s)
- 実験誤差として捨象する　discard [dismiss] … as experimental error(s)
- 測定誤差に由来するばらつき　variation [dispersion] due to measurement error(s)
- その値は我々の観測の誤差の範囲内にはいる． The value「is [falls, lies] within the error「bounds [limits] of our observation.
- 理論的な値と誤差の範囲内で一致する　agree with the theoretical value within the error「limits [bounds]
- 距離の誤差を見積もる　estimate the error in the distance
- ±0.5 の誤差を見込む　allow a margin of error of plus or minus 0.5
- ±1% 程度の誤差は避け得ないようである． Errors of plus or minus 1 percent or so seem to be unavoidable.
- 光度に系統誤差を引き起こす　cause [produce, introduce, lead to, result in] a systematic error in the luminosity
- 測定誤差　① a measurement error ② an error「in [of] measurement
- 実験誤差　an experimental error
- 系統誤差　a systematic error
- 統計誤差　a statistical error
- 偶然誤差　① a random error ② a sporadic error
- 相対誤差　a relative error
- 絶対誤差　an absolute error
- 誤差の伝播 [伝搬]　① propagation of errors ② error propagation

コサイン　〔余弦〕a cosine
- コサイン x　the cosine of x　★$\cos x$ と書く．

ごじ【五次】　① quintic ② fifth-degree ③ fifth-order
- 五次方程式　① a quintic equation ② an equation of the fifth degree [⇨ほうていしき]

こすう【戸数】　the number of「houses [dwellings, families, households]
- 戸数 300 ばかりの村　a village of about 300 houses
- その市は戸数 6,000，人口は 2 万である． There are 6,000 houses and 20,000 inhabitants in the city.

こすう【個数】　the number《of apples》

コスト　cost [⇨第 1 部・40-3 費用]

コセカント　〔余割〕a cosecant

こぜに

- コセカント x　the cosecant of x　★cosec x と書く．

こぜに【小銭】　① change　② small change　③ loose change　④ loose money
⑤ loose cash　[⇨第 1 部・40-6-3 小銭]

ごぜん【午前】　the morning [⇨第 1 部・32-1-2 午前と午後]
- 午前 8:00　① 8:00 in the morning　② 8:00 a.m.

コタンジェント　〔余接〕a cotangent
- コタンジェント x　the cotangent of x　★cot x と書く．

…ごと【…毎】
- 5 分ごとに　① every five minutes　② at intervals of five minutes
- 1 メートルごと　① every meter　② at intervals of one meter　③ at one-meter intervals
- 2 日めごとに　〔隔日に〕① every two days　② every other day
- メンバーが 1 人増すごとに　for each additional member
- ひと雨ごとに　① every time it rains　② with every rainfall
- 1 kg 増すごとに 100 円の割合で加算する　add ¥100 for every additional kilogram
- 人口を国ごとに示す　① show [indicate] the population by country　② show [indicate] the population of each country
- 月ごとの歳入　① monthly revenue　② revenue「a [per, each] month　③ revenue on a monthly basis　④ revenue calculated by the month
- 3 年ごとの　triennial [⇨第 1 部・36-4 …年ごとの]
- 夜ごとの悪夢　① a nightmare *one* has every night　② a recurrent nightmare
- 日曜ごとの集会　① meetings (held) every Sunday　② regular Sunday meetings
- 国ごとの特殊事情　the special circumstances of each country
- 県ごとの 18 歳人口　〔表の説明〕18-year-old population by prefecture
- 結果は計器ごとに変わりうる．
  ① The results may vary depending on the instrument.
  ② The results may vary from instrument to instrument.　★from … to … では名詞は無冠詞．

ことし【今年】　① this year　② the current year　③ the present year
- 今年中に　① this year　② during this year　③ before the end of「this [the] year　④ before the year is out　⑤ in the course of this year
- その作業は今年中続きます．
  ① The work will continue for the rest of the year.
  ② The work will continue until the end of this year.
- 今年いっぱい　① (for) the whole of this year　② throughout the present year

- ③ until the end of this year
- 今年の夏　① this summer　② (the) summer this year　③〔過ぎ去った〕last summer　④〔過ぎ去った〕this past summer　⑤〔来たるべき〕next summer　⑥〔来たるべき〕this coming summer
- 今年も残すところわずかとなった.
  ① There are only a few days (left) until the end of the year.
  ② The year is drawing to a close.
  ③ It is nearly the end of the year.
  ④ The year is almost over.

…こみ【…込み】　[⇨さんにゅう]

- 送料込みの価格　a price including「(the cost of) shipping [freight, postage]
- 配達料込みのお値段です．　The price includes delivery.
- 手数料込みでいくらですか．　How much is it including fees?
- サービス料込みで　service charges included
- 運賃, 保険料込み値段　① cost inclusive of shipping and insurance　② cost, insurance and freight [CIF]
- 運賃, 保険料および為替費用込み値段　cost, insurance, freight and exchange [CIF & E]
- 荷造り運賃込みトン 10 万円　① 100,000 yen per ton, including packing and freight　② 100,000 yen per ton, C & F
- 諸掛かり込みで　all charges paid
- 税込み　⇨ぜい
- 風袋込み　⇨ふうたい

ゴルフ　golf [⇨第 1 部・50-3 ゴルフ]

…ごろ【…頃】　〔だいたいの時間〕① about …　② around …

- 8 時ごろ　(at) about eight (o'clock)　★at about のように at を入れるのは誤りとする見解もあるが, 現実にはよく使われる.
- 来月の 10 日ごろ　① on「about [around] the tenth of next month　② next month on「about [around] the tenth
- 18 世紀の終わりごろ　toward [around] the end of the 18th century
- チョーサーは 1343 年ごろに生まれた．　Chaucer was born「in about 1343 [around 1343, in 1343 or so, c. 1343, circa 1343]．★circa《略 c.》はラテン語の前置詞で around の意味に相当する.

こん【根】　① a root　② a radical

- 多項式の根　a root of a polynomial
- 4 乗根　a fourth root [⇨第 1 部・54-6 累乗根]

こんげつ【今月】　① this month　② the current month　③ the present month [⇨第 1 部・31-2-4 今月]

こんご

こんご【今後】 ① in the future [《英》in future] ② from now on
- 今後数日間［数週間，数か月間，数年間］　for a few ⌈days [weeks, months, years] ahead [from now]
- 今後 2 年のうちに　within the next two years

こんごう【根号】　a radical sign

…こんしき【…婚式】　[⇨第 1 部・36-5 …周年]

こんしゅう【今週】　this week [⇨第 1 部・31-3 週]
- 今週か来週　this week or next (week)
- 今週中に　① during this week　② some time this week　③ before the end of the week　④ before the week ⌈ends [is out]　⑤ in the course of ⌈the [this] week
- 今週の土曜日　① next [this, this coming] Saturday　② Saturday (of) this week
- 今週私はずっと病気で寝ていた.
  ① I have been sick in bed ⌈the whole (of this) [all this] week.
  ② I've spent the whole of this week sick in bed.
  ③ I've spent all of this week sick in bed.

さ行

さ【差】　(a) difference ［⇨第 1 部・54-2 引き算 54-2-2］
- A と B の差　the difference between A and B
- その 2 数の差　the difference of these two numbers

…さい【…歳】　… years old ［⇨第 1 部・38. 年齢］

さいあく【最悪】　worst ［⇨第 1 部・15. 順位・順番の表現 15-2-1］

さいかい【最下位】
- 最下位である　①〔ランキングで〕rank lowest ② be lowest in rank ③〔競技で〕be at the bottom 《of the league》［⇨第 1 部・15. 順位・順番の表現 15-2-1］
- 最下位ビット　the least significant bit 《略 LSB》

さいけつ【採決】　① a ballot ② a vote ［⇨第 1 部・16. 投票・選挙の表現］

さいこ【最古】　oldest
- 最古級の…　one of the oldest … ［⇨ 15. 順位・順番の表現 15-2-1 (4)］

さいご【最後】
- 最後の　① last ② final
- 最後から 2 番目のランナー　① the second runner from the end ② the next-to-last runner ［⇨第 1 部・15. 順位・順番の表現 15-2-1］
- 到着は彼が最後だった．　① He was the last to arrive. ② He arrived last.
- 最後の 5 分が大事だ．　It's the last five minutes (of effort) that「decides the outcome [counts].

さいこう【最高】　［⇨第 1 部・14. 最高と最低］
- 最高の　① highest ② maximum ③〔最良の〕best
- 過去最高を記録する　① hit [set, mark] a record high ② hit [set, mark] an all-time high ③ hit [set] an all-time record ④ hit [set] a new record ⑤ hit [set] a new high ［⇨第 1 部・14-1 最高，14-2 過去最高］
- 世界最高のビル［世界一の高層ビル］　the「tallest [highest] building [skyscraper] in the world
- 世界最高記録　a world record
- 国内最高記録　a national record
- 最高の条件　① the best conditions ② the most desirable circumstances
- 彼の年収は最高 1,000 万円と最低 700 万円の間を上下している．　His「yearly [annual] income「varies [fluctuates] from a high of 10,000,000 yen to a low of 7,000,000 yen [between 10,000,000 and 7,000,000 yen].
- 平均株価が今年最高を記録した．　The stock average rose to its highest level this year.

さいこうきゅう

- **最高気温** ① the maximum temperature ② 〔天気予報で〕today's high [⇨第1部・45-1-3 気温]
- 昨日の最高気温は何度でしたか. What was the high (temperature) yesterday?
- **最高血中濃度** maximum blood concentration《記号 Cmax》
- **最高血中濃度到達時間** ① the time to maximum blood concentration ② the time to reach peak concentration《記号 Tmax》
- **最高限度** ① an upper limit ② a ceiling
- 最高限度を定める set a ceiling《on …》
- **最高時速** ① maximum [top] speed ② maximum「kilometers [miles] per hour
- **最高税率** the maximum rate《for income taxes》
- **最高速度** maximum [top] speed [velocity]
- 最高速度を出す take《a car》to its「maximum [top] speed [velocity]
- その機の最高速度は時速 800 キロである.
  ① The maximum speed of the plane is 800 kilometers per hour.
  ② The plane has a maximum speed of 800 kilometers per hour.
  ★「その機の最大速度」というときは the がつくが, ②の「時速 800 キロという速度」のように 1 つの数値を表わすときは a になる.
- 最高速度の改善 improving (the) maximum speed ★概念として「最大速力の改善」をいうときは無冠詞でもよい. 特定の飛行機などについてであれば the がつく.
- **最高幹部** the top executives
- 国権の**最高機関** the highest organ of state authority
- **最高傑作** ① a work of the highest quality ② a masterpiece ③ a masterwork ④ *one's* magnum opus
- **最高実力者** the most「powerful figure [influential person]
- **最高指導者** ① the paramount leader ② the supreme leader
- **最高責任者** the chief executive
- **最高法規** the supreme law (of the land)

さいこうきゅう【最高級】

- **最高級の** ① of the highest「grade [order] ② top-level [-ranking] ③ first-rate ④ of the「best [highest] quality ⑤ best ⑥ finest ⑦ topflight ⑧ choicest ⑨ top-of-the-line ⑩ top-of-the-range ⑪ top-drawer ⑫《口》topnotch
- **最高級品** ① an article of the highest quality ② the「finest [best] goods
- そのカメラは最高級品に数えられている. That camera is one of the best (there is).

さいころ a die ★複数形は dice. ただし, 今では dice を単数形に使って a dice ということもある. ゲームで使う 2 つ組のさいころは定冠詞を付けて the dice

という.
- さいころを振る　① roll a die　② throw a die
- さいころを振って5が出た.
  ① I rolled a die and got 5.
  ② I rolled a 5.
  ③ I got 5 on rolling a die.
  ④ I got 5 on a roll of a die.
- さいころの出た目の数　the number (of spots) showing on a die
- さいころを振ったときの目の数　the number of spots on a roll of a die
- さいころを振って1が出る確率　the probability of「rolling [getting] a 1 on a roll of a die
- さいころを振って1が出るのは1/6の確率しかない.　There is only a one-in-six probability that you roll a one on one roll of a die.
- さいころを10個振ったとき，一つも4が出ない確率を求めなさい.　Find the probability of getting no 4 when you roll ten dice.

さいしょ【最初】　[⇨第1部・15. 順位・順番の表現]
- 最初の単語　the first word
- 最初の4つの列　the first four columns
- 最初に来る　① come first　② be the first to come
- ホワイトハウスに住んだ最初のファーストレディ　the first First Lady「to live [who lived] in the White House
- 最初に話す人をくじで決める　decide who speaks first by drawing lots
- リストの最初に君の名が出ている.　Your name tops the list.

さいしょう【最小】
- 最小の　① smallest　② minimum　③〔最小限の〕minimal
- 世界最小のモーター　the smallest motor in the world
- 5つの信号のうちノイズが最小の信号　the signal with the smallest noise among the five
- 損失を最小にする戦略　a strategy to minimize losses
- 最小の努力で最大の効果を上げる　achieve a maximum of efficiency at a minimum of effort
- **最小二乗法**　① the least squares method　② the method of least squares
- **最小致死量**　the minimum lethal dose
- **最小有効量**　〔薬物の〕① the minimum effective dose　② the minimum therapeutic dose
- 必要**最小限**の情報　the minimum necessary information
- 最小限の費用で思い切り楽しむ　enjoy *one*self to the full at minimal expense
- 最小限にとどめる　① minimize　② keep 《the costs》 to a minimum

- 最小限に見積もる　① make a lowest estimate ② estimate at a minimum

さいしょう【最少】
- 最少の　① fewest ② least ③ minimum ④ minimal
- 最少失点　the fewest「points [runs, goals] allowed ★run は野球など，goal はサッカーなどにいう．
- 彼はこのピンチを最少失点で切り抜けた．　He managed to get through the tough spot giving up only one run.
- 最少催行人数　the minimum required number of participants

さいじょう【最上】
- 最上の　① best ② finest ③ highest 《quality》 ④ supreme ⑤ superb ⑥ superlative ⑦ of the first order ⑧《口》topnotch
- 最上階　① the top「floor [story] ② the highest「floor [story] ③〔高級アパート〕a penthouse
- 最上階層ドメイン　〖電算〗a top-level domain
- 最上級　① the best quality ② the finest quality [⇨さいこうきゅう] ③〖文法〗the superlative (degree)

さいじょうい【最上位】
- 最上位ビット　the most significant bit《略 MSB》
- 最上位機種の　① top-of-the-line ② top-of-the-range

さいしょうこうばいすう【最小公倍数】　the「least [lowest] common multiple《略 LCM, l.c.m.》
- 2, 6, 10 の最小公倍数は 30 だ．　The least common multiple of 2, 6, and 10 is 30.

サイズ　size
- 服のサイズ　clothing sizes [⇨第 1 部・44-3 婦人服のサイズ]
- 画像のサイズ　the size of an image
- 標準サイズ　a standard size
- コンパクトサイズの　① compact-size(d) ② compact
- てのひらサイズの　① palm-size ② palm-top
- サイズを測る　measure the size
- サイズを指定する　specify the size
- 用紙サイズを設定する　set the paper size
- 最大サイズを制限する　limit the maximum size
- 所望のサイズに拡大する　enlarge to a desired size
- サイズの縮小　reduction in size
- すべてのブロックは同じサイズだ．　All the blocks are (of) the same size.

- 画面のサイズは 1400×1050 だ．　The screen size is 1400×1050.

さいせん【再選】　reelection［⇨第 1 部・16-10 再選・多選］

さいそく【最速】
- 最速の　fastest
- その投手は自己最速の 157 キロを記録している．　That pitcher has set a personal best of 157 kilometers an hour.

さいた【最多】
- 最多の　the most (numerous)
- その年の真夏日は，東京では過去 10 年間で最多の 66 日を記録した．　That summer Tokyo had 66 tropical days, the highest number in a decade.
- **最多当選**　《a politician》elected the most times
- **最多得点**　the most「points［runs, goals］scored　★run は野球など，goal はサッカーなどにいう．［⇨第 1 部・49. 野球の数字表現 49-16］

さいだい【最大】
- 最大の　① greatest　② largest　③ biggest　④ maximum　⑤ maximal
- 世界最大の木造建築　the world's largest wooden building
- 日本最大の　① Japan's largest …　② the largest … in Japan
- 国内最大の　① the nation's largest …　② the largest … in the country
- 史上最大の　the「greatest《mistake》［worst《disaster》, biggest《army》］in history
- 3 社のうち加入者数が最大のプロバイダー
  ① the provider with the greatest number of subscribers among the three
  ② the provider whose number of subscribers is greatest among the three
- アジアで最大の自動車輸出国　the largest car exporting nation in Asia
- 今世紀最大の発見　the greatest discovery of this century
- 最大の収入源　① the largest source of revenue　② the biggest source of income
- 最大の原因　① the main cause《of …》　② the principal factor《in …》
- 最大級の…　one of the largest …［⇨ 15. 順位・順番の表現 15-2-1 (4)］
- **最大値**　①the maximum value　②the maximum　★数学では極大値と区別して absolute maximum, global maximum ともいう．
- $x \geq 1$ についての $f(x)$ の最大値　the maximum value of $f(x)$ for $x \geq 1$
- 単位円上での $3x + 4y$ の最大値　the maximum value of $3x + 4y$ on the unit circle
- 理論上の最大に達する　reach a theoretical maximum
- 電圧が最大になるとき　when the voltage is at its maximum
- 惑星と太陽の間の距離が**最大になる**点を遠日点という．

さいだい

① The point where the distance between a planet and the sun **is「greatest [at its maximum]**」is called the aphelion.
② A planet's point of「**greatest [maximum]**」distance from the sun is called the aphelion.

- 曲線が**最大になる**点　①the point at which the curve **has a maximum**　② the「**maximum [highest]**」point on the curve
- 関数 $y = -x^2 + 4x$ は $x = 2$ で**最大値をとる**[**最大になる**].
  ① The function $y = -x^2 + 4$ **assumes a maximum** at $x = 2$.
  ② The function $y = -x^2 + 4$ **has「a [its] maximum** at $x = 2$.
- 2 点間の最小距離が**最大になるように**点を配置する　distribute [arrange] points **so as to maximize** the minimum distance between any pair of points
- $f(x)$ の値を**最大にする** x の値を求めよ．　Find the value of x which **maximizes** $f(x)$.
- 平均処理量を**最大にする**戦略　a strategy to **maximize** the average throughput
- 電圧は**最大で** 700 V になる．　The voltage is 700 V **at its maximum**.
- **最大で** 5 年続く　continue for **a maximum of** five years
- このソフトウェアは**最大** 2 台のコンピューターにインストールすることができます．　This software may be installed on **a maximum of** two computers.
- 太陽電池のエネルギー変換効率は**最大でも** 30% だ．
  ① **The highest** energy conversion efficiency of solar cells is 30 percent.
  ② The energy conversion efficiency of solar cells is 30 percent **at best**.
- この船の**最大**乗客数は何人ですか．　What is **the maximum** number of passengers this ship is allowed to carry?
- **最大圧力**　the maximum pressure
- 4 MPa の最大圧力に耐える　withstand a maximum pressure of 4 MPa　★一つの数値を挙げるときには不定冠詞がつく．
- **最大加速度**　the maximum acceleration
- **最大許容線量**　the maximum permissible dose《略 MPD》
- **最大許容濃度**　the maximum permissible concentration
- **最大酸素摂取量**　the maximum oxygen uptake
- **最大持続生産量**　the maximum sustainable yield《略 MSY》
- **最大出力**　the maximum (power) output
- 最大出力で　①at full power　②at maximum power
- **最大静止摩擦力**　the maximum static friction force
- **最大耐(薬)量**　the「maximum [maximal] tolerated dose
- **最大風速**　the maximum wind speed [⇨ふうそく]
- **最大限**に利用する　make maximum use of
- **最大限**の譲歩をする　make the「maximum [largest possible] concession(s)

- 最大限の努力をする　make the「maximum [greatest possible] effort
- 建築費は7億円が最大限だ．　Construction costs must not「exceed [run over] 700 million yen.

さいだいこうやくすう【最大公約数】　① the greatest common divisor 《略 GCD, g.c.d.》② the greatest common「factor [measure] ③ the highest common factor ④ 〔複数の意見の共通部分〕the greatest common「factor [denominator]
- 20と16の最大公約数は4だ．　The greatest common divisor of 20 and 16 is 4.
- 政治家は国民の最大公約数的な意見を尊重すべきだ．　Politicians should respect「the greatest common denominator [the consensus] of public opinion.

さいたかね【最高値】　① an all-time high (price) ② a record high (price) [⇨第1部・14. 最高と最低]
- この日の最高値　① the day's highest price ② the day's high ③ the highest price of the day
- この株は先月つけた最高値のほぼ半値にまで落ち込んだ．　The stock has fallen from last month's all-time high to about half (price).
- 株価が最高値を更新した．　Share prices reached「a record high [a new high].

さいたん【最短】
- 最短の　shortest
- 北海道新幹線は東京－新函館北斗間を最短4時間2分で結ぶ．　The Hokkaido Shinkansen links Tokyo and Shin-Hakodate-Hokuto in four hours and two minutes at the fastest.

さいちょう【最長】
- 最長の　longest
- 素潜りの最長記録　a record for the longest free dive
- 契約期間は最長5年まで延長できる．　The contract period can be「extended [renewed] up to a maximum of five years.

さいてい【最低】　[⇨第1部・14. 最高と最低]
- 最低の　① minimum ② lowest ③ rock-bottom ④ 〔最悪の〕worst　★rock-bottom は「底値」「どん底」などの含意．
- 過去最低を記録する　① hit [set, mark] a record low ② hit [set, mark] an all-time low ③ hit [set] a new low [⇨第1部・14-5 最低，14-6 過去最低]
- 歴代内閣で最低の支持率　the lowest level of support for any cabinet in history
- 最低15万円が支給される．　A minimum of [Not less than] ¥150,000 is supplied.
- 全治には最低1か月必要だ．　It will take at least a month to recover completely.
- 建築費は最低5,000万円は要するだろう．　At a minimum you'll need 50

million yen for construction costs.
- 最低限これだけは守ってほしい．　I want you to keep to this ⌜at the very least [if nothing else]⌟.
- **最低気温**　① the ⌜minimum [lowest] temperature　② 〔天気予報で〕《today's》low [⇨第1部・45-1-3 気温]
- **最低限度**　a lower limit
- **最低合格点**　① a minimum passing grade　② a cutoff point
- **最低条件**　a minimum ⌜condition [requirement]⌟
- **最低生活水準**　a minimum standard of living
- **最低年齢**　the minimum age

さいど【彩度】　〔色の鮮やかさ〕saturation

さいねんしょう【最年少】　youngest [⇨ 38. 年齢 38-2]

さいねんちょう【最年長】　oldest [⇨ 38. 年齢 38-2]

さいはんばいかかく【再販売価格】　a resale price [⇨第1部・40-2-4 価格にまつわる術語]

さいひんち【最頻値】　a mode

ざいむしょひょう【財務諸表】　financial statements [⇨第1部・41. 英文会計]

さいやすね【最安値】　① an all-time low (price)　② a record low (price) [⇨第1部・14. 最高と最低]
- 株価が最安値をつけた．
  ① Share prices have reached an all-time low.
  ② The stock market has registered an all-time low.
- 株価が最安値を更新した．　Share prices have reached ⌜a record low [a new low]⌟.

サイン　〔正弦〕a sine
- サイン x　the sine of x　★$\sin x$ と書く．

さき【先】

1 〔先端〕① the point 《of a pencil》　② the tip 《of a finger》　③ the nib 《of a pen》　④ the end 《of a pole》　⑤〔先頭〕the head　⑥ the front

2 〔早い順番〕
- 先に　① earlier　② ahead　③ before　④〔最初〕first

3 〔前方〕
- 先に　① ahead　② beyond
- 2キロ先に　① two kilometers ahead　② two kilometers on　③ two kilometers down 《the road》

- その村は 2 キロ先だ. That village is two kilometers ahead.
- 博多はまだずっと先だ. Hakata is still a long way off.
- 箱根は小田原の何キロぐらい先ですか. About how many kilometers beyond Odawara is Hakone?
- 新宿より 3 つ先の駅 the third station beyond Shinjuku
- 彼女はうちから 3 軒先に住んでいる.
  ① She lives three houses beyond us.
  ② She lives three doors down from us.
- 名古屋より先へは行ったことがない. I haven't ever been beyond Nagoya.
- 暗くて 1 メートル先も見えない. It's so dark we can't see a meter ahead of us.
- 我々は世の中より 10 年先を走っているのだ. We are (racing) ten years ahead of the rest of the world.
- その家は花屋の先か手前か. Is the house on the other side or this side of the florist's?

4 〔将来〕the future
- これから先 ① after this ② hereafter ③ in (the) future ④ from now on
- この先数か月 for months to come
- 今から 10 年先 ① ten years from now ② ten years hence
- 50 年先の日本 ① Japan 50 years from now ② Japan 50 years in the future
- それは何年も先のことだ. That is years「away [ahead].
- 誕生日はまだ 5 日先だ. My birthday is still five days away.
- そんなに先のことまで考えていない. I haven't thought so far ahead.
- 10 手先を読む see ten moves ahead

さきおととい【一昨昨日】 three days ago [⇨第 1 部・31-5-2「先…」]

さきおととし【一昨昨年】 three years ago [⇨第 1 部・31-5-2「先…」]

さくげん【削減】 ① reduction ② trimming ③ retrenchment ④ cutting (back) ⑤ scaling back ⑥ slimming down [⇨第 1 部・13-5 減少・低下を表わす各種表現]
- 削減する ① reduce ② cut (back) ③ retrench ④ trim ⑤ scale back ⑥ pare (back [down]) ⑦ slim down
- 大幅な削減 ① a drastic reduction ② a drastic cut

さくじつ【昨日】 yesterday [⇨第 1 部・31-5-2「先…」]

さくねん【昨年】 last year [＝きょねん] [⇨第 1 部・31-5-2「先…」]
- 昨年同期 ① the year-ago period ② the「same [corresponding] period (of) a year ago [⇨どうき]

さげどまる【下げ止まる】 ① stop falling ② bottom out ③ hit rock bottom [⇨

第 1 部・14-7 底]

サッカー ① soccer ② (association) football [⇨第 1 部・50-2 サッカー]

さっかく【錯角】 alternate (interior) angles
- 2 本の平行線に 1 本の直線が交わるとき，**錯角**の大きさは等しい． If two parallel lines are cut by a transversal, then **alternate interior angles** have equal measures.

ざひょう【座標】 a coordinate [⇨たてじく，よこじく]
- 右手座標系　a right-handed coordinate system
- デカルト座標(系)で　① in Cartesian coordinates ② in the Cartesian coordinate system
- 極座標を用いて　using [in terms of, by means of] polar coordinates
- x 座標　an x-coordinate
- 座標軸　① an axis of coordinates ② a coordinate axis
- 座標変換　(a) coordinate transformation

さぶん【差分】 (finite) differences
- 差分法　(the) calculus of finite differences
- 差分法による熱伝導方程式の数値解法　numerical solution of the heat equation by (the method of) finite differences
- 差分方程式　a difference equation
- 差分絶対値和　the sum of absolute differences 《略 SAD》

さへん【左辺】 the left(-hand) side 《of an equation》《略 LHS, l.h.s.》

さようそ【作用素】 an operator

さらいげつ【再来月】 ① the month after next ② two months from now [⇨第 1 部・31-5-1「来…」]
- 来月か再来月　next month or the month after

さらいしゅう【再来週】 ① the week after next ② two weeks from now [⇨第 1 部・31-5-1「来…」]

さらいねん【再来年】 ① the year after next ② two years from now [⇨第 1 部・31-5-1「来…」]
- 来年か再来年　next year or the year after

さんエルディーケー【3LDK】　⇨第 1 部・46-3 住居

さんかく【三角】　⇨さんかくけい
- **三角錐**　① a triangular pyramid ② a trigonal pyramid
- **三角柱**　a triangular prism

さんかくかんすう【三角関数】　① a trigonometric function ② 《口》 a trig function

- 三角関数の公式　① trigonometric ⌈identities [formulae]　②《口》trig ⌈identities [formulae]

さんかくけい【三角形】　a triangle [⇨第 1 部・58-2 …角形，58-4 基本的な図形の性質，58-5 面積の公式]
- 三角形の頂点　a vertex of a triangle
- **鋭角三角形**　an acute triangle
- **鈍角三角形**　an obtuse triangle
- **正三角形**　an equilateral triangle
- **二等辺三角形**　an isosceles triangle
- **直角三角形**　a right triangle
- **直角二等辺三角形**　an isosceles right triangle
- **不等辺三角形**　a scalene triangle
- **球面三角形**　a spherical triangle

さんげん【三元】
- 三元合金　a ternary alloy
- 三元触媒　〔車の排ガス中の一酸化炭素・炭化水素・窒素酸化物を無害化する触媒〕a three-way catalyst
- 三元電解質　a ternary electrolyte

さんじ【三次】　①〔第 3 の〕third　② tertiary　③〔3 乗冪に関係する〕cubic　④ third-degree　⑤〔一般に次数が 3 の〕third-order
- 三次曲線　a cubic (curve)
- 三次構造　〔タンパク質の〕tertiary structure
- 三次産業　a tertiary industry
- 三次式　a cubic (expression)
- 三次下請け　tertiary subcontractors
- 三次消費者　a tertiary consumer
- 三次多項式　a cubic polynomial
- 三次反応　third-order reaction
- 三次方程式　① a cubic (equation)　② an equation of the third degree

さんじげん【三次元】　three dimensions [⇨じげん]
- 三次元の　① three-dimensional　② 3-D
- 三次元の世界　a three-dimensional world
- 三次元の流れ　a three-dimensional flow
- 三次元構造　(a) three-dimensional structure
- 三次元で　in three dimensions

さんじょう

- 三次元への一般化　generalization to three dimensions

さんじょう【三乗】　a cube ［⇨第 1 部・54-5 累乗 54-5-2, ⇨りっぽう］

さんしん【三振】　a strikeout ［⇨第 1 部・49-9 三振・三者凡退］

さんしん【三進】

- **三進法**　① the ternary system (of notation)　② base three　★ base three は「基数が 3」の意.

さんせん【三選】　election for a third term ［⇨第 1 部・16-10 再選・多選］

さんだい…【三大…】　⇨…だい【…大】

ざんだか【残高】　① the balance　② the remainder

- 口座の**残高**は 20 万円だ．　**The balance** of the bank account is 200,000 yen.
- 3 月末日時点で 40 億ドルの**現金残高**がある
  ① have **a cash balance** of four billion dollars as of March 31
  ② have four billion dollars **in cash** as of March 31
- その会社は**債務残高**が 3 億円ある．
  ① **The outstanding debt** of the company is 300 million yen.
  ② The company has 300 million yen **in debt outstanding**.
  ③ The company has **outstanding debts totaling** 300 million yen.
- **受注残高**は 2,000 万円だ．　**The backlog** (**of orders**) is 20 million yen.
- テレホンカードの**残高**　〔残り度数〕① **the number of units** (**available**) on a telephone card　② the **balance** on a telephone card
- 繰り越し残高
  ①〔前期からの〕**the**「**amount of money**〔**balance**〕**brought forward**《from the previous term》
  ②〔次期への〕**the**「**amount of money**〔**balance**〕**carried forward**《to the next term》

さんど【三度】　three times ［⇨第 1 部・36. 回数・頻度の表現］

- 三度に一度は　once in three times
- 三度 (三度) の食事　① three (regular) meals (a day)　② three daily meals
- 彼は賭け事が三度の飯よりも好きだ．　He「enjoys［likes］gambling more than anything else.
- 二度あることは三度ある．　⇨にど

さんとうぶん【三等分】　trisection

- 三等分する　① cut［divide］… into three equal parts　② divide … equally among three　③ trisect
- 一般角を三等分する　trisect a general angle
- 辺 AB を**三等分する点**で A に近いほうが C である．　**The point of trisection** of AB nearer to A is C.

さんにゅう【算入】　[⇨…こみ]

- 算入する　① count《in [among] …》② add《in …》③ include (in the calculation) ④ reckon《in …》
- 未決勾留の日数は本刑に算入することができる．　The number of days of detention pending trial may be incorporated in the main sentence.

関連表現

- うち（の従業員）はパートを入れて 15 人です．　We have 15 people on the payroll, including part-timers.
- 利息を入れて［入れずに］10 万円払わなければならない．　I have to pay one hundred thousand yen,「including [excluding] interest.
- すべてを入れて費用は 5000 円です．　It costs 5,000 yen, everything included.
- 預金を入れても 10 万円しか残っていない．　I have only one hundred thousand yen left, including what I have in the bank.
- 試験の合格者は私を入れて 10 人でした．　Ten applicants passed the examination, myself among them.
- 私は家から会社まで, 電車の乗り換えの時間を入れてだいたい 1 時間かかる．　It takes me approximately one hour to get to work, including time spent changing trains.
- 建築費は外構工事を含めて総額 4000 万円になる．　Building expenses will amount to forty million yen, including exterior work.
- うちのサッカー部は新 1 年生を含めても部員がやっと 12 人です．　Even if we「include [count] the new first-year students, our soccer club barely comes to twelve members.

さんばいかくのこうしき【三倍角の公式】　〔三角関数の〕a triple-angle formula

さんばんしょうぶ【三番勝負】　① a three-game match ② a three-bout contest ③〔どちらかが 2 勝すれば終わりになる〕a best-of-three match ④ a rubber

- ブリッジの三番勝負をする　play a rubber of bridge

さんへいほうのていり【三平方の定理】　the Pythagorean theorem

ざんりょう【残量】

- テープ残量　the time remaining on a tape
- バッテリー残量　remaining battery life［⇨第 1 部・51-2 バッテリー・充電・放電］

…じ【…次】　① degree ② order［⇨いちじ, にじ, さんじ, よじ, ごじ, こうじ］

★degree は多項式の最高冪などに, order は級数や近似などに使う．

- n 次多項式　① a polynomial of degree n ② a polynomial of the nth degree ③ an nth-degree polynomial
- x について 2 次である　① be of the second degree in x ② be of degree two in x ③ be quadratic in x

…じ

- テイラー級数の 2 次の項　a second-order term in a Taylor series
- h の 2 次の項を無視する　ignore second-order terms in h
- 右辺を 2 次までで打ち切る　truncate the right-hand side to second order
- …の展開式を 2 次まで計算する　calculate the expansion of … up to second order
- h の 1 次までで［1 次の項までとって］…を評価する　evaluate … to first order in h
- ［化学反応で］エチレンについて 1 次である　be first order in ethylene

degree, order 以外の「…次」の表現

▶ 多項式・代数方程式
　linear（一次），quadratic（二次），cubic（三次），quartic（四次），quintic（五次）

▶ その他の各分野［⇨第 1 部・61-5-11 …個組］
　primary（一次），secondary（二次），tertiary（三次），quaternary（四次）
　primary coil（一次コイル），secondary coil（二次コイル）
　primary consumer（『生態』一次消費者），secondary consumer（二次消費者），tertiary consumer（三次消費者）
　primary industry（一次産業），secondary industry（二次産業），tertiary industry（三次産業）
　primary structure（タンパク質の一次構造），secondary structure（二次構造），tertiary structure（三次構造），quaternary structure（四次構造）
　primary alcohol（第一級アルコール），secondary alcohol（第二級アルコール），tertiary alcohol（第三級アルコール）
　primary amine（第一級アミン），secondary amine（第二級アミン），tertiary amine（第三級アミン），quaternary ammonium salt（第四級アンモニウム塩）

…じ【…時】

1　［時刻］⇨第 1 部・32-1 時刻

- 午前 4 時に　① at four (o'clock) in the morning　② at 4 a.m.
- 午後 4 時に　① at four (o'clock) in the afternoon　② at 4 p.m.

2　［方角］

- 23h05m（23 時 5 分）　twenty-three hours five minutes ［⇨せっけい］
- 金星は 8 時の位置から太陽面に入った．　Venus entered the sun's disk at the 8 o'clock position.
- 7 時の方向に敵機．　There's an enemy plane at seven o'clock.

しあさって　three days from now ［⇨第 1 部・31-5-1「来…」］

ジー【G】　［加速度の単位］① g［G］② one gravity ［⇨かそくど］

- 3 G の加速度　acceleration of「3 g［3 G, 3 gravities,《口》3 gees］
- 急降下から機首を上げる際には 9 G もの慣性力がパイロットの体にかかることがある．　In pulling out of a dive, a pilot may be subjected to an inertial

force as high as 9 G.
- Gの力 ① G-force ② g-force

シーベルト 〔線量当量の単位〕a sievert《記号 Sv》

ジーメンス 〔コンダクタンスの単位〕a siemens《記号 S》

じえいかん【自衛官】
▶(( ))内は米軍における呼称との対応の目安.
- 陸上自衛隊　the Ground Self-Defense Force《略 GSDF》
- 陸上幕僚長《大将》　General
- 陸将《中将》　Lieutenant General
- 陸将補《少将》　Major General
- 一等陸佐《大佐》　Colonel
- 二等陸佐《中佐》　Lieutenant Colonel
- 三等陸佐《少佐》　Major
- 一等陸尉《大尉》　Captain
- 二等陸尉《中尉》　First Lieutenant
- 三等陸尉《少尉》　Second Lieutenant
- 海上自衛隊　the Maritime Self-Defense Force《略 MSDF》
- 海上幕僚長《大将》　Admiral
- 海将《中将》　Vice Admiral
- 海将捕《少将》　Rear Admiral
- 一等海佐《大佐》　Captain
- 二等海佐《中佐》　Commander
- 三等海佐《少佐》　Lieutenant Commander
- 一等海尉《大尉》　Lieutenant
- 二等海尉《中尉》　Lieutenant Junior Grade
- 三等海尉《少尉》　Ensign
- 航空自衛隊　the Air Self-Defense Force《略 ASDF》
- 航空幕僚長《大将》　General
- 空将《中将》　Lieutenant General
- 空将補《少将》　Major General
- 一等空佐《大佐》　Colonel
- 二等空佐《中佐》　Lieutenant Colonel
- 三等空佐《少佐》　Major
- 一等空尉《大尉》　Captain
- 二等空尉《中尉》　First Lieutenant

- 三等空尉《少尉》 Second Lieutenant

ジオプトリ a diopter ★日本語の「ジオプトリ」はドイツ語の Dioptrie より.
- 5D［5 ジオプトリ］のレンズ ① a 5D lens ② a 5-diopter lens

★ジオプトリはレンズの度の単位．メートル単位で測った焦点距離の逆数で定義され，たとえば 0.2 m なら 5 ジオプトリ（5D）となる．凸レンズではプラス，凹レンズではマイナスで表わす．めがねの場合，正であれば遠視，負で −3D くらいまでが軽度の近視，−3D〜−6D くらいが中程度の近視，その先が強い近視に相当する．

…しか ① only … ② but … ③ no more than … ④ as few as … ⑤ as little as … ［⇨第 1 部・20.「…も」「…しか」「たった」］
- 10 個**しか**ない．
  ① There are **only** ten.
  ② There are **but** ten.
  ③ There are **no more than** ten.
  ④ There are **as few as** ten.

しか【市価】
- これは市価 8 万円する． ① This has a market value of ¥80,000. ② This is quoted at ¥80,000.

じか【時価】 ［⇨第 1 部・40-2-6 時価］
- 時価総額 ⇨第 1 部・39-3 株 39-3-7

じかい【次回】 the next time
- 次回（に）〔次の機会に〕next time
- 次回の the next
- 次回の上演 the next performance
- 次回に延ばす［回す，譲る］ ① put … off until (the) next time ② postpone … until (the) next time

しかく【四角】 ⇨しかくけい
- **四角錐** a quadrangular pyramid
- **四角柱** a quadrangular prism

しかく【視角】 ① a visual angle ② an angle of vision ③ an angle of view ④ an optic angle
- 0.5 度以上**視角をなす**構造なら解像できる． Features that **subtend** more than 0.5 degree are resolvable.

しかくけい【四角形】 ① a quadrilateral ② a tetragon ［⇨第 1 部・58-2 …角形］
- 平行四辺形は向かい合う辺が互いに平行な**四角形**である． A parallelogram is **a quadrilateral** whose opposite sides are parallel to each other.
- 正方形は 4 つの辺が等しく，4 つの角が直角である**四角形**である． A square

じかん

じかん【時間】

1 〔時刻と時刻の間の期間・その長さ〕① time ② hours ★時刻の意味と区別して a period of time，また長さなら the length of time などと言える．
★時間の長さの単位は時間 (hour；⇨**2**)，分 (minute)，秒 (second)．

- ストップウォッチで時間を計る　① measure (the) time with a stopwatch ② time 《a person》 with a stopwatch
- 時間を5分延長する　extend the time「by [for] five (more) minutes
- 時間を10分短縮する　shorten [reduce] the time by 10 minutes
- 食事の時間は12時から1時までです．　Your mealtime is from 12「until [to] 1 o'clock.
- パルスの間の時間　①〔間隔〕the time between (successive) pulses　② the interval between (successive) pulses　③〔継続時間〕the time during a pulse　④ the duration of a pulse

…する時間

- その機械が使用される時間（の長さ）　the「amount [length, duration] of time the machine is used
- 私が居眠りした時間　① the time I spent (in) dozing　② the (length of) time I was dozing
- いつもならテレビを見る時間を読書にあてる　devote time to reading that *one* would otherwise spend watching TV
- 気温が30℃を超えていた時間　the time during which the temperature was above 30℃
- 経過した時間　① elapsed time　② the time (that has) elapsed
- 通勤時間　(*one's*) commuting time

制限時間

- 制限時間は2時間．
 ① There is a two-hour time limit.
 ② The time limit is two hours.
 ③ You have two hours 《to *do*》.
- 《競技などで》規定の時間内に　① within the fixed time　② within the appointed time　③ within the prescribed time

…時間

- 勤務時間中に　during working hours
- 営業時間　① office hours　② business hours
- 営業時間：午前9時から午後5時まで．〔掲示〕
 ① Open from 9 a.m. to 5 p.m.
 ② Office hours: from 9 a.m. to 5 p.m.

じかん

  ③ Business hours: 9 a.m.-5 p.m.
- 日照時間 〔日が照っている時間〕① hours of「sunlight [sunshine] ② the duration of sunshine ③ sunshine duration
- 1日の平均日照時間は冬は6.5時間，夏は10.5時間です．　The average daily amount of sunshine is 6.5 hours in the winter and 10.5 hours in the summer.
- 当地の日照時間は年平均2,500時間である．　This area has an annual average of 2,500 hours of sunlight.
- 夏至のあと昼の時間は短くなっていく．　After the summer solstice, daylight hours decrease.
- 睡眠時間　① sleeping hours ② sleeping time
- 総睡眠時間　total hours of sleep
- 連続した睡眠時間　the amount of uninterrupted sleep
- 一晩に8時間から9時間の睡眠時間をとったほうがいい．　You should get eight to nine hours of sleep per night.
- 睡眠時間を減らす　① cut down on sleep ② sleep less
- そのドラマの放送時間は月曜から金曜までの午後5:30から6:00までだ．
  ① The drama is aired from 5:30 p.m. to 6:00 p.m. Monday to Friday.
  ② The drama is aired from Monday to Friday from 5:30 p.m. to 6:00 p.m.
  ③ The air time of the drama is from 5:30 p.m. to 6:00 p.m. Monday to Friday.
  ④ The time slot of the drama is from 5:30 p.m. to 6:00 p.m. Monday to Friday.
- 労働時間　① working hours ② the hours of labor [⇨ろうどうじかん]

時間がある / ない

- まだだいぶ時間がある．
  ① We still have plenty of time.
  ② There is still plenty of time.
- 時間がまだ余っている．
  ① There is still some time left.
  ② We still have some more time.
- 午後には時間が多少あく．　I have some time to spare in the afternoon.
- 時間が足りない　do not have enough time 《for …, to *do*》
- 美術館に出かける時間の余裕がない．　I have no time to spare for visiting the gallery.
- 時間のあるときにやればいいさ．　You can do it when you have (the) time.
- 時間を作る　make time 《for …》
- 時間をかせぐ　① play for time ② buy time
- 時間不足　① a lack of time ② time poverty
- 「開演まで何時間ありますか」「あと2時間あります」　How「many more hours [much longer] before the curtain goes up? — Two (more) hours.

じかん

所要時間 [⇨第 1 部・26. 数量に関する疑問文 26-5-2]
- 所要時間　①the time required　②the time taken
- 時間がかかる　①take (a lot of) time　②require (a lot of) time
- 時間のかかる作業　a time-consuming task
- このパソコンが起動するのにかかる時間　①the time required for this PC to boot up　②the time it takes this PC to boot up　③this PC's boot-up time
- それに多くの時間をかける　①put a lot of time into it　②devote a lot of time to it　③spend a lot of time on it　④put many hours into it
- いくら時間をかけてもよい．　You can take as much time as you like.

節約・無駄
- 時間を節約する　①save time　②economize on time
- 時間節約のため　①to save time　②for the sake of time
- この道具を使えば時間が大いに省ける．　Using this tool [This tool] will save you a lot of time.
- 時間を無駄にする　waste time
- 一つ一つ点検するのは時間の無駄だ．　Checking them one by one is a waste of time.

時間的
- 時間的な　①temporal　②chronological　③… in terms of time
- 時間的制約がある　①have a time restriction　②be restricted in time

その他
- 交渉が決裂するのも時間の問題だ．　A breakdown in the negotiations is (only) a「question [matter] of time.
- 時間をさかのぼる　go back in time

2 〔単位〕an hour
- 2 時間 34 分 56 秒　①2 hours, 34 minutes, (and) 56 seconds　②2hr. 34 min. 56 sec.　③2:34:56
- 1 時間は 60 分である．
  ①There are 60 minutes in an hour.
  ②One hour has 60 minutes.
- 3 時間の行程 [距離]　①three hours'「journey [distance]　②〔徒歩で〕a three-hour walk　③〔車で〕a three-hour drive　④〔電車で〕a three-hour train ride　⑤〔飛行機で〕a three-hour flight
- 5 時間で　in five hours
- 8 時間の睡眠　eight hours of sleep
- 何時間も続けて　for hours (on end)
- 24 時間　⇨にじゅうよじかん

じかん

- 時間当たりの生産量　① production per hour　② hourly productivity
- 2時間待ちだ．　It's [There's] a two-hour wait.
- 1週間当たりのテレビ視聴時間数　the number of hours spent watching television per week

3 〔時刻〕① time　② the hour　★**1** と区別して time of day ともいえる．〔⇨じこく〕

- その時間には私は家にいた．　I was home at that time.
- 毎日同じ時間に　at the same time every day
- 開店［閉店］時間　opening [closing] time
- 出発［到着］時間　① a departure [an arrival] time　② the time of「arrival [departure]
- 日本［現地］時間　⇨第1部・32-3 時差

…する時間

- 寝る時間　① bedtime　② (the) time for going to bed
- もうそろそろ学校へ行く時間だ．　It's about time「to leave [you left] for school.
- 食事の時間です．　It's time to eat.
- 窓口が閉まる時間　the time a counter closes
- 音楽会の開始時間が変更になった．
  ① The concert's starting time has (been) changed.
  ② The starting time for the concert has been rescheduled.

定刻

- 時間どおりに　① on time　② punctually　③ like clockwork　④ as regularly as clockwork　⑤ on schedule　⑥《口》on the dot　⑦ on the nose　⑧〔定刻に〕at the「appointed [fixed, scheduled] time
- 予定の時間が来たが会議はまだ始まらない．　The scheduled time has come, but the meeting hasn't begun yet.
- 飛行機は時間どおりに到着した．　The airplane arrived「on schedule [on time].
- バスは時間どおり運行している．
  ① The bus is running「on time [on schedule].
  ②《英》The bus is running「to time [to schedule].
- 時間になったら教えてくれ．
  ① Tell me when it's time.
  ② Tell me when the time comes.

定刻の前後

- 時間すれすれに駆け込んできた．　He rushed in just in time.
- 時間前に着いた．　I「got [was] there ahead of time.
- …の時間に間に合う　be in time for …

- 時間に間に合わせる　① get … ready [done] in time　② get … ready [done] by the time appointed
- 時間に遅れる　① be late　② be not in time
- 約束の時間に 10 分遅れた．　I was ten minutes late for the appointment.
- もうとっくに閉店時間が過ぎていた．　It was already well past closing time.

時間変数

- 時間の関数　a function of time
- 時間を追って温度を記録する　record temperature over time
- 時間とともに減少する　① decrease over time　② decrease with time
- 時間依存性　time dependence
- 時間依存の　time dependent
- 時間的変動　① variation in time　② variation over time
- 時間微分　① a time derivative　② a derivative with respect to time
- 時間積分　① a time integral　② an integral with respect to time
- 時間分解能　① time resolution　② temporal resolution
- 時間平均　time average

4　〔学校の授業時間〕① an hour　② a period　③ a lesson　④ a class
- 2 時間目に数学がある．　We have mathematics (in the) second hour [period].
- 体育の授業は何時間目ですか．　What period is PE [physical education]?
- 次は何の時間だったっけ．　What was the next lesson?
- 歴史の時間に　① during the history lesson　② during the history hour
- 週 12 時間の授業を受け持っている．　I have [teach] 12 periods a week.

しき【式】　① an expression　② a formula　③〔方程式〕an equation　④〔等式〕an equality　⑤〔不等式〕an inequality　★formula の複数形は formulas, formulae　〔⇨第 1 部・55. 式の読み方，56. 式の書き方，57. 式変形の英語〕
- 式の値　the value of an expression
- 式を評価する　evaluate an expression
- けい子さんの持っている本の数を式で表わす　write a mathematical expression for the number of books Keiko has
- 式を立てる　① set up an equation　② construct an equation
- 未知数に関するこの式をもう一方の方程式に代入する　substitute this expression for the unknown in the other equation

しきそう【色相】　〔色合い〕a hue

しきゅう【四球】　① a base on balls　② a walk　〔⇨第 1 部・49. 野球の数字表現〕

じきゅう【時給】　① payment by the hour　② an hourly wage　③ hourly earnings

[⇨第1部・40-5-2 収入]

じくう【時空】 space-time
- 時空中のワームホール　a wormhole in space-time
- 時空の幾何学　the geometry of space-time
- 漸近的に平坦な時空　① an asymptotically flat space-time　② a space-time that is asymptotically flat　★幾何学的考察の対象としては可算

じくたいしょう【軸対称】　① axial symmetry　② axisymmetry
- 軸対称な　① axially symmetric　② axisymmetric
- 軸対称な磁場　an axisymmetric magnetic field
- 軸対称流　an axisymmetric flow
- 軸対称の(中心)軸　① the axis of axial symmetry　② the axis of axisymmetry

シグマ　a sigma　★標準偏差 (standard deviation) のこと.
- この理論値は実験結果**より4シグマ大きい**．　This theoretical value is **4 sigmas greater than** the experimental result.　★誤差分布が正規分布とすれば，4シグマ誤差がある確率は正規分布の性質から0.006%なので，誤差のために偶然その値になったのではなく，有意な差があると考えるのが妥当であるという意味．
- 結果は**4シグマ以上**の統計的有意さをもっている．　The result has a statistical significance of **more than 4 sigmas**.
- エラーボックスは**3シグマの誤差範囲**を表わす．　The error box defines **the 3 sigma error range**.
- **1シグマの不定性**は断面積の不定性を反映している．　**The 1 sigma uncertainties** reflect the uncertainties in the cross sections.
- **3シグマの等高線**　《標準偏差の3倍の誤差を見込んだ領域の境界線》**a 3 sigma contour**

じげん【次元】

1 ①〔空間の〕dimension　②〔群の表現の〕dimensionality
- 2 [3] 次元では　in "two [three] dimensions
- 4次元以上では　① in four or more dimensions　② in more than three dimensions
- 任意の次元で　in any number of dimensions
- 4次元での量子論　the quantum theory in four dimensions
- 高次元への拡張[一般化]　extension [generalization] to higher dimensions
- 2次元の絵　a picture in two dimensions
- 3次元的に記録される　be recorded in three dimensions
- 1次元運動　motion in one dimension
- 1次元自由粒子　a free particle in one dimension

- SU(5) の 15 次元表現　a 15-dimensional representation of SU(5)
- 無限次元のヒルベルト空間　a Hilbert space of infinite dimensions
- その空間の次元は有限 [2] である．　The dimension of the space is ⌈finite [two]⌋.
- 空間 3 次元と時間 1 次元　three dimensions of space and one of time
- 2 つの空間次元は無視し，1 つの空間次元のみを示す　suppress two spatial dimensions and show only one spatial dimension
- 第 3 の次元方向への投影　a projection in the third dimension

[⇨いちじげん，にじげん，さんじげん，よじげん，こうじげん，たじげん]

2〔物理量の〕dimension

- （さまざまな）物理量の次元　dimensions for physical quantities
- 拡散率は，長さかける速度の次元をもっている．　The diffusivity has dimensions of length times velocity.
- 長さの 2 乗割る時間の次元をもつ量　a quantity with dimensions of length squared divided by time
- 長さの逆数の次元をもつ量　a quantity having the dimensions of reciprocal length
- 無名数の次元をもつパラメーター　a parameter which has the dimensions of a pure number
- 無次元量［パラメーター］　a dimensionless ⌈quantity [parameter]⌋

しげんすう【四元数】　a quaternion

じこく【時刻】　① time ② hour ③ time of day [⇨じかん 3, 第 1 部・32-1 時刻]

- ただ今の時刻は 2 時 30 分です．　The time (now) is 2:30.
- 約束の時刻　① the appointed time ② the appointed hour
- そのプロセスが始まった時刻　① the time ⌈at which [when]⌋ the process started ② the time ⌈at which [when]⌋ the process was begun
- 録画を開始する時刻　① the time to start recording ② the time at which to start recording ③ the time when recording should be started
- もうそろそろ月が昇ってもいい時刻だ．　It's about time for the moon to rise.
- 指定された時刻になるとゲートを開く　① open the gate at the specified time ② open the gate when the specified time is reached
- 所定の時刻より 2 分早く　two minutes before the predetermined time
- 時刻 t_0 よりあとでできるだけ早い時刻に　① at the earliest possible time subsequent to time t_0 ② as soon as possible after time t_0
- （炊飯器の）ごはんの炊き上がりの時刻を合わせる
  ① set the timer (on the rice cooker) for when *one* wants the rice to be cooked
  ② set the timer (on the rice cooker) for the time the rice should be ready

しごと

- 現在時刻　the current time
- 開始時刻　① the starting time　② the start time
- 終了時刻　① the finishing time　② the ending time　③ the end time　④〔作動停止などの時刻〕the stop time
- 出発時刻　the departure time
- 到着時刻　the arrival time
- 発着時刻　arrival and departure times《of trains》
- 試合開始時刻　① the starting time of a match　② the time a match begins
- 時刻合わせ　① setting the time　② setting the clock

しごと【仕事】　work

- 気体によってなされる仕事　work done by a gas
- 加えられた力によってなされる仕事はいくらか．　How much work is done by the applied force?
- 1ジュールは1ニュートンの力が1メートルにわたってはたらいたときにされる仕事に等しい．　One joule is equal to the work done by a force of one newton acting through one meter.
- 熱を仕事に変える　convert heat into work
- 熱の仕事当量　the mechanical equivalent of heat
- 仕事量　① work　② the amount of work　★エネルギー・電力量と同じ次元で単位は joule《記号 J》．
- 仕事率　〔単位時間当たりになされる仕事量〕power　★電力と同じ次元で単位は watt《記号 W》．

じこベスト【自己ベスト】　[⇨第1部・14. 最高と最低]

- 自己最高［ベスト］記録　① *one's* best record　② *one's* best performance　③ a [*one's*] personal best
- 自己ベストを更新する　① better [beat] *one's* previous「best [record, time, height, distance]　② better *one's* best performance　③ improve on *one's* best score

じさ【時差】　① (a [the]) difference in time　② a [the] time difference　② a [the] time differential [⇨第1部・32-3 時差]

ししゃごにゅう【四捨五入】　rounding (off) [⇨第1部・10-2 四捨五入]

- 四捨五入して整数にする［小数第一位を四捨五入する］　① round (off)《fractions》to「whole numbers [integers, units]　② round (off)《3.45》to the nearest「whole number [integer, unit]

ししゃすう【死者数】　① the number of deaths　② a [the] death toll [⇨にんずう]

ししゅつ【支出】　① (an) expenditure　② (an) expense　③ (a) disbursement　④ (an) outgo　⑤ outgoings　⑥ (an) outlay [⇨第1部・40-5 収入と支出]

しじょう【史上】
- 史上最大の… ① the greatest … in history ② the biggest … in history［⇨第1部・15. 順位・順番の表現 15-2-1］

じじょう【二乗・自乗】 a square［⇨第1部・54-5 累乗 54-5-1, ⇨へいほう］

ししょうしゃすう【死傷者数】 ①the number of casualties ②the toll of dead and injured［⇨にんずう］

しじりつ【支持率】 ① an approval rating ② a public approval rating ③ a popularity rating
- 42パーセントの内閣**支持率** a forty-two percent **approval rating** for the administration
- 大統領**支持率**はなんとか2桁を維持している． **The approval rating** of the President is barely staying at the two-digit level.
- 世論調査では首相の**支持率**は高かった． The opinion polls gave the Prime Minister high **approval ratings**.
- 新内閣の**支持率**は上がる［下がる］一方だ．
① More and more［Fewer and fewer］people are **supporting** the new Cabinet.
② **The approval rating**［**Support**］for the new Cabinet keeps going「up［down］.

しすう【指数】
1 ①〔目安となる数字〕an index ② an index number
★index の複数形は indexes, indices. ただし，x_i のような「添え字」の意味では indices, 「索引」の意味では indexes が普通.
- 先行指数 ① a leading index ② a leading indicator
- 物価指数 a price index

2 〔冪乗の〕an exponent
- 指数分布 (an) exponential distribution
- 指数法則 laws of exponents
- 指数関数 an exponential function
- 宇宙の指数関数的な膨張 exponential expansion of the universe
- x について指数関数的に減少［減衰］する decrease［decay, diminish］exponentially in x
- 時間とともに指数関数的に増大する increase［grow］exponentially with time

じすう【次数】 ①〔多項式などの〕a degree ②〔級数の項・化学反応などの〕an order［⇨…じ【…次】］

しぜんすう【自然数】 a natural number［⇨せいすう 数の集合］

じそく【時速】

- 時速 500 マイル　500 miles per hour《記号 500 mph》
- 時速 20 キロで　at (a「velocity [speed] of) 20 kilometers「an [per] hour《記号 20 km/h》
- 時速 80 キロ出していた．
  ① We were driving 80 kilometers an hour.
  ② We were doing 80 kilometers an hour.
  ③ We were going at 80 kilometers an hour.
  ④ We were moving at 80 kilometers an hour.
- 時速を 80 キロに制限する　limit the speed to 80 kilometers an hour
- 当機はただ今時速 960 キロでシベリア上空を飛行中です．　We are now flying over Siberia at a speed of 960 kilometers an hour.

しそくえんざん【四則演算】　the four arithmetic operations(: addition, subtraction, multiplication, and division) [⇨第 1 部・54. 加減乗除]

したまわる【下回る】　① be「less [lower] than …　② be [fall] below …　③ be [fall] short of … [⇨第 1 部・13. 比較・差・増減 13-1-3]

しちょうりつ【視聴率】　① a rating　② a program rating　③ an audience rating　④ a popularity rating　⑤ a viewing rate

- その番組の**平均視聴率**は 20% だった．
  ① The program had an average audience rating of 20%.
  ② The program averaged a 20 rating.

★ 日本の視聴率調査はビデオリサーチ社が行なっている．2000年までは米国系のニールセン社も日本で調査を行なっていた．アメリカでは世帯ごとの視聴率のほかにテレビを見ている世帯の中での割合（シェアまたは視聴占拠率という）が発表され，しばしば 11.2/21 のように併記される（21 がシェアを表わす）．したがって，a 11.2/21 Nielsen rating のような表現もある．

- その試合は**最高視聴率** 13% だった．　The game「had [drew] a peak rating of 13%.
- その番組は視聴率週間 1 位を達成した．　The program achieved the highest audience rating of the week.
- その番組は視聴率全国第 1 位に躍進した．　The program soared to number one in the nationwide ratings.
- 高視聴率　① high TV ratings　② high television viewership　③ a high audience rating
- 視聴率がある率を割ればシリーズ打ち切りになるかもしれない．　If the ratings fall below a certain percentage, the series might be discontinued.
- **視聴率調査**　① audience measurement　② audience research　③ a ratings survey
- **世帯視聴率**　a household audience rating　★一般にいう「視聴率」のこと．

- **個人視聴率**　an individual audience rating
- **瞬間最高視聴率**　a maximum instantaneous audience rating 《of 75%》 ★ビデオリサーチ社の調査は1分単位であり，この語は正式な用語ではない．
- 瞬間最高視聴率60%を記録する　record a maximum instantaneous audience rating of 60%
- **延べ視聴率**　a gross rating point 《略 GRP》

じっかくけい【十角形】　a decagon [⇨第1部・58-2 …角形]

じっかんじゅうにし【十干十二支】　the「sixty-year [sexagenary] cycle of (the combination of) the ten calendar signs and the twelve zodiac signs [⇨第1部・37-6 十干十二支]

しつぎょうりつ【失業率】　① an unemployment rate　② a jobless rate
- 2003年のドイツの失業率は9.8%だった．
  ① Germany's unemployment rate for 2003 was 9.8%.
  ② The unemployment rate in Germany for 2003 was 9.8%.
- 史上最悪の失業率　the worst unemployment (rate)「ever [on record, in history]
- 中高年の失業率　the unemployment rate for the middle-aged and elderly
- 失業率が高い［低い］．　Unemployment [The unemployment rate] is「high [low]．
- 失業率が上昇する．　Unemployment [The unemployment rate] goes up [rises]．
- 失業率が低下する．　Unemployment [The unemployment rate] comes down [falls]．
- 失業率が5%を割った．　The unemployment rate fell below 5%.
- 失業率を下げる　lower [reduce, bring down] unemployment [the unemployment rate]

じっこん【実根】　a real root

じつじく【実軸】　the real axis
- 実軸の正の部分に零点を1つもつ　have one zero on **the positive real axis**

じっしつ【実質】
- 実質の　〔名目に対して〕real
- 実質で　in real terms
- 実質値　① the real「value [amount, figure]　② the actual「value [amount, figure]
- 実質1%のGDPの成長を目指す　aim for a real GDP growth rate of 1%
- 昨年度，その国の経済は実質で2%成長した．　Last year the nation's economy grew (by) 2% **in real terms**.

じっしん

- 今年度第1四半期における国内総生産の年率に換算した伸び率は**実質で** 10% と高かった. The annualized growth rate of the gross domestic product in the first quarter of this year was as high as 10% **in real terms**.
- 実質金利　the real interest rate
- 実質(経済)成長率　① a real (economic) growth rate　② a growth rate in real terms
- 実質国民所得　(a [the]) real national income
- 実質国民総生産　(a [the]) real gross national product 《略 RGNP》
- 実質所得　real income

じっしん【十進】

- 十進の　① decimal　② denary
- **十進法**　① the decimal system (of notation)　② decimal notation　③ base 10　★ base 10 は「基数が 10」の意.
- **十進数**　a decimal number
- 二進法の 1111 は十進法では 31 だ.
  ① The binary number 1111 is 31 in decimal notation.
  ② The base-two number 1111 is 31 in base ten.

じっすう【実数】　a real「number [quantity]」[⇨せいすう 数の集合]

- 実数と虚数　real numbers and imaginary numbers
- 実数解　a real root
- 実数体　a real number field
- 実数値の関数　a real-valued function
- 実数部　=じつぶ

じっせん【実線】　① a solid line　② a full line [⇨てんせん]

しつど【湿度】　humidity [⇨第 1 部・45-3 湿度]

- 湿度は現在 80% です.　The humidity is 80 (percent) now.

じつぶ【実部】　the real part 《of a complex number》

しつりょう【質量】　mass [⇨第 1 部・42-10 重さと質量]

- 質量の保存　conservation of mass
- 質量と光度の相関関係　correlation between mass and luminosity
- 球殻上に対称に分布する質量　mass distributed symmetrically over a spherical shell
- 質量 m, 電荷 q の試験粒子　a test particle of mass m and charge q
- 電子の約 200 倍の質量の粒子　a particle with a mass of about 200 times the electron mass
- 4 kg の質量をもつ　have a mass of 4 kg

- 異なる質量をもつ　have different masses
- ばねの端に取り付けられた質量　a mass on the end of a spring
- 質量のある　massive
- 質量のない　massless

しはらい【支払い】　payment［⇨第 1 部・40-6-2 支払いに関係する表現］

しはんき【四半期】　a quarter［⇨どうき］

- 第 1［第 2，第 3，第 4］四半期　《in》the「first［second, third, last］quarter《of the year》　★見出しなどでは Q1 2016, 1Q 2016 のように略すこともある．
- 暦四半期　a calendar quarter　★暦年に基づく四半期で，1〜3 月期を第 1 四半期とする．
- 会計四半期　a fiscal quarter　★会計年度に基づく四半期で，6 月決算なら 7〜9 月期が第 1 四半期となる．
- 当四半期　① the current quarter ② the latest quarter　★後者は「最新の四半期」の意．
- 前四半期　the previous quarter
- 来四半期，翌四半期　the next quarter
- 四半期初日　the first day of a quarter
- 四半期末　the end of a quarter
- 四半期ベースで　on a quarterly basis
- 四半期ごとの　quarterly
- 四半期業績［収益］　quarterly earnings
- 四半期決算　① quarterly settlement ②〔その結果〕quarterly results ③ quarterly earnings ④ a quarterly report［⇨第 1 部・41-2 決算の表現］
- 7 四半期連続で　① for seven consecutive quarters ② for seven quarters in a row ③ for seven quarters in succession ④ for seven quarters running

関連表現

- 1-3 月期　the January to March quarter

しひょう【指標】　① an indicator ② a barometer ③〔一般に，示すもの〕an indication ④ a measure ⑤〘数〙a character ⑥ a characteristic

- 景気回復の指標　① an indicator of economic recovery ② a barometer of economic recovery
- 生活水準の指標　an indicator［a measure］of the standard of living

しほう【四方】

- 100 メートル四方の敷地　a site 100 meters「square［on a side］　★ 100 square meters になると 100 平方メートルであり，正方形だとすると 10 メートル四方である．
- 1 キロ四方の中にコンビニが 15 店もある．　There are as many as fifteen

convenience stores in an area one kilometer「square [on a side].

- 20 センチ四方の布　①a cloth with sides of twenty centimeters　②a cloth with twenty-centimeter sides

じめい【自明】　① trivial　② self-evident

- 自明でない　nontrivial
- その方程式は自明でない整数解をもたない．
  ① The equation has no nontrivial「integer [whole number] solutions.
  ② The equation has no nontrivial solutions in integers.

しめきり【締め切り】　a deadline [⇨第 1 部・35. 期日・期限の表現]

しめんたい【四面体】　⇨第 1 部・58. 図形の基本表現 58-3

しゃえい【射影】　a projection

- 射影する　project
- **正射影**　an orthogonal projection
- 正射影する　orthogonally project
- **射影演算子**　a projection operator
- **射影幾何学**　projective geometry
- **射影空間**　a projective space

…じゃく【…弱】　①a little「less than [fewer than, under, short of] …　②slightly「less than [fewer than, under, short of] … [⇨第 1 部・9-4「…足らず」]

- 1 マイル弱　① a little less than a mile　② a short mile

しゃくど【尺度】　①a scale　②a gauge　③a yardstick　④a measure　⑤a (measuring) rule

- …を測る尺度になる　①be [constitute] a measure [a barometer, an index, an indicator] of …　② be a yardstick for …
- マグニチュードは地震の規模を表わす**尺度**である．　Magnitude is **a scale** that indicates the strength of an earthquake.
- 公約が実行されたかどうかが政治家の手腕や誠実度を測る**尺度**になる．
  Whether or not their public promises have been put into practice is **the gauge** by which to measure the capability and trustworthiness of politicians.

しゃこう【斜交】

- 斜交座標　① oblique coordinates　② skew coordinates
- 斜交軸　an oblique axle

しゃせん【車線】　a (traffic) lane [⇨第 1 部・59-7-2 トリビア]

- 4 車線の道路　a four-lane road
- 片側 2 車線の道路　① a road with two lanes in each direction　② 《英》a two-lane dual carriageway

しゃぞう【写像】 (a) mapping
- 一対一の写像　(a) one-to-one mapping
- 上への写像　(an) onto mapping
- A から B への上への写像　a map from A onto B

しゃっかんほう【尺貫法】 ① the traditional Japanese system of measurement ② (the system of) measuring length by *shaku* and weight by *kan* ③ the *shakkan-ho* system [⇨第 1 部・28-8 日本の伝統単位]

しゃへん【斜辺】 a hypotenuse
- ピタゴラスの定理によれば，直角三角形の**斜辺**の平方は他の二辺の平方の和に等しい．　The Pythagorean theorem states that the square of **the hypotenuse** of a right triangle is equal to the sum of the squares of the other two sides.

しゅい【首位】 《occupy [hold, have]》 (the) first place [⇨第 1 部・15-2 順位]

しゅう【週】 a week [⇨第 1 部・30-4 曜日, 31-3 週]
- 彼の新著は 5 週連続で売り上げ 1 位を記録している．
  ① His new work has been the top seller for five weeks running.
  ② His new work has been at the top of the best-seller list for five consecutive weeks.

じゅう【十】　ten ★「じゅっ…」については「じっ…」で配列．「十」は古典仮名遣いでは「じふ」であり，その促音便は「じゅっ」ではなく「じっ」が本来の形．「納」（古典仮名遣いで「なふ」）から「納付」（のうふ）のほかに納豆（なっとう）のような読みが生じ，「立」（古典仮名遣いで「りふ」）から「建立」（こんりゅう）のほかに「立春」（りっしゅん）のような読みが生じたのと同様である．

じゅういちかくけい【十一角形】 a undecagon [⇨第 1 部・58-2 …角形]

しゅうえき【収益】 ① earnings ② proceeds ③ returns ④ gains ⑤ a profit
- 収益を上げる　① realize a profit ② make a profit ③ turn out a profit ④ achieve a profit ⑤ attain a profit ⑥ chalk up a profit
- 音楽会の**収益**は全部被災者の救済に充てられる．　All **the proceeds** from the concert will be used for the relief of those stricken by the disaster.
- **収益性**　profitability
- 収益性指標　a profitability index [⇨第 1 部・41-1-5 収益性指標]
- **収益率**　〔投資に対する収益の割合〕① a rate of return (on investment) ② an earning(s) rate
- 高収益率　① a high rate of return ② high returns ③ high profitability
- 高収益率の　① high-profit ② highly profitable
- **株価収益率**　〔株価と利益の比〕a price-earnings ratio 《略 P/E ratio, PER》

- **投資収益率**　return on investment《略 ROI》
- **総収益率**　① 〔株価上昇と配当による利益の投資に対する割合〕a total rate of return　② 〔不動産の営業純利益の総投資額（諸費用含む）に対する割合〕free and clear return

じゅうかい【重解】　① a multiple root　② equal roots　③ repeated roots　④ 〔二重解〕a double root

しゅうかくだか【収穫高】　① the yield　② the crop
- 予想収穫高　① an estimated crop　② an estimated yield

しゅうかん【週間】　a week ［⇨第 1 部・31-3 週］
- 3 週間にわたって　① for three weeks　② over three weeks

しゅうき【周期】　① a period　② a cycle
- 振り子の周期　the period of a pendulum
- 3 年周期で　① with a period of three years　② on a three-year cycle
- ある**周期**で振動する　oscillate **with a** certain **period**
- この信号は 2.5 秒の**周期がある**．　This signal **has a period of** 2.5 seconds.
- 10 **周期**の長さである　be 10 **periods** long
- その火山の**活動には周期性がある**．
  ① That volcano **is periodically active**.
  ② That volcano **is active at regular intervals**.
- 周期関数　a periodic function
- 周期的に　① periodically　② cyclically
- 周期的に起きる地震　periodically occurring earthquakes
- 非周期的な　① aperiodic　② acyclic
- 周期性　periodicity
- 周期性鬱病　periodic depression

しゅうき【終期】　① the「closing [last, final] days [years, period]　② the end　③ the close
- 事業計画の終期　the final period of the business plan

しゅうきゅう…【週休…】　［⇨ろうどうじかん］
- 週休 2 日制　① a five-day week　② 〔企業などの〕《米》a five-day workweek　③ 《英》a five-day working week　④ 〔学校の〕a five-day school week　⑤ a week with two days off
- 週休 2 日制を導入する　introduce a five-day workweek system
- 我が社は週休 2 日制だ．
  ① We are on a five-day workweek.
  ② We work a five-day week.
  ③ We work five days a week.

④ We have two days off a week.
- 我が社は隔週週休 2 日制だ．
  ① We work a five-day week every other week.
  ②〔土曜日が隔週で休日〕We get every other Saturday off.
- 隔週週休 2 日制　〔土曜日が隔週で仕事日〕a system in which every other Saturday is a workday
- 完全週休 2 日制　① a regular five-day workweek ② a fully implemented five-day workweek

しゅうごう【集合】　a set
- $2n-1$ の形の数の集合　the set of numbers of the form $2n-1$
- 偶数の集合　the set of even numbers
- 有理数の集合　the set of rational numbers
- 要素［元］を明示的に列挙することによって集合を定義する　define a set by explicitly listing its「elements［members］
- **部分集合**　a subset
- **真部分集合**　a proper subset
- **補集合**　① a complementary set ② a complement
- **無限集合**　an infinite set
- **有限集合**　a finite set
- **集合論**　set theory

じゅうこん【重根】　① a multiple root ② equal roots ③ repeated roots ④〔二重根〕a double root

しゅうし【収支】　income［earnings, revenue］and「expenditure(s)［expenses］〔⇨第 1 部・40-5 収入と支出〕
- 貿易収支　① a balance of trade ② a trade balance
- 熱収支　(a) heat balance
- (二酸化) 炭素収支　〔森林などの〕① the carbon (dioxide) balance ② the carbon (dioxide) budget ③ the net carbon (dioxide) emissions

じゅうしょ【住所】　① *one's* address ② *one's* place of residence〔⇨第 1 部・46-1 住所〕

じゅうしん【重心】　①〔幾何学的図形の〕a centroid ②〔物質の〕a center of mass
- 重心系　a center-of-mass system
- 三角形の 3 つの中線は**重心**で交わる．　The three medians of a triangle meet **at the centroid**.
- **重心**は中線を 2:1 の比に分ける．　**The centroid** divides a median in a ratio of 2:1.

じゅうせきぶん【重積分】 a multiple integral

しゅうそく【収束】 convergence
- 収束する converge
- 収束性を判定する determine the convergence 《of a series》
- 収束性を改善する［よくする］ improve the convergence 《of the iterative calculation》
- その冪級数が収束するような x の値 values of x for which the power series is convergent
- 収束の速い［遅い］級数 a「rapidly [slowly] convergent series

じゅうだい【十代】 ★teenager などの英語は厳密には -teen の語尾をもつ年齢範囲 (13歳から19歳) に使い，10歳から12歳は含まない．［⇨ティーン，第1部・38. 年齢 38-3］
- 十代の人 ①a person between the ages of ten and nineteen ②a teenager ③a teen
- 十代後半の人 ① a person between the ages of fifteen and nineteen ② a person in「his [her] late teens ★② は下記のように「十代の終わり」の意．
- 十代の初めの［に］ in *one's* early teens
- 十代の半ばの［に］ ① in *one's* mid-teens ② in *one's* middle teens
- 十代の終わりの［に］ in *one's* late teens
- 彼は十代の終わりだ． He is in his late teens.
- 彼女は十代で結婚した． She got married while she was (still) in her teens.

じゆうど【自由度】 a degree of freedom
- 空間内での剛体には6つの自由度がある． A rigid body in space has six degrees of freedom.
- n 自由度の系 a system with n degrees of freedom
- 2自由度のジャイロ a two-degree-of-freedom gyro
- 有限自由度 a finite number of degrees of freedom

じゅうにおん【十二音】
- 十二音技法 〔音楽〕① the twelve-tone technique ② twelve-tone serialism ③ twelve-note composition ④ dodecaphony
- 十二音音楽 twelve-tone music

じゅうにかくけい【十二角形】 ① a dodecagon ② a duodecagon ［⇨第1部・58-2 …角形］

じゅうにし【十二支】 ① the twelve (annual) zodiac signs ② the twelve signs of the「Chinese [Oriental] zodiac ［⇨第1部・37-4 十二支］

しゅうにゅう【収入】 ①(an) income ②earnings ③〔歳入〕revenue ④〔売り上

げ〕proceeds ⑤〔入金〕receipts〔⇨第1部・40-5 収入と支出〕
- **興行収入**　⇨こうぎょうしゅうにゅう
- **潜在総収入**　〔不動産資産からの〕potential gross income《略 PGI》
- **実効総収入**　effective gross income《略 EGI》★PGI から空き室・未回収による損を差し引いたもの．さらに運営経費を差し引いたものが営業純利益 (net operating income, NOI) になる．

しゅうねん【周年】
- 5 周年祭　the fifth anniversary〔⇨第1部・36-5 …周年〕

しゅうはすう【周波数】　(a) frequency
- 周波数 f の音波を発生させる　produce sound waves of frequency f
- 周波数 1 kHz の正弦波信号　a sinusoidal signal having a frequency of 1 kHz
- 弦の振動の基本周波数　the fundamental frequency of vibration of a string
- その結晶は，100 kHz の**周波数**で振動するようにつくられている．　The crystal is designed to oscillate at **a frequency** of 100 kHz.
- それらの弦は，それぞれ 440 Hz, 660 Hz の基本**周波数**をもっている．　Those strings have fundamental **frequencies** of 440 Hz and 660 Hz, respectively.
- うなりの周波数は 2 つの音波の**周波数**の差に等しい．
  ① The beat frequency is equal to the **frequency** difference between the two sound waves.
  ② The beat frequency is equal to the difference in **frequency** of the two sound waves.
- 入力ビームの和または差の**周波数**をもつビームを生成する　generate a beam with (**a frequency** equal to) the sum or difference of the frequencies of the input beams
- 交流に対しては抵抗は**周波数**が増すとともに増大する．　For alternating current, resistance increases with increasing **frequency**.
- テレビのチャンネルというのは，ある特定の局からの信号を伝えるために割り当てられた電波の**周波数**の帯域のことである．　A TV channel is a band of radio **frequencies** allocated to carry signals from a particular station.
- フレーム周波数〔フレームレート〕は NTSC では 30 fps, PAL/SECAM では 25 fps だ．　The frame rate is 30 fps for NTSC and 25 fps for PAL/SECAM. ★fps は frames per second の略．

しゅうまつ【週末】　a weekend〔⇨第1部・31-3-4 週末〕

しゅうよう【収容】　①accommodation ②reception ③seating ④housing ⑤〔病院への〕hospitalization
- 収容する　①〔旅行者を〕accommodate《travelers》②〔観客を〕seat《a number of people》③〔患者を〕receive [take in]《a patient》④〔被災者を〕house《victims》
- このホテルは約 1500 人の客を収容できる．

- ① This hotel can accommodate about 1,500 guests.
- ② This hotel has accommodation(s) for about 1,500 guests.
- 新講堂は1000人収容できる．　① The new hall seats 1,000.　② The new auditorium has a seating capacity of 1,000.
- 収容(能)力　①〔劇場などの〕a seating capacity 《of 500》 ②〔ホテルなどの〕(sleeping) accommodation(s) 《for 200 people》 ③〔駐車場の〕a parking capacity 《of 200》
- この劇場の収容力はどのくらいですか．　① What is the seating capacity of this theater?　② How many people can this theater seat?

しゅうりつ【収率】　a yield
- 75%〜85%の範囲の収率が達成される．　Yields in the range from 75% to 85% are achieved.
- **理論収率**　a theoretical yield
- **量子収率**　〔光反応の〕a quantum yield
- **核分裂収率**　a fission yield
- **粗収率**　a crude yield

しゅうりょう【収量】　a yield
- 10アール当たり収量　〔作物の〕the (crop) yield per 10 ares
- 乾物収量　a dry-matter yield
- 生草［青刈］収量　① a fresh yield　② a green yield
- 種子収量　a seed yield

じゅうりょう【重量】　weight　[⇨第1部・42-10 重さと質量]

ジュール〔エネルギー・仕事・熱量の単位〕a joule 《記号 J》

じゅうろくしん【十六進】
- 十六進の　hexadecimal
- **十六進法**　① the hexadecimal system (of notation)　② hexadecimal notation　③ base 16　★ base 16 は「基数が16」の意．
- **十六進数**　a hexadecimal number
- 30は**十六進数**では1Eとなる．
  ① The number 30 is 1E in **hexadecimal** (**notation**).
  ② The number 30 is 1E in **base 16**.
- 計256通りの文字が**十六進数**では2桁で表わせる．　A total of 256 characters can be represented with two digits in **hexadecimal** (**notation**).

★十六進数であることは下付きの16で示したり，コンピュータ言語では0x…，…h，&H… のように示したりする．たとえば十六進数の4Aは $4A_{16}$ のほか，C言語やJavaでは0x4A，一部のアセンブラでは4Ah，一部のBASICでは&H4Aなどと書かれる．

しゅくしゃく【縮尺】 a scale
- 縮尺 5 万分の 1 〔地図などの記載〕Scale: 1/50,000 ★分数 1/50,000 のほかに比 1:50,000 で表わしたり，One inch equals 10 miles.（1 インチは 10 マイルを表わす）のように文で対応を示したり，縮尺バーで図的に示したりする．
- 縮尺 5 万分の 1 の地図　①a map drawn on a scale of 1 to 50,000　②a 1:50,000 map ★1:50,000 は one to fifty thousand と読む．
- 1/25,000 という縮尺がある地図　a map with a scale of 1:25,000
- 地図の縮尺　①a map('s) scale　②the scale of a map
- 縮尺図　a map on a reduced scale
- 大縮尺の地図［縮尺の大きな地図］　a large-scale map
- 小縮尺の地図［縮尺の小さな地図］　a small-scale map
- 大縮尺の地図では　on a large-scale map
- 小縮尺で描く　draw 《a map》「on [at] a small scale
- その村を見つけるにはもっと大縮尺の地図が必要だ．　You need a larger-scale map to locate that village.
- ★大縮尺の地図は小縮尺の地図よりも同じ対象をより大きく表示する．縮小率が小さいほうが「…分の 1」のような比の値が大きい（「5 千分の 1」のほうが「5 万分の 1」より大きい）ためである．日本語でも英語でも縮尺の大小と縮小率の大小が混同されやすいので注意．
- ゼロ戦の縮尺 24 分の 1 の模型　a「one-twenty-fourth [1/24, 1:24] scale model of a Zero fighter
- 日本の戦艦「大和」を実際の大きさ 263 メートルから 1 メートルに縮尺した模型　a model of the Japanese battleship Yamato scaled down to a length of 1 meter from the real-life 263 meters
- 1 フィートを 3/4 インチに縮尺したミロのヴィーナスの模刻　a replica of the Venus de Milo, scaled 3/4 inch to the foot ★3/4 inch は three-quarters of an inch または three-fourths of an inch と読む．

しゅくしょうりつ【縮小率】　①a degree of reduction　②a reduction 《of 50%》　③a reduction ratio ［⇨ばいりつ］

しゅすう【種数】　a genus

じゅっかくけい【十角形】　⇨じっかくけい

しゅっしょうりつ【出生率】　①a birthrate　②natality
- 出生率が高い［低い］．　The birthrate [Natality] is「high [low].
- 出生率の低下　①a drop in the birthrate　②a decline in natality
- 年々**出生率**が低下している．　**The birthrate** [**Natality**] is「going down [dropping, declining] year by year.
- 晩婚化とともに**出生率**が極端に落ち込んでいる．
①With later marriage, there is a drastic decline in **the birthrate**.

② As people postpone marriage, **the birthrate** is declining precipitously.
- 日本の**出生率**はますます低くなりつつある．
  ① **The birthrate** in Japan is getting lower and lower.
  ② **The birthrate** in Japan is dropping further and further.
  ③ **The birthrate** in Japan is going down and down.
- 今年は都市部でわずかながら**出生率**が回復した． Urban **birthrates** have recovered slightly this year.

じゅっしん【十進】 ⇨じっしん

しゅっぴ【出費】 ① expenses ② expenditure ③ (an) outlay ［⇨第 1 部・40-5-3 支出］

じゅみょう【寿命】 ① life ② *one's* life span ③ *one's* lifetime ④ the span of life ⑤ *one's* (natural)「term [duration] of「life [existence] ⑥ the length of *one's* days ⑦ *one's*「lease [tenure] of life

- 平均寿命 ⇨第 1 部・25-8 平均寿命
- ゾウの寿命 an elephant's life span
- 電球の寿命 the life of an electric lightbulb
- 自動車の寿命 the expected life span of automobiles
- ダムの寿命 a dam's (effective) life span
- 自由中性子の寿命は約 15 分である． The lifetime of a free neutron is about 15 minutes.
- 寿命が長い ① be long-lived ② have [enjoy] a long life (span) ★long-lived の lived は /livd/ と /laivd/ の両様の発音がある．
- 寿命が短い ① be short-lived ② have [enjoy] (only) a short life (span)
- 医者の話では彼の寿命はあと 1 年だそうだ． The doctor says that he has only a year to live.
- 大型の動物は概して小動物より寿命が長い． In general the life span of large animals is longer than that of smaller animals.
- 一般に女性は男性より長命だ． In general women live longer than men.
- 日本人女性は年々平均寿命が延びている． Year by year Japanese women are living longer on average.
- ツルは寿命が長い． Cranes live to a great age.
- 寿命が来る［尽きる］ ①〔人〕the end of *one's* days has come ②〔物〕exceed [reach] its life span
- 「惜しい人を亡くした」「これが寿命だったんだよ」 His death is a great loss. — His time had come.
- **有効寿命**［**有用寿命**］ useful life ［⇨たいようねんすう］
- **設計寿命** a design service life
- **貯蔵寿命** shelf life ［⇨第 1 部・35-4 賞味期限・消費期限］

- こまめに掃除をすればフィルターの**寿命**を延ばすことができる．　If you diligently clean it, you can increase **the life** of a filter.
- 周辺温度の変化は電池の**寿命**を縮めることがある．　Changes in the surrounding temperature can shorten **the life** of a battery.

関連表現
- 長命　① a long life　② longevity　③ macrobiosis
- 短命　① a short life　② a brief span of life
- その政権は比較的短命だった．　That government was comparatively short-lived.

じゅん【順】　order [⇨じゅんじょ，じゅんばん，第1部・15-4 順番]

じゅん…【純…】　〔利益などの〕① net　② clear
- 純収入　net income
- 純利　a net profit
- 純増　① a net increase　② net growth
- 純損　① dead loss　② a net loss
- 純益　① a net「profit [gain]　② a clear「profit [gain]　③ a pure「profit [gain]　④ net proceeds
- 純益100万円を得る　net [gross, clear, realize] a profit of one million yen
- 50万円の純益がある　have a net gain of 500,000 yen
- 1年に1千万円の純益を上げる　net ten million yen a year
- 1年に2割5分の純益を上げる　net 25 percent a year
- 業務純益　a net business profit

じゅんい【順位】　① order　② ranking　③ standing　④ placing　⑤ precedence　⑥〔レースの〕position [⇨第1部・15-2 順位]

じゅんきょすう【純虚数】　a pure imaginary number

じゅんじょ【順序】　① order　② sequence [⇨第1部・15-4 順番]
- 訪問順序を決める　① decide [fix] the「order [sequence] of visits　② decide [fix] the「order [sequence] in which《each destination》will be visited
- 指名された順序で　in the order named
- 数字の順序が乱れている．　The numbers are out of order.
- リストのこの2つの名前は**順序が逆だ**．　These two names on the list are **in the wrong order**.
- ステップ4とステップ5の**順序**は重要でない．
  ① **The order** of steps 4 and 5 is not important.
  ② Steps 4 and 5 are interchangeable.
- この検索では，入力した単語が隣接して，指定した通りの**順序**で出てこなければならない．　In this search, the terms you enter must「appear [be] adjacent

and in **the order** you specify.
- **順序体**　an ordered field
- **順序対**　an ordered pair
- **全順序集合**　① a totally ordered set　② a linearly ordered set
- **半順序集合**　a partially ordered set

じゅんど【純度】　purity

じゅんばん【順番】　①〔順序〕order　②〔輪番〕a turn　[⇨第 1 部・15-4 順番]
- 文字が選択される順番　the order in which the letters are selected
- 国名表記の順番　the order in which the names of countries are「listed [cited]
- 指名された順番に　in the order named
- 受け取った順番に　in the order received
- どういう順番にこれらの町を訪問するのがいちばんいいですか．　What is the best order (in which) to visit these towns?
- 順番を逆にする　① reverse the order　② invert the order
- 順番を待つ　① await [wait (for)] *one's* turn　②〔客として〕wait for service
- 順番が来た．　① Now it's my turn.　② My turn has come.
- **順番に**
〔順序よく〕① in order　② in regular order　③ in due order　④ in sequential order
〔代わる代わる〕⑤ in turn　⑥ by turns
〔輪番式に〕⑦ in rotation　⑧ by rotation
- 順番に歌う［スピーチをする］　sing [make speeches] in turn
- 部員が順番に夕食を作る．　Each member of the club takes turns cooking dinner.
- 順番に並べる　put … in order
- 数字が順番になっていない．　The numbers are not in sequential order.
- 順番に診ますのでもう少しお待ちください．　Consultations are carried out in order, so please wait a little longer.
- 順番に願います．　In order, please.
- オランダの国旗は**上から順番に**赤，白，青だ．　The national flag of the Netherlands is, **in order from the top**, red, white and blue.

じゅんりえき【純利益】　① a net profit　② a net gain　③ net proceeds　[⇨第 1 部・41-1-3 損益計算書]

じゅんれつ【順列】　a permutation
- 10 個のものから 3 つを選んで並べる**順列**の数　① the number of **permutations** of 3 objects out of 10　② the number of **permutations** of 10 things taken 3 at a time　★「並べる」の意は permutation（順列）の語に含まれているので

訳出する必要はない．
- 4つの異なる文字の順列の総数　the total number of permutations of four different letters

しょう【商】　the quotient ［⇨第1部・54-4 割り算 54-4-2］
- 64 を 17 で割ると，商は 3 で余りは 13 だ．　When you divide 64 by 17, the quotient is 3 and the remainder is 13.

…しょう【…勝】　［⇨第1部・50-1 勝敗］
- 3 勝 1 敗　① three victories「and ［against］one defeat　② three wins「and ［against］one defeat　③ three wins and one loss　④ a three-one record
- 日本シリーズは 7 戦で先に 4 勝したほうが優勝だ．
① The Japan Series goes to the team that wins four out of seven games.
② The Japan Series is a best-of-seven championship.

…じょう【…条】　① an article　② a section ［⇨第1部・48. 法律・条約］
- 第 24 条 1 項 1 号　Article 24, paragraph (1), item (i)
- 第 15 条において規定されている　be「provided ［stipulated］under Article 15
- 第 15 条によって課される　be「charged ［imposed］under Article 15

…じょう【…乗】　［⇨第1部・54-5 累乗］
- 10 の 2 乗 (10^2)　10 squared
- 10 の 3 乗 (10^3)　10 cubed
- 10 の 4 乗 (10^4)　① 10 (raised) to the power (of) four　② 10 (raised) to the fourth　③ 10 (raised) to the fourth power　④ the fourth power of 10

…じょう【…畳】　［⇨第1部・46-3 住居］
- 10 畳の間　a ten-mat (tatami) room

じょうい【上位】　［⇨第1部・15-2-1 順位一般，16-1 票数］
- 上位にランクされる　① be highly ranked　② be ranked high

しょうけい【小計】　a subtotal ［⇨第1部・24-2 小計］

しょうげん【象限】　a quadrant
- その点は第一象限にある．　The point lies in the first quadrant.

じょうげん【上限】　① the upper limit　② the maximum　③ a cap　④ a ceiling　⑤〚数〛the supremum　⑥ the least upper bound
- 貸金業者の利息の**上限**　**the upper limit** on interest rates charged by money-lenders
- 運動量の不確定性に対する**上限**（値）　**an upper limit**「on ［for］the uncertainty of the momentum
- この定数に対する実験的な**上限**　the experimental **upper limit** for this constant

...じょうこん

- この定数に対する最良の**上限** the best **upper limit** for this constant
- **上限（金）額** **the maximum amount** (**of money**)
- 老人医療費負担額の**上限** **the maximum** charge for medical treatment of the elderly
- 大学間で互換できる単位数の**上限** **the maximum** allowable number of credits exchangeable between universities
- 150万円が**上限**になっている． **The upper limit** is set at ¥1.5 million.
- 残業時間の**上限**を設定する set **a maximum** number of hours of overtime
- 免税額の**上限**を引き上げる raise **the limit** on tax exemptions
- 放射性炭素年代測定の結果は従来考えられていた**年代の上限**より1000年さかのぼるものだった．
  ① Radiocarbon dating yielded a date 1000 years earlier than the previously considered **earliest limit of the date**.
  ② The result of radiocarbon dating predated the previously considered **earliest date** by 1000 years.

…じょうこん【…乗根】 ［⇨第1部・54-6 累乗根］

- x の n 乗根 the nth root of x

じょうざん【乗算】 multiplication ［⇨第1部・54-3 かけ算］

しょうじ【正時】 《on》 the hour (sharp)

- 正時の時報 a time signal on the hour
- 毎正時に every hour on the hour

しょうじゅん【昇順】 ascending order

- 単語［数字］を昇順に並べる arrange「words［figures］in ascending order
- 昇順になっている be in ascending order

じょうじゅん【上旬】 ① early 《June》 ② the first ten days 《of June》 ③ the first third 《of June》 ［⇨第1部・33-2「初頭」「末」「旬」］

じょうしょう【上昇】

1 ［物理的な高さの］① a rise ② a climb ③ an ascent ④ ascension

- 海面の上昇 a rise in (the) sea level

2 ［値などの］① a rise ② a climb ③ an increase ④ an ascent ⑤ an upswing ⑥ an upturn ［⇨第1部・13-4 増加・上昇を表わす各種表現，13-2-2 増減の程度］

- 上昇する ① rise ② climb ③ ascend ④ go up
- 血圧の上昇 a rise in (*one's*) blood pressure
- 物価の上昇 ① a rise［an increase］in prices ② a price「rise［increase］ ③ rising prices

- 温度の上昇　① (an) increase「in〔of〕temperature　② a rise in temperature　③ (a) temperature increase
- 上昇率　① a rate of increase　② an increasing rate

しょうすう【小数】　① a decimal fraction　② a decimal［⇨第 1 部・52. 小数］

しょうすう【少数】　① a small number　② a few［⇨第 1 部・19-3 少数］

じょうすう【乗数】　a multiplier
- 負荷に対する乗数　a multiplier for the load
- 被乗数　a multiplicand

しょうてん【焦点】

1〔光学の〕① a focus　② a focal point　★focus の複数形は foci, focuses.
- レンズ［カメラ］の焦点　the focus of a「lens［camera］
- 焦点が合っている　be in focus
- 焦点が合っていない　be out of focus
- この写真は背景に**焦点が合って**しまって被写体がぼやけている．　In this photograph, the background is **in focus**, while the subject is blurred.
- **焦点を合わせる**　① **focus**《a telescope on an object》　② **adjust the focus**《of a lens》
- 彼の顔にカメラの**焦点を合わせる**　**focus** a camera **on** his face
- …に焦点を合わせる　bring … into focus
- 焦点に集まる　converge into a focus
- 焦点距離　① a focal distance　② a focal length
- 焦点深度　① the depth of a focus　② a focal depth
- 焦点面　a focal plane

2〔二次曲線の〕a focus
- 楕円上の任意の点から 2 つの**焦点**までの距離の和は一定である．　The sum of the distances from any point on an ellipse to the two **foci** is a constant.
- 放物線の軸に平行に入射した光線は反射されて**焦点**と呼ばれる 1 点に集まる．　Incident rays parallel to the axis of a parabola are reflected and gather at one point called **a focus**.

しょうど【照度】　illuminance　★単位はルクス（lux）＝ルーメン毎平方メートル（lumen per square meter）［⇨第 1 部・27. 単位］

しょうなり【小なり】
- A 小なり B．　A is less than B．　★$A<B$ のこと．
- A 小なりイコール B．　A is less than or equal to B．　★$A \leq B$ のこと．
- 小なり記号　a less-than symbol

しょうひきげん【消費期限】 ① a use-by date ② an expiration date ③ an expiry date ［⇨第1部・35-4 賞味期限・消費期限］

しょうべき【昇冪】 ascending powers
- x の昇冪の順で　in ascending powers of x

じょうほう【乗法】 multiplication ［⇨第1部・54-3 かけ算］

じょうほうしゅうせい【上方修正】 ① (an) upward revision ② (an) upward adjustment ③ (a) revision upward(s)
- 上方修正する　① revise upward(s) ② adjust upward(s) ③ make an upward revision ④ make an upward adjustment
- 収益予測を上方修正する　① make an upward revision of an earnings forecast ② revise an earnings forecast upward

しょうみ【正味】
- 正味の　① net ② clear
- 正味の重量　① (a) net weight ② (a) weight net
- 正味の数量　① (a) net quantity ② (a) quantity net
- 正味100グラム入り．〔ラベルなどの文句〕100 grams net.
- 正味売上高　① net sales ② net proceeds
- 正味8時間働く　work for eight full hours
- 正味1万円もうける　① clear ¥10,000 ② net ¥10,000 ③ get ¥10,000 net

しょうみきげん【賞味期限】 ① a "best before" date ② a "best if used by" date ③ a date of minimum durability ④《俗に》an expiry date ⑤ an expiration date ［⇨第1部・35-4 賞味期限・消費期限］

じょうよ【剰余】

1 〔余分〕① (a) surplus ② an overplus ③ a remainder

2 〔除算の余り〕① a remainder ② a residue ［⇨第1部・54-4-3 余り］

しょうりつ【勝率】 ① a percentage of wins ② a winning percentage《略 WPCT》③ the percentage of wins to the total number of「matches［games］

しょうりょう【少量】 ① a small amount ② a little ［⇨第1部・19-4 少量］

しょうわ【昭和】 ⇨第1部・29-5 元号

しょきち【初期値】 an initial value
- ウインドーサイズの**初期値を**デフォルト値に**セットする**　**set the initial** size of the window to the default value

しょこう【初項】 the first term《of a sequence》

じょさん【除算】 division ［⇨第1部・54-4 割り算］

じょすう【序数】 an ordinal number ［⇨第 1 部・4. 序数］

じょほう【除法】 division ［⇨第 1 部・54-4 割り算］

しりょく【視力】 ① sight ② eyesight ③ vision ④ visual power ⑤ visual acuity

- 私の視力は(両目とも) 1.0 [0.5] です.
 ① My eyesight (in both eyes) is「1.0 [0.5]」.
 ② I have a visual acuity of「1.0 [0.5]」(in both eyes).
 ③ I have「20/20 [20/40]」vision in both eyes. ★20/20, 20/40 はそれぞれ twenty-twenty, twenty-forty とも表記する.

- その仕事につくには裸眼で視力 0.1 以上が条件だ.
 ① To get that job you must have eyesight of at least 0.1 without glasses.
 ② A condition of that job is having at least 0.1 vision without glasses.

★ 1.0, 2.0 などの日本の視力表示は見分けることのできる最小の視角の逆数を使っている(見るものの大きさは角度で表わすが,小さな視角は実際の長さに比例し,距離に反比例する). 視力検査で使う輪のことはランドルト環 (Landolt ring, Landolt C) といい,この間隙の長さの視角が 1 分 (1°の 1/60) のときの視力が 1.0 である.

一方,アメリカでは標準視力を 20/20, その半分の視力を 20/40 などと表示する. これは, 被験者が 20 フィートの距離から見えるものを標準視力の人なら何フィートの距離から見えるかを表わしている. 分子は常に 20 で, 分母が大きいほど視力が悪いことになる. この「分数」は Snellen fraction という. アメリカの視力検査では E, C, F, P などと文字がさまざまな大きさで示された表 (Snellen chart という) を使う.

スネレンの定義した標準視力は 5 分角を見分けることのできる視力であり, スネレン視力表の文字の大きさは線の太さの 5 倍になっているので, 標準視力 20/20 はほぼ日本でいう 1.0 の視力に対応する.

- 視力検査 ① an eyesight test ② optometry
- 視力検査医 an optometrist
- 視力 (検査) 表 ① an eyesight test chart ② an eye chart
- 視力を検査する test 《a person's》 eyesight
- 普通の視力がある have normal「vision [eyesight]」
- 視力が衰え [落ち] 始めている. My eyesight has begun to fail (me).
- 視力減退 weakening of *one's* eyesight
- 視力が弱い ① have「bad [weak, poor]」eyesight ② be weak-sighted
- 視力の弱い人 ① a weak-sighted person ② a person with poor eyesight
- 視力を失う ① lose *one's* eyesight ② lose the use of *one's* eyes
- 視力を回復する ①〔失明した人が見えるようになる〕recover *one's* sight
 ②〔低下した視力がよくなる〕*one's* eyesight「recovers [gets better again]」

シリング a shilling ［⇨第 1 部・39-1-4 ポンド］

じんこう【人口】 ① a population ② the number of inhabitants

- その町の人口は5万人だ．
  ① The town has a population of 50,000.
  ② The residents of the town number 50,000.
  ③ Fifty thousand people live in the town.
- 東京の人口は1,000万以上である．
  ① The population of Tokyo is more than ten million.
  ② Tokyo has a population of over ten million.
- 市の人口は100万人に達した． The population of the city reached a million.
- 人口が多い［少ない］ have a「large［small］population
- 人口が最大の州 ① the state with the largest population ② the largest state「in［by］population
- 人口が増加する increase［grow, gain］in population
- この町は人口が増えた． The population of this town has grown.
- 人口がどんどん増えている． The population is steadily rising.
- 人口が減る［減少する］ decrease［diminish, decline］in population
- その町は人口がどんどん減っている． The population of the town is decreasing rapidly.
- 戦争と飢饉で国の人口が半減した． War and famine halved the country's population.
- その時点までには人口の2割以上が65歳以上になるだろう． By that time, more than twenty percent of the population will be 65 or older.
- 人口が密集している地域 a「densely populated［crowded］district
- インターネット人口 ① the Internet population 《of Japan》 ② the number of 《female》 Internet users
- 十八歳人口 ① the 18-year-old population ② the population of 18-year-olds

じんこうみつど【人口密度】 population density
- 人口密度が高い［低い］ ① be「densely［sparsely］populated ② be「thickly［thinly］peopled
- その地方の人口密度は1平方キロにつき100人である． The density of population in the region is 100「people［inhabitants］per［to a］square kilometer.

しんちょう【身長】 ① height ②《文》stature ③《競泳》a length［⇨第1部・43-1 身長］

しんど【震度】 seismic intensity［⇨第1部・45-6 震度とマグニチュード］

しんどうすう【振動数】 (a) frequency［⇨しゅうはすう］

しんぶんすう【真分数】 a proper fraction［⇨第1部・53. 分数］

すい【錐】 ①〔角錐〕a pyramid ②〔円錐〕a cone

すいせん【垂線】 a perpendicular (line)

- 垂線の足　the foot of a perpendicular
- PからABに下ろした[引いた]**垂線**の長さ　the length of **the perpendicular** from P to AB
- 垂線を引く　draw a perpendicular
- 三角形の3つの**頂点から各対辺に引いた垂線**が交わる点をその三角形の垂心という．The point where the three **altitudes** of a triangle meet is called the orthocenter of the triangle.　★「頂点から対辺に引いた垂線」を英語では altitude（高さ）という．

すいちょく【垂直】

- 垂直な　① perpendicular　② at right angles《to …》　③〔水平に対して〕vertical［⇨えんちょく］
- …**に垂直な線を引く**　① draw a line **perpendicular to**《a given line》　② draw a line **at right angles to**《a given line》
- **互いに垂直な** 2 方向　two **mutually perpendicular** directions
- 地球の自転軸が**公転面に対して垂直**でないために季節が生じる．Seasons occur because the axis of rotation of the earth is not **perpendicular to the**「**plane of revolution**［**ecliptic**］.
- 頂点 A を通って**対辺に垂直な線**　a line through vertex A **perpendicular to the opposite side**
- その壁は**床に垂直**ではなかった．The wall was not「**plumb**［**perpendicular**］**to the floor**.
- ディスク**に垂直な方向に動く**　move in a direction **perpendicular to** the disk
- 2 線が**垂直に交わる**．Two lines「**cross**［**meet**］**at right angles**.
- 菱形の対角線は互いに他を**垂直に二等分する**．The diagonals of a rhombus **perpendicularly bisect** each other.
- それら2つの格子点を結ぶ直線の垂直二等分面　① a perpendicular「bisector[bisecting] plane of the line between those two lattice points　② a perpendicular plane「at [through, passing through] the midpoint of the line between those two lattice points
- 垂直安定板　① a vertical stabilizer　② a (tail) fin
- 垂直運動　a vertical movement
- 垂直感染　〔妊婦から胎児への〕vertical「infection [transmission]
- 垂直距離　a vertical distance
- 垂直同期　vertical synchronization
- 垂直二等分線　a perpendicular bisector
- 垂直尾翼　① a (tail) fin　② a vertical「fin [tail]　③〔安定板〕a vertical stabilizer

すいてい【推定】　① (an) estimation　② (a) presumption　③ (an) inference

ずいはん

★数値の推定に使うのは estimation. presumption は何らかの根拠に基づいてそうみなすこと，inference は論理的な推論．presumption と似た語に assumption があるが，これはとりあえずそう想定すること．

- 推定する　① estimate　② presume　③ infer
- (損害などが) …と推定されている　be estimated at …
- 先ほどの地震はマグニチュード6.4と推定されます．　The earthquake a little while ago is estimated at magnitude 6.4.
- 推定500人の住人　an estimated 500 residents　★500 residents をひとまとまりと考えて an がついている．
- 約500人が国境を越えたと推定されている．　It is estimated that about 500 people crossed the border.
- 推定値　① an estimate　② an estimated value
- 誤差の推定値　① an error estimate　② an estimated error
- 推定位置　the estimated position 《of a boat》
- 推定患者［死亡者］数　the estimated number of「patients [casualties]」
- 推定小売価格　an estimated retail price [⇨第1部・40-2-4 価格にまつわる術語]
- 推定死亡時刻　the estimated time of death
- 推定年代　the estimated era 《of an object》
- 推定年俸　an estimated annual salary 《of ¥30 million》
- 推定量　an estimator
- 不偏推定量　an unbiased estimator
- 最尤推定値　a maximum likelihood estimate
- 推定無罪　presumption of innocence

ずいはん【随伴】 an adjoint
- 自己随伴行列《エルミート行列》　a self-adjoint matrix
- 随伴演算子［作用素］　an adjoint operator
- (ある) 演算子の随伴 (演算子)　the adjoint of an operator

すう【数】 a number [⇨かず]
- 負の数　① a negative number　② a minus number
- 学生数　① the number of students　② an enrol(l)ment 《of 1,000》
- 語数　① the number of words　② a word count
- 語数30の文　① a sentence of 30 words (in length)　② a 30-word sentence
- 有権者数と投票者数　the number registered and the actual number of voters
- 不景気で倒産件数が増えた．
  ① The number of bankruptcies「rose [went up]」on account of the recession.
  ② Bankruptcies increased in number due to the recession.

すうおく

- 砂糖のグラム数　the number of grams of sugar
- その電球のワット数　the wattage of the bulb
- 数平均　a number average
- 数密度　number density

すうおく【数億】　［⇨第1部・8-2「数十」など］
- 数億の　① several hundred million …　② a few hundred million …

すうし【数詞】　〚文法〛a numeral

すうじ【数字】　① a figure ② a numeral ③ a digit ④ a number ★numeral は概念としての数 (number) を書き表わしたものをいう．よって 3 や 125 も numeral であるし，ローマ数字も numeral である．文法用語の数詞を numeral というのも「数を書き表わしたもの」という原義から理解できる．digit は 125 のような数を表わす個々の数字 1, 2, 5 を指す．

- 有効数字　significant figures
- 3桁の数字　a three-digit figure
- 3で終わる数字　a number ending in 3
- 正確な数字　exact [precise] figures
- 不景気はこれらの数字に如実に現われている．　The recession is clearly reflected in these figures.
- 天文学的数字　astronomical figures
- その地震による死者は大変な数字になる見込みだ．　The number of dead from the earthquake is expected to「reach [mount up to] a huge figure.
- 数字の 8　①「the「number [numeral] 8　②〔8 の字形〕《shaped like》a figure (of)「8 [eight]
- 数字の上では　① numerically　② in figures　③ in terms of numbers
- 数字を示す［挙げる］　give [cite] figures
- 具体的な数字を掲げて政策目標とする　set out specific figures (to be achieved) as a policy target
- 適当な数字を並べて暗証番号とする　choose an arbitrary series of numbers as *one's* PIN
- 史上最悪の数字を記録する　record the worst figures in history
- アラビア数字　an Arabic「numeral [number]
- ローマ数字　a Roman「numeral [number]　［⇨第1部・3. ローマ数字］
- 2桁の数は科学技術文献ではしばしば数字で書かれるが，それ以外では通例スペルアウトされる．　While two-digit numbers are often written in「numerals [figures] in scientific and technical writing, in other contexts they are usually spelled out.

すうしき【数式】　① a mathematical expression ② a numerical expression ③ a numerical formula［⇨第1部・55. 式の読み方, 56. 式の書き方, 57. 式変形の英語］

すうじゅう【数十】［⇨第1部・8-2「数十」など］
- 数十の　① several tens of …　② a few tens of …　③ several dozen …　④ a few dozen …

すうせん【数千】［⇨第1部・8-2「数十」など］
- 数千の　① several thousand …　② a few thousand …

すうち【数値】　a numerical value
- ハッブル定数の数値としての値　the numerical value of the Hubble constant
- 入力行を数値としてソートする　sort the input lines numerically
- 光マイクロ秒の単位で表わした電気的な距離は，マイクロ秒で表わした伝送時間と数値的に等しい．Electrical distance in light microseconds is numerically equal to transmission time in microseconds.
- 数値で表わす　① express numerically　②〔評価する〕evaluate
- 数値を示す　① show data　② show statistics
- 数値計算　①(a) numerical「calculation［computation］　②〔物理現象などの〕＝数値実験
- 数値データ　numeric(al) data
- 数値目標を設定する　set a numerical target
- 数値制御　numerical control《略 NC》
- 数値制御工作機械　a numerically controlled［an NC, a computer-controlled］machine tool
- 数値制御旋盤　a numerically controlled［an NC, a computer-controlled］lathe
- 数値制御ロボット　a numerically controlled［an NC, a computer-controlled］robot
- 数値解　a numerical solution
- 数値解析　(a) numerical analysis
- 数値実験　(a) numerical simulation
- 数値積分　numerical integration
- 数値予報　〔気象の〕numerical weather prediction
- 数値流体力学　① numerical hydrodynamics　② numerical fluid dynamics
- 微分方程式を数値的に積分する　integrate a differential equation numerically

すうちょくせん【数直線】　a number line

すうひゃく【数百】［⇨第1部・8-2「数十」など］
- 数百の　① several hundred …　② a few hundred …

すうまん【数万】 ［⇨第1部・8-2「数十」など］
- 数万の ① several tens of thousands of … ② a few tens of thousands of …

すうれつ【数列】 ① a sequence ②〔規則的に進行する〕a progression
- 次の漸化式で指定される数列　the sequence specified by the following recurrence relation［⇨ぜんかしき］
- その数列の一般項を求めよ．　Find the general term of the sequence.
- n が大きくなったときその**数列**は収束する．　As n increases, the **sequence** converges.
- n が大きくなったときその**数列**は発散する．　As n increases, the **sequence** diverges.
- n が大きくなったときその**数列**は2つの値の間を振動する．　As n increases, the **sequence** oscillates between two values.
- **等差数列**　an arithmetic progression
- **等比数列**　a geometric progression
- 等比数列をなす　form a geometric progression
- **無限数列**　an infinite sequence

すうろん【数論】 ① number theory ② the theory of numbers
- 数論学者　a number theorist
- 数論的な　number theoretical

スカラー　a scalar
- 結果はスカラーになる．　The result is a scalar.
- 2つのスカラーの積　the product of two scalars
- …にスカラーを乗じる　multiply … by a scalar
- **スカラー積**　a scalar product
- **スカラー倍**　①〔演算〕scalar multiplication ②〔結果〕a scalar multiple《of a vector》
- **スカラー量**　a scalar quantity
- エネルギーは**スカラー**量である，すなわち方向によらない．　Energy is **a scalar quantity**, that is, it is independent of direction.

…すぎる【…過ぎる】 ① over- ② too … ③ … to excess ④ … to a fault ⑤ overly …［⇨第1部・21. 過不足の表現］
- それでは2人多すぎだ．　That's two people too many.
- 3センチ長すぎる　be three centimeters too long
- 20分早く来すぎる　come twenty minutes too early

すくない【少ない】 ① (a) few ② (a) little［⇨第1部・19. 多少の表現］

すくなくとも【少なくとも】 ① at least ② at the least ③ at the lowest ④〔控え

めに言って〕to say the least (of it)
- 開票に少なくとも 3 時間はかかる．　Ballot [Vote] counting will take at least three hours.
- 少なくとも 10,000 円はするだろう．
  ① It will cost at least ¥10,000.
  ② It will cost ¥10,000 at the (very) least. ★② は「どんなに少なく見積もっても」という強調のニュアンスがある．
- 彼女の年収は少なくとも 1000 万円は下らないはずだ．　Her annual income can't be any less than ¥10 million.

スコア　a score [⇨てん, 第 1 部・49. 野球の数字表現 49-4]
- 5 対 3 のスコアで試合に勝つ　win a game by a score of 5 to 3

スチルブ　〔輝度の CGS 単位〕a stilb 《記号 sb》

…ずつ
- 1 つずつ　① one by one　② one at a time
- 2 人ずつ　① two by two　② two at a time　③ by twos
- 3 人に 1 つずつ　one to every three persons
- 1 人 1,000 円ずつ寄付する　① contribute ¥1,000 per person　② contribute ¥1,000 each
- 1 日 3 回, 1 回に 3 錠ずつ飲む　take three pills [each time [together, all at once] three times a day
- 1 キロずつ袋に入れる　pack one kilogram in each bag
- 半額ずつ納入する　pay in two equal installments
- 階段を 2 段ずつ昇る　climb [go up] the stairs two at a time
- 札を 10 枚ずつ数える　count out bills in groups of ten
- 2, 3 人ずつ来た．　They came by twos and threes.
- 少しずつ　① little by little　② bit by bit　③ inch by inch　④ by [in] dribbles [driblets]　⑤ piecemeal　⑥〔薬など〕in small doses　⑦〔徐々に〕gradually　⑧ by degrees

ステラジアン　〔立体角の単位〕a steradian 《略 sr》
- 球面全体は 4π **ステラジアン**に相当する．　The entire sphere corresponds to 4π **steradians**.

ストークス〔動粘性率の CGS 単位〕a stokes 《記号 St》

ストップだか【ストップ高】　⇨第 1 部・39-3 株 39-3-4

ストップやす【ストップ安】　⇨第 1 部・39-3 株 39-3-4

スリー　three
- スリーアウト　three outs [⇨第 1 部・49. 野球の数字表現 49-8]

- スリーカード　《トランプ》three of a kind
- スリーサイズ　⇨第1部・43. 身体計測 43-6
- スリーバント　① a bunt on the third strike ② a bunt with two strikes ③ a two-strike bunt ［⇨第1部・49. 野球の数字表現 49-7］
- スリーピース　a three-piece (suit)
- スリーベース（ヒット）　①《hit》a triple ② a three-base hit ［⇨第1部・49. 野球の数字表現 49-11］

すんぽう【寸法】　①〔長さ〕length ②〔大きさ〕measure ③ measurements ④ dimensions ⑤ size ［⇨第1部・42. 大きさ・重さ］

せい【正】
- 正の　① positive ② plus
- 正の数　a positive number
- 正電荷　(a) positive charge
- 正になる　become positive
- 2階微分が**正**であればグラフは下に凸である．　If the second derivative is **positive**, the graph is「convex downward(s)［concave upward(s)］.
- この関数は常に**正**である．　This function is always **positive**.
- ベクトル *B* は *z* 軸の正方向を向いている．
  ① The vector *B* points in **the positive *z* direction**.
  ② The vector *B* points in **the direction of the positive *z*-axis**.
  ③ The vector *B* points in **the positive direction of the *z*-axis**.

ぜい【税】　① a tax ②〔物品税〕a duty
- たばこの値段には税金が 60 パーセントほど含まれている．
  ① The price of cigarettes includes「about 60% tax［a tax of about 60%］.
  ② About sixty percent of the price of a packet of cigarettes is tax.
- 毎月の給料から 3 万円ほど税金に差し引かれる．
  ① Every month about ¥30,000 is deducted from my pay for tax.
  ② There is a tax deduction of ¥30,000 or so from my monthly pay.
- 税込みの［で］　①〔税引き前〕before tax ② before「deduction［payment］of tax ③ pretax ④〔税加算後〕⇨税込み価格
- 税引きの［で］　① after tax ② after「deduction［payment］of tax
- 税込み給与　① pretax pay ② *one's* pretax「salary［wages］③ pay［a salary, wages］before (deduction of) tax
- 税引き［手取り］給与　① take-home pay ② pay after (deduction of) tax
- 税込み 40 万円の月給　① pretax monthly pay of ¥400,000 ② a salary of ¥400,000 before (deduction of) tax
- 税引き前利益　① profit before tax ② pretax profit
- 税引き後利益　① profit after tax ② after-tax profit

- 税引き後利回り　a net yield
- 税込み価格〔内税価格〕　① the posttax price　② the price「after [including] tax」③ a tax-inclusive price　④ a price that includes tax
- 税抜き価格〔外税価格〕　① a tax-exclusive price　② a price that does not include tax
- 内税方式　(the system of) tax-inclusive pricing
- 外税方式　(the system of) tax-exclusive pricing
- これらの商品は内税です．
  ① The (posted) prices of these goods include tax.
  ② Tax is included in the price of these goods.
- これらの商品は外税です．
  ① The (posted) prices of these goods do not include tax.
  ② Tax is not included in the price of these goods.
- 節税　① reducing *one's* taxes　② (a) tax saving　③《米》tax avoidance
- 脱税　① tax evasion　② tax dodging　③ (a) tax fraud　④ evasion of taxes　⑤ cheating on *one's* taxes
- 税率　① the rate of taxation　② tax rates　③〔関税の〕a tariff
- 消費税率の引き上げ　① an increase in consumption tax rates　② increasing [putting up, raising] consumption tax rates　③ a consumption tax「increase [rise, hike]」

せいき【世紀】　a century〔⇨第 1 部・29-7 世紀〕

- 21 世紀　① the twenty-first century　② the 21st century
- 20 世紀に　① in the twentieth century　② in the 20th century
- 今世紀　① this century　② the present century
- 前世紀　the last century
- 19 世紀の中ごろに　① in the middle of the nineteenth century　② in the mid-nineteenth century
- 20 世紀の最初の四半期に　in the first quarter of the twentieth century
- 18 世紀の後半に　in the second half of the eighteenth century
- それは2世紀の間忘れられていた．　It was forgotten for two centuries.　★「世紀」を絶対的な時代ではなく「100 年間」という時間の単位として使っている例．

せいき【正規】

- 正規曲線　① a normal curve　② a Gaussian curve
- 正規分布　① a normal distribution　② a Gaussian distribution
- その変数は正規分布にしたがう．
  ① The variable「has [follows]」a normal distribution.
  ② The variable is normally distributed.

- 正規分布曲線　a normal distribution curve

せいきちょっこう【正規直交】　orthonormality
- 正規直交関数　an orthonormal function
- 正規直交基底　an orthonormal basis
- 正規直交系　an orthonormal system

せいけい【西経】　(the) west longitude ［⇨けいど］

せいげん【正弦】　a sine
- 正弦関数　a sine function
- 正弦曲線　a sine curve
- 正弦定理［法則］　the law of sines
- 正弦波　① a sine wave ② a sinusoidal wave
- 正弦波電流　a sinusoidal current

ぜいこみ【税込み】　⇨ぜい

ぜいしゅう【税収】　① tax revenue(s) ② (a) tax yield ③ (the) revenue from taxation
- 2007年度の税収　fiscal 2007 tax revenues
- 40兆円の税収　tax revenues of ¥40 trillion
- それは1兆円の税収をもたらすだろう．　It will bring ¥1 trillion in tax revenues.
- 税収見積もり　estimated tax revenue(s)
- 税収の落ち込み　a「decrease [drop, plunge] of tax revenues
- 税収不足を穴埋めする　cover up the tax revenue shortfall

せいじょ【整除】　exact divisibility ［⇨第1部・54-4 割り算 54-4-4］
- 整除する　① divide evenly ② divide exactly
- p は x, y, z のいずれも整除しない．
  ① p exactly divides none of x, y, or z.
  ② Neither x nor y nor z can be divided by p exactly.
  ③ Neither x nor y nor z is divisible by p.
- 整除できる　be (evenly [exactly]) divisible 《by …》

せいすう【整数】　① an integer ② a whole number ③ an integral number
- 正の整数　a positive integer
- 負の整数　a negative integer
- 負でない整数　a nonnegative integer ★正の整数および0
- 0でない整数　a nonzero integer
- 5桁の整数　a 5-digit integer

せいすう

- 符号つき［なし］整数　〘電算〙a signed [an unsigned] integer
- 連続する整数　consecutive integers
- 3 で割り切れる整数　an integer divisible by 3
- n を整除する正の整数　a positive integer that divides n
- x を超えない最大の整数　the greatest integer not exceeding x
- 512 より小さな整数値　an integer value「less [smaller] than 512
- 半整数　a half-integer [⇨はんせいすう]
- あらゆる整数に対して　for all integers
- …となるような整数 n が存在する．　There exists an integer n such that ….
- R を複素数 $a+bi$ のなす環とする．ここで，a, b は**整数**である．　Let R be the ring of complex numbers $a+bi$, where a and b are **integers**.
- 原子質量単位で表わした同位体の質量は非常に**整数に近い**．　The masses of isotopes expressed in atomic mass units are very **nearly whole numbers**.
- 磁気量子数は $-l$ から l までの**任意の整数値**を取ることができる．　The magnetic quantum number can **assume any integer value** from $-l$ to l.
- **整数解**　① an integer solution　② a whole number solution
- その方程式は自明でない**整数解**をもたない．
  ① The equation has no nontrivial「**integer [whole number] solutions**.
  ② The equation has no nontrivial solutions **in integers**.
- **整数係数**　① an integer coefficient　② an integral coefficient
- 整数係数の多項式　a polynomial with integer coefficients
- 整数係数の代数方程式　an algebraic equation with integer coefficients
- **整数変数**　an integer variable
- **非整数次元**　noninteger dimension
- 経帯時は，一般にグリニッジ標準時とは**整数時間**だけずれている．　Zone times generally differ by **a whole number of hours** from GMT.
- ハドロンは**整数電荷**をもつ．　Hadrons have **integral electric charge**.
- **整数倍**　① an integral multiple 《of …》　② an integer multiple 《of …》　③ a whole number multiple 《of …》
- 基本振動数の**整数倍**の振動数　a frequency that is「**a whole number [an integer, an integral] multiple** of the fundamental frequency
- 波長の**整数倍**　① **an integral number of** wavelengths　② **a whole number of** wavelengths
- 電子の角運動量は $\hbar$ 単位の**整数倍**に量子化されている．　The angular momentum of the electron is quantized to be「**an integral number [a whole number] of units** of $\hbar$. ★$\hbar$ は h-bar と読む．
- **整数比**　① an integer ratio　② an integral ratio
- 軌道の共鳴は 2 つの天体の公転周期が**簡単な整数比**のときに起こる．　Or-

bital resonance occurs when two bodies have periods of revolution that are「**in a simple integer ratio [in a ratio of small whole numbers**].

- **整数分の一**　　an integral submultiple《of …》

▶ **数の集合**

　自然数　 a natural number《1, 2, 3, ...》

　整数　① an integer　② a whole number《−2, −1, 0, 1, 2, ...》

　有理数　 a rational number《分数で表わせる数；整数・有限小数・循環小数》

　無理数　 an irrational number《有理数でない実数》

　代数的数　 an algebraic number《有理数係数の多項式の根になる数；$\sqrt{2}$ など》

　超越数　 a transcendental number《代数的数でない実数；π など》

　実数　 a real number《有理数＋無理数》

　虚数　 an imaginary number《虚数単位 $i = \sqrt{-1}$ を含む数》

　複素数　 a complex number《実数と虚数単位で表わせる数》

★英語の whole number は「整数」「0 または正の整数」「自然数（正の整数）」を指すことがある．

せいせつ【正接】　 a tangent

せいそく【正則】

- 正則な　 regular
- 正則行列　① a regular matrix　② a nonsingular matrix　③ an invertible matrix
- 正則関数　 a regular function

せいていち【正定値】

- 正定値の　 positive-definite

せいど【精度】　① accuracy　② precision　★正しい値に近いことが accuracy，細かい桁まで求まることが precision．

- その測定の精度　 the accuracy of the measurement
- 精度を維持する　 maintain accuracy
- 目標は 90 パーセントの精度だ．　 The goal is 90 percent accuracy.
- 精度は 60 パーセントに落ちた．　 The accuracy dropped to 60 percent.
- 90 パーセントの精度で人間の発話を理解する　 understand human speech with 90 percent accuracy
- ピンポイントの高精度を必要とする　 require pinpoint precision
- 値を倍精度で計算する　 calculate a value in double precision

ぜいぬき【税抜き】　⇨ぜい

ぜいびき【税引き】　⇨ぜい

せいひれい【正比例】　direct proportion
- …に正比例する　be in direct proportion to …

せいほうけい【正方形】　a square
- 1 辺が 2 センチの正方形　① a square with 2 cm sides　② a square with a side length of 2 cm　③ a square 2 cm on a side　④ a square with sides 2 cm「long [in length]
- **正方形**は 4 つの辺が等しく，4 つの角が直角である四角形である．**A square is a quadrilateral with four equal sides and four right angles.**

せいまいぶあい【精米歩合】　① head rice yield　② rice milling yield
- 大吟醸酒は精米歩合 50% 以下の最高品質の酒だ．*Daiginjo* is top-quality sake brewed from rice grains milled to 50 percent of weight or less.

せいれき【西暦】　① the Christian Era　② Anno Domini《略 A.D.》　③〔グレゴリオ暦〕the Gregorian calendar ［⇨第 1 部・29. 年・年度・元号・世紀 29-3］
- 西暦 2000 年に　① in 2000　② in the year 2000

セカント〔正割〕a secant
- セカント x　the secant of x　★ sec x と書く．

せき【積】　a product ［⇨第 1 部・54-3 かけ算 54-3-2］
- x と y の積　the product of x and y

せきい【赤緯】　declination
★天文学の赤道座標（equatorial coordinates）の一つ．赤道からの角度を 23° 25′ のように表わして twenty-three degrees twenty-five minutes と読む．南側は負の値で表わす．［⇨せっけい］

せきさん【積算】　addition
- 積算する　add up
- 積算距離　(an) accumulated distance
- 積算距離計　〔車の走行距離計〕an odometer
- 積算電力計　① a watt-hour meter　②〔家庭の電気メーター〕an electricity meter
- 積算線量計　an integrating dosimeter
- 積算発電量　cumulative electricity「production [generation]
- 積算（被曝）線量　① a cumulative [an accumulated] radiation dose　② a cumulative [an accumulated] dose of radiation
- 年間積算線量　① an annual「cumulative [accumulated] radiation dose　② a [the] cumulative [accumulated] dose of radiation for「a [the] year

せきぶん【積分】　① integration　②〔積分したもの・式〕an integral　③〔分野〕integral calculus

せきぶん

- 積分する　integrate
- 積分を実行する　① carry out [perform] (an) integration ② integrate
- 被積分関数　an integrand
- 積分記号　① the sign of integration ② the integral sign《記号∫》
- 未知関数が積分記号の中に現われる方程式　an equation where the unknown function occurs under an integral sign
- 積分定数　a constant of integration
- 時間に関する積分　integration「over [with respect to] time
- ラグランジアンの時間(に関する)積分　① the time integral of the Lagrangian ② the integral of the Lagrangian with respect to time
- 積分変数を変換する　change the variable of integration
- 積分はこの2つの変数に関して行なわれるものとする．　The integration is to be performed over these two variables.
- 0からx[無限大]までのtに関する$\exp(-t^2)$の積分　the integral from 0 to「x [infinity] of $\exp(-t^2)$ with respect to t
- 全空間にわたってとった積分　the integral taken over all space
- 面上での積分　the integral over a surface
- (線)積分は，反時計方向にとる．　The integral is taken in the counterclockwise direction.
- エネルギーは力を経路に沿って積分したものに等しい．　The energy is equal to the integral of the force along the path.
- 力を，それが作用する期間にわたって時間積分したもの　the time integral of the force over the period during which it operates
- その積分を評価するのは難しい．　The integral is difficult to evaluate.
- 球対称な場合には，積分は解析的に求めることができる．　In the spherical case, the integral can be found analytically.
- 時間積分　a time integral
- 空間積分　a space integral
- 運動量積分　a momentum integral
- 線積分　① a line integral ② a contour integral
- 面積分　a surface integral
- 体積積分　a volume integral
- 置換積分　integration by substitution
- 部分積分　integration by parts
- 数値積分　numerical integration
- 楕円積分　an elliptic integral
- リーマン積分　a Riemann integral

- リーマン積分可能な　Riemann integrable
- ルベーグ積分　a Lebesgue integral
- 積分強度　〖化〗〔スペクトルなどの〕an integrated intensity
- 積分線量　〖物〗an integrated dose
- 積分不等式　an integral inequality
- 積分方程式　an integral equation
- 積分変換　an integral transform
- 積分路　a path of integration
- 積分可能な　integrable
- 2乗可積分な　square-integrable
- 2乗可積分な関数　① a square-integrable function ② a function whose absolute value squared has a finite integral

せし【セ氏】　① Celsius《記号 C》② centigrade《記号 C》[⇨第1部・45-1 温度]
- セ氏30度　thirty degrees「Celsius [centigrade]《記号 30°C》

ゼタ…　[10^{21}] zetta- [⇨第1部・27-4 SI 接頭語]

せっけい【赤経】　right ascension [⇨せきい]
　★天文学の赤道座標 (equatorial coordinates) の一つ．赤道に沿った 360° を 24h で表わし，23h05m (23時5分) のように表わして twenty-three hours five minutes と読む．1時 = 15° = 60分なので，赤経の1分は角度でいうと 15分 (1/4°) になる．赤緯の「分」は普通の角度の 1分 (1/60°) なので′の記号を使うが，赤経の分には記号 m が使われる．

せっし【摂氏】　⇨せし

せっせん【接線】　① a tangent (line) ② a tangential line
- (円上の) 点Pにおけるその円の接線　the tangent to the circle at P
- (円外の) 点Pからその円に引いた接線の長さ　the length of the tangent from P to the circle
- 接線応力　tangential stress
- 接線方向　the tangential direction
- 接線速度　tangential velocity
- 接線加速度　tangential acceleration

ぜったいち【絶対値】　① an absolute value ② a modulus　★modulus の複数形は moduli．
- x の絶対値　the absolute value of x　★$|x|$ と書く．
- 複素数の絶対値　the modulus of a complex number
- 電子の電荷の絶対値　the absolute value of the charge on an electron

- 電圧の絶対値　① the absolute value of the voltage　② the absolute voltage value　③ the absolute voltage
- 絶対値が1の定数　a constant of absolute value one
- 絶対値が1の複素数　a complex number of unit「magnitude [modulus]」
- 絶対値が1より大きい数　① a number whose absolute value is greater than one　② a number「of [with an] absolute value「greater [larger] than one　③ a number greater than one in absolute value
- 公比の絶対値が1より大きい幾何級数　① a geometric series the absolute value of whose common ratio is greater than one　② a geometric series with a common ratio greater than one in absolute value
- …の絶対値をとる　take the absolute value of …
- 絶対値(をとる)関数　the modulus function

ぜったいれいど【絶対零度】　absolute zero
- 絶対零度における完全結晶固体を考える　consider perfect crystalline solids at absolute zero
- 絶対零度よりかなり高い臨界温度　critical temperatures well above absolute zero
- これは絶対零度よりたった7度上で起こる．　This occurs only 7 degrees above absolute zero.
- 絶対零度には到達できないということ　the unattainability of absolute zero

せってん【接点】　① a point of contact　② a point of tangency
- その円と辺 AB の接点　the point of contact of the circle with the side AB

せつへいめん【接平面】　a tangent(ial) plane

せっぺん【切片】　an intercept
- y 切片　① the y-intercept　② the intercept on the y-axis
- 傾きが m で **y 切片が c** の直線　the line with「slope [gradient] m and **intercept c on the y-axis**

せばんごう【背番号】　① a player's number　② a uniform number [⇨第1部・49. 野球の数字表現 49-17]

ゼプト…　[10^{-21}] zepto- [⇨第1部・27-4 SI 接頭語]

セルシウスど【セルシウス度】　⇨せ

ゼロ　① zero　② nought　③ naught　④ nothing　⑤ nil [⇨れい, いち]
- ▶数字を読み上げるときには oh ともいう．競技の点数の場合は nothing (テニスでは love) という．
- ▶00は double zero, double oh と読むこともある．1900などは nineteen hundred のように読むこともある．
- ▶数詞形容詞として使うときは，後続の名詞は zero grams など複数形が普通．

ゼロ

- 10^{19} は 1 のあとに 0 が 19 個続く数だ．　The number 10^{19} is 1 followed by 19 zeros.
- 0 と 1 の数列　a sequence of zeros and ones　★数字としての 0 は可算名詞．
- **全部 0 の符号語**　① an **all-zero** codeword　② a codeword **consisting of zeros**
- 0 に何をかけても 0 だ．　Zero multiplied by any number is zero.
- 非対角成分は 0 だ．　The off-diagonal elements are zeros.
- $f(x)$ の 1 階微分が **0 になる** x の値を求めよ．　Find the value of x for which the first derivative of $f(x)$「**equals 0**［**vanishes**］．
- 0 になることのない　① nonvanishing　② nowhere vanishing
- 秤の目盛りを 0 に合わせる　set the「scale(s)［balance］to zero
- その変数は 0 に初期化される．　The variable is initialized to 0.
- 正規表現 a*b は **0 個以上の** a に b が続いたものにマッチする．　The regular expression "a*b" matches **zero or more** "a"s followed by a single "b".
- 配列の要素は 0 から番号が付けられている．
  ① The elements in an array are numbered from zero.
  ② The elements in an array are numbered starting「from［with, at］zero.
  ③ The elements in an array are counted from zero.
- **ゼロオリジンの配列**　a zero-based array
- 添え字はゼロオリジン，すなわち最初の要素が添え字 0 になることに注意．　Note that indices are zero-based; that is, the first element has an index of zero.
- 最上行が第 0 行，左端の列が第 0 列である．　The top row is row 0 and the leftmost column is column 0.
- ゼロから出発する　start from「zero［nothing, scratch, the very beginning］
- 本番ではミスをゼロにしなければならない．
  ① There must be absolutely no mistakes in the actual performance.
  ② There must not be a single mistake in the actual performance.
- 僕の化学の知識はゼロに等しい．　I know「almost［practically, as good as］nothing about chemistry.
- その確率はほとんどゼロだ．　The probability is almost zero.
- 私の貯金は限りなくゼロに近い．
  ① My savings are as close as they can get to zero.
  ② I have「practically［essentially］nothing「in savings［saved］．
  ③ I have only infinitesimal savings.
- 0 次のモーメント　a zero-［zeroth-］order moment
- ゼロ・エミッション・カー［ビークル］〔無公害車〕a zero-emission vehicle 《略 ZEV》
- ゼロ回答　〔賃上げの〕a「reply［counteroffer］of a zero wage increase (from management)
- ゼロ期　〚医〛〔癌の初期，上皮内癌〕stage zero

- ゼロ金利政策　a zero-interest-rate policy
- ゼロクーポン債　a zero-coupon bond
- ゼロゲーム　〔無得点で負けること〕a love「game［set］
- ゼロ歳児　① a baby under 12 months of age　② baby in its first year
- ゼロ歳児の平均余命　the average life expectancy at birth［⇨第1部・25-8 平均寿命］
- ゼロサムゲーム　a zero-sum game
- ゼロ成長　zero growth
- 経済［人口］のゼロ成長　zero「economic［population］growth
- ゼロ年代　'00s ★このように書くことはできるが，英語では口頭でどう言うかについてのコンセンサスはない．［⇨第1部・29-6 …年代］
- ゼロ発信　〔電話で外線発信するための数字〕a zero prefix
- 外線はゼロ発信です．　You have to dial zero (first) for an outside line.
- ゼロベースの予算編成　zero-base(d) budgeting《略 ZBB》
- ゼロベースで見直す　① make a zero-based review《of …》② reexamine … from scratch　③ reexamine …, taking nothing for granted

せん【千】　a［one］thousand［⇨第1部・1. 基数］
- 3000　three thousand
- 2199　two thousand, one hundred, and ninety-nine
- 1600　① one thousand, six hundred　② sixteen hundred
- 何千という生徒　thousands of students［⇨第1部・8. 漠然とした大きな数］
- 1000 分の 1　① one one-thousandth　② one thousandth

関連表現
- 千里の道も一歩から．　A journey of a thousand miles starts with a single step.
- 恋する者には千里も一里．
  ① Love laughs at distance.
  ② People in love don't care how far they have to go to meet each other.
- 一騎当千のつわもの　① a match for a thousand　② an「unbeatable［invincible］warrior　③ a mighty「warrior［champion］
- 一攫千金　① making a fortune at one stroke　② getting rich quick　③ making a killing ★a killing は口語で「大もうけ」の意.
- 一日千秋の思いで待つ　wait impatiently《for …》
- 一日千秋の思いでした．　It was an eternity for me.

せん【銭】　a sen ★単複同形
- 102 円 95 銭　102.95 yen
- 金利は日歩 3 銭の割合だ．　The interest is (at the rate of)「three sen［0.03 yen］a［per］day.

せん【線】 a line [⇨ちょくせん]
- 幅［太さ］0.5 mm の線　a line 0.5 mm「wide［thick］
- 細い線　a thin line
- 太い線　a thick line
- 線で結ぶ　①connect《two points》with a line ②make［draw］a line between《two points》
- 線を引く　draw a line
- 実線　①a solid line ②a full line
- 破線　①a broken line ②a dashed line
- 点線　①a dotted line ②a broken line ③〔切取線〕a perforated line
- 一点鎖線　①a dash-dotted line ②a dot-dash line
- 点線の円　a dotted circle

せん…【先…】　last《week》[⇨第 1 部・31-5-2「先…」]

ぜんかい【前回】　①the last time ②the last occasion ③the previous time ④the previous occasion
- 前回の　①the last《session》②the previous《meeting》③the preceding《decision》
- 前々回の　①the《game》before last ②two《elections》ago ②the last《meeting》but one
- 前々回のお手紙　your letter before last
- 前回会ったときは…　(The) last time《we》met, …

ぜんかしき【漸化式】　①a recursion「formula［relation］②a recursive「formula［relation］③a recurrence「formula［relation］
- この数列は次の**漸化式**で定義される．　This sequence is defined by the following **recursive formula**.

ぜんき【前期】　①the early period ②the first term ③the first half year ④〔2 学期制の〕the first semester ⑤《生物》〔細胞分裂の〕the prophase
- 17 世紀前期　①the early seventeenth century ②the early part of the seventeenth century
- 前期比　⇨第 1 部・13-3 比較の基準の表現

せんきょ【選挙】　(an) election [⇨第 1 部・16. 投票・選挙の表現]

ぜんきん【漸近】
- 漸近的な　asymptotic
- 漸近的に　asymptotically
- 漸近する［漸近的に近づく］　approach asymptotically
- 漸近解　an asymptotic solution

- 漸近級数　an asymptotic series
- 漸近線　① an asymptote　② an asymptotic line
- 漸近展開　(an) asymptotic expansion

せんけい【線形】

- 線形の　linear
- 線形性　linearity
- 銀河までの距離と銀河の後退速度との間の**線形関係**　**the linear relationship** between the distance to a galaxy and its recession velocity
- A と B の間に**線形関係**が見出せる．
  ① **A linear relation** can be found between A and B.
  ② A and B are **linearly related**.
- 音速は温度に対して**線形に変化する**．　The speed of sound **changes linearly** with temperature.
- 線形より速く増大する　increase [grow] faster [more] than linearly
- **線形演算子**　a linear operator
- **線形写像**　(a) linear mapping
- **線形解析**　(a) linear analysis
- **線形近似**　(a) linear approximation
- **線形代数**　linear algebra
- **線形独立**　linear independence
- **線形従属**　linear dependence
- **線形空間**　(a)「linear [vector]」space
- **線形回路**　a linear circuit

せんげつ【先月】　last month [⇨第 1 部・31-5-2「先…」]

- 先月 5 日に　on the fifth of last month
- 先月号　〔雑誌などの〕last month's issue

ぜんげつ【前月】　① the month「before [earlier]」② the previous month

…ぜんご【…前後】　[⇨第 1 部・9. 概数]

- 30 前後の男　① a man of about thirty　② a man of thirty or so　③ a man of something like thirty　④ a thirtyish man
- 10 メートル前後はありそうなクジラが見えた．　We saw a whale「some [about, around, roughly, approximately]」ten meters long.
- 10 日前後かかるかもしれない．　It might take「ten days or so [something like ten days]」.

せんじつ【先日】　① the other day　② some days ago　③ a few days ago

ぜんじつ【前日】　① the day before　② the previous day　③ the preceding day [⇨

第 1 部・31-6-2「前…」]

せんしゅう【先週】　last week [⇨第 1 部・31-5-2「先…」]
- 先週の月曜　① last Monday　② Monday (of) last week　③ a week ago on Monday [⇨第 1 部・31-5-4 last … の使用例]

ぜんしゅう【前週】　① the week「before [earlier]　② the previous week

せんせきぶん【線積分】　① a line integral　② a contour integral

せんせんげつ【先々月】　① the month before last　② two months ago [⇨第 1 部・31-5-2「先…」]
- 先々月の 10 日　① two months ago on the tenth　② the tenth of the month before last

ぜんぜんげつ【前々月】　two months「before [earlier]

ぜんぜんじつ【前々日】　① two days before　② two days earlier

せんせんしゅう【先々週】　① (the) week before last　② two weeks ago [⇨第 1 部・31-5-2「先…」]
- 先々週の水曜日　① Wednesday of the week before last　② Wednesday two weeks ago

ぜんぜんしゅう【前々週】　two weeks「before [earlier]

ぜんぜんねん【前々年】　two years「before [earlier]

せんそ【線素】　a line element

せんたいしょう【線対称】　① line symmetry　② axial symmetry　③ bilateral symmetry
- 線対称である　have [possess] line symmetry
- 線対称な図形　a figure with line symmetry

センチ…　〔10^{-2}〕centi- [⇨第 1 部・27-4 SI 接頭語]

センチメートル　a centimeter《= 1/100 m；記号 cm》[⇨メートル，第 1 部・27-2 SI 基本単位]
- 平方センチメートル　a square centimeter《記号 cm^2》
- 立方センチメートル　a cubic centimeter《記号 cm^3》

セント　a cent《記号 ¢》[⇨第 1 部・39-1-2 ドル，39-1-3 ユーロ]

せんねん【先年】　① (in) past years　② some [a few] years ago　③ formerly　④ in the past

ぜんねん【前年】　① the year「before [earlier]　② the preceding year　③ the previous year
- 前年比　⇨第 1 部・13-3 比較の基準の表現

ぜんひてい【全否定】 〚文法〛total negation ［⇨第1部・22-5 部分否定と全否定］

ぜんびぶん【全微分】 a total differential
- 全微分方程式　a total differential equation

ぜんぶ【全部】 ① all ② the whole ［⇨第1部・22-4-4 全部］

せんぶん【線分】 ① a segment (of a line) ② a line segment
- 点 A, B を結ぶ線分の中点　the midpoint of the (line) segment joining the points A and B
- 線分 AB の垂直二等分線　a perpendicular bisector of (line) segment AB
- 線分描画　〚電算〛line drawing

そいんすう【素因数】 a prime factor ［⇨いんすう］
- n の異なる素因数の数　the number of different prime factors of n
- 大きな整数の素因数をみつける　find the prime factors of a large integer
- **素因数分解**　① factorization into primes ② factorization into prime numbers ③ prime factorization ④〔その結果〕a prime factorization
- 24 を素因数分解しなさい．
  ① Factor the number 24.
  ② Find the prime factorization of 24.
- 126,356 は $2 \times 2 \times 31 \times 1019$ に素因数分解できる．　The number 126,356 can be factored into $2 \times 2 \times 31 \times 1019$.

…ぞう【…増】
- 3 割増になる　increase (by) 30 percent ［⇨第1部・13-2-2 増減の程度］

ぞうえき【増益】 ① (an) increase in profit(s) ② (a) profit increase ③ profit growth ［⇨第1部・41-2 決算の表現］

ぞうか【増加】 ① (an) increase ② (a) gain ③ augmentation ④ rise ［⇨第1部・13-4 増加・上昇を表わす各種表現，13-2-2 増減の程度］
- 増加する　① increase ② rise ③ grow ④ swell ⑤ multiply ⑥ be augmented
- 数［重さ］が増加する　increase in「number［weight］
- 3 割増加する　increase (by) 30 percent
- 年に 3% 増加する　① increase by 3% per year ② increase at (the rate of) 3% per year
- 増加率　① a rate of increase ② an increasing rate

ぞうかかんすう【増加関数】 an increasing function 《of ［in］x》
- 単調増加関数　a「monotone［monotonic］increasing function
- 狭義の［厳密な］増加関数　a strictly increasing function ★変化率が 0 にならず常に増加する関数．変化率が 0 または正のものは「非減少関数」．

539

そうがく

- 非増加関数　a non-increasing function　★変化率が0または負.

そうがく【総額】　① the total　② the total「amount［sum］　③ the sum total［⇨第1部・24-1 合計・総計・総額］

そうかん【相関】　correlation
- 相関がある，相関する　① be correlated ⟪with［to］…⟫　② correlate ⟪with［to］…⟫
- 有意な［強い］相関　a「significant［strong］correlation
- おおまかな相関関係　a rough correlation
- 正［負］の相関　a「positive［negative］correlation
- 価格と性能の間の密接な相関関係　a close correlation between price and performance
- 銀河の赤方偏移と我々からの距離との間の相関関係　a correlation between the redshift of a galaxy and the galaxy's distance from us
- その量はそのクォークの質量と相関している［相関がある］．　The quantity is correlated with the mass of the quark.
- 主系列星については質量と光度の間に相関がある［あるようだ］．　There「is［appears to be］a correlation between mass and luminosity for main-sequence stars.
- 化学物質と症状との間に相関があることを示している　indicate a correlation between the chemicals and the symptoms
- AとBの間の相関関係を確立する　establish a correlation between A and B
- **相関関係**があっても因果関係があるとは限らない．　**Correlation** does not imply causation.［⇨いんがかんけい］
- 喫煙が肺癌と**相関がある**だけでなく，実際その原因となるということは十分確立されている．　It is well established that cigarette smoking not only **correlates** with lung cancer but actually causes it.
- 2つの変数の間に高い**相関関係があっても**，一方が他方の原因であるとは限らない．アイスクリームの売り上げと日射病で倒れる人の数の間に**相関**があったとしても，アイスクリームが日射病を引き起こすということにはならないのである．　Even if two variables are highly **correlated**, it does not necessarily mean that one causes the other. **A correlation** between ice cream sales and the number of cases of sunstroke does not mean that ice cream causes sunstroke.
- すべての誤差は互いに**相関がない**と仮定している．　All the errors are assumed to be **uncorrelated**.
- 相関は見出されなかった．　No correlation was found.

そうき【早期】　an early stage［⇨第1部・33-2「初頭」「末」「旬」］

そうきょくせん【双曲線】　a hyperbola
- 直角双曲線　a rectangular hyperbola

- 双曲線関数　a hyperbolic function

そうけい【総計】　① the total ② the total「amount [sum] ③ an aggregate《of …》[⇨第 1 部・24-1 合計・総計・総額]

そうこうきょり【走行距離】　① the distance traveled ② the distance covered《in a given time》③ (a) mileage ★英語の mileage には走行距離（単位は km など）と一定の燃料消費当たりの走行距離（単位は km/l など）の両方の意味がある．後者については⇨ねんぴ．

- 走行距離計〔自動車などの〕① an odometer ② a mileage「indicator [recorder] ③《英》a mil(e)ometer ④《口》《have 1,000 kilometers on》the clock
- この車の走行距離は 1 万キロだ．　This car's odometer reads 10,000 kilometers.
- 走行距離 2 万 km の中古自動車
  ① a used car that has been driven 20,000 kilometers
  ② a used car with 20,000 kilometers on「it [the odometer]
- その車の走行距離はどのくらいですか．
  ① How far has the car been driven?
  ② What sort of mileage has the car done?
  ③ What is your mileage《in kilometers》?
- 1 日の平均走行距離は何マイルですか．　What is your average mileage per day?
- 1 日 150 マイルの走行距離　a daily mileage of 150 (miles)
- 燃料 1 リットル当たりの走行距離はどのくらいか．
  ① What is the mileage per liter of fuel?
  ② What mileage does your car do per liter of fuel?

そうじ【相似】　① (a) similarity ② (a) similitude

- …に相似である　be similar to …
- 相似形　① a similar figure ② a like figure
- 2 つの**相似な多角形**の面積の比は任意の対応する辺の比の 2 乗に等しい．
  The ratio of the areas of two **similar polygons** is equal to the square of the ratio of the lengths of any two corresponding sides.
- **相似比**　a ratio of similitude
- **自己相似**　self-similarity
- レイノルズの**相似則**　the Reynolds **similarity**

ぞうしゅう【増収】　① an increase「of [in] revenue [income, receipts] ② growth of earnings

- 増収分　an increment「of [in] revenue [income, receipts]《resulting from …》
- 二期連続の増収増益　an increase in both income and profits for two successive periods [⇨第 1 部・41-2 決算の表現]

そうすう【総数】 ① the total ② the total number ③ the aggregate number [⇨第 1 部・24-1 合計・総計・総額]
- 総数はいくらになりますか． What does it amount to「in all [altogether, in total]?
- 総数 100 になる．
  ① The total「is [amounts to] one hundred.
  ② There are one hundred in all.
  ③ They total a hundred.
- 参加者の総数は 500 名を超えた．
  ① The total number of participants surpassed 500.
  ② More than 500 people attended altogether.

ぞうだい【増大】 (an) increase [⇨第 1 部・13-4 増加・上昇を表わす各種表現，13-2-2 増減の程度]
- 増大する ① become [grow] larger ② mount ③ rise ④ increase
- 増大させる ① enlarge ② increase ③ swell《the total》④ expand
- 被害者数の増大 (an) increase in the number of victims

そうつい【双対】 duality
- 双対な dual
- 双対空間 (a) dual space

そうとう【相当】 ⇨第 1 部・18-3 相当

そうば【相場】 ① the market (price) ② the current price ③ going rate [⇨第 1 部・39-2 外国為替]
- 円相場 ① the yen exchange rate ② the exchange rate「for [of] the yen ③ the「price [value] of the yen ④ the yen

ぞうばいりつ【増倍率】 a multiplication factor

ぞうぶん【増分】 an increment
- 増分 10 で増加する increase in increments of 10

そえじ【添え字】 ①〔一般に下付きの〕a subscript ②〔a_i や $a[i]$ の〕an index [⇨第 1 部・55. 式の読み方 55-3]
- 配列 $a[i]$ の添え字 i the「subscript [index] i for the array $a[i]$
- 共変添え字 a covariant index《of a tensor》
- 反変添え字 a contravariant index《of a tensor》
- 上付き添え字 ① a「superior [superscript] letter [figure] ② a superscript

そくど【速度】 ① (a) speed ② (a) velocity ③ (a) rate
  ★日英語とも，力学では velocity（速度）は大きさと向きをもつベクトル量であるのに対し，speed（速さ）は向きに関係ない速さをいう．したがって，等

そくど

速円運動 (uniform circular motion) のことを circular motion at a constant speed ということはできるが，circular motion at a constant velocity というと円運動では速度の向きは絶えず変わっているので形容矛盾になる．しかし，科学技術分野を含め一般に velocity（速度）を speed（速さ）と同義に用いることは多い．

★ 空間的移動以外の速さの場合は speed または rate を使うのが普通．
★ 以下，「高速」「低速」などの関連表現も扱う．

- 40 km/s の速度で　① with [at] a velocity of 40 km/s ② with [at] a speed of 40 km/s
- 時速 100 キロの速度を出している　go at a speed of 100 kph ★ kph は kilometers per hour の略．
- その粒子が標的に当たる速度　the velocity at which the particle hits the target
- 一定の速度で運動する　① move「with [at] (a) uniform velocity ② move「with [at] (a) constant velocity
- 光には有限の**速度**がある．　Light has a finite **speed**.
- このロケットなら光速の 10 分の 1 の最大**速度**が得られるはずだ．　This rocket would reach a maximum **velocity** of one tenth the speed of light.
- 水中では粒子は光速よりも速い**速度**で運動することができる．
  ① In water, a particle can move with **a speed** greater than the speed of light.
  ② In water, a particle can move faster than light.
- 地面［系の重心］**に対する**ボールの**速度**　the velocity of the ball **relative to**「the ground [the center of mass of the system]
- 対気速度　(an) airspeed
- 対地速度　(a) ground speed
- **小さい速度に対しては**空気抵抗は速度に比例する．　**For small velocities**, (the) air resistance is proportional to (the) velocity.
- 高速で　《move [operate, etc.]》at high speed
- 低速で　《move [operate, etc.]》at low speed
- 低速では　at low velocities
- 最高［最大］速度で走行する　① go [travel, run] at (the) maximum speed ② run at「full [top] speed
- 速度を増す［上げる］　① increase speed ② gather speed ③ put on speed ④ get up speed ⑤ gain (in) speed ⑥ speed up ⑦ gear up ⑧ gather pace ⑨ accelerate
- 速度を減じる［落とす］　① decrease speed ② reduce speed ③ decelerate ④ lose speed ⑤ slow down ⑥ gear down
- ノズルでガスを**超音速**に加速する　accelerate gas **to supersonic velocities** in the nozzle
- 初**速度**　initial velocity

そくど

- 地球の引力圏を脱するために必要な**初速度** **the initial velocity** necessary to escape the gravitational attraction of the earth
- 初期位置と**初期速度**がわかっているときに物体の運動を決定する　determine the motion of a body when the initial position and **the initial velocity** are known
- **終速度**　final velocity
- **制限速度**　① 《at》regulation speed　② 《within》the speed limit
- 制限速度時速 50 キロ．〔掲示〕Speed limit: 50 (kph).
- 彼は制限速度を 20 キロ超えた．
  ① He exceeded the speed limit by 20 km/h.
  ② He was (driving) over the speed limit by 20 km/h.
  ③ He was (driving) 20 km/h over the speed limit.
  ④ He broke the speed limit by 20 km/h.
- 彼女は制限速度をどれくらい超えたのですか．　How「fast [much, far]」over the speed limit did she go?
- **平均速度**　① average speed　② average velocity
- **速度計**　① a speedometer　② a speed indicator

▶ **移動の速さ以外の速度**

- 液体の分子が膜を通して拡散する速度　the rate at which liquid molecules diffuse through the membrane
- 入力速度　〔文字の〕① input speed　② speed of input
- 処理速度を 50% 増加させる　increase processing speed by 50 percent
- 燃焼速度　①《化》〔燃焼の速さ〕a burning rate　②《物》〔燃焼面の広がる速さ〕a burning velocity
- 上り[下り]速度　《電算》an upstream [a downstream] bandwidth [speed, performance]
- 反応速度　(a) reaction rate
- 変形速度　〔ひずみの進行する速さ〕(a) rate of strain
- 膨張速度　the speed of expansion
- 速度定数　《化》① a rate constant　② a rate coefficient
- 速度方程式　《物》a rate equation

そくど【測度】　a measure
- 測度空間　a measure space

そくめん【側面】　① the side　② the flank　③ an aspect　④ a dimension　⑤〔横顔〕a profile　⑥〔立体の〕a side face　⑦ a lateral face
- 角錐の側面は三角形だ．
  ① A side of a pyramid is a triangle.
  ② The sides of pyramids are triangles.

- 側面図　① a side「view [elevation]　② a lateral「view [elevation]　③ a profile
- 右側面図　a right side「view [elevation]

そくめんせき【側面積】　a lateral area

そこ【底】　〚相場〛a「(rock-)bottom [bedrock] price [⇨第1部・14. 最高と最低]
- 底を打つ　① hit bottom　② bottom out
- 消費低迷は底を打った．　The consumption slump has hit bottom.
- 景気は底を打ったと見ていいだろう．　It is probably fair to say that the economy has bottomed out.
- 底を割る　〚底値より下がる〛① break (the) bottom　② go [sink] below the bottom line
- 底堅い　① show a steady tone　② be firm in tone
- 相場は底堅く推移した．　The market showed a steady change.

そこいれ【底入れ】　① reaching bottom　② bottoming out [⇨第1部・14. 最高と最低]
- 底入れする　① touch [reach] the (rock-)bottom price　② reach [strike, hit] (the) bottom　③ bottom out
- 市況はおそらく底入れしている．　The market has probably「reached bottom [bottomed out].
- 底入れ感　a sense that the market has bottomed out

そこね【底値】　① a (rock-)bottom price　② a bedrock price [⇨第1部・14. 最高と最低]
- 底値に達する　reach [strike] (the) bottom
- 物価は目下底値だ．　Prices are now at「rock bottom [their bottom].
- 鉄鋼株は今が底値だ．　Steel stocks have bottomed out.
- 鉄道株は底値安定．　Railway stocks remain near the bottom.

そこわれ【底割れ】　① breaking the bottom　② sinking even deeper　③ a double recession [⇨第1部・14. 最高と最低]
- 底割れする　① break (the) bottom　② sink even further
- 株価が底割れした．　Stock prices hit new lows.

そすう【素数】　a prime (number)
- 13 は素数である．　13 is (a) prime.
- $2p-1$ が素数となるような素数 p　**a prime p for which $2p-1$ is also (a) prime**
- 次の数のうち素数はどれか．　Which of the following numbers「is [are] prime?
- 素数でない数　① a number that is not prime　②〔合成数〕a composite number

そてん

- 素数の分布　the distribution of prime numbers
- 素数定理　the prime number theorem

そてん【素点】 ① a raw score ② an unadjusted score

そのいち【其の一】 ① the first … ② part one

- 日本映画論 (その一)　Japanese Film: Part 1

それぞれ　① each ② respectively [⇨第 1 部・63-13「それぞれ」の用法]

そろばん【算盤】　an abacus　★複数形は abacuses, abaci.

関連表現

- 願いましては 12 円なり，34 円なり，56 円なり，引いては 78 円なり，加えて 90 円では．　Starting with twelve yen, add thirty-four yen, fifty-six yen, subtract seventy-eight yen, and add 90 yen. That's all.
- ご名算．　① That's right. ② Correct. ③ You got it right.

そんえき【損益】　① profit and loss ② loss and gain [⇨りえき]

- 損益を確定する　realize *one's* gains or losses
- 損益なし．
  ① The profit and loss are on a par.
  ② 《We》 broke even.
- **損益分岐点**　a break-even point 《略 BEP》
- 損益分岐点分析　a break-even analysis
- 損益分岐点比率　〔損益分岐点の現在の売上高に対する比〕a break-even point ratio
- **損益計算書**　① an income statement ② a profit and loss statement ③ a profit and loss account [⇨第 1 部・41. 英文会計]

関連表現

- **安全余裕**　〔現在の売上高が損益分岐点を超える額〕a margin of safety
- 安全余裕率，M/S 率　〔安全余裕の現在の売上高に対する比〕a margin of safety ratio　★(安全余裕率) = 1 - (損益分岐点比率) である．

た行

ダース a dozen
- 1ダースの鉛筆　a dozen pencils　★このほうが a dozen of pencils より普通
- 5ダースの卵　five dozen eggs　★このほうが five dozen of eggs より普通.
- 数ダースのハンカチ　several [a few] dozen handkerchiefs
- 5ダースのビール　five dozen「bottles [cans] of beer
- 2ダース入りの箱　a box containing two dozen　★この場合 dozen は名詞だが，数詞，many, several (some を除く)などのあとでは単数形を用いる.
- あそこの卵2ダース　two dozen of the eggs over there　★特定のものの一部を指す場合には of を使う.
- 何ダースもの…　dozens of …
- 1ダースごとに詰める　pack in dozens
- ダースいくらで売る　sell by the dozen
- 鉛筆は何ダースありますか.　How many dozen pencils are there?

たい【体】 a field

タイ

1〔同点〕a tie
- タイに終わる　① end in a ((2-2)) tie ② tie
- タイにする　tie the score ((with a homer))
- 5勝5敗のタイに持ち込む　bring the game to a「5-5 [five-all, five-each] tie
- スミスの見事なゴールでタイになった.　Smith tied the game with a brilliant goal.
- 両チームは3対3のタイとなった.　The two teams tied (at)「3:3 [three all].
- 4対4のタイスコアであった.　The「game [score] was tied at「4 all [4 to 4].

2〔同順位〕a tie
- 世界[日本]タイ記録　《a「time [score]》equaling [tying (with)] the「world [Japanese] record
- 世界タイ記録を出す　equal [tie, match] the world record
- アリスはボブとともに2位[首位]タイだった.　Alice「tied [was tied] with Bob for「second place [the lead].

…たい…【…対…】

1 ①〔対抗〕… versus … ((略: v., vs.)) ② between … and …
- ジャイアンツ対タイガース　① the Giants versus the Tigers ② the Giants vs. the Tigers
- アントラーズ対レッズ戦　① an Antlers-(versus-)Reds (soccer) game ② a

(soccer) game between the Antlers and the Reds
- 日本対イラン戦　a Japan-Iran match
- グローバリズム対ナショナリズムの対立　a struggle between globalism and nationalism
- 地対空ミサイル　① a ground-to-air missile　② a surface-to-air missile

2 〔得点〕… to … [⇨第 1 部・49. 野球の数字表現 49-5]
- 0 対 7 の大差で負ける　lose by the massive margin of zero to seven
- 30 対 40 で私たちの勝ち［負け］です．　We「won［lost］, thirty (points) to forty.
- ハーフタイムでの得点は 3 対 1 だった．　The score at halftime was 3-1.
- 彼女のホームランで 3 点入って 5 対 2 になった．　Her homer scored three runs, making it 5 to 2.
- その法案は 200 票対 150 票で可決された．　The bill was passed by a vote of 200 to 150. [⇨第 1 部・16. 投票・選挙の表現]

3 〔比率〕… to … [⇨第 1 部・22-3 相対比率]
- 酢としょうゆを 1 対 1 の割合で混ぜる　mix one part of vinegar「with［and］one part of soy sauce
- このクラスは 3 対 2 の割で女子のほうが多い．　In this class girls outnumber boys by three to two.
- 三角形の 3 辺の比を 2 対 5 対 7 とする．　Assume the sides of the triangle are in the ratio two to five to seven.
- 信号対雑音比　a signal-to-noise ratio 《略 SNR》
- 費用（対）効果　《improve》cost-effectiveness

だい…【第…】　[⇨だいいち，だいに，だいさん]
- 第 2　① number two 《略 No. 2》　② the second 《略 2nd》[⇨…ばん，…め，第 1 部・4. 序数]
- 第 4 条第 3 項　the third「paragraph［clause］of Article IV [⇨第 1 部・48. 法律・条約]
- 第 5 課　Lesson 5

…だい【…大】　[⇨…きょう]

▶ major を使う例
- 四大大会　〔テニスなどの〕① the four major annual tournaments　② the four majors
- 三大国際映画祭　the three major international film festivals
- 三大栄養素　〔炭水化物・タンパク質・脂肪〕the three major nutrients (of carbohydrates, proteins, and fat)
- 三大生活習慣病［成人病］〔癌・心疾患・脳血管疾患〕the three major adult

diseases (of cancer, heart disease, and cerebrovascular disease)
- 三大発明 〔火薬・羅針盤・活版印刷術〕 the three major inventions (of gunpowder, the compass, and the printing press)
▶ big を使う例
- 三大自動車メーカー［ビッグスリー］〔米国の〕the Big Three
- ビッグフォー［四大銀行，etc.］ the Big Four
- 四大公害裁判 the four big pollution trials
▶ great を使う例（畏敬の念がこもる）
- 三大テノール the three great tenors
- シェイクスピアの四大悲劇 Shakespeare's four great tragedies
- 四大文明 the four great ancient civilizations of the world(: Mesopotamian, Indus, Chinese, and Egyptian)
- 二大スター夢の共演 a dream joint performance by the two great stars
▶ largest を使う例（客観的に最大）
- 三大都市 the three largest cities 《of Japan》
- 四大工業地帯 the four largest industrial zones
- 四大漁場 the four largest fishing grounds in the world
▶ その他
- 二大政党制 a two-party system
- 四大トーナメント 〔テニス・ゴルフの〕the four Grand Slam tournaments

…だい【…代】

1 〔当主など〕

- 初代大統領 the first president
- 先代の社長 ① the last president ② the previous president
- 先々代の社長 ① the last-but-one president ② the president before last
- 7代目の主人 the seventh-generation proprietor 《of a shop》
- 池坊派の直系15代目 ① the 15th in the direct line of heads of the Ikenobō school (of flower arrangement) ② the 14th direct descendant of the founder of the Ikenobō school
- 2代目若乃花 ① Wakanohana II ② Wakanohana the second
- 第2代バッキンガム公爵 the second Duke of Buckingham ★George Villiers, second Duke of Buckingham のように個人名と同格にするときは無冠詞にすることが多い．
- 「このお店は古いんですか」「8代目になります」 Is this an old store? — It's been in our family for eight generations.
- 何代目 ⇨第1部・26. 数量に関する疑問文 26-10 何番目
- 何代も続いた旧家 an ancient family that goes back for generations

2 〔年代の範囲〕⇨第 1 部・29. 年・年度・元号・世紀 29-6
- 1930 年代に　in the 1930s
- 1990 年代に入ってかなりたつまで　until well into 1990s

3 〔年齢の範囲〕⇨第 1 部・38. 年齢
- 40 代の男　a man in his forties

…だい【…台】　[⇨第 1 部・9-3「…台」]
- 50 台の数字　a number in the fifties
- 15,000 円台に達する　① touch [rise to] the level of 15,000 yen　② reach [hit] the 15,000-yen「mark [level]

だいいち【第一】　① the first　② number one《略 No. 1》　③ the foremost
- 第一の　① first　② initial　③ foremost　④ primary
- 五月の第一土曜日　the first Saturday in May
- 第一楽章　the first movement
- 第一条　Article 1 [⇨第 1 部・48. 法律・条約]
- 第一走者　〔リレーの〕the lead-off runner
- 第一泳者　〔リレーの〕the lead-off swimmer
- アメリカチームの第一走者[泳者]は…だった．　The United States (relay) team was led off by ….
- 第一希望　*one's* first「preference [choice]
- 第一志望校　① *one's* first choice of school　② the school *one* wants to go to
- 第一鉄[銅]の　〖化〗ferrous [cuprous]
- 酸化第一銅　〖化〗cuprous oxide
- 第一に　① first　② firstly　③ first of all　④ in the first place

たいおん【体温】　① temperature　② body temperature [⇨第 1 部・45-1 温度]

たいかく【対角】

1 〔対する角〕the opposite angle

2 〔対角線に関係する〕⇨たいかくせん
- 対角行列　a diagonal matrix
- 非対角行列　a nondiagonal matrix
- 対角要素　a diagonal element
- 非対角要素　an off-diagonal element
- 対角化　diagonalization
- 対角化する　diagonalize《a matrix, an operator》
- 同時対角化可能な　simultaneously diagonalizable

たいかくせん【対角線】　a diagonal (line)

- 一辺の長さが2の立方体の**対角線の長さ**　**the length of a diagonal** of a cube whose edges have length 2
- 多角形[n角形]の**対角線の本数**　**the number of diagonals** in「a polygon [an n-gon]
- 対角線を引く　draw a diagonal (to the opposite angle)
- 平行四辺形の**対角線は互いに他を二等分する**．　**Diagonals** of a parallelogram **bisect each other**.
- 菱形の**対角線は直交する**．　**Diagonals** of a rhombus **are perpendicular to each other**.

だいけい【台形】　①《米》a trapezoid　②《英》a trapezium　★trapezium の複数形は trapeziums または trapezia.
★《英》での trapezoid と《米》での trapezium は不等辺四角形の意で，英米で台形と不等辺四角形の用法が逆になっている．
- **台形**の面積を求める　find the area of **a trapezoid**
- **台形**の面積は上底足す下底かける高さ割る2である．
  ① The area of **a trapezoid** is found by multiplying the「height [altitude]」by the sum of the two bases and dividing by two.
  ② The area of **a trapezoid** is half the product of its height and the sum of the (lengths of the two) bases.
  ③ The area of **a trapezoid** is the average of the parallel sides times the height.
- **台形公式**　〔定積分の〕the trapezoidal rule
- **等脚台形**　an isosceles trapezoid
- 等脚台形の底角は等しい．　The base angles of an isosceles trapezoid are congruent.

だいさん【第三】　① the third　② number three《略 No. 3》　③ the tertiary
- 第三の　① third　② tertiary
- 第三に　① third　② thirdly　③ in the third place

たいしゃくたいしょうひょう【貸借対照表】　a balance sheet〔⇨第1部・41. 英文会計〕

たいじゅう【体重】　① *one's* weight　② *one's* body weight〔⇨第1部・43-2 体重〕

たいしょう【対称】　symmetry
- 対称な図形　a symmetric(al) figure
- このグラフは x 軸に関して**対称**である．　This graph is **symmetric**「about [around, with respect to]」the *x*-axis.
- 地球は赤道に関して**対称**ではない．　The earth is not **symmetric**「about [around, with respect to]」the equator.
- パルス波形はピークの前後で**対称的に**下がっている．　The pulse waveform

falls off **symmetrically**「about [from] the peak.

- 原点のまわりに**対称的な**区間 an interval **symmetric** about the origin
- グラフがそのまわりに**対称**になる点の座標 the coordinates of the point about which the graph is **symmetric**
- これらは**対称的な**配置で取り付けられている． These are「attached [mounted] in a **symmetrical** arrangement.
- このテンソルは添え字の巡回置換について**対称**である． This tensor is **symmetric** with respect to cyclic permutations of the indices.
- **回転対称** rotational symmetry
- 回転対称な rotationally symmetric
- 6回回転対称 six-fold rotational symmetry
- **球対称** spherical symmetry [⇨きゅうたいしょう]
- **軸対称** ① axial symmetry ② axisymmetry [⇨じくたいしょう]
- **線対称** ⇨せんたいしょう
- **点対称** ⇨てんたいしょう
- **対称の中心** a center of symmetry
- **対称軸** ① an axis of symmetry ② a symmetry axis
- **対称面** ① a plane of symmetry ② a symmetry plane
- **対称性** symmetry
- 系の基本的な対称性 the fundamental symmetries of a system
- 八面体の対称性の(なす)群 the group of symmetries of an octahedron
- **非対称性** asymmetry
- **対称関数** a symmetric function
- **対称行列** a symmetric matrix
- **対称式** a symmetric expression

たいすう【対数】 a logarithm《記号 log》

- 3の対数 the logarithm of 3 ★log 3 と書く．
- 10を底とする x の対数 ① the logarithm of x to the base 10 ② the base-10 logarithm of x ★$\log_{10} x$ と書く．
- 対数の底 the base of a logarithm
- 対数の底を変換する change a logarithm from one base to another
- 両辺の対数を取る take「logarithms [《口》logs] of both sides《of the equation》
- 対数はすべて10を底としている． All logarithms are to (the) base 10.
- 対数目盛りで 《plot …》on a logarithmic scale
- 時間スケールは対数目盛りである． The time scale is logarithmic.

- 対数的に　logarithmically
- x の対数でしか増大しない　increase only logarithmically with x
- **片〔半〕対数の**　semilogarithmic《graph》
- **常用対数**　a common logarithm
- **自然対数**　a natural logarithm
- 自然対数の底　the base of natural logarithms《記号 e》
- **対数関数**　a logarithmic function
- **対数微分**　① logarithmic differentiation　②〔微分したもの〕a logarithmic derivative
- **対数表**　① a table of logarithms　② a logarithmic table　③《口》a log table
- 5桁〔位〕対数表　① a five-figure logarithmic table　② a five-place logarithmic table
- **対数平均**　a logarithmic mean
- **対数方眼紙**　① logarithmic (coordinate) paper　②《口》log paper

だいすうてきすう【代数的数】　an algebraic number〔⇨せいすう 数の集合〕

たいせき【体積】　(a) volume〔⇨第1部・42-9 体積・容積, 58-6 体積の公式〕
- その立方体の体積は 64m³ だ．　The volume of the cube is「64 m³〔64 cubic meters〕.
- 体積を求める　find the volume《of …》
- 体積積分　a volume integral
- 体積要素　〔積分の〕a volume element
- 体積百分率　① volume percentage　② percentage by volume　③ cubical percentage〔⇨第1部・22-1-10 重量比・体積比など〕
- 体積速度　(a) volume velocity
- 体積抵抗率　(a) volume resistivity
- 体積弾性率　a bulk modulus
- 体積膨張係数　a coefficient of cubical expansion

たいちょうかく【対頂角】　① vertically opposite angles　② vertical angles

だいなり【大なり】
- A 大なり B．　A is greater than B．★$A>B$ のこと．
- A 大なりイコール B．　A is greater than or equal to B．★$A \geq B$ のこと．
- 大なり記号　a greater-than symbol

だいに【第二】　① the second　② number two《略 No. 2》
- 第二の　① second　② secondary
- アメリカ第二の都市　America's second「most important〔largest〕city
- 五月の第二土曜日　the second Saturday in May

- 第二鉄の 〖化〗 ferric
- 第二銅の 〖化〗 cupric
- 酸化第二銅 〖化〗 cupric oxide
- 第二に ① second ② secondly ③ in the second place
- その町はあやうく第二のチェルノブイリになるところだった． The town narrowly escaped becoming another Chernobyl.

だいにゅう【代入】 ① substitution ② 〖電算〗 assignment
- 代入する ① substitute ② 〖電算〗 assign 《a value to a variable》
- x に a を代入する　substitute a for x
- その値を方程式の未知数に**代入する**　**substitute** the value for the unknown in the equation　★substitute A for B の元来の意味は「A を B の代わりに用いる」であるので，次のような場合には for は使えない．
- その値をもとの方程式に**代入する**　**substitute** the value ⌈in [into] the original equation
- 代入演算子 〖電算〗 an assignment operator
- 代入式 〖電算〗 an assignment expression
- 代入文 〖電算〗 an assignment statement

たいぶんすう【帯分数】　a mixed number [⇨第 1 部・53. 分数]

タイマー　a timer
- タイマーできっかり 2 分測って麺をゆでる　boil the noodles for exactly two minutes using a kitchen timer
- タイマーを 6 時にセットした．　I set the timer for six o'clock.

たいようねんすう【耐用年数】 ① life ② service life ③ useful life ④ working life ⑤ fatigue life ⑥ wear life ⑦ 《have 20》 years of durability [⇨じゅみょう]
- 木造住宅の耐久年数はせいぜい 50 年だ．　A wood house lasts for at most 50 years.
- 耐用年数は 8 年である　last (not more than) eight years
- 耐用年数の長い住宅　a long-lived house
- 耐用年数を過ぎた洗濯機　① a washing machine that has reached the end of its (useful) life ② a worn-out washing machine

たいりょう【大量】　a large amount of [⇨第 1 部・19-2 多量]

ダイン〔力の CGS 単位〕a dyne 《= 10^{-5} ニュートン；記号 dyn》

だえん【楕円】 ① an ellipse ② an oval　★oval は「卵形」だが日常語としては楕円を指すこともある．
- 楕円の ① elliptic(al) ② oval
- **楕円**上の任意の点から 2 つの焦点までの距離の和は一定である．　The sum

of the distances from any point on **an ellipse** to the two foci is a constant.
- 楕円運動　elliptic motion
- 楕円関数　an elliptic function
- 楕円軌道　an elliptical orbit
- 楕円曲線　an elliptic curve
- 楕円積分　an elliptic integral
- 楕円体　an ellipsoid
- 回転楕円体　① an ellipsoid of revolution　② a spheroid
- 楕円柱　① a cylindroid　② an elliptic cylinder

たがいにそ【互いに素】
- 互いに素である　①《p and q are》relatively prime　② coprime
- p は q と互いに素である．　p is (relatively) prime to q.
- それらは互いに素と仮定してよい．　They can be assumed (to be) relatively prime.
- 互いに素な集合　disjoint sets

たかくけい【多角形】　a polygon ［⇨第 1 部・58-2 …角形］
- 正多角形　a regular polygon

たかさ【高さ】

1 ①〔高いこと〕height　② tallness　③〔垂直方向の長さ〕(a) height　④〔高度〕(an) altitude　⑤ (an) elevation　⑥ a level［⇨第 1 部・42-5 高さ，42-6 縦・横・高さ〕
- 三角形の高さ　① the height of a triangle　② the length of the altitude of a triangle　★この altitude は「高さを表わす線分」（頂点から底辺に下ろした垂線）のこと．

2 〔値・程度が大きいこと〕
- 技量の高さ　a (high) level of skill
- 請求書を見てその代金の高さに目をむいた．　When I saw the bill, I was astounded at「the price［how expensive it was］．
- この湖の汚染度は 10 年前の 5 倍もの高さだ．
① The (level of) pollution in the lake is five times「higher than［as high as, worse than］(it was) ten years ago.
② The lake is five times more polluted than (it was) ten years ago.

3 〔音声の高低〕(a) pitch
- カラオケのキーの高さを調節する　adjust the pitch of a karaoke tune
- 1 オクターブ上の高さの音　a note an octave higher

たかだか【高々】　① at most　② at the most　③ at best　④ at the (very)「outside

[utmost] ⑤〔単に〕merely ⑥ just ⑦〔たったの〕only ⑧ but ⑨ no more than …
- n 次多項式の根は高々 n 個しかない.
  ① A polynomial of degree n has at most n roots.
  ② There are at most n roots for an nth-degree polynomial.
- 高々可算個の不連続点　at most countably many discontinuities
- x の高々 2 次の関数　a function of at most second degree in x
- 連続する 0 の数を高々 2 つに制限する　limit the number of consecutive 0s to at most 2
- 高々 5,000 円　① ¥5,000 at most　② no more than ¥5,000
- 高々 2 万円の損だろう.　The loss will not be more than ¥20,000.
- 飛行機が発明されてから高々 100 年にすぎない.
  ① It is a mere hundred years since the airplane was invented.
  ② It is no more than a century since the airplane was invented.

たかっけい【多角形】　⇨たかくけい

たかどまり【高止まり】　⇨第 1 部・13. 比較・差・増減 13-6

たかね【高値】　a high price [⇨さいたかね, 第 1 部・40. 料金・価格・収支 40-2-2]

…たく【…択】　⇨たくいつ

たくいつ【択一】
- 二者択一［二択］　① a choice [choosing] between two「things [alternatives]　② a choice of one or the other　③ (a choice of) two alternatives
- 五者択一［五択］　① a choice [choosing] from [among, from among] five　② choosing one out of five alternatives
- 三者択一［三択］の問題　① a three-choice question　② a three-item multiple-choice question　③ a question with three choices
- 択一式の問題　a multiple-choice question

たくさん【沢山】
- たくさんの　①〔数〕many …　② a large number of …　③〔量〕much …　④ a large amount of …　⑤〔数・量〕a lot of …　⑥ lots of …　⑦ plenty of … [⇨第 1 部・19-1 多数, 19-2 多量]

たこうしき【多項式】　① a polynomial (expression)　② a multinomial (expression)
- 実係数の x の多項式　a polynomial in x with real coefficients
- 複素係数の x の多項式　a polynomial in x with complex coefficients
- 整数係数の多項式　a polynomial with integer coefficients
- 1 次多項式　① a linear polynomial　② a first-degree polynomial
- 2 次多項式　① a quadratic polynomial　② a second-degree polynomial

- 3次多項式　① a cubic polynomial　② a third-degree polynomial
- n 次多項式　① a polynomial of degree n　② a polynomial of the nth degree　③ an nth-degree polynomial
- 高次多項式　higher-degree polynomials
- 低次の多項式に因数分解できる5次式　a quintic that「factors [factorizes]」into lower degree polynomials
- 多項式時間で計算可能である　be computable in polynomial time

たじげん【多次元】
- 多次元解析　multidimensional analysis
- 多次元尺度法　multidimensional scaling《略 MDS》
- 多次元表現　multidimensional representation

たしざん【足し算】　① addition　② adding up［⇨第1部・54-1 足し算］

だじゅん【打順】　the batting order［⇨第1部・49. 野球の数字表現 49-6］

たす【足す】　① add　②〔合計する〕add up　③ do addition　④ do a sum［⇨第1部・54-1 足し算］
- 2足す4は6.　①Two and four「make [are]」six.　②Two plus four「is [equals]」six.

たすう【多数】

1〔数の多さ〕
- 多数の　① many …　② a large number of …　③ a number of …　④ numbers of …　⑤ a great number of …　⑥ an enormous number of …　⑦ a huge number of …　⑧ a vast number of …　⑨ a lot of …　⑩ lots of …　⑪ plenty of …［⇨第1部・19-1 多数］

2〔票などの過半数・最多〕
- 賛成多数で可決する　① approve by a majority　② approve by a majority vote
- 理事会はその提案を5対3の賛成多数で承認した.　The board voted 5-3 in favor of the proposal.
- 賛成(者)多数. よって動議は可決いたしました.　The ayes have it. I declare the motion passed.
- 投票で**多数になった**が過半数には至らなかった.　They **won a plurality of votes** but fell short of a majority.［⇨第1部・16-3 過半数］
- 3分の2の多数　⇨第1部・16-4 3分の2の多数
- **安定多数**〔与党が全常任委員会の委員長を出した上に委員の半数以上を占められる国会の議席数〕① a stable majority　② a secure majority　③ a solid majority　④ a comfortable majority
- **絶対安定多数**〔与党が全委員会の委員長を出した上に委員の過半数を占められる国会の議席数〕an absolute stable majority

- 2000年から2014年までの衆議院では，全480議席中，**安定多数**は252，**絶対安定多数**は269だった．　In the House of Representatives from 2000 to 2014, **a stable majority** meant 252 and **an absolute stable majority** 269 out of the total of 480 seats.
- **不特定多数**の人　① an unspecified large number of people　② large numbers of the general public　③ 《open to》 the (general) public　④ many unspecified individuals
- 不特定多数の人が集まる場所　a place where large numbers of the general public gather

だすう【打数】　at bats［⇨第1部・49. 野球の数字表現 49-13］
- 5打数3安打である　① have three hits in five at bats　② be「three for five [3-for-5]」

たせん【多選】　election many times［⇨第1部・16-10 再選・多選］

たたいいち【多対一】　many-to-one 《relationship, mapping, correspondence》

たっする【達する】　① reach　② amount to …　③ come (up) to …　④ run [mount, add] up to …　⑤ work out at …　⑥ number［⇨第1部・2-4 数値を呈示する各種表現］
- 川幅はところによって2キロにも達する．
  ① In places the river is as wide as two kilometers.
  ② In places the river is a full two kilometers wide.
  ③ In places the river reaches a width of two kilometers.
- その時船の速さは30ノットに達していたものと思われる．　It is likely that the boat was「doing as much as [going a full]」thirty knots at the time.
- 成長した闘牛の体重は500キロから700キロに達する．　A full-grown fighting bull can weigh「anything [anywhere]」from 500 to 700 kilos.

たっせいりつ【達成率】　① achievement　② percentage achievement　③ fulfillment　④ performance　★achievement は達成，fulfillment は成就，performance は実績の意だが，適切な文脈ではその度合いを表わす．
- 目標達成率　① the degree of target achievement　② the target achievement (level)　③ the percentage achievement of a「target [goal]」
- 目標に対する達成率［実績］を評価する　evaluate performance against goals
- 月間目標達成率は90%だった．
  ① Ninety percent of the monthly target was reached.
  ② 《They》 reached 90% of the monthly target.
- 売り上げは1,600万円で，目標達成率は80%だった．　The sales were ¥16 million, fulfilling 80% of their target.
- 基準(学力)達成率　the percent 《of second graders》 meeting (learning) standards

たった　① only　② just　③ merely　④ mere　⑤ 《文》 but［⇨第1部・20.「…も」

「…しか」「たった」]
- **たった** 10 個**しか**ない．
  ① There are **only** ten.
  ② There are **but** ten.
  ③ There are **no more than** ten.
  ④ There are **as few as** ten.
- たった3日間　just [only, no more than, a mere, but] three days
- たった1分の差で列車に間に合わなかった．　I missed the train by just「a [one] minute.

…だて【…建て】

1〔建物〕⇨…かい【…階】

2〔通貨〕⇨えん2

たてじく【縦軸】　①the axis of ordinates　②the「vertical [ordinate] axis　③the y axis　★ordinate は縦軸の座標の意.

- このグラフは**縦軸**が平均体重，横軸が年齢を表わしている．　In this graph **the vertical axis** shows average weight, and the horizontal axis (shows) age.
- 応力とひずみがそれぞれ横軸，**縦軸**として示されている．　Stress and strain are plotted as「abscissae and **ordinates** [x and y], respectively.
- 縦軸に濃度を取る　plot density on the「vertical [ordinate, y] axis
- 圧力を縦軸に取って温度に対する関係をグラフにする　①plot [graph] pressure as the ordinate against temperature as the abscissa　② plot [graph] pressure against temperature
- 横軸に時間，縦軸に速度を取ってグラフを描く　draw a graph with time as the abscissa and velocity as the ordinate
- 辺AB は縦軸上にあるものとする．　Assume that the side AB lies on the「vertical [ordinate, y] axis.

たて・よこ【縦・横】　⇨第1部・42-6 縦・横・高さ，59-2 縦・横

- 縦2m, 横1m の板
  ① a board (measuring) two meters by one (meter)
  ② a board two meters long and one (meter) broad
  ③〔立てて使う場合〕a board two meters「tall [high] and one (meter) wide

だてん【打点】　a run batted in [⇨第1部・49. 野球の数字表現 49-14]

- 彼は2打点入れた．
  ① He batted in two「runs [runners].
  ② He drove in two「runs [runners].

ためんたい【多面体】　a polyhedron　★複数形は polyhedra, polyhedrons.

- 多面体の　polyhedral
- 多面体の一つの面　one face of a polyhedron

- 正多面体 a regular polyhedron

たようたい【多様体】 a manifold
- n 次元多様体 an n-dimensional manifold

…たらず【…足らず】 ① a little less than … ② a little under … ③ (just) short of … ④ (just) inside of … [⇨第 1 部・9-4「…足らず」]

だりつ【打率】 a batting average [⇨第 1 部・49. 野球の数字表現 49-12]
- 彼の打率は 3 割 2 分 5 厘である． He has a batting average of .325. ★.325 は three twenty-five と読む．

たりない【足りない】 [⇨第 1 部・21-1 不足]

〈対象物が主語〉 ① be not enough ② be insufficient ③ be deficient ④ be inadequate ⑤ be lacking ⑥ be in short supply

〈人などが主語〉⑦ be short of … ⑧ be shy of … ⑨ be deficient in … ⑩ lack ⑪ be lacking in …
- 1,000 円に 10 円足りない． I'm ten yen「short [shy] of a thousand (yen).

たりょう【多量】
- 多量の ① much … ② a large amount of … ③ a large quantity of … ④ a large volume of … [⇨第 1 部・19-2 多量]

たりる【足りる】 ① be enough ② be sufficient ③ be adequate ④ suffice [⇨たりない]
- ケーブルの長さは 5 メートルあれば足りる． Five meters of cable will suffice.
- 夕食は 2,000 円もあれば足りる． Two thousand yen or so will be sufficient for the evening meal.
- 水は 1 リットルで足りますか． Will one liter of water be enough?

だん【段】

1 〔段階をなすもの〕① a step ② a stage
- 上から 2 番目の段 ① the next to the top stair ② the top stair but one
- (多段式) ロケットの第 1 段 the「first [bottom]」stage of a rocket
- 階段を数段降りる go down several steps of the stairs
- 2 段ずつ階段を上る go up the「stairs [steps]」(taking them) two at a time

2 〔上下階層をなすもの〕
- 10 段のウェディングケーキ a ten-tier(ed) wedding cake
- 押し入れの上の段 the upper shelf of a wall closet
- その本は (本棚などの) 一番下の段に置いてあるよ． The book's on the bottom shelf.
- 3 段重ねの重箱 a three-tier(ed) box

- 菓子箱を開けてみると中は2段重ねになっていた． I opened the box of candies to find there were two layers.

3 〔印刷物の欄〕a column (of print)
- 3段の記事　①〔英字新聞などの〕a three-column article ②〔邦文の〕a three-tier article
- 2段組み　a double-column「setting [layout]」
- 3段抜きの見出し　a three-column heading
- この新聞は10段になっている．　This newspaper has ten (horizontal) columns to the page.

4 〔九九の〕a multiplication table
- 〔九九の〕八の段　the eight times table
- 五の段まで全部覚えた．　I've remembered up to my five times table.

5 ①〔等級〕a grade ②a class ③a rank ④a level ⑤〔級と区別して〕a dan ⑥a degree〔⇨きゅう【級】〕
- （碁・将棋などの）9段（の人）　①a ninth-degree (shogi [go]) player ②a ninth-dan (shogi [go]) player ③a nine-dan (shogi [go]) player
- 彼は柔道［剣道］2段だ．　He has a second dan in「judo [kendo]」.
- 彼女は何段ですか．　What「dan [grade, rank]」is she?
- 同じ段位の選手どうしの試合　a match between two players of the same rank

たんい【単位】　a unit

1 〔測る基準〕〔⇨第1部・27. 単位，28. 伝統単位〕
- 長さの単位　a unit of length
- 重さの単位　a unit of weight
- MKS単位で表わされた量　a quantity expressed in MKS units
- SI単位で表わされた量をCGS単位に変換するにはこの因子をかける．　A quantity in SI units is multiplied by this factor to convert it to CGS units.
- nm単位で表わした波長　the wavelength in「nm [nanometers]」
- **ミリ単位で測る**　measure … **in (units of) millimeters**
- **SI単位で書く**　write《a formula》**in SI units**
- **ミリ単位の精度で測る**　measure … **with an accuracy down to units of millimeters**
- 会合は**秒単位まで時間ぴったりに**開会した．　The meeting opened **on time to the second**.
- 単位をそろえる　①unify units ②make units consistent
- 単位を間違えて計算する　calculate「with [using]」the wrong unit
- 電荷の**SI単位**はクーロンである．　**The SI unit**「of [for]」charge is the cou-

たんい

lomb.
- 日本の**貨幣の単位**は円である． **The monetary unit** of Japan is the yen.
- ヨーロッパ共通の**通貨単位**ユーロは 1999 年に導入された． The common **unit** of European **currency**, the euro, was introduced in 1999.
- $\hbar$ を単位として半奇数のスピンをもつ粒子　a particle that has odd-half-integer spin **measured in units of** $\hbar$.
- 特に指定のない限り大きさはすべて**波長を単位として**表わす．　Unless otherwise specified, all dimensions will be **in units of wavelengths**.
- L はオーディオデータの**サンプル（数）単位で**のフレーム長である．　L is the frame length of the audio data「**in samples**〔**in units of samples**, **in number of samples**〕.
- この表の人口は **1,000 単位で**示してある．　The population in the table is「shown〔expressed〕**in (units of) thousands**.
- 単位：千円　① units: ¥1,000　② units: ¥000　③ units: ¥000s　④ yen in thousands　⑤ amounts in thousands　★④の yen は複数形で，ドルなら dollars in thousands となる．⑤は表に ¥159 などと「円」が示されている場合．
- 単位：千人　① units: 1,000　② units: 000　③ units: 000s
- **国際〔SI〕単位**　an「international〔SI〕unit
- **単位系**　a system of units
- SI 単位系で表わす　express … in SI units
- 用いる単位系によって変わる　depend on the system of units used
- **基本単位**　① a basic unit　②〔標準〕a standard unit　③〖物〗〔一連の単位のもとになる〕a fundamental unit　④〔SI 単位系で組立単位に対し〕a base unit　⑤〔通貨の〕a basic (monetary) unit
- **組立〔誘導〕単位**　〔基本単位から構成される〕a derived unit
- **補助単位**　① an auxiliary unit　②〔1995 年までの SI 単位系で〕a supplementary unit　③＝補助通貨単位
- **補助通貨単位**　① a subunit　② a fractional (monetary) unit

2〔基準となる大きさ〕
- 単位面積　a unit area
- 単位質量　a unit mass
- 単位面積当たりの収穫　a harvest per unit (of) area
- 単位時間に単位面積を通過する粒子の数　the number of particles passing through a unit area per unit time
- 2 単位の正電荷をもつ　carry two units of positive charge
- **単位円**　① a unit circle　②〔円板〕a unit disk
- **単位行列**　① an identity matrix　② a unit matrix
- **単位元**　① an identity (element)　② a unit element　③ a unity

- 乗法に関する単位元　a multiplicative identity
- **単位電荷**　a unit charge
- **単位ベクトル**　a unit vector
- **単位胞**　〚結晶〛a unit cell

3〔扱い上のひとまとまり〕
- 彼女は**億単位の金**を動かせる．　She has control over (**money in the**) **hundreds of millions of yen**.
- 列車のスケジュールは**秒単位**で組まれている．　Trains are scheduled **down to the second**.
- 家族を**社会の単位**とみなす　regard the family as **the basic unit of society**
- **グループ単位**で自由研究をする　do free study **in groups**
- その会社の株式買い付けの**単位は 10 株**だ．　The company's shares may be applied for **in blocks of ten**.
- これらのカップは **4 個単位**で販売しています．　These cups are sold **in sets of four**.

4〚教育〛① a unit　② a point　③ a credit
- フランス語を 2 **単位**取る　① take French for two **credits**　② take two **credits**「of [in] French　★① は履修登録することを表わす．
- 週 2 時間の講義で 4 **単位**与える　give four **credits** for a lecture of two hours per week
- 一年を通して履修した場合，講義科目は **4 単位**，演習科目は **2 単位**となる．When taken for a full year, lecture courses「are worth [carry]」**four credits** and seminar courses **two**.
- 卒業するための**単位**が足りない　do not have「enough [sufficient]」**credits** to graduate
- 彼は卒業に必要な**単位**が取れなかった．　He failed to earn enough **credits** to graduate.
- この授業は専門科目の**単位**になる．　This class **qualifies for credit** in your major.
- 授業を聴講してもいいが**単位にはならない**．　You may audit the course, but you **will not receive credit** (**for it**).
- **単位**を取ったことを証明する　① certify that《a student》has received **credit**　② credit《a student with two units for physics》
- 1 年で 40 **単位**を取る　take 40 **units** in a year
- **単位**を落とす　① fail **a credit**　② lose **a credit**

たんか【単価】　① a unit cost　② a unit price［⇨第 1 部・40-2-5 単価］

たんげつ【単月】　a single month
- 単月過去最高額［値］　monthly record highs

- 単月過去最高だった昨年 9 月の 5 兆円 ① last September's monthly record of 5 trillion yen ② last September's record for a single month of 5 trillion yen
- 9 月の米貿易赤字は単月としては過去最大の赤字額を更新した． The US trade deficit for September was the highest for any month on record.

たんこうしき【単項式】 a monomial (expression)

タンジェント〔正接〕a tangent
- タンジェント x the tangent of x ★tan x と書く．

たんちょう【単調】
- 単調な ① monotone ② monotonic
- 単調性 monotonicity
- 単調関数 a monotone function [⇨ぞうかかんすう，げんしょうかんすう]

たんねんど【単年度】 a single fiscal year [⇨第 1 部・29-4 年度]

ちいき【値域】 the range 《of a function》

ちか【地価】 ①〔売買価格〕the price of land ② land prices ③〔評価額〕the value of land ④ land value(s)
- 地価が上がった． The price of land [Land prices] rose [increased].
- 新しい鉄道ができてから地価がだいぶ上がった． Land has appreciated greatly [Land prices have gone up considerably] since the new railway was built.
- 地価高騰 ① soaring [spiraling, skyrocketing] land prices ② a「jump [steep rise] in land prices
- 地価公示 (the) official「posting [listing] of land「prices [values]
- 公示地価 ① official land values ② government-declared[-assessed] land value(s) ③ listed [posted] land prices
- 公示地価と土地の実勢価格には開きがあるのが普通である． There is usually a difference between the「officially assessed [government-declared] value of land and the real price of land.

ちかん【置換】 ①〔置き換え〕(a) substitution ② (a) replacement ③〔並べ替え〕(a) permutation
- A を B で置換する   ① substitute B for A ② replace A with B
- 入力ビットの置換   a permutation of the input bits
- n 個のものの可能な置換の数   the number of possible permutations of n things
- この写像は単なる置換である． This map is a simple permutation.

チップ a tip
- チップを渡す   give 《a maid》 a tip
- チップを 5 ドル渡す   ① give a tip of five dollars ② tip 《the bellboy》 five dol-

lars
- 少しのチップ　a small tip
- 多すぎるくらいのチップ　a more-than-adequate tip
- チップをはずむ　① give a generous tip ② tip「generously [lavishly]」

チャンネル　a channel ［⇨第 1 部・51. 電池・テレビ 51-4］
- 4 チャンネルで　on Channel 4

ちゅうおうち【中央値】　a median

ちゅうき【中期】　① the middle period ②〘生物〙〔細胞分裂の〕the metaphase
- 17 世紀中期　① the mid-seventeenth century ② the middle part of the seventeenth century

ちゅうじゅん【中旬】　①the middle《of June》②mid-《June》③the second ten days《of June》④ the second third《of June》［⇨第 1 部・33-2「初頭」「末」「旬」］

ちゅうしん【中心】　a center
- P を中心とする円　① a circle centered on P ② a circle with center P ③ a circle「having [with] its center at P ④ a circle with P as its center
- 与えられた点を中心とする円を描く　draw a circle around a given center
- 中心角　〔円周角に対する〕① an angle at the center ② a central angle

ちゅうせん【中線】　a median

ちゅうてん【中点】　① the midpoint ② the middle point ③ the median (point)

ちょう【兆】　①《米》a [one] trillion ②《英》a [one] billion ［⇨第 1 部・7. 大きな数］

…ちょう【…超】　① more than … ② greater than … ③ higher than …　④ larger than …　⑤ above …　⑥ over …　⑦ exceeding …　⑧ … plus ［⇨第 1 部・12.「以上」「以下」等の表現，11. 数値範囲の表現］
- 50 億円超の年間売上高　annual revenue of over ¥5 billion
- 1,000 億ドル超の対米貿易黒字　a $100 billion-plus trade surplus with the U.S.
- その会社の資産総額は 5 億円超だ．
  ① The company has assets valued at more than ¥500 million.
  ② The company has more than ¥500 million in assets.
- 2,000 万円超に達すると見込まれている．
  ① It is expected to total more than ¥20 million.
  ② It is likely to exceed ¥20 million.
- 損失は 1 億円超にふくらんだ．　Losses「piled up [ballooned] to more than ¥100 million.
- 10N [ニュートン] 超の荷重　a load of more than 10「N [newtons]

- 400 cc 超 750 cc 以下の排気量　① displacement of more than 400 cc and less than or equal to 750 cc　② displacement from 400 cc (exclusive) to 750 cc (inclusive)

ちょうえつすう【超越数】　a transcendental (number)　[⇨せいすう 数の集合]

ちょうか【超過】　① excess　②〔余剰〕surplus
- 超過する　① exceed …　② be in excess《of …》　③ be above …　④ be over …　⑤ be more than …
- 制限時間を超過する　exceed [go over] the time limit
- 規定の重量を大幅に超過する　greatly exceed the regulation weight
- 予算を超過する　go over the budget
- 輸出に対する輸入量の超過　a surplus of imports over exports
- 死亡数に対する出生数の超過　a surplus of births over deaths
- 超過重量　excess weight
- 超過請求　① an excess charge　② an overcharge

ちょうかく【頂角】　〔二等辺三角形の〕a vertex angle
- 底角が 70° の二等辺三角形の**頂角**を求めよ．　Find the measure of **the vertex angle** of an isosceles triangle whose base angles are 70°.

ちょうかんすう【超関数】　① a distribution　② a hyperfunction

ちょうきかかんすう【超幾何関数】　a hypergeometric function

ちょうきょくめん【超曲面】　a hypersurface

ちょうくうかん【超空間】　①〔高次元空間〕(a) hyperspace　②〔空間の集合〕(a) superspace.

ちょうてん【頂点】　① a vertex　② an apex
- ★多角形・多面体の一般の頂点は vertex. apex は二等辺三角形や角錐の頂部の頂点. ★vertex の複数形は vertexes, vertices, apex の複数形は apexes, apices.
- 三角形の頂点　a vertex of a triangle
- A は AB＝AC の二等辺三角形 ABC の**頂点**である．　A is **the「vertex [apex]** of an isosceles triangle ABC in which AB＝AC.
- 二等辺三角形の**頂点**から底辺の中点までの線分　the segment from **the「vertex [apex]** of an isosceles triangle to the midpoint of the base
- ある**頂点**を通ってその対辺に垂直な線　a line through **a vertex** perpendicular to the opposite side
- ある**頂点**からその対辺の中点への線分　a (line) segment from **a vertex** to the midpoint of the opposite side
- 隣り合う頂点　consecutive [adjacent] vertices
- 点 A, C は平行四辺形 ABCD の**向かい合う頂点**である．　The points A and C

are **opposite vertices** of a parallelogram ABCD.
- 立方体は6つの面，12の辺，8の**頂点**をもつ．　A cube has 6 faces, 12 sides, and 8 **vertices**.
- 円錐の**頂点**から底面までの距離　the distance from **the apex** of a cone to the base

ちょうど　① just　② exactly　③ precisely　[⇨第1部・18-4「ちょうど」「ぴったり」]

ちょうへいめん【超平面】　a hyperplane

ちょうほうけい【長方形】　a rectangle
- 3 cm×4 cm の長方形　① a rectangle 3 cm by 4 cm　② a rectangle 3 cm×4 cm　③ a 3×4 cm rectangle

ちょうめ【丁目】　⇨第1部・46-1 住所

ちょくせき【直積】　① a direct product　② 〔デカルト積〕a Cartesian product

ちょくせん【直線】　① a line　② a straight line
- 点 A，B を結ぶ直線　the line joining the points A and B
- これらの2直線の交点を通る直線　a line through the intersection of these two lines
- 傾き m，y 切片 c の直線　the line with「slope [gradient] m and intercept c on the y-axis
- どの2つも平行でない3直線　three lines, no two of which are parallel
- 辺 AB はこの直線上にある．　The side AB lies along this line.
- 同一直線上にある　① be collinear　② lie on the same line
- その線は直線であることが期待される．　The line is expected to be straight.
- f のグラフは直線になる．　The graph of f will be a straight line.
- 直線運動　① linear motion　② straight-line motion
- 直線分子　a linear molecule

ちょくわ【直和】　a direct sum

ちょっかく【直角】　a right angle
- 直角である　① be at right angles (to each other)　② be of「90 degrees [90°]《to …》
- 直角に交わる　intersect [cross] at right angles
- 直角をなす　① form a right angle　② make a right angle《with …》
- 2直角より大きな角　an angle larger than two right angles

ちょっけい【直径】　a diameter
- 直径 10 cm の円　a circle with a diameter of 10 cm

- 直径 46 cm, 幅 1.5 cm の環状の溝　a circular groove 46 cm in diameter and 1.5 cm wide
- 直径 1 m, 幅 28 cm のタイヤ　a tire 1 m in diameter and 28 cm wide
- その木は直径 2 メートルある.
  ① The tree is two meters「across [in diameter].
  ② The tree has a diameter of two meters.
  ③ The tree measures two meters in diameter.
- その木は直径いくらありますか.
  ① What is the diameter of the tree?
  ② What does the tree measure across the middle?
  ③ What does the tree measure from one side to the other?
- 外側からみた直径　an「outside [external, outer] diameter [⇨がいけい]
- 内側の直径　an「inside [internal, inner] diameter [⇨ないけい]
- 《天体などの》角直径　an angular diameter
- A, B を直径の両端とする円　a circle with A and B as endpoints of the diameter
- 直径が最大になるところの断面　the cross-section at which《its》diameter is greatest

関連表現

- 山径　〔雄ねじの〕a major diameter
- 谷径　〔雄ねじの〕a minor diameter
- さしわたし 5 キロの湖　a lake 5 kilometers across

ちょっこう【直交】

- 直交する　①〔幾何学的に〕intersect [cross, meet] at right angles　②be [lie] at right angles《to …》　③〔関数どうしが〕be orthogonal
- 直交化　orthogonalization
- 直交性　orthogonality
- 正規直交　⇨せいきちょっこう
- 直交関数系　orthogonal functions
- 直交行列　an orthogonal matrix
- 直交座標　Cartesian coordinates
- 直交変換　orthogonal transformation

ツー　two

- ツーアウト　two outs [⇨第 1 部・49. 野球の数字表現 49-8]
- あこがれの俳優とのツーショット　a photograph taken together with a favorite actor　★英語の a two-shot は放送業界用語で役者 2 人が映るカットをいう.
- 白地に青のラインの入ったツートンカラーの車体　a two-tone body of white with a blue「line [band]

- ツードア車　a two-door car
- ツーピース　a two-piece「dress [suit]
- ツービート　two-beat 《rhythm》
- ツーベース (ヒット)　①《hit》a double　②a two-base hit [⇨第 1 部・49. 野球の数字表現 49-11]
- ツーペア　〘トランプ〙two pairs
- ツーランホーマー　《hit》a two-run homer
- 2 ストロークエンジン　a 2-stroke engine

つうさん【通算】　①a total of …　②overall …　③career …
- 通算 20 年以上　for a total period of twenty years or more
- 勤務年数を通算すると 15 年になる．　All together I have been at my job for 15 years.
- 通算勝率　an overall winning percentage
- 通算打率　〘野球〙*one's* career batting average [⇨第 1 部・49. 野球の数字表現 49-16]
- 本刑に通算する　include 《previous confinement》in the calculation of the regular penalty
- 未決 30 日通算 1 年の禁錮　one year's imprisonment with thirty days deducted for time served before conviction

つうぶん【通分】　reduction to a common denominator [⇨第 1 部・53. 分数]
- 通分する　①reduce [change, convert]《fractions》to a common denominator　②write《fractions》with a common denominator
- 3/4 と 1/3 を足すにはまず通分する必要がある．　To add 3/4 and 1/3 you need first to change the fractions to a common denominator

つき【月】　a month [⇨第 1 部・30-1 月名，31-2 月]

つぎ【次】
- **次の**…　①the next …　②the following …　③the ensuing …　④the coming …
- 次の日　①the next day　②the following day　③the day after
- 次の夏　①the next summer　②the following summer
- (その) 次の日曜　(the) next Sunday [⇨第 1 部・31-5-3 next … の使用例]
- 次の次の日曜　《on》the Sunday after next
- 次の次の駅　①the station after the next (one)　②the next station but one
- その単語の先頭文字に対しアルファベットで次の文字で始まる単語　a word starting with the letter that comes next in the alphabet after the first letter of that word
- 朔望月は新月から次の新月までの期間だ．　The synodic month is the period

…づけ

between successive new moons.
- **次に**　① next　② (and) then　③ after 《that》　④ 《文》 subsequently
- …の次に　① after …　② following …
- 次に会ったときには…　The next time 《we》 met, …
- (地位が) **…の次**にくる　① be second to …　② rank「next [second] to …　③ be ranked「after [just below] …
- 大阪は東京の次に人口が多い．　Osaka is second「to [after, behind] Tokyo in population.
- 大正の次が昭和，その次が平成である．　After Taisho comes Showa, and after that Heisei.
- 大臣の発言は次のとおり．　The minister's statement was as follows.
- 参会者には次の顔ぶれがあった．　Among those present were the following.
- 次から次へと　① one after「the other [another]　② in succession　③ in turn　④ in sequence

…づけ【…付け】　⇨第 1 部・30-5 …付け

つよさ【強さ】　① strength　② intensity　③ power [⇨ きょうど]
- 風の強さ　① the strength of the wind　② the wind speed
- 電場の強さ　electric field strength
- 電流の強さ　① current strength　② current intensity
- 圧縮強さ　compressive strength
- 引っ張り強さ　tensile strength
- 曲げ強さ　bending strength
- 剪断強さ　shear strength

つりせん【釣り銭】　change [⇨第 1 部・40-6-4 おつり]

つれて　⇨第 1 部・13-4-3 相関

ディーケー【DK】　⇨第 1 部・46-3 住居

ていいん【定員】

1　〔乗り物や施設の収容人員数〕① (fixed) capacity　② the seating capacity 《of a theater》　③ the passenger capacity 《of a car》 [⇨…のり]
- 定員 6 人　① Carrying capacity: 6　② Seating capacity: 6
- 定員 [席数] 500 の映画館　① a movie theater capable of seating 500　② a movie theater with a seating capacity of 500　③ a 500-seat movie theater
- この映画館の定員は 50 名だ．　This movie theater seats 50 people.
- このバスの定員は 40 名だ．
  ① This bus has a passenger capacity of 40.
  ② This bus has a carrying capacity of 40 passengers.

③ This bus has 40 seats.
④ This bus carries 40 passengers.
⑤ This bus accommodates 40 passengers.
⑥ This bus is for 40 passengers.
⑦ Up to 40 people may ride this bus.
⑧ No more than 40 people may ride this bus.

- 定員10名のかご4台からなるエレベーターシステム
①an elevator system consisting of four elevator cars, each with a passenger capacity of 10 people
②an elevator system with four 10-passenger cars
- このエレベーターの定員は何人ですか． What is the maximum number of passengers for this elevator?
- 説明会には定員の3倍の150名が集まった． ①Three times the capacity, or 150 people, showed up for the information session. ②One hundred fifty people showed up for the information session, which was three times the capacity.
- その列車の混み具合は定員の120パーセントだった． The train was carrying 20 percent more passengers than the official capacity.
- このバスは定員以上の乗客を乗せている． This bus is overloaded.
- フェリー沈没事故の原因は乗客の定員オーバー［超過］だった．
①The cause of the ferry's sinking was overloading (of passengers).
②The ferry sank because too many passengers were on board.

2 〔学校などの受け入れ人数〕a quota

- 生徒募集定員 ①a quota (for admission) ②the number of students to be admitted ③enrollment ④registration
- 幼稚園の募集定員 the「quota [fixed number]」of children being accepted for places in a kindergarten
- 定員の約1割を社会人枠で募集する ①seek to take in approximately a tenth of the quota from among adults ②set a 10-percent quota for adult admissions
- 今春，大学の約30％が定員割れとなった． This spring, approximately 30 percent of universities did not meet their enrollment goals.
- 受験者が定員に満たない学校もある． There are even some schools that do not have enough examinees to fill the quota for admission.
- あの高校は追加募集を行なってようやく定員を充足した． By offering a second round of applications, that high school barely managed to meet its enrollment goal.
- 文学部の定員を減らす lower the Faculty of Literature quota
- 定員削減 ①a cutback in a quota ②cutting down on a quota
- 定員以上に入学を許可する ①allow [permit] an intake of students over the quota ②allow [permit] more students to enroll than originally planned

関連表現

- 人種的マイノリティーのための入学枠　an admission quota for racial minorities

3 〔所定の受け入れ人数〕the「prescribed [designated, fixed] number of applicants
- クラス定員は5名です．
  ① Class enrollment will be limited to five students.
  ② Up to five students may enroll in the class.
- 申込者が定員に達し次第，募集を打ち切らせていただきます．　Applications will close when the prescribed number of applicants is reached.
- 応募者はまだ定員に達していない．　We are still short of the designated number of applicants.
- 定員を超える応募者があった．　We had more applicants than the number of positions available.
- 参加者が定員を割ったので今回のヨーロッパツアーは中止となった．　The number of participants was below the minimum required, so the planned tour of Europe was canceled.

関連表現

- 最少催行人数　the minimum required number of participants

4 〔所定の構成人数〕① the「regular [fixed, prescribed] number of staff [level of staffing] ② the「full [definite] number of personnel ③ the full strength《of a staff》[⇨ていすう]
- この病院は医師・看護師とも定員を満たしていない．
  ① This hospital does not have the prescribed number of doctors and nurses.
  ② This hospital is understaffed by both doctors and nurses.
- 各行政機関の職員の定員は法律で定められている．　The prescribed number of workers in each administrative organ is fixed by law.
- 定員減　a drop in the「regular [fixed, prescribed] number of staff
- 定員削減　① a cutback in the「regular [fixed, prescribed] number of staff　② cutting down on the「regular [fixed, prescribed] number of staff　③ a staff reduction
- 定員外の臨時職員　① a temporary extra worker ② extra help
- 定員を満たしていない大隊　an understrength battalion

ティーン　★-teen の語尾をもつ年齢範囲 (13歳から19歳) を指す．[⇨じゅうだい，第1部・38. 年齢 38-3]
- ティーン (エージャー)　① a teenager ② a teen
- ハイティーンの少年　a boy in his late teens
- ローティーンの少女　a girl in her early teens
- ミドルティーン (の人)　a mid-teen

- ハイティーンに人気のあるファッション　(a) fashion popular「among [with] kids in their late teens

ディオプトリ　⇨ジオプトリ

ていか【低下】　①a fall ②a decline ③a drop ④a dip ⑤(a) decrease ⑥lowering ⑦〔価値・値段の〕depreciation ⑧〔品質の〕deterioration
- 低下する　①fall (off) ②drop (off) ③decrease ④sink ⑤decline ⑥go down《in price》⑦come down ⑧depreciate
- 出生率の低下　a「decline [drop, fall] in the birthrate
- 視力の低下を食い止める　①check [halt] a decline in *one's* eyesight ②check [halt] the deterioration of *one's* eyesight
- 川の水位が低下しはじめた．　The water level of the river began to「fall [go down]．

ていか【定価】　①the list price ②the marked price ③the labeled price ④the regular price ④the fixed price〔⇨第1部・40-2-4 価格にまつわる術語〕
- 定価の2割引きで　at a 20 percent discount off the「list [marked] price

ていかく【定格】　(a) rating
- 定格電流　a rated current
- 定格電力　a rated power
- 定格負荷　a rated load
- 電力定格　a power rating
- 電流の定格を超えたら　if the current rating is exceeded
- 絶対最大定格　an absolute maximum rating
- 定格を超える電圧　a voltage exceeding the rating
- 連続使用定格　a continuous-duty rating
- 定格10Aのリレー　a relay rated at 10 A
- 定格負荷の75%　75% of the rated load
- 定格動作温度は75℃である　①have a rated operating temperature of 75℃ ②be rated for 75℃

ていかく【底角】　a base angle
- **底角**が70°の二等辺三角形の頂角を求めよ．　Find the measure of the vertex angle of an isosceles triangle whose **base angles** are 70°.

ていがく【低額】
- 低額の所得　(a) low income
- 低額の貯金　small savings
- 低額貨幣　①low-denomination「notes [coins, currency] ②notes [coins, currency] of low denomination

- 低額宿泊所　① low-cost lodging　② a low-cost shelter

ていがく【定額】　① a fixed amount　② the required amount　③ a flat sum
- 定額請負　〘土木〙 a fixed-sum contract
- 定額課税　① fixed-amount taxation　② a flat tax
- 定額料金制　the flat-rate system

ていぎいき【定義域】　the domain 《of a function》

ていすう【定数】

1 〔定められた数〕[⇨第 1 部・16-7 定数]
- 定数の半数　〔議席の〕half the seats
- 定数 1 の選挙区　a single-member「constituency [(electoral) district]

2 〔変化せず一定である数〕a constant
- ほとんど[本質的に]定数である　be「nearly [essentially] constant
- 光の速さはあらゆる観測者に対して定数である．　The speed of light is a constant for all observers.
- 定数倍を除いて…に等しい　① equal to … up to a constant multiple　② equal to … up to a factor
- 任意定数　an arbitrary constant

ディスク　① a disk　② a disc [⇨第 1 部・51-5 録画]

ていせきぶん【定積分】　a definite integral

ていそくすう【定足数】　a quorum [⇨第 1 部・16-8 定足数]

ていへん【底辺】　a base
- 三角形の面積は**底辺**かける高さ割る 2 である．　The area of a triangle is **the base** times the height divided by two. [⇨第 1 部・58-5 面積の公式]

ていめん【底面】　a base
- 底面の半径が 2 cm，高さが 12 cm の円錐　a cone with base radius 2 cm and height 12 cm

ていめんせき【底面積】　the area of a base
- 角錐の体積は**底面積**かける高さかける 1/3 である．　The volume of a pyramid is one third the product of **the area of its base** and the height.

デカ…　〔10〕deca- [⇨第 1 部・27-4 SI 接頭語]

デカルトざひょう【デカルト座標】　Cartesian coordinates

できだか【出来高】

1 〔作物の収穫高〕① (a) yield　② (a) crop

2 〔生産高〕① (an) output　② (a) turnout　③ (a) production

- 出来高仕事　piecework
- 出来高払い〔給〕　①piecework payment　②payment at (a) piece rate　③payment at (a) piecemeal rate　④〔特にプロスポーツ選手などの〕performance pay　⑤performance-related pay　⑥performance-based pay　⑦performance incentives　⑧performance bonuses　⑨〔建設工事などにおける〕progress payment
- 出来高払いで働く　①work on a piece(-rate) basis　②work by the piece
- 出来高払い制　①a piecework system　②a performance-based pay system　③〔保険医療における〕a fee-for-service system

3 〔取引高〕①(a) (trading) volume　②(a) turnover
- 東京証券取引所の今日の出来高　today's「volume [turnover]」at the Tokyo Stock Exchange
- 200万株の1日当たり平均出来高　an average daily volume of two million shares

デシ…　〔10^{-1}〕deci-〔⇨第1部・27-4 SI 接頭語〕

デシベル　〔強度比の表示の単位〕a decibel《＝1/10 ベル；記号 dB》

★デシベルは対数スケールであり，振幅が10倍になると（強度は100倍）デシベル値は20上がる．電気通信や音響分野では特定の基準強度を定めてデシベル値を強度の絶対値の表示に用いることもある．

- デシベルで表わした強度　an intensity expressed in decibels
- 信号を3デシベル減衰させる　attenuate a signal by 3 decibels
- +3デシベルの利得は出力電力が入力の2倍であることを示す．　A gain of +3 decibels indicates that the output power is double the input.　★強度が2倍になるとデシベル値は $10\log_{10} 2 ≒ 3$ だけ上がる．

テスラ　〔磁束密度の単位〕a tesla《記号 T》

てどり【手取り】　①take-home pay　②take-home wages　③spendable earnings〔⇨第1部・40-5-2 収入〕

テラ…　①〔10^{12}〕tera-　②〔テラバイト〕a terabyte〔⇨第1部・27-4 SI 接頭語〕

テレビ　①television　②TV〔⇨第1部・51. 電池・テレビ〕
- 20型のテレビ　①a 20-inch TV　②a 20″ TV　③a 20-inch diagonal TV　★数値は画面の対角線の長さを表わす．

てん【点】

1 a point
- 点Aを通る直線　a straight line (passing) through point A
- その曲線で y が1になる点　the point on that curve at which y equals one

2 〔試験などの評点〕①a grade　②a score　③points　④《英》a mark　★grade, mark は試験の得点のほか学期末の成績の意もある．〔⇨てんすう〕

てん

- 英語は70点だった． I got 70 in English.
- 70点台を取る　score in the seventies
- よい[悪い]点を取る　get a「good [bad] grade [score,《英》mark]《on a test》
- 数学の点がよかった[悪かった]． I got a「good [bad] grade [《英》mark] in math.
- 0点を取る　① get [score] zero《in math》 ② receive a「grade [《英》mark] of zero
- 100点を取る　① get 100　② score 100
- 100点満点で51点取る　① get 51 out of 100　② obtain 51 points out of a possible 100
- 満点を取る　① get a perfect score　② do perfectly《on a test》　③《英》get a full mark　④《英》get full marks
- **100点満点で答案を採点する**　① grade [《英》mark] examination papers **on the basis of 100 points**　② grade [《英》mark] examination papers **on a maximum of 100 points**　③ grade [《英》mark] examination papers **out of 100**　④ grade [《英》mark] examination papers **on a scale of 0 to 100**
- 今日の算数のテスト**何点**だった？　**What was your score** on the math test today?
- 最高点　〔試験などの〕① the highest score　② the best score　③《英》top marks
- 最高点を取る　get the highest「score [《英》marks]

3 〔競技の得点〕① a point　② a score　③ a run　④ a goal　★run は野球など，goal はサッカーなどについていう．[⇨…たい…，てんすう，とくてん，どうてん，タイ，てんさ，第1部・49. 野球の数字表現 49-4, 49-5]
- 点を取る[入れる]　① score　② score a point　③ score a run　④ score a goal
- 5点取る　① score 5 points　② score 5 runs　③ score 5 goals
- …より多く得点する　① outscore …　② outpoint …
- やっと点が入った． We finally scored (a「point [run, goal])!
- 1点返す　① get [claw] back one point　② retrieve a point
- 点が取れない　be unable to「score [rack up, chalk up] any points
- 点が取れずに終わる　① end without scoring a (single) point　②〔双方無得点〕end [finish] in a scoreless draw
- (相手に)点を許す[取られる]　① lose a point《to *one's* opponent》　② go down a point《to *one's* opponent》
- 追加点を許す　yield [concede] another [an additional, an extra] point [run, goal]
- 最後まで相手チームに点を入れさせなかった． They held the other team scoreless right to the end.

- 勝っていたのに最後に3点入れられて逆転負けした．　We were ahead, but they scored three「points [runs] at the end to beat us.
- だめ押しの1点を加える　① add [score] an insurance「run [goal] ② pad the score with an extra「run [goal] ③《This goal》puts the game out of reach.
- 8回裏にスクイズでだめ押しの1点が入った．　An insurance run came in with a squeeze play in the bottom of the eighth (inning).
- 点は5対1だ．　① The score is 5 to 1. ② The score stands at 5 to 1.
- 今タイガース何点？　① What's the Tigers' score? ② How many points do the Tigers have?
- あと20分の時点でフランスが12点リードしていた．
  ① The French led by 12 points with 20 minutes to go.
  ② The French were 12 points ahead with 20 minutes to go.

でんあつ【電圧】　(a) voltage
- ボルトで測った電圧　(a) voltage (measured) in volts
- 電極間に20Vの電圧がかけられる．　A voltage of 20 volts is applied between the electrodes.
- 端子間の電圧　the voltage between the terminals
- コイルの両端の間の電圧　the voltage across the coil
- 逆方向に加えられた電圧　the voltage applied in the reverse direction
- 導体中に誘起された電圧　the voltage induced in the conductor
- 90から200Vの入力電圧　an input voltage of 90 to 200 volts
- 50Ωの抵抗に1Aの電流を流すのに必要な電圧　the voltage needed to cause a current of 1 A to flow in a 50-ohm resistor
- 100Vの電圧がかけられ, 200 mAの電流が流れている抵抗器　a resistor with a voltage of 100 volts applied across it and passing a current of 200 mA
- 高電圧　(a) high voltage
- 低電圧　(a) low voltage
- 非常に高い電圧がかかっている電線　a wire carrying a very high voltage
- 正電圧　(a) positive voltage
- 負電圧　(a) negative voltage
- 電圧を150Vに上げる　increase [raise] the voltage to 150 volts
- 電圧を下げる　decrease [lower] the voltage
- 電池の電圧が1.1Vにまで低下する．　The cell voltage「drops [falls] to 1.1 volts.
- 一次コイルの電流の変化によって，二次コイルの両端の間の電圧に変化が生じる．　A change in the current through the primary coil will produce a change in voltage across the secondary coil.
- これらの電池の電圧が下に挙げてある．　The voltages for these batteries are

でんい

given below.
- 2つの入力電圧を比較する　compare two input voltages

でんい【電位】 electric potential
- 電流は**電位**の高い点から低い点へと流れる．　Electric current flows from a point of higher **potential** to one of lower **potential**.
- 大地を基準として，それらの導体は大きさが等しく極性が反対の**電位**になっている．　With respect to ground, those conductors are at equal **potential** but opposite polarity.
- …を接地**電位**にする　set … at ground **potential**
- フィラメントは負の高**電位**に保たれている．　The filament is「held [maintained]」at a high negative **potential**.

でんいさ【電位差】 ① potential difference ② difference of potential
- 50 Ω の抵抗に 2 A の電流が流れると 100 V の**電位差**が生じる．　A current of 2 amperes in a 50-ohm resistor produces **a potential difference** of 100 volts.
- 2点間の**電位差**　**the potential difference** between two points
- 1 V の**電位差**で粒子を加速する　accelerate a particle **through a potential difference** of 1 volt
- 1 V の**電位差**に逆らって電子を動かすのに必要なエネルギー　the energy required to move an electron through **a potential difference** of 1 volt
- 接触電位差　contact potential (difference)
- 電位差計　a potentiometer
- 電位差滴定　potentiometric titration

てんかい【展開】

1 〔たたんだ物の〕① unfolding ②〔圧縮データの〕decompression ③ extraction ④ unpacking ⑤〔配備〕deployment ⑥〔立体図形を平面上に表現すること〕development［⇨てんかいず］
- 円錐は平面に展開できる．　Cones can be developed into a plane.
- 展開可能な曲面《可展曲面》　a developable surface

2 〔事態の進展〕① development ② evolution ③ unfolding

3 〔式の〕expansion
- $(a+b)^2$ を展開すると $a^2+2ab+b^2$ になる．
  ① Expand $(a+b)^2$, and you will get $a^2+2ab+b^2$.
  ② The expansion of $(a+b)^2$ is $a^2+2ab+b^2$.
  ③ The expression $(a+b)^2$ expands into $a^2+2ab+b^2$.
- フーリエ級数に展開する，フーリエ展開する　expand (…) into a Fourier series

- z の冪で展開する　expand ⋯ in powers of z
- v/c について［v/c の冪に］展開する　expand (⋯) in (powers of) v/c
- この点のまわりの冪級数に展開する　expand (⋯) into a power series around this point
- ポテンシャルを $R=R_0$ のまわりで展開する　expand the potential around $R=R_0$
- f の x の逆の冪での展開式　an expansion of f in inverse powers of x
- 小さな x に対して展開する　expand (⋯) for small x
- x が小さいときの f の展開式　an expansion of f for small x
- その関数を運動量演算子の固有関数で展開する《固有関数を基底として展開する》　expand the function in terms of the eigenfunctions of the momentum operator
- 級数展開　(a) series expansion

てんかいず【展開図】　① a net　② a development　③ a pattern

- 角柱の展開図　a net of a prism
- 立方体には 11 通りの展開図がある．　There are 11 nets for a cube.
- 上図のうち，下の展開図を折ってできるさいころの図でありうるのはどれか．　Which of the pictures above could be a view of a die made by folding the「pattern［net］shown below?
- 円錐の展開図は底面になる円と側面になる扇形からなる．　The net of a cone consists of a circle that gives the base and a sector that gives the lateral surface.

てんさ【点差】　① a point difference　② a point spread　③〔野球などで〕a run difference　［⇨第 1 部・49-5 点差］

- 点差を縮めて 3 対 2 にする　cut the deficit to 3-2
- 点差を 5 対 2 まで広げる　① widen the lead to 5-2　② boost the lead to 5-2
- 1 点差を守りきる　hold［hang］onto a one-point lead
- 後半になって点差がさらに開いた．　Once into the second half the「point difference［point spread］grew even wider.

でんしボルト【電子ボルト】　〔素粒子などのエネルギーの単位］an electronvolt《記号 eV》

てんすう【点数】

1　〔試験などの評点］① a grade　② a score　③《英》a mark　［⇨てん］

- 点数が 50 点未満の人　those who scored less than fifty
- 点数がよければ［悪ければ］　if you get a「good［bad］grade［《英》mark］《in history》
- 彼はすべての科目で点数が私より高かった．

① He scored higher than me in every subject.
② He got better「grades [《英》marks] than me in every subject.
- 前回のテストより点数が上がった[下がった]．　I got a「higher [lower] grade [《英》mark] on the test than last time.
- **点数をつける**　① **grade** [**rate**, 《英》**mark**]《an assignment, a paper, a movie, etc.》② **give**「**grades** [《英》**marks**] ③ **award points**
- 今日の試合に自分で点数をつけるなら何点ぐらいだと思う？　If you had to grade your own performance today, how many points would you give yourself?

2〔競技などの得点〕① points ② a score ③〔野球の〕runs [⇨てん]

3〔診療の〕health insurance points

4〔交通違反などの〕① traffic violation points ② endorsement points
- 点数切符　a traffic violation ticket
- 違反の点数が6点になると免許停止になります．　If you accumulate 6 traffic violation points, your license will be suspended.

5〔品物の数〕the number of「articles [items]
- 帳簿と現物との点数が一致しない．　The number of items does not tally with the entry in the book.
- お買い上げ点数は5つですね．　So you'll take five (of them) altogether?
- この展示会の出品点数は500を超える．　This exhibition has more than five hundred items on display.

てんせん【点線】　① a dotted line ② a broken line ③〔切取線〕a perforated line
- クーポン券は**点線の所から**切り取ること．　The coupon should be torn **off along the perforated line**.
- 点線を引く　draw a dotted line
- 点線の円　a dotted circle
- 理論的な曲線は点線で示されている．　The theoretical curve is shown「by [with] a dotted line.

テンソル　a tensor
- 2階テンソル　① a tensor of「order [rank] two ② a tensor of the second「order [rank] ③ a second-order[-rank] tensor
- 応力テンソルの成分　the components of a stress tensor
- 曲率テンソルを縮約して得られる2階テンソル　a second-rank tensor formed by contracting the curvature tensor

てんたいしょう【点対称】　point symmetry
- 点対称である　have [possess] point symmetry
- **点対称な図形**はある点のまわりに180°回すともとの図形に一致する．　If **a**

figure with point symmetry is rotated 180° about a certain point, it coincides with the original figure.

でんち【電池】 ① a battery ② a cell［⇨第 1 部・51-1 電池］

てんちょうかく【天頂角】 a zenith angle
- 鉛直面内における天頂と対象との間の角は**天頂角**と呼ばれる． The angle in a vertical plane between the zenith and an object is called **the zenith angle**.

てんもんがくてき【天文学的】
- **天文学的**数字に達する　① reach an **astronomical**「figure [sum］② run (in)to astronomical「figures [numbers］③ be astronomical

てんもんたんい【天文単位】〔距離の単位〕an astronomical unit《≒1 億 5000 万 km；記号 au》
- 海王星は太陽からの平均距離 30 天文単位のところを回っている． Neptune orbits the sun at an average distance of 30 astronomical units.
- 木星の平均軌道半径は何天文単位か． What is the average radius of Jupiter's orbit in astronomical units?

でんりゅう【電流】 ① (an) electric current ② (a) current
- アンペアで測った電流　(a) current (measured) in amperes
- 数百アンペアのオーダーの大電流　a very large current of the order of magnitude of several hundred amperes
- その 50 Ω の抵抗を流れる電流　the electric current「passing [flowing］through the 50-ohm resistor
- R_2 を流れる電流は R_1 を流れる電流の 2 倍だ． The current through R_2 is twice the current through R_1.
- 20 Ω の抵抗に 100 V の電圧をかけると 5A の電流が流れる．
① A voltage of 100 V across a 20-ohm resistor causes 5 A of current to flow.
② When a voltage of 100 V is applied across a 20-ohm resistor, 5 A of current will flow.
- …に電流を流す　① a current is sent through … ② send a current through … ③ let a current flow through … ④ allow a current to flow through …
- その導線は 0.1 A までの電流を流すことができる． The wire can carry a current up to 0.1 A.
- 電流を 300 mA に制限する　limit the current to 300 mA
- 電源から 1.2 A の電流を引き出す　draw 1.2 A of current from the power supply
- 電力は電圧に電流をかけたものだ． Power is voltage multiplied by current.
- 電流は電圧割る抵抗だ．〔オームの法則〕Current is voltage divided by resistance.
- 回路中の任意の点に流れ込む電流はその点から流れ出る電流に等しい．〔キ

ルヒホッフの法則〕 The current「entering [flowing into] any point in a circuit is equal to the current「leaving [flowing out of] that point.
- 並列に接続した抵抗を流れる全電流は各抵抗を流れる電流の和に等しい. The total current flowing through resistors connected in parallel is equal to the sum of the currents flowing through each resistor.
- 大電流　a「large [high, powerful, strong] current
- 小電流　a「small [low, weak] current
- 低電流では　at low currents
- 電流の強さ　① current intensity ② current strength ③ the intensity of a current ④ the strength of a current
- 電流を発生させる [誘導する]　produce [induce] an electric current
- ずっと大きな電流を流せるようにする　allow a much larger current to flow
- 超伝導体でできたリングの電流は永久に流れ続ける.　An electric current in a ring made of a superconductor will keep flowing forever.
- 電流が流れない.　No current flows.

でんりょく【電力】　① electric power ② power ③〔漠然と電気の意で〕electricity
- 10 ワットの電力を散逸 [消費] する　dissipate [consume] a power of 10 watts
- ワットで表わした電力の大きさ　the amount of power in watts
- その抵抗が消費する電力は何ワットか.　How much power in watts does the resistor「use [consume]?
- 電力会社　① a power company ② an electric power company ③ an electric company ④ an electricity company
- 電力計　a wattmeter
- 積算電力計　① a watt-hour meter ②〔家庭の電気メーター〕an electricity meter
- 電力需要　① (electric) power demand ② electricity demand
- 電力消費 (量)　① (electric) power consumption ② electricity consumption
- 電力ピーク　(the) peak load
- 電力不足　① an electric power shortage ② a power shortage ③ a shortage of electricity

でんりょくりょう【電力量】　electric energy
- 電力量計　① an electric energy meter ② an electricity meter ③ a watt-hour meter
- 1 ワット時の電力量　① one watt-hour of electricity ② one watt-hour of electric energy
- 1 ワットの電灯が 1 時間に消費する電力量が 1 ワット時である.　The amount of electric energy consumed by a one-watt light「over [for a period of] one

でんわばんごう

hour is one watt-hour.
- 両方とも同じ電力(量)を消費する．　Both consume the same amount of power.　★amount of power は「電力量」と「電力の大きさ」の両方の意味がありうるので注意．

でんわばんごう【電話番号】　①a telephone number　②a phone number［⇨第1部・46. 住所と電話番号］

ど【度】

1〔角度〕a degree［⇨ひゃくはちじゅうど］
- 12 度 34 分 56 秒　12 degrees, 34 minutes, and 56 seconds　★12°34′56″ と書く．
- 45 度の角　①an angle of 45 degrees　②a 45-degree angle
- 45 度の角度で　at an angle of 45 degrees
- 5°傾ける　①tilt 5 degrees　②tilt by 5 degrees　③tilt through 5 degrees
- ピサの斜塔は**4度傾いている**．　The Leaning Tower of Pisa **leans 4 degrees**.
- 軸は表面**に対して**正確に**90度**ではない．　The shaft is not exactly **90°**「**with respect to** [**relative to**] the surface.
- 偏光面を偏光器**に対して90度の角度に**する　make the polarization plane **at an angle of 90 degrees with respect to** the polarizer
- 2つのブロックを45度ずらして重ねる　stack one block on another offset「by 45 degrees [at a 45-degree angle]
- **鉛直線に対して**5°**傾いている**　be inclined at an angle of 5°「**from (the) vertical** [**off (the) vertical, to the vertical, with respect to the vertical, relative to the vertical**]
- 地軸は地球の公転軌道面に垂直な線**に対して 23.5 度**傾いている．　The earth's axis is tilted **23.5 degrees**「(**away**) **from** [**with respect to**] the perpendicular to the plane of its orbit around the sun.
- **360度**回転できる　can rotate **360 degrees**
- 360 度の眺め［視野］　a (full) 360-degree view
- 360 度パノラマ写真　①a 360-degree panoramic photograph　②〔技術〕360-degree panoramic photography　③〔撮影〕panoramic 360-degree imaging
- 円筒表面の周囲 360 度の方向に均等に分布している　be uniformly distributed 360 degrees around the circumference of the cylinder's surface

2〔経緯度〕a degree［⇨いど，けいど］
- 北緯 51 度にある　be at latitude 51°N　★51°N は fifty-one degrees north と読む．
- 17 度線で　at the 17th parallel (of latitude)

3〔温度〕a degree［⇨第 1 部・45-1 温度，28. 伝統単位 28-7］
- セ氏 8 度　eight degrees「Celsius [centigrade]《記号 8°C》

- マイナス［プラス］3度　three degrees「below [above]」zero

4〔アルコール飲料の容量パーセント〕percent alcohol (by volume)《記号 % または % ABV》［⇨とうど］

- ワインは通常 **14 度**までだ．　Wine is typically up to **14 percent alcohol**.
- ビールのアルコール分は一般に **4 度から 7 度**の範囲だ．
  ① Beer contains alcoholic contents generally in the range of **4 to 7 percent alcohol**.
  ② Beer generally contains **between 4 and 7 percent alcohol**.

★英米ではアルコール分を proof で表わすこともある．100 (%) proof は米国では 50%(1/2)，英国では約 57%(1/1.75) に当たる．

- プルーフ度が 80 の酒は**アルコール分 40 度**である．　An 80-proof liquor is **40 percent alcohol**.
- このウイスキーは **40 度**だ．　This whiskey is **80 (percent) proof**.
- **度の強い**ウイスキー　**high-proof** whiskey［⇨どすう］

5〔レンズの屈折力〕(a) power

- 度が 5D［5 ジオプトリ］のレンズ　① a 5D lens　② a 5-diopter lens［⇨ジオプトリ］
- このめがねは**度が合っていない**．　These lenses are **not the right strength** for my eyes.
- **度の強い**めがね　strong glasses
- めがねの**度を強くする**　**use stronger** lenses

6〔度合い〕① a degree　② an extent

- 習熟度　①〔学習内容の〕a degree of (academic) achievement　②〔技術の〕a degree of mastery　③ a skill level
- 難易度　① the「degree [level]」of difficulty　② how difficult《a task》is
- 理解度　① comprehension　② how well《a subject》has been understood
- 重要度　(the degree of) importance
- 優先度　priority
- 解像度　resolution
- 硬度　(a) hardness

▶専門語では -ity で終わるものも少なくない．［⇨りつ］

- アルカリ度　(an) alkalinity
- 易動度　(a) mobility
- 電気伝導度　(an) electric conductivity
- 偏光度　a degree of polarization

7〔音程〕

- 長三度　a major third

…とう

- 短三度　a minor third
- 完全四度　a perfect fourth
- 完全五度　a perfect fifth
- 減五度　① a diminished fifth　② tritone
- 増四度　an augmented fourth
- ドとミの間の音程は長三度だ．　The interval from C to E is a major third.
- 彼は**1オクターブと七度**の声域がある．　His voice has a range of **an octave and a seventh**.
- 減七の和音は**4つの短三度**を重ねたものだ．　A diminished seventh consists of **four minor thirds** on top of each other.
- ドからミは**何度**ですか．　**What is the interval** from C to E?

8〔回数〕a time ［⇨第1部・36. 回数・頻度の表現〕

- 1度　① one time　② once
- 1, 2度　once or twice
- 2, 3度　two or three times
- 1度ならず(2度3度)　① more than once　② on more occasions than one　③ repeatedly
- 3度に1度は　① one time out of three　② once in three times

…とう【…等】

1〔順位〕

- 競走で2等になる　① take second place in a race　② come out second in a race　③ be runner-up in a race
- 1等賞　① the first prize　② the gold medal
- 2等賞　the second prize
- 1等賞受賞者　a first-prize winner
- 1等賞を取る　① win (the) first prize　② take first place
- 1等賞は伊藤氏の手に落ちた．　The first prize went to Mr. Ito.

2〔格〕

- 1等車　a first-class〔carriage [car]
- 1等乗客[船客]　a first-class passenger
- 1等寝台　① a first-class sleeping compartment　② a first-class berth
- 1等船室　a first-class cabin
- 2等切符　a second-class ticket
- 2等運賃　a second-class fare
- 1等で行く　go [travel] first-class
- 2等で行く　① go [travel] second-class　② go second　③〔船〕go [travel]

cabin-class
- 3等で旅行する　① go [travel] third(-class)　②〔船〕travel (in the) steerage

3〔その他一般に等級〕① a class　② a grade　③ a degree
- 1 [2, 3] 等　the「first [second, third] class [grade]
- 一等機関士　a first engineer
- 一等航海士　① a first mate　② a chief officer
- 二等航海士　① a second mate　② a second officer
- 一等 [二等，三等] 書記官　〔大使館などの〕a「first [second, third] secretary
- 一等陸佐など　⇨じえいかん
- 1 等星　① a star of the first magnitude　② a first-magnitude star
- 2 等星　① a star of the second magnitude　② a second-magnitude star
- 2.5 等星　a star of magnitude 2.5

どうい【胴囲】　*one's* waist measurement [⇨第 1 部・43-4 ウエスト]

どういかく【同位角】　the corresponding angle
- 2本の平行線に1本の直線が交わるとき，**同位角**の大きさは等しい．　If two parallel lines are cut by a transversal, then **corresponding angles** have equal measures.

どうかんすう【導関数】　① a derivative　② a derived function
- 2階導関数　① a second derivative　② a second-order derivative　③ a derivative of the second order.
- $f(x)$ のすべての（階数の）導関数が $x = a$ の近傍で連続であれば　if all the derivatives of a function $f(x)$ are continuous in the vicinity of $x = a$

とうき【騰貴】　① a rise ((in prices))　② an advance ((in the Nikkei index))　③ (an) appreciation ((of [in] land values))　④ a jump ((in land prices))　⑤ a leap [⇨第 1 部・13-4 増加・上昇を表わす各種表現]

どうき【同期】　① the same period　② the equivalent period　③ the comparable period [⇨しはんき，第 1 部・13-3 比較の基準の表現]
- 昨年同期　① the year-ago period　② the「same [corresponding] period a year ago　③ the「same [corresponding] period last year
- 前年同期　① the year-before period　② the「same [corresponding] period a year earlier
- 前年同期の売上げ　sales for the same period a year earlier
- 昨年同期比で
  ① compared「with [to] (the figures for) the same period「a year ago [last year]
  ② compared with the year-ago period
  ③ on a year-on-year basis
- 前年同期比で

① compared「with [to] (the figures for) the same period the previous year
② compared with the year-before period
③ on a year-on-year basis
- 前年同期に比べて 32 パーセントの月次売り上げ増　a 32 percent rise in sales for the month as compared with「the same period (of) the previous year [the year-ago period]
- 会社の売り上げは昨年の同期に比較して 3 割上昇した．　The company's sales were up by 30 percent compared with the same period last year.
- 売り上げは前年同期の 2.7 倍に増えた．　Sales were 2.7 times higher than in the same period a year earlier.
- パソコン売上高は 3 か月連続で前年同期割れが続いている．　Sales of computers have been lower than for the equivalent periods last year for three months running.

とうきゅう【等級】　① a class　② a grade　③ an order　④ a rank　⑤ a degree　⑥〔星の〕a magnitude　⑦〔船員の〕a rating
- 1, 2, 3 と等級がある　be graded 1, 2, (or) 3
- その航空会社は 3 つの等級がある．　There are three classes of service on that airline.
- 等級を付ける [等級に分ける]　① classify　② grade　③ rank　④ graduate　⑤〔船員・船舶の〕rate
- 品質により細かに等級を設けてある　be finely graded according to quality
- 視等級　〘天〙(an) apparent magnitude
- 絶対等級　〘天〙(an) absolute magnitude
- 等級順に並べる　arrange《articles》by grade

とうけい【東経】　(the) east longitude [⇨けいど]

とうけい【統計】

1　① statistics　②〔データの数字〕figures
★statistics は「統計学」および物理学でいう粒子の「統計」の意味では単数扱いだが，統計データの意味では複数扱い．単数形 a statistic は「統計量」（個々の統計データから算出される平均値・標準偏差など）の意．
- …の統計を取る [集める]　① collect [gather] statistics「on [about, concerning] …　② take [get] the statistics「on [for, of] …　③ prepare [compile] the statistics「on [for, of] …
- 降雨に関する**統計**は 200 年近くにわたって取られている．　**Statistics** on rainfall have been kept for nearly 200 years.
- その都市の**昼間人口統計**　**the daytime population statistics** for the city
- …から (集めてきて) 編集した**統計**　**statistics** compiled from …
- より多くの**統計**をもたらす　bring in more **statistics**

どうけい

- 比較的とぼしい**統計データ**　relatively poor **statistics**
- 小さな統計［データ数の少ない統計］　small statistics
- これについては**統計**がない．　There are no 「**figures** ［**statistics**］available concerning this「point ［question］.
- その**2組の統計**には著しい違いがあった．　There was a marked disagreement between the **two sets of statistics**.
- 統計（の示すところ）によれば　① according to the statistics　② the figures 「show ［teach us, disclose］that …　③ statistics show that …
- 統計上は　① statistically　② according to the statistics　③ in the statistics
- この統計を一目見れば…ということがわかるだろう．　A glance at these statistics will show that …
- 最新の統計に基づく計算　calculations based on the latest statistics
- **死亡統計**　① mortality statistics　② statistics of mortality
- **出生統計**　① birth statistics　② statistics of births
- **人口動態統計**　① vital statistics　② demographic statistics
- **人口統計**　population statistics
- **統計データ**　statistical data
- **統計表**　① a statistical table　② a statistical chart
- **統計的有意性**　statistical significance
- **統計分析**［**解析**］　(a) statistical analysis

2〘物〙statistics

- **ボーズ‐アインシュタイン統計**がなりたつ．　The **Bose-Einstein statistics** applies.
- **古典統計**によって記述される　be described by **classical statistics**

どうけい【同型】〔写像〕(an) isomorphism

- 群 U(2) は SU(2)×U(1) と**同型である**．　The group U(2) is **isomorphic** to SU(2)×U(1).
- 次数 10 で，どの 2 つも**同型**でないアーベル群の集合　a collection of Abelian groups, each of order 10, no two of which are **isomorphic**
- V から W への写像 f は**同型（写像）**である．　The map f of V to W is an **isomorphism**.
- 複素数とこの形の 2×2 行列の間には**同型写像**が存在する．　There exists an **isomorphism** between complex numbers and 2×2 matrices of this type.

どうけい【動径】　a radius

- 動径方向の速度　radial velocity
- 動径方向の加速度　radial acceleration
- **動径** OP, OQ と弧 PQ で囲まれる面積　the area bounded by **the radius vec-**

tors OP, OQ and the arc PQ

- (惑星の) **動径**は同じ時間内に等しい面積を掃く． **The radius vector** (of a planet) sweeps out equal areas in「equal time intervals [equal times].
- 動径ベクトル　a radius vector

とうごう【等号】　① an equal(s) sign　② a sign of equality

★日本語では「イコール」という特別な読み方があるが，英語では $A=B$ は「A は B に等しい」という普通の表現として読むので，たとえば A equals B. または A is equal to B. と読める．文の一部として使われている場合は，たとえば For $n=2$, this simplifies to … なら For n equal to 2, … と読める．[⇨第1部・55. 式の読み方]

とうざいなんぼく【東西南北】　north, south, east, and west [⇨第1部・59-5 東西南北]

どうじ【同次】　homogeneity
- 同次式　a homogeneous expression
- 同次対称式　a homogeneous symmetrical expression

どうじ【同時】　[⇨第1部・33-3 同時]
- 同時に　① at the same time　② simultaneously 《with …》　③ in the same instant　④ concurrently 《with …》　⑤ in concurrence 《with …》　⑥ synchronously

とうしき【等式】　an equality

どうしんえん【同心円】　a concentric circle

どうすう【同数】　as many as [⇨第1部・18-2「同数の」]
- 賛否同数, 可否同数　⇨第1部・16-2 キャスティングボート

どうてん【同点】　① 《have》 the same score 《at halftime》　② a tie　③ a draw [⇨タイ]
- 彼は他の5選手と同点で6位だった．　He tied with five others for sixth place.
- 同点になる　① tie with …　② draw with …　③ 〖ゴルフ〗halve 《a match》
- 同点にする　① tie the score 《at 14-14》　② even the score　③ level the score　④ tie the game　⑤ draw the game
- 3対3の同点にする　tie 《the game》 at three-all
- 同点に終わる　finish [end] in a「draw [tie]
- 5対5の同点に終わる　①〈試合が主語〉end in a「draw [tie], five to five　②〈チームが主語〉play to a five-all draw　③ play to a five-to-five tie
- 4位は同点の三者 A, B, C であった．　There was a three-way tie for fourth place among A, B, and C.

とうど【糖度】　① sugar content　② a Brix value

とうひょう

★比重や屈折率の測定値を糖分の百分率に換算したもの（水以外の成分が主として糖分である場合）．Brix は比重を百分率に換算する代表的な方式である Brix scale から．
- 糖度 15 度［15%］のりんご　an apple with a sugar content of「15% [15 degrees Brix, 15° Brix, 15° Bx]

とうひょう【投票】　①voting　②balloting　③a vote　④a poll　⑤a ballot　⑥〔国民投票など〕a referendum［⇨第 1 部・16. 投票・選挙の表現］

とうひょうりつ【投票率】　①(a) voter turnout　②a turnout (of voters)　③a turnout rate　④a voting rate［⇨第 1 部・16-6 投票率］
- 投票率は 49.16% だった．　Voter turnout stood at 49.16%.

どうまわり【胴回り】　*one's* waist measurement［⇨第 1 部・43-4 ウエスト］

とうりょう【当量】　①an equivalent　②an equivalent weight
- 2 当量の酢酸が 1 当量の水を失う．　Two equivalents of acetic acid lose one equivalent of water.
- これは加えた水酸化ナトリウムが 5 ミリ当量になるまで続く．　This continues until 5 milliequivalents of sodium hydroxide has been added.
- 1 リットルの溶液に溶けている溶質の当量数　the number of equivalents of a solute dissolved in one liter of solution
- 硫酸の当量を計算する　calculate the equivalent (weight) of sulfuric acid
- 当量の水酸化カリウムを加える　add an equivalent「amount [quantity]」of potassium hydroxide
- 化学当量　a chemical equivalent
- 熱の仕事当量　the mechanical equivalent of heat

どうるいこう【同類項】　①a like term　②terms which are alike　③a similar term
- 同類項をまとめる　①collect like terms (together)　②combine like terms

とくいてん【特異点】　①a singular point　②a singularity
- この解では y 軸近くに特異点が現われる．　In this solution a singularity appears near the y-axis.
- 時空の特異点　a space-time singularity
- 裸の特異点　a naked singularity
- **特異点**では物理法則は成り立たなくなる．　The laws of physics break down at **a singularity**.
- そこに含まれる物質は**特異点**にまで圧縮される．　Matter therein is compressed into **a singularity**.

とくてん【得点】　①a point　②a score　③a run　④a goal［⇨てん，第 1 部・49. 野球の数字表現］
- 総得点　a total score

- 高得点　①〔スポーツで〕a「high [good] score　②〔試験などの〕a good「grade [score]　③《英》high [good] marks
- 試験で高得点を取った．　① He「got [obtained] a high score on the examination.　② He did very well「on [in] the exam.
- 得点数　① the runs scored　② the goals scored [⇨第1部・49. 野球の数字表現 49-16]
- 大量得点　heavy scoring
- 大量得点する　①〔野球で〕score a lot of runs　②〔サッカーで〕score a lot of goals
- 4試合連続得点を記録する　score in four games in a row
- 得点争いの首位に立つ　be the leading scorer
- 得点差　the difference in scores [⇨てんさ]
- 最少得点差　the smallest point margin

とくひょう【得票】　[⇨第1部・16-1 票数]
- 得票する　① get votes　② win votes　③ gain votes　④ poll votes
- 彼の得票は10万票であった．　He polled 100,000 votes.
- 最も多く得票する　get the most votes
- 彼のほうが得票が少なかった．　He received fewer votes.

どくりつ【独立】　independence
- …とは独立である　be independent of …
- 互いに独立して動作できる．　They can operate independently of one another.
- **一次独立**　linear independence
- **独立変数**　an independent variable
- 誤差が ΔA と ΔB である2つの**独立**な測定値 A と B を足したとき，全体の誤差は $\sqrt{\Delta A^2 + \Delta B^2}$ となる．　When two **independent** measurements A and B with errors ΔA and ΔB are added together, the overall error is $\sqrt{\Delta A^2 + \Delta B^2}$.

とけい【時計】　① a clock　② a watch [⇨第1部・32. 時刻と時間]
- この時計は3分進んでいる．　This「clock [watch] is three minutes fast. [⇨第1部・32-2 時計]

としょぶんるいほう【図書分類法】　a system of library classification

★代表的なものに下記がある．
- 日本十進分類法　the Nippon Decimal Classification 《略 NDC》
- デューイ十進分類法　the Dewey Decimal Classification 《略 DDC》
- 国立国会図書館分類表　the National Diet Library Classification 《略 NDLC》
- 米国議会図書館分類表　the Library of Congress Classification 《略 LCC》

★NDC は DDC をもとにした000から999までの数字による分類．NDLC と LCC は英字と数字の組み合わせを使用．

どすう【度数】

1 〔回数〕① (the number of) times ② frequency
- 度数分布　frequency distribution
- 度数分布曲線　a frequency distribution curve
- テレホンカードの**残り度数**　① **the number of units (available)** on a telephone card ② the **balance** on a telephone card
- このテレホンカードはあと**5度数**しか残っていない．　This phone card has only **five call units** left on it.

2 〔程度〕
- アルコールの度数　① the percentage of alcohol ② the alcoholic content ③ the proof ［⇨ど］
- レンズの度数　the power of a lens

とつたかくけい【凸多角形】　a convex polygon

トップ ［⇨第1部・15. 順位・順番の表現 15-2-1 (2)］
- ランキングでトップである　① hold [have] the「No. 1 [top] ranking ② hold [have] the first place in the ranking

とどく【届く】　reach ［⇨第1部・13. 比較・差・増減 13-1-3］

どのくらい　① how much ② how long ［⇨第1部・26. 数量に関する疑問文］

トランプ　① (playing) cards ② a card game ［⇨第1部・50-4 トランプ］

ドル　a dollar《記号 $》［⇨第1部・39-1-2 ドル］

トン　a ton《= 1000 kg》［⇨第1部・28. 伝統単位 28-3］
- トン数　tonnage
- 石炭3トン　three tons of coal
- 5,000トンの汽船　① a steamer of 5,000 tons (burden [burthen]) ② a 5,000-tonner
- この船は何トンですか．　What is the tonnage of this ship?

どんかく【鈍角】　an obtuse angle
- **鈍角三角形**　an obtuse triangle

な行

ないかく【内角】 an interior angle
- 三角形の内角の和は 180° である.
  ① The sum of the angles of a triangle is 180°.
  ② The three (interior) angles of a triangle add up to 180 degrees.

ないけい【内径】 ① the「internal [inside, inner] diameter ②〔鉄砲などの内筒の〕the caliber ③〔口径〕the bore

ないし【乃至】

1〔または〕or ★法律文などでは「ないし」の語は普通 **2** の意味.
- 修士号取得**ないし**はこれと同等の学識を有する者を求む.　We are looking for「somebody [a candidate, a person] with a master's degree **or** equivalent (qualification).

2〔…から…まで〕from … to … [⇨…まで]
- 第 12 条**ないし**第 16 条の規定　the provisions of Articles 12 **to** 16 inclusive
- 10 年**ないし**終身の懲役　penal servitude ranging from (a minimum of) ten years **to** life
- 完治までには半年**ないし**一年かかるだろう.　A complete cure will take six months **to** a year.

ないしん【内心】 an incenter
- 三角形の内接円の中心はその三角形の**内心**と呼ばれる.　The center of the incircle of a triangle is called **the incenter** of the triangle.
- 三角形の 3 つの角の二等分線は**内心**で交わる.　The three angle bisectors of a triangle meet **at the incenter**.

ないせき【内積】 an inner product
- 内積空間　an inner product space

ないせつ【内接】
- 内接する　① be inscribed 《in a circle》 ② touch 《the sides》 internally
- 内接円　an inscribed circle
- 内接多角形　an inscribed polygon

ないぶん【内分】 interior division
- AB を *m:n* の比に内分する　divide AB internally in the ratio *m:n*
- 内分点　an internally dividing point

なか…【中…】 ⇨第 1 部・31-4-4 中…日

ながさ【長さ】 (a) length [⇨第 1 部・42-1 長さ]
- 長さ 5 メートルのケーブル　① a cable five meters long　② a five-meter-long

cable ③ a cable of five meters
- 長さ30文字以下のパスワード ① a password at most 30 characters「in length [long] ② a password less than or equal to 30 characters in length ③ a password with length no more than 30 characters
- 長さ30秒のビデオ映像 a video footage of 30 seconds in length [⇨じかん]
- 今の時期, 昼間の長さはどのくらいですか.
① How long does daylight last at this time of year?
② How long is the day at this time of year?
- 中断した長さだけその期間を延長する extend the period by the length of the interruption

ななかくけい【七角形】 a heptagon [⇨第1部・58-2 …角形]

ナノ… [10^{-9}] nano- [⇨第1部・27-4 SI 接頭語]
- 可視光は約390〜700ナノメートルの波長をもつ. Visible light has wavelengths (ranging) from about 390 to 700 nanometers.
- 5〜10ナノメートルの直径をもつカーボンナノチューブ carbon nanotubes having diameters of 5–10 nanometers

…なん…【…何…】 ① -odd ② -plus ③ -some [and some] ④ -something ⑤ something over ⑥ just over [⇨第1部・9-2「…何」「…数」「…余り」など]
- 50何年前 ① fifty-some years ago ② fifty-odd years ago

なんい【何位】 ⇨第1部・26. 数量に関する疑問文 26-10-4

なんい【南緯】 (the) south latitude [⇨いど]

なんおく【何億】
- 何億(も)の hundreds of millions of … [⇨第1部・8. 漠然とした大きな数]

なんかい【何回】

1 〔疑問〕① how many times ② how often
- 一年に何回出張しますか. How many business trips do you take a year?
- 何回さいころを振れば, 少なくとも1回1が出る確率が1/2を上回りますか. How many times do you have to throw a die in order for the probability of getting one at least once to be greater than 1/2?
- このディスクは何回書き換えできますか. How many times can you rewrite the disc?
- 彼はこれまで何回無断欠勤しましたか. How「often [many times] has he missed work without permission?
- 何回使えるか the number of times it can be used
- 何回言ったらわかるんだ. How many times do I have to tell you?

2 〔数字の幅〕

- 何回か　① a number of times　② several times　③ a few times　④ a couple of times
- そこには何回か行ったことがある．　I've been there a number of times.
- 何回も　① many times　② time and time again　③ time after time　④ over and over
- 何回も言ったじゃないか．　I've told you over and over.
- 何回言っても彼は覚えない．　No matter how many times I tell him, he doesn't learn.
- 何回でも（好きなだけ）　① as many times as you「like ［wish］　② as often as you「like ［wish］　③ any number of times
- 何回でも繰り返して使える．　You can use it any number of times.

なんかい【何階】　⇨…かい【…階】

なんかいめ【何回目】　⇨なんどめ

なんかげつ【何か月】

1〔疑問〕how many months
- 何か月かかりますか．　How many months does it take?
- それは何か月前のことですか．
  ① How many months has it been since then?
  ② How many months ago did it happen?
  ③ How long ago did it happen?
- 今妊娠何か月目ですか．　How many months pregnant are you?［⇨第1部・38-5 妊娠・出産］

2〔数字の幅〕
- 何か月か　① some months　② several months　③ a few months
- 1年と何か月か　a year and some months

なんがつ【何月】　what month (of the year)
- 今何月だっけ？
  ① Hey, what month (of the year) is it now?
  ② What's the month now?
- 何月に実施されますか．
  ① In what month will it take effect?
  ② When will it take effect?
- 誕生日は何月ですか．　What month is your birthday (in)?

なんさい【何歳】　how old ［⇨第1部・26. 数量に関する疑問文 26-6］
- その赤ん坊は何歳ですか．　How old is the baby?
- 何歳であっても　at any age
- 勉強は何歳から始めても遅すぎるということはない．

なんじ

① It's never too late to study, no matter at what age you begin.
② You're never too old to begin studying.
- 50 何歳かの時に　in *one's* 50-somethingth year

なんじ【何時】　① what time ② when［⇨第1部・26. 数量に関する疑問文 26-5, 32. 時刻と時間］

- 何時ですか.
  ① What time is it?
  ② What's the time?
  ③ Do you have the time? ★Do you have the time? は時計を持っていますかという形で婉曲的に時間を聞く表現で，通りすがりの人に聞く場合などにおいて比較的ぶしつけでないとされる.
- 今朝家を出たのは何時ごろですか.　About what time did you leave the house this morning?
- 明日の打ち合わせは何時からにしましょうか.　What time should we start the meeting tomorrow?
- 明日は何時までに来ればいいですか.　(By) what time should I be here tomorrow?
- （窓口などが）何時から何時までやってますか.
  ① What time do you open and close?
  ② What hours are you open?
  ③ What are your 《store's》 hours?
- 目覚まし時計，何時に合わせとく？　What time should I set the alarm for?
- 何時のバスで来るかな.　I wonder which bus she'll be on.
- 夜何時でもいいから結果が出たら電話をくれ.　It doesn't matter how late it is. Just call me when you know the results.

なんじかん【何時間】　［⇨第1部・26. 数量に関する疑問文 26-5］

1 〔疑問〕① how many hours ② how long

- 到着まであと何時間かかりますか.
  ① How many hours will it be till we arrive?
  ② How「many more hours［much more time］will it take before we arrive?
  ③ How much longer will it take for us to get there?

2 〔数字の幅〕

- 何時間か　① some hours ② several hours ③ a few hours
- 何時間も　① for hours ② for hours together ③ for hours on end ④ for hour after hour ⑤ for any number of hours

なんじゅう【何十】

- 何十（も）の　① tens of … ② dozens of … ③ scores of …［⇨第1部・8. 漠然とした大きな数］

なんじょう【何乗】　⇨第1部・54-5 累乗 54-5-5

なんぜん【何千】

- 何千(も)の thousands of … ［⇨第1部・8. 漠然とした大きな数］

なんちゃく【何着】 ⇨第1部・26. 数量に関する疑問文 26-10 何番目

なんてん【何点】

- 今タイガース何点？
  ① What's the Tigers' score?
  ② How many runs do the Tigers have?
- 今日の算数のテスト何点だった？ What was your score on the math test today?
- 君は彼の作品に何点入れますか. How do you「score [rate]」his work?

なんど【何度】

1 〔温度〕

- 昨夜は(熱が)何度ありましたか. What was your temperature last night?
- 冷凍庫の中の温度は何度ですか. What's the temperature inside a freezer?
- 室温はセ氏で今何度ですか. What is the room temperature in (degrees)「Celsius [centigrade]」?
- 水の沸点はカ氏で何度ですか.
  ① What is the boiling point of water in Fahrenheit?
  ② At how many degrees Fahrenheit does water boil?
- その金属は何度で溶けますか. At what temperature does the metal melt?

2 〔角度〕

- その坂の勾配は何度ですか.
  ① What is the gradient of that slope in degrees?
  ② How steep in degrees is that slope?
  ③ How many degrees is that slope?

3 〔回数〕① how many times ② how often ［⇨なんかい【何回】］

なんどめ【何度目】 ［⇨第1部・26-10 何番目］

- 来日はこれで何度目ですか. How many times have you come to Japan, including this time?
- 何度目かの失敗でようやくあきらめた.
  ① After failing any number of times, he eventually gave up.
  ②《口》After failing for the umpteenth time, he finally gave up.

なんにち【何日】 ［⇨第1部・26. 数量に関する疑問文 26-5］

1 〔日数〕① how many days ② how long

- 何日でも，何日間でも ① for any number of days ② for as many days as you like
- 何日も for many days

- 有給休暇は1年に何日もらえますか.
  ① How many days of paid「vacation [leave] do you「get [receive] per year?
  ② How many paid vacation days do you「get [receive] per year?

2〔日付〕
- 今日は何日ですか.
  ① What day of the month is it?
  ② What's the date today?
  ③ What date is it today?
- 誕生日は何日ですか.
  ① What day《in April》is your birthday?
  ② When is your birthday?
- 新学期は何日からですか.
  ① When will the new (school) term begin?
  ② On what date will the new (school) term begin?

なんにん【何人】

1〔疑問〕how many (people)〔⇨ 26. 数量に関する疑問文 26-1〕

2〔数字の幅〕
- 何人か ① some people ② several people ③ a few people ④ a number of people ★a number of は多数の意味にもなるので注意.
- 何人でも雇います.　We'll hire「as many as [however many] we can.
- 何人でもいい.　Any number of people will do.

なんねん【何年】〔⇨第1部・26. 数量に関する疑問文 26-5〕

1〔年数〕① how many years ② how long
- それを達成するのに何年かかりますか.　How many years [How long] will it take to achieve it?
- その苗木が実をつけるまでに何年かかりますか.
  ① How many years [How long] does it take for the seedlings to bear fruit?
  ② How many years [How long] does it take before the seedlings bear fruit?
- その患者は手術後何年間生きましたか.　How many years [How long] did the patient survive after the operation?
- あの建物は築何年ですか.　How old is that building?
- そのご友人に会ったのは何年ぶりのことでしたか.　After「how long [how many years] did you see that friend of yours?
- 何年もの間 ① for (many) years ② over the years ③ for years and years
- 今年の米は何年来の不作だった.　This year's rice crop was the worst in many years.

2〔年号〕what year
- 今年は(西暦)何年ですか.　What year is this?

- 今年は平成何年ですか． What year of Heisei is this?
- モーツァルトは何年生まれですか． In what year was Mozart born?
- そのワインは何年物ですか． What year is that wine (from)?

なんねんせい【何年生】 ⇨第1部・47-2 …年生

なんばい【何倍】
- ロシアの面積は日本の何倍ですか．
  ① How many times larger is Russia than Japan?
  ② How much larger is Russia than Japan?
- 三角形の辺の長さを5倍したとき，面積は何倍になるか． By what factor does the area of a triangle increase if the lengths of all sides are multiplied by five?
- 26を何倍すれば100を超えるか． By what factor should 26 be multiplied to get a number greater than 100?

なんばん【何番】

1 〔番号〕 what number
- ファクスは何番ですか． What is your fax number?
- 長嶋の背番号は何番ですか． What's Nagashima's number?
- 〔間違い電話に対して〕何番におかけですか．
  ① What number are you trying to reach?
  ② What number are you calling?
- 〔ゴルフで〕何番のアイアンを使いますか． What number iron will you use?
- 成績はクラスで何番ですか． What is your class rank? [⇨第1部・26-10 何番目]

2 〔対戦〕
- 何番でも将棋をさす play one game of shogi after another.
- 横綱と当たったことは何番ありますか． How many times have you faced yokozuna?

なんばんめ【何番目】 ⇨第1部・26-10 何番目

なんびゃく【何百】
- 何百（も）の hundreds of … [⇨第1部・8. 漠然とした大きな数]

なんふん【何分】 ① how many minutes ② how long [⇨第1部・26. 数量に関する疑問文 26-5]
- このパスタは何分ゆでますか[ゆで時間は何分ですか]．
  ① How long should I boil this pasta?
  ② How long does it take to cook this pasta?
  ③ What is the cooking time for this pasta?
- 4時何分かの列車 ① a train at something after four ② the four-something

train

なんまん【何万】
- 何万（も）の　tens of thousands of … [⇨第1部・8. 漠然とした大きな数]

なんめい【何名】　how many (people) [⇨ 26. 数量に関する疑問文 26-1]

なんようび【何曜日】　[⇨第1部・26. 数量に関する疑問文 26-5]
- 今日は何曜日ですか．　What day of the week is it today?
- 明日は何曜日ですか．
  ① What day of the week is it tomorrow?
  ② What day is tomorrow?
- ピアノのレッスンは**何曜日**ですか．　What day of the week is your piano lesson?
- 日曜以外は何曜日でもいい．
  ① Any weekday will do.　★「土日以外は」の意になることも多いので注意.
  ② Any day but Sunday will do.
  ③ I'll be available on any day but Sunday.

にい【二位】　[⇨第1部・15-2 順位]
- 2位である　① rank [be, stand, be ranked, be placed] second　② hold (the) second place　③ be (the) runner-up　④ be No. 2

にか【二価】　[⇨いっか]
- 二価の　① bivalent　② divalent　③ diatomic
- 二価関数　a two-valued function
- 二価アルコール　dihydric alcohol
- 二価染色体　a bivalent chromosome

にげん【二元】
- 二元一次方程式　a linear equation「with [in] two「unknowns [variables]
- 二元連立方程式　simultaneous equations in two unknowns
- 二元化合物　a binary compound
- 二元合金　a binary alloy
- 二元性　① dualism　② duality
- 二元説［論］　dualism
- 二元的　① dual　② dualistic
- 二元接着剤　a two-part adhesive

にし【西】　west [⇨第1部・59-5 東西南北]

にじ【二次】　①〔2つめの〕second　② secondary　③〔2乗冪に関係する〕second-degree　④ quadratic　⑤〔一般に次数が〕second-order [⇨…じ【…次】]
★quadratic は語源的には「4」であるが，「四角形」→「正方形」→「2乗」と

いう関連による用法である．

▶ second を使うもの
- 第二次世界大戦　① World War II　② the Second World War
- 二次面接　a second(-stage) interview

▶ secondary を使うもの
- 二次イオン化　secondary ionization
- 二次宇宙線　① secondary cosmic rays　② (cosmic-ray) secondaries
- 二次エネルギー　secondary energy
- 二次汚染　secondary contamination
- 二次温度計　a secondary thermometer
- 二次感染　(a) secondary infection
- 二次コイル　a secondary coil
- 二次構造　〔タンパク質の〕the secondary structure
- 二次災害　a secondary disaster
- 二次産業　a secondary industry
- 二次産品［製品］　secondary products
- 二次試験　a secondary examination
- 二次消費者　《生態》a secondary consumer
- 二次資料　a secondary source
- 二次性徴　a secondary sexual characteristic
- 二次電池　① a secondary cell　② a secondary battery
- 二次被害　secondary damage

▶ quadratic, degree を使うもの
- x の 2 次式　a quadratic in x
- $P(x)$ が 2 次式なら　If $P(x)$ is a quadratic …
- x について 2 次である　① be of the second degree in x　② be of degree two in x　③ be quadratic in x
- x^2 の係数が 1 の 2 次式　a quadratic in which the coefficient of x^2 is ⌈one [unity]⌋
- 二次関数　a quadratic function
- 二次曲線　① a quadratic curve　② a curve of the second ⌈degree [order]⌋　③ a conic ［⇨えんすいきょくせん］
- 二次曲面　① a quadric　② a ⌈quadric [quadratic]⌋ surface　③ a surface of the second ⌈degree [order]⌋　④ a conicoid　★quadric は曲面を表わす式のように 2 変数以上の場合に使う．
- 二次不等式　a quadratic inequality
- 二次方程式　① a quadratic equation　② a quadratic　③ an equation of the sec-

ond degree
- 二次方程式の解の公式　the quadratic formula　★$x=(-b\pm\sqrt{b^2-4ac})/2a$ というもので，読み方は x equals minus b plus or minus the square root of b squared minus four a c「divided by [all over] two a など.
- 二次ふるい法　〔素因数分解法〕the quadratic sieve
▶ order を使うもの
- 二次の効果　the second-order effects
- 二次相転移　second-order phase transition
- 二次反応　a second-order reaction
▶ その他の表現
- 二次的著作物　derivative work
- 二次募集　① additional recruitment　② a second phase of recruitment

にじげん【二次元】　two dimensions [⇨じげん]
- 二次元の　① two-dimensional　② 2-D
- 二次元の流れ　a two-dimensional flow
- 二次元 NMR スペクトル　a two-dimensional NMR spectrum
- 二次元クロマトグラフィー　two-dimensional chromatography
- 二次元系　a two-dimensional system
- 二次元で　in two dimensions
- 二次元への投影　projection「into [to] two dimensions

にじゅうしせっき【二十四節気】　the 24 seasonal divisions of the year in the old lunar calendar [⇨第 1 部・37-3 二十四節気]

にじゅうよじかん【二十四時間】　24 hours
- 24 時間の介護サービス　① a 24-hour(-a-day) nursing service　② a nursing service operating 24 hours a day　③ an around-the-clock nursing service
- 当店は 24 時間営業です．
  ① We are open 24 hours (a day).
  ② We are open around the clock.
- 24 時間態勢で警戒に当たる　① keep watch 《on a building [for criminal activity]》 on a 24-hour basis　② keep watch 24 hours a day　③ start an around-the-clock「guard [alert]

にじょう【二乗】　a square [⇨第 1 部・54-5 累乗 54-5-1, ⇨へいほう]

にしん【二進】
- 二進法　① the binary system (of notation)　② base two　★base two は「基数が 2」の意.
- 二進数　a binary number

- 5 は二進法では 101 と書く．
  ① Five is written 101 in binary notation.
  ② Five is written 101 in base two.

にだい…【二大…】 ⇨…だい【…大】

にち【日】

1 〔日付〕［⇨第 1 部・30-2 月日〕
- 2007 年 6 月 21 日　①《米》June 21(st), 2007　②《英》21(st) June 2007

2 〔時間の長さ〕a day［⇨第 1 部・31-4 日］
- 15 日間　fifteen days

にち【二値】

- 二値の　① binary　② two-valued

にっすう【日数】　the number of days［⇨第 1 部・31-4-2 日数］

にディーケー【2DK】　⇨第 1 部・46-3 住居

ニト　〔輝度の単位〕a nit ★SI 単位系ではカンデラ毎平方メートル（candela per square meter）［⇨第 1 部・27. 単位］

にど【二度】　① twice　② two times［⇨第 1 部・36. 回数・頻度の表現］

- 週に 2 度　twice a week
- 二度三度と　① again and again　② repeatedly
- 同じ過ちを二度繰り返すな．　Don't「repeat the same mistake［make the same mistake twice］.
- あの人の招待を二度も断っては大変失礼だ．　It would be very rude to refuse his invitation「a second time［yet again］.
- あの事件には驚いたが事件の場所を聞いて二度びっくり．　I was surprised at the incident, and when I heard where it happened, I was shocked「again［a second time, even more］.
- 二度あることは三度ある．　① What happens twice will happen three times. ②〔悪いことが〕Misfortunes never come alone.　③ Disasters come in threes. ④ When it rains, it pours.
- こんなことが二度あろうとは考えられない．　I cannot imagine such a thing happening again.
- 彼は部下の失敗を二度までは許す．（三度めは許さない）　① He allows the people working under him to make the same mistake no more than twice. ② He tolerates the same mistake at most twice from the people under him.
- 二度は言わないからよく聞け．　I'm not going to「say it again［repeat myself］, so listen carefully.
- もう二度とこういうことはいたしません．　① I will never do it again.　② I promise never to do it again.

- 二度とない機会　an opportunity of a lifetime
- **二度手間**　① a botched job (that has to be done all over again) ② a waste of time
- 指示通りにしないと二度手間になるよ．　If you don't follow the instructions, you'll have to「do it all over again［start again from scratch］.
- 必要な書類を忘れて市役所に行ったので二度手間になってしまった．　Since I forgot to take the necessary papers to the city hall, it turned into an enormous waste of time.
- 今朝は**二度寝**して起きたのは昼すぎだった．　This morning I slept in and didn't get up until after noon.
- **二度塗り**　① double coating ② a double coat 《of paint》
- ニス［ペンキ］を二度塗りする　give《a board》two coats of「varnish［paint］

にとうぶん【二等分】　bisection

- 二等分する　① divide … into two equal parts ② cut … in half ③ bisect《a line》
- 二等分線　a bisector
- 垂直二等分線　a perpendicular bisector
- 角の二等分線　① an angle bisector ① a bisectrix
- 三角形の3つの**角の二等分線**は内心と呼ばれる1点で交わる．　The three **angle bisectors** of a triangle meet at a point called the incenter.

にゅうさつ【入札】　bidding ［⇨第1部・39-4 入札・オークション］

ニュートン　〔力の単位〕a newton《記号 N》

…にん【…人】

- みなで10人いる．　There are 10 people in all.
- うちは6人家族です．　① There are six (people) in our family. ② We are a family of six.
- 私たちは6人きょうだいだ．　① There are six children (in our family). ② There are six of us kids.
- 私は3人きょうだいの真中です．　I am the middle (one) of three children.
- 1部屋に8人寝る　sleep eight to a room

にんき【任期】　① *one's* term of「office［service］② *one's* period of「office［service］③ *one's* tenure (of office) ④〔協会員などの〕a term of membership ⑤〔議長などの〕a presidency ⑥ a chairmanship［第1部・16-10 再選・多選］

- 衆議院議員の任期は4年だ．　The tenure of office for a member of the House of Representatives is four years.
- 任期6年の議席　a seat with a term of six years
- 任期満了の日　the date of termination of *one's* office

にんしん

- 彼は本月3日で任期満了となる． His term「expires [comes to an end, ends] on the third of this month.
- 大統領は任期がまだ5か月ほどある． The President has about five months more to serve.
- 任期の残りが1年もない大統領がその施策を推進するのは適切ではない． It is not appropriate for a president with less than a year「remaining [left] in office [in his term]」to push that measure.
- 任期中に　during *one's* term
- 任期半ばで　in the middle of *one's* term
- 任期前半［後半］　the「first [second] half of *one's*「term [tenure] of office
- 任期切れ［任期満了］　the「expiry [expiration] of a term of office
- 任期を終える［勤めあげる］　① complete *one's* term of service　② serve out *one's* time　③ serve *one's* (full) time　④ wind up 《*one's* navy service, etc.》
- 任期いっぱい勤める　serve out *one's* term
- 委員長の任期を延長する　extend the term of the committee chair

関連表現

- 彼女は3期続けて町長を務めた． She served three consecutive terms as mayor of the town.
- テキサス州出身の1期目の上院議員　a first-term senator from Texas

にんしん【妊娠】　[⇨第1部・38-5 妊娠・出産]
- 妊娠6か月である　① be six months「pregnant [《口》along, gone, on the way]　② be in the sixth month of pregnancy

にんずう【人数】　the number of「persons [people]
- おおよその人数　an approximate number (of people)
- 人数は100人です．　① There are 100 (people, of them).　② They are 100「in number [strong].　③ They number 100.
- 搭乗客のうち生存が確認されている人数は25人です．　① Twenty-five survivors from among the passengers have been confirmed.　② The number of confirmed survivors among the passengers is 25.
- 大［小］人数のグループ　a「large [small] group
- 人数が増える　increase in number
- 野球をやるには人数が足りなかった．
  ① We didn't have the numbers「for [to play] baseball.
  ② There weren't enough of us「for [to play] baseball.
- この人数ではとても今日中には終わらない． With「this (small) number of [so few] people, we won't finish today.
- 人数を数える　① count the number of people　② count 《the participants [the audience, etc.]》　③ count heads　④ count noses　⑤ do a head count

にんずう

- (必要な)人数をそろえる　① get (together) [gather] the 「required [necessary] number (of people)　② make up the number(s)
- 人数合わせに未経験者まで入れてチームを編成した．　We made up the numbers for a team by including those with no experience.
- 採用予定人数　the number (of people) scheduled to be hired
- 参加人数　① the number of participants　② the number of people 「present [attending, taking part]　③ an attendance 《of 100 people》
- ツアーの参加人数　the number of people 「on [taking part in] a tour
- 参加人数の多少にかかわらずガイド2人が同行します．　Irrespective of 「the number of participants [numbers]，two guides will accompany the group.

関連表現

- 就業者数　the number of 「employees [the employed]
- ▶ attendance (出席者数)，membership (会員数)，enrollment (登録者数)，casualties, toll (死傷者数) など，number を使わずに人数を表わす語もいろいろある．
- 現在会員数　① the present membership (of the society)　② the number of members presently on the books
- 登録会員数　the number of registered members
- 当会の会員数は 1000 名を超える．
  ① The society has more than 1,000 members.
  ② The society has a membership of over 1,000.
- 会員数は頭打ち状態だ．　Membership has 「peaked [reached a limit].
- 会員数を制限することにした．　We decided to limit the membership 《to 1,000》.
- 在籍者数　① an enrollment 《of 2,000 students》　② the number of (registered) 「persons [students, members]
- 死者数　① the number of deaths　② the number of (the) dead　③ a death toll 《of thirty-five》　④ the death toll
- 民間人死者数　① the number of civilian deaths　② the civilian death toll
- 死傷者数　① the toll of casualties　② the toll of dead and injured
- その火災の死傷者数は 150 人に達した．　The 「casualties [toll] in the fire reached 150 people.
- 我が軍の損害は死者 50 名，負傷者 300 名だった．　Our 「casualties [losses] were 50 killed and 300 wounded.
- 自動車所有者数　① the number of people with cars　② 《an increase in》 automobile [car] ownership
- 読者数　①〔新聞などの読者の総数〕readership　②〔発行部数〕circulation
- 入場者数　① attendance 《at …》　② a gate
- 開園以来の延べ入場者数　total [cumulative] attendance since opening (of the

- その病気の発症者数は 50 万人に上った． ① The number of people with symptoms of the disease was 500,000. ② Half a million people developed symptoms of the disease.
- 来館者数 ① attendance 《at a「museum [library]》 ② the number of visitors 《to a「museum [library]》
- 正月三が日の人出予想 a forecast of the likely turnout 《at temples and shrines》 during the first three days of the New Year
- 何人 how many (people) [⇨第 1 部・26. 数量に関する疑問文 26-1]

ね【値】 a price [⇨第 1 部・40-2 価格・値段，39-4 入札・オークション]

ネーパー 〔自然対数による強度比の表示の単位〕a neper

ねだん【値段】 a price [⇨第 1 部・40-2 価格・値段]
- この牛肉の値段は 100 グラム 2,000 円だ．
  ① The price of this beef is ¥2,000 per 100 grams.
  ② This beef costs ¥2,000 per 100 grams.

ねつようりょう【熱容量】 ① heat capacity ② thermal capacity [⇨ひねつ]

ねん【年】

1 〔時間の長さ〕a year [⇨第 1 部・31-1 年]
- 3 年 5 か月 three years and five months
- 半年 ① half a year ② a half year ③ six months

2 〔年次〕[⇨第 1 部・29. 年・年度・元号・世紀]
- 1945 年に in 1945
- 1945 年以前は before 1945
- 1945 年は日本にとって新しい出発点だった． The year 1945 was a new starting point for Japan.
- 平成 10 年に ① in the 10th year of Heisei ② in the 10th year of the Heisei era
- 私にとって歴史年号を暗記するのはたいへんだった． It was hard for me to memorize historical dates.

3 〔学年〕⇨第 1 部・47. 学校

ねんがっぴ【年月日】 [⇨第 1 部・30-2 月日]
- 製造年月日 a date of manufacture

ねんしゅう【年収】 ① an annual income ② a yearly income [⇨第 1 部・40-5 収入と支出]

ねんしょう【年商】 ① a yearly turnover ② an annual business volume
- 年商 100 万ドルである ① turn over a million dollars a year ② do over a million dollars of business a year

…ねんせい

- 彼はたった 10 年で小さな学習塾を年商 5 億円の予備校にした．　In a mere ten years he turned the little cram school into a preparatory school with an annual turnover of ¥500 million.

…ねんせい【…年生】　⇨第 1 部・47. 学校

…ねんだい【…年代】　⇨第 1 部・29-6 …年代

ねんど【年度】　⇨第 1 部・29-4 年度

ねんぴ【燃費】　① fuel consumption　② fuel economy　③ fuel efficiency　④ (fuel) mileage

★英語の mileage には走行距離（単位は km など）と一定の燃料消費当たりの走行距離（単位は km/l など）の両方の意味がある．［⇨そうこうきょり］

★以下，関連表現も含めて扱う．

- この車は時速 60 キロでリッター当たり 20 キロ走る．
  ① This car「gives［goes, does, gets］20 kilometers to the liter (traveling) at 60 km/h.
  ② This car runs 20 kilometers on one liter of gasoline at 60 km/h.

★日本では燃料 1 リットル当たりのキロ数 (km/l) で表わすが，アメリカでは 1 ガロン当たりのマイル数 (mpg: miles per gallon) で表わす．mpg で表わされた数字は約 1/3 倍すれば km/l の表示になる．ヨーロッパでは 100 km 当たりのリッター数 (l/100 km) などを使うので，数値が小さいほどいいことになる．

- この車は 1 ガロン当たり何マイル走りますか．　What mileage does this car do per gallon?
- あなたの車の燃費はどのくらいですか．
  ① What (sort of) mileage are you getting?
  ② What is your mileage 《in kilometers per liter》?
- この車は燃費がいい［悪い］．
  ① This car gets「good［poor］mileage.
  ② I get「good［poor］mileage out of this car.
- 低燃費　① low fuel consumption　②《get》good mileage
- 燃費のよい車［低燃費車］　① a fuel-efficient car　② a car that「gets［gives］good mileage
- 燃費の悪い車　① a fuel-inefficient car　② a car that gets low mileage　③《口》a gas guzzler
- 燃費を改善する［低燃費化する］　① improve［reduce］fuel consumption　② improve「fuel economy［fuel efficiency, mileage］　③ make《cars》more fuel efficient
- **燃費**が 1 ガロン 27 マイルから 34 マイルに向上した．　**Mileage** has「increased［risen］from 27 to 34 mpg.
- **燃費**が 25% よくなる　get 25 percent better「**gas**［《英》**petrol**］**mileage**

- この新製品のオイルを使えば車の**燃費**がよくなります．　You'll get more **mileage** out of your car with this new brand of oil.

ねんぽう【年俸】　① an annual salary　② a yearly stipend［⇨第 1 部・40-5-2 収入］

ねんれい【年齢】　age［⇨第 1 部・38. 年齢］

のうど【濃度】　① (a) concentration　② (a) level
- その NaOH 溶液の濃度は 4%［1 M, 40 g/L］だ．　The concentration of the NaOH solution is「4%［1 M, 40 g/L］.
- 水溶液 A と B は同じ濃度だ．　The aqueous solutions A and B have the same concentration.
- モル濃度［パーセント］で表わした溶液濃度　solution concentrations expressed「as molarities［in percent］
- 溶液中での溶質粒子の濃度　the concentration of solute particles in the solution
- 反応物と生成物の濃度　the concentrations of the reactants and products
- 空気中のダイオキシン濃度　dioxin levels in the air
- (運転者の) 血液中のアルコール濃度を測定する　measure《a driver's》blood alcohol level(s)
- 濃度が高い［低い］　① be at (a)「high［low］concentration　② be at (a)「high［low］level
- 濃度が高いと有毒で命にかかわることもある．　It is poisonous and can be fatal「at［in］high concentrations.
- 雨水中にごく低濃度で存在する　occur in rain in very low concentrations
- 特定の濃度の溶液は当量の溶質と溶媒を混ぜて調製できる．　A solution with a specific concentration can be prepared by mixing appropriate amounts of solute and solvent.
- 既知［未知］濃度の塩基溶液　a base solution of「known［unknown］concentration

▶ **濃度の単位**

重量パーセント濃度 (weight percentage)…全体に対する着目物質の重さの割合《記号 %》

(容量) モル濃度 (molarity)…溶液 1 リットル中の溶質のモル数《記号 M》

規定度 (normality)…溶液 1 リットル中の溶質のグラム当量数《記号 N》(NaOH の 1M は 1N だが，1M の H_2SO_4 は 2N に相当する)

重量モル濃度 (molality)…溶媒 1000 g に対する溶質のモル数《記号 mol/kg》

モル分率 (mole fraction)…全体に対する着目物質のモル数の比《記号 %》

その他，微量の汚染物質の濃度を表わすのに，ppm, ppb, ppt で表わしたり，

ノット

単位体積に含まれる質量を mg/m³, μg/m³, ng/m³, pg/m³ で表わしたりするなどさまざまな単位が使われる.

ノット 〔船や海流の速度の単位〕a knot
- 27 ノットで進む　① move [go] at 27 knots　② move [go] at a speed of 27 knots
- この船は23ノット出せるように造られている.　This ship is designed to ⌈do [make]⌋ 23 knots.

のべ【延べ】 [⇨第1部・24-4 延べ]
- 延べ35,000人　a total of 35,000 people
- 延べ日数　① a total number of (working) days　② total man-days

のぼる【上る】 ① reach　② amount to …　③ come (up) to …　④ run [mount, add] up to …　⑤ work out at …　⑥ number [⇨第1部・2-4 数値を呈示する各種表現]
- 数億円に上る負債　debts amounting to several hundred million yen

…のり【…乗り】 [⇨ていいん]
- 1人乗りの　① single-seated　② for one　③ for a single ⌈person [user, rider, driver, pilot]⌋
- 1人乗りの飛行機　a single-seater (plane)
- 2人乗りの飛行機　a two-seater (plane)
- 4人乗りの自動車[馬車, etc.]　a four-seater
- 5人乗りの自動車　① a five-seater (car)　② a car for five　③ a car for four passengers
- 2人乗りの自転車　① a tandem (bicycle)　② a bicycle (built) for two
- 1人乗りのカヌー　① a one-man canoe　② a one-person canoe　③ a canoe for one
- 自転車の2人乗り　① riding two to a bicycle　② doubling up on a bicycle　③ two people riding a bicycle at the same time

関連表現
- 単座機　① a single-seat plane　② a single-seater
- 複座機　① a two-seat plane　② a two-seater　③ a double-seater

ノルマ　a ⌈work [production]⌋ quota　★日本語のノルマはロシア語に由来する. 英語の norm も「規範」「基準生産量」の意はあるが, 日常的によく使われるのは quota などである.
- 1日のノルマ　a daily quota
- 月間ノルマ　a monthly quota
- ノルマを課す　① assign a quota　② impose a quota　③ set a quota　④ give 《a

person》a certain amount of work to do
- 私たちの仕事にはノルマがある． In our job we have quotas to fulfill.
- 仕事のノルマがきつい．
  ① It's tough meeting my quotas.
  ② It's tough getting through the tasks I'm allotted.
- ノルマに縛られている　① be tied down by quota requirements　② be tied down by the need to fulfill a quota
- (人が) ノルマを果たす [達成する，こなす]　① meet a quota　② fulfill a quota　③ complete a quota　④ meet the full quota　⑤ fulfill the full quota　⑥ complete the full quota　⑦ finish the work assigned to *one*
- 販売ノルマの 80% に達する　reach 80% of the sales quota
- ノルマに 20% 不足する　fail to「fill [fulfill]」the quota by 20 percent
- ノルマを超える　exceed a quota

ノルム　a norm
- ベクトルのノルム　the norm of a vector
- ノルムが 1 のベクトル　a vector whose norm is 1

は行

バージョン　a version《略 ver., v.》
- 初期のバージョン　an early version
- 2.0 より前のバージョン　① versions「earlier [lower]」than 2.0　② versions before 2.0
- 2.0 より新しいバージョン　versions「later [higher]」than 2.0
- バージョン 2.0 以上　version 2.0 or「above [later, higher, beyond]」
- バージョン 2.0 以下　version 2.0 or「lower [earlier]」
- バージョン 3.0 の時点では　as of version 3.0
- そのソフトは今バージョン 5.0 だ．　The software is now「in [at]」version 5.0.
- 現行[最新]バージョンは 6.0 だ．　The「current [latest, newest]」version is 6.0.
- ソフトのバージョンはいくつですか．　What version is your software?
- バージョン番号　a version number

パーセク　〔距離の単位〕a parsec《= 3.26 光年；記号 pc》

パーセント　percent《記号 %》[⇨第 1 部・22. 割合，23. 確率と可能性]
- 住民の 80%　eighty percent of the residents
- 70% の削減　a 70 percent reduction
- 100% の確実性　a 100 percent certainty
- 彼女は 99% の確率で勝つだろう．　She has a 99% chance of winning.
- 50% の確率で吸収される可能性がある．　There is a 50 percent chance of being absorbed.
- 90% の精度　90 percent accuracy
- 彼女が正しいと 100% 確信している．　I'm 100 percent sure that she is right.

パーミル　① per mil　② per mill《記号 ‰》[⇨第 1 部・22-1-3 パーミル]

バール　〔圧力の単位〕a bar《= 10^5 Pa；記号 bar》

バーン　〔素粒子反応の断面積の単位〕a barn《= 100 fm^2；記号 b》

ばい【倍】

1　〔…倍〕① times　② -fold　③ by a factor of …　④ multiplied by … [⇨第 1 部・17. …倍]
- 2 倍　① two times　② double　③ twice　④ twofold
- 3 倍　① three times　② threefold　③ treble　④ thrice
- 市場価格の 2.5 倍で　at 2.5 times the market price
- A は B の 3 倍の長さである．
  ① A is three times as long as B.

ばいかくのこうしき

② A is three times the length of B.
③ A is three times longer than B.
- 10 倍になる　① increase by a factor of ten　② increase (by) ten times　③ increase tenfold　④ show [achieve, etc.] a tenfold increase　⑤ show [achieve, etc.] a ten times increase　⑥ be multiplied by ten　⑦ become [get] ten times「bigger [larger, etc.]」⑧ become [get] ten times as「big [large, etc.]」
- 2π の数倍　a few times 2π
- 100 倍小さい　① 100 times smaller　② be a factor of 100 smaller
- 4 倍速　〖電算〗quad speed
- 40 倍速　〖電算〗40X speed　★ forty times speed または 40 speed などと読む.

2 〔2 倍〕
- 倍にする　double
- 倍になる　① double　② be doubled　③ double itself
- (金を) 倍にして返す　repay「double [twice] the original amount」
- 倍の　① double　② twice　③ two times　④ twofold
- これは元の値段の倍だ．　This costs double what it did before.
- それは金が倍かかる．　It would cost twice as much.
- この方法は時間が倍かかる．　This method takes twice as much time.
- パン生地が倍にふくらんだ.
  ① The dough expanded to twice its size.
  ② The dough doubled in size.
- 新しいモデルの収容力［容量］は旧型の倍だ．　The new model has double the capacity of the original.

ばいかくのこうしき【倍角の公式】　〔三角関数の〕a double-angle formula

ばいすう【倍数】　a multiple
- 6 は 2 と 3 の倍数だ．　6 is a multiple of both 2 and 3.
- 数の各桁の合計が 3 の倍数だったらその数は 3 の倍数だ．　If the sum of the digits of a number is a multiple of three, the number is a multiple of three.

はいとう【配当】　a dividend ［⇨第 1 部・39-3 株 39-3-8］

ばいりつ【倍率】

1 ①〔拡大する度合い〕magnification　②〔拡大する能力〕magnifying power　③ magnifying capacity
- ズーム倍率　① a zoom level　② a zoom factor　③ zoom magnification　④ a zoom percentage　⑤ how much zoom is applied
- 倍率を上げる［下げる］　increase [reduce] magnification
- 高倍率の　① high power《lens》② high magnification《lens》
- 《コピー機の》倍率を＋または－キーで調整してください．　Adjust the (en-

largement/reduction) ratio with the + or − key.
- 倍率 10 倍の双眼鏡　① binoculars with a magnification of「10x [10 times]」② 10x [10-power] binoculars
- 倍率 1 万倍で撮影した顕微鏡画像　① a microscopic image taken at 10,000 power ② a 10,000X microscopic image ③ a microscopic image magnified 10,000 times

関連表現［⇨かくだいりつ，しゅくしょうりつ］
- 100 倍に拡大する　magnify … 100 times
- どのくらいの縮小率でコピーしますか．　How much do you want the copy reduced?
- 拡大縮小は 25% から 400% までできます．　You can zoom up to 400% or down to 25%.

2〔応募者と定員の数の比率〕a competition rate
- 5 倍の倍率　a competition rate of 5 to 1
- 倍率 20 倍の狭き門
① a forbidding acceptance rate of one in twenty applicants
② a very competitive situation in which only one in twenty applicants is accepted
- 倍率が高い試験　a highly competitive examination ★competitive は「競争の激しい」「競争力のある」の意味があるが，ここでは前者．
- 倍率が低そうな学校を受験する　take an examination at a school with a higher「acceptance rate [pass rate]」
- 求人倍率　⇨きゅうじんばいりつ

はいる【入る】
- このびんには 2 リットル入る．　This bottle holds two liters.
- この部屋には 100 人入れる．　① This room can accommodate a hundred people. ② This room「holds [has a capacity of]」one hundred.

はく【泊】　⇨第 1 部・31-4-3 1 泊 2 日

パスカル　〔圧力の単位〕a pascal《記号 Pa》

バスト　① *one's* bust measurement ② the measurement around the bust［⇨第 1 部・43-3 胸囲］

はせん【破線】　① a broken line ② a dashed line［⇨てんせん］

はちかくけい【八角形】　an octagon［⇨第 1 部・58-2 …角形］

はちぶんめ【八分目】　eight-tenths［⇨…ぶんめ］

はちょう【波長】　(a) wavelength
- 380 nm の波長をもつ　have a wavelength of 380 nm

- 240-320 nm の波長をもつ紫外光　ultraviolet light「with [having] wavelengths [a wavelength] between 240 and 320 nm
- 2つの波長の比　the ratio of two wavelengths
- 1波長の4分の1　① a quarter wavelength　② a quarter of a wavelength
- 3波長分の長さである　be three wavelengths long
- 波長の半分より小さな空隙　a gap smaller than half the wavelength
- 特に指定のない限り大きさはすべて**波長を単位として**表わす．　Unless otherwise specified, all dimensions will be **in units of wavelengths**.
- それらはエネルギーの大半を可視光と赤外線の**波長領域**で放出している．They radiate most of their energy in the visible and infrared **wavelengths**.
- 波長が長い［短い］　① have a「long [short] wavelength　② the wavelength is「long [short]
- 波長が同じだ　① be equal in wavelength　② be of the same wavelength
- ごく短波長の電磁波　electromagnetic radiation of very short wavelength
- 与えられた波長の光　light of a given wavelength
- 与えられた波長での数次にわたる測定　multiple measurements at a given wavelength
- 波長の異なる光で見た太陽の画像　images of the sun as seen in different wavelengths of light
- 多くの高エネルギーガンマ線源は他の**波長**で観測されている天体と対応づけられていない．　Many energetic gamma-ray sources have not been correlated with objects observed at other **wavelengths**.
- 広い波長範囲にわたって　over a wide range of wavelengths
- 塵はこれらの**波長**（の電磁波）に対して透明である．　The dust is transparent to these **wavelengths**.
- 波長の測定　measurement of wavelength
- 波長の変化を測定する　measure the change in wavelength

はつ【初】　the first ［⇨第1部・15. 順位・順番の表現］
- 日本人初の宇宙飛行士　the first Japanese astronaut
- 世界初の商業宇宙飛行　the world's first commercial space flight
- 私の初の海外旅行　my first trip abroad
- 史上初の有人宇宙船を打ち上げたのは旧ソ連だ．　It was the former Soviet Union that launched the first manned space vehicle in history.

バッテリー　a battery ［⇨第1部・51. 電池・テレビ］

はば【幅】　① width　② breadth　③〔範囲〕range ［⇨第1部・42-2 幅］
- 幅は10メートルある．
  ① It is ten meters「wide [across].
  ② It is ten meters in width.

③ It has a width of ten meters.

はやさ【速さ】　① (a) speed　② (a) velocity ［⇨ そくど【速度】］

パラメーター　a parameter
- BUFFERS パラメーターを 20 に設定する　set the BUFFERS parameter to 20
- このモデルは自由パラメーターは一つだけである．　This model has only one free parameter.

ばりき【馬力】　horsepower 《略 hp, h.p., HP, H.P.》★単複同形
- メートル馬力［仏馬力］　a metric horsepower

★1 メートル馬力は 75 重量キログラム・メートル毎秒（約 735.5 W）．日本の計量法ではメートル法に基づくこの仏馬力が内燃機関の分野で使用が定められている．日本での略語 PS はドイツ語 Pferdstärke から．1782 年にジェームズ・ワットが最初に定義した馬力はヤード・ポンド法に基づき 550 重量ポンド・フィート毎秒（約 745.7 W）とされており，日本では「英馬力」と呼ばれる．

- そのエンジンは 200 馬力ある．
  ① The engine produces 200 hp.
  ② The engine delivers 200 hp.
  ③ The engine has a capacity of 200 hp.
- 300 馬力のエンジン　a「300-horsepower［300 hp］engine
- 馬力のある自動車　a high-powered car
- 馬力時　a horsepower hour 《略 hph, HpH》

パリティー　(a) parity
- **パリティー**が逆の 2 つの粒子［状態］　two「particles［states］with opposite「parity［parities］
- 弱い相互作用では**パリティー**は保存されない．　**Parity** is not conserved in weak interactions.
- ［データチェック用］**パリティー**は通例 0 に設定される．　**Parity** is usually set to 0.
- その系は確定した**パリティー**をもつ．　The system has a definite **parity**.

はる【張る】

1　［角度を見込む］subtend
- 太陽の赤道半径が地球に対して張る角　the angle at the earth subtended by the equatorial radius of the sun
- 星の視差とは，その星の位置に対して地球と太陽の平均距離が張る角である．　The parallax of a star is **the angle at** the star **that is subtended by** the mean distance between the earth and the sun.
- その面が光源に対して張る立体角　the solid angle which the surface subtends at the source

2 〔ベクトル空間の基底となる〕span
- 有限個の要素**によって張られる**ベクトル空間　a vector space **spanned by** a finite number of elements.
- その空間は X, Y の2つのベクトル**によって張られる**.　The space **is spanned by** two vectors X and Y.
- これらの固有関数**によって張られる**線形空間の次元　the dimension of the linear space **spanned by** these eigenfunctions
- 3次元空間**を張る**ベクトル　vectors **spanning** a three-dimensional space

はん【半】　(a) half［⇨第1部・17-9 半分］
- 9時半　① half past nine ② half after nine［⇨第1部・32-1 時刻］
- 1時間半　① an hour and a half ② one and a half hours
- 2キロ半　① two and a half kilometers ② two kilometers and a half
- 1倍半　① one and a half times ② half as「much［many］again《as …》 ③ half again as「many［much］《as …》［⇨第1部・17. …倍］
- 1ダース半　a dozen and a half
- 半周期ごとに　every half period
- 半回転　① one half revolution ② one half rotation
- 半日　① half a day ② a half day
- 半年　① half a year ② a half year ③ six months

…ばん【…番】　［⇨いちばん］

1 〔番号〕① number ② No.
- 5番　① number five ② No. 5
- **50番以降の**番号札をお持ちの方はこちらにお並びください.　Those of you holding numbers **fifty and above** please「form a line［stand in line］here.
- 1番に田中さんからお電話です.　〔電話の取り次ぎ〕You have a call from Mr. Tanaka on 1.
- 1番線で列車を待つ　wait for the train on platform number one
- 列車は3番線にくる［から出る］　The train「arrives at［leaves from］platform number three.
- この前買った宝くじは，一等の当選番号と1番違いだった.　The lottery ticket I bought a while back was only one number away from the first-prize number.
- 何番　⇨なんばん
- 5番アイアン　a five iron［⇨第1部・50-3 ゴルフ］

2 〔順位・順序〕① a ranking ② a position ③ a standing［⇨第1部・15. 順位・順番の表現］
- 私は3番だった.　I was third (from the top).

はんい

- *k*番目のセル　the *k*th cell
- 1番で卒業する　graduate top
- 6番目にゴールインする　reach the goal sixth
- 1番打者　the leadoff batter ［⇨第1部・49-6 打順］
- 試験で10番上がる　go up ten places in an examination
- 右から3番目の男　① the third man from the right　② the man three (positions) from the right
- 何番目　⇨第1部・26-10 何番目

関連表現

- 上から指定されたセル数のところにある．　It is (located at) a designated number of cells from the top.

3〔勝負などの回数〕① a game　② a round　③ a bout

- 1番やる　① play [have] a game 《of go》　② have a bout 《of wrestling》
- 3番勝つ［負ける］　win [lose] three games 《straight, in succession》
- 3番勝負　a three-game match ［⇨さんばんしょうぶ］
- 結びの一番　the last (sumo) bout of the day
- スパニッシュダンスを3番踊ってみせる　give [dance] three Spanish dances

4〔曲・歌詞の数〕

- 『ローレライ』の**1番**の歌詞　(the) ⌈lyrics [words]⌉ to **the first verse** of *Lorelei*.
- **2番**の歌詞が思い出せない．　I can't remember the words of **the second verse**.
- 狂言**百番**集　(a collection of) **100** kyogen ⌈**pieces** [**dramas**]⌉

はんい【範囲】　① a range　② a scope ［⇨第1部・11. 数値範囲の表現，12.「以上」「以下」等の表現］

- xの値は10から20の範囲内である．　The value of x is within a range of ⌈10 to 20 [10-20]⌉.
- 70から80の範囲にはいる　① fall ⌈in [within]⌉ the range of ⌈70 to 80 [70-80]⌉　② fall ⌈in [within]⌉ the range from 70 to 80
- 広い範囲の温度にわたって一定である．　It is constant over a wide range of temperatures.
- 狭い範囲に限られている　① be confined within narrow limits　② be limited to a narrow range
- 変動の範囲　the range of ⌈variation [fluctuation]⌉
- 本発明の範囲　the scope of the present invention
- 大統領権限の範囲を規定する　define the limits of presidential power
- 予算の範囲内に収める　① keep expenditure within the limits of *one's* budget　② do not go over (the) budget

- マウスを使って範囲を指定する　define [mark, specify] an area with a mouse
- 彼の読書の範囲は広い．
  ① His reading is wide-ranging.
  ② He reads a wide range of books (and magazines).

はんき【半期】

1 〔1年の半分からなる期〕a half year
- 上［下］半期　the 「first [second] half of the year
- 上半期決算報告　the balance sheet for the first half (year)
- 下半期の決算　the final account for the second half
- 半期ごとの　① semiannual ② half-yearly
- 半期ごとに　① semiannually ② half-yearly
- 半期に一度の大バーゲン　a grand sale held twice a year

2 〔1期の半分〕a half term

はんきすう【半奇数】　① an odd-half integer ② a half odd integer ③ an odd multiple of 1/2 ［⇨はんせいすう］

はんけい【半径】　a radius ★複数形は radii, radiuses.
- 半径5センチの円を描く　draw [describe] a circle with a radius of five centimeters
- 底面の半径が r，高さが d の円柱　a cylinder with base radius r and height d
- その建物から半径30キロ以内に　① within a 30-kilometer radius of that building ② within 30 kilometers of that building

ばんごう【番号】　a number
- 7桁の番号　① a seven-digit number ② a seven-figure number
- **電話番号の末尾が3**の聴取者　those listeners whose **telephone numbers end in (a) 3**
- **登録番号**によって識別する　identify … by **the registration number**
- 番号の若い　low-numbered
- 番号の大きい　high-numbered
- 番号順に並ぶ　line up in numerical order
- **チケットの番号順に**入場する　be admitted **in the order of the number on** *one's* **ticket**
- **ケッヘル番号順の**モーツァルトの作品リスト　① a list of Mozart's works **sorted by Köchel number** ② a list of Mozart's works **in the order of their Köchel numbers**
- 番号付け　numbering
- 番号を付ける［振る］　① number ② assign a number 《to …》 ③ give a number 《to …》

はんすう

- 番号付けされていない ① unnumbered ② numberless
- これらの本にはみな**番号が打ってある**.
  ① All these books **are numbered**.
  ② All these books **bear serial numbers**.
- リストの番号を振りなおす renumber a list
- **続き番号**
  〔連続する番号〕① consecutive numbers ② running numbers ③ sequential numbers ④ numbers in sequence
  〔宝くじの連番〕⑤ 《10 lottery tickets with》 consecutive numbers ⑥ numbers in sequence
- **続き番号でない** 1 万円札で 1 億円 ¥100 million in ¥10,000 bills **with non-sequential serial numbers**
- **通し番号** ① a serial number ② a sequential number
- その秘密文書は 1 部ごとに**通し番号**が印刷されている. Every copy of the confidential document has **a serial number** printed on it.
- **製造番号** the manufacturer's serial number 《on a camera》
- **電話番号** ① a telephone number ② a phone number ［⇨第 1 部・46. 住所と電話番号］
- **当選番号** ① the winning number(s) ② the lucky number(s)
- **部屋番号** a room number
- **郵便番号** ① 《米》 a「zip [ZIP] code ② 《英》 a postcode ③ a postal code ［⇨第 1 部・46. 住所と電話番号］
- 7 桁の数字の郵便番号 a seven-digit zip code

はんすう【半数】 ① half the number ② half 《of the members》

- 参議院議員は 3 年ごとに半数が改選になる. Half the members of the House of Councillors are reelected every three years.
- 半数を超えている ① be more than half the number ② be in [have, obtain] a majority ［⇨第 1 部・16. 投票・選挙の表現 16-3 過半数］
- 半数体 〖生物〗 a haploid

はんせいすう【半整数】 a half-integer ［⇨はんきすう］

- 半整数の half-integral
- 半整数スピンをもつ粒子 a particle with a half-integer spin
- フェルミオンは半整数のスピンをもつ. Fermions have half-integer spin.

はんたいしょう【反対称】 antisymmetry

- 反対称な antisymmetric
- 反対称行列 an antisymmetric matrix
- 反対称化 antisymmetrization

- 反対称化する　antisymmetrize

ばんち【番地】　⇨第 1 部・46-1 住所

はんちょくせん【半直線】　① a ray　② a half line

ハンデ　a handicap［⇨第 1 部・50-3 ゴルフ 50-3-2］
- ハンデ 20 のゴルファー　① a 20-handicap player　② a 20-handicapper

はんてん【反転】　① inversion　② reversal

★inversion は鏡に映すような反転，reversal は矢印の向きを逆にするような反転をいうことが多い．
- 空間反転　(space) inversion
- 反転対称性　inversion symmetry
- 時間反転　① time reversal　② time reflection
- 時間反転不変性　① time reversal invariance　② time invariance　③ time symmetry
- 単位円に関する反転　① inversion in the unit circle　② inversion with respect to the unit circle
- 反転中心　① a center of inversion　② an inversion center
- 位相反転　① phase inversion　② phase reversal
- 反転増幅器　an inverting amplifier
- 反転分布　①〔現象〕population inversion　②〔系〕an inverted population
- 反転ラマン効果　the inverse Raman effect

はんとう【反騰】　① a rebound　② a rally［⇨第 1 部・13-4 増加・上昇を表わす各種表現］
- 反騰する　① rally　② rebound
- 株価の急反騰　a sharp rebound in stock prices

はんばいきげん【販売期限】　① sell-by date　②《米》a pull-by date［⇨第 1 部・35-4 賞味期限・消費期限］

はんぴれい【反比例】　① an inverse「proportion [ratio]　② a reciprocal「proportion [ratio]
- …に反比例する　① be in inverse proportion to …　② be inversely proportional to …
- 引力は距離の自乗**に反比例して**弱くなる．
  ① The force of gravitation「weakens [declines] **at the inverse** square of the distance.
  ② The force of gravitation「weakens [declines] **in inverse proportion to** the square of the distance.
  ③ The force of gravitation「weakens [declines] **inversely proportionally to** the square of the distance.

はんぶん【半分】 ① (a) half ② 〖法〗(財産などの) a moiety ［⇨第 1 部・17-9 半分］

はんぶんすう【繁分数】 ① a compound fraction ② a complex fraction ［⇨第 1 部・53. 分数］

はんべつしき【判別式】 a discriminant

はんらく【反落】 ① a fallback 《in stock prices》 ② a correction ③ a setback ［⇨第 1 部・13-5 減少・低下を表わす各種表現］
- 反落する ① fall [drop, slip] back ② fall [drop, retreat] after 《hitting a record high》
- 反落がある there is a correction 《in stock prices》
- 急反落 a sharp correction
- 小反落 ① a slight setback ② a small correction

ひ【比】

1 〔比率〕(a) ratio ［⇨第 1 部・22. 割合］
- A と B の比 [A の B に対する比] ① the ratio of A to B ② the ratio between A and B ③ the ratio $A:B$ ★$A:B$ は A to B または $A B$ と読む.
- 社員の男女比は男が 6 で女が 4 だ.
  ① The ratio of men to women in the company is six to four.
  ② There are six men to every four women in the company.
- メンバーの男女比はどのくらいですか.
  ① What is the ratio of male to female members?
  ② What is the ratio of men to women among the members?
- 信号対雑音比 a signal-to-noise ratio 《略 SNR》
- 質量光度比 〖天〗a mass-to-light ratio

2 〔比較の基準〕［⇨第 1 部・13-3 比較の基準の表現］
- 前年比で 1 割減 a ten percent drop「on [compared with] last year

…ひ【…費】 ① (an) expense ② (a) cost ［⇨第 1 部・40-3 費用, 41-1-3 損益計算書］

ピーエイチ【pH】 〔水素イオン指数〕pH ★potential of hydrogen の略.
- pH が 4.4 の溶液 a solution with a pH of 4.4
- pH の大きな変化 ① a large change in pH ② a large pH change
- ほぼ一定の pH を維持する maintain an approximately constant pH
- その溶液の pH は 7 より大きい. The pH of the solution is greater than 7.
- その溶液の pH はいくらですか. What is the pH of the solution?
- 色の変化が見られる指示薬の pH 範囲 the pH range of an indicator during which a color change can be seen

ピー・ピー・エム【ppm】 ppm ★parts per million の略. ［⇨第 1 部・22-1-4 ppm／ppb／ppt］

ピー・ピー・ティー【ppt】 ppt ★parts per trillion の略. ［⇨第 1 部・22-1-4 ppm／ppb／ppt］

ピー・ピー・ビー【ppb】 ppb ★parts per billion の略. ［⇨第 1 部・22-1-4 ppm／ppb／ppt］

ひかかん【非可換】
- 非可換な　noncommutative
- 非可換群　① a non-Abelian group ② a noncommutative group

ひかく【比較】 (a) comparison ［⇨第 1 部・13. 比較・差・増減］

ひかさん【非可算】
- 非可算無限個の　① uncountably infinite ② an uncountably infinite number of

ひがし【東】 east ［⇨第 1 部・59-5 東西南北］

ひきあてきん【引当金】 ① a reserve fund 《to cover an expected loss》 ② money set aside 《for …》
- 貸し倒れ引当金　① an allowance for doubtful accounts ② a loan loss reserve ③ a bad debt reserve ④ a bad debt provision ⑤ a bad debt allowance ⑥ a provision for bad debts ⑦ a reserve for bad debts ⑧ an allowance for bad debts
- 損失引当金　① a loss reserve fund ② a provision for loss
- 退職給付引当金　① a reserve for (employees') retirement benefits ② an allowance for (employees') retirement benefits ★かつての退職給与引当金に代わるもので, 企業年金の給付分も対象.
- 退職給与引当金　a reserve for (employees') retirement「payments [allowance]
- 役員退職慰労引当金　a reserve for「directors' [officers'] retirement「allowance [bonus]

ひきざん【引き算】 subtraction ［⇨第 1 部・54-2 引き算］

ひく【引く】 ① subtract ② take away ③ take off ④ deduct ［⇨第 1 部・54-2 引き算］
- 13 引く 8 は 5.　13 minus 8 is 5.

ピコ… 〔10^{-12}〕pico- ［⇨第 1 部・27-4 SI 接頭語］
- このインクジェットプリンターの印刷ヘッドは体積 2〜4 ピコリットルの液滴を噴出する.　The printing head of this inkjet printer ejects ink droplets between 2 and 4 picoliters in volume each.

ひこうかんど【非好感度】 how negatively … is viewed

- その候補者の非好感度は 61% だった. ① Negative views of the candidate were 61%. ② Sixty-one percent had 「a negative [an unfavorable] view of the candidate. ③ Sixty-one percent viewed the candidate negatively. ④ The proportion of people negatively viewing the candidate was 61%.
- その国は非好感度 1 位だった.　The country attracted the most negative ratings.

ひさしぶり【久しぶり】 [⇨…ぶり]

- 久しぶりに　① after a long 「time [interval, break, silence, absence, separation] ② for the first time in a long time
- 久しぶりに雨が降った.　It rained for the first time in quite a while.
- 彼は久しぶりに家に帰った.　He returned home after a long absence.
- 彼から久しぶりにメールが来た.　I received an e-mail from him after a long silence.
- 親子は久しぶりに顔を合わせた.　The father and son met after a long separation.
- この地を訪れるのは本当に久しぶりだ.　I haven't been in this area for ages.
- お久しぶりです.
  ① I haven't seen you 「for a long time [for an age].
  ② It is a long time since I saw you last.
  ③ It's been quite a time since we met.
  ④《略式》Long time no see.
  ⑤ It's sure been a while.

ひしがた【菱形】 ① a rhombus ② a rhomb ③ a lozenge ④ a diamond (shape)
★rhombus の複数形は rhombuses, rhombi.

- 菱形の　① rhombic ② rhombiform ③ diamond-shaped ④ lozenge-shaped
- 菱形の対角線は直交する.　The diagonals of a rhombus intersect at right angles.
- 菱形模様　① a diamond pattern ② a lozenge pattern

ひじゅう【比重】 specific gravity [⇨みつど]

- **比重**とは,物質の質量と,同体積の水の質量との比である.　**Specific gravity** is the ratio of the mass of a 「substance [material] to the mass of an equal volume of water.
- 4℃における水の**比重**は 1.0 だ.
  ① **The specific gravity** of water at 4℃ is 1.0.
  ② Water at 4℃ has **a specific gravity** of 1.0.
- 鉛は鉄よりも**比重**が大きい.　Lead has a 「higher [greater] **specific gravity** than iron.
- さまざまな金属の**比重**の表　a table showing **the specific gravities** of various metals

ヒストグラム

- **比重**を計る　measure [determine] **the specific gravity**《of …》
- 比重計　① a hydrometer　② a gravimeter　③ a densitometer　④ a densimeter　⑤〔液体の〕an areometer
- 世界経済において日本の占める比重　the relative importance of Japan in the world economy

ヒストグラム　a histogram

ひせんけい【非線形】

- 非線形な　nonlinear
- 光の強度に対して**非線形に**変化する　vary **nonlinearly** with light intensity
- **非線形性**　nonlinearity
- **非線形方程式**　a nonlinear equation
- **非線形回路**　a nonlinear circuit
- **非線形増幅器**　a nonlinear amplifier
- **非線形効果**　nonlinear effects
- **非線形光学**　nonlinear optics

ひたいしょう【非対称】　asymmetry

- 非対称な　asymmetric(al)

ピタゴラスのていり【ピタゴラスの定理】　the Pythagorean theorem

ひだり【左】　the left［⇨第 1 部・59-1 左右］

ひだりて【左手】

- 左手系　a left-hand system
- 左手の法則　the left-hand rule

ひづけ【日付】　① a date　② dating［⇨第 1 部・30-2 月日］

- 日付を 4 桁の数字で入力してください．　Enter the month and day in four digits.

ぴったり　exactly［⇨第 1 部・18-4「ちょうど」「ぴったり」］

ビット　a bit

- 最上位ビット　the most significant bit《略 MSB》
- 最下位ビット　the least significant bit《略 LSB》
- 64 ビットプロセッサー　a 64-bit processor
- RGB の各色が 8 ビットで表わされる．　Each color of RGB is represented「by [with, in] 8 bits.

ビットコイン　〔仮想通貨〕(a) bitcoin

- ミリ［マイクロ］ビットコイン　a「millibitcoin [microbitcoin]
- 当時，1 ビットコインの価値は約 600 米ドルだった．　At the time, the value

of one bitcoin was about 600 US dollars.
- 50 ビットコイン (300 万円相当) を失う　lose 50 bitcoins (worth three million yen)

ヒットチャート　the charts ［⇨第 1 部・15. 順位・順番の表現 15-2-3］
- イギリスのシングルヒットチャート第 1 位になる　hit [reach] No. 1 on the UK singles charts

ヒップ　① *one's* hip measurement　② the measurement around the hips ［⇨第 1 部・43-5 ヒップ］

ひとしい【等しい】　① equal …　② be equal 《to …》　③〔同じ〕the same 《amount》　④〔等価〕be equivalent 《to …》　⑤〔同一〕be identical ［⇨第 1 部・18. 同等・相当］
- 128 ビットは 16 バイトに等しい．　128 bits「equals [is equal to, is equivalent to] 16 bytes.
- 線分 A と B は長さが等しい．
  ① Line A「is [has] the same length as line B.
  ② Lines A and B are equal in length.
  ③ Lines A and B are of identical length.
  ④ Lines A and B have the same length.
- 日本は面積でドイツにほぼ等しい．
  ① Japan and Germany are roughly the same「size [area].
  ② Japan is roughly the same size as Germany.
  ③ Japan has roughly the same area as Germany.
  ④ Japan is more or less equivalent to Germany in area.
  ⑤ Japan is more or less as big as Germany.
- これを 0 に等しいとする　let this be equal to zero
- 円の半径に等しい長さの弧　an arc equal in length to the radius of the circle

ひねつ【比熱】　specific heat ［⇨ねつようりょう］
- 比熱の大きい［小さい］　of「high [low] specific heat

ひのえうま【丙午】　⇨第 1 部・37-6 十干十二支

ひふ【非負】
- 非負の　〔0 または正〕nonnegative
- 非負の整数　a nonnegative integer

びぶん【微分】　① differentiation　②〔微分したもの〕a derivative　③〔分野〕differential calculus
- 微分する　differentiate
- その式を x で微分する　differentiate the expression with respect to x
- 座標の時間に関する微分　differentiation of the coordinate with respect to

- y に関する f の微分　the derivative of f with respect to y
- ダッシュは y に関する微分を表わす．　The prime denotes differentiation with respect to y.
- f の $x=a$ における微分　the derivative of f at $x=a$
- 1 階時間微分　① the first-order time derivative　② the first-order derivative with respect to time
- 2 階微分　the second(-order) derivative
- n 階微分　① the nth(-order) derivative　② the derivative of order n
- 高階微分　a higher(-order) derivative
- 空間微分　a spatial derivative
- 方向微分　a directional derivative
- 微分演算子　a differential operator
- 微分形式　a differential form
- 微分係数[商]　a differential ⌈coefficient [quotient]
- 微分断面積　a differential cross section
- 微分積分　differential and integral calculus
- 偏微分　⇨へんびぶん
- **微分方程式**　a differential equation
- 1 階 [2 階] 線形微分方程式　① a linear differential equation of the ⌈first [second] order　② a first-[second-]order linear differential equation
- 常微分方程式　an ordinary differential equation
- **微分可能な**　differentiable
- 2 回微分可能な　twice differentiable
- 無限回微分可能な　infinitely differentiable
- その区間上で連続微分可能な関数　a continuously differentiable function on the interval
- f は連続な微分をもつものとする．　Let f have a continuous derivative.
- いたるところ微分不可能な連続関数　a continuous function which is nowhere differentiable

ひゃく【百】　a [one] hundred [⇨第 1 部・1. 基数]

- 200　two hundred
- 365　three hundred (and) sixty-five
- 何百もの　hundreds of … [⇨第 1 部・8. 漠然とした大きな数]

関連表現

- 両者は五十歩百歩だ．

① There is ｢little [not much] difference between the two.
② There is little to choose between them.
③ It is six of one and half a dozen of the other.
④ One is as bad as the other.
⑤ One is not much better than the other.
- 百聞は一見にしかず.
  ① One picture is worth ｢a thousand [ten thousand] words.
  ② There's nothing like seeing for oneself.
  ③ Seeing for oneself is (far) better than hearing about something. ★これに似た英語の諺 Seeing is believing. は「自分の目で見てこそ信じられる」といった意味で使う.
- 一罰百戒　① punishing one while giving a warning to hundreds　② making an example of one

ひゃくはちじゅうど【180度】

1 〔角度〕① one hundred and eighty degrees　② 180 degrees
- 三角形の3つの角の合計は**180度**である.　The sum of the three angles of a triangle is **180 degrees**.

2 〔正反対〕
- 180度の転換をする　① take [make, do] a 180-degree turn　② make [do] a complete ｢about-face [《英》about-turn]　③ change 180 degrees　④ make a ｢complete [total, radical] change　⑤ completely reverse 《a policy, a course of action》
- 180度態度を変える　① change *one's* attitude 180 degrees　② change *one's* attitude completely

ひゃくぶんりつ【百分率】　(a) percentage [⇨第1部・22-1-2 百分率／パーセント]

ひよう【費用】　①(an) expense　②(an) expenditure　③(a) cost　④(an) outlay [⇨第1部・40-3 費用]

ひょう【表】　① a table　② a list
- 表にする　① make … into a table　② show … as a table　③ make a table of …　④ make [show] a list of …　⑤ list　⑥ tabulate　⑦ put into tabular form
- 表に載せる　① put … in a ｢table [list]　② add … to a ｢table [list]
- 表に載っている　① be listed　② be in a ｢table [list]　③ be ｢included [placed] in [on] a list
- 詳細は下表のとおり.　Details are given in the table below.
- 表の第5列の3行目の数字　the figure ｢on the third line [in the third row] of the fifth column in the table [⇨ぎょう]

ひょう【票】　a vote [⇨第1部・16. 投票・選挙の表現]

- その法案は 200 票対 150 票で可決された．　The bill was passed by a vote of 200 to 150.
- その候補者は 20 万票を得た．　The candidate「got［obtained, polled］two hundred thousand votes.

びょう【秒】

1 〔時間の単位〕a second ⟪= 1/60 分 = 1/3600 時間；記号 s, sec., ″⟫

- （シャッタースピード）100 分の 1 秒で写真を撮る　take a「photograph［picture］at a hundredth of a second
- 1 秒の何分の 1 まで正確な時計　a watch that is accurate to (within) a fraction of a second
- 5 秒ルール　〔落とした食べ物でも 5 秒以内に拾えばきたなくないという考え〕the five-second rule　★形容詞句をなすので second は単数形．

2 〔角度の単位〕a second ⟪= 1/60 分 = 1/3600 度；記号 sec., ″⟫

ひょうかがく【評価額】

- 評価額 1000 万円の絵　a painting「valued［assessed］at ten million yen

びょうかく【秒角】　① an arc second　② a second of arc

ひょうし【拍子】　〔音楽〕

- 4 分の 2 拍子　① ⟪in⟫ two-four time　② ⟪米⟫ two-four meter
- 4 分の 3 拍子　① ⟪in⟫ three-four time　② three-quarter time　③ ⟪米⟫ three-four meter　④ waltz time

ひょうじかかく【表示価格】　①〔カタログ記載価格〕a list price　②〔店頭小売表示価格〕a displayed retail price　③ a sticker price［⇨第 1 部・40-2-4 価格にまつわる術語］

ひょうじゅんじ【標準時】　standard time［⇨第 1 部・32-3 時差］

ひょうじゅんへんさ【標準偏差】　(a) standard deviation

- **標準偏差**は平均からの偏差の 2 乗を平均したものの平方根である．　**The standard deviation** is the square root of the average squared deviation from the mean.
- 正規分布では得点の約 68% が**平均から 1 標準偏差以内にある**．　In a normal distribution, about 68% of the scores **are within one standard deviation of the mean**．［⇨シグマ］★約 68%（約 3 分の 2）のデータは平均から 1 標準偏差の範囲内，95% のデータは平均から 2 標準偏差の範囲内にある．
- 娘の点が 87 点でその試験の平均点が 80 点だったとする．標準偏差が 10 ならその子の点は**平均から 1 標準偏差の**範囲内で，それほどすごいことではないかもしれない．　Suppose that your daughter's score was 87 and the average score on the test was 80. If the standard deviation was 10, her score was **within one standard deviation of the average**, which may not be so impressive.

- 一方，**標準偏差**が5だったとすると，その子は非常によくやったということを意味することになる．すべての得点の84%は85点以下のはずだからである． On the other hand, if **the standard deviation** was 5, this would indicate that she did very well, because 84% of all scores would be below the score of 85. ★ 84 = 68 + 32/2（次例参照）
- すべての得点の約68%は**平均から1標準偏差以内で**，残りの32%の半分は平均より1標準偏差以上低いはずである． About 68% of all scores should be **within one standard deviation of the average** and half of the remaining 32% should be more than one standard deviation below the average.

ひょうすう【票数】 ①〔票の数〕the number of votes ②〔票決力〕(a) voting strength ［⇨第1部・16-1 票数］

ひょうすう【標数】 a characteristic

びょうそく【秒速】
- 秒速20メートルで　at (a「velocity [speed] of) 20 meters「per [a] second

ひょうてん【氷点】 ①(a) freezing point ②an ice point ［⇨第1部・45-1 温度］

ひょうめんせき【表面積】 a surface area
- 半径 r の球の**表面積**は $4\pi r^2$ である． **The surface area** of a sphere of radius r is $4\pi r^2$. ★ $4\pi r^2$ は four times pi times r squared などと読む．

びり ①(the) last ②(the) bottom ［⇨第1部・15. 順位・順番の表現 15-2-1］

ひりつ【比率】 ①(a) ratio ②(a) percentage ［⇨第1部・22. 割合］
- 3対2の比率である．
  ① They are in a ratio of three to two.
  ② They are in a ratio 3:2.
- 3対1の比率を示す　indicate a ratio of three to one
- 5:5:3の比率　①《at》a five-five-three ratio ②《at》a ratio of 5:5:3
- 合格者のうち女性の比率が年々高くなってきている． The percentage of women among successful examinees has been increasing yearly.

ひれい【比例】 (a) proportion
- …に比例する　① be proportional to … ② be in proportion to …
- …に比例して増加する　increase [rise, grow] in proportion to …
- その素子は光の強度に**比例する**電流を生じる． The device「produces [generates] a current (which is) **proportional to** the intensity of the light.
- 応力のひずみに対する [応力とひずみの間の] **比例関係**　① **the proportionality** of stress to strain ② **the proportionality** between stress and strain
- 後退速度と距離の間には**比例関係がある**． There is a proportionality between recession velocity and distance.
- 富が増すの**に比例して**，彼は寛大さを失っていった．
  ① **As** his wealth grew, his generosity shrank.

② 《文》 **In proportion as** his wealth grew, his generosity shrank.
③ He grew wealthier and meaner **at the same time**.
- **正比例** direct proportion
- **反比例** inverse proportion [⇨はんぴれい]
- **比例式** ① a proportional expression ② a proportion
- **比例式**において, 外項の積と内項の積は等しい. In **a proportion**, the product of the extremes is equal to the product of the means.
- **比例定数** ① a constant of proportionality ② a proportionality constant ③ a proportionality factor

ひれいはいぶん【比例配分】
① (a) pro rata allocation ② (a) proportional「allotment [allocation] ③ (a) proportional distribution ④ apportionment ⑤〔線形補間〕 (a) linear interpolation

- 議席は各政党の得票率**に応じて比例配分する**.
① Seats **are「allotted [apportioned]** to each party **according to** the number of votes it gets.
② Each party **receives a number of** seats **which is proportional to** its share of the vote.

- 利益は出資額**に応じて比例配分する**.
① Profits distributed「**are [shall be] proportional to** the investment.
② Profits「**are [shall be] apportioned according to** the investment.
③ Profits **are distributed pro rata to** the investment.

- その点の座標を**比例配分**で求める
① **use linear interpolation to** find the coordinates of the point
② find the coordinates of the point **by linear interpolation**

ひろさ【広さ】

1 ①〔面積〕 (an) area ②〔広がり〕 (an) extent [⇨第1部・42-8 面積]
- 庭の広さ the size of the garden

2 ①〔幅〕 width ② breadth [⇨第1部・42-2 幅]

ひんしつほじきげん【品質保持期限】 ⇨第1部・35-4 賞味期限・消費期限

ひんど【頻度】 frequency [⇨第1部・36. 回数・頻度の表現]

- 高い [低い] 頻度 high [low] frequency (of occurrence)
- パスワードを変更する頻度
① the frequency with which you change your password
② the frequency with which your password is changed
③ how「frequently [often] you change your password
④ how「frequently [often] your password is changed
⑤ the frequency of changing passwords

ふ【負】

- 負の ① negative ② minus
- 負の数　a negative number
- 負でない整数　a nonnegative integer ★0 または正の整数
- 負電荷　(a) negative charge
- 負になる　become negative
- 負の遺産　a negative legacy 《of the Cold War》

…ぶ【…分】

1 〔十分の一〕

- 桜はまだ一分咲き程度だ．　The cherry blossoms are just beginning to come out.
- 桜は今が五分咲きだ．　Half the cherry blossoms are open.
- 六［七, 八, 九］分立て　〔生クリームの泡立ての固さ〕soft ［slightly firm, moderately firm, very firm］《whipped cream》
- 三分［五分, 七分］搗き米　① rice from which「thirty percent ［fifty percent, seventy percent］ of the bran has been removed　② thirty percent ［fifty percent, seventy percent］ polished rice
- 七分粥　① rice porridge that is three parts water to seven parts rice　② thick rice porridge
- 七分丈　three-quarter (length)《sleeves, dress》
- 七分袖　① three-quarter sleeves　② bracelet sleeves
- 工事は6分通り完成した．　The work is more than half finished.［⇨くぶどおり］
- 九分九厘　⇨くぶくりん

2 〔1割の十分の一；1%〕［⇨第1部・22. 割合 22-1-1 歩合］

- 3割5分　thirty-five percent ［⇨…わり］
- 8分の利子　eight-percent interest
- 5分利付き公債　five-percent bonds

ぶあい【歩合】　percentage ［⇨第1部・22. 割合］

- 売り上げに対して2割の歩合を出す　〔手数料〕allow ［give］ a commission of 20 percent on sales
- 精米歩合　⇨せいまいぶあい

ファラド　〔静電容量の単位〕a farad《記号 F》

フィート　feet ★単数形は a foot《=12インチ, 30.48 cm；記号 ft. または′》［⇨第1部・28. 伝統単位 28-1］

- 3フィート5インチ　① three feet five inches　② 3 ft. 5 in.　③ 3′5″
- 彼は身長5フィート6インチだ．　★英米では身長の単位にはフィート, イ

ンチを使うことが多い（⇨第 1 部・28. 伝統単位）.
① He is five feet six inches (tall [in height]).
② He is five「foot [feet] six. ★数詞のあとでは複数形として feet, foot のどちらも用いられる.
③ He is five-six. ★口頭ではこのように数字のみをいうことが多い.

- その山は29,028フィートの高さだ． The mountain is 29,028 feet high. ★数字が大きいときの複数形には foot は使わず feet が普通.
- 6,000フィートの山　a 6,000-foot mountain ★数詞がついて形容詞になるときには単数形 foot となる．[⇨第 1 部・1-2-6 数詞が複合形容詞をつくる場合]
- 身長6フィートの女性　① a six-foot-tall woman ② a woman six feet tall ③ a six-foot woman
- 10 フィートの棒　a ten-foot pole
- 平方フィート　a square foot《記号 sq. ft.》
- 立方フィート　a cubic foot《記号 cu. ft.》

ふうそく【風速】　① wind speed ② wind velocity [⇨第 1 部・45-5 風速, 37-7 気象用語]
- 現在の風速は3メートルです． The wind is blowing (at) three meters per second.

ふうたい【風袋】　①〔商業〕〔包装重量〕a tare (weight) ②〔包装〕the packing ③ the packaging ④ the wrapping ⑤〔箱の類の〕a package ⑥ a parcel ⑦ a container
- 風袋込みで　① gross ② in gross weight
- 風袋抜きで　① net ② in net weight
- これは風袋込みでちょうど200グラムです． This weighs exactly 200 grams gross.
- 重さを量る時は風袋を入れないようにしなさい． When you weigh it, make sure you don't include the「wrapping paper [packaging].
- 風袋を計る　① weigh the packaging ② tare

フーリエへんかん【フーリエ変換】　① a Fourier transform ② (a) Fourier transformation ③〔変換したもの〕a Fourier transform
- フーリエ変換を施す　perform [do] a Fourier transform《on …》
- 入力信号のフーリエ変換　the Fourier transform of the input signal
- 信号のフーリエ変換を計算する　compute the Fourier transform of a signal
- **フーリエ変換**は信号を時間領域から周波数領域に変換する数学的操作である． A **Fourier transform** is a mathematical operation that transforms a signal from the time domain to the frequency domain.
- フーリエ変換された信号　a Fourier-transformed signal

- フーリエ変換された画像　a Fourier-transformed image
- 単一周波数の信号は**フーリエ変換すると**1つのピーク**になる**．　A signal with a single frequency would be **Fourier transformed to** a single peak.
- デジタル画像を**フーリエ変換すること**　**Fourier transformation** of the digital images
- フーリエ解析　Fourier analysis
- フーリエ級数　a Fourier series
- フーリエ係数　a Fourier coefficient
- フーリエ成分　a Fourier component
- フーリエ積分　a Fourier integral
- フーリエ展開　a Fourier expansion

フェムト…　〔10^{-15}〕femto- 〔⇨第1部・27-4 SI接頭語〕

- 数フェムト秒のレーザーパルスを使って化学反応を研究する　study chemical reactions with a laser pulse「that lasts for〔with a duration of〕a few femtoseconds

フォト　〔照度のCGS単位〕a phot《記号 ph》

フォン　〔音の大きさのレベルの単位〕a phon　★純音の知覚的な大きさを表わす．〔⇨ホン〕

ふかく【俯角】　①a dip　②an angle of depression　③〔地磁気の〕a (magnetic) dip 〔⇨へんかく〕

ふかさ【深さ】　depth 〔⇨第1部・42-4 深さ〕

- そのプールは深さが2メートルある．　The pool is two meters「deep〔in depth〕.

ふくい【腹囲】　①(the) girth of the abdomen　②ventral girth　③abdominal girth 〔⇨第1部・43-4 ウエスト〕

ふくごう【複号】　①a plus or minus sign　②a double sign

- 複号は同順とする．　Both upper or both lower signs should be chosen in the double signs.
- 複号の上のものが音源が観測者から遠ざかる場合，下のものが音源が近づいてくる場合を表わす．　The top signs represent the source receding from the observer, and the bottom signs the source approaching the observer.

ふくすう【複数】

- 複数の　①plural　②multiple　③more than one　④two or more　⑤〔技術文で〕a plurality of　⑥a multiplicity of
- 同じ結果を与える複数の異なる k の値がある．　There are different values of k which give the same result.　★日本語では「複数の」を入れないと There is a different value of k which gives the same result.（同じ結果を与えるもう一つの異なる k の値がある）と区別できないが，英語は values という複数形を使

えば訳出する必要はない.
- 複数のコンピューターを接続するネットワーク　① a network connecting computers　②〔技術文で〕a network connecting a plurality of computers
- 本を複数のグループに分類する　classify books into (several) groups
- 複数の関係者によると　according to several「sources [people] involved
- 複数回　① several times　② multiple times　③ more than once　④ two or more times　⑤〔技術文で〕a plurality of times
- 複数回答　multiple answers
- 複数形　〖文法〗the plural (form)
- 複数年契約　a multiyear contract
- 複数年(度)方式　a multiple-fiscal-year system

ふくそ【複素】

- 複素の　complex
- **複素関数**　a complex function
- **複素共役**　a complex conjugate
- アステリスクは複素共役を表わす.　The asterisk denotes a complex conjugate.
- $\bar{z}$ は z の複素共役を表わす.　$\bar{z}$ denotes the complex conjugate of z.
- 方程式の複素共役をとる　take the complex conjugate of the equation
- **複素数**　⇨ふくそすう
- **複素平面**　⇨ふくそへいめん
- **複素変数**　a complex variable
- **複素表示**　(a) complex representation
- **複素振幅**　a complex amplitude
- **複素電流**　a complex current
- **複素インピーダンス**　(a) complex impedance
- **複素誘電率**　a complex dielectric constant
- **複素屈折率**　① a complex refractive index　② a complex index of refraction

ふくそすう【複素数】　a complex number［⇨せいすう 数の集合］

- 複素数値の関数　a complex-valued function
- 複素数平面　＝ふくそへいめん
- 複素数の絶対値［ノルム］　the「modulus [norm] of a complex number

ふくそへいめん【複素平面】　① the complex plane　② the Gaussian plane

- 複素平面上の距離　distance in the complex plane
- 複素平面上に点を表わす　plot points in the complex plane

ふくめる【含める】 ⇨さんにゅう 関連表現, …こみ

ふくり【複利】　compound interest
- 複利の計算をする　calculate [compute] compound interest
- 年当たりの利回り 2% は 6 か月ごとの**複利計算がされる**．　The equivalent annual rate of 2% will **be compounded** twice a year.
- 72 の法則は，**複利の利率**を x, 元金が倍になる年数を y として $y=72/x$ というものだ．　The Rule of 72 states that $y=72/x$, where x is **the compound interest rate** and y is the number of years needed to double the principal.

ふごう【符号】

1 ① a code 《⇨コード》 ② 〔記号〕a mark ③ a sign ④ a symbol

2 〔正負の〕a sign
- 符号は正［負］である．　The sign is「positive [negative].
- 符号が逆である　be of the opposite sign
- 大きさが等しく符号が逆である　be equal in magnitude but opposite in sign
- **異符号**の電荷［イオン］　a charge [an ion] **of the opposite sign**
- 2 つの電荷は異なる**符号**をもつ．　The two charges **have opposite signs**.
- 2 つの電荷は同じ**符号**をもつ．　The two charges **have the same sign**.
- 符号が変化［反転］する　the sign「changes [reverses]
- その関数は $x=0$ で**符号を変える**．　The function「**changes** [**reverses**] **sign** at $x=0$.
- 2 つの関数の**符号が一致する**　**the signs** of the two functions **coincide**
- ここでは電子電荷 e を負とする**符号の取り方**を採用している．
  ① We use **the sign convention** that the electron charge e is negative.
  ② In **the sign convention** adopted here, the electron charge e is taken to be negative.
  ③ **The sign convention** used here is such that the electron charge e is negative.

ふじんふく【婦人服】　women's clothing［⇨第 1 部・44-3 婦人服のサイズ］

ふそく【不足】　① (a) shortage　② (a) deficiency［⇨第 1 部・21-1 不足］

ぶっか【物価】　(commodity) prices［⇨第 1 部・40-2-7 物価］
- 先月の**消費者物価指数**は前年同月比 3% の上昇となった．　Last month's **consumer price index** was three percent higher than for the same month last year.

ふってん【沸点】　a boiling point 《略 bp》
- 沸点に達する　① reach boiling point　② come to a boil
- 沸点上昇　① (a) boiling-point elevation　② (an) elevation of the boiling point

ふていせきぶん【不定積分】　an indefinite integral

- 関数 $\exp(-x^2)$ は初等関数の範囲では**不定積分**はない． The function $\exp(-x^2)$ has no **indefinite integral** in terms of elementary functions.

ふとうごう【不等号】 ① an inequality「sign [symbol] ②〔＞形の (左に開いている)〕a greater-than symbol ③〔＜形の〕a less-than symbol

- 不等号の向きを変える　reverse (the「direction [order, sense] of) the inequality sign
- 不等号の向きを保存する　preserve the「direction [order, sense] of the inequality
- 不等式の両辺に負の数をかけると，不等号の向きが変わる．　Multiplying both sides of an inequality by a negative number reverses the「direction [sense, order] of the inequality.
- ★日本語では「大なり（＞）」「小なり（＜）」「大なりイコール（≧）」「小なりイコール（≦）」といった特別な読み方があるが，英語ではA＞Bを「AはBより大きい」とするなど普通の表現として読む．基本は次の通り．
  A＞B　A is greater than B.
  A＜B　A is less than B.
  A≧B　A is greater than or equal to B.
  A≦B　A is less than or equal to B.
  文の途中に出てくる場合は次のように適宜文法構造に合わせて読む．
  This holds only for $n > 2$. → This holds only for n greater than 2.
  [⇨第1部・55. 式の読み方]

ふとうしき【不等式】　an inequality

- 不等式の解　the solution (set) of an inequality
- 不等式を解く　solve an inequality
- 次の不等式をみたす　satisfy the following inequality
- 絶対不等式　an「unconditional [absolute] inequality
- 条件不等式　① a conditional inequality ② an inequation

ぶどまり【歩留まり】　① a yield ② a yield rate [⇨ふりょうりつ]

- その新技術の導入で歩留まりが85％に上がった．　The introduction of the new technology brought yields up to 85%.

ぶぶんひてい【部分否定】　〚文法〛partial negation [⇨第1部・22-5 部分否定と全否定]

ぶぶんぶんすう【部分分数】　partial fractions

- 部分分数で表わす　express《a rational function》in partial fractions
- 部分分数に分解する　decompose《a rational function》into partial fractions
- 部分分数分解［展開］　decomposition [expansion] into partial fractions

ブラジャー　① a bra ② a brassiere [⇨第1部・44-2 ブラジャーのサイズ]

プラス　plus

プラスアルファ

- 3 **プラス** 5 は 8.
  ① Three **plus** five「is [makes, equals] eight.
  ② Three **and** five「are [make, equal]eight.
- マイナス 3 かけるマイナス 4 は**プラス** 12.　Minus 3 times minus 4「is [equals]**plus** 12.
- 今朝は**プラス** 3 度だった.
  ① The temperature was **plus** three (degrees) this morning.
  ② The temperature was three (degrees) **above zero** this morning.
- **プラスの値**　① a **positive** value　② a **plus** value　③ a value **greater than zero**　④ a value **above zero**
- 今月の決算は 568,000 円の**プラス**だった.　At the「settlement [close] of accounts for this month, we were ¥568,000 **in the black**.
- **プラスになる**　① become **positive**　② go **above zero**　③ rise **above zero**
- 経済成長率がやっと**プラス**になった.　The economic growth rate has finally moved into **plus figures**.
- **プラス記号**　a **plus** (sign)
- 電池の**プラス**とマイナスを図の通りの向きにして入れる　insert the batteries with the **plus** and minus terminals aligned as illustrated
- 500 円**プラス**して 2,500 円ではどうだい.　How about **adding** ¥500 and making it ¥2,500?

プラスアルファ　① a little more (than usual)　② a bit more (than usual)　③ some extra　④ a little extra

- 周りの長さ**プラスアルファ**くらいのひも　a piece of string long enough to go round《the bundle》**with a little to spare**
- 今やそのレコーダーは 1 万円**プラスアルファ**くらいの値段で買える.　You can buy the recorder now for **not much more than** ¥10,000.
- 交通費**プラスアルファ**くらいのお金だけ持っていけばいい.　All you need to take is enough money for your fare **plus a little extra**.
- 基礎年金に加えて**プラスアルファが付く**.　**A certain amount is added** on top of the basic pension.

★野球の「アルファ付き」については⇨第 1 部・49. 野球の数字表現 49-1

プラスマイナス　① plus and minus　② plus or minus [⇨ふくごう]　★±の記号が使えない場合は+/−と書く (/が「または」の意味になる).

- 誤差として**プラスマイナス** 5 を見込む　allow a margin of error of **plus or minus** 5
- その価格の変動幅は**プラスマイナス 10% の範囲内に**ある.　The price is fluctuating **within a range of 10% in either direction**.
- それでは結果として**プラスマイナスゼロ**だ.
  ① That would mean **no gain or loss** after all.

② So we come out **even** in the end.
- **プラスマイナス** 3 歳くらいの違いはあるとして，その男は 27, 8 歳に見えた. The man looked 27 or 28, **give or take** about three years. [⇨第 1 部・9. 概数 9-1]

…ぶり

★「…ぶり」は英語では「ここ…の間で初めて」と発想する．「間」に当たる語を下記の用例の lapse, break, interval, separation, silence, absence などのように的確に選べば生きのよい表現になる．「長い期間のうちで初めて」といえば「久しぶり」を表現できる．[⇨ひさしぶり]

- 5 年ぶりに　① for the first time in five years　② for the first time since five years「ago [before]　③ after「a lapse [a break, an interval] of five years　★ago は現在を基準にして，before は過去のある時点を基準にしての表現．
- 10 年ぶりで兄弟に会う　see *one's* brother for the first time「in ten years [after ten years' separation]
- 2 年ぶりで彼から便りがあった．　I heard from him for the first time「in two years [after two years' silence].
- 君と会うのは，高校卒業以来実に 30 年ぶりだよな．　This really must be the first time we've met since graduating from high school thirty years ago.
- 1 年ぶりで酒を飲む　drink sake after a year's abstinence
- 3 年ぶりに帰省する　come home after three years' absence
- そのご友人に会ったのは**何年ぶり**のことでしたか．　**After**「**how long** [**how many years**] did you see that friend of yours?
- 今回の我が校の優勝は 1999 年以来**8 年ぶり**の快挙である．　This win for our school is our **greatest** feat「**since** we won **eight years ago** in 1999 [**since** our victory of 1999, **eight years ago**].
- これは **10 年ぶり**の暑さだ．
  ① This is the warm**est** weather we have had「**for** [**in**] **ten years**.
  ② This is the hot**test** it has been **in ten years**.
- **10 年ぶり**に行ってみたら，その町は以前とはだいぶ様子が違っていた．
  ① I had**n't** been there **for ten years**, and the town seemed to have changed a good deal.
  ② It was my **first** trip there **in ten years**, and the town seemed to have changed a good deal.
  ③ It was my **first** visit there **since ten years ago**, and the town seemed to have changed a good deal since then.

関連表現
- 3 年来の低水準　① the lowest level in three years　② a fresh three-year low

ふりょうりつ【不良率】　① a defect rate　② the「fraction [proportion] defective　③〔百分率〕the percent defective [⇨ぶどまり]

- 1% 未満の不良率　a defect rate less than 1 percent

ふれんぞく【不連続】 discontinuity
- 不連続の　discontinuous
- その関数は $x=0$ で**不連続**である．　The function is **discontinuous** at $x=0$.

プロット
- データをグラフ上にプロットする　① plot the data on a graph ② graph the data
- A を B の関数としてプロットする　plot A as a function of B
- A を B に対してプロットする　plot A against B

ふん【分】

1 〔時間の単位〕a minute 《= 1/60 時間；記号 m., min., ′》〔⇨第 1 部・32. 時刻と時間〕
- 15 分　① fifteen minutes ② a quarter (of an hour)
- 4 時 15 分　① a quarter「past [after] four ② four fifteen 《4:15》
- 5 時 15 分前　① a quarter「to [before,《米》of] five ② four forty-five 《4:45》
- 30 分　① thirty minutes ② half an hour ③《米》a half hour
- 1 時 30 分　① half past one ② one thirty (1:30)
- 45 分　① forty-five minutes ② three quarters of an hour

2 〔角度の単位〕a minute 《= 1/60 度；記号 min., ′》

…ぶん【…分】

1 〔相当〕①…'s worth of ② for … 〔⇨…まえ 1〕
- 牛肉 1 万円分　ten thousand「yen's [yen] worth of beef
- 数か月分の食料　① several months' supply of food ② several months' worth of food ③ enough food for several months
- 3 日分の着替え　① extra clothes for three days ② three changes of clothes
- （食物の）4 人分　① four helpings ② four servings
- 5 人分の弁当　lunches for five people
- 3 日分の薬　medicine for three days
- 2 人分食べる　eat enough for two
- 1 日分の糧食　a day's ration
- 1 日分の薬を 3 度に分けて飲む　split the daily dosage into three parts
- 3 日分の仕事　① three days' work ② three days of work ③ three days' worth of work
- 3 人分の仕事　an amount of work「sufficient for [requiring] three people
- 3 人分の仕事をする　do the work of three people

- レモン3個分のビタミン　① the vitamins of three lemons　②《contain》as much vitamins as three lemons　③ the vitamin content of three lemons
- 東京ドーム7つ分の広さ　seven times the area of Tokyo Dome
- 1フレーム分のオーディオデータ　one frame's worth of audio data
- 何世帯分の電気を発電するか　how many households worth of electricity《it》generates
- 1日で例年の7月1か月分の雨が降った．　The usual amount of rain for the whole month of July fell in just one day.
- 今月分の新聞代　① this month's newspaper bill　② the newspaper bill for this month
- 今月分の給料　① this month's「salary [pay, wages]　②《my》salary for the month　③《my》pay for「this [the current] month

2〔分数〕⇨第1部・53. 分数

ぶんいすう【分位数】　a quantile

- q分位数　a q-quantile　★昇順に並べたデータ値の集合においてデータ値の数をq等分したそれぞれの点の値．
- 四分位数　a quartile　★「二分位」はメジアン（中央値）という．
- 十分位数　a decile
- 百分位数　a percentile
- 第k百分位数　the kth percentile　★「下から百分のk」の順位．
- 第50百分位数はメジアンと等価だ．　The 50th percentile is equivalent to the median.
- 百分位スコア［百分順位］　① a percentile score　② a percentile rank　★百分位数で表わした順位．

ふんかく【分角】　① an arc minute　② a minute of arc

ぶんし【分子】

1〔分数の〕a numerator［⇨第1部・53. 分数］

2〔物質の構成単位〕a molecule

- 水の分子は1個の酸素原子と2個の水素原子から成る．　A water molecule is formed of one oxygen atom and two hydrogen atoms.

ぶんすう【分数】　① a fraction　② a fractional number［⇨第1部・53. 分数］

ふんそく【分速】

- 分速20メートルで　at (a「velocity [speed] of) 20 meters「per [a] minute

ぶんどき【分度器】　a protractor

ぶんぷ【分布】　distribution

- 分布する　① be distributed　② range《from one place to another》

ぶんぽ

- 動植物の（地理的）分布　the geographical distribution of plants and animals
- 体内での放射性同位体の分布　the distribution of radioisotopes in the body
- 素数の分布　the distribution of prime numbers
- 電子密度の空間分布　the spatial distribution of the electron density
- ニュートリノイベントの天頂角分布　the zenith angle distribution of neutrino events
- ラザフォードは大角度で散乱された α 粒子の角度分布を測定した．Rutherford measured the angular distribution of alpha particles scattered at large angles.
- 理想気体分子の速度分布　the velocity distribution of molecules in an ideal gas
- 大気中の温度の異常な垂直分布　an unusual vertical distribution of temperature in the atmosphere
- 分布の一様性　uniformity in distribution
- 非一様な分布　(a) non-uniform distribution
- b クォーク生成の非対称な分布を生じる　give rise to an asymmetric distribution for b-quark production
- 平均が μ, 標準偏差が σ のガウス分布　a Gaussian distribution with mean μ and standard deviation σ
- その分布の平均値のまわりの広がり　the spread of the distribution around the mean
- $v=a$ のところにピークをもつ速度分布になる　have a velocity distribution with its peak at $v=a$
- 他の原子核は陽子と同じようなエネルギー分布を示す．The other nuclei show an energy distribution similar to that of the protons.
- その変数は正規分布に従う．
  ① The variable「has [follows]」a normal distribution.
  ② The variable is normally distributed.
- 決まった時間区間内に発生するそのような事象の数はポワソン分布に従う．The number of such events occurring in a fixed time interval follows a Poisson distribution.
- 各瞬間の大きさがガウス分布に従って決まるランダム雑音　a random noise whose instantaneous magnitudes occur according to the Gaussian distribution
- 分布関数　a distribution function
- 分布曲線　a distribution curve
- 連続分布　(a) continuous distribution
- 離散分布　(a) discrete distribution

ぶんぼ【分母】　a denominator ［⇨第 1 部・53. 分数］

…ぶんめ【…分目】

- コップに八分目ぐらい入れなさい．　Fill the glass four-fifths full.
- 腹八分目にしておく　〔控えめ〕① be moderate in eating　② avoid stuffing *one*self completely full
- 「グラスの何分目まで入れましょうか」「7分目くらいまで入れてください」How full do you want your glass? — Fill it about seven-tenths full.

へいきん【平均】　① an average　② a mean　[⇨第1部・25. 平均]

- 平均では［平均して, 平均すると］　① on average　② on an average　③ on the average
- このサイトは**平均して**1日に1000件ほどのアクセスがある．
  ① This site is accessed **on average** 1000 times a day.
  ② This site receives **an average of** 1000 hits a day.
  ③ This site **averages** 1000 hits a day.
- 平均点　〔試験の得点〕the average「grade［《英》mark］[⇨第1部・25-6 平均点]
- 平均年齢　the average age《of the members》[⇨第1部・25-7 平均年齢]
- 平均寿命　①〔人の〕the average life span《of Japanese people》② the average longevity《of human beings》③ the average life expectancy (at birth)　④〔放射性核種などの〕the mean lifetime　[⇨第1部・25-8 平均寿命]
- 平均的　①〔平均値の〕mean　② average　③〔普通の〕ordinary　④ normal　⑤ general　[⇨第1部・25-9 平均的]

へいこう【平行】　[⇨へいこうせん]

- 平行な　parallel
- …と平行に線を引く　draw a line parallel to …
- その道は海岸線とほぼ平行に走っている．　The road runs「almost [nearly] parallel to the coastline.
- 直線 *l* は直線 *m* と**平行である**．　Line *l* **is parallel**「**to** [**with**] line *m*.
- ある点を通って, 与えられた直線に**平行な**直線はただ一つだけ引ける．
  ① Only one line can be drawn **parallel to** a given line through a point not on this line.
  ② For a given point outside a given line, only one line can be drawn through the point **parallel to** the given line.
- 凸レンズは入射する**平行光線**を集束させる．　A convex lens causes incoming **parallel (light) rays** to converge.
- その2つの電子は**平行**[**反平行**]**スピン**をもつ．　The two electrons have「**parallel** [**antiparallel**] **spins**.
- 平行からのわずかなずれ　slight deviations from parallelism
- 平行性　parallelness
- 平行性のいいビーム　① a well-collimated beam　② a highly parallel beam

へいこういどう

- 平行性の誤差　errors in the parallelism
- 平行六面体　a parallelepiped

へいこういどう【平行移動】 translation [⇨へいしん]

- その曲線を x 軸に接するように**平行移動させる**　**translate** the curve so that it is tangent to the x-axis
- x 軸方向への単位長さの**平行移動**　**translation** by a unit「distance [length]」in the x direction
- (1回の) **平行移動**とそれに続く回転　**a translation** followed by a rotation

へいこうしへんけい【平行四辺形】 a parallelogram

- **平行四辺形**の面積は底辺かける高さである．　The area of **a parallelogram** is「the product of its base and height [base times height]」.
- 菱形は 4 辺が等しい**平行四辺形**である．
  ① A rhombus is **a parallelogram** with four equal sides.
  ② A rhombus is an equilateral **parallelogram**.
- **平行四辺形**の対角線は互いに他を二等分する．　The diagonals of **a parallelogram** bisect each other.
- 四角形は向かい合う角が等しければ**平行四辺形**である．　A quadrilateral is **a parallelogram** if its opposite angles are congruent.

へいこうせん【平行線】 parallel lines [⇨へいこう]

- 平行線の公理　the parallel postulate
- 線 l に対し，点 A を通る平行線を引く　draw a line through point A parallel to line l
- 平行線は交わることはない．　Parallel lines never meet.

関連表現

- 平行線をたどる　① pursue [go along, move along, be on] parallel tracks
  ② do not get [fail to get] any closer (to agreement)　③ get nowhere
- 話し合いは平行線をたどるばかりだった．
  ① The talks got nowhere.
  ② The talks didn't bring agreement any closer.
  ③ There was no progress (in the negotiations).
- 両者の話し合いは最後まで平行線をたどった．　Their talks led to no agreement to the end.

へいしゅうごう【閉集合】 a closed set

へいしん【並進】 translation [⇨へいこういどう]

- 並進させる　translate
- 時空中での並進　translations in space-time
- 並進運動　translation

- 並進運動のエネルギー　energy of translational motion
- 並進対称性　translational symmetry
- 並進不変性　translational invariance
- 並進不変性のある　translationally invariant

へいせい【平成】　⇨第 1 部・29-5 元号

へいねん【平年】

1　〔うるう年でない年〕a common year
- 西暦 1700 年はユリウス暦ではうるう年だがグレゴリオ暦では平年になる．　The year 1700 was a leap year in the Julian calendar and a common year in the Gregorian calendar.

2　〔例年〕① a normal year　② an average year
- 平年値　〔気温などの〕the average year value　★気象庁では 1981 年～2010 年の 30 年間の平均値 (the 1981–2010 average) (10 年毎に更新) を平年値として使っている．
- 今年の降雨量は平年並みの見込みである．　This year's rainfall is expected to be normal.
- 今年の夏はあまり気温は上がらず平年よりも平均して 1 度から 2 度ほど低くなるでしょう．　This summer's temperatures will not be very high; they will be an average of one or two degrees lower than normal.
- 平年作　① a normal ⌈crop [harvest]　② an average ⌈crop [harvest]
- 今年の米作は平年作を上回る [下回る] 見込み．　This year's rice crop is expected ⌈to be better than [to fall short of] (the) average.

へいほう【平方】　〔2 乗〕a square [⇨第 1 部・54-5-1 2 乗]
- 4 平方メートル　4 square meters　★4 meters square というと「4 メートル四方」の意味なので面積は 16 平方メートルになる．
- x^2+x [右辺] を平方完成する　complete the square on ⌈x^2+x [the RHS]
- 平方数　a square number
- 平方剰余　a quadratic residue
- 平方非剰余　a quadratic non-residue

へいほうこん【平方根】　a square root [⇨第 1 部・54-6 累乗根]
- 4 の平方根は 2 である．$((\sqrt{4}=2))$　① The (square) root of 4 is 2.　② Root 4 is 2.

へいめん【平面】　a plane
- 3 点 A, B, C を含む平面　the plane containing the three points A, B, and C
- 直線 l と点 A を含む平面　the plane containing the line l and the point A
- 同一平面上にある　① lie in the same plane　② be coplanar
- 直線 l はその平面上 [内] にある．　The line l lies in the plane.

- 動きは xy 平面内である． The motion is in the x-y plane.
- その球に接する平面 a plane tangent to the sphere
- z 軸に垂直な平面 a plane perpendicular to the z-axis
- 点 P から平面までの距離 the distance of the plane from point P
- その平面の法線 the normal to the plane
- 法線ベクトル $\boldsymbol{n} = (a, b, c)$ をもつ平面の方程式は $ax + by + cz = k$ の形になる．
  The equation of a plane with normal vector $\boldsymbol{n} = (a, b, c)$ is in the form $ax + by + cz = k$.
- 点 Q はその平面に関して点 P と同じ側にある． Point Q is on the same side of the plane as point P.
- 平面幾何学 plane geometry
- 平面角 a plane angle
- 平面曲線 a plane curve
- 平面鏡 a plane mirror
- 平面図 ① a plan ② a ground plan ③ a floor plan ④ an ichnography
- 平面図形 a plane figure
- 平面波 a plane wave

ページ【頁】 a page

- 123 ページ ①〔ページ番号〕page 123 《略 p. 123》 ②〔ページ数〕123 pages 《略 123 pp.》
- 3 ページに on page 3
- 24 ページに続く． Continued on page 24.
- 10 ページの図をご覧ください． See the chart on page 10.
- 90 ページを開く［開ける］ ① open 《the book》 at [to] page 90 ② find page 90
- 教科書の 12 ページを開いてください． Open your textbooks to page 12.
- 123 ページから 128 ページ ① pages 123 to 128 ② 《米》 pages 123 through 128 ③ pages 123-128 《略 pp. 123-128》
- 10 ページから 15 ページまで予習してきなさい． Prepare pages 10「to [《米》through] 15.
- 3 ページの上から 10 行目に ① on the 10th line from the top of page 3 ② on page 3, line 10 from the top
- 15 ページ 19 行目から 16 ページ 5 行目まで ① page 15, line 19 to page 16, line 5 ② from the 19th line of page 15 to the 5th line of page 16 ③ from line 19 on page 15 to line 5 on page 16
- 21 ページ以降に記載されている説明 ① the explanation beginning on page 21 ② the explanation on p. 21ff. ★ff. は and the following pages（および後続ページ）の意．単数の場合は f.（and the following page）となる．

- 8 ページの小冊子　a pamphlet of eight pages
- 第 1 巻は 362 ページある．　The first volume「covers [numbers, runs to, extends to] 362 pages.
- その本は本文が 120 ページで，注が 20 数ページある．　The book「contains [consists of] 120 pages of text and 20-odd pages of notes.
- 参考文献は 362 ページから始まる．　The references begin on page 362.

ベース
- 時価 [簿価] ベースで　on a「market [book] value basis
- 今年の売り上げは，金額ベースで 10% 増，台数ベースで 5% 増となった．　Sales this year resulted in a ten-percent increase in value terms and a five-percent increase in units.
- ドルベースで 5% の利回りといっても，ドル安がそれ以上に進めば元本割れになる．　Even with dollar-based interest of five percent, if dollar depreciation exceeds that figure, it results in a loss of principal.

べき【冪】　power [⇨第 1 部・54-5 累乗 54-5-4]

べきじょう【冪乗】　⇨第 1 部・54-5 累乗

ヘクタール　〔面積の単位〕a hectare 《= 10000 m^2；記号 ha》

ヘクト…　〔10^2〕hecto- [⇨第 1 部・27-4 SI 接頭語]

ヘクトパスカル　〔圧力の単位〕a hectopascal 《= 100 Pa；記号 hPa》

ベクトル　a vector
- 列ベクトル　a column vector
- 行ベクトル　a row vector
- ベクトルの成分　① components of a vector　② elements of a vector
- ベクトルの大きさ [ノルム，絶対値，長さ]　the「magnitude [norm, modulus, length] of a vector
- 速度は**ベクトル量**であり，大きさと方向をもつ．　Velocity is **a vector quantity** and has both magnitude and direction.
- z 軸方向の**単位ベクトル**　**the unit vector** in the direction of the z-axis
- 単位ベクトルは**大きさ 1 のベクトル**である．　A unit vector is **a vector that has a magnitude of one**.
- **あるベクトル**とそれ自身とのドット積　the dot product of **a vector** with itself
- ベクトル関数　a vector function
- ベクトル空間　(a) vector space
- ベクトル積　a vector product
- ベクトル場　a vector field

ベクレル　〔放射能の単位〕a becquerel 《記号 Bq》

ベスト best

- **ベストセラー** ① a best-seller ② a best-selling book ③ a top seller ④ a blockbuster
- 決定的ベストセラー　a runaway best-seller
- ベストセラーの第1位　① the「No. 1 [top]」best-seller ② best-seller No. 1 ③ No. 1 in a best-seller list
- **ベストドレッサー**　a best-dressed「man [woman]」
- **ベストフォー**　① the top four ②〔準決勝出場選手〕a semifinalist
- ベストフォーに進出する　① reach the semifinals ② win *one's* way to the semifinals
- **ベストエイト**　① the top eight ②〔準々決勝出場選手〕a quarterfinalist
- **ベストナイン**　〖野球〗① the nine players voted best of the year in their respective positions ② the all-star nine ③〔日本プロ野球の〕the Best Nine
- ベストナインに選ばれる　be voted into [make] the「all-star nine [Best Nine]」
- **ベストテン**　① the top ten ② the ten best … ③〖野球〗the「top ten [ten best]」hitters 《for the season》 [⇨第1部・15. 順位・順番の表現 15-2-1]
- **ベストイレブン**　〖サッカー〗① an all-star eleven ② an all-star「soccer [《英》football]」team
- **ベストオブスリー**〔3戦中先に2勝したほうを勝者とする方式〕best-of-three
- **ベストオブファイブの試合**〔5戦[セット]中先に3勝したほうを勝者とする試合〕① a best-of-five (match [contest, series]) ② a best-of-five set match
- ベストオブファイブで3-2で負けた.　《We》lost 3-2 in a best-of-five.
- ベストオブファイブ方式　a best-of-five format
- **ベストオブセブンシリーズ**　a best-of-seven series

ペタ…　〔10^{15}〕peta- [⇨第1部・27-4 SI接頭語]

- 2008年にアメリカのスーパーコンピューターが1ペタフロップスの演算速度を達成した.　In 2008, an American supercomputer achieved a processing speed of one petaflops.

…べつ【…別】　classified by …

- 府県別人口　population by prefecture
- 体重別選手権　① a championship ranked by weight ② a championship with separate weight rankings
- 国別に分ける　classify 《foreign residents》by nationality
- 輸入品名を国別に示す　show [indicate] imports by country
- 《外国人労働者数に関し》国別では中国人が約32万人と最も多く全体の35.5パーセント, それにベトナム, フィリピン, ブラジルが続く.　By country, the number of Chinese workers is the highest, at about 320,000, or 35.5 per-

cent of the total, followed by workers from Vietnam, the Philippines, and Brazil.

ペニー a penny ★複数形は pence [⇨第 1 部・39-1-4 ポンド]

ベル 〔強度比の表示の単位〕a bel《記号 B》[⇨デシベル]

ヘルツ 〔振動数の単位〕a hertz《記号 Hz》 ★単複同形

へん【辺】

1 〔方程式の〕a side [⇨うへん,さへん,りょうへん]

2 〔多角形の〕① a side ② a member

- 三角形の 3 辺　the three sides of a triangle ★三角形には辺が 3 つしかないので 3 辺といえば一意的に決まり,したがって定冠詞がつく.
- 四角形の向かい合った 2 辺　two opposing sides of a quadrilateral
- その角に対する辺　〔三角形で〕① the side opposite the angle ② the side which subtends the angle
- 2 角とその間の辺　two angles and the included side
- 2 辺とそのはさむ角　two sides and the included angle
- 1 辺が 2 センチの正方形　① a square with 2 cm sides ② a square with a side length of 2 cm ③ a square 2 cm on a side ④ a square with sides 2 cm「long [in length]
- 3 辺の長さの合計　the sum of the lengths of three sides
- 斜辺の長さが c,角 A に対する辺の長さが a,それに隣接する辺の長さが b の直角三角形　a right triangle with hypotenuse of length c, side opposite A of length a, and side adjacent of length b
- 辺 AB は辺 DE の 3 倍である．　Side AB is three times as long as side DE.

へんいき【変域】 〔変数の〕a domain

へんかく【偏角】

1 〔進行方向変化の〕① an angle of deviation ② an angle of deflection

- 小さな**偏角** x については tan $x ≒ x$ が成り立つ．　For small **angles of deviation** x, tan x is approximately equal to x.

2 ①〔地磁気の〕(magnetic) declination ②〔航海用語として〕variation

- この機器は**偏角と俯角**を両方とも測ることができる．　This instrument can measure both **magnetic declination and dip**.

3 〔複素平面での〕① an argument ② an amplitude

- 極座標では複素数は**絶対値と偏角**で表わされる．　In polar coordinates, a complex number is represented by its **modulus and argument**.

へんかん【変換】 ① change ② conversion ③ transformation ④ a transform

へんさち

- 変換する ① change ② convert ③ transform

▶ **電子工学上の変換**

- データ変換　data conversion
- 入力信号のデジタル信号への変換　transformation [conversion] of an input signal to a digital signal
- 音をデジタルパルスに変換する　convert [transform] sound into digital pulses
- テキストデータをシフト JIS からユニコードに**変換する**　**convert** text data from Shift-JIS to Unicode
- 電気音響変換器　an electroacoustic transducer

▶ **数学上の変換**

- 行列 M による変換　transformation with matrix M
- ベクトル空間 V 上での線形変換　linear transformation on a vector space V
- その変換(のもと)で不変である　be invariant under the transformation
- その変換は…を不変に保つ．　The transformation leaves … invariant.
- 座標変換　(a) coordinate transformation
- 線形変換　(a) linear transformation
- 恒等変換　the identity transformation
- 直交変換　(an) orthogonal transformation
- ユニタリー変換　(a) unitary transformation
- フーリエ変換　⇨ フーリエへんかん
- ローレンツ変換　(a) Lorentz transformation
- 双子の座標を別の慣性系にローレンツ変換する　Lorentz transform the coordinates of the twins to another inertial frame
- ローレンツ変換のもとで不変である　be invariant under Lorentz transformations

▶ **その他**

- 自動車は化石燃料のエネルギーを運動エネルギーに**変換する**．　The automobile「**converts** [**transforms**]」fossil-fuel energy into kinetic energy.

へんさち【偏差値】　① a standard score ② a standardized score ③ a T-score

- 日本でいう偏差値とは得点分布全体を平均が 50，標準偏差が 10 となるように調整した標準化得点です．　The deviation value, as so called in Japan, is a standardized score adjusted so that the overall distribution of scores has an average of 50 and a standard deviation of 10.
- 偏差値偏重教育　① education that stresses studying and passing exams to raise one's ranking ② academic cramming

★得点のよしあしを見るのに平均との差(偏差)を使うことがあるが，平均点が 80 点の試験で 87 点を取ったとしても，標準偏差が 10 の場合と 5 の場合

とでかなり意味が違う（⇨ひょうじゅんへんさ）．平均との差を標準偏差で割れば統一的な評価尺度となる．そのように規格化した得点を統計学ではZ-score（Zスコア）という．Z-scoreはどんな得点分布でも平均0，標準偏差1に揃えて比較できるようにするものである．$10 \times Z + 50$ により平均点が50，標準偏差が10となるようにしたものはT-score（Tスコア）といい，日本で言う「偏差値」はこれに当たる．

なお，「偏差値」は日本語独特の表現で，文字通りに英訳した deviation value は得点と平均との差（偏差）の値と解されるのが普通．standard score は Z-score を指すことが多い．「偏差値偏重」など値そのものを問題にしない文脈では適宜意訳することが好ましい．

このほか英語圏でしばしば使われるものに percentile score（百分位スコア）または percentile rank（百分順位）というものがある．［⇨ぶんいすう］

ペンス　pence　★単数形は penny［⇨第1部・39-1-4 ポンド］

へんすう【変数】 a variable

- 独立変数　an independent variable
- 従属変数　a dependent variable
- 0 から 1 までの間の**ランダム変数**　**a random variable** between 0 and 1
- 変数に値を代入する　substitute a value for a variable
- **二変数関数**　a function of two variables
- **変数分離**　separation of variables
- **変数分離**を使って球対称シュレーディンガー方程式を解く　① use **separation of variables** to solve a spherical Schrödinger equation　② solve a spherical Schrödinger equation by (**the technique of**) **separation of variables**
- 積分における**変数変換**　**change of variables** in integrals
- 代入により**変数変換**して積分を求める　find an integral by using a substitution to **change the variable**
- この**変数変換**のためのヤコビアン　the Jacobian matrix for this **change of variables**

へんせい【編成】

- 10両編成の列車　① a train (made up) of ten「carriages [《米》cars]　② a train ten「carriages [《米》cars] long　③ a「ten-carriage [《米》ten-car] train
- 次の電車は 8 両編成で参ります．　The next train will have eight「carriages [《米》cars].
- 1 編成当たり 8 両　8「carriages [《米》cars] per train
- 新型車両は 1 編成のみ運行されている．　Only one formation of the new「carriages [《米》cars] is in operation.
- 40 人で 1 クラスを編成する　① make up a class with forty students　② put forty students in a class
- 2 個中隊に編成する　organize … into two companies

へんどうかんすう【偏導関数】 a partial derivative

へんびぶん【偏微分】 ① partial differentiation ② 〔微分したもの〕a partial derivative
- x について偏微分する　differentiate partially with respect to x
- 偏微分方程式　a partial differential equation
- 放物型偏微分方程式　a parabolic (partial) differential equation
- 双曲型偏微分方程式　a hyperbolic (partial) differential equation
- 楕円型偏微分方程式　an elliptic (partial) differential equation

へんぶんほう【変分法】 ①〚数〛the calculus of variations ②〚物〛the variational method

ヘンリー　〔インダクタンスの単位〕a henry《記号 H》　★複数形は henries と henrys がある.

ポアズ　〔粘性率の CGS 単位〕a poise《記号 P》

ポイント

1　〔得点〕a point
- その技はポイントが高い．　That trick is given high points.
- 《ボクシングなどで》ポイントで勝つ　① outpoint《an opponent》② win on points
- ポイントを取る［かせぐ］　win [get, score] a point
- ポイントを失う　lose a point

2　〔百分率の差〕a (percentage) point ［⇨第 1 部・22-1-9 ポイント］
- 割合は **10 ポイント**上がって 70% から 80% になった．　The percentage rose **(by) 10 points**, from 70 percent to 80 percent.

3　〔購入額に応じて与えられる点数〕a point
- 購入額の 10% 分がポイント化される．
  ① Ten percent of your purchases are converted into points.
  ② You get 1 point for every 10 yen spent. ★この訳は 1 ポイントが 1 円に相当することを想定している.
- ポイントをためる　save up points

4　〔活字の大きさ〕point
- 9 ポイントの活字　(a) 9-point type
- 12 ポイントで印刷する　print in 12-point
- 12 ポイントの行間　① 12-point leading ② 12-point line spacing

ほう【法】　a modulus　★複数形は moduli.
- 87 は 10 **を法として** 7 に合同である．　87 is congruent to 7 **modulo** 10.

★modulo は英語では「…を法として」の意の前置詞.
- **n を法とする**算術　① **modulo** n arithmetic　② arithmetic **modulo** n
- すべての算術計算は n を**法として**行なわれる．　All arithmetic is performed **modulo** n.
- 異なる**法**を使って計算を繰り返す　repeat the calculation using a different **modulus**
- **法による**還元　**modular** reduction

ほういかく【方位角】　① an angle of direction　②〖数〗an azimuth　③〖測量〗bearing　④ an azimuth (angle)

ぼうぎょりつ【防御率】　an earned run average［⇨第1部・49. 野球の数字表現 49-15］

ほうこう【方向】　① a direction　② bearings［⇨第1部・59. 方向・向き］

ほうせん【法線】　a normal (line)
- その点における面の法線　the normal to the surface at the point
- 与えられた点からその曲線に下ろした法線　the normal to the curve from a given point
- 法線影　a subnormal
- 法線応力　(a) normal stress
- 法線速度　(a) normal velocity
- 法線加速度　(a) normal acceleration
- 法線微分　a normal derivative
- 法線ベクトル　a normal vector

ほうていしき【方程式】　an equation
- 文章題についての**方程式**を立てる　① construct **an equation** for a word problem　② set up **an equation** for a word problem　③ translate a word problem into **an equation**
- 方程式を解く　solve an equation
- 方程式の解　① a solution「of［to］an equation　② a root of an equation
- 方程式の両辺に2をかける　multiply both sides of the equation by 2
- 方程式の左辺［右辺］　the「left［right］(-hand) side of an equation
- **一次方程式**　① a linear equation　② an equation of the first degree
- **二次方程式**　① a quadratic equation　② a quadratic　③ an equation of the second degree
- **三次方程式**　① a cubic equation　② an equation of the third degree
- カルダノによる三次方程式の解の公式　① Cardano's formula for solving cubic equations　② Cardano's cubic formula

- **四次方程式** ① a quartic equation ② an equation of the fourth degree
- **五次方程式** ① a quintic equation ② an equation of the fifth degree
- 五次方程式の一般解を四則演算と累乗根だけで表わす公式はない． ① There is no formula that expresses the general solution of a quintic equation involving only the four arithmetic operations and the extraction of roots. ② A general quintic equation cannot be solved by radicals.
- **n次方程式** ① an equation of degree n ② an equation of the nth degree ③ an nth-degree equation
- n次方程式は多重度も数えてn個の根を複素平面上にもつ． An equation of degree n has n roots in the complex plane counting multiplicity.
- **高次方程式** higher-degree equations
- **線形方程式** a linear equation
- **非線形方程式** a nonlinear equation
- **一元方程式** an equation in one variable
- **二元一次方程式** a linear equation in two variables
- **代数方程式** an algebraic equation
- **連立方程式** simultaneous equations
- **二元連立方程式** simultaneous equations in two unknowns

★英語では複数形でいうのが普通の方程式も多い．電磁場のマクスウェル方程式は4つのベクトル方程式で表わされるのが一般的で，Maxwell('s) equations と複数形でいう．重力場のアインシュタイン方程式は1つのテンソル方程式で書かれるが成分の立場からは複数の方程式をまとめて書いたものであり，Einstein('s) equation(s) としばしば複数形が使われる．

ほうぶつせん【放物線】 a parabola

- その放物線は下に凸である． The parabola is vertex down.
- 放物線(状)の parabolic
- 放物線運動 a parabolic「motion [movement]」
- 放物線軌道 a parabolic「orbit [track]」

ほうぶつめん【放物面】 a paraboloid

- 放物面の paraboloidal
- 放物面鏡 a parabolic mirror

ぼうらく【暴落】 ① a slump ② a (sharp) break ③ a crash ④ a heavy「fall [decline]」⑤ a tremendous drop ⑥ a nosedive [⇨第1部・13-5-2 急減・急落]

ほうりつ【法律】 ⇨第1部・48. 法律・条約

ボーナス a bonus

- 月給3か月分のボーナス a bonus equivalent to three months' pay

★英米でのボーナスは日本でいうボーナスとはかなり異なる．日本では夏・

冬の年2回，社員全員に支払われるのが普通だが，英米のボーナスはあくまでも臨時の「特別賞与」であり，特別な貢献をした個々の従業員に与えられる．

ぼか【簿価】 a book value ［⇨第1部・40-2 価格・値段］
- 簿価ベースで　on a book value basis

ほかく【補角】 ① a supplementary angle ② the supplement 《of an angle》

ほくい【北緯】 (the) north latitude ［⇨いど］

ほし【星】 ［⇨第1部・15-3 格付けと星］
- 三つ星のホテル［星三つのホテル］　① a three-star hotel ② a hotel with three stars ③ a hotel with a three-star rating

ほすう【補数】 ① a complement ② a complement number

ポテンシャル (a) potential
- 固体球殻の内部の**重力ポテンシャル**　**the gravitational potential** inside a solid sphere
- **イオン化ポテンシャル**の低い原子　atoms with a low **ionization potential**
- 磁場は**スカラーポテンシャル**を用いて書くこともできる．　The magnetic field may be written in terms of **a scalar potential**.
- 周期ポテンシャル　a periodic potential
- ポテンシャル井戸　a potential well
- ポテンシャル障壁　a potential barrier
- ポテンシャル面　a potential surface
- ポテンシャルエネルギー　potential energy

…ほど【…程】

1 〔概数〕［⇨第1部・9. 概数］
- 1週間ほど　about a week
- 3年ほどの間　for something like three years
- 3時間ほどで　in about three hours

2 〔比較・程度〕
- てのひらほどの大きさの機器　① a device about the size of the palm of your hand ② a roughly palm-sized device
- 今年は去年ほど暑くない．　This year is not「so [as]」hot as last year.

3 〔…するほど〕⇨第1部・13-4-3 相関

ほとんど ① almost all ② nearly all ［⇨第1部・22-4-3 ほとんど］

ボルト 〔電圧の単位〕a volt 《記号 V》［⇨でんあつ，でんいさ］
- ボルト数　voltage

- ボルトアンペア　a volt-ampere《記号 VA》

ホン　〔騒音レベルの単位〕a phon　★日本独自の単位であり，純音の知覚的な大きさを表わすフォンとは異なる．計量法の改正により日本でも国際単位であるデシベルを使うことになり，1997年以降は猶予期間も終わってデシベルに統一されている．ここでいうデシベル値は各周波数の音圧を人の知覚上の特性で補正をしたもので，ホンで表わしたものと数値は同じになる．このような単位で表わす騒音レベルは学術的には A-weighted sound pressure level (A 特性補正した音圧レベル) という．

- これらの地域では騒音の基準は昼間は 50 ホン以下，夜間は 40 ホン以下である．　The maximum permissible noise level in these areas is 50 phons during the day and 40 phons at night.

ポンド

1　〔重量単位〕a pound《常衡は 16 オンス，約 454 g；金衡は 12 オンス，約 373 g；記号 lb.》[⇨第 1 部・28. 伝統単位 28-3]

- 20 ポンド　20 pounds《記号 20 lbs. または 20 lb. または 20#》
- ポンドいくらで売る　sell by the pound

2　〔通貨単位〕a pound《記号 £》　★英貨を特に a pound sterling，俗語で a quid ともいう．[⇨第 1 部・39. 通貨と為替 39-1-4]

- 10 ポンド　10 pounds《£10》

ま行

まい…【毎-】 ① every ② each ③ apiece ④ per
- 毎秒　per second ［⇨まいびょう，まいふん，まいじ］
- 毎土曜日　every Saturday

マイクロ…　〔10^{-6}〕 micro- ［⇨第 1 部・27-4 SI 接頭語］

まいじ【毎時】　① every hour ② per hour ③ an hour
- 毎時 20 マイルの速力で　① at a speed of 20 miles an hour ② at 20 mph

マイナス　minus ［⇨ふ］
- 気温はマイナス 20 度だった.
  ① The temperature was **minus** 20 (degrees).
  ② The temperature was 20 (degrees) **below zero**.
- 7 マイナス 5 は 2.　Seven **minus** five ｢is [equals]｣ two.
- マイナスの値　① a negative value ② a minus value ③ a value less than zero ④ a value below zero
- マイナス記号　a minus (sign)
- マイナスになる　① become negative ② fall below zero
- マイナスする　〔引き算する〕① subtract ② take away
- 今年第二四半期の経済成長率はマイナスに転じた.　In the second quarter of the current year the economy's growth rate fell into negative figures.

まいびょう【毎秒】　① every second ② per second ③ a second
- 毎秒 100 m の速度で　at (a speed of) 100 meters per second
- 毎秒 1 万回転で回転する　rotate at 10,000 ｢rps [revolutions per second]｣
- 動画を毎秒 25 フレームの速度で表示する　display video at a rate of 25 frames per second
- メートル毎秒　〔速さの単位〕meters per second 《記号 m/s》
- メートル毎秒毎秒　〔加速度の単位〕① meters per second squared ② meters per second per second 《記号 m/s^2》
- 加速度の単位はメートル毎秒毎秒である.
  ① The unit of acceleration is meters per second squared.
  ② The unit of acceleration is meters per second per second.

まいふん【毎分】　① every minute ② per minute ③ a minute
- 毎分 45 回転で回転する　rotate at 45 ｢rpm [revolutions per minute]｣
- 成人では安静時に心臓は毎分約 70 回鼓動する.　The heart beats about 70 times per minute at rest in adults.

マイル　a mile 《＝約 1.6 km》［⇨第 1 部・28. 伝統単位 28-1］
- 1 時間に 4 マイル行く　go [cover, do, make] four miles in an hour

…まえ

- 時速50マイル ① 50 miles per hour ② 50 mph
- マイル数　mileage [⇨そうこうきょり]
- 平方マイル　a square mile

…まえ【…前】

1 ① for … ②〔食事の〕a helping ③ a serving ④ a cover ⑤ a portion [⇨…ぶん]

- 1人前の料理　① a serving for one person ② a helping for one person ③ a portion for one person
- 料理2人前　① two helpings of food ② two servings of food
- 分量は4人前．〔レシピで〕① 4 servings. ② Serves 4. ③ Makes 4. ④ Serving size: 4.
- これは6人前になる．
  ① This is enough for six people.
  ② This can serve six.
- 食事を1人前出す　serve a meal for one person
- すし1人前　one portion of sushi
- ステーキを2人前食べる　eat two portions of steak
- 1人前ずつ土鍋で煮る　boil each serving separately in an earthen pot

2〔時間的に先行〕① before ② ago [⇨第1部・31-7「…前」「…後」]

マクスウェル　〔磁束のCGS単位〕a maxwell 《= 10^{-8} ウェーバー；記号 Mx》

マグニチュード　magnitude [⇨第1部・45-6 震度とマグニチュード]

- M6［マグニチュード6］の地震　a magnitude 6 earthquake

まける　① discount ② give [allow, make] a discount ③ take [cut] off 《(5%)》[⇨第1部・40-4 割引]

まじわる【交わる】　① cross ② intersect ③ meet ④ join

- 直角に交わる　meet at a right angle
- 2直線が**交わる**角度　**the angle at which** two lines「**meet [intersect]**
- 線分ABは点Pにおいて線分CDと**交わる**．
  ① The line AB **intersects** the line CD at point P.
  ② The lines AB and CD **intersect** at point P.
- そのグラフは x 軸と2回**交わる**．The graph **cuts** the x-axis twice.

またした【股下】　①〔ズボンの筒の内側の，股から裾までの丈〕an inseam ②〔人の〕an inside leg measurement ③ *one's* inside leg [⇨第1部・43. 身体計測]

- 股下80センチのズボン　① trousers with an inside leg (measurement) of 80 cm ② trousers with an inseam (measurement) of 80 cm

まっき【末期】　① the「last [closing] years [period, days] ② the end ③ the close

④ the「last［terminal］stage ⑤〖生物〗〔細胞分裂の〕the telophase
- 政権末期の政治的混乱　political confusion in the last days of a government
- 戦争末期の食糧不足　the food shortage toward the end of the war
- 平安時代末期の貴族社会　noble society at the end of the Heian period
- 明治の末期　the late Meiji era

まったんかかく【末端価格】　①〔小売価格〕a retail price ②an end price ③〔麻薬などの〕a street price ④a street value［⇨第1部・40-2-4 価格にまつわる術語］
- その覚醒剤は末端価格で1グラム3万円する．
  ① The street price of the stimulant is ¥30,000 a gram.
  ② The stimulant is selling on the street for ¥30,000 a gram.

マッハ　Mach《略 M》
- マッハ1　Mach 1
- マッハ3で飛ぶ　fly at Mach 3
- マッハ数　a Mach (number)

…まで【…迄】

1〔値の上限〕up to …　★上限の値を含むことが多いが，そのことを明示するには up to and including … または up to … inclusive という．上限を含めたくないときは up to but not including … または up to but excluding … または up to … exclusive といえる．［⇨げんど］
- 300 ページまでの本　a book of up to 300 pages
- 10,000 K までの温度　① a temperature of up to 10,000 K ② temperatures up to 10,000 K
- 定形郵便は 25 グラムまで 82 円です．　Postage for standard-size mail is ¥82 for up to 25 grams.
- 会社から 100 万円まで借りられる．　I can get a loan of up to ¥1 million from my company.
- 一度に借りられるのは 10 冊までです．　Up to ten books can be borrowed at one time.
- 応募は 1 人 4 口までです．　Entries limited to four per person.
- N 個までの連続する整数　up to N consecutive integers
- 項目には 100 までのシリアル番号が振ってある．　The entries are「assigned［given］serial numbers running to 100.
- そのタイミングはクロック周期の半分までは本来あるべきところから動くことができる．　The timing can move up to half a clock cycle away from where it should be.
- 下は 100 mV までの電圧に応答する必要がある．　It must respond to volt-

…までに

ages down to 100 mV.

▶「…から…まで」の表現 [⇨第 1 部・11. 数値範囲の表現]

- 50 から 100 までの値　① values from 50 to 100　② values from 50 through 100《米用法》　③ values「50 to 100 [50-100]」　④ values from 50 up to 100　⑤ values ranging from 50 to 100　⑥ values between 50 and 100

2〔期間の終端〕① till …　② until … [⇨第 1 部・35. 期日・期限の表現]

- ゆうべは 11 時まで起きていた．　I was up until eleven last night.
- その金属を溶け始めるまで加熱する　heat the metal until it starts to melt
- いつまでかき混ぜている必要がありますか．
  ① How long do I have to stir this?
  ② Till when do I have to stir this?
- 解決するまで　pending the settlement《of the dispute》
- 今年 3 月 31 日までの 1 年間に　during「the year [the one-year period] ending [ended] March 31 this year　★ending は 3 月 31 日の前でも後でも使えるが，ended は 3 月 31 日より後に使うのが普通.
- 戦争がいつまで続くか誰にもわからなかった．　No one could tell how long the war would continue.
- 「いつまで延期になったのですか」「10 月 10 日に延期されました」　How long [Until when] has it been postponed? — Until October 10.

…までに【…迄に】　① by …　② no later than …　③ not later than …　④ before … [⇨第 1 部・35-2 …までに]

- …するまでに　① by the time …　② before …
- 3 時までに　① by three (o'clock)　② before three
- 出発の 15 分前までに　by fifteen minutes before departure
- 日曜までに　by Sunday
- 明日の朝までに　by tomorrow morning
- 期限までに　by the deadline
- 遅くとも明日のこの時間までには着くはずだ．　At the latest it should be here by tomorrow at this time.
- 申込書は 10 月 31 日までに到着のこと．　Applications must be received no later than October 31.
- テスト開始 10 分前までに着席しなさい．　Be in your seats no later than 10 minutes before the test begins.
- 水が沸騰するまでに野菜の下ごしらえをする　prepare the vegetables while the water is heating
- 私の新しいパソコンは立ち上がるまでに時間がかかる．　My new PC takes a long time to start up.

まるまる　full [whole, entire]《week》[⇨第 1 部・20-1「…も」]

まるめる【丸める】 round (off) [⇨第1部・10. 位取りと四捨五入・切り上げ・切り捨て]
- 小数点以下を丸める　round off《a sum》to the nearest whole number
- 信号値を最も近い量子化された値に丸める　round a signal value to the nearest quantized value

まん【万】 ten thousand [⇨第1部・1. 基数]
- 2万　twenty thousand
- 3万6000　thirty-six thousand
- 1万7000　seventeen thousand
- 26万　two hundred (and) sixty thousand
- 100万　a [one] million
- 1000万　ten million
- 何万という人　tens of thousands of people [⇨第1部・8. 漠然とした大きな数]
- 数百万円　① several million yen ② a few million yen

まん…【満…】 [⇨第1部・38-4 満年齢と数え年]
- 満15歳になる　① turn fifteen (years old) ② attain *one's* fifteenth year ③ complete *one's* fifteenth year

まんがく【満額】 the full amount
- 満額回答〔労働組合などの要求に対する〕　① acceptance in full (of a union's demand) ② a completely satisfactory response (to a salary demand)
- 満額支給　《pension》payment in full

まんき【満期】

1〔手形など〕maturity《略 mat.》.
- 満期になる　① mature ② reach maturity ③ fall [be, become] due
- もうじき保険が満期を迎える．　The insurance policy will soon mature.
- 満期前の解約　cancellation before maturity
- 10年満期の定期預金　a ten-year time deposit
- 10年満期の日本国債　① a ten-year Japanese government bond《金融報道では 10-year JGBs と略記することもある》② a Japanese government bond with a maturity of ten years ③ a Japanese government bond with a ten-year maturity
- この定期預金は3か月で[この25日で]満期だ．　This time deposit matures「in three months' time [on the 25th of this month].
- 満期償還　redemption「at [on] maturity
- 満期手形　a matured bill

- 満期配当　a maturity dividend
- 満期日　① the date of maturity ② the due date
- 満期返戻金　a refund at maturity
- 満期利回り　〔債券などの〕a yield to maturity 《of 6%》《略 YTM》

関連表現
- 10年物の国債利回り　①(a) yield on ten-year government bonds ②(a) yield on government bonds with a maturity of ten years

2〔契約など〕expiry《of a contract》[⇨第1部・34. 期間の表現 34-3]

3〔任期など〕expiration《of a term》[⇨にんき]

まんてん【満点】　① a perfect score ②《英》full marks [⇨てん]

みぎ【右】　the right [⇨第1部・59-1 左右]

みぎかたあがり【右肩上がり】　[⇨第1部・13-4-5 右肩上がり]
- 右肩上がりの経済成長　a continuously growing economy

みぎて【右手】
- 右手系　a right-hand system
- 右手の法則　the right-hand rule

みちすう【未知数】　① an unknown quantity ② an unknown

みつど【密度】　density [⇨ひじゅう]
- 水銀の**密度**は水の 13.6 倍だ．　**The density** of mercury is 13.6 times that of water.
- 土星の平均**密度**は 0.7 g/cm^3 で，太陽系の惑星で最も低い．　The average **density** of Saturn is 0.7 g/cm^3, the lowest of all the planets in the solar system. ★0.7 g/cm^3 は zero point seven gram(s) per cubic centimeter と読む．
- 密度計　① a densimeter ② a densitometer
- エネルギー密度　energy density
- ビット密度　bit density
- 人口密度　⇨じんこうみつど
- 数密度　number density
- 線密度　linear density
- 面密度　① surface density ②〔磁気ディスクの〕areal density

みなみ【南】　south [⇨第1部・59-5 東西南北]

みまん【未満】　① less than … ② fewer than … ③ lower than … ④ smaller than … ⑤ below … ⑥ under … [⇨第1部・12.「以上」「以下」等の表現，11. 数値範囲の表現]
- 10人未満の人　① fewer than 10 people ②《口》less than 10 people　★量で

なく数の場合には less よりも fewer が好まれる．
- 5ミリ未満の長さ　a length of less than 5 millimeters　★量を表わす単位は可算名詞であっても fewer より less が普通．
- 5歳未満の小児　children under five (years of age)

みょうごにち【明後日】　the day after tomorrow [⇨あさって]

みょうにち【明日】　tomorrow [⇨あした]

ミリ…　① [10^{-3}] milli-　② [ミリメートル] a millimeter [⇨第1部・27-4 SI 接頭語]

ミリバール [圧力の単位] a millibar 《= 1/1000 バール = 1 ヘクトパスカル；記号 mb》　★現在はヘクトパスカルを使う．

むげん【無限】　infinity
- 無限の　infinite
- 無限に　infinitely
- 無限に続く　continue without end
- **無限個の**解がある．
  ① There is [《The equation》has] **an infinite number of** solutions.
  ② There are [《The equation》has] **infinitely many** solutions.
- n が**無限大に近づくときの**数列の極限値　the limit of a sequence as n **tends to infinity**
- 等比数列の公比が1以上であれば**無限大までの和**は存在しない．　If the common ratio of a geometric series is greater than 1, the **sum to infinity** does not exist.
- そのような星は理論的には**密度無限大**の点にまで崩壊する．　Theoretically, such a star will collapse into a point of **infinite density**.
- 無限小の　① infinitesimal　② infinitely small
- 単位電荷を**無限遠から**その点まで動かす際になされる仕事 [動かすのに必要な仕事]　the work done in moving [the work needed to move] a unit positive charge **from infinity** to the point
- その2直線は**無限遠で交わる**．　The two lines **meet at infinity**.
- 光源は**無限遠にある**と考えられる．　The light source can be considered to **lie at infinity**.
- 無限遠点　① a point at infinity　② an infinite point
- 無限遠直線　a line at infinity
- 無限級数　an infinite series
- 無限数列　an infinite sequence
- 無限次元の　infinite dimensional

むりかんすう【無理関数】　an irrational function

むりすう【無理数】 ① an irrational (number) ② a surd ［⇨せいすう 数の集合］
- 答えは無理数のままとせよ．　Leave ［Give］ your answer in surd form.

★英語の数学の教科書でよく見られる surd の語は，アラブの数学者フワーリズミーが有理数の「有音」に対して無理数を「無音」と記述したのがラテン語で surdus と直訳されたのがそもそもの始まりである．「ばかげた」の意の absurd も surd が語源になっており，「調子外れの」といった原義から派生した．

…め【…目】
- 8 番目の人　the eighth person ［⇨…ばん，だい…，第 1 部・15. 順位・順番の表現］
- 10 万人目の入場者　the 100,000th visitor 《to the exhibition》
- 3 日目の夕方に　on the evening of the third day　★日程表などでは 3 日目を Day Three, Day 3 のように書くこともできる．
- 上京後 4 年目に　four years after 《they》 came up to Tokyo
- この前のときからちょうど **1 年目**にまた同じことが起こった．　The same thing happened again exactly **one year** to the day after it last occurred.　★to the day は「日付まで同じ」ことを意味する．
- その本の **15 ページ目**の写真　the photo on **page 15** of that book
- 角から **5 軒目**の家　the **fifth** house from the corner
- 彼はその酒屋の向こう，**4 軒目**に住んでいる．　He lives in the **fourth** house beyond the sake shop.
- 彼女の家は私の家から**北へ 3 軒目**です．　She lives **three doors north** of my house.
- うちから **2 軒目**の家　the house **next door but one** to us
- あの彗星は **7 年目**ごとに現われる．
  ① That comet appears (**once**) **every seven years**.
  ② That comet appears **every seventh year**.
- 「あなたいくつ食べた？」「これで 3 つ目だよ」　How many have you eaten? — This is ʼ**my** ［**the**］ **third**.
- 彼女は主演 **2 作目**でアカデミー賞を獲得した．　She won an Academy Award **for her second starring role**.
- これで 5 つ目！　That's five!
- 偶数番目　⇨ぐうすう
- 奇数番目　⇨きすう【奇数】
- 何番目　⇨第 1 部・26-10 何番目

…めい【…名】　《twenty》 people ［⇨…にん］

めいじてき【明示的】
- 明示的な　explicit

- このポテンシャルは明示的には時間に依存しない． This potential does not depend on time explicitly.［⇨よう］

めいど【明度】 ① lightness ② brightness ③ value ④ luminosity ★明度は色相（hue）・彩度（saturation）とともに色の三要素だが，色を定義する色空間によって呼称が異なる．HSL［＝HLS］色空間では lightness, HSV［＝HSB］色空間では value または brightness を使う．マンセル表色系では lightness または value を使うのが一般的．［⇨きど］

めいもく【名目】
- 名目の 〔実質に対して〕nominal
- 名目で in nominal terms
- 名目値 ① a nominal value ② a nominal amount ③ a nominal figure
- 名目価格 〔額面価格〕a nominal value
- 名目金利 a nominal (interest) rate
- 名目（経済）成長率 a nominal (economic) growth rate
- 名目国民所得 (a [the]) nominal national income
- 名目国民総生産 (a [the]) nominal gross national product《略 NGNP》
- 名目所得 nominal income
- 名目賃金 nominal wages
- 名目利回り a nominal yield

メートル a meter《＝100 cm；記号 m》［⇨第 1 部・27-2 SI 基本単位］
- メートル法 the metric system (of measurement)
- メートル法を採用［実施］する adopt [implement] the metric system
- メートル毎秒 〔速さの単位〕meters per second《記号 m/s》
- メートル毎秒毎秒 〔加速度の単位〕① meters per second squared ② meters per second per second《記号 m/s^2》
- 平方メートル a square meter《記号 m^2》
- 立方メートル a cubic meter《記号 m^3》

メガ… ①〔10^6〕mega- ②〔メガヘルツ〕a megahertz ③〔メガバイト〕a megabyte［⇨第 1 部・27-4 SI 接頭語］

メジアン 〔中央値〕the median

メッシュ

1 〔網目〕a mesh
- 粗いメッシュ a coarse mesh
- 細かいメッシュ a fine mesh
- 2 インチのメッシュ［目］の網 a net with two-inch meshes

- 80×80のメッシュの格子　a grid with 80×80 meshes
- 10 kmのメッシュサイズ《網目の単位の大きさ》　a mesh size of 10 km
- シミュレーションの誤差はメッシュの大きさに依存する．　The error of the simulation depends on the mesh size.
- ハリケーンのシミュレーションは水平方向 10 km のメッシュ上で行なわれた．　The simulation of the hurricane was [performed [run]] on a 10-km horizontal mesh.

2〔網目・粒子の大きさの単位〕★網・篩・濾膜などの1インチ当たりの開口の数を表わす．粉・粒子に使うときにはそのような開口を通過するものをいう．この表示は Tyler Equivalent, Tyler Mesh Size などと呼ばれる．
- 20 メッシュのスクリーン　a 20-mesh screen
- 40 メッシュの粉末　40-mesh powder
- 20 メッシュの粉は 20 メッシュのスクリーンを通過する粒子からなる．　A 20-mesh powder consists of particles that pass through a 20-mesh screen.
- 100 メッシュの粒子は 10 メッシュの粒子より細かい．　100-mesh particles are finer than 10-mesh particles.
- 50 メッシュより小さな粒度　particle sizes smaller than 50 mesh
- メッシュ数が大きいほど粉の粒度は小さい．　The larger the mesh number, the smaller the particle size of the powder.

めやす【目安】　①〔指標となるもの〕an indication　② a measure　③〔見当〕an estimate　④〔一応の標準となるもの〕a standard　⑤ a guideline
- 費用の目安　①〔見当〕an estimation of fees　② estimated expenses　③ an estimate of costs　④〔標準値〕standard fees　⑤ average expenses
- 販売台数が売上高の一応の**目安**となる．　The number sold can be used as [**a rough estimate** [**an indication, a measure**]] of the monetary sales volume.
- 売り上げ目標 1 億円というのはあくまで**目安**だから，そうこだわる必要はない．　You don't have to be a stickler for the sales target of ¥100,000,000, for it is, after all, **a tentative one**.

めんせき【面積】　(an) area　[⇨第 1 部・42-8 面積, 58-5 面積の公式]
- 面積が 60 平方メートルある　① be 60 square meters in area　② measure 60 square meters

めんせきぶん【面積分】　a surface integral

…めんたい【…面体】　[⇨第 1 部・58. 図形の基本表現 58-3]
- 四面体　a tetrahedron

めんたいしょう【面対称】　symmetry with respect to a plane
- 面対称である　① have [possess] symmetry with respect to a plane　② be symmetrical with respect to a plane

- 面対称な立体 a solid that has a plane of symmetry

…も ① as「many [much] as … ② no「fewer [less] than … ③〔距離〕as far as … ④〔長さ〕as long as …〔⇨第1部・20.「…も」「…しか」「たった」〕
- 10個もある．
  ① There are **as many as** ten.
  ② There are **no fewer than** ten.

モード 〔最頻値〕a mode

もくひょう【目標】 ① a target ② a goal ③ an object ④ an objective ⑤ an aim
★数値的な目標には target または goal がよい．goal は定性的・定量的いずれの目標にも使い，最終的な到達点の含意がある．object は努力・行動・希望などが向けられる対象，objective は達成すべき内容，aim は意図している・狙っている内容．以下の用例では特に明記していない場合でも適宜入れ換えて使える場合もある．
- 月間目標 a monthly target
- 月間販売目標 ① a monthly sales target ② a sales target for the month
- 長期目標 ① a long-term「target [objective, aim] ② a long-range objective
- 中期目標 ① a medium-term「target [objective] ② an intermediary「target [objective]
- 中長期目標 a medium- to long-term「target [objective]
- 年間売上高100億円の長期目標 a long-term goal of ¥10 billion in annual sales
- CO_2 排出削減目標
  ① the target for the reduction of CO_2 emissions
  ② the CO_2 emission reduction target
  ③ the target amount of reduction for CO_2 emissions
  ④ the targeted cuts in CO_2 emissions
  ⑤ the target of cutting 《5%》「in [from] CO_2 emissions
  ⑥ the reduction in CO_2 emissions sought by 《the government》
- 目標を設定する set a target
- …を目標にする ① aim at … ② set *one's* sights on … ③ have … as an object ④ set the goal at … ⑤ state *one's* objective of …
- 1割増産を目標とする set [fix] a「goal [target] of a ten-percent increase in production
- 1か月で5キロやせるという目標を立てた．I set a「target [goal] of losing 5 kg in a month.
- その会社が現在掲げている10%増益の長期目標 the company's current long-term target of 10% profit growth
- 2012年までに2割の営業利益率達成を目標にする ① aim to attain a 20% operating profit margin by 2012 ② set a goal of a 20% operating profit margin

by 2012 ③ aim for a 20% operating profit margin by 2012
- その社は売り上げ目標を達成した． The company「reached [attained, achieved, met] its sales「target [goal].
- 売り上げが目標に達した [到達した]． The sales reached the「target [goal].
- 売り上げが目標を上回った． ① The sales exceeded the「target [goal]． ② The sales were above the「target [goal].
- 売り上げが目標に達しなかった [目標を下回った]．
 ① The sales「were [fell] short of the「target [goal].
 ② The sales did not reach the「target [goal].
 ③ The sales were below the「target [goal].
- 売り上げは同社が掲げていた 1,000 万円の目標に至らない見込みだ．
 ① The sales will not reach the ¥10 million goal that the company had「set [aimed to meet].
 ② The sales will be less than the ¥10 million that the company had sought.
- 目標まであと 3,000 円だ．
 ① We have another ¥3,000 (to go) before we reach the target.
 ② We have yet to collect ¥3,000 to reach the target.
- 目標にまだ 3,000 円足りない． We are still ¥3,000 short of the target.
- 売り上げ目標　a sales target
- 業績目標　① a business performance target ② an earnings target
- 生産目標　① a production target ② an output target ③ a goal for output
- 月産目標額　the target (figure) for monthly output
- 貯蓄目標額　a savings target
- 輸出目標額　an export target
- 研究目標　a research objective
- 学習目標　the aim of study
- 数値目標　a numerical target
- 目標水準　① the target level ② the targeted level
- 目標達成率　⇨たっせいりつ

モル a mole《記号 mol》
- 2 モル　two moles《記号 2 mol》
- **2 モルの窒素**　**two moles of** nitrogen
- **酸素原子のモル数**　**the number of moles of** oxygen atoms
- 1 g の水素が燃焼すると何モルの水が発生しますか． **How many moles of** water will be produced when 1 g of hydrogen is burned.
- **モル濃度**　① (a) molarity ② (a) mole concentration
- 溶液のモル濃度　the molarity of a solution
- モル濃度で表わされた濃度　concentration expressed as molarity

モル

- **重量モル濃度** (a) molality
- **容量モル濃度** (a) molarity

★(容量)モル濃度(molarity)は溶液 1 リットル中の溶質のモル数《記号 M》，重量モル濃度(molality)は溶媒 1000 g に対する溶質のモル数《記号 mol/kg》．[⇨のうど]

- **モル吸収係数** a molar absorption coefficient
- **モル凝固点降下** a molal freezing point depression constant ★溶媒 1 kg に溶質 1 mol が溶けているときの数値で表わすので molal を使う．
- **モル沸点上昇** a molal boiling point elevation constant
- **モル比熱** ① molar heat (capacity) ② molar specific heat
- **モル百分率** a mole percentage

や行

ヤード a yard 《= 3 フィート，0.9144 m；記号 yd.》[⇨第 1 部・28. 伝統単位 28-1]
- 1 ヤードいくらで売る　sell by the yard
- ヤード数　yardage
- 平方ヤード　a square yard《記号 sq. yd.》
- 立方ヤード　a cubic yard《記号 cu. yd.》

やきゅう【野球】　baseball [⇨第 1 部・49. 野球の数字表現]

やく【約】　[⇨第 1 部・9. 概数]
- 約 100 冊の本　① about 100 books　② approximately 100 books　③ roughly 100 books　④ around 100 books

やくすう【約数】　① a divisor　② a measure
- 7 は 42 の約数である．　7 is a divisor of 42.

やくぶん【約分】　reduction [⇨第 1 部・53. 分数]
- 約分する　① reduce　② cancel
- 最も簡単な分数に約分する　① reduce to a fraction in its lowest terms　② reduce to the lowest terms
- 約分できる　reducible
- 約分できない　irreducible

やすね【安値】　a low price [⇨さいやすね，第 1 部・40. 料金・価格・収支 40-2-2]

ゆうこうきかん【有効期間】　①〔期間〕the term of validity　② the period of validity　③ the period for which《a ticket》is「valid [good]　④〔期限〕the expiry date　⑤ the expiration date [⇨第 1 部・34-4 有効期間]

ゆうこうすうじ【有効数字】　a significant figure
- その値の**有効数字**は 3 桁である．　The value is correct to three **significant figures**.
- その値は**有効数字** 3 桁で[まで]与えられている．　The value is given to three **significant figures**.
- 誤差を有効数字 1 桁に切り上げる　round up the error to 1 significant figure
- 有効数字の桁数　the number of significant figures

ゆうてん【融点】　a melting point《略 mp》

ゆうど【尤度】　likelihood

ゆうびんばんごう【郵便番号】　①《米》the「zip [ZIP] code　②《英》the postcode

③ the postal code [⇨第 1 部・46-2 郵便番号]

ゆうりか【有理化】
- 有理化する　rationalize
- $10/\sqrt{2}$ の分母を有理化する　① rationalize the denominator of $10/\sqrt{2}$ ② write $10/\sqrt{2}$ with a rational denominator

ゆうりかんすう【有理関数】　a rational function

ゆうりすう【有理数】　a rational (number) [⇨せいすう 数の集合]

ユーロ　a euro《記号 €》[⇨第 1 部・39-1-3 ユーロ]

ゆかめんせき【床面積】　① the floor area　② the floor space

ユニタリー　unitary
- ユニタリー行列　a unitary matrix
- ユニタリー演算子　a unitary operator
- ユニタリー変換　(a) unitary transformation

ゆみがた【弓形】　a segment

よう【陽】
- その関数は t に**陽に**依存する．　The function **explicitly** depends on t.
- その方程式には時間変数が**陽には**現われない．　The time variable does not appear **explicitly** in the equation.
- x を**陽に**含まない関数　a function that does not contain x **explicitly**
- 解を**陽な形で**求める　find the solution **explicitly**
- $J(z)$ は簡単な式で**陽に**表わせる．　There is a simple **explicit** formula for $J(z)$.

ようかいど【溶解度】　solubility
- 水に対する食塩の溶解度　the solubility of salt in water
- 水に対する溶解度が高い　be highly soluble in water
- 炭酸ナトリウムは炭酸カルシウムよりはるかに溶解度が高い．　Sodium carbonate is much more soluble than calcium carbonate.
- 溶解度曲線　a solubility curve
- 溶解度係数　a solubility coefficient
- 溶解度積　a solubility product

ようかんすう【陽関数】　an explicit function
- 変数 y は x の陽関数として与えられて［書かれて］いる．　The variable y is 「given [written]」as an explicit function of x.

ようせき【容積】　capacity [⇨第 1 部・42-9 体積・容積]
- 容積トン　a measurement ton
- 容積トン数　measurement tonnage

ようせきりつ【容積率】 ① a floor-area ratio 《略 FAR》 ② the ratio of total floor area to site area ［⇨第 1 部・46-3 住居］

ようび【曜日】 a day of the week ［⇨第 1 部・30-4 曜日］
- 3 月 10 日の火曜日に ①《米》on Tuesday, March 10 ②《英》on Tuesday 10 March ［⇨第 1 部・30-2 月日］
- 16 日の火曜日に on Tuesday the 16th

ようりょう【容量】 capacity
- ディスク容量 (a) disk (storage) capacity
- バッテリー容量 (a) battery capacity ［⇨第 1 部・51-2 バッテリー・充電・放電］
- 容量オーバー ①〔電気回線などの〕an electrical overload ②〔一般に, 許容量を上回ること〕an overload ③ an overflow ④ oversaturation ⑤ (an) excess
- 静電容量 (electrical) capacitance
- 熱容量 ① heat capacity ② thermal capacity
- 容量性リアクタンス capacitive reactance
- 容量分析 ① volumetric analysis ② volumetry

よかく【余角】 ① a complementary angle ② the complement 《of an angle》

よくげつ【翌月】 ① the next month ② the following month

よくじつ【翌日】 ① the next day ② the following day ③ the day after ［⇨第 1 部・31-6-1「翌…」］

よくしゅう【翌週】 ① the next week ② the following week

ヨクト… 〔10^{-24}〕yocto- ［⇨第 1 部・27-4 SI 接頭語］

よくねん【翌年】 ① the next year ② the following year ③ the year after

よくよくげつ【翌々月】 two months later

よくよくじつ【翌々日】 two days later

よくよくしゅう【翌々週】 two weeks later

よくよくねん【翌々年】 two years later

よげん【余弦】 a cosine
- 余弦定理［法則］ the law of cosines

よこじく【横軸】 ① the axis of abscissa(s) ② the horizontal axis ③ the x axis
★abscissa は横軸の座標の意で「切り取られた」の意のラテン語から. 複数形は abscissas または abscissae.
- 横軸は…を表わす. The horizontal axis ｢represents［shows］…
- 時間を横軸として描かれる［プロットされる］ be plotted against time as the

abscissa
- 時系列は，通例時間を**横軸**に，関数値を縦軸にとって描かれる．
  ① A time series is usually plotted with time along **the horizontal axis** and the values of the function along the vertical axis.
  ② A time series is usually plotted with time as **the abscissa** and the values of the function as the ordinate.

よこばい【横ばい】 [⇨第 1 部・13-6 横ばい]
- 横ばいである　① remain at the same level　② show no (marked) fluctuations

よさん【予算】　a budget
- 2007 年度予算案を可決する　pass the budget for「fiscal 2007［FY 2007, the fiscal year 2007］
- 来年度予算総額　the total budget for the coming fiscal year
- 生徒会の予算　the budget for the student council
- その計画の年間予算はどのくらいですか．　What is the annual budget for the program?
- 日本の国家予算は約 80 兆円だ．　Japan's national budget is about 80 trillion yen.
- 2000 年度の米国の連邦予算は 1.8 兆ドルだった．　The United States federal budget for fiscal 2000 was $1.8 trillion.
- 衆議院は昨日 82.9 兆円の予算を可決した．　The House of Representatives passed「an 82.9 trillion yen budget［a budget of 82.9 trillion yen］yesterday.
- プロジェクトは 5,000 万円で予算が組まれた．　The project was budgeted at fifty million yen.
- 予算が 80 兆円を下回ったのは 8 年ぶりのことだった．　It was the first time in eight years that the budget fell below 80 trillion yen.
- これはウガンダの国家予算より多い．　This is more than Uganda's national budget.
- 今年度の活動費の予算がもう 5 万円しか残っていない．　Only ¥50,000 remains of our budget for activity expenses this fiscal year.
- 今年度の予算で…を行なう　finance《a project》out of this year's budget
- …を予算に計上する［組み入れる］　① appropriate［include, add］… in the budget　② set down … in the「budget［estimate］　③ provide for … in the budget
- それには予算がついていない．
  ① No appropriation for it can be made from the budget.
  ② It has no budgetary appropriation.
- 予算の執行　① budget「implementation［execution］　② implementation［execution］of a budget
- 予算を減額する　reduce a budget

- 予算を増額する　increase a budget
- 予算を切り詰める［削る］　①cut down [reduce] a budget　②make a retrenchment in the budget
- 予算の削減　①budget cuts　②cuts「in [to] a budget　③a budget reduction　④a reduction「in [of] appropriations　⑤a reduced「budget [appropriation]《for capital equipment》
- 予算案　①a draft budget　②〔議案〕a budget bill　③a bill of budget
- 1年分の予算を使い切る　use up the year's budget funds
- 支出を予算内で収める　keep expenditures within the budget
- 予算をオーバー［超過］する　①go beyond the estimate　②go over (the) budget　③exceed [be in excess of] the「budget [estimate]　★「予定費用」の意味では an estimate; an estimated cost などを使うことが多い．
- 国家予算　the national budget
- 防衛予算　a defense budget
- 補正予算　①〔増額・減額・組み替えなど〕a supplementary budget　②〔修正された全体〕a revised budget
- 暫定予算　a provisional budget
- 月次予算　a monthly budget
- 予算配分　budgetary allocations

関連表現

- 概算要求　①a budgetary request　②an estimated budget request　③a skeleton (budget)「demand [proposal]　④a request for budgetary appropriations

よじ【四次】　①quartic　②biquadratic　③fourth-degree　④fourth-order

- 四次曲線　a quartic (curve)
- 四次式　a quartic (expression)
- 四次方程式　a quartic (equation)

よじげん【四次元】　four dimensions［⇨じげん］

- 四次元の　four-dimensional
- 四次元空間　(a) four-dimensional space
- 四次元世界　①a four-dimensional world　②a world of four dimensions

ヨタ…　〔10^{24}〕yotta-［⇨第1部・27-4 SI 接頭語］

…より　［⇨第1部・13. 比較・差・増減］

- AはBよりも長い．　A **is longer than** B.

よんだい…【四大…】　⇨…だい【…大】

ら行

らい…【来…】 next 《week》[⇨第 1 部・31-5-1「来…」]

…らい【…来】

1 〔継続期間〕for …
- 30 年来の友人　a friend of thirty years' standing
- 数年来ひどい腰痛に悩まされている．　I've been suffering from a bad backache for the past several years.
- 先日来病気で寝込んでいる．　I've been ill in bed for the past couple of days.

2 〔考慮対象期間〕since …
- 昨年来の高水準　the highest level since last year
- 20 年来の大雪　①the heaviest snowfall in twenty years　②the heaviest snowfall that ｢we [they] have had for the past twenty years
- 今年の夏は 60 年来の暑さだ．　This summer has been the hottest in sixty years.
- 今年の米は何年来の不作だった．　This year's rice crop was the worst in many years.

らいげつ【来月】 next month [⇨第 1 部・31-5-1「来…」]
- 来月 1 日に　on the first of next month
- 来月か再来月　next month or the month after

らいしゅう【来週】 next week [⇨第 1 部・31-5-1「来…」]
- 来週の月曜日に　①on Monday next week　②next Monday　③《英》on Monday next [⇨第 1 部・31-5-3 next … の使用例]

らいねん【来年】 ① next year　②《in》the coming year [⇨第 1 部・31-5-1「来…」]
- 来年の春　next spring
- 来年の 1 月　① next January　②《in》January next year　③《英》《in》January next
- 来年の今ごろ　about this time next year
- 来年は私も 50 だ．　I'll ｢be [turn] fifty next year.

らくさつ【落札】 a successful bid [⇨第 1 部・39-4 入札・オークション]

ラジアン a radian
- ラジアンで表わした角度　an angle expressed in radians
- 一周，すなわち 360° は 2π **ラジアン**に等しい．　A full ｢circle [turn], or 360 degrees, equals 2π **radians**.　★360°＝2π のように書く．ラジアンには単位記号は付けないのが普通．

- 1°は何ラジアンですか.
  ① How many radians is one degree?
  ② How many radians are there in one degree?

ラッキーセブン the lucky seventh (inning) [⇨第1部・37-6 トリビア: 縁起のいい数・悪い数]

ラド 〔吸収線量の単位〕a rad《記号 rad》★SI 単位はグレイ（gray）.

ランキング (a) ranking [⇨第1部・15-2 順位]
- 世界ランキング2位である　be ranked second in the world

らんすう【乱数】 ① random numbers ②〔無作為に選んだ一つの数〕a randomly chosen number ③ a randomly chosen value ④ a random number ⑤ a random value
- 乱数を発生させる　generate random numbers

りえき【利益】 ①(a) profit ② gain(s) ③ returns [⇨しゅうえき, 第1部・41-1-3 損益計算書]
- 利益と損失　profits and losses [⇨そんえき]
- 利益が少ない　① give [yield] little profit ② have a「narrow [small, slim] margin of profit ③ do not pay much
- 利益を上げる　①〈事物が主語〉bring [yield, fetch] a profit ②〈人が主語〉make [gain, obtain, earn] a profit
- 利益になる　① profitable ② lucrative ③ paying ④ remunerative
- 経費がかかりすぎて**利益**が出なかった.　There was too much overhead, so there was no **profit**.
- 今期は売り上げ・**利益**とも過去最高を記録した.　In this term the company's sales and **profit(s)** marked an all-time high.
- **当期利益**　profits for the term
- **営業利益**　operating income
- **営業純利益**　net operating income《略 NOI》
- **粗利益**　① a gross profit ② a gross margin
- **純利益**[**純益**]　① a net「profit [gain] ② a clear「profit [gain] ③ a pure「profit [gain] ④ net proceeds
- 50万円の**純益**がある　have **a net gain** of five hundred thousand yen
- 1年に1千万円[2割5分]の純益を上げる　net「ten million yen [25 percent] a year
- 純益100万円を得る　net [gross, clear, realize] a profit of one million yen
- **要求利益率**　① required return ② a required rate of return《略 RRR》
- **売上利益率**　〔利益（総利益または純利益）の純売上高に対する比率〕① the ratio of profit to net sales ② the sales-profit rate ③ the profit margin

- **自己資本利益率** 〔純利益の自己資本に対する比率〕return on equity《略 ROE》

りえきじょうよきんけいさんしょ【利益剰余金計算書】 a statement of retained earnings [⇨第 1 部・41. 英文会計]

りさん【離散】
- 離散的な　discrete
- 離散的なエネルギー準位　discrete energy levels
- 離散変数　a discrete variable
- 離散量　a discrete quantity
- 離散化　discretization
- 離散化する　discretize

りし【利子】　interest《on a「loan [deposit]」》[⇨りりつ, きんり]
- 1,000 ドルに対する利子　the interest on $1,000
- 公債の利子　interests on public bonds
- 5 パーセントの利子で金を借りる　borrow money at 5% interest
- 高い [低い] 利子で金を貸す　lend money at「high [low] interest
- 無利子で貸す　① lend 《him》 money free of interest ② lend 《him》 money without interest ③ lend 《him》 money interest-free
- あの銀行に預金すると利子はどれくらいですか.　How much interest do they give at that bank?
- 定期預金の利子はいくらですか.
  ① What is the interest rate on time deposits?
  ② What interest is「paid [allowed]」on time deposits?
- 利子がつく　① yield interest ② bear interest
- 6 パーセントもの利子がつく預金　a deposit「drawing [carrying, bearing, paying]」as much as 6% interest
- 預金してもたいして利子はつかない.　① If you「make a deposit [deposit money]」in the bank, it won't「earn [yield]」much interest. ② A deposit in the bank won't earn you much interest.
- 5 パーセントの利子を取る　charge 5% interest
- 利子を取って金を貸す　lend [put out] *one's* money at interest
- 年 2 回利子を元金に繰り入れる　compound interest semiannually

りしょくりつ【離職率】　① a job separation rate ② a separations rate ③ (employee [worker, staff]) turnover

▶ 米国労働省の求人労働移動調査 (JOLTS: Job Openings and Labor Turnover Survey) の発表する統計には quits rate (退職率) および layoffs and discharges rate (解雇率) があり separations rate または turnover はこの両方を含む.

[⇨ きゅうじんばいりつ]
- 三年離職率　a ((high)) rate of employees leaving work within three years

りしんりつ【離心率】〔二次曲線の〕eccentricity

りつ【率】　①〔単位量・単位時間に対する割合〕a rate　②〔占める割合〕a proportion　③ a share　④ a percentage　⑤ a ratio　⑥ a rate　⑦〔確率〕(a) probability　[⇨ 第1部・13-4-6 増加率・上昇率, 13-5-4 低下率・減少率, 22. 割合]

▶**時間変化の割合の「…率」は rate**

- 成長率　a growth rate
- 人口増加率　a population growth rate
- 増加率　① a rate of increase　② an increasing rate

★rate は速度を表わすのにしばしば使う：reaction rate（反応速度），decay rate（崩壊率，崩壊速度），transmission rate（伝送速度），bit rate（ビットレート）．

▶**単位量に対する大きさの「…率」も rate**

- 換算率　a conversion rate
- 1ドル100円の換算率で　at (the conversion rate of) ¥100 to the dollar
- 利益率　a rate of return
- 利率　an interest rate
- 割引率　a discount rate
- 5倍の競争率　a competition rate of 5 to 1

▶**何倍であるかを表わす因子はしばしば factor を使う**

- 増幅率　an amplification factor
- 乗車率　a (passenger) load factor

▶**「占める割合」「利益や負担を分かち合う割合」の意では share**

- 市場占有率　a (market) share
- 負担率　a [*one's*] share of ((the costs))
- 医療費の個人負担率　① the patient's (percentage) share of medical expenses　② the patient's copayment (percentage) for medical expenses

▶**占める割合の「…率」も複合語としては rate が多い**

- 失業率　an unemployment rate　[⇨ しつぎょうりつ]
- 出生率　a birthrate　[⇨ しゅっしょうりつ]
- 普及率　a penetration rate
- 五年生存率　a five-year survival rate
- 稼働率　① an operating rate　② a utilization rate　③ a capacity utilization rate　[⇨ かどうりつ]
- 成功率　a success rate

▶**説明的に表現する場合は ratio, percentage などを使うことが多い**

- 合格率　① the ratio of successful applicants　② the (examination) pass rate
- 勝率　the percentage of wins
- 正答率　the percentage of correct answers
- 労働分配率　〔企業の付加価値に対する人件費の比率〕the ratio of labor costs to value added　★英語の labor share [wage share] は一国の GDP に対する被雇用者に還元される割合(厳密にはいくつかの異なる定義がある)をいうが, これも「労働分配率」と訳されている.
- 売上高人件費率　the ratio of labor costs to sales
- 大学進学率　① the college-going rate　② the percentage of students enrolling in universities

▶ **評価・格付けの意味は rating**

- 支持率　① an approval rating　② a popularity rating [⇨しじりつ]
- 視聴率　a rating [⇨しちょうりつ]

▶ **抽象名詞を単に「…の度合い」の意味で使うことも多い**

- 70% の変換率が達成される．　Seventy percent conversion is achieved.
- 電圧変動率　voltage regulation
- 死亡率　(a) mortality
- 乳児死亡率　(an) infant mortality
- 投票率　①(a) voter turnout　② a turnout (of voters)　③ a turnout rate　④ a voting rate [⇨第 1 部・16-6 投票率]
- 回転率　(a) turnover (rate) [⇨かいてんりつ]

▶ **物理では接尾辞 -ity をもつ語も多い**

- 拡散率　(a) diffusivity
- 帯磁率　(a) susceptibility
- 抵抗率　(a) resistivity
- 透磁率　(a) permeability
- 反射率　①(a) reflectance　②(a) reflectivity
- 分極率　(a) polarizability

★次のように, 物理量・物性としては不可算, 値としては可算.

- 透磁率は SI 単位系ではヘンリー毎メートルで測る．　Permeability is measured in henrys per meter in SI units.
- 真空は透磁率 1 である．　Vacuum has a permeability of 1.

▶ **慣習的に index, constant 等を使う語も多い**

- 屈折率　a refractive index
- 誘電率　① a dielectric constant　②(a) permittivity
- 粘性率　① a coefficient of viscosity　② a viscosity coefficient
- 膨張率　① a coefficient of expansion　② an expansion coefficient

りったいかく

- 弾性率　a modulus of elasticity
- 体積弾性率　a bulk modulus
- ヤング率　Young's modulus
- 曲率　(a) curvature
- 仕事率　(a) power
- 圧縮率　⇨あっしゅくりつ
- 打率　a batting average〔⇨第 1 部・49-12 打率〕

▶「…率」という名詞表現にこだわらずに訳すこともできる

- 7% の経済成長率を維持する　① maintain an economic growth rate of 7 percent　② keep economic growth at 7 percent
- 経済成長率 3% という政府の想定　① the government's assumption that the economic growth rate will be 3 percent　② the government's assumption that the economy will expand by 3 percent
- 落札率が 90% を超えていた.〔落札額が予定価格の 90% 超〕　The winning bid price was above 90% of the bid ceiling.

りったいかく【立体角】

- 光源の（視点における）**立体角**　**the solid angle** subtended by the source
- ステラジアンは，球の半径の 2 乗に等しい球面上の面積**に対する立体角**である．　A steradian is **a solid angle subtending** an area on the surface of a sphere equal to the square of the sphere's radius.

リットル　a liter《記号 l, L, ℓ》

★記号 l が数字の 1 とまぎらわしいことからアメリカ，カナダ，オーストラリアでは大文字の L の使用が一般化しており，接頭辞がつくときにも mL, μL などと記される．イギリスを含むそれ以外の国では小文字の l が普通．日本の学校教育では 21 世紀初頭まで筆記体の ℓ がよく使われた．

りっぽう【立方】〔⇨第 1 部・54-5 累乗〕

- 100 立方メートル　100 cubic meters

りっぽうこん【立方根】　a cube root〔⇨第 1 部・54-6 累乗根〕

- 125 の立方根は 5 だ．　The cube root of 125 is 5.

りまわり【利回り】　① (a) yield (on investments)　② (an) investment yield　③ interest　④ return(s)　⑤ profits

- 10 年米国債の利回り　the yield on the ten-year treasury
- 利回り 5 分の債券　a bond with a yield of 5%
- その債券は年 6 分の利回りになる．　This bond「yields [bears, pays] interest of 6% a year.
- ドルベースで 5% の利回りといっても，ドル安がそれ以上に進めば元本割れになる．　Even with dollar-based interest of five percent, if dollar deprecia-

tion exceeds that figure, it results in a loss of principal.
- 利回りがよい [悪い]　yield [bear] a「good [bad] return
- 高利回りの投資　① an investment「yielding [bearing] high interest　② a high-interest investment
- 投資の利回りを計算する　compute the yield on investments
- 債権利回りの低下　a drop in bond yields
- (株の) 配当利回り　dividend yield
- 税込み [税引き] 利回り　pretax [after-tax] yield
- 満期利回り　yield to maturity

りょう【量】　① (a) quantity　② (an) amount　③ volume
- 適正な量　a proper amount《of food, of exercise》
- 膨大な量の　① an enormous amount of …　② a vast amount of …
- 必要な量の食物繊維　the necessary amount of dietary fiber
- たったこれだけの量でレモン3個分のビタミンがとれます．Just this「much [amount] will give you the vitamins of three lemons.
- 量が増える　gain in「quantity [volume]
- 量が減る　diminish in「quantity [volume]
- 量が多い　be large in quantity
- 量が少ない　be small in quantity
- 質量ともに　both in quality and in quantity
- そのプロセスが必要としている特定のリソースの量を判別する　determine「the amount of [how much of] a particular resource the process needs

…りょう【…料】　① a charge　② a rate　③ a fee ［⇨第1部・40-1 料金］

りょうが【凌駕】　［⇨第1部・13. 比較・差・増減 13-1-3］
- 凌駕する　① surpass　② exceed

りょうがえ【両替】　［⇨第1部・40-6-3 小銭，39-2 外国為替］
- 両替する　①〔外貨〕exchange《dollars into yen, American money into Japanese》　②〔小銭〕change《a 1,000-yen note》

りょうきん【料金】　① a charge　② a rate　③ a fee　④〔乗り物の〕a fare ［⇨第1部・40-1 料金］

りょうへん【両辺】　both sides《of an equation》

りりつ【利率】　① the rate of interest　② the interest rate ［⇨りし，きんり］
- 年利率　an annual interest rate
- 年1分の利率で金を借りる [貸す]　borrow [lend] money at the rate of「one percent per annum [1% p.a.]
- 想定元本に対する固定利率　a fixed-rate interest on a notional principal

- 利率を上げる raise [increase] the rate of interest
- 利率を下げる lower [decrease] the rate of interest
- 利率引き上げ ① a raise in interest rates ② an increase in interest rates
- 利率引き下げ ① a reduction in interest rates ② a decrease in interest rates

…りん【…厘】〔1割の1/100；0.1%〕[⇨第1部・22. 割合 22-1-1 歩合]
- 日歩5厘の利子 interest of 0.5 percent per day
- 3割4分5厘 ① 34.5 percent ② 0.345 [⇨…わり]

るい【塁】 ① a base ② a base bag [⇨第1部・49. 野球の数字表現 49-11]
- タイガースはノーアウトでランナー二塁，三塁だった．
  ① The Tigers had「men [runners]」on second and third with none out.
  ② There were Tigers on second and third with nobody out.

るいけい【累計】 ① the cumulative「total [number, amount]」《to date》 ② the accumulated「total [number, amount]」[⇨第1部・24-3 累計]

るいじょう【累乗】 ①〔演算〕exponentiation ②〔結果〕a power [⇨第1部・54-5 累乗 54-5-5]

るいじょうこん【累乗根】 a (power) root [⇨第1部・54-6 累乗根]
- 四則計算と**累乗根**を取る操作の有限の組み合わせからなる公式 a finite formula involving only the four arithmetic operations and the extraction of **roots**

ルート 〔平方根〕a square root
- ルート2 ① the square root of 2 ② root 2 ★$\sqrt{2}$

ルーメン 〔光束の単位〕a lumen《記号 lm》[⇨第1部・27. 単位]

ルクス 〔照度の単位〕a lux《記号 lx》 ★複数形は lux, luxes, luces がある．[⇨第1部・27. 単位]

れい【零】 ① zero ② naught ③ nought ④ nothing ⑤ nil [⇨ゼロ]
- 零歳児 ① a baby under 12 months of age ② a baby in its first year ★英語では zero years old とは言わない．
- 零時 ①〔午前零時〕(twelve o'clock) midnight ②〔正午〕noon ★英語では zero o'clock のような表現はない．[⇨第1部・32-1-4 零時と12時]
- ★zero hour という表現があるが，これは軍事用語で「作戦開始時刻」，また転じて口語で「決定的に重要な瞬間」といった意味で，カウントダウンして0になる瞬間ということに由来する．
- 00年代 the '00s ★このように書くことはできるが，英語では口頭でどういうかについてのコンセンサスはない．日本語では「ゼロ年代」という言い方がある．[⇨第1部・29-6 …年代]
- 0点のスコア a zero score [⇨れいてん]

- 0度　zero degrees　★degree が複数形になることに注意．［⇨ぜったいれいど］
- 0度より低い［高い］　below［above］zero
- 0次の項　a zero(th)-order term
- 熱力学の第零法則　the zeroth law of thermodynamics
- 零電流　a zero current
- 零因子　a zero divisor

れいてん【零点】

1〔試験の得点〕① (a) zero ② a mark of zero
- 0点を取る　① get (a) zero《in math》② receive a mark of zero
- 彼は教師としては0点だ．　As a teacher he is「a failure［useless］．

2〔競技得点〕① zero ② nil ③《口》《米》a goose egg ④《英》a duck ⑤ a duck's egg ⑥〖テニス〗love

▶テニスで得点が0のことを love といい，win a game at love（ラブゲームで勝つ）のようにいうが，俗説ではフランス語の l'oeuf が訛ったものといわれる．これは「卵」の意であり，他の egg を使った表現とも発想が共通している．しかし，実際は，何も求めず（得ず）に好きだからプレイするという意味からきたものとされる．

- 0点に終わる　①〔競技で〕《口》《米》get a goose egg ②《英》get a duck ③《口》《米》get skunked

3〔0になる点〕① a zero ② a node
- その関数は実軸の正の部分に零点を1つ持つ．　The function has one zero on the positive real axis.
- 零点エネルギー　〖物〗zero-point energy
- 零点振動　〖物〗zero-point vibration

レイノルズすう【レイノルズ数】　a Reynolds number
- 低レイノルズ数の流れ　fluid flow at low Reynolds numbers
- 大きな［高］レイノルズ数に対しては　for「large［high］Reynolds numbers
- レイノルズ数の大きな極限において　in the limit of large Reynolds number

レート　〔率〕a rate
- 為替レート　① a rate of exchange ② an exchange rate［⇨第1部・39-2 外国為替］
- 1ドル100円のレートで　at the (exchange) rate of 100 yen to the US dollar

れきだい【歴代】　all-time《record》［⇨第1部・15. 順位・順番の表現 15-2-1］
- 歴代記録　an all-time record
- 歴代興行記録　an all-time box-office record

- 歴代トップ 10　the all-time「top [best] ten《movies》
- 歴代 1 位 [トップ]　① (the) all-time number one　② (the) all-time first place
- 彼は食らった三振の数が歴代 1 位という記録の持ち主だ．　He holds the all-time record for「batter strikeouts [number of times struck out].
- 彼は通算出場試合数で（歴代）4 位だ．　He ranks fourth (all-time) in career games played.　★career が通算，all-time は史上通した歴代記録の意．

レム　〔線量当量の単位〕a rem　★SI 単位はシーベルト．

れんしょう【連勝】　① straight「victories [wins]　② consecutive「victories [wins]　③ successive「victories [wins]　④ a series of「victories [wins]　⑤ victory after victory　⑥ win after win　[⇨第 1 部・50-1-2 連勝・連敗]

れんぞく【連続】

1　〔つながっていること〕continuous …
- 連続関数　a continuous function
- 関数の連続性　the continuity of a function
- 連続変数　a continuous variable
- 連続極限では　in the continuous limit

2　〔隣り合う数であること〕consecutive …
- 連続する整数　consecutive integers
- 和が 36 となる 3 つの**連続する整数**を求めよ．
  ① Find the **three consecutive integers** whose sum is 36.
  ② What **three consecutive integers** add up to 36?
- 連続する奇数　consecutive odd numbers

3　〔一続きであること〕contiguous …
- そのファイルの内容はディスクの**連続したクラスター**に記憶されているのではない．　The contents of the file are not stored in **contiguous clusters** on the disk.
- **連続していないセクション**を指定することを許容する　allow **non-contiguous sections** to be specified
- その 20,000 ビットデータを**連続した 4 ビットセグメント** 5,000 個に分割する　divide the 20,000-bit data into 5,000 **contiguous 4-bit segments**
- n バイトの**連続したメモリーブロック**が必要とされる．　**A contiguous block of memory** of n bytes is required.
- 少なくとも 24 個の**連続するヌクレオチド**　at least 24「**contiguous [consecutive]** nucleotides

4　〔相続くこと〕succession [⇨第 1 部・13. 比較・差・増減 13-4-4, 13-5-3]

- 3 週間**連続で**　① for three weeks「running [straight, on end]　② for three「consecutive [successive, straight] weeks ★「21日間連続」という意味であればcontinuously や without stop を加えればよい.「(週間記録などの)3週連続」という意味であれば three times in three weeks「running [straight, on end] や three times in three「consecutive [successive, straight] weeks のように言うこともできる.

- **10年連続の**地価下落　a「fall [decline] in land prices「**for [over] 10 consecutive years**
- **6年連続で**増収増益だった.　《The company》reported increases in both revenue and profits **for the sixth「consecutive [straight] year**. ★for six consecutive years と違って最新(6年目)の決算に着目した表現.
- 理事は最大で**連続4期**務めることができる.　A director may serve a maximum of **four consecutive terms**.
- トーナメントで**連続優勝する**　**win two consecutive** tournaments
- **10試合連続**ヒット　hits **in 10 consecutive games** [⇨第1部・49. 野球の数字表現 49-16]

レントゲン　〔照射線量の単位〕a roentgen《記号 R》

れんぱい【連敗】　① successive defeats ② a series of reverses [⇨第1部・50-1-2 連勝・連敗]

れんぶんすう【連分数】　a continued fraction
- 連分数展開　continued fraction expansion

れんりつ【連立】
- これらの方程式を**連立させて**解く　solve these equations **simultaneously**
- **連立方程式**　(a「pair [set, system] of) simultaneous equations
- x と y の連立方程式　simultaneous equations in x and y
- 二元連立方程式　simultaneous equations in two unknowns
- **連立不等式**　① compound inequalities ② simultaneous inequalities ★日本語では複数の不等式をすべてみたす変数の範囲を求めるものを言うが, ①の英語は複数の不等式のどれかをみたす変数の範囲を求めるものも含む.

ろうどうじかん【労働時間】　① working hours ② the hours of labor ③〔延べ労働時間数〕man-hours
- 時間外の労働時間数　the number of hours of overtime work
- **労働時間**を8時間から10時間に延長する　lengthen **the working day** from 8 hours to 10

関連表現
- 8時間労働制　the eight-hour working day system
- 週40時間労働を定着させる　establish a 40-hour workweek
- フランスは2000年に**週35時間労働制**を導入した.　France adopted **a 35-**

- **hour workweek** in 2000.
- この工場は週5日，1日8時間労働である． In this factory, they work eight hours a day, five days a week.
- 3交代制の工場　a plant run in three shifts
- 週5日制［週休2日制］　①《introduce》a five-day-workweek system　②《work on》a five-day-workweek basis［⇨しゅうきゅう］

ローマすうじ【ローマ数字】　Roman numerals［⇨第1部・3. ローマ数字］

ろっかくけい【六角形】　a hexagon［⇨第1部・58-2 …角形］

わ行

わ【和】 ① the sum ②〔合計〕the sum total ③ the total (amount) [⇨第1部・54-1 足し算 54-1-3]

ワースト worst [⇨第1部・15. 順位・順番の表現 15-2-1]

ワット〔電力の単位〕a watt《記号 W》
- 60 ワットの電球　a 60-watt bulb
- 家庭用の 800 ワットの電子レンジ　① a household 800-watt microwave oven ② a household microwave oven with a power of 800 watts
- この電子レンジは 500 ワットです．　This microwave oven「consumes [delivers] 500 watts (of power).
- この電球は 40 ワットです．　This light bulb uses 40 watts (of power).
- ワット時　〔電力量の単位〕a watt-hour《記号 Wh》
- ワット数　wattage
- 1 ワットは 1 秒当たり 1 ジュールのエネルギー消費に等しい．　One watt equals the energy consumption of one joule per second.

…わり【…割】 ① 10 percent ② a tenth ③ one-tenth [⇨第1部・22-1-1 歩合]
- 2 割 7 分　27 percent
- 2 割 3 分 5 厘　① 23.5 percent ② 0.235 ③〔打率〕《a batting average of》.235 ★小数 0.235 は zero [《主に英》nought] point two three five と読むが，打率の場合は 0 を書かず two thirty-five と読む．
- 1 割未満　① below 10 percent ② under 10 percent ③ less than 10 percent ④ under a tenth ⑤ less than a tenth
- 8 割の確率で　① with a probability of 80 percent ② with an eight-in-ten chance
- 我がチームは 20 歳未満が **3 割**を占めている．
① Those under 20 years of age account for **30 percent** of this team's players.
② **Thirty percent** of the players on this team are under 20 years of age.

わりあい【割合】 ① a proportion ② a ratio ③ a rate ④ a percentage ⑤〔受け取る割合など〕a share [⇨第1部・22. 割合]
★ *a:b* のような相対比率を表わすのは proportion, ratio, 母数の中で占める比率を表わすのは percentage, proportion, ratio, rate (⇨りつ), 単位量当たりの大きさを表わすのは rate を使うことが多い．
- この会社は女性社員の**割合**が高い．　There is a high **proportion** of women employees in this company.
- 参加者の大きな**割合**を中高年が占めている．　A large **proportion** of participants are middle-aged and elderly people.
- この病気は **1,000 人に 1 人の割合**で現われる．

① This disease occurs **in one in a thousand**.
② This disease occurs **in one in every thousand**.
③ This disease affects **one in a thousand people**.
- 受験者 **10 人に 1 人の割合**で合格者が出た.
  ① **One out of ten** applicants passed the test.
  ② The pass rate was **one in ten**.
- 1 秒当たり 100 ギガビットの割合で　at the rate of 100 gigabits per second
- 月に1度の割合で　①at the rate of once a month　②as often as once a month
- 1 ドル 100 円の割合で換算する　convert at the rate of ¥100 to the dollar

わりかん【割り勘】　⇨第 1 部・40-6-2 支払いに関係する表現

わりきる【割り切る】　divide [⇨第 1 部・54-4 割り算 54-4-4]

わりきれる【割り切れる】　① can be (evenly [exactly]) divided《by …》② be (evenly [exactly]) divisible《by …》[⇨第 1 部・54-4 割り算 54-4-4]
- 30 は 6 で割り切れる.
  ① 30 can be divided by 6 (without a remainder).
  ② 30 is (exactly) divisible by 6.
  ③ 6 divides 30.
  ④ 6 will go into 30.
  ⑤ 6 is an aliquot part of 30.

わりざん【割り算】　division [⇨第 1 部・54-4 割り算]

わりびき【割引】

1　〔販売価格の〕①(a) discount　②(an) allowance　③price cutting [⇨第 1 部・40-4 割引]

2　〔手形の〕(a) discount
- 割引する　discount
- 手形を銀行で割引してもらう　get a bill discounted at a bank
- 手形の割引をする　discount a bill
- 債券を割引発行する　issue bonds at discount
- 割引歩合［率］　a discount rate

わる【割る】

1　〔割り算〕divide [⇨第 1 部・54-4 割り算]
- 6 割る 2 は 3.
  ① 6 divided by 2 gives 3.
  ② Divide 6 by 2 and you get 3.
  ③ 2 goes into 6 3 times.

2　〔下回る〕fall below …
- 仕入れ値を割って売る　sell below cost

- 株価が1,000円を割った銀行がある． The stock prices of some banks「broke [dropped below] the ¥1,000 level.
- 気温が零度を割った． The temperature fell below zero.

ワン ① one ② single
- ワンカット　one (continuous) shot
- その長いシーンはワンカットで撮影されている． That long scene was filmed in a single continuous shot.
- ワンクリック　〖電算〗one click
- ワンコインバス　a 100-yen flat-rate bus
- 減税案はたいてい他の分野の増税と**ワンセットになっている**．
  ① Tax reductions usually **come together with** increases somewhere else.
  ② Tax reductions **are** usually **accompanied by** increases somewhere else.
- ワンタッチだ． All you have to do is (just) push the button.
- ワンタッチ操作　① one-touch control ② one-button control
- ワンチップコンピューター　a single-chip computer
- ツーワン　two balls one strike ［⇨ 49. 野球の数字表現 49-7］
- ワンナウト［ワンアウト］　one (man) out ［⇨第 1 部・49. 野球の数字表現 49-8］
- ワンパスの処理　〖電算〗one-pass processing
- ホテルのワンフロアを借り切る　rent an entire floor at a hotel
- ワンペア　〖トランプ〗one pair
- ワンマンな［の］　①〔一人で行なう〕one-man《bus》②〔独裁的な〕autocratic ③ dictatorial
- ワンルームマンション　① a one-room apartment ② a one-room condo ③《米》a studio apartment ④《英》a studio flat ⑤《英》a bedsit ⑥ a bedsitter ⑦ a bedsitting room ［⇨第 1 部・46-3 住居］

ん 〔数字をぼかして言うときに用いて〕［⇨第 1 部・8-3「うん十」など］
- ン万円　some tens of thousands of yen

ENKYUSHA'S
GUIDE TO QUANTITATIVE EXPRESSIONS IN ENGLISH

研究社 英語の数量表現辞典 増補改訂版

2007 年 6 月	初版発行
2017 年 3 月 18 日	増補改訂版発行

KENKYUSHA
〈検印省略〉

編　者	研究社辞書編集部
発行者	関戸雅男
発行所	株式会社 研究社
	〒102-8152　東京都千代田区富士見 2-11-3
	電話　編集 03(3288)7711
	営業 03(3288)7777
	振替　00150-9-26710
	http://www.kenkyusha.co.jp
印刷所	研究社印刷株式会社

ISBN 978-4-7674-3480-3 C0582　　Printed in Japan
装丁　亀井昌彦